Alastair

Sawday's

Special Places
to Stay

British
Bed & Breakfast

4 Contents

The buildings

Beautiful as they were, our old offices leaked heat, used electricity to heat water and rooms, flooded spaces with light to illuminate one person, and were not ours to alter.

So in 2005 we created our own eco-offices by converting some old barns to create a low-emissions building. We made the building energy-efficient through a variety of innovative and energy-saving building techniques, described below.

Insulation We went to great lengths to ensure that very little heat can escape, by laying thick insulating board under the roof and floor and adding further insulation underneath the roof and between the rafters. We then lined the whole of the inside of the building with plastic sheeting to ensure air-tightness.

Heating   We installed a wood-pellet boiler from Austria, in order to be largely fossil-fuel free. The pellets are made from compressed sawdust, a waste product from timber mills that work only with sustainably managed forests. The heat is conveyed by water, throughout the building, via an under-floor system.

Water We installed a 6000-litre tank to collect rainwater from the roofs. This is pumped back, via an ultra-violet filter, to the lavatories, showers and basins. There are two solar thermal panels on the roof providing heat to the one (massively insulated) hot-water cylinder.

Photo: Tom Germain

Lighting We have a carefully planned mix of low-energy lighting: task lighting and up-lighting. We also installed sun-pipes to reflect the outside light into the building.

Electricity All our electricity has long come from the Good Energy company and is 100% renewable.

Materials Virtually all materials are non-toxic or natural. Our carpets are made from (80%) Herdwick sheep-wool from National Trust farms in the Lake District.

Doors and windows Outside doors and new windows are wooden, double-glazed and beautifully constructed in Norway. Old windows have been double-glazed.

We have a building we are proud of, and architects and designers are fascinated by. But best of all, we are now in a better position to encourage our owners and readers to take sustainability more seriously.

What we do

Besides having moved the business to a low-carbon building, the company works in a number of ways to reduce its overall environmental footprint.

Our footprint We measure our footprint annually and use it to find ways of reducing our environmental impact. To help address unavoidable carbon emissions we try to put something back: since 2006 we have supported SCAD, an organisation that works with villagers in India to create sustainable development.

Travel Staff are encouraged to car-share or cycle to work and we provide showers (rainwater-fed) and bike sheds. Our company cars run on LPG (liquid petroleum gas) or recycled cooking oil. We avoid flying and take the train for business trips wherever possible. All office travel is logged as part of our footprint and we count our freelance editors' and inspectors' miles too.

Our office Nearly all of our office waste is recycled; kitchen waste is composted and used in the office vegetable garden. Organic and fairtrade basic provisions are used in the staff kitchen and at in-house events, and green cleaning products are used throughout the office.

Working with owners We are proud that many of our Special Places help support their local economy and, through our Ethical Collection, we recognise owners who go the extra mile to serve locally sourced and organic food or those who have a positive impact on their environment or community.

Engaging readers We hope to raise awareness of the need for individuals to play their part; our Go Slow series places an emphasis on ethical travel and the Fragile Earth imprint consists of hard-hitting environmental titles. Our Ethical Collection informs readers about owners' ethical endeavours.

Ethical printing We print our books locally to support the British printing industry and to reduce our carbon footprint. We print our books on either FSC-certified or recycled paper, using vegetable or soy-based inks.

Our supply chain Our electricity is 100% renewable (supplied by Good Energy), and we put our savings with Triodos, a bank whose motives we trust. Most supplies are bought in bulk from a local ethical-trading co-operative.

For many years Alastair Sawday Publishing has been 'greening' the business in different ways. Our aim is to reduce our environmental footprint as far as possible, and almost every decision we make takes into account the environmental implications. In recognition of our efforts we won a Business Commitment to the Environment Award in 2005, and in 2006 a Queen's Award for Enterprise in the Sustainable Development category. In that year Alastair was voted ITN's 'Eco Hero'. In 2009 we were given the South West C+ Carbon Positive Consumer Choices Award for our Ethical Collection.

In 2008 and again in 2009 we won the Independent Publishers Guild Environmental Award. In 2009 we were also the IPG overall Independent Publisher and Trade Publisher of the Year. The judging panel were effusive in their praise, stating: "With green issues currently at the forefront of publishers' minds, Alastair Sawday Publishing was singled out in this category as a model for all independents to follow. Its efforts to reduce waste in its office and supply chain have reduced the company's environmental impact, and it works closely with staff to identify more areas of improvement. Here is a publisher who lives and breathes green. Alastair Sawday has all the right principles and is clearly committed to improving its practice further."

Becoming 'green' is a journey and, although we began long before most companies, we still have a long way to go. We don't plan to pursue growth for growth's sake. The Sawday's name – and thus our future – depends on maintaining our integrity. We promote special places – those that add beauty, authenticity and a touch of humanity to our lives. This is a niche, albeit a growing one, so we will spend time pursuing truly special places rather than chasing the mass market.

That said, we do plan to produce more titles as well as to diversify. We are expanding our Go Slow series to other European countries, and have launched *Green Europe*, both bold new publishing projects designed to raise the profile of low-impact tourism. Our Fragile Earth series is a growing collection of campaigning books about the environment: highlighting the perilous state of the world yet offering imaginative and radical solutions and some intriguing facts, these books will keep you up to date and well-armed for the battle with apathy.

Photo: Tom Germain

People are usually comforted to hear that I use this book myself! I rarely go anywhere without it, and have been known to simply avoid the places where there is nowhere 'Special' to stay. But of course I am missing out. There are dozens of towns that I should get to know, but which still lack a Sawday's B&B. So this is a plea: we are especially keen to learn of special places to stay in cities, to which more and more of you are going for your weekends.

It is uplifting to learn how many of our owners have embraced the food 'revolution'. I met an organic farmer in Scotland whose wife makes her own cheese and devotes the rest of her time to showing city kids what a farm is like. She depends on her local friends to buy it; together they are keeping a fine tradition alive. I wish there were enough of us to alter the economics of modern shopping, to create an alternative to the supermarkets' monopoly.

If we value good health, we should feed ourselves with good food. Increasing numbers of adults and children, in Britain and beyond, are developing type 2 diabetes, a disease directly linked to unhealthy lifestyles. Hundreds of our B&B owners are providing us with their own eggs, bread, fruit and vegetables, and sometimes more: their lamb, pork, chicken. Some make their own muesli; one I know grows the wheat to make his bread. This is wonderful stuff and I salute them all. In fact we have created a grand

Photo: Tom Germain

literary 'salute' in the shape of Eat Slow Britain, a loving romp through the landscape of great organic food producers and Special Places owners doing their bit to give us real food.

Thinking of the panache, style, fine food and brilliant hospitality with which you will be greeted in these places I end with a comforting quote from Frederic Raphael: "There's a sort of person who rushes out of his house to shake hands with you precisely in order not to have to take you inside". You won't meet him here.

Alastair Sawday

The seasons whirl by. Just weeks ago we embarked on a lovely, crunchy snowy walk into the Sawday's office. Now, as I write, there is a heat wave, beans are running up their poles and dogs are seeking a shady place for a snooze.

Another edition of British Bed & Breakfast will soon herald another autumn. Reassuringly our owners are a constant lot and are steadfast in their willingness to welcome guests, feed them exceptionally well and send them on their way restored.

They have always been industrious but more than ever the economy and concern about food miles is spurring on these B&B folk to grow their own food. It's the same for many of us: vegetable seed sales have exceeded flower seed sales for the past three years and the demand for allotments far outstrips the number available. Many of the owners in this guide are passionate about growing and rearing their own food, sourcing locally and eating with the seasons; they often send us splendid pictures of contented livestock and groaning veg plots.

Our B&Bers are offering all sorts of courses, too, from cookery and gardening to art and pottery. You will find wool producers, apple juice makers and craftspeople who are keen to pass on their knowledge and share their gardens, farms and studios. One owner grows twenty varieties of potato and another has a quarter-acre asparagus bed; the marmalade and jam makers are, of course, legion. Some produce their own honey or plant flowers to attract bees; protecting bees and considering them in our planting plan is something we should all seek to do, for the future of agriculture. Many of our B&Bs delight in introducing youngsters to their animals and their gardens; surely spending time among nature has to be one of the best ways to foster a willingness to seek out good food later in life.

Here at Sawday's we have a thriving vegetable plot worked on by a few stalwarts at lunchtime. On the other side of the lane, a section of field has been set aside for Sawday's Community Garden where an enterprising group of villagers has turned over the land with the help of a horse-drawn plough and a few rootling pigs and now they have neat rows of onions, beans and potatoes to share.

Photo of the 'French team', left: Tom Germain
Photo right: Upper Buckton, entry 430

Alongside are some busy hens – the work and the eggs are shared too. Fattening piglets and their mum take up the rest of the field – we swear they spend most of their day plotting how to escape into the veg patch.

At home we took on a couple of the piglets, too. They're an eye-catching mix of ginger and black and a mischievous pair. A public footpath runs past their field and it's amazing how much attention they get from passers-by. Every day people (some making a special visit) stop to chat to them and give them a scratch. Runners jog past and, without stopping, just call, "Pigs!" and then jog on, smiling; one walker goes past twice a day and we can hear her call, "See you in the morning, darlings!" People are delighted by pigs and seem to leave them happier, as if they've had some sort of therapy. We've got to know a few of these visitors and it's touching that many of them feel as if the piglets belong to them – "They

get a lot of visitors you know, but we think of them as 'ours'," they say. We're more than happy to share the joy of keeping them – it makes it all doubly rewarding.

Our Ethical Collection Awards celebrate owners who are providing locally sourced and organic food, safeguarding the environment or forging strong links with their communities. Check out the website entries of those people who have an Ethical Collection mention on their page to find out what good works they are up to, then set off to experience it all first-hand. There are many other owners doing just as much but who are, perhaps, too busy to apply. However, we hope their write-ups will set the scene for you.

There are many favourites still here and some wonderful additions this year: a relaxed farmhouse in Pembrokeshire with bantams laying your breakfast eggs, a grand castle on the Tamar with a vast walled kitchen garden, a funky London bakery with rooms above and plenty of B&Bs where you can come and go with your own key and even rustle up your own organic breakfast at a time to suit you.

Whether you set off on your travels in snow, rain or sunshine, we're sure you are going to have an inspiring, memorable time with these people, of whom we are very fond and firmly consider 'ours'.

Wendy Ogden

Photo: Bunkers Hill, entry 275

It's simple. There are no rules, no boxes to tick. We choose places that we like and are fiercely subjective in our choices. We also recognise that one person's idea of special is not necessarily someone else's so there is a huge variety of places, and prices, in the book. Those who are familiar with our Special Places series know that we look for comfort, originality, authenticity, and reject the insincere, the anonymous and the banal. The way guests are treated comes as high on our list as the setting, the architecture, the atmosphere and the food.

Inspections

We visit every place in the guide to get a feel for how both house and owner tick. We don't take a clipboard and we don't have a list of what is acceptable and what is not. Instead, we chat for an hour or so with the owner and look round. It's all very informal, but it gives us an excellent idea of who would enjoy staying there. If the visit happens to be the last of the day, we sometimes stay the night. Once in the book properties are re-inspected every four years or so, to keep things fresh and accurate.

Feedback

In between inspections we rely on feedback from our army of readers, as well as from staff members who are encouraged to visit properties across the series. This feedback is invaluable to us and we always follow up on comments. So do tell us whether your stay has been a joy or not, if the atmosphere was great

Photo: Fourteen, entry 207

or stuffy, the owners cheery or bored. The accuracy of the book depends on what you, and our inspectors, tell us. A lot of the new entries in each edition are recommended by our readers, so keep telling us about new places you've discovered too. Please use the forms on our website at www.sawdays.co.uk, or later in this book (page 437).

However, please do not tell us if the bedside light was broken, or the shower head was scummy. Tell the owner, immediately, and get them to do something about it. Most owners are more than happy to correct problems and will bend over backwards to help.

Far better than bottling it up and then writing to us a week later!

Subscriptions

Owners pay to appear in this guide. Their fee goes towards the high costs of inspecting, of producing an all-colour book and of maintaining our website. We only include places that we like and find special for one reason or another, so it is not possible for anyone to buy their way onto these pages. Nor is it possible for the owner to write their own description. We will say if the bedrooms are small, or if a main road is near. We do our best to avoid misleading people.

Disclaimer

We make no claims to pure objectivity in choosing these places. They are here simply because we like them. Our opinions and tastes are ours alone and this book is a statement of them; we hope you will share them. We have done our utmost to get our facts right but apologise unreservedly for any mistakes that may have crept in.

You should know that we don't check such things as fire regulations, swimming pool security or any other laws with which owners of properties receiving paying guests should comply. This is the responsibility of the owners.

Photo: Orchard Barn, entry 247

Finding the right place for you

All these places are special in one way or another. All have been visited and then written about honestly so that you can take what you like and leave the rest. Those of you who swear by Sawday's books trust our write-ups precisely because we don't have a blanket standard; we include places simply because we like them. But we all have different priorities, so do read the descriptions carefully and pick out the places where you will be comfortable. If something is particularly important to you then do check when you book: a simple question or two can avoid misunderstandings.

Maps

Each property is flagged with its entry number on the maps at the front. These maps are a great starting point for planning your trip, but please don't use them as anything other than a general guide – use a decent road map for real navigation. Most places will send you detailed instructions once you have booked your stay.

Ethical Collection

We're always keen to draw attention to owners who are striving to have a positive impact on the world, so you'll notice that some entries are flagged as being part of our "Ethical Collection". These places are working hard to reduce their environmental footprint, making significant contributions to their local community, or are passionate about serving local or organic food. Owners

have had to fill in a very detailed questionnaire before becoming part of this Collection – read more on page 430. This doesn't mean that other places in the guide are not taking similar initiatives – many are – but we may not yet know about them.

Sawday's Travel Club

We've launched a Travel Club, based around the Special Places to Stay series; you'll see a 💼 symbol on those places offering something extra to Club members, so to find out how to join see the inside front cover.

Symbols

Below each entry you will see some symbols, which are explained at the very back of the book. They are based on the information given to us by the owners. However, things do change: bikes may be under repair or a new pool may have been put in. Please use the symbols as a guide rather than an absolute statement of fact and double-check anything that is important to you – owners occasionally bend their own rules, so it's worth asking if you may take your child or dog even if they don't have the symbol.

Children – The 🤸 symbol shows places which are happy to accept children of all ages. This does not mean that they will necessarily have cots, high chairs, etc. If an owner welcomes children but only those above a certain age, we have put these details at the end of their write-up. These houses do not have the child symbol, but even these folk may accept your younger child if you are the only guests. Many who say no to children do so not because they don't like them but

Photo left: The Mount House, entry 621
Photo right: Bosvathick, entry 63

because they may have a steep stair, an unfenced pond or they find balancing the needs of mixed age groups too challenging.

Pets – Our 🐕 symbol shows places which are happy to accept pets. It means they can sleep in the bedroom with you, but not on the bed. Be realistic about your pet – if it is nervous or excitable or doesn't like the company of other dogs, people, chickens, children, then say so. Do let the owners know when booking that you intend to bring your pet – particularly if it is not the usual dog!

Owners' pets – The 🐈 symbol is given when the owners have their own pet on the premises. It may not be a cat! But it is there to warn you that you may be greeted by a dog, serenaded by a parrot, or indeed sat upon by a cat.

Quick reference indices

At the back of the book you'll find a number of quick-reference indices showing those places that offer a particular service, perhaps a room for under £70 a night, or owners who are happy for you to stay all day. They are worth flicking through if you are looking for something specific.

A further listing refers to houses within two miles of a Sustrans National Cycle Network route. Take your own bike or check if you can hire or borrow one from the owners before you travel, and enjoy a cycle ride on your break.

Types of places

Some houses have rooms in annexes or stables, barns or garden 'wings', some of which feel part of the house, some of which don't. If you have a strong preference for being in the throng or for being apart, check those details. Consider your surroundings when you are packing: large, ancient country houses may be cooler than you are used to; city places and working farms may be noisy at times; and that peacock or cockerel we mention may disturb you. Light sleepers should pack ear plugs, and take a dressing gown if there's a separate bathroom (though these are sometimes provided).

Some owners give you a front door key so you may come and go as you please; others like to have the house empty between, say, 10am and 4pm. If you would prefer not to wander far during the day then look for the places that have the 'Stay all day' quick reference at the back of the book.

Rooms

Bedrooms – We tell you if a room is a double, twin/double (ie with zip and link beds), suite (with a sitting area), family or single. Most owners are flexible and can juggle beds or bedrooms; talk to them about what you need before you book. Staying in a B&B will not be like staying in a hotel; it is rare to be given your own room key and your bed will not necessarily be made during your stay, or your room cleaned. Make sure you are clear about the room that you have booked, its views, bathroom and beds, etc.

Bathrooms – Most bedrooms in this book have an en suite bath or shower room; we only mention bathroom details when they do not. So, you may get a 'separate' bathroom (yours alone but not in your room) or a shared bathroom. Under certain entries we mention that two rooms share a bathroom and are 'let to same party only'. Please do not assume this means you must be a group of friends to apply; it simply means that if you book one of these rooms you will not be sharing a bathroom with strangers. If these things are important to you, please check when booking. Bath/shower means a bath with shower over; bath and shower means there is a separate shower unit.

Sitting rooms – Most B&B owners offer guests the family sitting room to share, or they provide a sitting room specially for guests. If neither option is available we generally say so, but do check. And do not assume that every bedroom or sitting room has a TV.

Photo left: Horsleygate Hall entry 103
Photo right: Lower End House, entry 590

Meals

Unless we say otherwise, a full cooked breakfast is included. Some owners – particularly in London – will give you a good continental breakfast instead. Often you will feast on local sausage and bacon, eggs from resident hens, homemade breads and jams. In some you may have organic yogurts and beautifully presented fruit compotes. Some owners are fairly unbending about breakfast times, others are happy to just wait until you want it, or even bring it to you in bed.

Apart from breakfast, no meals should be expected unless you have arranged them in advance. Although we don't say so on each entry – the repetition a few hundred times would be tedious – all owners who provide packed lunch, lunch or dinner need ADVANCE NOTICE. And they want to get things right for you so, when booking, please discuss your diet and meal times. Meal prices are quoted per person, and dinner is often a social occasion shared with your hosts and other guests.

Do eat in if you can – this book is teeming with good cooks. And how much more relaxing after a day out to have to move no further than the dining room for an excellent dinner, and to eat and drink knowing there's only a flight of stairs between you and your bed. Very few of our houses are licensed, but most are happy for you to bring your own drink.

Prices and minimum stays

Each entry gives a price PER ROOM for two people. We also include prices for single rooms, and let you know if there is a supplement to pay should you choose to loll in a double bed on your own.

Photo left: Lower Harton Farm, entry 131
Photo right: The Linen Shed, entry 276

The price range for each B&B covers a one-night stay in the cheapest room in low season to the most expensive in high season. Some owners charge more at certain times (during regattas or festivals, for example) and some charge less for stays of more than one night. Some owners ask for a two-night minimum stay at weekends and we mention this where possible. Most of our houses could fill many times over on peak weekends and during the summer; book early, especially if you have specific needs.

Booking and cancellation

You may not receive a reply to your booking enquiry immediately; B&Bs are not hotels and the owners may be away. When you speak to the owner double-check the price you will pay for B&B and for any meals.

Requests for deposits vary; some are non-refundable, especially in our London homes, and some owners may charge you for the whole of the booked stay in advance. Some cancellation policies are more stringent than others. It is also worth noting that some owners will take the money directly from your credit/debit card without contacting you to discuss it. So ask them to explain their cancellation policy clearly before booking to avoid a nasty surprise.

Payment

All our owners take cash and UK cheques with a cheque card. Few take credit cards but if they do, we have given them the

appropriate symbol. Check that your particular credit card is acceptable.

Tipping

Owners do not expect tips. If you have been treated with extraordinary kindness, write to them, or leave a small gift. Please tell us, too – we love to hear, and we do note, all feedback.

Arrivals and departures

Say roughly what time you will arrive (normally after 4pm), as most hosts like to welcome you personally. Be on time if you have booked dinner; if, despite best efforts, you are delayed, phone to give warning.

Closed

When given in months this means the whole of the month stated.

Photo: Bridge Cottage, entry 378

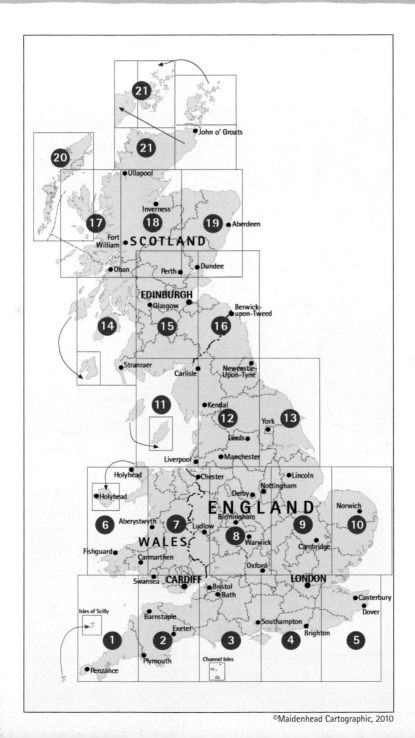

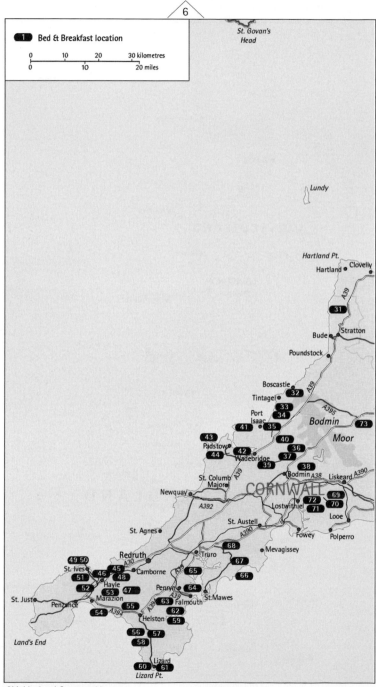

Bed & Breakfast location

0   10   20   30 kilometres
0   10   20 miles

©Maidenhead Cartographic, 2010

Map 2   25

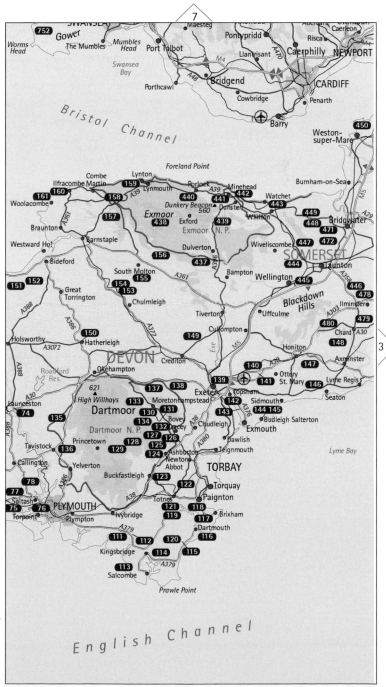

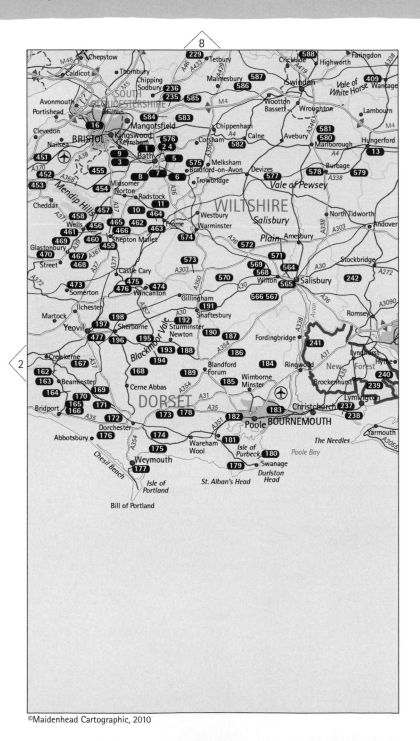

Map 4   27

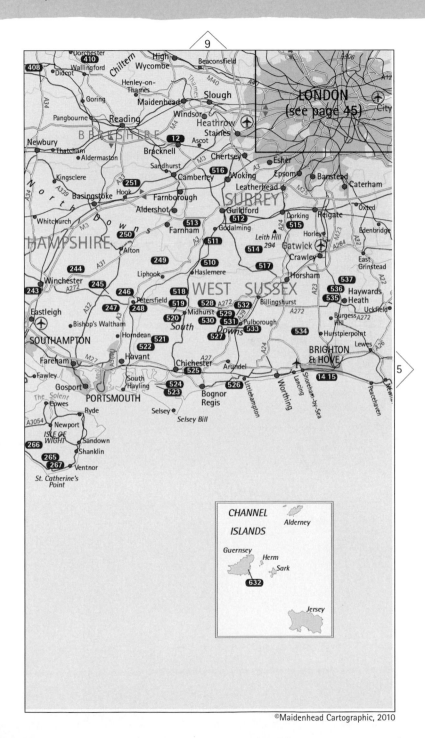

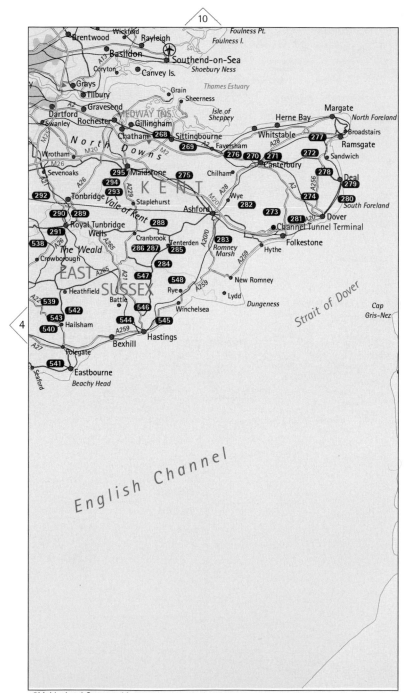

Map 6   29

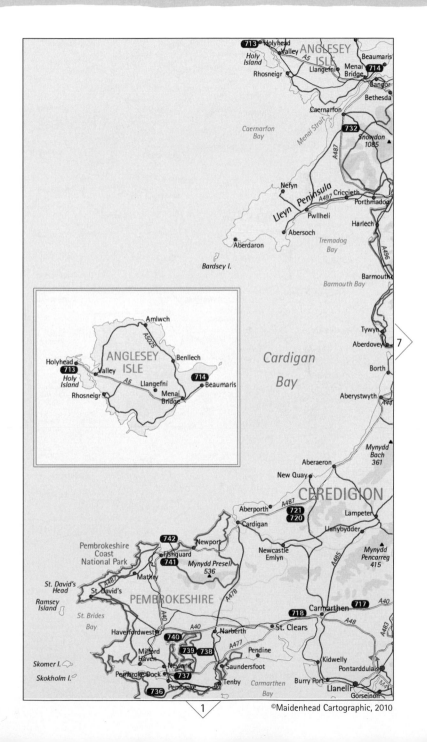

©Maidenhead Cartographic, 2010

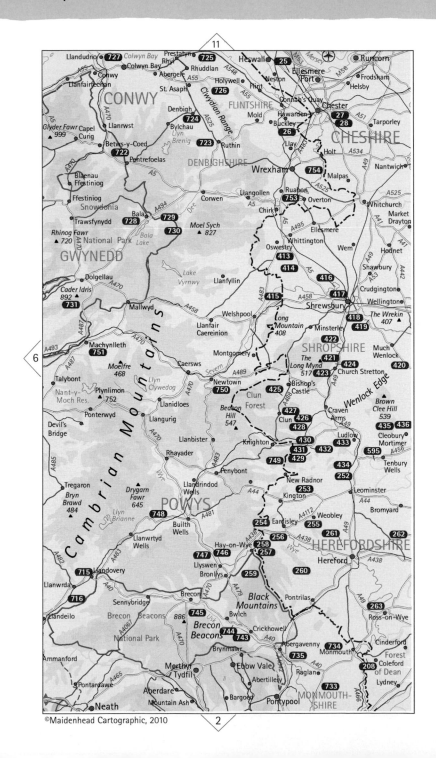

Map 8

31

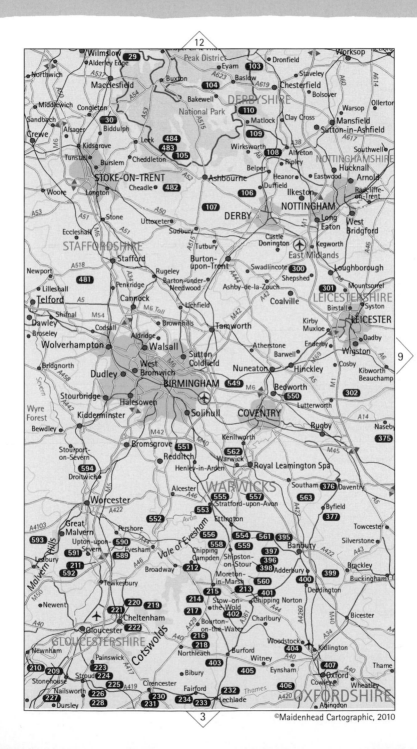

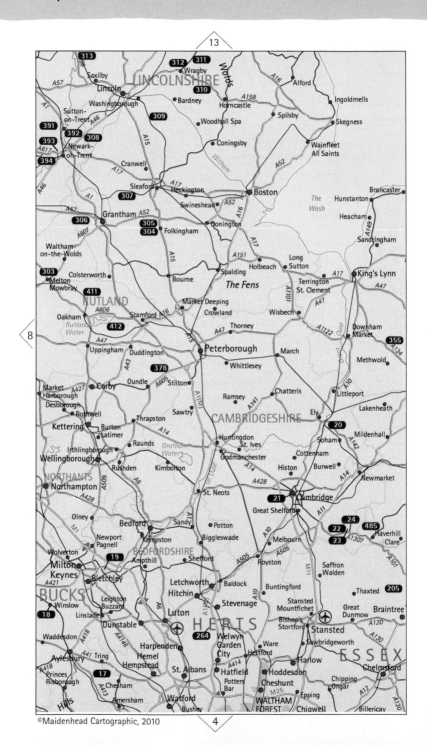

Map 10 33

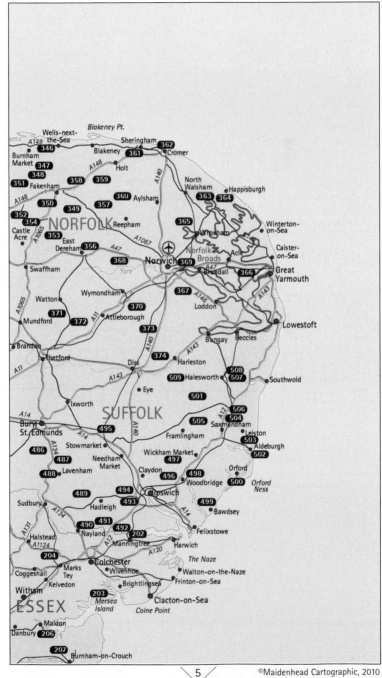

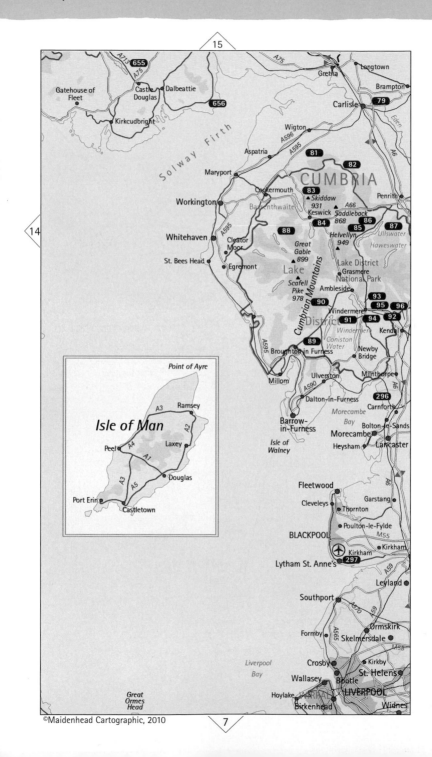

15

Gatehouse of
Fleet

A713 **655**
A75
Castle
Douglas   Dalbeattie
Kirkcudbright

A75
Gretna   Longtown
Brampton
656
Carlisle   **79**
Eden
A6

14

Wigton
A596
Aspatria   A595   **81**   **82**
Maryport

Solway Firth

CUMBRIA

Workington
Cockermouth   **83**
▲*Skiddaw*
931   A66   Penrith
Bassenthwaite   Keswick   *Saddleback*   **86**
84   *868*   **85**   **87**
88   *Helvellyn*   Ullswater
Whitehaven   Cleator   *949*   *Haweswater*
Moor   ▲
St. Bees Head   *Great*
Egremont   *Gable*   Lake District
899   Grasmere
▲   National Park
Lake   Ambleside   **93**
Scafell   **90**   **95**   **96**
Pike   Windermere   **92**
978   **91**   **94**   Kendal
A595   *District*   *Windermere*
Coniston
89   *Water*   Newby
Broughton-in-Furness   Bridge
Millom   Ulverston   Milnthorpe
A590   A6
Dalton-in-Furness   **296**
Carnforth
Morecambe
Barrow-   *Bay*   Bolton-le-Sands
in-Furness   Morecambe
Isle of   Heysham   Lancaster
Walney

Point of Ayre

A3
Ramsey
Isle of Man   A2
A4
Peel   Laxey
A1
A3   A5   Douglas
Port Erin
Castletown

Fleetwood
Garstang
Cleveleys   Thornton
Poulton-le-Fylde
M55
BLACKPOOL
Kirkham   Kirkham
297
Lytham St. Anne's
A59
Leyland
A570   A59
Southport
Ormskirk
Formby   A565   Skelmersdale   M58
Crosby   Kirkby
Liverpool   Wallasey   St. Helens
Bay   Bootle
Hoylake   **LIVERPOOL**
Great   Birkenhead   Widnes
Ormes
Head

Map 12   35

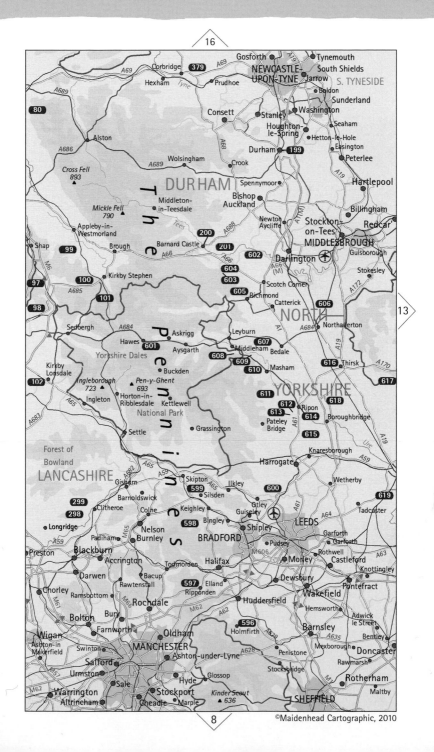

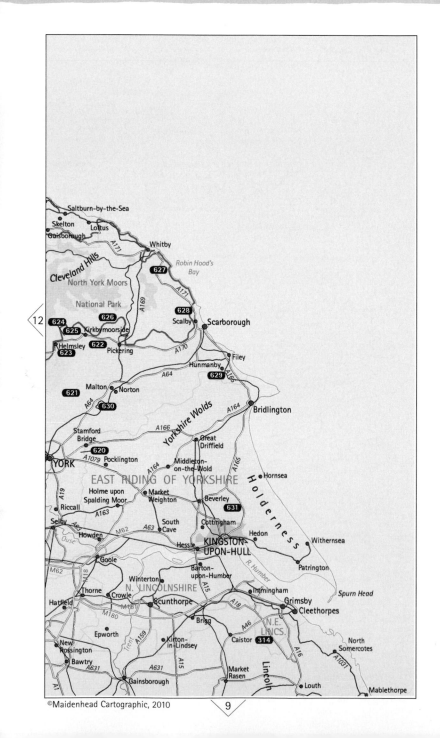

Map 14

37

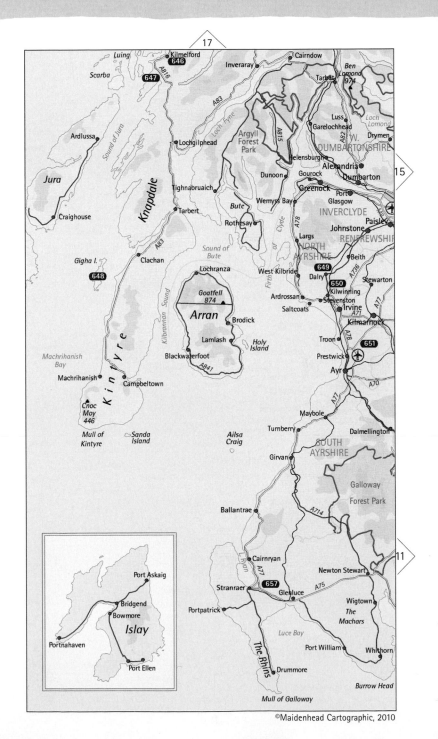

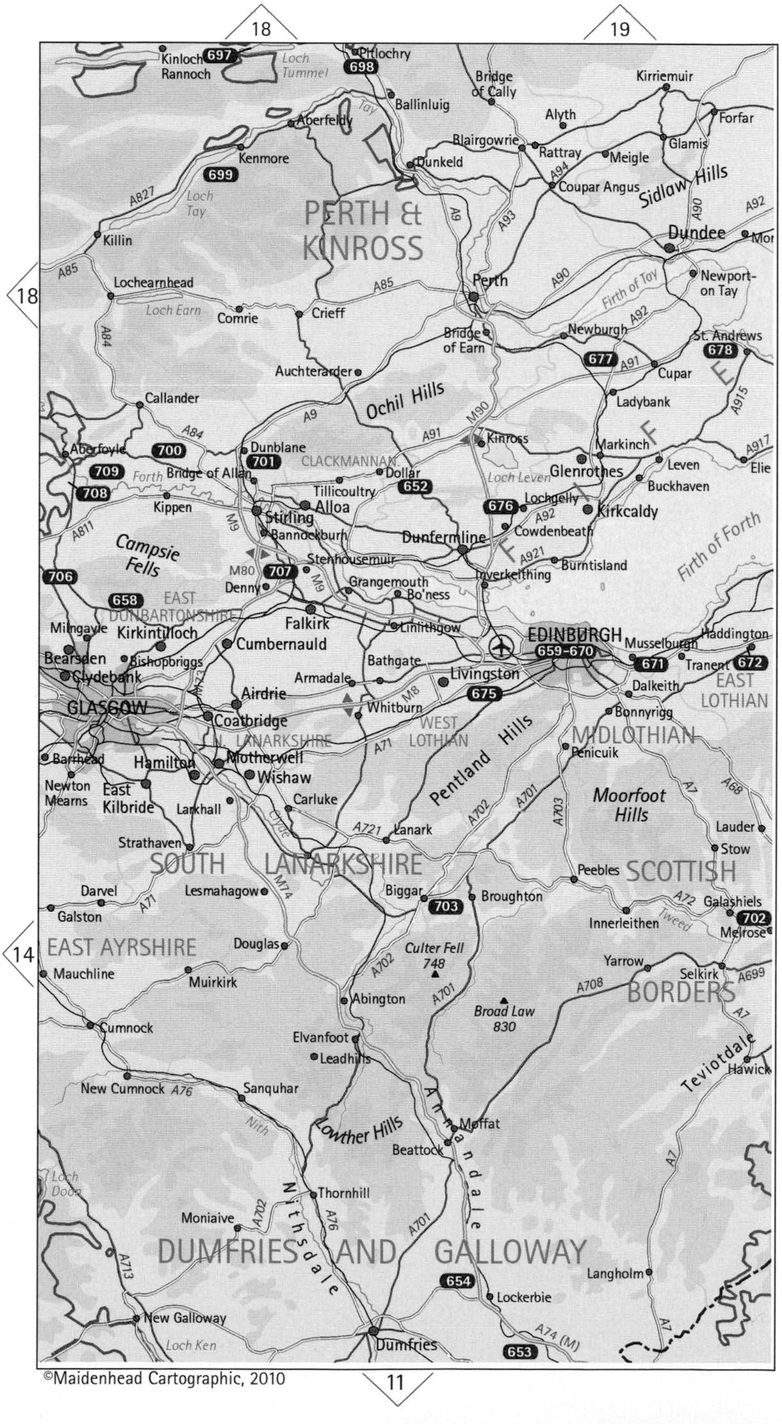

18

19

Kinloch 697
Rannoch
Loch Tummel 698
Pitlochry
Bridge of Cally
Kirriemuir
Ballinluig
Alyth
Forfar
Aberfeldy
Blairgowrie
Rattray
Meigle
Glamis
Kenmore
Dunkeld
Coupar Angus
Sidlaw Hills
A94
A90
A92
A827
699
Loch Tay
PERTH &
KINROSS
A9
A93
Dundee
Mor
Killin
A85
Newport-
on Tay
Lochearnhead
Perth
A90
Firth of Tay
A92
18
Loch Earn
Comrie
Crieff
A85
Newburgh
St. Andrews 678
A84
Callander
Auchterarder
Bridge
of Earn
677 A91
Cupar
F
A915
A9
Ochil Hills
Ladybank
Aberfoyle
700
Dunblane
701
A91
Kinross
Markinch
Leven
Elie
709
Forth
Bridge of Allan
CLACKMANNAN
Dollar
Glenrothes
708
Tillicoultry
652
Loch Leven
Buckhaven
Kippen
Alloa
676
Lochgelly
Kirkcaldy
Campsie
Fells
M9
Stirling
Bannockburn
Dunfermline
Cowdenbeath
A811
706
Stenhousemuir
A921
Burntisland
M80
707
Grangemouth
Inverkeithing
Firth of Forth
658
Denny
Bo'ness
EAST
DUNBARTONSHIRE
M9
Falkirk
Linlithgow
Milngavie
Kirkintilloch
Cumbernauld
EDINBURGH
Musselburgh
Haddington
Bearsden
Bishopbriggs
Armadale
Bathgate
659-670
671
Tranent
672
Clydebank
Airdrie
Whitburn
Livingston
Dalkeith
EAST
LOTHIAN
GLASGOW
Coatbridge
M8
675
Bonnyrigg
LANARKSHIRE
WEST
LOTHIAN
MIDLOTHIAN
Barrhead
Hamilton
Motherwell
A71
Penicuik
Moorfoot
Hills
Newton
Mearns
East
Kilbride
Wishaw
Carluke
A7
A68
Larkhall
Carluke
A702
A701
A703
Lauder
Strathaven
CLYDE
Lanark
Stow
SOUTH
LANARKSHIRE
A721
Peebles
SCOTTISH
Darvel
Lesmahagow
Biggar
Broughton
A72
Galashiels
702
Galston
703
Innerleithen
Tweed
Melrose
EAST AYRSHIRE
Douglas
Culter Fell
748
Yarrow
Selkirk
A699
Mauchline
Muirkirk
Abington
A702
A701
BORDERS
A708
A7
Cumnock
Elvanfoot
Broad Law
830
Hawick
New Cumnock A76
Leadhills
Sanquhar
Teviotdale
Nith
Lowther Hills
Moffat
A7
Beattock
Loch
Doon
Thornhill
A76
A701
Annandale
Moniaive
A702
Nithsdale
DUMFRIES AND GALLOWAY
Langholm
654
Lockerbie
New Galloway
A713
Loch Ken
Dumfries
653
A74 (M)

14

Map 16

39

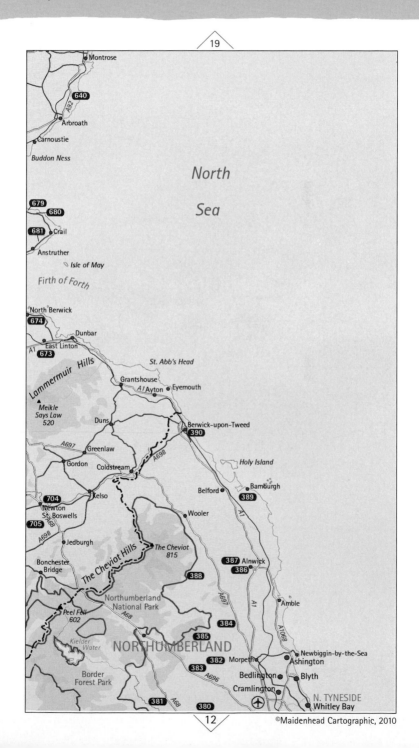

Montrose

640

Arbroath

Carnoustie

Buddon Ness

North

Sea

679
680

681 Crail

Anstruther

◇ *Isle of May*

Firth of Forth

North Berwick

674

Dunbar

East Linton

673

Lammermuir Hills

St. Abb's Head

Grantshouse

A1 Ayton ● Eyemouth

▲ *Meikle Says Law 520*

Duns

Berwick-upon-Tweed

390

A697

Greenlaw

Gordon

Coldstream

A698

Holy Island

Bamburgh

Belford ●

389

704

Kelso

Newton St. Boswells

705

A698

Jedburgh

The Cheviot Hills

Wooler

The Cheviot 815

387 Alnwick

386

Bonchester Bridge

388

Northumberland National Park

A697

A1

● Amble

A69

Peel Fell 602

384

A1068

Kielder Water

NORTHUMBERLAND

385

Newbiggin-by-the-Sea

382 Morpeth

Ashington

Border Forest Park

383 A696

Bedlington ●

● Blyth

Cramlington

381 A68

380

N. TYNESIDE
Whitley Bay

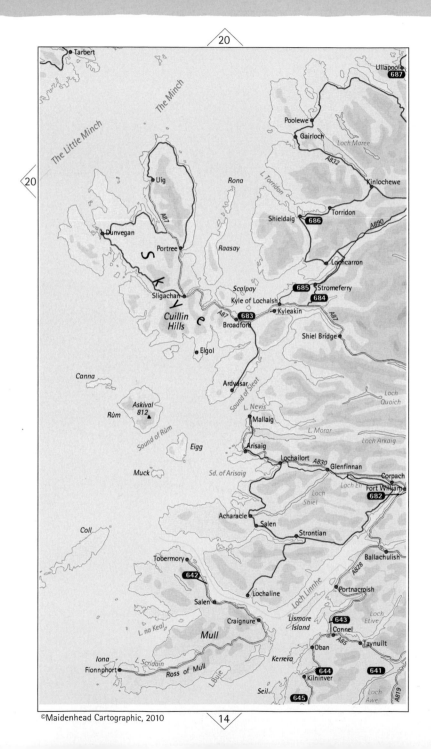

Map 18

41

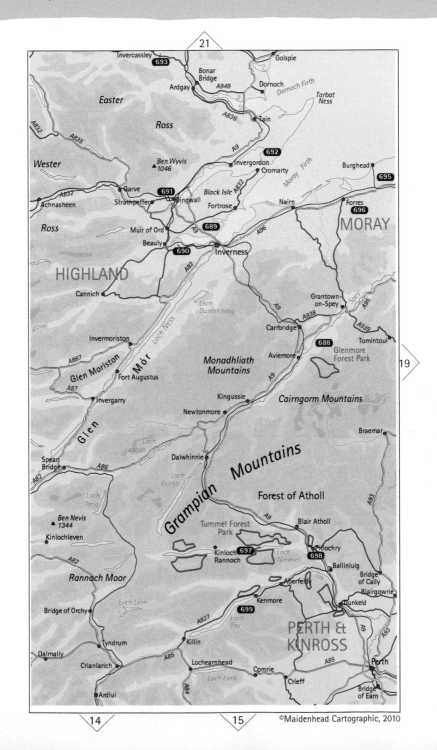

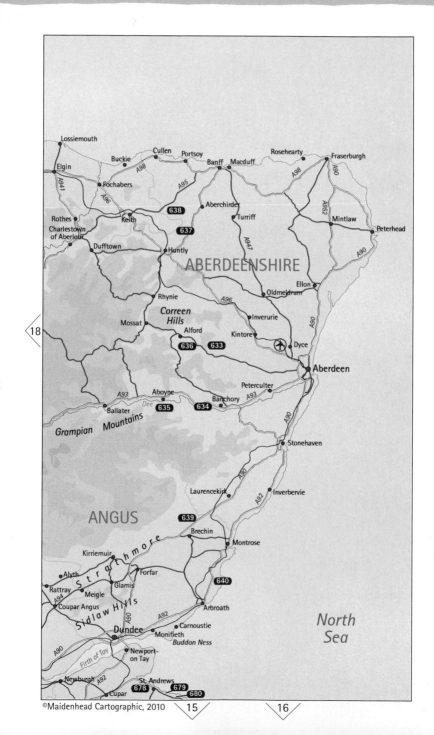

Map 20   43

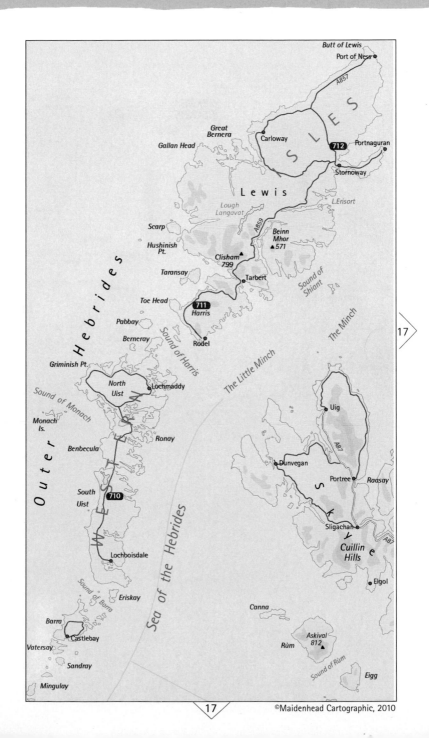

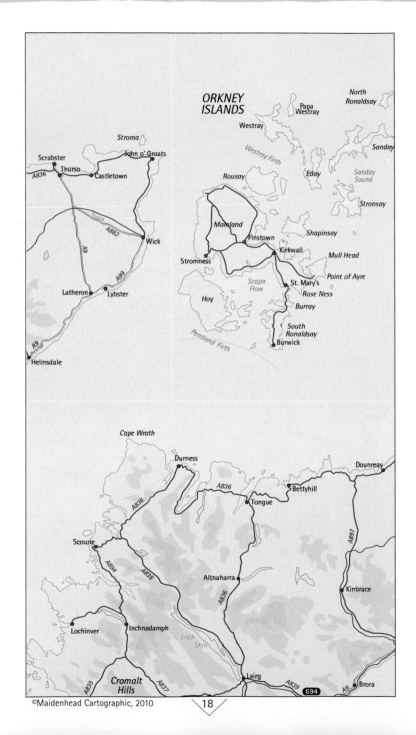

ORKNEY
ISLANDS

North
Ronaldsay

Papa
Westray

Westray

Stroma

Scrabster
Thurso
A836
Castletown
John o' Groats

Westray Firth

Sanday

Eday

Sanday
Sound

Rousay

Stronsay

A892

Mainland

Shapinsay

Finstown

Wick

Stromness

Kirkwall

Mull Head

A9

Scapa
Flow

St. Mary's

Point of Ayre

A99

Hoy

Rose Ness

Latheron
Lybster

Burray

A9

South
Ronaldsay
Burwick

Pentland Firth

Helmsdale

Cape Wrath

Durness

Dounreay

A838

A836

Bettyhill

Tongue

A897

Scourie

A894

A838

Altnaharra

A836

Kinbrace

Lochinver
Inchnadamph

Loch
Shin

A835

A837

Cromalt
Hills

Lairg

A839
694

A9
Brora

18

Map 22 45

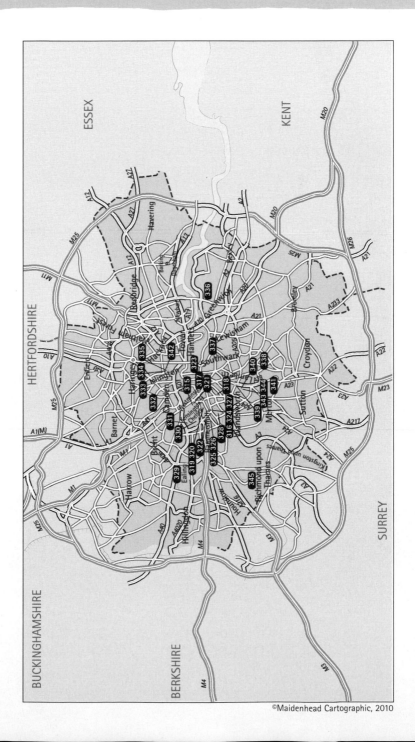

©Maidenhead Cartographic, 2010

England

Bath & N.E. Somerset

77 Great Pulteney Street

Elegant stone steps lead down past exotic ferns to a spacious garden flat in this broad street of grand Grade I-listed houses. Inside all is pale wood, modern art, bergère chairs and palms. Downstairs is a large, smart bedroom and bathroom with loads of books and its own door to a delightful small sunny garden. On fine mornings you breakfast here, or choose the gorgeous upstairs dining room: fine local bacon and sausages and fruit from the allotment. Ian is a keen cook so dinner will also be special, but there are lots of good places to eat – and shop – nearby. Henry may play the Northumbrian pipes for you if you ask nicely...

Price	£75–£100. Singles from £55.
Rooms	1 double.
Meals	Dinner £25. Packed lunch from £5
Closed	Rarely.
Directions	A4 into centre of Bath. Last house before Laura Place on south side of Great Pulteney St. Parking by arrangement; 7-minute walk from station.

Ian Critchley & Henry Ford
77 Great Pulteney Street,
Bath BA2 4DL
Tel   +44 (0)1225 466659
Email   critchford@77pulteneyst.co.uk
Web   www.77pulteneyst.co.uk

Entry   Map 3

Bath & N.E. Somerset

Bathwick Gardens

The period, hand-printed wallpaper is just one of the remarkable features of this elegant Grade I-listed house: Julian is an expert. The house, in one of Bath's finest Regency terraces, has been so beautifully restored that the BBC used its rooms for Jane Austen's *Persuasion*. Bedrooms are flooded with light and views are stunning; one stylish bathroom has marquina marble, cherrywood and ebony. Breakfast is taken in the family kitchen, or in the conservatory. For the adventurous, Mechthild serves up an Austrian alternative of cold meats and cheeses, fresh rye breads and homemade cakes. Herrlich! *Min. stay two nights weekends.*

Price	£95–£130. Singles £85.
Rooms	3 twins/doubles.
Meals	Pub/restaurant 300 yds.
Closed	Rarely.
Directions	A46 to Bath, then A4 for city centre. Left onto A36 over Cleveland Bridge, follow signs to Holburne Museum. Directly after museum, left. House on right.

3 nights for the price of 2 Mon-Thurs. Homemade Austrian cakes in room.

Mechthild Self von Hippel
Bathwick Gardens,
95 Sydney Place, Bath BA2 6NE
Tel   +44 (0)1225 469435
Email   visitus@bathwickgardens.co.uk
Web   www.bathwickgardens.co.uk

Entry 2   Map 3

14 Raby Place

A listed Regency house within walking distance of one of Europe's most beautiful cities. Muriel likes modern art and has filled the elegant rooms with stunning pictures and objects, antique chairs and lovely fabrics. Beautifully proportioned double bedrooms are graceful and spotless with laundered linen; one on the top (third) floor has fabulous views over the city to the Abbey, the small single has a piano in case you get the urge. Breakfast is organic, delicious, and eaten at a communal table in the dining room; chat to Muriel or bury your head in a paper. *Free parking permit for road outside.*

Price	£65–£70. Singles £35.
Rooms	5 doubles, family room, twin with separate shower, single with separate bath. Cot available.
Meals	Restaurant 8-minute walk
Closed	Never.
Directions	Bathwick Hill is turning off the A36 towards Bristol; look for signs to university. No. 14 or left as you go uphill, before left turn into Raby Mews.

Muriel Guy
14 Raby Place,
Bathwick
Bath BA2 4EH
Tel   +44 (0)1225 465120

The Bath Courtyard

You are a brisk ten-minute walk from the centre, but all is hushed in this Bath stone cottage, neatly tucked down a back lane. Shoes must be removed at the door; pad through to a dining room with a big mahogany table and interesting paintings, a large conservatory for breakfasts (homemade granola, fresh fruit salad, smoked salmon or a full English) and a long, rose-filled garden. Bedrooms are perfectly presented in pale yellows, with silk curtains, pocket-sprung mattresses and well-lit, ultra-modern bathrooms. Borrow bikes from Michael and his partner, and head for the tow path, or pedal into town for the shops and sights.

Price	£90–£110. Singles £75.
Rooms	2 doubles.
Meals	Pubs/restaurants 0.25 miles
Closed	Rarely.
Directions	M4 Bath signs. London Road, over river (Cleveland Bridge), past fire station. Right at next lights, left into Sydney Place. Vellore Lane 200 yds on right. Private parking is available.

Holistic massage from Tosh Jamir for stays of 3+ nights Mon–Thurs.

Michael Wilson
The Bath Courtyard,
38 Vellore Lane, Bath BA2 6JQ
Tel   +44 (0)1225 42474
Email michaelnwilson@gmail.com
Web   www.thebathcourtyard.co.uk

Bath & N.E. Somerset

Tolley Cottage

Breakfast on the patio on fine days and watch the barges pass the bottom of the gorgeous garden; raise your eyes to Bath Abbey on the skyline. This Victorian house is a ten-minute walk from city centre, spa and fine Georgian theatre. Sunny and bright, rooms are a comfortable mix of contemporary and classical; books, art and interesting glass pieces catch the eye. Bedrooms are small, calming and charming with elegant furnishings and long views; bathrooms sparkle. Judy does outstanding breakfasts; James, Master of Wine, can arrange tastings. Both are warm and relaxed, give attention to every detail and love sharing their home.

Ethical Collection: Food. See page 430.

Price	From £100. Singles from £90.
Rooms	2: 1 double, 1 twin.
Meals	Pubs/restaurants 10-minute walk.
Closed	Christmas.
Directions	Follow signs for American Museum & University up Bathwick Hill. Take 1st turn right to Sydney Buildings. House 200 yds on right. Free parking.

Half decanter of sherry in your room. 10% off room rate Mon–Thurs.

	Judy & James John
	Tolley Cottage,
	23 Sydney Buildings,
	Bath BA2 6BZ
Tel	+44 (0)1225 463365
Email	jj@judyj.plus.com
Web	www.tolleycottage.co.uk

Entry 5   Map 3

Bath & N.E. Somerset

55a North Road

Prepare yourself for a surprise. A short hop from Capability Brown-designed Prior Park, hidden down a narrow drive off one of Bath's less remarkable streets, is an architectural novelty — only the roof tiles give away the 1980s origins. Energetic owners Natalie and Guy offer you two completely private self-contained studios each with its own entrance, delightful small kitchen and elegant furniture. Find a charming mix of ultra-chic and traditional: oak floors, wool carpets, limestone tiles, old Irish bedheads and pure cotton linen. Natalie bring a very delicious breakfast to your room. *Ask about beauty & massage therapies.*

Price	From £110. Singles from £90.
Rooms	2 studios: 1 double, 1 twin, each with kitchen.
Meals	Pubs/restaurants within 1 mile.
Closed	Rarely.
Directions	Turn off North Road in Combe Down between (and on same side as) Farrs Lane and Hadley Road into wide driveway. Keep left. 55a is behind number 55.

10% off stays of 2 or more nights.

	Natalie & Guy Woods
	55a North Road,
	Combe Down,
	Bath BA2 5DF
Tel	+44 (0)1225 835593
Email	info@55anorthroad.co.uk
Web	www.55anorthroad.co.uk

Entry 6   Map 3

Bath & N.E. Somerset

Grey Lodge

In a conservation area, yet only a short drive from the centre of Bath, the views are breathtaking from wherever you stand. The steep valley rolls out ahead of you from most of the rooms, and from the garden comes a confusion and a profusion of scents and colours – a glory in its own right. The friendly and likeable Sticklands are conservationists as well as gardeners and have a Green Certificate to prove it. Breakfasts are a feast: bacon and eggs, cereals, home-grown jam, smoked fish and much more. Jane will tell you all about wonderful local gardens to visit.

Bath & N.E. Somerset

Manor Farm Barn

Duchy of Cornwall farmland stretches as far as the eye can see; the views from this converted barn – with light open-plan spaces – are splendid by any standards, but remarkable considering you are so close to Bath. There's much wildlife, too: sparrowhawks nest in the gable end, buzzards circle above the valley, and deer may gaze at you eating your breakfast. Giles, who pots, and Sue, who paints, are gentle and easy-going hosts; spruce guest rooms have built-in wardrobes, houseplants and excellent beds. For those in search of birdsong and country peace after a day on the hoof in Bath.

Price	£80-£90. Singles £50-£55.
Rooms	3: 2 twins/doubles, 1 family room.
Meals	Pubs/restaurants 2 miles.
Closed	Rarely.
Directions	From A36, 3 miles out of Bath on Warminster road, take uphill road by lights & viaduct. 1st left, 100 yds, signed Monkton Combe. After village, house 1st on left; 0.5 miles on.

 Free pick-up from local bus/train station. Taxi fare reimbursed up to £8.

 Use your Sawday's Gift Card here.

Jane & Anthony Stickland
Grey Lodge,
Summer Lane, Combe Down,
Bath BA2 7EU

Tel   +44 (0)1225 832069
Email greylodge@onebillnet.co.uk
Web   www.greylodge.co.uk

Entry 7   Map 3

Price	£60-£80. Singles £40-£50.
Rooms	2: 1 twin/double; 1 double with separate shower.
Meals	Pubs/restaurants 2.5 miles.
Closed	Christmas & New Year.
Directions	From Bath, A367 (Wells Rd). At Red Lion r'bout right (Bristol A4). Straight on, pass Culverhay School on left. After 100 yds left to Englishcombe. There, right after postbox to church, fork right, follow road; last on right.

10% off room rate Mon-Thurs. Free pick-up from local bus/train station.

Sue & Giles Barber
Manor Farm Barn,
Englishcombe,
Bath BA2 9DU

Tel   +44 (0)1225 424195
Email info@manorfarmbarn.com
Web   www.manorfarmbarn.com

Entry 8   Map 3

Bath & N.E. Somerset

Corston Fields Farm

In rolling agricultural land, a short hop from Bath, the Addicotts have given over swathes of their farm to indigenous wildlife. They have been 'green' for years, have won a Gold Award under the Duke of Cornwall's habitat scheme and use flax from their linseed crops to heat every room of this marvellous, stone-mullioned, listed farmhouse. Big sumptuous bedrooms (the best in the house) glow with ethnic and eclectic touches; bathrooms are delicious. Come for the setting, the farm trails, the romantic courtyard, the spectacular wildflower meadow – and delightful Gerald and Rosaline. *Minimum two nights at weekends.*

Price	From £94. Singles £60.
Rooms	4: 1 double; 1 double, 1 twin sharing bath (2nd room let to same party only). Annexe: 1 double.
Meals	Pub 300 yds.
Closed	Christmas & New Year.
Directions	From A4 west of Bath, A39 through Corston. 1 mile on, take right just before Wheatsheaf Pub (on right), Signed 200 yds along lane on right.

Gerald & Rosaline Addicott
Corston Fields Farm,
Corston,
Bath BA2 9EZ
Tel   +44 (0)1225 873305
Email   corston.fields@btinternet.com
Web   www.corstonfields.com

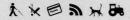

Entry 9   Map 3

Bath & N.E. Somerset

Melon Cottage Vineyard

Interesting, friendly hosts who are entirely natural and unbusinesslike make this place special; it's excellent value, too. The ancient Mendip-style 'long cottage' with mullioned windows and beams made of ships' timbers, fronted by a small vineyard, is temptingly close to Babington House, the treasures of Bath and Wells, the gardens and concerts at Stourhead, and Gregorian chant in Downside Abbey. Rooms are old-fashioned and cosy, the jams are homemade and the hosts the kindest you may meet. No sitting room, but tea in the walled garden is rich compensation. *Children over five welcome. Minimum two nights.*

Price	£60–£70. Singles £30.
Rooms	1 double/family.
Meals	Pubs 2 miles.
Closed	Rarely.
Directions	From Bath A367, Wells road, through Radstock. After 3 miles, at large r'bout, B3139 for Trowbridge. After 1.1 miles, and Charlton sign, right up 2nd driveway on right. Pink house at top, visible from road.

Virginia & Hugh Pountney
Melon Cottage Vineyard,
Charlton, Radstock,
Bath BA3 5TN
Tel   +44 (0)1761 435090
Email   meloncottage@hotmail.co.uk
Web   www.meloncottage.co.uk

Entry 10   Map 3

Bath & N.E. Somerset

Hollytree Cottage

Meandering lanes lead to this 16th-century cottage, with roses round the door, a grandfather clock in the hall and an air of genteel tranquillity. The cottage charm has been updated with Regency mahogany and sumptuous sofas. The bedrooms have views over undulating countryside; pretty bathrooms have oils and lotions. On sunny days breakfast is in the lovely garden room looking onto a colourful ornamental patio, sloping lawns, a pond, flowering shrubs and trees. A place to come for absolute peace, birdsong and walks; the joys of elegant Bath are 20 minutes away and Julia knows the area well; let her help plan your trips.

Price	£80–£90. Singles £45–£50.
Rooms	3: 1 double, 1 twin, 1 four-poster.
Meals	Pub/restaurant 0.5 miles.
Closed	Rarely.
Directions	From Bath, A36 to Wolverton. Just past Red Lion, turn for Laverton. 1 mile to x-roads; towards Faukland; downhill for 80 yds. On left, just above farm entrance on right.

10% off room rate Mon–Thurs.

Julia Naismith
Hollytree Cottage,
Laverton,
Bath BA2 7QZ
Tel   +44 (0)1373 830786
Email   jnaismith@toucansurf.com
Web   www.hollytreecottagebath.co.uk

Entry 11   Map 3

Berkshire

Whitehouse Farm Cottage

Once you get past the housing estates of Bracknell, this is a fabulous find. A 17th-century farmhouse with a delightful garden, and two charmingly converted buildings with their own entrances. Garden Cottage has a beamed drawing room downstairs and a gallery bedroom with creamy walls and a cast-iron bed. The Forge has the blacksmith's fireplace and lovely views onto the courtyard garden and its pebble mosaics. The single is in the house with its own comfortable sitting room. Locally sourced breakfasts with fresh bread are served in the house by friendly Keir and Louise, who are film prop makers.

Price	£75–£95. Singles £65–£85.
Rooms	3: 1 single & sitting room. The Forge: 1 double. Garden Cottage: 1 double & sitting room.
Meals	Pubs/restaurants within 1 mile.
Closed	Christmas & occasionally.
Directions	From A329, B3408 to Binfield. At 2nd traffic lights left into St Marks Rd. Then 2nd left Foxley Ln, 1st left Murrell Hill Ln. House 1st on right. Do not use postcode for satnav.

Keir Lusby
Whitehouse Farm Cottage,
Murrell Hill Lane, Binfield,
Bracknell RG42 4BY
Tel   +44 (0)1344 423688
Mobile   +44 (0)7711 948889
Email   garden.cottages@ntlworld.com

Entry 12   Map 4

Berkshire

Wilton House

With its handsome Queen Anne frontage, "the most ambitious house in Hungerford" (Pevsner) conceals medieval origins – and the roofline is pure Dickens. A classic townhouse in a charming market town, its interior is a panelled, soft-painted delight. Light floods through sash windows onto paintings and prints, books, antiques and wide, inviting sofas; bedrooms are understatedly elegant and relaxing; bathrooms are a good size. So is your (almost all local or organic) breakfast in the 18th-century dining room: the Welfares, and their labradors, look after you perfectly. *Children over eight welcome.*

Brighton & Hove

Lansdowne Guest House

Fun, refreshing and bang in the middle of Pimlico-by-Sea. This is Hove: grand white Regency villas and the promenade a hop away. In this 1920s mansion built for a lord's mistress, the Bundys occupy the first floor. Enter a big friendly living room with a fire for winter nights, a sprinkling of modern art and a superb spread for the morning: Asian or English. Your hosts are attentive, interesting, well-travelled and love meeting their guests. Up under the roof are low-ceilinged, stylish bedrooms and a landing with a comfortable sofa; bathrooms, cleverly compact, have lotions and bubbles. Brighton lies at your feet.

Price	From £78. Singles from £62.
Rooms	2: 1 double, 1 twin/double.
Meals	Packed lunch £5. Pub 100 yds.
Closed	Christmas.
Directions	M4 exit 14; A338 to A4; right for Marlborough, turning at Bear Hotel onto Salisbury road (A338). Over canal bridge into High St. House 200 yds past Town Hall on right.

Price	£75-£85. Singles from £65.
Rooms	2: 1 double, 1 twin/double.
Meals	Dinner from £20. Packed lunch from £7.50. Picnic hampers from £10.
Closed	Christmas & occasionally.
Directions	A23 to seafront, then right towards Hove. 2nd right after Brunswick Square into Holland Rd; right at 2nd lights. House 2nd left behind red brick wall. Street parking with visitor's voucher.

 10% off stays of 3 or more nights Mon-Thurs.

	Deborah & Jonathan Welfare
	Wilton House,
	33 High Street,
	Hungerford RG17 0NF
Tel	+44 (0)1488 684228
Email	welfares@hotmail.com
Web	www.wiltonhouse-hungerford.co.uk

	Diana Bundy
	Lansdowne Guest House,
	21 Lansdowne Road,
	Hove BN3 1FE
Tel	+44 (0)1273 773700
Email	lansdowneguesthouse@hotmail.co.uk
Web	www.lansdowneguesthouse.synthasite.com

✕ � 🔊 🐕 ⚲

🍴 💳 � 🔊

Entry 13   Map 3

Entry 14   Map 4

Brighton & Hove

4-5 Palmeira Square

Drift along Brighton seafront, and emerge into the Regency splendour of Palmeira Square. Susie with the twinkling eyes welcomes you into a fun, bohemian, ground-floor flat in Hove. Rooms are flooded with light, ceilings are high, furnishings have pizzazz (kilims on bamboo floors, funky chandeliers). Your bedroom is deep lilac and lovely, your bathroom (big shower, stylish toiletries) is Susie's. She has lived in Portugal, Brazil, Bordeaux, works from home and delivers a delicious breakfast to your door. Or, at a pretty seat in the window bay; turn your head and you'll catch the sea. *Minimum stay two nights.*

Price	£80-£90.
Rooms	1 double with shared bath.
Meals	Continental breakfast. Pub/restaurant 500 yds.
Closed	Rarely.
Directions	Seafront towards Hove. Right onto Adelaide Crescent (white Regency buildings) then immediate right, following road up into Palmeira Square. No 5 is just after Crescent becomes Square.

10% off room rate Mon-Thurs. Bottle of wine in room for returning guests.

Susie de Castilho
4-5 Palmeira Square,
Flat 1,
Hove BN3 2JA
Tel +44 (0)1273 719087
Email stay@2staybrighton.co.uk
Web www.2staybrighton.co.uk

Bristol

9 Princes Buildings

A super city base with jolly comfortable beds, charming owners and, without a doubt, the best views in Clifton. You are a short hop from the elegant Suspension Bridge, good restaurants, shops and pubs of the village and a ferry to whisk you to town or the station; yet all is quiet, green and leafy. Walk in to a big square hall, a drawing room with a peaceful feel and a veranda for gazing in fine weather. Your bedroom is fresh, light and traditional, one downstairs overlooks the garden and has a quirky 70s bathroom. Best of all, Simon and Joanna are easy-going and give you a breakfast cooked to order with homemade jams.

Price	From £80. Singles £50.
Rooms	4: 2 doubles, 1 twin/double; 1 twin/double with separate bath.
Meals	Pub/restaurant 100 yds.
Closed	Never.
Directions	In Bristol signs to Clifton and Clifton Suspension Bridge, just before bridge left down Sion Hill, past Avon Gorge hotel on right. House next to hotel with double red front doors.

Simon & Joanna Fuller
9 Princes Buildings,
Clifton,
Bristol BS8 4LB
Tel +44 (0)117 973 4615
Email info@9pb.co.uk
Web www.9pb.co.uk

Buckinghamshire

Field Cottage

Sue, relaxed and friendly, is the consummate professional: the fitted bedrooms are immaculate, chintzy and filled with treats, and the bathrooms pristine. She has also created a horticultural haven amid open fields (old-fashioned roses, a willow tunnel, colourful clematis). The peachy guest sitting room is neat and comfortable – doors swing open onto the garden and a patio suntrap – and you tuck into breakfast in the conservatory surrounded by peaceful pastoral views. It's walking distance across fields to the pub and to the Ridgeway National Trail, Britain's oldest road. *Children over 12 welcome.*

Buckinghamshire

Brook Hall

Delicious smells emanate from this handsome red-brick Queen Anne house – Stephen (who ran Raymond Blanc's cookery school at Le Manoir) and Joanna offer cookery courses here. Bedrooms have pretty bed covers, books and magazines; one bathroom has a huge period bath. Downstairs find a fine drawing room, polished wooden floors with rugs, interesting antique kitchen pieces and cookbooks galore. Dinner with other guests in the elegant dining room is a highlight— perhaps braised lemon sole with crab and Asian greens, or pigeon with celeriac and madeira. A scrumptious place for all who appreciate good local food and a friendly feel.

Price	£75. Singles £50.
Rooms	3: 1 double; 1 twin with separate shower; 1 single with separate bath/shower.
Meals	Pub 0.5 miles.
Closed	Christmas & New Year.
Directions	South on A413 from Wendover. Pass Jet station, left to Kings Ash, 2 miles on, left at x-roads, past pub; 0.5 miles on, sharp left onto bridlepath; 2nd gate along.

Price	£90-£110. Singles £60-£75.
Rooms	3: 1 twin/double; 1 double, 1 twin/double with shared bath.
Meals	Continental breakfast included, full English £5. Dinner, 3 courses, £28. Pub/restaurant across the road.
Closed	Christmas: two weeks mid-July & one week Easter.
Directions	On A413 between Buckingham (6 miles) and Aylesbury (12 miles), just off Market Square in Winslow, opposite car park to The Bell Hotel.
	10% off stays of 2 or more nights. 10% off one-day cookery courses.

Mike & Sue Jepson
Field Cottage,
St Leonards,
Tring HP23 6NS

Tel	+44 (0)1494 837602
Email	michael.jepson@lineone.net
Web	www.fieldcottagebandb.co.uk

Joanna Bulmer
Brook Hall,
9 Sheep Street, Winslow,
Buckingham MK18 3HL

Tel	+44 (0)1296 712111
Email	info@brookhall.net
Web	www.brookhall.net

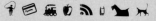

Buckinghamshire

South Lodge

Handy for the M1, this interestingly developed single-storey building appears pleasant enough. But clever Julia has introduced modern English art, dramatic lighting and contemporary furniture – a look to thrill minimalists. A dark slate corridor lit by fluorescent multicoloured ceiling sticks leads to big airy bedrooms with memory mattresses and hi-spec bathrooms; all generous, all different. Velux blinds are solar-powered, heating is underfoot, rainwater is harvested for loos. You have your own patio overlooking a colourful garden, you can walk to the Stables Theatre, and Woburn Abbey is nearby. Great for gatherings.

Price	£124–£136. Singles from £62.
Rooms	3: 2 doubles, 1 suite.
Meals	Supper, 2 courses, £18. Pubs/restaurants within 0.5 miles.
Closed	Occasionally.
Directions	Directions on website.

10% off stays of 2 or more nights.

Julia Cox
South Lodge,
33 Cross End, Wavendon,
Milton Keynes MK17 8AQ
Tel   +44 (0)1908 582946
Email   info@culturevultures.co.uk
Web   www.culturevultures.co.uk

Entry 19   Map 9

Cambridgeshire

The Old Hall

You'll feel spoilt in this stunning house, transformed phoenix-like by the charming Morbeys, who look after guests in style. Arrive to tea and homemade cake in the beamed sitting room with paintings, photographs, fresh flowers, soft places to unwind and a dreamy view of the cathedral. Sleep well in smart, large bedrooms (cleverly planted trees disguise any road noise) and wake to Ely sausages, hot waffles with maple syrup, or smoked salmon and scrambled eggs on ciabatta toast. Cambridge is a short train ride away but there is history galore here, a formal garden and 15 acres of parkland with lakeside walks. Excellent value.

Price	From £85. Singles from £85.
Rooms	3 doubles.
Meals	Pub/restaurant 1 mile.
Closed	Christmas & New Year.
Directions	From Ely A142 towards Newmarket, under railway bridge. After 1 mile entrance gates on left, signed. Do not use satnav.

Anthony & Alison Morbey
The Old Hall,
Stuntney,
Ely CB7 5TR
Tel   +44 (0)1353 663275
Email   stay@theoldhallely.co.uk
Web   www.theoldhallely.co.uk

Entry 20   Map 9

Cambridgeshire

Cambridge University

Buses, bicycles and punting on the Cam: huge fun when you're in the heart of it all. Enter the Great Gate Tower of Christ's College – as did John Milton in 1625 – to be wooed by tranquil, beautiful quadrangle gardens, breakfasts beneath portraits of hallowed masters, and a serene chapel. At smaller Sidney Sussex –1598-old with additions – you can play tennis in gorgeous gardens, picnic on perfect lawns and start the day with rare-breed sausages. More charm, and a candlelit chapel, at St Catherine's on King's Parade. Bedrooms and lounges are functional; well-informed porters are your first port of call. *12 colleges in total.*

Price	Doubles £80–£90. Twins £75–£120. Singles £41–£77.
Rooms	Sidney Sussex: 267 twins & singles. St Catherine's: 347 twins & singles. Christ's College: 150 singles, twins & doubles. Some share showers.
Meals	Breakfast included. Christ's College: no breakfast Sundays. St Catherine's: supper £6.
Closed	Mid-Jan to mid-March; May/June; Oct/Nov; Christmas. A few rooms available throughout year.
Directions	Website booking. Limited parking at a few colleges.

University Rooms
Cambridge University,
Cambridge
Web   www.cambridgerooms.co.uk

Entry 21   Map 9

Cambridgeshire

Springfield House

The former school house hugs the bend of a river, its French windows opening to delightful rambling gardens with scented roses, a yew garden, and a mulberry tree providing fruit for breakfast. Find interesting items from American history, maps and paintings; the conservatory, draped with a huge mimosa, is an exceptional spot for summer breakfasts. Bedrooms are large and comfortable, with interesting books, fresh flowers and garden or river views; one is reached by steep stairs. This is an old-fashionedly elegant home and Judith is an ever-thoughtful hostess. Good value and peaceful, yet close to Cambridge.

Price	£65–£70. Singles £45–£50.
Rooms	3: 2 doubles; 1 double with separate bath.
Meals	Pubs 150 yds.
Closed	Rarely.
Directions	A1307 from Cambridge, left into High St. 1st right after The Crown (on left) into Horn Lane. House on right next to chapel, before ford. Or bus no. 13 and 13A from Cambridge.

Judith Rossiter
Springfield House,
14–16 Horn Lane, Linton CB21 4HT
Tel   +44 (0)1223 891383
Email   fredrossiter@tiscali.co.uk
Web   www.springfieldhouse.org

Entry 22   Map 9

Cambridgeshire

Westoe Farm

Immerse yourself in miles of waving wheat, woodlands and sugar beet. The house is a flint-knapped oasis of deep comfort: you will find traditionally comfortable bedrooms and a large and attractive hall with a huge sitting-room that is yours; you may not want to go out if the stove is seductive and the weather not so. Generous Tim and Henrietta are a capable pair and you are well looked after: meats are local, the eggs are theirs, jams and honey are homemade. There's a fine, rose-filled garden and woods and fields; stroll around to your heart's content before a delicious dinner of home-grown vegetables and local game in season.

Price	£100. Singles £65.
Rooms	2 twins/doubles.
Meals	Dinner, 2 courses, £25. BYO. Pub/restaurant 1 mile.
Closed	Christmas & New Year.
Directions	A1307 to Linton, right at Bartlow crossroads through Bartlow, then 1 mile from village, house signed, 3rd farm track on right.

10% off stays of 2 or more nights Mon–Thurs.

Henrietta Breitmeyer
Westoe Farm,
Bartlow CB21 4PR
Tel +44 (0)1223 892731
Email enquire@bartlow.u-net.com
Web www.westoefarm.co.uk

Entry 23   Map 9

Cambridgeshire

The Old Chapel

Tardis-like, this 1823 converted chapel opens out to a series of lovely light rooms and a gorgeous garden with cows peeping over the fence. You have a large drawing room with a wood-burner, a dining room with a grand piano, a verdant conservatory, a fabulous library, even a sauna. Bedrooms are beautifully dressed with cream bedspreads, pale carpets, fine antiques and heaps of cushions; bathrooms have gleaming tiles and fresh flowers. Alex and Ian are both keen cooks and love entertaining; the vast kitchen, with arched chapel windows, has a huge table and food is sourced as locally as possible. Good fun.

Ethical Collection: Environment; Food.
See page 430.

Price	£75. Singles £50.
Rooms	2: 1 double; 1 single with separate bath.
Meals	Dinner £25. Pubs within walking distance. Restaurants 3 miles.
Closed	Rarely.
Directions	A1307 dir. Haverhill. Thro' Linton; after dual carriageway, left slip road into village. Left at sign of horse on green towards West Wickham. House 200 yds on left opposite thatched cottage.

Bucks Fizz with breakfast.

Alexandra & Ian Rose
The Old Chapel,
West Wickham Road, Horseheath,
Cambridge CB21 4QA
Tel +44 (0)1223 894027
Email alexchapel@btinternet.com
Web www.theoldchapelbandb.co.uk

Entry 24   Map 9

Cheshire

Goss Moor

Crunch up the gravelled drive to the big white house, a beautifully run family home. Bedrooms are light, bright and decorated in creams and blues; bathrooms are spotless and warm. Be cosseted by fluffy bathrobes, biscuits, decanters of sherry – all is comfortable and inviting. After a day's exploring the Wirral and Liverpool, historic Chester and the wilds of north Wales – a short drive all – return to a kind welcome from Sarah. Expect a generous and delicious breakfast by the sunny bay window, and, in the summer, feel free to enjoy the garden, its tennis court and pool.

Price	£80-£85. Singles £50-£55.
Rooms	2: 1 twin/double; 1 double with separate bath.
Meals	Occasional dinner with wine, £25. Pub/restaurant 2 miles.
Closed	Rarely.
Directions	From Chester, A540 north. After about 7 miles turn right to Willaston. Right at T-junc., then first left into Mill Lane. House is 9th on left.

Bottle of wine in your room.

Chris & Sarah White
Goss Moor,
Mill Lane, Willaston,
Neston CH64 1RG
Tel   +44 (0)1513 274000
Email   sarahcmwhite@aol.com
Web   www.gossmoor.co.uk

Entry 25   Map 7

Cheshire

The Mount

Britain at its best: rare trees planted in 1860, bountiful flowers, a pond, a vegetable garden and Rachel – delightful, warm and friendly. The Victorian house, built for a Chester corn merchant and furnished in a traditional style, has garden views from every light-filled window. You get an airy drawing room, a high-ceilinged dining room and comfortable, spacious, country-house bedrooms with attractive paintings and soft furnishings. A haven for garden buffs and walkers – and there's a tennis court too. Chester, North Wales and two airports are conveniently close. *Arrivals after 5pm.*

Price	£60. Singles £40.
Rooms	3: 2 doubles, 1 twin.
Meals	Pub/restaurant 5-minute walk.
Closed	Christmas & New Year.
Directions	A55 signed North Wales. A5104 Broughton; 2nd r'bout A5104 left Penyffordd. Thro' Broughton, cross A55, 2nd left Kinnerton Lane, signed Higher Kinnerton, 0.5 miles then left Lesters Lane. House on left.

Jonathan & Rachel Major
The Mount,
Higher Kinnerton,
Chester CH4 9BQ
Tel   +44 (0)1244 660275
Email   themount@higherkinnerton.com
Web   www.bandbchester.com

Entry 26   Map 7

Cheshire

Cotton Farm

Only a four-mile hop from Roman Chester and its 900-year-old cathedral is this sprawling, red-brick farmhouse. Elegant chickens peck in hedges, ponies graze, lambs frisk and cats doze. The farm, run by conservationists Nigel and Clare, is under the Countryside Stewardship Scheme – there are wildflower meadows, summer swallows and 250 acres to roam. Bedrooms are large, stylish farmhouse with lovely fabrics and touches of luxury (bath towels are huge), but best of all is the relaxed family atmosphere. Breakfasts are delicious and beautifully presented. *Stabling available. Children over ten welcome.*

Price	£75. Singles £52.
Rooms	3: 2 doubles, 1 twin.
Meals	Pub 1.5 miles.
Closed	Rarely.
Directions	A51 Chester-Nantwich. 1.5 miles from outskirts, after golf course on left, right, down Cotton Lane, signed Cotton Edmunds; 1.5 miles, left on sharp right-hand bend; 2nd drive on right.

Clare & Nigel Hill
Cotton Farm,
Cotton Edmunds,
Chester CH3 7PG
Tel   +44 (0)1244 336616
Email   echill@btinternet.com
Web   www.cottonfarm.co.uk

Entry 27   Map 7

Cheshire

Greenlooms Cottage

This pretty cottage was where the estate's chief hedger and ditcher lived. The smallholding has gone but the walnuts, quinces and garden pump remain – and the views still reach to the Peckforton Hills. Now it is a stylishly simple and fun place to stay, thanks to Deborah – traveller, ex-potter, fabulous cook – and Peter, furniture-maker and restorer. Follow your nose to the Aga-cosy kitchen where the best black pudding and bacon are waiting to fuel you for a day on the Cheshire cycle route. Return to two sweet bedrooms, one up one down: crisp white duvets, Floris soaps in simple walk-in showers, ethnic touches.

Price	£70. Singles from £47.
Rooms	2: 1 double, 1 twin.
Meals	Dinner, with wine, £25. Pub 3 miles.
Closed	Never.
Directions	A41 Whitchurch; south from Chester. After petrol station, 2nd left at antiques shop. On for 1.5 miles thro' village, right into Martins Lane; 1 mile on right.

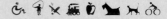 10% off stays of 2 or more nights.

Deborah Newman
Greenlooms Cottage,
Martins Lane,
Hargrave, Chester CH3 7RX
Tel   +44 (0)1829 781475
Email   dnewman@greenlooms.com
Web   www.greenlooms.com

Entry 28   Map 7

Cheshire

Harrop Fold Farm

Artists, foodies and walkers adore this antique-filled farmhouse with soul-lifting views. On the edge of the Peak District, the oldest building on the farm dates from 1694 (Bonnie Prince Charlie visited here!). The B&B part has a warm, peaceful breakfast room, a stone-flagged sitting room, a spectacular studio. Fresh flowers, antique beds, fine fabrics, hot water bottles with chic covers, bathrooms with fluffy robes: you get the best. Gregarious Sue and daughter Leah hold art and cookery courses so the food too is outstanding. Bedrooms have stupendous views – and flat-screen TV and DVD just in case they pall.

Ethical Collection: Food; Community. See page 430.

Price	£90. Singles £55.
Rooms	2 doubles.
Meals	Cookery demonstration & dinner £50. Dinner £30. Supper £15. Packed lunch available. Pub 0.25 miles.
Closed	Never.
Directions	B470 Macclesfield to Whaley Bridge. After 4 miles Highwayman pub; 0.25 miles further down track (rutted at top); on left, immed. before sharp right bend.

Local food/produce in your room.

Sue Stevenson
Harrop Fold Farm,
Rainow, Macclesfield SK10 5UU

Tel	+44 (0)1625 560085
Email	stay@harropfoldfarm.co.uk
Web	www.harropfoldfarm.co.uk

Cheshire

Lower Key Green Farm

Aga-cooked breakfasts with home-laid eggs and locally sourced food: just the thing to set you up for a day's walking round this organic farm or in the Peak District. This is an unusual, quirky farmhouse filled with reclaimed things, good art (both David and Janet's own work too), flagged floors, leather bucket chairs round a wood-burning stove and grand views. The bedroom has a cottagey simplicity; a Victorian washstand and a slipper bath add delight, as do homemade biscuits and sloe gin. The garden is filled with interest; take a book and a cuppa and sit peacefully here, or find a good pub nearby.

Price	£70. Singles £50.
Rooms	1 twin/double.
Meals	Pub 5-minute drive.
Closed	Rarely.
Directions	From A54, A523 towards Leek. Thro' Bosley village, turn right; after Queen's Arms pub, onto Tunstall Rd; 2nd farm on left after 0.5 miles.

Janet Heath
Lower Key Green Farm,
Bosley, Macclesfield SK11 0PB

Tel	+44 (0)1260 223278
Email	lowerkeygreen@hotmail.com
Web	www.lowerkeygreen.co.uk

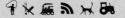

Cornwall

The Old Vicarage

The first sight of quirky chimneys – the spires of former owner Reverend Hawker's parish churches – sets the scene for a huge house packed with interest and steeped in Victoriana. Jill and Richard, both delightful, know the local history – and the cliff-top walks, which are glorious. Rooms are casually grand, dotted with *objets* – brass gramophone, magic lantern, eccentric Hawker memorabilia. Browse books in the study, play the grand piano, sip brandy over billiards. Bedrooms are country-house pretty, with most bathrooms refurbished, lawns well tended and views to the sea. Blissfully, mobiles don't work.

Price	£80. Singles £40.
Rooms	3: 1 double, 1 twin, 1 single.
Meals	Pub/tea rooms 5-10-minute walk.
Closed	December/January.
Directions	From A39 at Morwenstow, follow signs towards church. Small turning on right, just before church, marked 'public footpath'. Drive down to house.

Jill & Richard Wellby
The Old Vicarage,
Morwenstow EX23 9SR
Tel +44 (0)1288 331369
Web www.rshawker.co.uk

Entry 31   Map 1

Cornwall

The Old Parsonage

A spellbinding coastline, secret coves, spectacular walks. All this and a supremely comfortable Georgian rectory – with a drying room for wet togs to return to. Morag and Margaret have transformed the interior. Superb pitch pine floors and original woodwork add warmth and a fresh glow, the big engaging bedrooms (including one on the ground floor) have a quirky, upbeat mix of furniture and furnishings, and the bathrooms are pampering. In front of the house the land slopes away to the Atlantic, just a five-minute walk across a SSSI. There are plans afoot for the garden, which already has some pleasant corners.

Ethical Collection: Environment; Food
See page 430.

Price	From £80. Singles from £60.
Rooms	5 twins/doubles.
Meals	Packed lunch £5.95. Pub/restaurant 600 yds.
Closed	November-January.
Directions	In Boscastle head towards Tintagel on B3263. 500 yds after garage on left turn right into Green Lane. After bend, house 3rd on right.

Bottle of champagne for bookings of 2 nights or more.

Use your Sawday's Gift Card here.

Morag Reeve & Margaret Pickering
The Old Parsonage,
Forrabury, Boscastle PL35 0DJ
Tel +44 (0)1840 250339
Email morag@old-parsonage.com
Web www.old-parsonage.com

Entry 32   Map 1

Cornwall

Upton Farm

A restored farmhouse set back from the rugged coastline with unrivalled views, from Tintagel to Port Isaac and beyond... the sunsets are sublime. There's a games room and safe storage for surfers, slate slabs in the hall, gentle colours throughout, and bedrooms smart and traditional. From the depths of the sea-green sofa in your drawing room, breathe in those AONB views. Such seclusion, yet ten minutes across fields is the coastal path and, nearby, serious surfing, a great pub, a restaurant and more. Kick-start your day with Ricardo's signature muesli. *Minimum stay two nights. Children over eight welcome.*

Price	From £90.
Rooms	3: 2 doubles, 1 twin.
Meals	Pub/restaurant 1 mile.
Closed	Rarely.
Directions	South thro' Delabole, right into Treligga Downs Rd; right at T-junc. towards Trebarwith; Farm on right after 1 mile.

Elizabeth & Ricardo Dorich
Upton Farm,
Trebarwith PL33 9DG

Tel	+44 (0)1840 770225
Email	ricardo.dorich@homecall.co.uk
Web	www.upton-farm.co.uk

Entry 33   Map 1

Cornwall

Caradoc of Tregardock

A 200-acre farm with hens, sheep and wheeling gulls; lush fields roll down to a tidal beach. Children love it, artists come to paint, you can take the whole place and cook for yourself (the kitchen is super) or dig into something delicious, perhaps fresh lobster, roast lamb, lemon meringue pie. Janet lives in the farmhouse, you get a converted listed barn. Expect a warm country feel, the odd beam, seascapes on the wall, comfy bedrooms. The vast first-floor sitting room is open to the rafters, overlooks the Atlantic and has views of glorious sunsets. Total peace is guaranteed, the night sky can be amazing. *Cream teas.*

Price	£90-£130. Singles £45-£65. Whole house self-catering £475-£2,000 per week.
Rooms	4 twins/doubles.
Meals	Dinner, with wine, £35. Private chef available. Pub/restaurant 2 miles.
Closed	Never.
Directions	Take turn to Treligga off B3314; 2nd farm road, signed.

Janet Cant
Caradoc of Tregardock,
Treligga, Delabole PL33 9ED

Tel	+44 (0)1840 213300
Email	info@tregardock.com
Web	www.tregardock.com

Entry 34   Map 1

Cornwall

Tremoren

Views stretch sleepily over the Cornish countryside. You might feel inclined to do nothing more than wander the lovely garden or snooze by the pool, but the surfing beaches, the Camel Trail and the Eden Project are so close. The stone and slate former farmhouse has been smartly updated and your airy ground-floor bedroom comes with soft colours, pretty china, crisp linen, a comfortable bathroom. And its own cosy sitting room, full of books and interesting maps, leading to a flower-filled terrace – perfect for a pre-dinner drink. Lanie, bubbly and engaging, runs her own catering company; your dinner will be delicious!

Price	From £80.
Rooms	1 double & sitting room.
Meals	Dinner, 4 courses, £25. Inn 0.5 miles.
Closed	Rarely.
Directions	A39 to St Kew Highway through village; left at Red Lion. Down lane, 1st left round sharp right-hand bend. 2nd drive on right; signed.

Philip & Lanie Calvert
Tremoren,
St Kew,
Bodmin PL30 3HA
Tel +44 (0)1208 841790
Email la.calvert@btopenworld.com

Entry 35   Map 1

Cornwall

Higher Lank Farm

Families rejoice: you can only come if you have a child under five! Celtic crosses in the garden and original panelling hint at the house's 500-year history; bedrooms, newly decorated, have pocket sprung mattresses and large TVs. Nursery teas begin at 5pm, grown-up suppers are later and energetic Lucy will cheerfully babysit while the rest of you slink off to the pub. Farm-themed playgrounds are covered in safety matting and grass, there are piglets and chicks, a pony to ride, eggs to collect, a nursery rhyme trail, a sand barn for little ones and cream teas in the garden. Oh, and real nappies are provided!

Price	From £95. Singles by arrangement.
Rooms	3 family rooms.
Meals	Supper £20. Nursery tea £6.50. Pub 1.5 miles.
Closed	November-Easter.
Directions	A30 past Launceston. Right to St Brevard 4 miles. Across moor thro' Bradford, then first right. Humpback bridge and crossroads, turn left (no sign & not straight on to St Brevard). Follow road to bottom of hill; house signed opposite.

Lucy Finnemore
Higher Lank Farm,
St Breward, Bodmin PL30 4NB
Tel +44 (0)1208 850716
Email lucyfin@higherlankfarm.co.uk
Web www.higherlankfarm.co.uk

Entry 36   Map 1

Cornwall

Lavethan

A glorious house in the most glorious of settings: views sail down to the valley. It rambles on many levels and is part 15th-century: walls are stone, floors are flagged, stairs are oak. The sunny bedroom in the house is best, with its panelled walls and smart bathroom; bedrooms across the courtyard are very private with their own entrances and have pretty quilted bedspreads. Catherine, a warm hostess, has decorated in country style; the guest sitting room is hugely welcoming with books, flowers and piano. All this and acres of ancient woods, Celtic crosses and a heated pool in the old walled garden. *Children over ten welcome.*

Price	£90. Singles £50.
Rooms	3: 2 twins/doubles, 1 double.
Meals	Pub 0.25 miles.
Closed	Rarely.
Directions	From A30, turn for Blisland. There, past church on left & pub on right. Take lane at bottom left of village green. 0.25 miles on, drive on left (granite pillars & cattle grid).

Christopher & Catherine Hartley
Lavethan,
Blisland, Bodmin PL30 4QG
Tel   +44 (0)1208 850487
Email   chrishartley@btconnect.com
Web   www.lavethan.com

Entry 37   Map 1

Cornwall

Cabilla Manor

There's a treasure round every corner and an opera house in one of the barns. Instant seduction as you enter the old manor house out on the moor, brimful of interest and colour. Rich exotic rugs and cushions, artefacts from around the world, Louella's sumptuous hand-stencilled quilts, huge beds, coir carpets, garden flowers. There's a dining room crammed floor to ceiling with books, many of them Robin's (a writer and explorer) and a lofty conservatory for meals overlooking a semi-wild garden – with tennis and elegant lawns. The views are heavenly, the hosts wonderful and the final mile thrillingly wild.

Price	£80. Singles £40.
Rooms	4: 1 double; 1 double with separate bath; 1 double, 1 twin, sharing bath (let to same party only).
Meals	Dinner, 3 courses, £30. Pub 4 miles. Restaurant 8-10 miles.
Closed	Christmas.
Directions	6 miles after Jamaica Inn on A30, left for Cardinham. Through Millpool & straight on, ignoring further signs to Cardinham. After 2.5 miles, left to Manor 0.75 miles; on right down drive.

Robin & Louella Hanbury-Tenison
Cabilla Manor,
Mount, Bodmin PL30 4DW
Tel   +44 (0)1208 821224
Email   louella@cabilla.co.uk
Web   www.cabilla.co.uk

Entry 38   Map 1

Cornwall

Menkee

From this handsome Georgian farmhouse there are long views towards the sea; you're 20 minutes away from the coastal path and wild surf but you may not want to budge. Gage and Liz are deliciously unstuffy and look after you well: newspapers and a weather forecast appear with a scrumptious breakfast, your gorgeously comfortable bed is turned down in the evening and walkers can be dropped off and collected. The elegant house is filled with beautiful things, gleaming furniture, fresh flowers, roaring fires and pretty fabrics — all you have to do is slacken your pace and wind down. *Minimum stay two nights in high season.*

Ethical Collection: Food. See page 430.

Cornwall

Polrode Mill Cottage

A lovely, beamy, 17th-century cottage in a birdsung valley. Inside, flagged floors, Chesterfields, a wood-burner and a light, open feel. Your friendly young hosts live next door; they are working hard on the informal flower and vegetable garden, much of the produce is used in David's delicious homemade dinners, there's pumpkin marmalade and eggs from the hens. Bedrooms are cottage-cosy with stripped floors, comfy wrought-iron beds and silver cast-iron radiators; fresh bathrooms have double-ended roll tops. A slight hum of traffic can be heard outside, but inside is blissfully peaceful. *Minimum stay two nights in high season.*

Price	£80–£90. Singles from £40.
Rooms	2 doubles.
Meals	Pub/restaurant 1.3 miles.
Closed	Rarely.
Directions	A389 Bodmin-Wadebridge; 2.5 miles, then fork right on B3266; on for 2 miles for Camelford; 600 yds after St Mabyn turn-off, left down drive.

Price	£81–£90. Singles £60.
Rooms	3: 2 doubles; 1 double with separate bath.
Meals	Dinner, 3 courses, £30. Pub/restaurant 3 miles.
Closed	Rarely.
Directions	From A395 A39 towards Camelford. Through Camelford; continue on A39 to Knightsmill. From there, 1.8 miles on left-hand side.

Arrangement for St Enodoc golf (green fee excl.). Talk on Cornish gardens or coastal & moor walks over glass of wine.

Bottle of wine with dinner. Late checkout (12pm).

	Gage & Liz Williams
	Menkee,
	St Mabyn, Wadebridge PL30 3DD
Tel	+44 (0)1208 841378
Email	gagewillms@aol.com
Web	www.cornwall-online.co.uk/menkee

	Deborah Hilborne & David Edwards
	Polrode Mill Cottage,
	Allen Valley, St Kew, Wadebridge PL30 3NS
Tel	+44 (0)1208 850203
Email	polrode@tesco.net
Web	www.polrodeguesthouse.co.uk

Entry 39 Map 1

Entry 40 Map 1

Cornwall

Porteath Barn

What a spot! This upside-down house is elegantly uncluttered and cool with seagrass flooring and a wood-burner in the sitting room. Bedrooms – not vast – have fresh flowers, quilted bedspreads and there's an Italian marble shower room; the feel is private with your own doors to the lovely, large garden. Walks from here down a path with ponds will take you to Epphaven Cove and the beach at the bottom of the valley or to a good pub for supper if you're feeling hearty. The Bloors have perfected the art of B&B-ing, being kind and helpful without being intrusive. *Children over 12 by arrangement.*

Price	From £80. Singles by arrangement.
Rooms	3: 2 twins/doubles, each with separate bath or shower; 1 double sharing bath (let to same party only).
Meals	Pub 1.5 miles.
Closed	Rarely.
Directions	A39 to Wadebridge. At r'bout signed for Polzeath, then to Porteath Bee Centre. Through Bee Centre shop car park, down farm track; signed on right after 150 yds.

 Use your Sawday's Gift Card here.

Jo & Michael Bloor
Porteath Barn,
St Minver,
Wadebridge PL27 6RA
Tel   +44 (0)1208 863605
Email   m.bloor17@btinternet.com

Entry 41   Map 1

Cornwall

Roskear

Drive down the fields to this 17th-century working farmhouse, a blissfully peaceful escape. A large sitting room with log fire, a warm and smiling hostess, happy dogs, comfortable bedrooms, a cheerful Aga, fabulous estuary views – country life at its most charming. Delicious breakfasts are served on blue china, doors open to the garden on sunny days and there are acres of woodland and grassland to explore. Good restaurants include Rick Stein's, the ferry takes you to Rock, surfing is a short drive and the Camel cycle trail is nearby (hire bikes locally). Uncomplicated, good value B&B.

Price	From £70. Singles £35.
Rooms	2: 1 double with separate bath; 1 twin/double sharing bath (let to same party only).
Meals	Pubs/restaurants 0.5-6 miles.
Closed	Rarely.
Directions	Bypass Wadebridge on A39 for Redruth. Over bridge, pass garage on left, straight over roundabout, filter 1st right to Edmonton. By modern houses turn immed. right to Roskear over cattle grid.

Rosina Messer-Bennetts
Roskear,
St Breock, Wadebridge PL27 7HU
Tel   +44 (0)1208 812805
Email   rosina@roskear.com
Web   www.roskear.com

Entry 42   Map 1

Cornwall

Mother Ivey Cottage

So close to the sea that there are salt splashes on the windows! Exceptionally lovely hosts here and a simple refuge from crashing surf and Atlantic winds. The house was once a fish cellar for processing catches, and recently a film location. Look out of the window to the big blue below, swim to the lifeboat launch, barbecue on the beach, have breakfast in the summerhouse. The coastal path is stunning and you can walk to surfing beaches or just drop down to the quiet sandy bay beneath your window. Cultured, kind hosts and a relaxed atmosphere; bedrooms and bathrooms are not smart but come for the views. Families love it.

Price	From £70. Singles by arrangement.
Rooms	2 twins. Extra single bed.
Meals	Dinner from £25. Packed lunch from £5. Pubs/restaurants 3-5 miles.
Closed	Rarely.
Directions	From St Merryn, right for Trevose Head. Over sleeping policemen. After tollgate ticket machine, right thro' 2nd farm gate. On towards sea; cottage gate at end of track, on right.

	Phyllida & Antony Woosnam-Mills
	Mother Ivey Cottage,
	Trevose Head, Padstow PL28 8SL
Tel	+44 (0)1841 520329
Email	antony@trevosehead.co.uk
Web	www.trevosehead.co.uk

Entry 43   Map 1

Cornwall

Molesworth Manor

It's a splendid old place, big enough to swallow hoards of people, peppered with art and interesting antiques. There are palms and a play area in the garden, a drawing room with an honesty bar and an open fire for cosy nights, a carved staircase leading to bedrooms that vary in style and size – His Lordship's at the front, the Maid's in the eaves – and bathrooms that are lovely and pampering. The whiff of homemade muffins lures you downstairs in the morning, the Cornish Riviera and its food scene will ravish you later – you're in the heart of it all. A superb bolthole run by Geoff and Jessica, youthful and fun.

Price	£70-£110. Singles from £52.50.
Rooms	9: 7 doubles, 1 twin/double; 1 twin with separate shower.
Meals	Pubs/restaurants 2 miles.
Closed	November-January. Open off-season by arrangement for larger parties.
Directions	Off A389 between Wadebridge & Padstow. Entrance clearly signed; 300 yds from bridge in Little Petherick.

💼	10% off stays of 2 or more nights.

	Geoff French & Jessica Clarke
	Molesworth Manor,
	Little Petherick, Padstow PL27 7QT
Tel	+44 (0)1841 540292
Email	molesworthmanor@aol.com
Web	www.molesworthmanor.co.uk

Entry 44   Map 1

Cornwall

Calize Country House

Beneath wheeling gulls and close to blond beaches, the big square 1870 house has amazing views of skies and sea. Virginia Woolf's lighthouse is in the bay and winter seals cavort at the colony nearby. A fresh, uncomplicated décor brings the tang of the sea to every room. Artworks recall a world of surf; deckchair stripes clothe the dining table and dress the window; traditional sofas call for quiet times with a book. Upstairs, patterned or pale walls, practical bath or shower rooms, perhaps a sea view. Jilly and Nigel are testament to the benefits of sea air and look after you beautifully.

Ethical Collection: Environment; Food. See page 430.

Price	£80–£90. Singles £55.
Rooms	4: 2 doubles, 1 twin, 1 single.
Meals	Packed lunch £5. Pub 350 yds.
Closed	Rarely.
Directions	Exit A30 at Camborne (west) A3047. Left, then right at r'bout. Right on entering Connor Downs, then on for 2 miles. House on right after sign for Gwithian.

 Use your Sawday's Gift Card here.

Jilly Whitaker
Calize Country House,
Gwithian,
Hayle TR27 5BW
Tel   +44 (0)1736 753268
Email   jilly@calize.co.uk
Web   www.calize.co.uk

Cornwall

Treglisson

A short drive from St Ives, the glorious bay and some nifty surfing beaches. Inside the old farmhouse, all is calm and peaceful. Stephen and Heather are thoughtful, fun, easy-going and filled with enthusiasm for looking after you: large light bedrooms in soft colours, generous beds with lovely linen, modern white bathrooms, good art on the walls, a beautiful antique-marble hall floor. Cornish Aga-cooked breakfasts can be relished late if you prefer; in the evening, take a sundowner to the garden in summer or relax by the log fire in winter. There's a heated indoor pool too in the summer.

Price	£60–£80. Singles from £35.
Rooms	3: 1 double, 2 family rooms.
Meals	Pubs/restaurants 2–5 miles.
Closed	End of September to Easter.
Directions	A30 to Hayle; 4th exit on r'bout into Hayle. Left at mini r'bout into Guildford Rd; up hill for 1 mile. Turn left at green sign into lane.

Bottle of wine in your room. Free pick-up from local bus/train station.

Stephen & Heather Reeves
Treglisson,
Wheal Alfred Road,
Hayle TR27 5JT
Tel   +44 (0)1736 753141
Email   steve@treglisson.co.uk
Web   www.treglisson.co.uk

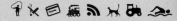

Cornwall

Drym Farm

Rural, but not too deeply: the Tate at St Ives is a 15-minute drive. The 1705 farmhouse, beautifully revived, is surrounded by ancient barns, a dairy and a forge, fascinating to Cornish historians. Jan arrived in 2002, with an enthusiasm for authenticity and simple, stylish good taste. French limestone floors in the hall, eclectic art on the walls, a roll top bath, a *bateau lit*, an antique brass bed. Paintwork is fresh cream and taupe. There are old fruit trees and young camellias, a TV-free sitting room with two plump sofas and organic treats at breakfast. Charming and utterly peaceful.

Price	£70-£90. Singles from £55.
Rooms	2 doubles.
Meals	Pubs/restaurants within 1-4 miles.
Closed	Rarely.
Directions	From A30 to Hayle; through Hayle to r'bout, left to Helston. At Leedstown, left towards Drym. Follow road until right turn to Drym. Farm fourth on lane, on right after Drym House.

Local food/produce in your room.

Jan Bright
Drym Farm,
Drym, Praze-an-Beeble,
Camborne TR14 0NU
Tel   +44 (0)1209 831039
Email   drymfarm@hotmail.co.uk
Web   www.drymfarm.co.uk

Entry 47   Map 1

Cornwall

House at Gwinear

An island of calm – it sits, as it has for 500 years, in its own bird-trilled acres a short drive from St Ives. The Halls are devoted to the encouragement of the arts and crafts which is reflected in their lifestyle. There's no stuffiness – just fresh flowers on the breakfast table, a piano in the corner, rugs on polished floors and masses of books. In a separate wing you have a cosy bedroom and sitting room and a fine view of the church from the bath. The big lawn-filled gardens are there for bare-footed solace, and you can have breakfast in the Italianate courtyard on sunny days.

Price	From £75.
Rooms	1 twin/double with separate bath & sitting room.
Meals	Dinner, with wine, from £29. Supper, with glass of wine, £20. Pub 1.5 miles.
Closed	Rarely.
Directions	From A30 exit Hayle (Loggans Moor r'bout); 100 yds left at mini r'bout; 400 yds left for Gwinear; 1.5 miles, top of hill, driveway on right, just before 30mph Gwinear sign.

Talk about St Ives artists with a glass of wine.

Charles & Diana Hall
House at Gwinear,
Gwinear,
St Ives TR27 5JZ
Tel   +44 (0)1736 850444

Entry 48   Map 1

Cornwall

Organic Panda B&B & Gallery

A five-minute walk from busy St Ives, with a panoramic view of the bay, boutique B&B in perfect harmony with this artistic spot; come for a bold scattering of modern art and a ten-seater rustic table. Spacious contemporary bedrooms have a laid-back style with organic linen, bamboo towels, chunky beds, white walls and raw-silk cushions. Shower rooms are small but perfectly formed. Andrea is an artist and theatre designer, Peter a photographer and organic chef; the food is delicious and bread home-baked. The most beautiful coastal road in all England leads to St Just. *Minimum stay three nights Christmas, Easter, July & August.*

Ethical Collection: Environment; Food. See page 430.

Price	£75–£130.
Rooms	3: 2 doubles, 1 twin.
Meals	Packed lunch £10. Restaurants nearby.
Closed	Rarely.
Directions	A3074 to St Ives. Signs to leisure centre; house behind 3rd sign, on left-hand bend.

Peter Williams & Andrea Carr
Organic Panda B&B & Gallery,
1 Pednolver Terrace,
St Ives TR26 2EL
Tel   +44 (0)1736 793890
Email   info@organicpanda.co.uk
Web   www.organicpanda.co.uk

Entry 49   Map 1

Cornwall

11 Sea View Terrace

In a smart row of Edwardian villas, with views over harbour, island and sea, is a delectable retreat. Sleek, softy coloured interiors are light and gentle on the eye – an Italian circular glass table here, a painted seascape there – deeply civilised. Bedrooms are perfect with crisp linen, vistas of whirling gulls, your own terrace; bathrooms are state-of-the-art. Rejoice in softly boiled eggs with anchovy and chive-butter soldiers for breakfast – or continental in bed if you prefer. Grahame looks after you impeccably and design aficionados will be happy. *Free admission to Tate Gallery & Barbara Hepworth Museum.*

Price	£90–£125. Singles from £65.
Rooms	3 suites.
Meals	Dinner, with wine, from £25 (groups only). Packed lunch £10. Pubs/restaurants 5-minute walk.
Closed	Rarely.
Directions	At Porthminster Hotel, signs for Tate; down Albert Rd, right just before Longships Hotel. Limited parking.

Grahame Wheelband
11 Sea View Terrace,
St Ives TR26 2DH
Tel   +44 (0)1736 798440
Email   info@11stives.co.uk
Web   www.11stives.co.uk

Entry 50   Map 1

Cornwall

Jamies

Breathe in the ocean views from this stylish 1920s villa. Airy bedrooms are hotel-smart with white bed linen, striped and checked curtains, fresh new bathrooms, a feeling of space and sea views; two have proper sitting areas. Crisp linen and silver at the breakfast table create an elegant mood – relish an exotic fruit salad in a perfect white room overlooking the bay, or admire some of artist Felicity's inspiring work. Generous, easy-going Felicity and Jamie are ex-hoteliers with a great sense of fun, the white sands of Carbis Bay are a five-minute walk, and St Ives lies just beyond. *Children over 12 welcome.*

Price	From £100. Singles £80.
Rooms	4: 3 twins/doubles, 1 suite.
Meals	Pub 3-minute walk. Restaurants 1.5 miles.
Closed	Rarely.
Directions	A30, then A3074 for St Ives. At Carbis Bay, Marshalls estate agents & Methodist church on left. Next right down Pannier Lane; 2nd right is Wheal Whidden; 1st house on left.

	Felicity & Jamie Robertson
	Jamies,
	Wheal Whidden, Carbis Bay,
	St Ives TR26 2QX
Tel	+44 (0)1736 794718
Email	info@jamiesstives.co.uk
Web	www.jamiesstives.co.uk

Entry 51   Map 1

Cornwall

The Old Vicarage

Artists will be inspired, not just with the proximity to St Ives but with Jackie's dazzling collection of her own and other artists' work. This is a light, airy, welcoming house whose big sash windows overlook a subtropical garden; wander at will after a grand breakfast of fresh fruit and local bacon and sausages. Bedrooms have soft coloured walls, deeply comfortable beds, period furniture and more lovely artwork adding spots of colour; bathrooms are gleaming and fresh. There's a sandy beach 20-minutes' walk away and you can join the coastal path just up the road. Wonderful house, lovely owners.

Price	From £80. Singles from £50.
Rooms	3: 1 twin; 1 double with separate bath, 1 single sharing bath (let to same party only).
Meals	Pubs 5-8 minute walk. Restaurants in St Ives 2.5 miles.
Closed	November, December & March.
Directions	A30 Penzance. At 2nd Hayle r'bout, A3074 St Ives. After Wyvale Garden Centre, over mini r'bout; right at next one & into Lelant. Brush End on left after Elm Farm sign. House at end.
	Free pick-up from local bus/train station.

	Jackie & Howard Hollingsbee
	The Old Vicarage,
	Brush End, Lelant,
	St Ives TR26 3EF
Tel	+44 (0)1736 753324
Email	bookings@oldvicaragelelant.co.uk
Web	www.oldvicaragelelant.co.uk

Entry 52   Map 1

Cornwall

Ennys

Prepare to be spoiled. A fire smoulders in the sumptuous sitting room, tea is laid out in the Aga-warm kitchen, bedrooms are luxurious (a king-size bed, an elegant modern four-poster, a powerful shower) and breakfasts are served at separate tables. The stylishness continues into the suites and everywhere there are fascinating artefacts from Gill's travels, designer fabrics and original art. The road ends at Ennys, so it is utterly peaceful; walk down to the river and along the old towpath to St Ives Bay. Or stay put: play tennis (on grass!) and swim in the heated pool sunk deep into the tropical gardens.

Price	£95–£145. Singles from £75.
Rooms	5: 3 doubles; 2 suites (doubles) each with kitchenette.
Meals	Pub 3 miles.
Closed	Rarely.
Directions	2 miles east of Marazion on B3280, look for sign & turn left leading down Trewhella Lane between St Hilary & Relubbus. On to Ennys.

Gill Charlton
Ennys,
St Hilary
Penzance TR20 9BZ
Tel   +44 (0)1736 740262
Email   ennys@ennys.co.uk
Web   www.ennys.co.uk

Entry 53   Map 1

Cornwall

Ednovean Farm

There's a terrace for each immaculate bedroom (one truly private) with views to the wild blue yonder and St Michael's Mount Bay, an enchanting outlook that changes with the passage of the day. Come for peace, space and the best of eclectic fabrics and colours, pretty lamps, gleaming copper, fluffy bathrobes and handmade soaps. The beamed, open-plan sitting/dining area is an absorbing mix of exotic, rustic and elegant; have full breakfast here (last orders nine o'clock) or continental in your room. A footpath through the field leads to the village; walk to glorious Prussia Cove and Cudden Point, or head west to Marazion.

Price	£90–£110.
Rooms	3: 2 doubles, 1 four-poster.
Meals	Pub 5-minute walk.
Closed	Christmas & rarely.
Directions	From A30 after Crowlas r'bout, A394 to Helston. 0.25 miles after next r'bout, 1st right for Perranuthnoe. Farm drive on left, signed.

Christine & Charles Taylor
Ednovean Farm,
Perranuthnoe,
Penzance TR20 9LZ
Tel   +44 (0)1736 711883
Email   info@ednoveanfarm.co.uk
Web   www.ednoveanfarm.co.uk

Entry 54   Map 1

Cornwall

The Gardens

Two old miners' cottages combine to create this small, modest, pretty home. Irish Moira, a retired midwife, adores flowers and her posies brighten every corner; Goff, a potter and painter, tends the vegetables. Both are charming and kind. Sweet snug bedrooms have patchwork quilts, cotton sheets, antique linen runners and plenty of books. One is on the ground floor overlooking the colourful cottage garden, two are up a narrow stair. Aga-cooked breakfasts and homemade jams are brought to the sun-streamed conservatory and there's homemade cake in the sitting room by the wood-burner. Great value.

Price	From £66. Singles £33–£37.
Rooms	3: 2 doubles; 1 twin/double with separate bath.
Meals	Packed lunch from £7.50. Pubs/restaurants 10-minute drive.
Closed	Christmas & New Year.
Directions	A394 Helston to Penzance, 2nd right after Lion & Lamb pub in Ashton for Tresowes Green. After 0.25 miles, sign for house on right.

Moira & Goff Cattell
The Gardens,
Tresowes, Ashton,
Helston TR13 9SY
Tel   +44 (0)1736 763299
Mobile +44 (0)7881 758191
Email   moira.cattell@gmail.com

Entry 55   Map 1

Cornwall

Chydane

Only the coastal path separates you from sand and sea. At the far end of the dreamy three-mile beach is Porthleven; West Penwith stretches into the distance. Come for super comfort, stylish art, magical views. No sitting room, but a chesterfield in the big elegant double, a superb bed, gorgeous linen, and a French balcony overlooking the waves. Bathrooms, too, are inviting, with thick white bathrobes, romantic candles, generous showers. Upstairs is a second double room with a porthole window; in the garden are teak-furnished terraces and a heated summerhouse. And cream teas for walkers in season. Wow. *Children over 12 welcome.*

Ethical Collection: Food. See page 430.

Price	From £100.
Rooms	2 doubles.
Meals	Meals by arrangement. Pub 200 yds.
Closed	Christmas.
Directions	From Helston A3083 to the Lizard. After 2 miles right to Gunwalloe. Right before Halzephron Inn. Chydane on right immediately above beach.

10% off room rate Mon-Thurs in low season.

Use your Sawday's Gift Card here.

Carla Caslin
Chydane,
Gunwalloe,
Helston TR12 7QB
Tel   +44 (0)1326 241232
Email carla.caslin@btinternet.com
Web   www.chydane.co.uk

Entry 56   Map 1

Cornwall

Halzephron House

A rambling white seaside cottage with a crenellated roof and the whiff of a gentleman's folly about it. Step in to a contemporary interior of thick wood floors, original paintings, velvet sofas and lots of fresh flowers: the Tower room in the house has its own white-walled sitting room overlooking the bay and, upstairs, a beautiful French bed. Peace seekers and lovers will choose to stay in the Cabin – a white painted wooden shack with roll top bath and porthole overlooking the garden – or the Observatory, a carefully designed funky space for two. Lucy and Roger give you super local breakfasts too. *Dogs welcome in Observatory & Cabin only.*

Price	£100–£120.
Rooms	3: Tower: 1 suite. Cabin: 1 suite. Observatory: 1 double.
Meals	Pub 0.25 miles.
Closed	Rarely.
Directions	From Helston head towards the Lizard. After 2 miles, right signed Gunwalloe. In village lane towards Church Cove passing Halzephron Inn on left. House at top of hill overlooking the sea.
	Key to 'secret' clifftop garden.

Lucy & Roger Thorp
Halzephron House,
Gunwalloe, Helston TR12 7QD
Tel +44 (0)1326 241719
Email lucy@halzephronhouse.co.uk
Web www.halzephronhouse.co.uk

Entry 57 Map 1

Cornwall

Halftides

Hugely enjoyable and special, surrounded by three acres with dazzling views down the coast and out to sea. Fresh funky bedrooms, not huge but filled with light, have gorgeous fabrics, crisp bedding, dreamy views; bathrooms (one a small pod-shower in the room) are sleek in glass and chrome. Susie is great fun, an artist and chef and gives you a delicious organic breakfast in the pretty, airy dining room. Take the coastal path north or south, visit the working harbour in the village, head for a swim down the private path to the beach below. A perfect place to relax and unwind. *Minimum stay two nights. Children over three welcome.*

Price	£95–£120. Singles £60–£75.
Rooms	3: 1 double; 1 double, 1 single sharing separate bath.
Meals	Pub 0.5 miles.
Closed	February.
Directions	A3083 to Lizard, right to Cury, 5 miles; past Poldhu beach & into Mullion. Right into Laflouder Lane, past 'no through road' sign. Ignore side road on right. 1st on right.

Charles & Susie Holdsworth Hunt
Halftides,
Laflouder Lane, Mullion, Helston TR12 7H
Tel +44 (0)1326 241935
Email halftides@btinternet.com
Web www.halftides.co.uk

Entry 58 Map 1

Cornwall

The Hen House

Greenies will be delighted: Sandy and Gary, truly welcoming, are passionately committed to sustainability and happy to advise on the best places to eat, visit and walk; there are OS maps on loan too. Enlightened souls will adore the spacious, colourful rooms, the bright fabrics, the wildflower meadow with inviting sun loungers, the pond, the tai chi, the fairy-lit courtyard at night, the scrumptious locally sourced breakfast, the birdsong. There's even a sanctuary room for reiki and reflexology set deep into the earth in this peaceful retreat. *Minimum stay two nights. Children over 12 welcome. Self-catering in Barn available.*

Ethical Collection: Environment; Food.
See page 430.

Price	£70–£85. Singles £60.
Rooms	3: 2 doubles. Barn: 1 double.
Meals	Pub/restaurant 1 mile.
Closed	Rarely.
Directions	A3083 from Helston, B3293 to St Keverne; left to Newtown-in-St Martin. After 2 miles, right at T-junc. Follow road for 2.3 miles then left fork. Round 7 bends then right at triangulation stone for Tregarne.

Reiki or reflexology therapy session per room on minimum stay of 7 nights.

Sandy & Gary Pulfrey
The Hen House,
Tregarne, Manaccan, Helston
TR12 6EW
Tel   +44 (0)1326 280236
Email   henhouseuk@aol.com
Web   www.thehenhouse-cornwall.co.uk

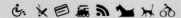

Entry 59   Map 1

Cornwall

Carmelin

The setting of this bungalow is sensational, gazing straight out to sea from the Lizard, England's most southerly point. Your peaceful bedroom shares the views, and leads into a sun room just for you: a sofa, a log-effect fire, a private entrance, more beautiful views. Breakfast – a spread of breads and pastries, fruits, eggs, freshly made yogurt and homemade jams – fights for your attention against the breaking waves and sparkling sea. John and Jane are gentle dog-loving people, seasoned B&B providers who enjoy their guests. Walk the coastal path, stroll to the pub for a meal. *French & German spoken.*

Price	From £90. Singles by arrangement.
Rooms	1 double with separate bath/shower & sitting room.
Meals	Pub/restaurant within walking distance.
Closed	Rarely.
Directions	From Helston to the Lizard; at Lizard Green, right, opp. Regent Café (head for Smugglers Fish & Chips); immed. right, pass wc on left. Road unmade; on for 500 yds; double bend; 2nd on right.

Bottle of wine in your room. Discounts on Jane & John's books.

Jane & John Grierson
Carmelin,
Pentreath Lane,
The Lizard TR12 7NY
Tel   +44 (0)1326 290677
Email   pjcarmelin@gmail.com
Web   www.bedandbreakfastcornwall.co.uk

Entry 60   Map 1

Cornwall

Landewednack House

The pug dogs will greet you enthusiastically and Susan will give you tea and biscuits in the drawing room of this immaculate house with a boutique hotel feel. Antony the chef keeps the wheels oiled and the food coming – treat yourself to green crab soup or succulent lobster; the wine cellar holds over 2,000 bottles so there's plenty of choice. Upstairs to bedrooms that are not huge and not all with sea views, but everything you could possibly need is there, from robes to brandy. The pool area is stunning, the garden is filled with interest and it's a three-minute walk to the sea. *Minimum stay two nights July & August.*

Price	From £110. Singles £55-£85.
Rooms	4: 3 doubles, 1 twin.
Meals	Dinner, 3 courses, £35.
Closed	Never.
Directions	From Helston, A3083 south. Just before Lizard, left to Church Cove. Follow signs for about 0.75 miles. On left behind French blue gates.

Susan Thorbek
Landewednack House,
Church Cove,
The Lizard TR12 7PQ
Tel +44 (0)1326 290877
Email luxurybandb@landewednackhouse.com
Web www.landewednackhouse.com

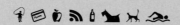

Entry 61   Map 1

Cornwall

Trerose Manor

Follow winding lanes through glorious countryside to find the prettiest, listed manor house, a warm family atmosphere and welcoming tea in the beamed kitchen. Large, light bedrooms, one with floor-to-ceiling windows, sit peacefully in your own wing and have views over the stunning garden. Both are dressed in pretty colours, have comfy seats for gazing and smartly tiled bathrooms. A sumptuous breakfast can be taken outside in summer, there are lovely walks over fields to river or beach, stacks of interesting places to visit and lots to read in the library for the lazy. Lovely. *French, German & Italian spoken.*

Price	£100-£125. Singles £70.
Rooms	2 doubles.
Meals	Pubs/restaurants within walking distance.
Closed	Rarely.
Directions	Left at Red Lion in Mawnan Smith. After 0.5 miles right down Old Church Road. After 0.5 miles house on right through white gate immediately after Trerose Farm.

Use your Sawday's Gift Card here.

Tessa Phipps
Trerose Manor,
Mawnan Smith,
Falmouth TR11 5HX
Tel +44 (0)1326 250784
Email info@trerosemanor.co.uk
Web www.trerosemanor.co.uk

Entry 62   Map 1

Cornwall

Bosvathick

A huge old Cornish house that has been in Kate's family since 1760, along with all the art, heavy furniture, Indian rugs, ornate plasterwork, pianos and even a harp. Historians will be in their element: pass three Celtic crosses dating from the 7th century before the long drive finds the imposing house (all granite gate posts and lions) and a rambling garden with grotto, lake, pasture and woodland. Bedrooms are simple and traditional, full of books and antiques; bathrooms are spick and span, one plain and functional, one new. Come to experience a 'time warp' and charming Kate's good breakfasts; close to Falmouth University too.

Price	From £80. Singles £40-£60.
Rooms	4: 1 twin/double, 1 twin, 2 singles. 2 bathrooms (each party has sole use of a bathroom).
Meals	Supper, with wine, £25. Packed lunch £5-£10. Pubs 2 miles.
Closed	Christmas, New Year & Easter.
Directions	From Constantine, signs to Falmouth. 2 miles, pass Bosvathick Riding Stables, next entrance on left. Drive thro' gateposts & green gate. A map can be sent to visitors.

Kate & Stephen Tyrrell
Bosvathick,
Constantine,
Falmouth TR11 5RD
Tel   +44 (0)1326 340103
Email   kate@bosvathickhouse.co.uk
Web   www.bosvathickhouse.co.uk

Entry 63   Map 1

Cornwall

Tregew Vean

Once the home of a packet skipper, this pretty Georgian slate-hung house stands in a sunny spot above Flushing. From the garden with its palms, agapanthus, olive and fig trees, you glimpse the Fal estuary. The house is fresh and elegant, with tenderly cared-for antiques and an entertaining straw hat collection in the hall; Sandra and Rodney – both chatty and charming – give you comfortable bedrooms in your own part of the house. Flushing is a ten-minute walk and in the village there are two pubs that do food and a restaurant on the quay. There's plenty to do and you can catch the passenger ferry to Falmouth.

Price	From £90. Singles £50.
Rooms	2 doubles, sharing bath (let to same party only).
Meals	Pubs/restaurants 0.25 miles.
Closed	Christmas.
Directions	From Penryn towards Mylor. After 1 mile right to Flushing. Entrance 1 mile down road on right, 40 yds before T-junc., opposite 'Give Way 40 yds' sign.

 10% off minimum 5 nights. Free pick-up from Penryn station.

Sandra & Rodney Myers
Tregew Vean,
Flushing,
Falmouth TR11 5TF
Tel   +44 (0)1326 379462
Email   tregewvean@aol.com
Web   www.tregewvean.co.uk

Entry 64   Map 1

Cornwall

Trevilla House

Come for the position: the sea and Fal estuary wrap around you, and the King Harry ferry gives you an easy reach into the glorious Roseland peninsula. Inside, find frog stencils in the bathroom, and faded, old-fashioned comfortable bedrooms – the twin with garden views and a sofa, the double with sea views. Jinty is warm and welcoming and rustles up delicious locally sourced breakfasts with homemade jams in the sunny conservatory that looks south over the sea. Trelissick Gardens and the Copeland China Collection are just next door; the Maritime Museum, Eden, Tate, cycling, watersports and coastal walks are close by.

Price	From £80. Singles £50.
Rooms	3: 1 twin; 1 double with separate bath/shower & sitting room. Extra single sharing bath (let to same party only).
Meals	Restaurants/pubs 1-2 miles.
Closed	Christmas & New Year.
Directions	A390 to Truro; A39 to Falmouth. At double r'bout with garage, left off 2nd r'bout (B3289); pass pub on left; at x-roads, left (B3289); 200 yds on, fork right to Feock. On to T-junc., then left; 1st on right.

Jinty & Peter Copeland
Trevilla House,
Feock,
Truro TR3 6QG
Tel   +44 (0)1872 862369
Email   jinty@trevilla.com
Web   www.trevilla.com

Entry 65   Map 1

Cornwall

Pine Cottage

The Cornish sea laps the steep quay of this narrow inlet's port, its blue horizon just visible from the window of the elegant bedroom high up on the coveside. A perfect spot to wake on a summer's morn. The house is as sunny as its owner, the guest bedroom charmingly informal with its hand-painted violet-strewn wallpaper, super big bed and shelves brimming with books. A handful of small open-top fishing boats slips out at dawn to bring back catches of crab and lobster. Clare will give you a splendid breakfast of warm fruit salad and organic or local produce whenever possible.

Price	£85.
Rooms	1 double.
Meals	Pub 100 yds. Restaurants within 5 miles.
Closed	Rarely.
Directions	From Tregony, A3078 to St Mawes. After 2 miles, at garage, left to Portloe. Thro' village to Ship Inn. Right fork after pub car park. Cottage immed. on left up drive.

Clare Holdsworth
Pine Cottage,
Portloe,
Truro TR2 5RB
Tel   +44 (0)1872 501385
Web   www.pine-cottage.net

Entry 66   Map 1

Cornwall

Hay Barton

Giant windows overlook many acres of farmland, well-stocked with South Devon cows and their calves. Jill and Blair look after you well with lovely homemade cake, granola and yogurt, sausages and bacon from the village; later, retire to the guest sitting room with log fire. Bedrooms are fresh and pretty with garden flowers, soft white linen on big beds, floral green walls and stripped floors. Gloriously large panelled bathrooms have long roll top baths and are painted in earthy colours. Guests can use the tennis court; you are near to good gardens and plenty of places to eat. *Minimum stay two nights in summer.*

Cornwall

Creed House

The big Georgian rectory is surrounded by one of Cornwall's loveliest gardens. Light pours into every elegant corner and your very lovely hosts give you fresh, bright, traditional bedrooms in a peaceful wing. Sheets are crisp, colours are serene and flowers are from the garden. Local breads, jams and seasonal fruit salads await you at breakfast — enjoyed in the cosy guest sitting room or the handsome dining room. A perfect place from which to explore not only the gardens and coastline of Cornwall, but the Eden Project too.

Price	£80. Singles £50.
Rooms	2 twins/doubles.
Meals	Pubs 1-2 miles.
Closed	Rarely.
Directions	A3078 from Tregony village towards St Mawes. After 1 mile, house on left, 100 yds down lane.

 Fruit bowl in your room.

Jill & Blair Jobson
Hay Barton,
Tregony,
Truro TR2 5TF
Tel   +44 (0)1872 530288
Email   jill@haybarton.com
Web   www.haybarton.com

Entry 67   Map 1

Price	£90.
Rooms	2: 1 double, 1 twin.
Meals	Continental breakfast (cooked sometimes available). Pub/restaurant 1 mile.
Closed	Christmas & New Year.
Directions	From St Austell, A390 to Grampound. Just beyond clock tower, left into Creed Lane. After 1 mile, left at grass triangle opp. church. House behind 2nd white gates on left.

Jonathon & Annabel Croggon
Creed House,
Creed, Grampound,
Truro TR2 4SL
Tel   +44 (0)1872 530372
Email   jrcroggon@btinternet.com
Web   www.creedhouse.co.uk

Entry 68   Map 1

Cornwall

Trussel Barn

Jo and Mike look after you beautifully: large, light bedrooms with super views, squashy pillows, state-of-the-art bathrooms, fancy dressing gowns, your own hidden-away fridge. They're keen on reducing their carbon footprint, too; drink water from their borehole, wander down to the wildlife pond, admire the vegetable and strawberry beds, tuck into a locally sourced breakfast cooked in an eco-Aga, ask about their plans for off-grid electricity – it's fascinating stuff. Explore acres of garden running down to a wildlife pond, hike the five miles to the coast, and come home to a roaring fire in the guest sitting room.

Ethical Collection: Environment; Food. See page 430.

Price	From £75. Singles from £55.
Rooms	2: 1 double; 1 double with separate bath.
Meals	Pubs/restaurants within 2 miles.
Closed	Rarely.
Directions	A38 Plymouth-Liskeard, then B3254 to St Keyne for 1.5 miles. Climb steep hill; at bend, 1st left into Trussel Barn. Or train to Liskeard, 2 miles.

	Jo Lawrence
	Trussel Barn,
	St Keyne,
	Liskeard PL14 4QL
Tel	+44 (0)1579 340450
Email	trusselbarn@me.com
Web	www.trusselbarn.com

Entry 69　Map 1

Cornwall

Botelet

The farmhouse at the end of the wild-flowered lane is an inspired synthesis of stone, wood, Shaker simplicity and comfy old chairs: the chicest of shabby chic. Rustic bedrooms reached by a steep stair have planked floors, antique beds and beautiful linen; the bathroom is below. Breakfasts – organic, home-baked, home-picked, vegetarian – are enjoyed at a scrubbed table by the Rayburn. Drink in the pure air, explore the farm, walk the wooded valley; return to a therapeutic massage in your room. Botelet has been in the family since 1860 and is quirky, friendly, artistic, huge fun. The yurts are amazing. *Over tens welcome.*

Price	From £70. Yurt £170 (2 nights).
Rooms	2: 1 double, 1 twin/double (with extra single), sharing bath. Yurts: each 1 double.
Meals	Continental breakfast (£10 for yurt). Pub 2 miles.
Closed	October to Easter.
Directions	From Liskeard on A38. At Dobwalls left fork, A390 for St Austell. After East Taphouse, left onto B3359 for Looe. After 2 miles, right, signed.

	The Tamblyn Family
	Botelet,
	Herodsfoot,
	Liskeard PL14 4RD
Tel	+44 (0)1503 220225
Email	stay@botelet.com
Web	www.botelet.com

Entry 70　Map 1

Cornwall

Collon Barton

Come for the lofty position on a grassy hillside, the heartlifting views over unspoiled countryside and the pretty creekside village of Lerryn. This 18th-century house is a working sheep farm and an artistic household (sculptures galore). Interesting and generous Anne and Iain give you eggs from their free-range chickens, traditional airy bedrooms in pink or blue and an elegant drawing room. Anne sells huge dried hydrangeas and, on sunny days, welcomes you with tea in the summer house. Wonderful riverside and coastal walks and good gardens; the Eden Project is 20 minutes away. *Children & pets by arrangement.*

Price	£80. Singles £40.
Rooms	2: 1 twin/double, 1 twin/double with dressing room & extra beds.
Meals	Pub 10-minute walk.
Closed	Rarely.
Directions	A390 to Lostwithiel. After Lostwithiel sign 1st left, signed Lerryn. 200 yds, left at 1st x-roads for Lerryn. After 2 miles, at top of hill, hard left signed Bodmin & Liskeard. Immed. right by 5-bar gate, stone farm lane.

Anne & Iain Mackie
Collon Barton,
Lerryn,
Lostwithiel PL22 0NX
Tel   +44 (0)1208 872908
Mobile   +44 (0)7721 090186
Email   annemackie@btconnect.com

Entry 71   Map 1

Cornwall

Higher Trebarret

A narrow drive winds through the middle of the beautiful Boconnoc Estate, crosses over the ford and lands you in charming Caroline's 17th-century cottage, in a half acre of well cared for gardens, rolling fields, woodland and glorious views from every corner. The sitting room is smart, elegant, full of flowers and antiques, huge comfortable sofas and lots of books. Cottagey bedrooms have the sun streaming in. You breakfast on local produce in the conservatory or deep pink dining room, the garden has open days in the spring, and the Eden Project and lovely sandy bays are nearby; the area is unspoilt. Perfect peace.

Price	£80. Singles £40.
Rooms	2: 1 double; 1 twin with separate bath.
Meals	Pub/restaurant 3 miles.
Closed	Rarely.
Directions	A38 to Dobwalls roundabout; A390 to Lostwithiel & St Austell. At East Taphouse, left to Looe, then 1st right to Lerryn, Counch's Mill. At T-junc. right, down lane. Drive on left signed on letterbox.

Carolyn Fortescue
Higher Trebarret,
Boconnoc,
Lostwithiel PL22 0RT
Tel   +44 (0)1208 872030
Email   c@fortescue.eclipse.co.uk

Entry 72   Map 1

Cornwall

Hornacott

The garden, in its lovely valley setting, has seats in little corners poised to catch the evening sun – perfect for a pre-dinner drink. The peaceful house is named after the hill and you have a private entrance to your wonderfully fresh and airy suite: a room with twin beds plus a large, square, high sitting room with windows that look down onto the wooded valley. With CD player, music, chocolates and magazines you'll feel beautifully self-contained. Jos, a kitchen designer, and Mary-Anne love having guests, and give you fresh local produce and free-range eggs for breakfast.

Price	From £80. Singles £50.
Rooms	2: 1 suite; 1 twin with separate shower.
Meals	Dinner, 3 courses, £20. BYO. Pubs/restaurants 4.5 miles.
Closed	Christmas.
Directions	B3254 Launceston-Liskeard. Through South Petherwin, down steep hill, last left before little bridge. House 1st on left.

Cornish produce. Luxury toiletries.

Jos & Mary-Anne Otway-Ruthven
Hornacott,
South Petherwin,
Launceston PL15 7LH
Tel   +44 (0)1566 782461
Email   stay@hornacott.co.uk
Web   www.hornacott.co.uk

Entry 73   Map 1

Cornwall

St Leonards House

Enjoy gardens, history, riding, fishing? John runs tailormade tours for groups and individuals, and knows Cornwall like the back of his hand; Jane is an embroiderer whose curtains add colour to the rooms. The twin, downstairs, overlooks the garden; the doubles are up; expect good mattresses, anti-allergic duvets, bath oils and waffle robes. Breakfast is served in a low-ceilinged dining room whose beams attest to the house's age and whose tiled floor is elegantly rugged. You are on the edge of Launceston, quaint capital of Cornwall, and close to the great beaches of Widemouth Bay, Crackington Haven and Bude.

Price	£80. Singles £50.
Rooms	3: 2 doubles, 1 twin.
Meals	Dinner £17. Cream tea £3.50. Pub/restaurant 2 miles.
Closed	Christmas & New Year.
Directions	From Launceston A30 towards Polson. Opp. rugby club take road to St Leonards. After 150 yds house is next to the Equitation Centre.

10% off stays of 2 or more nights.

John & Jane Marshall
St Leonards House,
Polson,
Launceston PL15 9QR
Tel   +44 (0)1566 779195
Email   enquiries@stleonardshouse.co.uk
Web   www.stleonardshouse.co.uk

Entry 74   Map 2

Cornwall

Buttervilla Farm

Gill and Robert are so good at growing vegetables (organically) they supply the local restaurants. They're pretty good at looking after you too, in a relaxed fashion, delivering breakfasts of rare-breed bacon, eggs from their own chickens and sweet home-grown tomatoes. No sitting room but bedrooms are comfortable and cared for with modern furniture, flat screen TVs and fresh coffee; bathrooms are smart with solar-powered showers and thick towels. Explore these 15 beautiful eco acres, spot woodpeckers and kestrels, stride the coastal path or head for the surf. *Soil Association certified organic smallholding.*

Ethical Collection: Environment; Food. See page 430.

Price	£75-£95.
Rooms	3 doubles.
Meals	Restaurants within 3 miles.
Closed	Rarely.
Directions	Turn by Halfway House at Polbathic for Downderry. House 400 yds up hill from inn, on left; signed before lane.

10% off 3 nights+ except July & August. Advance purchase Eden Project tickets.

Gill & Robert Hocking
Buttervilla Farm,
Polbathic, St Germans,
Torpoint PL11 3EY
Tel   +44 (0)1503 230315
Email   info@buttervilla.com
Web   www.buttervilla.com

Entry 75   Map 2

Cornwall

Erth Barton

Everyone is bowled over by this house; open to three tidal estuaries, it makes your heart leap. The manor house was once owned by the National Trust and is casually grand, with its own derelict chapel; a 14th-century fresco still clings to the walls. Relaxed Jenny and Nicholas, its privileged trustees, keep hens and two retrievers, and – in spite of the rabbits – grow salads and vegetables. Airy bedrooms have pretty linen, big beds and peaceful views; one has its own terrace for breakfast and afternoon tea. Pick quiet spots in the large garden, enjoy stunning walks. Historic houses abound. *Residential gardening courses.*

Price	£80-£100.
Rooms	5: 4 doubles; 1 twin with separate bath.
Meals	Dinner from £20. Pubs/restaurants 2 miles.
Closed	Rarely.
Directions	Plymouth, Tamar Bridge (A38); at 1st roundabout take exit Liskeard. Turn left Trematon, left Elmgate then right Elmgate. Right at White Cottage signed Erth Barton, keep straight on until the end.

Nicholas & Jenny Foster
Erth Barton,
Elmgate,
Saltash PL12 4QY
Tel   +44 (0)1752 841560
Email   nicholasfoster@btopenworld.com
Web   www.erthbarton.co.uk

Entry 76   Map 2

Cornwall

Lantallack Farm

You will be inspired here, in this heart-warming old Georgian farmhouse where generous Nicky runs one-to one-courses in landscape painting and sculpture. Find a straw-yellow sitting room with a log fire, books to read, a grand piano and bedrooms with deliciously comfortable beds; views are breathtaking across countryside, streams and wooded valleys. Breakfast in the walled garden on fine days: apple juice from the orchard and bacon and sausages from their own pigs. There are 40 acres to explore, a leat-side trail and a heated outdoor pool; marvellous. *Minimum stay two nights at weekends. Self-catering cottages available.*

Ethical Collection: Environment; Food; Community. See page 430.

Price	From £100. Singles by arrangement.
Rooms	2: 1 double; 1 double with separate bath.
Meals	Pubs/restaurants 1 mile.
Closed	Rarely.
Directions	A38 thro' Saltash, continue 3 miles. At Landrake 2nd right at West Lane. After 1 mile, left at white cottage for Tideford. House 150 yds on, on right.

A bottle of Lantallack apple juice on checkout.

Nicky Walker
Lantallack Farm,
Landrake,
Saltash PL12 5AE
Tel +44 (0)1752 851281
Email enquiries@lantallack.co.uk
Web www.lantallack.co.uk

Entry 77 Map 2

Cornwall

Pentillie Castle

So many temptations: woodland gardens that tumble down to the Tamar, a walled Victorian kitchen garden still being restored, a magnificent Victorian bathing hut… and Pentillie beef cattle, uniquely theirs, grazing either side of the great drive up to the handsome house. Bedrooms are smart, spacious and deeply comfortable, bathrooms pamper. Ted and Sarah, with daughter Sammie, have mastered that delicate balancing act between luxury and stuffiness, bringing out one and banishing the other. It's the sort of place where you gasp at the perfection of it all and then throw your shoes off before diving into the sofa.

Price	£120–£200.
Rooms	9: 8 twins/doubles, 1 four-poster suite.
Meals	Dinner from £25.
Closed	Rarely.
Directions	Cross Tamar River into Cornwall on A38. Right onto A388. 3.1 miles, then right at Paynters Cross. Entrance within 100 yds.

Bottle of wine with dinner on first night.

Sammie Coryton
Pentillie Castle,
St. Mellion,
Saltash PL12 6QD
Tel +44 (0)1579 350044
Email contact@pentillie.co.uk
Web www.pentillie.co.uk

Entry 78 Map 2

Cumbria

Warwick Hall

Warwick Hall stands on the River Eden, facing east towards the hills, with one of the best salmon beats in the country. Basil Hume used to fish here, Bonnie Prince Charlie once stayed, though not in the comfort you can expect. Vast windows flood the house with light, breakfast is taken in a dining room with river views, a beautiful sitting room is warmed by an open fire. Bedrooms – some entered through a lovely rod room – are excellent (super beds, candles in the bathroom, books, fine views). The house stands in 270 acres, with a private 2-mile river walk; the food is delicious, the atmosphere relaxed. *Min. stay two nights at weekends.*

Price	£118-£175.
Rooms	6: 1 double, 3 twins/doubles, 2 suites.
Meals	Dinner, 2-4 courses, £25-£30. Restaurant 1 mile.
Closed	Rarely.
Directions	M6, junc. 43, then A69 east. After 2 miles, pass town sign and on left down hill before bridge.

10% off room rate Mon-Thurs. No charge for dogs.

	Val Marriner
	Warwick Hall,
	Warwick-on-Eden,
	Carlisle CA4 8PG
Tel	+44 (0)1228 561546
Email	info@warwickhall.org
Web	www.warwickhall.org

Entry 79   Map 11

Cumbria

Sirelands

Sirelands, once a gardener's cottage, stands among rhododendrons and spreading trees on a sunny slope, a stream trickling by: a stunning spot. The Carrs have lived here for years and the house has a relaxed and homely feel. Enjoy home-grown produce at dinner on a polished table, then retire to the sitting room, delightful with log basket, honesty bar, flowers and books. Sash windows overlook the wooded garden, visited by roe deer, red squirrels and various birds. Bedrooms and bathrooms are pleasant, peaceful and spotless; one loo has an amazing view! Friendly Angela loves cooking and treats you to tea and homemade cake.

Price	£90.
Rooms	2: 1 twin; 1 double with separate bath/shower.
Meals	Dinner, 2-3 courses, £22-£27.50. Pubs within 4 miles.
Closed	Christmas & New Year.
Directions	M6 north to junc. 43; A69 Newcastle; 3 miles to traffic lights. Right, on to Heads Nook; house 2 miles after village.

	David & Angela Carr
	Sirelands,
	Heads Nook, Brampton,
	Carlisle CA8 9BT
Tel	+44 (0)1228 670389
Mobile	+44 (0)7748 101513
Email	carr_sirelands@btconnect.com

Entry 80   Map 12

Cumbria

Boltongate Old Rectory

The setting of this lovely old house could hardly be more pastoral. Many of its rooms face south and have superb views, with mountains and fells beyond. History has created an intriguing house full of unexpected corners; the old rectory dates from around 1360 but bedrooms are freshly contemporary and have super big beds. Gill cooks in imaginative 'bistro' style, David knows his wines and you eat by candlelight in a 16th-century room. They're relaxed and charming and, when the place is full, create a fabulous house-party feel. Outside, red squirrels and well-fed rabbits, a croquet lawn and stunning Skiddaw.

Ethical Collection: Environment; Food; Community. See page 430.

Price	From £104. Singles from £90.
Rooms	3: 1 double, 1 twin/double; 1 double with separate bath.
Meals	Dinner, 3 courses, £33. Pub 10-minute drive.
Closed	Christmas & New Year.
Directions	B5305 to Wigton; at A595, left. After 5 miles, left to Boltongate. Left at T-junc.; in village, signs for Ireby; down hill, last driveway on left.

Gill & David Taylor
Boltongate Old Rectory,
Boltongate,
Wigton CA7 1DA
Tel   +44 (0)1697 371647
Email   boltongate@talk21.com
Web   www.boltongateoldrectory.com

Entry 81   Map 11

Cumbria

Daffodil & Daisy

Who wouldn't love it here? Teen and David, young and friendly, live in a bright-white-and-pale-green farmhouse in soaring countryside with the waggiest dog, wandering hens, ducks and geese, their own pigs. They also care about feeding you well: homemade cakes, mouthwatering breakfasts and delicious suppers. Through your own entrance find private suites with enormous, pillow-filled beds, fresh flowers, pink bubbly, fruit and cosy robes; there's an adjoining door for families. Bathrooms are spanking new; outside are a wood-fired hot tub and pizza oven. Generous and fun. *£10 discount if you come without a car.*

Price	£150. Singles £110.
Rooms	2 doubles.
Meals	Packed lunch from £9. Supper from £15. Pub within 1 mile.
Closed	Rarely.
Directions	M6 exit 41, take B5305 to Wigton. 7 miles then left Hesket Newmarket, 2nd right Hallfield. Pass farm in dip, at brow of hill turn right in front of dry stone wall into lane to house.

A basket of home-grown produce (goose fat, marmalade, free-range eggs, sloe gin).

David & Teen Fisher
Daffodil & Daisy,
Banks Farm, Hesket Newmarket,
Wigton CA7 8HR
Tel   +44 (0)1697 478137
Email   banksfarm@mac.com
Web   www.daffodilbanksfarm.co.uk

Entry 82   Map 11

Cumbria

Willow Cottage

Gaze across rooftops through tiny windows towards the towering mass of Skiddaw, the Lakes' third highest mountain. Here is a miniature cottage garden with sweet peas, herbs, vegetables and flowers... all suitably rambling. Roy and Chris have kept most of the old barn's features: wooden floorboards, wonderful beams. Dried flowers, pretty china, antique linen, glowing lamps and patchwork quilts, a collection of christening gowns... dear little bedrooms have panelled bathrooms and old pine furniture. TV is delightfully absent, classical music plays and you are in the heart of a farming village.

Price	£65–£70. Singles £50.
Rooms	2: 1 double, 1 twin.
Meals	Packed lunch £5. Pub 300 yds.
Closed	December/January.
Directions	From Keswick A591 towards Carlisle (6.5 miles) right for Bassenthwaite village (0.5 miles). Straight on at village green, house on right.

Roy & Chris Beaty
Willow Cottage,
Bassenthwaite,
Keswick CA12 4QP
Tel   +44 (0)1768 776440
Email   chriswillowbarn@googlemail.com
Web   www.willowbarncottage.co.uk

Entry 83   Map 11

Cumbria

Howe Keld

Dismiss all thoughts of the chintzy Keswick guest house: David and Val have swept through with carpets made of Herdwick sheep wool, bedroom furniture made by a local craftsman, gorgeous fabrics, striking wallpaper and smart bathrooms with green slate. It's luxurious but not flashy, and there's a cosy sitting room in primary colours crammed with local info; theatre, shops and restaurants are all strolling distance (choose rooms at the front if you need total quiet). Fill up at breakfast on home-baked bread, freshly made smoothies or a jolly good fry-up. *Minimum stay two nights at weekends, three on bank holidays.*

Ethical Collection: Environment. See page 430.

Price	£80–£130. Singles £45-60.
Rooms	14: 13 doubles, 1 single.
Meals	Pub/restaurant 300 yds.
Closed	Part December including Christmas. Most of January excluding New Year.
Directions	From Penrith (junc. 40 on M6) west on A66, 18 miles until r'bout with A591. Left towards Keswick. After 800 yds left at junc. On to mini r'bout in high street (600 yds), then right. After 600 yds right into The Heads.
	A bottle of wine in your room for stays of 3 or more nights Sun-Thurs.

David Fisher
Howe Keld,
5/7 The Heads,
Keswick CA12 5ES
Tel   +44 (0)1768 772417
Email   david@howekeld.co.uk
Web   www.howekeld.co.uk

Entry 84   Map 11

Cumbria

Lowthwaite

Leave your worries behind as you head up the lanes to the farmhouse tucked into the fell. Jim, ex hiking guide from Tanzania, and Danish Tine moved with their daughters in 2007 and give you four peaceful bedrooms in the view-filled barn wing. Handsomely chunky twin beds are of recycled dhow wood, crisp light bathrooms sport organic soaps and you wake to the smell of homemade bread; breakfasts are fine spreads of Danish and English. In a garden full of bird feeders and pheasants a stream trickles through one of the guest terraces, and there are endless fells to explore. A treat for peace-seekers and families.

Price	£60–£85. Singles £40–£65.
Rooms	4: 2 twins/doubles, 2 family rooms.
Meals	Packed lunch £6. Supper from £12. Dinner £15–£25. Pubs 2.5 miles.
Closed	Christmas.
Directions	Penrith M6 junc. 40, A66 towards Keswick. Left opposite B5288 onto Matterdale road. After 1.25 miles, left after Walloway Farm. Up hill, then right signed 'Lowthwaite 1'.

Tine & Jim Boving Foster
Lowthwaite,
Matterdale,
Penrith CA11 0LE
Tel   +44 (0)1768 482343
Email info@lowthwaiteullswater.com
Web   www.lowthwaiteullswater.com

Entry 85   Map 11

Cumbria

Greenah

Tucked into the hillside off a narrow lane, this 1750s smallholding is surrounded by fells, so is perfect for walkers. Absolute privacy for four friends or family with your own entrance to a beamed and stone-flagged sitting room with wood-burning stove, creamy walls and cheery floral curtains. Warm bedrooms have original paintings, good beds, hot water bottles, bathrobes and a sparkling bathroom – which has a loo with a remarkable view. Malcolm is a climber; Marjorie is totally committed to organic food so you get a fabulous breakfast and good advice about the local area. Fell walking is not compulsory!

Ethical Collection: Food. See page 430.

Price	£80–£88. Singles £52.
Rooms	2: 1 double, 1 twin sharing shower (let to same party only).
Meals	Pubs/restaurants 3 miles.
Closed	Rarely.
Directions	M6 junc. 40 follow A66 west. Left for Matterdale; after 1.5 miles, left signed Dacre. Up hill, right fork to Lowthwaite, house 100 yds on right.

Marjorie & Malcolm Emery
Greenah,
Mattterdale,
Penrith CA11 0SA
Tel   +44 (0)1768 483387
Email info@greenah.co.uk
Web   www.greenah.co.uk

Entry 86   Map 11

Cumbria

Whitbysteads

Swing into the yard of a gentleman's farmhouse at the end of a drive lined with gorse, stone walls and sheep. It's a working farm, so lots going on with four-wheel drives, dogs, busy hens and relaxed bustle. Victoria does styles and periods well: warm rugs, flowery sofas with plain linen armchairs, modern family paintings. The main bedroom is sumptuous and stylish, the smaller room simpler; bathrooms are wonderfully vintage, eclectic and big. Great hosts who make you feel instantly at home here; enjoy the breathtaking views over the fells – easy for the M6 too. Dress up in the evening for dinner at Sharrow Bay. *Garden open for NGS.*

Price	£100–£110.
Rooms	3: 1 double; 1 double, 1 twin with shared bath.
Meals	Children's tea available £5. Pub 0.5 miles.
Closed	Rarely.
Directions	Exit 39 M6. A6 north, thro' Askham village, turn left up hill past postbox, over cattle grid and fork left. House is about 1 mile up - on top of the hill to the left.

	Victoria Lowther
	Whitbysteads,
	Askham,
	Penrith CA10 2PG
Tel	+44 (0)1931 712284
Email	info@gnap.fsnet.co.uk
Web	www.whitbysteads.org

Entry 87   Map 11

Cumbria

New House Farm

The large comfy beds, the extravagant baths, the linen, the fabrics, the pillows – comfort par excellence! The renovation is impressive, too; the plasterwork stops here and there to reveal old beam, slate or stone. A trio of the bedrooms are named after the mountain each faces; Swinside brings the 1650s house its own spring water. The breakfast room has a wood-burner, hunting prints and polished tables for Hazel's breakfasts to fuel your adventures, the sitting room sports fireplaces and brocade sofas, and walkers will fall gratefully into the hot spring spa. Luxurious, and huge fun. *Children over six welcome.*

Price	£140–£180. Singles £70–£120.
Rooms	5: 2 doubles, 1 twin/double. Stables: 2 four-posters.
Meals	Lunch from £6 (April–November). Dinner, 3–5 courses, £30–£37. Packed lunch £8. Pubs 2.5 miles.
Closed	Never.
Directions	A66 to Cockermouth, then B5289 for Buttermere. Signed left 2.5 miles south of Lorton.

	Bottle of Moët champagne for bookings of 2 or more nights.

	Hazel Thompson
	New House Farm,
	Lorton,
	Cockermouth CA13 9UU
Mobile	+44 (0)7841 159818
Email	hazel@newhouse-farm.co.uk
Web	www.newhouse-farm.com

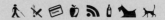

Entry 88   Map 11

Cumbria

Cockenskell Farm

Sara loves her house and hill farm garden with its wild rhododendrons and damson orchard; it sits at the southern end of Lake Coniston. Inside are beamed bathrooms and faded lemon quilts, old pine, patterned walls and idiosyncratic touches of colour. Relax with a book in the conservatory, stroll through the magical garden or tackle a bit of the Cumbrian Way which meanders through the fields to the back. On sunny days lovely Sara will give you breakfast in the garden with the birds. History seeps from every pore, the place glows with loving care and to stay here is a treat. *Children over 12 welcome.*

Price	£90. Singles from £45.
Rooms	3: 1 twin; 1 twin with separate bath; 1 single sharing bath.
Meals	Packed lunch £5. Pubs 2-4 miles.
Closed	November-February.
Directions	In Blawith, opp. church up a narrow lane, through farmyard. Right after cattle grid, over fell, right at fork through gates & up drive.

Late checkout (12pm). Free picnic and maps for walkers.

Sara Keegan
Cockenskell Farm,
Blawith,
Ulverston LA12 8EL
Tel +44 (0)1229 885217
Email keegan@cockenskell.fsnet.co.uk
Web www.cockenskell.co.uk

Cumbria

Yew Tree Farm

Everything here is special: 600 acres of sheep and cattle, a farmhouse once owned by Beatrix Potter, a spinning gallery on the side of the barn, one of the best known buildings in the Lakes. Jon farms the rising hills, Caroline (a member of the Mountain Rescue team) looks after guests with great warmth. Inside, ancient panelling, vast flagstones and William Morris wallpaper shine. There's a fire at breakfast (home-cured bacon, home-laid duck eggs), Ms Potter's furniture, letters from Wordsworth and Ruskin in a cabinet. Bedrooms are traditional with original wood, smart fabrics and views of the valley. Unmissable.

Price	£104-£124. Singles £70.
Rooms	3: 1 double, 1 four-poster; 1 four-poster with separate bath.
Meals	Dinner, 3 courses, £30; supper £15 (min. 6).
Closed	Rarely.
Directions	From M6 junc. 36, then A591 for Windermere. 17 miles then outside Ambleside left at lights, then left onto A593 for Coniston. After 5 miles house signed on right.

10% off stays of 4 nights.

Jon & Caroline Watson
Yew Tree Farm,
Coniston LA21 8DP
Tel +44 (0)1539 441433
Email info@yewtree-farm.co.uk
Web www.yewtree-farm.com

Cumbria

Low Fell

The family is great fun, their warmth is infectious and their well-orchestrated house is packed with maps, lists, books and guides. Bedrooms are bright, sunny, pretty, with elegant patterned or checked fabrics, heavenly big beds, plump pillows, warm towels; the suite up in the loft is a super hideaway and you overlook trees animated with birds. Tuck into warm homemade bread and Aga pancakes at breakfast, warm your toes by the fire in winter, relax in the lovely secluded garden with a glass of wine in summer. The house is a five-minute stroll from the lake and bustling Bowness. *Children over ten welcome.*

Price	£78-£104. Half price for children.
Rooms	2: 1 double, 1 family suite (1 double, 1 twin).
Meals	Pubs/restaurants 200 yds.
Closed	Christmas.
Directions	Directions sent on confirmation of booking.

 20% off dinner at Lindeth Howe Hotel (incl. use of leisure facilities). 20% off Mountain Goat Tours.

Louise & Stephen Broughton
Low Fell, Ferney Green,
Bowness-on-Windermere,
Windermere LA23 3EW
Tel +44 (0)1539 445612
Email louisebroughton@btinternet.com
Web www.low-fell.co.uk

Entry 91   Map 11

Cumbria

Gillthwaite Rigg

All is calm and ordered in this light, airy and tranquil Arts and Crafts house. Come for nature and to be surrounded by countryside – you may spot a badger or deer. Find panelled window seats, gleaming oak floors, leaded windows, wooden latched doors and motifs moulded into white plaster. Homely bedrooms with large beds, reached via a spiral staircase, have an uncluttered simplicity and mountain and lake views. Banks of books, wood-burners and kind, affable hosts add cheer. Rhoda and Tony are passionate about conservation and wildlife in their 14 acres of garden and woodland. *Babies & children over six welcome.*

Price	£70-£80. Singles £55.
Rooms	2: 1 double, 1 twin/double.
Meals	Pubs/restaurants 1 mile.
Closed	Christmas & New Year.
Directions	M6 junc. 36; A590 & A591 to r'bout; B5284 (signed 'Hawkshead via ferry') for 6 miles. After golf club, right for Heathwaite. Bear right up hill past nursery. Next drive on right; central part of manor.

 Guided woodland walks & badger watching. Maps loaned & help planning local trips.

Rhoda M & Tony Graham
Gillthwaite Rigg,
Heathwaite Manor,
Lickbarrow Road,
Windermere LA23 2NQ
Tel +44 (0)1539 446212
Email tony_rhodagraham@hotmail.com

Entry 92   Map 11

Cumbria

Fellside Studios

Off the beaten tourist track, a piece of paradise in the Troutbeck valley: seclusion, stylishness and breathtaking views. Prepare your own candlelit dinners, rise when the mood takes you, come and go as you please. The flower beds spill with heathers, hens cluck, and there's a decked terrace for continental breakfast in the sun – freshly prepared by your gently hospitable hosts who live in the attached house. In your studio apartment you get oak floors, slate shower rooms, immaculate kitchenettes with designer touches, DVD players, comfy chairs, luxurious towels. Wonderful. *Minimum stay two nights.*

Price	£70–£90. Singles from £45.
Rooms	2 studios: 1 double, 1 twin/double & kitchenette each.
Meals	Pub/restaurant 0.5 miles.
Closed	Rarely.
Directions	From Windermere, A592 north for 3 miles; after bridge, immed. before church, left signed Troutbeck; 300 yds, 1st house on right.

Monica & Brian Liddell
Fellside Studios,
Troutbeck,
Windermere LA23 1PE

Tel	+44 (0)1539 434000
Email	brian@fellsidestudios.co.uk
Web	www.fellsidestudios.co.uk

Entry 93   Map 11

Cumbria

Gilpin Mill

Come to be seriously spoiled. Down leafy lanes is a pretty white house by a mill pond, framed by pastures and trees. Steve took a year off to build new Gilpin Mill, and Jo looks after pigs, hens, labs and guests – beautifully. In the country farmhouse sitting room young oak beams span the ceiling and a slate faux-lintel sits above the log fire. Bedrooms are equally inviting: beds are topped with duckdown, luscious bathrooms are warm underfoot. Alongside is a lovely old barn where timber was made into bobbins; in the mill pond is a trout ladder and dam, soon to provide power for the grid. And just six cars pass a day!

Price	£70–£95. Singles £50–£60.
Rooms	3: 1 double, 2 twins/doubles.
Meals	Pub 2.5 miles.
Closed	20-30 December.
Directions	Kendal to Windermere, 1st roundabout B5284 to Crook. Left at Crook church, follow signs to Winster; house is on the river.

Jo & Steve Ainsworth
Gilpin Mill,
Crook,
Kendal LA8 8LN

Tel	+44 (0)1539 568405
Email	info@gilpinmill.co.uk
Web	www.gilpinmill.co.uk

Entry 94   Map 11

Cumbria

Middle Reston

A proper Edwardian summer house in the heart of the Lakes (Windermere is the nearest) set high and with mature rhododendrons. Inside is crammed with beautiful dark furniture, Turkish rugs, gorgeous paintings and oak overmantels; there is a comfortable drawing room which you may use. Two traditional bedrooms have claret walls and dark carpets; the yellow attic room is more modern; all are a good size and entirely quiet. Ginny and Simon are great fun and give you a stylish breakfast by a blazing fire with the newspapers; then explore the magic outside — woods, gardens, fabulous views of the mountains.

Cumbria

Summerhow House

In four acres of fine landscaping and fun topiary is a large and inviting home of flamboyant wallpapers and shades of aqua, lemon and rose. Stylish but laid-back, grand but unintimidating, both house and hosts are a treat. Bedrooms have gilt frames and marble fireplaces, Molton Brown goodies and garden views, there are two sitting rooms to retreat to and breakfasts to delight you — fruits from the orchard, eggs from Sizergh Castle (John's family home). Two miles from Kendal: hop on the train to the Lakes. Walkers, sailors, skiers, food-lovers, dog-lovers will be charmed... aspiring actors too (talk to Janey!).

Price	£90-£110.
Rooms	3: 1 double with shower; 2 twins sharing bath.
Meals	Pub 1 mile.
Closed	Christmas & occasionally.
Directions	A591 Kendal-Windermere; 500 yds past 2nd Staveley turning, turn right by small blue bicycle sign, then immediately hard left up drive.

Price	£80-£120. Singles £50-£69.
Rooms	2: 1 double, 1 twin.
Meals	Pub/restaurant 1.5 miles.
Closed	Occasionally.
Directions	M6, junc. 36 for Kendal. Then follow signs for A6 Shap & on outskirts of Kendal, as 40mph zone ends, immediate next right at white gates. House signed on wall next to gate.

 10% off room rate Mon-Thurs. Free pick-up from local bus/train station.

	Simon & Ginny Johnson
	Middle Reston,
	Staveley,
	Kendal LA8 9PT
Tel	+44 (0)1539 821246
Email	simonhj@btinternet.com
Web	www.lake-district-accomodation.com

	Janey & John Hornyold-Strickland
	Summerhow House,
	Shap Road,
	Kendal LA9 6NY
Tel	+44 (0)1539 720763
Email	stay@summerhowbedandbreakfast.co.uk
Web	www.summerhowbedandbreakfast.co.uk

Entry 95   Map 11

Entry 96   Map 11

Cumbria

Low Jock Scar

Those who like to be made a bit of a fuss of will settle in well here: a cheerful greeting from John and Roslyn comes with homemade cake in the garden, or the guest sitting room with its books and maps, and log fire for chilly days. Roslyn is a keen cook and spoils you with seasonal and local produce in the sun room with its lovely garden views. Gloriously peaceful and comfortable bedrooms have pretty fabrics; all are a good size and filled with light. Stride those hills, explore Kendal with its interesting shops and theatre, or just find a seat in the garden by the river, watch the wildlife go by and unruffle yourself.

Price	£70-£95. Singles £46-£65.
Rooms	5: 3 doubles, 2 twins.
Meals	Dinner £23. Pubs/restaurants 6-8 miles.
Closed	Rarely.
Directions	From Kendal, A6 to Penrith. After 6 miles, sign on left for Low Jock Scar. From north M6 junc. 39 to A6 south; after 9 miles sign on right for Low Jock Scar.

John & Roslyn Flackett
Low Jock Scar,
Selside, Kendal LA8 9LE
Tel   +44 (0)1539 823259
Email   info@lowjockscar.co.uk
Web   www.lowjockscar.co.uk

Entry 97   Map 12

Cumbria

Lapwings Barn

In the back of most-beautiful-beyond, down narrow lanes, this converted barn is a gorgeous retreat for two – or four. Delightful generous Gillian and Rick give you privacy and an upstairs sitting room with log stove, sofa and a balcony with views. Bedrooms (separate entrances) are elegantly rustic with sweeping beams and modern, stone-tiled bathrooms. Breakfast is delivered: sausages and bacon from their Saddlebacks, eggs from their hens, superb homemade bread and marmalade. Stroll along lowland tracks, watch curlews and lapwings, puff to the top of Whinfell. Ambleside and Beatrix Potter's house are near. One of the best.

Ethical Collection: Food. See page 430.

Price	£50-£90. Singles from £35.
Rooms	Barn: 2 twins/doubles & sitting room.
Meals	Packed lunch £5. Pub/restaurant 3.5 miles.
Closed	Rarely.
Directions	A685 Kendal-Appleby. 500 yds after Morrison's petrol left signed Mealbank; over hill after Mealbank, after 2nd bridge at Patton, middle road of 3. After Borrans Farm, left fork; 0.25 miles on left.

 Late checkout (12pm). 20% off our marmalades, sausages, bacon & eggs.

 Use your Sawday's Gift Card here.

Rick & Gillian Rodriguez
Lapwings Barn,
Whinfell, Kendal LA8 9EQ
Tel   +44 (0)1539 824373
Email   stay@lapwingsbarn.co.uk
Web   www.lapwingsbarn.co.uk

Entry 98   Map 12

Cumbria

Drybeck Hall

Looking south to fields, woodland and beck this Grade II* listed, 1679 farmhouse has blue painted mullion windows and exposed beams. Expect a deeply traditional home with good furniture, an open fire and pictures of Anthony's predecessors looking down on you benignly; the family has been in the area for 800 years. Comfortable bedrooms have pretty floral fabrics and oak doors; bathrooms are simple but sparkling. Lulie is relaxed and charming and a good cook: enjoy a full English with free-range eggs in the sunny dining room, and home-grown vegetables and often game for dinner. A genuine slice of history.

Price	£86. Singles £45.
Rooms	2: 1 double, 1 twin.
Meals	Dinner, 3 courses, £25. Pub/restaurant 4 miles.
Closed	Rarely.
Directions	From A66 south on B6260. After Hoff take 2nd left signed Drybeck, left at bottom of hill, then left at fork. House on left.

 Free pick-up from local bus/train station.

Lulie & Antony Hothfield
Drybeck Hall,
Appleby-in-Westmorland CA16 6TF
Tel +44 (0)1768 351487
Email lulieant@aol.com
Web www.drybeckhall.co.uk

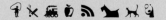

Cumbria

Coldbeck House

An old mill leat runs through the garden – elegant with trees, populated by woodpeckers and red squirrels; at breakfast they feed by the window. Belle's forte is her cooking and Richard assists with walks; both are natural hosts. The dignified 1820s house with Victorian additions has sanded and polished floors, antiques and splendid stained glass, a guest sitting room with a log-burning stove and a country-house feel. Bedrooms are delightful: fresh flowers, homemade biscuits, towels to match colourful walls. It's peaceful here, on the edge of a village with a green, and you are in unsurpassed walking country.

Price	£85-£95. Singles £55-£60.
Rooms	3: 2 doubles, 1 twin.
Meals	Dinner for groups, 2-4 courses, £20-£30. Pub within 5-minute walk.
Closed	Christmas.
Directions	M6 exit 38; A685 to Kirkby Stephen; 6 miles, then right to Ravenstonedale. 1st left opp. Kings Head pub; drive immed. on left.

10% off room rate Mon-Thurs.

Use your Sawday's Gift Card here.

Belle Hepworth
Coldbeck House,
Ravenstonedale, Kirkby Stephen CA17 4LW
Tel +44 (0)1539 623407
Email belle@coldbeckhouse.co.uk
Web www.coldbeckhouse.co.uk

Cumbria

A Corner of Eden

In the listed farmhouse surrounded by Cumbrian hills and infinite sky, tradition and comfort luxuriously combine. The sitting room has a cosy log fire; the dining room is red and gold; bedrooms glow with designer fireplaces and wooden floors – in one is a contemporary four-poster. Ochres, golds and rich fabrics embellish all, along with robes and slippers for shared bathrooms. Engaging Richard and Debbie live in the barn and show a passion for detail: sloe gin in the rooms, barbours by the door, an honesty bar and home-bakes in the dairy. Offset any indulgence by a walk to the pub – across three glorious fields.

Ethical Collection: Environment. See page 430.

Price	£130.
Rooms	4: 3 doubles, 1 twin, all sharing 2 bathrooms.
Meals	Dinner, 3 courses, £30. Pub 1 mile.
Closed	Christmas.
Directions	M6 junc. 38, signs for Brough on A685. Right into Ravenstonedale; through village until The Fat Lamb, then right. After 0.5 miles left to Stennerskeugh, keep bearing left.

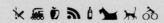

Bottle of wine with 2-night stay.

Debbie Temple & Richard Greaves
A Corner of Eden,
Low Stennerskeugh, Ravenstonedale,
Kirkby Stephen CA17 4LL
Tel   +44 (0)1539 623370
Email enquiries@acornerofeden.co.uk
Web   www.acornerofeden.co.uk

Cumbria

Lavender House

An 1850s house – the local vet's for many years – a comfortable stroll away from the centre of the bustling little market town with its interesting shops and pubs; John can collect you if you come by train. Tea and homemade cake are served in the yellow sitting room – admire Diana's lovely paintings on the walls – with comfy chairs and a fire on chilly days. Bedrooms are bright, with vibrant cushions and antique furniture; bathrooms have big mirrors, thick towels and plenty of soaps and bubbles. On sunny mornings try a Manx kipper on the roof terrace with its 'Mary Poppins' views and smart potted plants.

Ethical Collection: Food. See page 430.

Price	£70–£80. Singles from £40.
Rooms	2: 1 double; 1 twin/double with separate bath.
Meals	Packed lunch £6. Pub/restaurant 150 yds.
Closed	Rarely.
Directions	M6 junc. 36; A65 Kirkby Lonsdale. After 6.5 miles, left at r'bout. Pass Booth's supermarket. Right at junc. House 50 yds on left; park in drive.

Bottle of organic wine with 2-night stay. 10% off stays of 2+ nights.

Use your Sawday's Gift Card here.

John & Diana Craven
Lavender House,
17 New Road,
Kirkby Lonsdale LA6 2AB
Tel   +44 (0)1524 272086
Email info@lavenderhousebnb.co.uk
Web   www.lavenderhousebnb.co.uk

Derbyshire

Horsleygate Hall

Hens and guinea fowl animate the charming old stable yard, and the gardens are vibrant and fascinating, with stone terraces and streams, hidden patios, modern sculptures and seats in every corner... the Fords, attentive and kind, encourage you to explore. Inside the 1783 house, Margaret has created yet more charm. There is a warm, timeless, harmonious feel, with worn kilims on pine boards, striped and floral wallpapers, deep sofas and pools of light. Breakfast is served round a big table in the old schoolroom – homemade jams and oatcakes, garden fruit, eggs from the hens. Special. *Children over five welcome.*

Price	£70–£80. Singles from £50.
Rooms	3: 1 double; 1 family room, 1 twin sharing bath.
Meals	Pub/restaurant 1 mile.
Closed	23 December–4 January.
Directions	M1 exit 29; A617 to Chesterfield; B6051 to Millthorpe; Horsleygate Lane 1 mile on, on right at the bottom of lane. House 25 yds on left.

5% off stays of 2 or more nights.

Robert & Margaret Ford
Horsleygate Hall,
Horsleygate Lane,
Holmesfield S18 7WD
Tel   +44 (0)1142 890333

Entry 103   Map 8

Derbyshire

River Cottage

Well-travelled Gilly and John have restored their large house – built in the 1740s – and given it a fresh modern twist. Interiors are light and airy; modern wallpapers, soft furnishings, mirrors and antiques give each room a charm of its own. There's the little village to explore and a lovely, tiered garden with the duck-and-trout-filled river Wye idling past; easy to forget the busy A6 when settled here with a cup of tea or glass of wine. Fishing can be arranged and you are ten minutes from Chatsworth. Many guests come by bus: it stops outside the house. *Minimum two nights at weekends Easter-October.*

Price	£90–£135. Singles from £85.
Rooms	4: 3 doubles; 1 double with separate bath.
Meals	Pubs 600 yds.
Closed	10 December–10 February.
Directions	On northern edge of Ashford village, 1.5 miles N of Bakewell on A6. Buses from Nottingham, Matlock, Manchester & Buxton stop outside the door.

Bottle of wine in your room.

Gilly & John Deacon
River Cottage, The Duke's Drive,
Ashford-in-the-Water,
Bakewell DE45 1QP
Tel   +44 (0)1629 813327
Email info@rivercottageashford.co.uk
Web   www.rivercottageashford.co.uk

Entry 104   Map 8

Derbyshire

Alstonefield Manor

Country manor house definitely, but delightfully understated and cleverly designed to look natural. Local girl Jo spoils you with warm, homemade scones and tea when you arrive, on the lawns overlooking the rolling hills, or in the elegant drawing room with its soft tones and warming fire. Bedrooms have a painted wooden floor, antique iron bed or large bay window and all have garden views; wood panelled bathrooms have showers or a roll top tub. Wake to birdsong – and a candlelit breakfast with local bacon and Staffordshire oatcakes. After a game or two of badminton or croquet, take supper at The George in the village. A joy.

Price	£80-£150.
Rooms	3: 1 double; 2 doubles each with separate bath.
Meals	Pub 100 yds.
Closed	Christmas & occasionally.
Directions	A515 north out of Ashbourne; 6 miles, left into Alstonefield. Over the bridge (river Dove) and up hill. Take 1st left on entering village, go towards the church. House on right.

10% off room rate Mon-Thurs. Bottle of wine in your room.

Robert & Jo Wood
Alstonefield Manor,
Alstonefield,
Ashbourne DE6 2FX
Tel   +44 (0)1335 310393
Email stay@alstonefieldmanor.com
Web   www.alstonefieldmanor.com

Entry 105   Map 8

Derbyshire

Park View Farm

An amazing farm stay, run by hospitable hosts. Daringly decadent, every inch of this plush Victorian farmhouse brims with flowers, sparkling trinkets, polished brass, plump cushions and swathes of chintz. The rooms dance in swirls of colour, frills, gleaming wood, lustrous glass, buttons and bows – it is an extravagant refuge after a long journey. New-laid eggs from the hens for breakfast, fresh fruits and homemade breads accompany the grand performance. The solid brick farmhouse sits in 370 organic acres and Kedleston Hall Park provides a stunning backdrop. *Children over eight welcome.*

Ethical Collection: Food. See page 430.

Price	£80-£90. Singles £50-£60.
Rooms	3: 2 doubles; 1 double with separate bath.
Meals	Pub/restaurant 1 mile.
Closed	Christmas.
Directions	From A52 & A38 r'bout west of Derby, A38 north, 1st left for Kedleston Hall. House 1.5 miles past park on x-roads in Weston Underwood.

10% off stays of 2 or more nights in a double en suite room, Mon-Thurs.

Linda Adams
Park View Farm,
Weston Underwood,
Ashbourne DE6 4PA
Tel   +44 (0)1335 360352
Email enquiries@parkviewfarm.co.uk
Web   www.parkviewfarm.co.uk

Entry 106   Map 8

Derbyshire

Hungry Bentley Barn

Off a lane in the tranquil Dales, a beautiful, light-filled, modern interpretation of a barn conversion, renovated by Jane and Brian. Genial and relaxed, she breeds dressage horses and walls are hung with equine prints and oils; his passion is vintage cars... a spin in the Bentley may be offered. Find pale chintzy sofas by a huge fireplace, and a grand piano on a toasty warm floor. Up handcrafted oak stairs is a small library of books and maps: a lovely spot to read. Uncluttered cream bedrooms have high ceilings, oak timbers and sandstone floors; bathrooms are fabulous. Wake to rare breed sausages and homemade preserves.

Price	From £78.
Rooms	3: 1 double, 2 four-posters.
Meals	Pubs/restaurants 1.5 miles.
Closed	Christmas, New Year & January.
Directions	From A50 take A515 to Ashbourne. After 4 miles right at Howard Arms (closed) on corner. House 1 mile on right, next to Bentley Hall.

10% off stays of 2 or more nights.

Jane Boothroyd
Hungry Bentley Barn,
Derby Lane, Alkmonton,
Ashbourne DE6 3DJ
Tel   +44 (0)1335 330296
Email   bandb@hungrybentleybarn.co.uk
Web   www.hungrybentleybarn.co.uk

Entry 107   Map 8

Derbyshire

Mount Tabor House

On a steep hillside between the Peaks and the Dales, a chapel with a peaceful aura and great views. Enter a hall where light streams through stained-glass windows – this is a relaxed, easy place to stay with a distinctive and original interior. Breakfast, served in a dining room with open stone walls, is mainly from the village shops, and as organic as possible; you can eat on the balcony in summer. Enjoy a delicious dinner in or walk to the pub, then retire to a luxurious bed. Rooms, thanks to charming Fay, are as inviting as can be, and bathrooms a treat. *Usually minimum stay two nights at weekends.*

Price	£85. Singles £60.
Rooms	2: 1 double, 1 twin/double.
Meals	Occasional dinner, £25. Pubs 100 yds.
Closed	Rarely.
Directions	M1 exit 26; A610 towards Ripley. At Sawmills, right under r'way bridge, signed Crich. Right at marketplace onto Bowns Hill. Chapel 200 yds on right. Can collect from local stations.

10% off room rate Mon-Thurs. Bottle of wine with dinner first night.

Fay Whitehead
Mount Tabor House,
Bowns Hill, Crich,
Matlock DE4 5DG
Tel   +44 (0)1773 857008
Mobile   +44 (0)7813 007478
Email   mountabor@msn.com

Entry 108   Map 8

Derbyshire

Manor Farm

Between two small dales, close to great houses (Chatsworth, Hardwick Hall, Haddon Hall), lies this cluster of ancient farms and church; welcome to the 16th century! Simon and Gilly, warm, delightful and fascinated by the history, have great green plans for the romantic old wing. The Elizabethan kitchen, arched and atmospheric, is where you are served breakfast, scrumptious and organic. There's a 'book exchange' in the old milking parlour, one bedroom, cosy and quaint, overlooks the church, and another has a super big bathroom. The pretty garden swoops to fields and distant river. *Children over six welcome.*

Ethical Collection: Environment; Food; Community. See page 430.

Price	£65-£75. Singles £40-£55.
Rooms	3: 1 double, 1 twin/double; 1 double with separate bath.
Meals	Pubs 5-10 minute drive.
Closed	Rarely.
Directions	From M1 exit 28. A38 then A615 dir. Matlock. Thro' Wessington, after 1 mile right at Plough pub, then 3rd left . Down Dethick Lane 1 mile.

	Simon & Gilly Groom
	Manor Farm,
	Dethick,
	Matlock DE4 5GG
Tel	+44 (0)1629 534302
Email	gilly.groom@w3z.co.uk
Web	www.manorfarmdethick.co.uk

Entry 109   Map 8

Derbyshire

Tinkersley Cottage

Sarah has painstakingly reassembled two run-down cottages at the very top of a hill, with the giddiest views over the Peak district's loveliest parts. You can tell she's a stylist: here are pretty stripes and florals, painted wood panelling, chandeliers and shabby chic, Farrow and Ball colours. The comfy and restful bedroom, with antique linen, painted French bed and the fantastic views, is gloriously private with its own entrance up steps from the pretty terraced garden. Sarah is bright and bubbly and loves having guests: breakfast comes from Chatsworth farm shop (you can walk there) or Bakewell farmers' market.

Price	£80.
Rooms	1 suite.
Meals	Pubs/restaurants within 1 mile.
Closed	Never.
Directions	A6 Bakewell to Matlock. Through Rowsley, East Lodge Hotel on left, after 0.5 miles Barn Lane on left. House at top of hill.

 10% off room rate Mon-Thurs. 10% off stays of 2 or more nights.

	Sarah Copley
	Tinkersley Cottage,
	Tinkersley,
	Rowsley,
	Matlock DE4 2NJ
Mobile	+44 (0)7802 494814
Email	sarahcopley16@hotmail.co.uk

Entry 110   Map 8

Devon

Orchard Cottage

Tucked into a quiet village corner, this is the last cottage in a row of three. Walk through the pretty garden, past seats that (sometimes!) bask in the sun and down to your own entrance and terrace… you may come and go as you please. Your bedroom is L-shaped and large, with a comfortable brass bed and a super en suite shower; it is spotless yet rustic. The Ewens are friendly and fun, their two spaniels equally so and you are brilliantly sited for Dartmoor, Plymouth, the sand and the sea. Breakfasts in the beamed dining room are generous and delicious; this is excellent value B&B.

Price	From £60. Singles £45.
Rooms	1 double.
Meals	Pubs 300 yds.
Closed	Christmas.
Directions	A379 from Plymouth for Modbury. On reaching Church St at top of hill, before Modbury, fork left at Palm Cross, then 1st right by school into Back St. Cottage 3rd on left, past village hall.

	Maureen Ewen
	Orchard Cottage,
	Back Street, Palm Cross Green,
	Modbury PL21 0RF
Tel	+44 (0)1548 830633
Mobile	+44 (0)7979 558568
Email	moewen@talktalk.net

Entry 111   Map 2

Devon

Annapurna

Rural bliss: the garden of this pretty, cream-painted longhouse surrounded by munching cows and happy hens looks down the folded valley to the steeple of Modbury Church. Inside, Carol and Peter spoil you with blueberry pancakes, organic home-baked bread, home-laid eggs and charming bedrooms with a fresh, country feel. Choose independence in the annexe with your own sitting room, or sleep in the main house; each room is lovely with garden flowers, good beds and sparkling bath or shower rooms. Fabulous walking starts from the door and you are close to the watery delights of Salcombe and Dartmouth.

Ethical Collection: Food. See page 430.

Price	£65–£75. Singles £30–£40.
Rooms	3: 1 twin/double; 1 single with separate bath. Annexe: 1 double & sitting room.
Meals	Pubs/restaurants 1 mile.
Closed	Rarely.
Directions	A38 Modbury & Ermington. After 1.5 miles approx. Kittaford Cross straight on, thro' California Cross. After 2.4 miles left down unmarked lane. House 300 yds on right.

A 'spoil yourself' day: massage, seaweed bath & scented candles (reduced rate of £25).

	Carol Farrand & Peter Foster
	Annapurna,
	Mary Cross,
	Modbury PL21 0SA
Tel	+44 (0)1548 831299
Email	carolfarrand@tiscali.co.uk
Web	www.annapurna-devon.co.uk

Entry 112   Map 2

Devon

Rafters Barn

A delightful and peaceful 300-year-old barn along the narrowest of lanes and with soaring views from the valley to the sea. This is big sailing country but mostly agricultural so you will avoid the madding crowds. You have a comfy guest sitting room with big sofas and a wood-burner that belts out the heat, neat bedrooms in bright colours with pretty touches, tiled bathrooms that gleam and a great big breakfast in the open hallway. Elizabeth is thoughtful and smiley and will point you to the best beaches and places to eat in Salcombe. Or let her cook for you – with produce fresh from farmers' markets.

Price	From £75.
Rooms	3: 1 double, 1 twin; 1 double with separate bath.
Meals	Dinner from £20 (October-March only). Pubs/restaurants 4 miles.
Closed	Christmas & New Year.
Directions	A381 dir. Salcombe. Just before Hope Cove sign, right to Bagton & S. Huish. Follow lane for 1 mile; 30 yds past saw mill, right up farm lane; at bottom on left.

Elizabeth Hanson
Rafters Barn,
Holwell Farm, South Huish,
Kingsbridge TQ7 3EQ

Tel	+44 (0)1548 560460
Email	raftersdevon@yahoo.co.uk
Web	www.raftersdevon.co.uk

Entry 113   Map 2

Devon

Washbrook Barn

Hard not to feel happy here – even the blue-painted windows on rosy stone walls make you want to smile. Inside is equally sunny. The barn – decrepit until Penny bought it six years ago – rests at the bottom of a quiet valley. She has transformed it into a series of big light-filled rooms with polished wooden floors, pale beams and richly coloured walls lined with fabulous watercolours: the effect is one of gaiety and panache. No sitting room as such, but armchairs in impeccable bedrooms from which one can admire the rural outlook. The beds are divinely comfortable and the fresh bathrooms sparkle.

Price	From £75. Singles £50.
Rooms	3: 1 double; 1 double, 1 twin, each with separate bath/shower.
Meals	Dinner occasionally in winter. Pubs/restaurants 10-min. walk.
Closed	Christmas & New Year.
Directions	From Kingsbridge quay to top of Fore St; right into Duncombe St; on to T-junc.; left to Church St. Right into Belle Cross Rd; 150 yds, right into Washabrook Lane; 250 yds left; at bottom on right.

 10% off stays Mon-Thurs.

Penny Cadogan
Washbrook Barn,
Washabrook Lane,
Kingsbridge TQ7 1NN

Tel	+44 (0)1548 856901
Email	penny.cadogan@homecall.co.uk
Web	www.washbrookbarn.co.uk

Entry 114   Map 2

Devon

Strete Barton House

Contemporary, friendly, exotic and exquisite: French sleigh beds and Asian art, white basins and black chandeliers, and a garden with sofas for the views. So much to love, and the coastal path right outside the door. Your caring hosts live the dream, running immaculate B&B by the sea, in an old manor house at the top of the village. Breakfasts are exuberantly local (village eggs, sausages from Dartmouth, honey from the bay), there's a wood-burner in the sitting room and Kevin and Stuart know exactly which beach, walk or pub is perfect for you. *Minimum stay two nights in summer. Pets in cottage only.*

Ethical Collection: Food; Community. See page 430.

Price	£90–£140. Singles £80.
Rooms	6: 3 doubles, 1 twin; 1 twin with separate shower. Cottage: 1 suite & sitting room.
Meals	Pub/restaurant within 50 yds.
Closed	Rarely.
Directions	From Dartmouth, A379 to Kingsbridge. At mini r'bout, left onto A379 signed Stoke Fleming. A379 to Strete, then right into Totnes Rd. House 20 yds up hill on right.

Free pick-up from local bus/train station.

Use your Sawday's Gift Card here.

Stuart Litster & Kevin Hooper
Strete Barton House,
Totnes Road,
Strete, Dartmouth TQ6 0RU
Tel   +44 (0)1803 770364
Email info@stretebarton.co.uk
Web   www.stretebarton.co.uk

Entry 115   Map 2

Devon

Nonsuch House

The photo says it all! You are in your own crow's nest, perched above the flotillas of yachts zipping in and out of the estuary mouth: stunning. Kit and Penny are great fun and look after you well; Kit is an ex-hotelier, smokes his own fish fresh from the quay and knocks out brilliant dinners. Further pleasures lie across the water: a five-minute walk brings you to the ferry that transports you and your car to the other side. Breakfasts in the conservatory are a delight, bedrooms are big and comfortable and fresh bathrooms sparkle. *Children over ten welcome. Minimum stay two nights at weekends. Disabled ramps available.*

Ethical Collection: Food. See page 430.

Price	£110–£150. Singles £85–£125.
Rooms	4: 3 twins/doubles, 1 double.
Meals	Dinner, 3 courses, £35. (Not Tues/Wed/Sat.) Pub/restaurant 5-minute walk & short boat trip.
Closed	Rarely.
Directions	2 miles before Brixham on A3022, A379. After r'bout, fork left (B3205) downhill, through woods, left up Higher Contour Rd, down Ridley Hill. At hairpin bend.

Bottle of wine with dinner on first or second night. Late checkout (12pm).

Kit & Penny Noble
Nonsuch House,
Church Hill,
Kingswear, Dartmouth TQ6 0BX
Tel   +44 (0)1803 752829
Email enquiries@nonsuch-house.co.uk
Web   www.nonsuch-house.co.uk

Entry 116   Map 2

Devon

The White House

Gaze on the sparkling estuary from the comfort of your bed in this very friendly, very relaxing house at the top of the hill – filled with books and art. There's classical music and Hugh's homemade bread at breakfast, and a real fire for your sitting room in winter. Fresh, pretty bedrooms have sherry, chocolates, bathrobes and opera glasses for views; more village and estuary views from the garden terrace. A ferryman transports you to Agatha Christie's house just across the river: shake the bell opposite the Inn! Another ferry takes you to Dartmouth – catch the river boat on to Totnes. *Children by arrangement.*

Price	£90. Singles £60.
Rooms	2 doubles.
Meals	Pubs a short walk.
Closed	Christmas.
Directions	Off A3122 at Sportsman's Arms. After approx. 3 miles down hill into Dittisham, sharp right immed. before Red Lion. Along The Level, up hill & house entrance opp. at junc. of Manor St & Rectory Lane.

	Hugh & Jill Treseder
	The White House,
	Manor Street,
	Dittisham TQ6 0EX
Tel	+44 (0)1803 722355
Email	jilltreseder@btinternet.com

Entry 117 Map 2

Devon

Old Mill Farm

Position, position, position. Dazzling sunsets, resident kingfisher, the occasional seal, total seclusion; painters and birdwatchers will think they have died and gone to heaven. The approach is stunning: from the top of the hill you descend to the estuary's edge, and find a hugely refitted house with Elizabethan origins and glamorous Robert and Kate. Bedrooms are spacious, plush, stylish; bathrooms have thick fluffy towels and one has a bath with the best-ever view. Breakfast is posh (eggs benedict, home-baked croissants, kippers) and eaten in the river room with slate floor, French windows and… views. A treat.

Price	£100–£135.
Rooms	3 doubles.
Meals	Pub less than a mile.
Closed	January/February.
Directions	From Brixham road into Galmpton, straight through (Greenway Road), with primary school on right. Up hill out of village, right at 'No Through Road' sign, down lane. Entrance on left.

	10% off stays Mon-Thurs. Transport to foot ferry.

	Robert & Kate Chaston
	Old Mill Farm,
	Greenway, Galmpton TQ5 0ER
Tel	+44 (0)1803 842344
Email	enquiries@oldmillfarm-dart.co.uk
Web	www.oldmillfarm-dart.co.uk

Entry 118 Map 2

Devon

Riverside House

The loveliest 18th-century house with wisteria growing up its walls and the tidal river estuary bobbing past with boats and birds; dip your toes in the water while sitting in the garden. Felicity, an artist, and Roger, a passionate sailor, give you pretty bedrooms with paintings, poetry, little balconies, wide French windows and binoculars – spot swans at high tide and herons when the river goes down. Stroll to the pub for quayside barbecues and jazz in summer; catch the ferry from Dittisham to Agatha Christie's house; discover delightful Dartmouth. Kayaks and inflatables welcome by arrangement. *Min. two nights at weekends.*

Price	From £75. Singles from £60.
Rooms	2: 1 double; 1 double with separate shower.
Meals	Packed lunch £6. Pubs 100 yds.
Closed	Rarely.
Directions	In Tuckenhay, pass Maltsters Arms on left to 2nd thatched house on left, at right angle to road. Drive past, turn at bridge and return to slip lane.

 Bottle of wine in room for stays of 2 or more nights. Use of slipway.

Felicity & Roger Jobson
Riverside House,
Tuckenhay,
Totnes TQ9 7EQ
Tel   +44 (0)1803 732837
Email   felicity@riverside-house.co.uk
Web   www.riverside-house.co.uk

Entry 119   Map 2

Devon

Lower Norton Farmhouse

Hard to believe the downstairs bedroom was a calving pen and its smart bathroom the dairy. Now it has a seagrass floor and a French walnut bed. All Glynis's rooms are freshly decorated, and she and Peter are the most amenable hosts, genuinely happy for you to potter around all day should you wish to do so. For the more active, a yacht on the Dart and a cream Bentley are to hand, with Peter as navigator and chauffeur – rare treats. Return to gardens, paddocks, peaceful views, super dinners and a big log fire. Off the beaten track, a tremendous find. *Children over ten welcome.*

Price	From £70. Singles £60.
Rooms	3: 2 doubles, 1 twin.
Meals	Dinner, 2 courses, £25. Lunch £9. Packed lunch £7. Pub/restaurant 1.5 miles.
Closed	Rarely.
Directions	From A381 at Halwell, 3rd left signed Slapton; 4th right after 2.3 miles signed Sherford, Kingsbridge at Wallaton Cross. House down 3rd drive on left.

Bottle of wine with dinner on first night.

Peter & Glynis Bidwell
Lower Norton Farmhouse,
Coles Cross, East Allington,
Totnes TQ9 7RL
Tel   +44 (0)1548 521246
Email   enquiries@lowernortonfarmhouse.co.uk
Web   www.lowernortonfarmhouse.co.uk

Entry 120   Map 2

Devon

Avenue Cottage

The tree-lined approach is steep and spectacular; the cottage sits in 11 wondrous acres of rhododendron, magnolia and wild flowers with a lily-strewn pond, grassy paths and lovely views over the river. Find a quiet spot in which to read or simply sit and absorb the tranquillity. Richard is a gifted gardener, and the archetypal gardener's modesty and calm have penetrated the house itself – it is uncluttered, comfortable and warmed by a log fire. The old-fashioned twin room has a big, faded bathroom with a faux-marble basin and a balcony with sweeping valley views; the pretty village and pub are a short walk away.

Price	£60–£80. Singles £40–£50.
Rooms	2: 1 twin/double; 1 double sharing shower.
Meals	Pub 0.5 miles.
Closed	Rarely.
Directions	A381 Totnes to Kingsbridge for 1 mile; left for Ashprington; into village, then left by pub ('Dead End' sign). House 0.25 miles on right.

Richard Pitts
Avenue Cottage,
Ashprington,
Totnes TQ9 7UT
Tel   +44 (0)1803 732769
Email   richard.pitts@btinternet.com
Web   www.avenuecottage.com

Entry 121   Map 2

Devon

Manor Farm

Sarah is a happy gardener, producing vegetables that will find their way into your (excellent) dinner, and raspberries for your muesli. She keeps bees and hens too, so you can have honey and eggs for breakfast, served in a super red dining room. The farmhouse, facing a communal courtyard, twists and turns around unexpected corners thanks to ancient origins, and its good traditional bedrooms in bright farmhouse colours are reached via two separate stairs – nicely private. Sarah and Michael's labs are charming and the village is pure Devon: surrounded by apple orchards and with two good pubs for eating out.

Price	From £70. Singles £45–£50.
Rooms	2: 1 double; 1 twin with separate bath/shower.
Meals	Dinner £17–£23. Packed lunch £5. Pubs 500 yds.
Closed	Rarely.
Directions	From Newton Abbot, A381 for Totnes. After approx. 2.5 miles, right for Broadhempston. Past village sign, down hill & 2nd left. Pass pub on right & left after high stone wall into courtyard.

Sarah Clapp
Manor Farm,
Broadhempston,
Totnes TQ9 6BD
Tel   +44 (0)1803 813260
Email   mandsclapp@btinternet.com

Entry 122   Map 2

Devon

Kilbury Manor

You can stroll down to the Dart from the garden and onto their little island, when the river's not in spate! Back at the Manor — a listed longhouse from the 1700s — are four super-comfortable bedrooms, the most private in the stone barn. Your genuinely welcoming hosts (with dogs Dillon and Buster) moved to Devon to renovate a big handsome house and open it to guests. Julia does everything beautifully so there's organic smoked salmon for breakfast, baskets of toiletries by the bath, the best linen on the best beds and a drying room for wet gear — most handy if you've come to walk the Moor. Spot-on B&B.

Price	£75-£90. Singles from £50.
Rooms	4: 2 doubles. Barn: 1 twin/double; 1 double with separate bath.
Meals	Pubs/restaurants 1.5-4 miles.
Closed	Rarely.
Directions	Leaving A38, left for Totnes. After 0.5 miles, right over river on narrow bridge; follow lane over railway bridge then immed. left into Colston Rd. House 0.25 miles on left.

Julia & Martin Blundell
Kilbury Manor,
Colston Road,
Buckfastleigh TQ11 0LN
Tel   +44 (0)1364 644079
Email   info@kilburymanor.co.uk
Web   www.kilburymanor.co.uk

Entry 123   Map 2

Devon

Agaric Rooms at Tudor House

A merchant's townhouse now happily given over to rooms for the Agaric Restaurant. Sophie and Nick are young, fun and very clever: in these mostly large, individually styled rooms, fabrics are plush, colours innovative and bathrooms have roll tops. A breakfast room is cool with leather and palms; full English or anything else you want is delivered here. Don't come without booking into the restaurant for fabulous modern British cooking — then stagger two steps down the street to your well-earned bed. Ashburton bustles with good food shops, antiques and books.

Price	£110-£135. Singles £50.
Rooms	4: 2 doubles, 1 family, 1 single.
Meals	Owners' restaurant next door. Packed lunch from £10 for 2.
Closed	Rarely.
Directions	From A38 follow signs to Ashburton. North Street is the main street, house is on the right after the Town Hall.

10% off room rate Mon-Thurs.
10% off stays of 2 or more nights.

Sophie & Nick Coiley
Agaric Rooms at Tudor House,
36 North Street,
Ashburton TQ13 7QD
Tel   +44 (0)1364 654478
Email   eat@agaricrestaurant.co.uk
Web   www.agaricrestaurant.co.uk

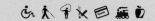

Entry 124   Map 2

Devon

Penpark

Clough Williams-Ellis of Portmeirion fame did more than design an elegant house; he made sure it communed with nature. Light pours in from every window and the views are long, across rolling farmland to Dartmoor and Hay Tor. The big double has a comfy sofa and its own balcony; the private suite has arched French doors to the garden and an extra room for young children. Antiques and heirlooms, African carvings, silk and fresh flowers – it is deeply traditional and comforting. Your generous hosts have been doing B&B for years; they and their two springer spaniels look after you well.

Price	From £76. Singles by arrangement.
Rooms	3: 1 family suite; 1 twin/double with separate bath; 1 double with separate shower.
Meals	Pub 1 mile.
Closed	Rarely.
Directions	A38 west to Plymouth; A382 turn off; 3rd turning off r'bout, signed Bickington. There, right at junc. (to Plymouth), right again (to Sigford & Widecombe). Over top of A38 & up hill; 1st entrance on right.
	10% off stays of 2 or more nights Mon-Thurs. Lift to local pubs.

Madeleine & Michael Gregson
Penpark,
Bickington, Ashburton TQ12 6LH
Tel   +44 (0)1626 821314
Email maddy@penpark.co.uk
Web   www.penpark.co.uk

Entry 125   Map 2

Devon

Hooks Cottage

At the end of a long bumpy track, the hideaway mine captain's house may have few original features but the woodland setting is gorgeous. Mary and Dick have a finely judged sense of humour; labradors Archie and Cobble will charm you. It is simple, rural, close to the Moors, with woodland birds and a gentle river to unwind stressed souls. Carpeted bedrooms have a faded floral charm and pretty stream views; bathrooms are plain. Enjoy local sausages and Mary's marmalade for breakfast, a lovely garden and amazing bluebells in spring; walks from the house are sublime. Your horse is welcome too.

Price	£60-£65. Singles £40.
Rooms	2: 1 double en suite (wc across landing); 1 twin with separate bath.
Meals	Pub/restaurant 2 miles.
Closed	Rarely.
Directions	From A38, A382 at Drumbridges for Newton Abbot; 3rd left at r'bout for Bickington. 2.7 miles on, down hill, right for Haytor. Under bridge, 1st left & down long, bumpy track, past thatched cottage to house.

Mary & Dick Lloyd-Williams
Hooks Cottage,
Bickington,
Ashburton TQ12 6JS
Tel   +44 (0)1626 821312
Email hookscottage@yahoo.com

Entry 126   Map 2

Devon

Bagtor House

What a setting! A ten-minute walk and you're on top of the moor. Enfolded by garden, fields and sheep, the 15th-century house with the Georgian façade is the last remaining manor in the parish. Find ancient beauty in granite flagstones, oak-panelled walls, great fireplaces glowing with logs, country dressers brimming with china. Sue looks after hens, geese, labs, guests, grows everything and makes her own muesli. She gives you a large and elegant double room with an antique brass bed and, steeply up the stairs, a big attic-cosy suite perfect for families. Warm, homely, spacious, civilised, and close to beautiful Hay Tor.

Ethical Collection: Environment; Food. See page 430.

Price	From £76. Singles by arrangement.
Rooms	2: 1 double, 1 family room, each with separate bath/shower.
Meals	Restaurants/pubs 1.5 miles.
Closed	Never.
Directions	From A38 to Plymouth, A382 turn off at r'bout, 3rd exit to Ilsington; up through village, 2nd left after hotel (to Bickington), 1st crossroads right to Bagtor, 0.5 miles, on right next to Farm.

Late checkout (12pm).
Lift to local pubs.

Sue & Nigel Cookson
Bagtor House,
Ilsington, Bovey Tracey TQ13 9RT
Tel   +44 (0)1364 661538
Email   sawreysue@hotmail.com
Web   www.bagtormanor.co.uk

Entry 127   Map 2

Devon

Corndonford Farm

An ancient Devon longhouse and an engagingly chaotic haven run by warm and friendly Ann and Will, along with their Shire horses and Dartmoor ponies. Steep, stone circular stairs lead to bedrooms: bright lemon walls, a four poster with lacy curtains, gorgeous views over the cottage garden and a bathroom with a beam to duck. A place for those who want to get into the spirit of it all – maybe help catch an escaped foal, chatter to the farm workers around the table; not for fussy types or Mr and Mrs Tickety Boo. Good for walkers too – the Two Moors Way footpath is on the doorstep. *Children over ten by arrangement.*

Ethical Collection: Food. See page 430.

Price	£60-£70. Singles £35.
Rooms	2: 1 four-poster; 1 twin with separate bath.
Meals	Pub 2 miles.
Closed	Rarely.
Directions	From A38 2nd Ashburton turn for Dartmeet & Princetown. In Poundsgate pass pub on left; 3rd right on bad bend signed Corndon. Straight over x-roads, 0.5 miles, farm on left.

Late checkout (12pm).
Drive in carriage with pair of Dartmoor Hill ponies.

Ann & Will Williams
Corndonford Farm,
Poundsgate,
Newton Abbot TQ13 7PP
Tel   +44 (0)1364 631595
Email   corndonford@btinternet.com

Entry 128   Map 2

Devon

Heron Cottage

Folded into a valley in an idyllic corner of Dartmoor is a freshly renovated riverside B&B. One of two adjoining 18th-century cottages, it's light and airy inside, with one white-walled guest bedroom in the house and the other outside, down by the river – new, wooden and triple-glazed, with shower rooms modern and white. Your hosts – outgoing, musical, hospitable and well-travelled – give you delicious breakfasts (local sausages, homemade bread) at flexible times and perhaps on the veranda in summer, overlooking the roses. There's a wood-burner in the living room and the Two Moors Way runs right by the door.

Price	£70–£75. Singles £55.
Rooms	2: 1 double. Garden: 1 double.
Meals	Pub 3 miles.
Closed	Rarely.
Directions	Bovey Tracy to Widecombe, then Postbridge road for 1.2 miles, then 1st left to Jordan. Left again, down to bottom of hill. Cottage on bend.

Sue Bottomley
Heron Cottage,
Jordan,
Widecombe-in-the-Moor,
Newton Abbot TQ13 7PN
Tel   +44 (0)1364 631596
Email   sue@patrickgarvey.demon.co.uk

Entry 129   Map 2

Devon

Hammerslake Cottage

Be seduced by narrow lanes and high hedges before you arrive at this smartly painted 16th-century farm worker's cottage on the edge of Dartmoor. You are surrounded by a tranquil garden with twittering birds, a trickling stream and dramatic views; breakfast out here in summer, on eggs from Caroline's hens, local bacon, kedgeree. Two bedrooms (one with a balcony) are smartly dressed with big beds, goosey pillows, fresh flowers and chocolate, the third is a frill-free space for kids with bunks, comics and games. Tents can be put up in the garden, trees can be climbed; this is an affable place with a lovely owner.

Price	£70–£80.
Rooms	3: 2 doubles, 1 bunk room.
Meals	Pub 1 mile.
Closed	Rarely.
Directions	From Lustleigh, left down lane to T-junc.; right for North Bovey, Pethybridge & Cleave. On for 1 mile, to blind bend with thatched cottage on right. Next house on right, set back from road, signed 'B&B'.

Caroline Byng
Hammerslake Cottage,
Ellimore Road, Lustleigh,
Newton Abbot TQ13 9SQ
Tel   +44 (0)1647 277547
Email   caroline.byng@btinternet.com
Web   www.lustleighbedandbreakfast.co.uk

Entry 130   Map 2

Devon

Lower Harton Farm

The views from the lovely living room/conservatory reach to the sea at Torbay. Warm friendly Sue keeps her just-moved-into house in apple-pie order and is delighted to share it with guests. Make the most of an immaculate TV snug with a wood-burning stove, big comfy beds in fresh peaceful bedrooms, deep white tubs in shiny new bathrooms, and heavenly views from every sparkling window. You can take tea in thatched Lustleigh (two miles), and walk to the moors from the door. Breakfasts are flexible and feature eggs from the hens, and there's a great little pub in the village.

Price	£70-£100. Singles £50.
Rooms	3: 1 double; 1 double, 1 twin sharing bath (let to same party only).
Meals	Pub/restaurant 2 miles.
Closed	Christmas, New Year & occasionally.
Directions	Bovey Tracey to Moretonhamstead; left Lustleigh. Left opp. Dairy then 0.5 miles to T-junc. Right, 1.3 miles, then left into Lower Harton drive.

 10% off room rate.

	Sue Clark
	Lower Harton Farm,
	Lustleigh,
	Newton Abbot TQ13 9SG
Tel	+44 (0)1647 277472
Email	sue21clark@yahoo.co.uk
Web	www.lowerhartonfarm.co.uk

Entry 131   Map 2

Devon

Highfield House

Come for complete peace in the Dartmoor National Park and be bowled over by the glorious garden. Helen is charming and her smart contemporary house gleams; light floods in through huge windows and the south-facing terrace runs the length of the house. Large bedrooms with armchairs are sumptuous, one has its own roof terrace with views of the moor; bathrooms are sparkling and modern. The birds sing, the pale oak floors are heated from underneath and the locally sourced breakfast is generous. Wonderful walks start at the end of the garden and the pretty village has a friendly pub serving good food.

Price	£75-£85. Singles £60-£70.
Rooms	3: 1 double, 2 twins/doubles.
Meals	Pub 300 yds. Restaurants within 5 miles.
Closed	Christmas & New Year.
Directions	A382 past Bovey Tracey, left to Lustleigh. Over railway bridge, into village; 3 bungalows & steep hill on right. Up hill & house 7th on left.

  10% off stays of 3 or more nights.

	Helen Waterworth
	Highfield House,
	Mapstone Hill, Lustleigh,
	Newton Abbot TQ13 9SE
Tel	+44 (0)1647 277577
Email	helen@highfieldhousedevon.co.uk
Web	www.highfieldhousedevon.co.uk

Entry 132   Map 2

Devon

Cyprian's Cot

A charming terraced cottage of 16th-century nooks and crannies and beams worth ducking. The setting is exquisite: the garden leads into fields of sheep, the Dartmoor Way goes through the town and the Two Moors Way skirts it. Shelagh, a lovely lady, gives guests their own sitting room with a fire, lit on cool nights; breakfasts, served in the cosy dining room, are fresh, free-range and tasty. Up the narrow stairs and into simple bedrooms – a small double and a tiny twin. A perfect house and hostess, and a perfect little town to discover, with its pubs, fine restaurant and delicatessen, organic shop and tearoom.

Price	£60. Singles from £30.
Rooms	2: 1 twin;
	1 double with separate bath.
Meals	Pubs/restaurants 4-minute walk.
Closed	Rarely.
Directions	In Chagford pass church on left; 1st right beyond Globe Inn opposite. House 150 yds on right.

10% off stays Mon-Thurs.

Shelagh Weeden
Cyprian's Cot,
47 New Street, Chagford,
Newton Abbot TQ13 8BB
Tel   +44 (0)1647 432256
Email   shelaghweeden@btinternet.com
Web   www.cyprianscot.co.uk

Entry 133   Map 2

Devon

Easdon Cottage

Replenish your soul in this newly decorated, light and beautifully proportioned cottage; if the charming big double in the house is taken, you may stay in the nearby barn. Both have tranquillity and delightful moor views. Inside are wood-burners in the dining and drawing rooms, and an enchanting mix of good pictures, oriental rugs, books, plants and some handsome Victorian finds. You are in a classic Devon valley, Dartmoor lies beyond, and the sweet cottage garden is filled with birds. Liza and Hugh's veggie and vegan breakfasts are imaginative and delicious. *Children & pets by arrangement. Reduction for four nights or more.*

Ethical Collection: Environment; Food. See page 430.

Price	From £70.
Rooms	1 twin/double.
Meals	Occasional supper £10–£20. Pub/restaurant 3 miles.
Closed	Rarely.
Directions	A38 from Exeter; A382 for Bovey Tracey. There, left at 2nd r'bout for Manaton; 2 miles beyond Manaton, right at x-roads for M'hampstead. 0.5 miles on, right, signed Easdon. On left up track.

Liza & Hugh Dagnall
Easdon Cottage,
Long Lane,
Manaton TQ13 9XB
Tel   +44 (0)1647 221389
Email   easdondown@btopenworld.com
Web   www.easdoncottage.co.uk.

Entry 134   Map 2

Devon

Burnville House

Granite gateposts, Georgian house, rhododendrons, beechwoods and rolling fields of sheep: that's the setting. But there's more. Beautifully proportioned rooms reveal subtle colours, elegant antiques, squishy sofas and bucolic views, stylish bathrooms are sprinkled with candles, there are sumptuous dinners and pancakes at breakfast. Your hosts left busy jobs in London to settle here, and their place breathes life – space, smiles, energy. Swim, play tennis, walk to Dartmoor from the door, take a trip to Eden or the sea. Or... just gaze at the moors and the church on the Tor and listen to the silence, and the sheep.

Price	From £75. Singles £50.
Rooms	3 doubles.
Meals	Dinner from £19. Pub 2 miles.
Closed	Rarely.
Directions	A30 Exeter-Okehampton; A386 dir. Tavistock. Right for Lydford opp. Dartmoor Inn; after 4 miles (thro' Lydford), Burnville Farm on left (convex traffic mirror on right).

Victoria Cunningham
Burnville House,
Brentor,
Tavistock PL19 0NE
Tel +44 (0)1822 820443
Email burnvillef@aol.com
Web www.burnville.co.uk

Entry 135   Map 2

Devon

Mount Tavy Cottage

Joanna and Graham, a lovely Devon couple, have worked hard to restore this former gardener's bothy, Graham making much of the furniture himself. Pretty bedrooms in the house have stripped floorboards, a four-poster or half-tester bed, and deep, free-standing baths. Two other simpler bedrooms, each with a big shower, are across the courtyard in the garden studios; here you can be completely independent, or trot over to the house for a delicious breakfast. Outside are ponds – one with a breezy pagoda for summer suppers – and a walled Victorian garden. Tavistock is a short walk. *Arrivals after 5pm, unless previously arranged.*

Price	From £70. Singles from £35.
Rooms	4: 1 double, 1 four-poster, both with separate bath. 2 studios: 1 twin/double & kitchenette each.
Meals	Dinner, 3 courses, £20. Pub 2 miles.
Closed	Rarely.
Directions	From Tavistock B3357 towards Princetown; 0.25 miles on, after Mount House School, left. Drive past lake to house.

G H Moule
Mount Tavy Cottage,
Tavistock PL19 9JL
Tel +44 (0)1822 614253
Email mounttavy@btinternet.com
Web www.mounttavy.co.uk

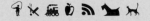

Entry 136   Map 2

Devon

Higher Eggbeer Farm

Over 900 years old and still humming with life: pigs, cows, ponies, rabbits and chickens share the rambling gardens. Sally Anne and William are artistic, fun, slightly wacky and charming. It's an adventure to stay, so keep an open mind: the house is a historic gem and undeniably rustic. Huge inglenook fireplaces, interesting art, books, piano, wellies, muddle and charm. Your lovely hosts will take children to feed animals and collect eggs, and will babysit. Be wrapped in peace in your own half of the house (with beautiful drawing room), immersed in a magnificent panorama of forest, hills and fields of waving wheat.

Price	£65–£75. Singles £42.
Rooms	3: 2 twins/doubles sharing bath (2nd room let to same party only); 1 double sharing owners' bath. Self-catering option.
Meals	Restaurants 5-minute walk.
Closed	Rarely.
Directions	A30 to Okehampton. After 10 miles left exit into Cheriton Bishop; 1st left after Old Thatch pub, signed Woodbrooke. Down & up hill; road turns sharp left but you don't. Right down private lane.

Sally Anne & William Selwyn
Higher Eggbeer Farm,
Cheriton Bishop,
Exeter EX6 6JQ
Tel   +44 (0)1647 24427

Entry 137   Map 2

Devon

Brook Farmhouse

Tuck yourself up in the peace and quiet of Paul and Penny's whitewashed, thatched cottage, surrounded by glorious countryside. Inside find a charming sitting room with a huge inglenook, good antiques, fresh flowers, and comfy sofa and chairs; breakfast here on homemade apple juice, eggs from the owners' hens and delicious local bacon and sausages. Up the ancient spiral stone stairs is your warm, beamed bedroom with smooth linen, chintzy curtains, lots of cushions. You are near Dartmoor and can reach the Devon beaches and the north Cornish coast; perfect for hearty walkers, birdwatchers, surfers and picnic-lovers.

Price	£70. Singles £40.
Rooms	1 double with separate bath.
Meals	Pub 2 miles.
Closed	Christmas & New Year.
Directions	In Tedburn village turn into North Park Rd opp. garage, then right at T-junc. after bridge. House on right after 1.4 miles at bottom of steep hill.

Paul & Penny Steadman
Brook Farmhouse,
Tedburn St Mary,
Exeter EX6 6DS
Tel   +44 (0)1647 270042
Email   penny.steadman@btconnect.com
Web   www.brookfarmhouse.2day.ws

Entry 138   Map 2

Devon

The Garden House

Refulgent! An extraordinary restoration of a 1930s house, carried out with passion. Bedrooms are sumptuous: beds plump with cushions, fabrics smooth, colours vibrant, scents divine. The exuberance reaches the garden; Jane's energy among the pots, quirky topiary and tulips is almost palpable. A huge collection of books are stacked hither and thither, the chandeliers sparkle, homemade cakes abound, candles flicker and there's a vast choice of locally sourced breakfasts, beautifully served. It may not be minimalist but it is deeply comfortable, good-humoured and an easy walk into the city.

Price	£85–£90. Singles £50–£60.
Rooms	2: 1 double, 1 twin.
Meals	Restaurant 8-minute walk. Pubs nearby.
Closed	Rarely.
Directions	M5 junc. 30 for city centre & university. Behind old Debenhams, Longbrook St into Pennsylvania Rd. Thro' lights, 2nd left into Hoopern Ave; house at end on left.

David & Jane Woolcock
The Garden House,
4 Hoopern Avenue, Pennsylvania,
Exeter EX4 6DN
Tel +44 (0)1392 256255
Email david.woolcock1@virgin.net
Web www.exeterbedandbreakfast.co.uk

Entry 139   Map 2

Devon

Larkbeare Grange

Expectations rise as you follow the tree-lined drive to the immaculate Georgian house… and are met, the second you enter. The upkeep is perfect, the feel is chic and the whole place exudes well-being. Sparkling sash windows fill big rooms with light, floors shine and the grandfather clock ticks away the hours. Expect the best: good lighting, goose down duvets, contemporary luxury in fabric and fitting, the fabulous suite — perfect for a small family, flexible breakfasts and lovely views from the bedrooms at the front. Charlie, Savoy-trained, and Julia are charming and fun: you are in perfect hands.

Ethical Collection: Environment. See page 430.

Price	£95–£165. Singles from £80.
Rooms	4: 2 doubles, 1 twin/double, 1 suite.
Meals	Pub 1.5 miles.
Closed	Rarely.
Directions	From A30 Exmouth & Ottery St Mary junc. At r'bouts follow Whimple signs. 0.25 miles, right; 0.5 miles, left signed Larkbeare. Grange 1 mile on left.

 Upgrade when available or 10% off stays Sun-Thurs. (Phone bookings only.)

 Use yourSawday's Gift Card here.

Charlie & Julia Hutchings
Larkbeare Grange,
Larkbeare, Talaton,
Exeter EX5 2RY
Tel +44 (0)1404 822069
Email stay@larkbeare.net
Web www.larkbeare.net

Entry 140   Map 2

Devon

Lower Allercombe Farm

Horses in the paddock and no-frills bedrooms at this down-to-earth, very friendly B&B. Don't expect twinsets and pearls; Susie, ex-eventer, may greet you in two-tone jodphurs instead. She and Lizzie (her terrier) live at one end of the listed longhouse, guests at the other. There's a sitting room with horsey pictures and cosy wood-burner, and bedrooms upstairs that reflect the fair price. You'll feast on home eggs and tomatoes in the morning, and rashers from award-winning pigs. Very handy for Exeter, the south coast and Dartmoor; the airport is ten minutes away, the A30 is one mile. *Stabling available.*

Price	£60-£70. Singles £40-£50.
Rooms	3: 1 double, 1 twin; 1 double with separate bath.
Meals	Pub/restaurant 2 miles.
Closed	Rarely.
Directions	From Exeter junc. 29, M5. A30 towards Honiton. At Daisymount exit to Ottery St Mary, B3180 off r'bout. 200 yds, then right to Allercombe. 1 mile until x-roads, then right. House 50 yds on right.

Susie Holroyd
Lower Allercombe Farm,
Rockbeare,
Exeter EX5 2HD
Tel   +44 (0)1404 822519
Email holroyd.s@gmail.com
Web   www.lowerallercombefarm.co.uk

Devon

Beach House

Lapping at the riverside garden is the Exe estuary, wide and serene. Birds and boats, the soft hills beyond, a gorgeous Georgian house on the river and kind hosts who have been here for years. The garden is pretty with quirky rooster-shaped topiary and old apple trees; you may have a locally sourced breakfast in the conservatory or in the dining room, with raspberries and blackberries in season. Relax on comfy chairs in bedrooms with antique white bedspreads, charmingly old-fashioned bathrooms and estuary views. Cycle into Exeter, for culture and cathedral; the RSPB reserve is just five minutes away.

Price	From £80. Singles £50.
Rooms	2: 1 twin, 1 double.
Meals	Pubs/restaurants 8-minute walk.
Closed	December-March.
Directions	M5 exit 30; signs to Exmouth. Right at pub. After 1 mile, immed. left after level crossing. At mini r'bout, left down The Strand. House last on left by beach.

Trevor & Jane Coleman
Beach House,
45 The Strand,
Topsham,
Exeter EX3 0BB
Tel   +44 (0)1392 876456
Email janecoleman45@hotmail.com

Devon

Varnes

Catch the train to this tidy village on the estuary, with its winding streets and picture book cottages; there are super walks and a cycle path from here. You stay in a long, white-painted house, hunkered in a dip with a large, pretty garden; the well-travelled Finneys give you comfortable, bright, uncluttered bedrooms (one has its own sitting room) with lots of pictures, hot water bottles, fresh milk, feather duvets, modern bathrooms and a feeling of independence in your own wing. All is peaceful and quiet; breakfast is mainly locally sourced and is taken in the sunny conservatory. *Well-behaved dogs by arrangement.*

Price	£60-£65. Singles £45.
Rooms	2: 1 double, 1 twin.
Meals	Pub/restaurant 30 yds.
Closed	Christmas.
Directions	From junc. 30 M5, A376 towards Exmouth. After 5 miles, right at traffic lights by Saddlers Arms. After 0.75 miles, right into 1st open gateway after parish church.

Chris Finney
Varnes,
Church Road,
Lympstone EX8 5JT
Tel   +44 (0)1395 276999
Email   chris@varnes16.freeserve.co.uk
Web   www.varnes.co.uk

Entry 143   Map 2

Devon

Pebbles

Once owned by the Duchess of Westminster, this neat 1920s house has spectacular views of sea, surf and seagulls. Gentle, friendly Humfrey and Rosemary have mixed old with new, fun art with recycled pieces. Bedrooms, with big comfy beds, face the sea; spotless bathrooms sport robes and good lotions. The Sail Loft has two plantation chairs and a sweet extra room with twin beds; two rooms have their own little conservatories. Breakfast is a spread: fruit compotes, homemade muesli, good bacon. Stride the coast path, visit castles, spot dolphins from the conservatory, soak up those huge views. *Min. two nights weekends April-Sept.*

Price	From £89. Singles from £79.
Rooms	3: 1 twin/double; 2 twins/doubles each with separate bath.
Meals	Pubs/restaurants within 100 yds.
Closed	Rarely.
Directions	From Exeter A30 or M5 to junc. 30. A365 signed Exmouth. Left on B3179 signed Budleigh Salterton. Into town, thro' high street. On right next to tourist information centre.

Humfrey & Rosemary Temple
Pebbles,
16 Fore Street,
Budleigh Salterton EX9 6NG
Tel   +44 (0)1395 442417
Email   stay@bedandbreakfastbythebeach.com
Web   www.bedandbreakfastbythebeach.com

Entry 144   Map 2

Devon

Simcoe House

In a gracious seaside setting, this 18th-century villa was the summer home of General Simcoe – look up the history in the local museum. There are stunning views from wide windows in the big inviting sitting room, so find a book and settle by the fire. Bedrooms, sunny and lovely, have good art, fresh flowers and fabulous vistas; the newest is in the coach house, open-plan, restful and reached via an outside spiral stair. Enjoy the garden with its subtropical palms and the terrace with its rooftop views. A charming home with wonderful owners, in strolling distance from beach and town. *Children over ten welcome.*

Devon

Glebe House

Set on a hillside with fabulous views over the Coly valley, this late-Georgian vicarage is now a heart-warming B&B. The views will entice you, the hosts will delight you and the house is filled with interesting things. Chuck and Emma spent many years at sea – he a Master Mariner, she a chef – and have filled these big light rooms with cushions, kilims and treasured family pieces. There's a sitting room for guests, a lovely conservatory with a vintage vine, peaceful bedrooms with blissful views and bathrooms that sparkle. All this, two sweet pigmy goats, wildlife beyond the ha-ha and the fabulous coast a hike away.

Price	From £80. Singles from £70.
Rooms	3: 1 double, 1 twin.
	Coach house: 1 studio &
	kitchenette.
Meals	Pubs/restaurants 5 minute walk.
Closed	Christmas.
Directions	M5 junc. 30 onto A376. Then
	B3179 to Budleigh Salterton (approx.
	8 miles). Into town centre then left
	opposite The Creamery, onto Fore
	Street Hill. 150 yds on right and
	through white gates into car park.
	Steps lead to front door.

Price	From £70. Singles £45.
Rooms	3: 1 double, 1 twin/double,
	1 family.
Meals	Pubs/restaurants 2.5 miles.
Closed	Christmas & New Year.
Directions	A375 from Honiton; left opposite
	Hare & Hounds on B3174 to
	Seaton. 2nd left to Southleigh,
	1.5 miles. In village 1st left to
	Northleigh; 600 yds, drive on left.

 10% off stays of 3 or more nights.

Use your Sawday's Gift Card here.

Jane & John Crosse
Simcoe House,
8 Fore Street Hill,
Budleigh Salterton EX9 6PE
Tel   +44 (0)1395 446013
Email   simcoehouse@hotmail.co.uk
Web   www.simcoehouse.co.uk

Emma & Chuck Guest
Glebe House,
Southleigh,
Colyton EX24 6SD
Tel   +44 (0)1404 871276
Email   emma_guest@talktalk.net
Web   www.guestsatglebe.com

Entry 145   Map 2

Entry 146   Map 2

Devon

West Colwell Farm

Devon lanes, pheasants, bluebell walks *and* sparkling B&B. The Hayes clearly love what they do; ex-TV producers, they have converted this 18th-century farmhouse and barns into a cosy, warm and stylish place to stay. Be charmed by original beams and pine doors, heritage colours and clean lines. Bedrooms feel self-contained, two have terraces overlooking the wooded valley and the most cosy is tucked under the roof. Linen is luxurious, showers are huge and breakfasts (Frank's pancakes, lovely bacon, eggs from next door) are totally flexible. A pretty garden in front, beaches nearby, peace all around. Bliss.

Price	From £75. Singles £55.
Rooms	3 doubles.
Meals	Restaurants 3 miles.
Closed	December/January.
Directions	3 miles from Honiton; Offwell signed off A35 Honiton–Axminster road. In centre of village, at church, down hill. Farm 0.5 miles on.

Frank & Carol Hayes
West Colwell Farm,
Offwell,
Honiton EX14 9SL
Tel   +44 (0)1404 831130
Email stay@westcolwell.co.uk
Web   www.westcolwell.co.uk

Entry 147 Map 2

Devon

Applebarn Cottage

A tree-lined drive leads to a long white wall, and a gate opening to an explosion of colour – the garden. Come for a deliciously restful place and the nicest, most easy-going hosts; the wisteria-covered 17th-century cottage is full of books, paintings and fresh flowers. Bedrooms – one in an extension that blends in beautifully – are large, traditional, wonderfully comfortable, and the views down the valley are sublime. Patricia trained as a chef and dinners at Applebarn are delicious and great fun. Breakfast, served in a lovely oak-floored dining room, includes a neighbour's homemade honey. *Minimum stay two nights.*

Price	£76–£80. Half-board option (dinner) £60–£63 p.p.
Rooms	2 suites.
Meals	Pub/restaurant 3 miles.
Closed	Mid-November to mid-March.
Directions	A30 Chard to Honiton. Left at top of hill, Wambrook & Stockland. Straight on at next x-roads (Membury); 0.75 miles, left, Cotley & Ridge. Past Hartshill Boarding Kennels; signed 2nd right.

 Bottle of wine with dinner for stays of 4+ nights. 5% off 2nd and subsequent stays.

Patricia & Robert Spencer
Applebarn Cottage,
Bewley Down,
Axminster EX13 7JX
Tel   +44 (0)1460 220873
Email paspenceruk@yahoo.co.uk
Web   applebarn.wordpress.com

Entry 148 Map 2

Devon

The Devon Wine School

Alastair and Carol run their wine school from this delightfully rural spot where the night sky still twinkles, and look after you to perfection. Chill out in an open-plan sitting/dining room with wooden floors, smart chesterfields, Xian terracotta warriors, claret walls. Choose from bedrooms in the house, or brand new ones in a separate building; all are light, unfussy and elegant with swish bathrooms. Work up an appetite on the hard tennis court: food is taken seriously and sourced locally, the wine is a joy and reasonably priced, the atmosphere is house party style; relaxed and friendly. *Children over eight welcome.*

Price	From £85. Singles by arrangement.
Rooms	5: 1 double, 1 twin. Old Dairy: 3 doubles.
Meals	Dinner from £29.50. Occasional lunch. Pub 1 mile.
Closed	Rarely.
Directions	From Cadeleigh, 1.5 miles to Postbox Cross, turn left to Cheriton Fitzpaine. Follow road to Redyeates Cross x-roads, then right, house is 150 yds on left down track.

10% off stays of 2 or more nights. Bottle of house wine with dinner on first night.

Alastair & Carol Peebles
The Devon Wine School,
Redyeates Farm, Cheriton Fitzpaine,
Crediton EX17 4HG
Tel +44 (0)1363 866742
Email alastair@devonwineschool.co.uk
Web www.devonwineschool.co.uk

Entry 149　Map 2

Devon

Raymont House

Delightful to be in the heart of a historic little town with a Tuesday market and good pubs yet close to the wilds of Dartmoor. This is civilised B&B: your charming hosts give you one bedroom (or, if you're a party, three), peaceful, pretty and serene, and a wow of a bathroom that mixes period features with beautiful modern fittings. No guest sitting room but TVs, homemade biscuits, delicious breakfasts, dressing gowns and fresh flowers... The breakfast room is warmed by a wood-burner, there's a drying room for wet gear, you're on the Tarka Trail and near to RHS Rosemoor. Great value.

Price	From £70. Singles £45–£55.
Rooms	3: 2 doubles, 1 single all sharing bath (let to same party only).
Meals	Pub/restaurant 50 yds.
Closed	Christmas & New Year.
Directions	From Okehampton, signs to Hatherleigh for 6 miles. At r'bout, right thro' Hatherleigh to top of Market Street. House on left.

 Use your Sawday's Gift Card here.

Jan & Alan Toogood
Raymont House,
49 Market Street, Hatherleigh,
Okehampton EX20 3JP
Tel +44 (0)1837 810850
Email alan.toogood@yahoo.co.uk
Web www.raymonthouse.co.uk

Entry 150　Map 2

Devon

Leworthy Barton

Biscuits, scones, sweet vases of hedgerow flowers. Breakfasts are left for you to cook and come courtesy of Rupert's Tamworth pigs and happy hens; bread and jams are homemade, wellies and waxed jackets are on tap. Rupert is a busy farmer and designer who chooses to give guests what he would most like himself. So… you have the whole of the stables, tranquil, beautifully restored and with field and sky views. Downstairs is open-plan, with kitchen and log-burner; up are sloping ceilings, wooden floors, big bed, soft towels. It's cosy yet spacious, stylish yet homely, and the Atlantic coast is the shortest drive.

Ethical Collection: Food. See page 430.

Price	£80. Singles £60.
Rooms	Barn: 1 double, sitting room & kitchen.
Meals	Pub 3 miles.
Closed	Never.
Directions	A39 to Woolfardisworthy. At T-junc. in village, left. 0.5 miles left to Stibb Cross. Over bridge bear right, then left. Uphill, right towards Leworthy & Mill; 0.5 miles; on left.

Rupert Ashmore
Leworthy Barton,
Woolsery,
Bideford EX39 5PY
Tel   +44 (0)1237 431140

Entry 151   Map 2

Devon

Beara Farmhouse

The moment you arrive at the whitewashed farmhouse you feel the affection your hosts have for the place. Richard is a lover of wood and a fine craftsman – every room echoes his talent; he also created the pond that's home to mallards and geese. Ann has laid brick paths, stencilled, stitched and painted, all with an eye for colour; bedrooms and guest sitting room are delectable and snug. Open farmland all around, sheep, pigs and hens in the yard, the Tarka Trail on your doorstep and hosts happy to give you 6.30am breakfast should you plan a day on Lundy Island. Readers love this place. *Minimum stay two nights June-September.*

Price	£70. Singles by arrangement.
Rooms	2: 1 double, 1 twin.
Meals	Pub 1.5 miles.
Closed	20 December-5 January.
Directions	From A39, left into Bideford, round quay, past old bridge on left. Signs to Torrington; 1.5 miles, right for Buckland Brewer; 2.5 miles, left; 0.5 miles, right over cattle grid & down track.

Ann & Richard Dorsett
Beara Farmhouse,
Buckland Brewer,
Bideford EX39 5EH
Tel   +44 (0)1237 451666
Web   www.bearafarmhouse.co.uk

Entry 152   Map 2

Devon

Hillbrow House

You could be forgiven for thinking this 'house on the hill' is genuine Georgian – but it's mostly new, with a deep veranda and glorious views over the golf course (and, on a clear day, to distant Dartmoor). The light, uncluttered rooms are neat as a pin with coordinated colours, thick fabrics, antiques and your own upstairs studio sitting room; bedrooms have feather pillows, proper blankets and luxurious bathrooms. Golfers and walkers will be in paradise, surfers can reach Croyde easily and a plethora of gentler beaches lie in the other direction. Stoke up on delicious homemade granola for breakfast.

Price	From £85. Singles £50.
Rooms	2: 1 double; 1 double with separate bath.
Meals	Dinner, 3 courses, £25. Pubs/restaurants within walking distance.
Closed	Christmas.
Directions	Take B3226 from South Molton for 5 miles. Turn right for Chittlehamholt, left at T-junc., then through village. House is last on right.
	10% off room rate Mon-Thurs. Free pick-up from local bus/train station.

Clarissa Roe
Hillbrow House,
Chittlehamholt,
Umberleigh EX37 9NS
Tel   +44 (0)1769 540214
Email   clarissaroe@btinternet.com
Web   www.hillbrowhouse.com

Entry 153   Map 2

Devon

Lower Hummacott

Charming decorative touches, antique furniture, fresh fruit and handmade chocolates: you'll find thoughtful extras in the bedrooms (one with a gorgeous king-size bed) and in the guest sitting rooms. Plus delicious organic and traditionally reared meat, vegetables and eggs, fresh fish, homemade cakes... As if that were not enough, the Georgian farmhouse has formal landscaped gardens in seven acres of grounds with woodland, streams, ponds, wildlife and orchard hens. Liz, a weaver, and Tony, a professional artist (there's a gallery by the house) are charming and friendly and look after you brilliantly. Great value.

Price	£68.
Rooms	2 doubles & sitting rooms.
Meals	Dinner £27 (Sunday & Monday only). Pub/restaurant 1.5 miles.
Closed	Rarely.
Directions	0.5 miles east of Kings Nympton village is Beara Cross; go straight over marked to Romansleigh for 0.75 miles; Hummacott is 1st entrance on left; down drive & 1st house on left.

Tony & Liz Williams
Lower Hummacott,
Kings Nympton,
Umberleigh EX37 9TU
Tel   +44 (0)1769 581177
Email   tony@tonywilliamsart.co.uk
Web   www.tonywilliamsart.co.uk

Entry 154   Map 2

Devon

Catsheys

Folded into the Devon hills, this open 30-year-old house is full of light and surprises. Lovely likeable David and Rosie are designers and their home is a hymn to contemporary texture and colour. Bedrooms are superb – a French sleigh bed here, a chic 60s armchair there, new art, crisp linen, ethnic treasures. Bathrooms are pure delight. Surrounded by bluebell woods and badgers, the garden has flowers for your room and a solar-heated pool for summer swims. After breakfast of homemade granola and fresh laid eggs, surf the north Devon coast, ramble the two moors, walk the Tarka Trail. Special. *Over 12s welcome. Min. two nights bank hols.*

Price	From £95. Singles from £60.
Rooms	2: 1 twin/double, 1 double.
Meals	Pubs within 3 miles.
Closed	Rarely.
Directions	From South Molton, B3137 for 4.5 miles; right at Odam Cross to Romansleigh; next left at Buckham Cross signed 'No Through Road'; steep hill, over ford, 2nd right, house on left at top of hill.

Jar of Rosie's secret recipe homemade chutney. Single guests half double room rate.

Rosie & David Ames
Catsheys,
Romansleigh,
South Molton EX36 4JW
Tel   +44 (0)1769 550580
Email rooms@catsheys.co.uk
Web   www.catsheys.co.uk

Entry 155   Map 2

Devon

Sannacott

On the southern fringes of Exmoor you're in peaceful countryside with hidden valleys. The Trickeys breed national hunt racehorses from their Georgian style farmhouse; downstairs is a happy mix of casual countryside living, antiques, open fires and family pictures. Bedrooms are traditional, clean and comfortable, some have lovely long views across rolling hills and trees. Clare bakes her own bread, most produce is organic or local and there's a pretty bird-filled garden to wander through. Great for walkers with the North Devon coastal path nearby: riders, birdwatchers and nature lovers will be happy too.

Price	£70-£80. Singles £45.
Rooms	3: 1 double; 1 twin/double sharing bath/shower. Annexe: 1 twin.
Meals	Occasional dinner, 3 courses, £20. Pub 5 miles.
Closed	Rarely.
Directions	M5 J27; A361 for Barnstaple, past Tiverton, 15.5 miles; right at r'bout (signed Whitechapel). 1.5 miles to junc., right towards Twitchen & N. Molton; 1.5 miles to 3rd on left, black gates.

10% off stays of 2 or more nights. Local food/produce in your room.

Clare Trickey
Sannacott,
North Molton EX36 3JS
Tel   +44 (0)1598 740203
Email mctrickey@hotmail.com
Web   www.sannacott.co.uk

Entry 156   Map 2

Devon

Bratton Mill

Breakfast is locally sourced and superb; in summer, eat by the Exmoor trout stream to almost deafening birdsong. Absolute privacy down the long track to a thickly wooded and beautifully secluded valley: watch for dragonflies, red deer, buzzards and the flash of the kingfisher. To the backdrop of the rushing stream is the house, painted white and filled with treasure – including Marilyn who spoils you: elegant china, fresh flowers, a warm bathroom, crisp linen and a comforting decanter of port. There are strolls or hikes straight from the door. Wonderful. *Self-catering cottage & folly available.*

Price	£95. Singles £60.
Rooms	1 twin/double. Children's rooms available.
Meals	Pub within walking distance.
Closed	Rarely.
Directions	From Bratton Fleming High Street turn right into Mill Lane. Down road for 0.5 miles thro' railway cutting; turn right.

 Free entry to Arlington Court. A drink before dinner each night of stay.

	Marilyn Jacobs Holloway
	Bratton Mill,
	Bratton Fleming,
	Barnstaple EX31 4RU
Tel	+44 (0)1598 710026
Email	contact@brattonmill.co.uk
Web	www.brattonmill.co.uk

Entry 157 Map 2

Devon

Beachborough Country House

A gracious 18th-century rectory with stone-flagged floors, lofty windows, wooden shutters, charming gardens. Viviane is vivacious and spoils you with dinners and breakfasts straight from the Aga; dine in the kitchen or in the elegant dining room with twinkling fire. Hens cluck, horses whinny but otherwise the peace is deep. Ease any walker's pains away in a steaming roll top tub; big airy bedrooms are fresh as a daisy with Turkish rugs and great views – admire them from the window seats. There's a games room for kids in the outbuildings and Combe Martin is a short hop for a grand beach day. Huge fun. *Dogs £5 per stay.*

Ethical Collection: Food; Community. See page 430.

Price	From £75. Singles £50.
Rooms	3: 1 twin/double, 2 doubles.
Meals	Dinner, 2-3 courses, from £19. Pub 3 miles.
Closed	Rarely.
Directions	From A361 take A399 for 12 miles. At Blackmoor Gate, left onto A39. House 1.5 miles on right.

 Waived charge for dogs, or decanter of port.

Use your Sawday's Gift Card here.

	Viviane Clout
	Beachborough Country House,
	Kentisbury,
	Barnstaple EX31 4NH
Tel	+44 (0)1271 882487
Email	viviane@beachborough.freeserve.co.uk
Web	www.beachboroughcountryhouse.co.uk

Entry 158 Map 2

Devon

North Walk House

Come for the organic, local food: jazz-enthusiasts Kelvin and Liz are passionate cooks, serving candlelit dinners in the large bistro-style dining room at one convivial table; try Appledore sea bass or braised Exmoor beef. Bedrooms, all with sea views, have brass beds, stripped floors, local art, modern pine and TVs; bathrooms are brand new with tiles from Provence – all is clean, comfortable and informal but not state of the art. A paved terrace at the front is fine for a cup of coffee, or a glass of wine, and a look at the view. Great for coastal path walkers and foodies. *Minimum stay two nights.*

Ethical Collection: Food. See page 430.

Price	From £80. Singles £50.
Rooms	5: 4 doubles, 1 twin.
Meals	Packed lunch £6.50. Dinner, 4 courses, from £26.50. Pub/restaurant 0.25 miles.
Closed	January.
Directions	A39 from Barnstaple to Lynton Town Hall. From there, left turn at the church down North Walk. Third hotel on left.

Bottle of wine with dinner on first night.

Use your Sawday's Gift Card here.

Kelvin Jacobs & Liz Hallum
North Walk House,
North Walk,
Lynton EX35 6HJ
Tel   +44 (0)1598 753372
Email walk@northwalkhouse.co.uk
Web   www.northwalkhouse.co.uk

Entry 159   Map 2

Devon

Southcliffe Hall

An Argentinian chandelier, antique French radiators, a rediscovered Victorian garden; this is a grandly idiosyncratic house with inherited eccentric touches. Overlooking the sea and originally the Manor House, each floor resounds with history. Charming Kate and Barry will give you dinner in the panelled dining room, and local produce for a delicious breakfast. Bedrooms are vast with rich carpets, big beds, antique flourishes; bathrooms are unique – roll top baths to Victorian high-level cisterns. Spot deer in the woodland, walk to rock pools, hike to great beaches; the view of the bay is fabulous.

Ethical Collection: Food. See page 430.

Price	£100. Singles by arrangement.
Rooms	2 twins/doubles.
Meals	Dinner, 3 courses, £30. Pub 5-minute walk.
Closed	Rarely.
Directions	From A361, B3343 towards Woolacombe. Turn right, through Lincombe, into Lee. Long drive to house is on left, between village hall and red telephone box.

Kate Seekings & Barry Jenkinson
Southcliffe Hall,
Lee EX34 8LW
Tel   +44 (0)1271 867068
Email stay@southcliffehall.co.uk
Web   www.southcliffehall.co.uk

Entry 160   Map 2

Devon

Victoria House

Beachcombers, surfers and walkers will be in their element in this Edwardian seaside villa where each bedroom has a magnificent view. Choose between the two in the main house (with sofas) and the beach-hut annexe with a big romantic deck facing the sea. Heather is lively and fun, she and David are ex-RAF and go out of their way to give you the best; bathrooms are state of the art, breakfasts are a tour de force – fruits, yogurts, waffles, eggs benedict or the full Monty. No garden but you are on the coastal road to Woolacombe (of surf and kite surfing fame) and the beach is a ten-minute walk. A top spot.

Ethical Collection: Food. See page 430.

Price	£90–£140.
Rooms	3: 1 double, 1 twin/double. Annexe: 1 double.
Meals	Pubs/restaurants 200 yds.
Closed	Rarely.
Directions	From B3343, right for Mortehoe. Through village & past the old chapel. Down steep hill, with the bay ahead; house 3rd on left.

 Late checkout (12pm).

Heather & David Burke
Victoria House,
Chapel Hill, Mortehoe,
Woolacombe EX34 7DZ
Tel   +44 (0)1271 871302
Email heatherburke59@fsmail.net
Web   www.victoriahousebandb.co.uk

Entry 161   Map 2

Dorset

Bowes House

A great place to blow the cobwebs away. The light, airy and spacious 1980s house with wide country views is at the end of a track, just where it peters out into a bridleway. With a gorgeous big garden and an orchard It's a great place for families... Lisa and Jeremy have two young sons, a dog, cats, geese and a clutch of hens. No traffic – just the occasional passing horse – and walking from the door. Lisa is seriously eco-minded, so a wood has been planted to fuel the fires and the Rayburn; breakfast is local, homemade and often organic. Super comfy bedrooms, too; the twin has Spanish bedheads.

Ethical Collection: Environment. See page 430.

Price	From £60.
Rooms	3: 1 double; 1 twin, 1 single sharing bath (let to same party only).
Meals	Pub 540 yds.
Closed	Rarely.
Directions	A3066 from Beaminster to Mosterton. From south of the village, right immed. before Eeles Pottery into Bowes Lane. House last on left. Crewkerne station 5-min. walk.

Lisa & Jeremy Purkiss
Bowes House,
Bowes Lane, Mosterton,
Beaminster DT8 3HN
Tel   +44 (0)1308 868862
Email info@boweshousebandb.com
Web   www.boweshousebandb.com

Entry 162   Map 3

Dorset

Wooden Cabbage House

Leafy lanes and a private drive lead you to Martyn and Susie's beautifully restored keeper's cottage, hidden deep in rolling countryside on the Dorset border. Leave the hubbub behind, savour the valley views, relax in this spacious stylish home, filled with fresh flowers, fine antiques and paintings, and country-house charm in cosy bedrooms. Eat al fresco on the terrace or in the verdant garden room, or by the Aga in winter – the breakfast and home-cooked suppers are delicious. The Lees are fabulous hosts – nothing is too much trouble. Great local walks and the Jurassic coast is half-an-hour away.

Price	From £90. Singles £65.
Rooms	3: 2 doubles, 1 twin.
Meals	Dinner, 3 courses with coffee & wine, £35. Pub/restaurants 3 miles.
Closed	Rarely.
Directions	3 miles S of Yeovil on A37, turn west to Closworth. Continue on this road, past turn to Halstock; 200 yds on right, over cattle grid. House down drive on left.

 A jar of Susie's homemade marmalade or jam, or free pick-up from Yeovil station.

Martyn & Susie Lee
Wooden Cabbage House,
East Chelborough,
Dorchester DT2 0QA
Tel   +44 (0)1935 83362
Email   relax@woodencabbage.co.uk
Web   www.woodencabbage.co.uk

Entry 167   Map 3

Dorset

Holyleas House

This is a fabulous house, comfortable and easy; Tia and her two friendly dogs are genuinely welcoming. You breakfast by a log fire in the elegant dining room in winter: free-range eggs, bacon and sausages from the farmers' market, homemade jams and marmalade. Sleep in light, softly-coloured bedrooms with lovely views across the well-tended gardens, and spotless bathrooms. Walkers and explorers will be happy: return to a roaring fire and a good book in the drawing room. It's a short hop to the pub for supper and Tia is happy to babysit too. *Minimum stay two nights in high season & at weekends.*

Price	£80-£90. Singles £40.
Rooms	3: 1 double, 1 family room; 1 single with separate bath.
Meals	Pub a short walk.
Closed	Christmas & New Year.
Directions	From Dorchester, B3143 into Buckland Newton over x-roads; Holyleas on right opp. village cricket pitch.

Bottle of wine in your room.

Use your Sawday's Gift Card here.

Tia Bunkall
Holyleas House,
Buckland Newton,
Dorchester DT2 7DP
Tel   +44 (0)1300 345214
Email   tiabunkall@holyleas.fsnet.co.uk
Web   www.holyleashouse.co.uk

Entry 168   Map 3

Dorset

Fullers Earth

Such an English feel: the village with pub, post office and stores, the walled garden with fruit trees beyond (source of perfect compotes and breakfast jams), the gentle church view. This listed house – its late-Georgian face added in 1820 – was where the Cattistock huntsmen lived; the unusual thatched stables alongside housed their steeds. Guests share a large and lovely sitting room in sand, cream and dove-blue; carpeted bedrooms have a lofty feel; the resplendent coastline – at times dramatic, at other times softly serene – is yours to discover, and Wendy and Ian will always plan your walks with you.

Price	£90–£95. Singles from £65.
Rooms	2 doubles.
Meals	Pub 500 yds.
Closed	Christmas.
Directions	From A37 take Cattistock turning downhill to T-junc. Left thro' village. Pub on left. After 90° right-hand bend, 5th house on right.

🧳 5% off stays of 3 or more nights Mon-Thurs.

Wendy Gregory
Fullers Earth,
Cattistock,
Dorchester DT2 0JL
Tel   +44 (0)1300 320190
Email stay@fullersearth.co.uk
Web   www.fullersearth.co.uk

🏹 🚂 📶 🐾

Entry 169   Map 3

Dorset

Gray's Farmhouse

Rosie greets you with tea and cake – in the lovely garden on warm days. This former shooting lodge has flagstones and vibrant art on aqua walls; Rosie paints, Roger writes poetry. Light, peaceful bedrooms have goose down, crisp cotton sheets (and blankets if you prefer); the guest sitting room has contemporary furnishings, music, books, maps and a fridge; you can picnic here too. Breakfast well on homemade or local produce, sometimes in the conservatory with its long views over the valleys of Hardy county. Walk the Jurassic coast or wander the bird-rich woods and wonderful footpaths from the house. *Minimum stay two nights.*

Price	£70–£95. Singles from £60.
Rooms	2: 1 double, 1 double/family.
Meals	Pub 3 miles.
Closed	Rarely.
Directions	A356 from Dorchester, left at 1st sign for T. Porcorum. Through, & up hill 1 mile. Ignore right turn, cont. thro' village; on 1 mile, right signed Powerstock & Hooke. Under bridge, 0.3 miles, left at unmarked x-roads.

🧳 Bottle of wine in your room.

Rosie & Roger Britton
Gray's Farmhouse,
Toller Porcorum,
Dorchester DT2 0EJ
Tel   +44 (0)1308 485574
Email rosieroger@farmhousebnb.co.uk
Web   www.farmhousebnb.co.uk

🍴 🏹 🐾

Entry 170   Map 3

Dorset

Frampton House

A grand Grade II*-listed house in parkland landscaped by Capability Brown... and two labradors, Potter and Dumble, to greet you as you scrunch up the gravel. Beyond the Georgian façade lies a delicious mix of English and Gallic styles. Bedrooms combine comfort with outstanding views, a magnificent four-poster in one, everywhere fine linen and plump pillows. Georgina is a portrait painter and a food and arts writer. Breakfasts, served in the conservatory, are true-blue English, with spectacular bangers. Log fires in the drawing room in winter, tea on the terrace in summer, dinners accompanied by French wines.

Price	£90.
Rooms	3: 2 twins/doubles, 1 four-poster.
Meals	Dinner, 3 courses with wine, £25. Pub 2 miles.
Closed	Rarely.
Directions	A37 Dorchester-Yeovil; A356 for Crewkerne & Maiden Newton. In Frampton, left at green; over white bridge; left, opp. Frampton Roses. 'Private' track to house, signed 3rd on left.

Georgina & Nicholas Maynard
Frampton House,
Frampton,
Dorchester DT2 9NH
Tel   +44 (0)1300 320308
Email   maynardryder@btconnect.com
Web   www.frampton-house.co.uk

Entry 171   Map 3

Dorset

Whitfield Farm Cottage

Jackie and David make light of the practicalities of B&B; they and their 200-year-old cottage have much character and charm. Breakfast in the large, stone-tiled, beamed kitchen, or in the walled courtyard in summer. The twin with garden access and its own shower is immaculate in its fresh white and blue checks; the sitting room is cosy with comfy sofas and pretty coral-checked cushions, inglenook fireplace and window seats. Minutes from the main road but with a rural feel; the Frome – beloved by local fishermen – is 150 yards away and you can fish here for £35 a day. *Minimum stay two nights at weekends.*

Price	£80-£85. Singles £50.
Rooms	1 twin/double.
Meals	Pubs/restaurants 1.25 miles.
Closed	Christmas & Easter.
Directions	From r'bout at top of Dorchester, west on B3150 for 100 yds. Right onto Poundbury Rd (before museum); 1 mile; over another road; 2nd track on right by house sign. Cottage set back from road.

Bottle of wine in your room. Free pick-up from local bus/train station.

Jackie & David Charles
Whitfield Farm Cottage,
Poundbury Road,
Dorchester DT2 9SL
Tel   +44 (0)1305 260233
Email   dcharles@gotadsl.co.uk
Web   www.whitfieldfarmcottage.co.uk

Entry 172   Map 3

Dorset

The White Cottage

Strolling distance from lovely old Athelhampton House and its gardens is this thatched cottage where Lindsay and Mark are slowly becoming self-sufficient. You will be well fed: home-grown vegetables, bacon from the pigs, eggs from Clarissa the chicken. It's a lively young-family household with gorgeous bedrooms, super linen, fresh flowers, plump pillows, chocolates; generous bathrooms have thick towels and eco-friendly lotions. The suite has its own entrance and a big comfortable sitting room. Help feed the animals and enjoy the river Piddle running through the garden – fish for brown trout but please put them back!

Price	£70-£120. Singles from £50.
Rooms	3: 1 double, 1 suite for 2-4 (with sofabed); 1 twin with separate bath.
Meals	Dinner £16-£18. Pub 1 mile.
Closed	Never.
Directions	A35 exit Athelhampton & Puddletown; signs for Athelhampton House. Left at lights in Puddletown; house 200 yds on right, after Athelhampton House.

	Lindsay & Mark Piper
	The White Cottage,
	Athelhampton,
	Dorchester DT2 7LG
Tel	+44 (0)1305 848622
Email	bookings@white-cottage-bandb.co.uk
Web	www.white-cottage-bandb.co.uk

Entry 173   Map 3

Dorset

Yoah Cottage

Rosemary makes delicate terracotta figures, Furse creates bold, glazed works in clay; their thatched, cob-walled, rambling house is a jaw-dropping gallery of modern art, ceramics, tapestries. The cottage garden's colours complete the vibrant picture. A private guest wing holds a country-pretty double and L-shaped twin under the eaves, sharing a bathroom (with friends or family). Breakfast is next to the couple's studio; Rosemary will also whip up a Swedish-style supper on a tray if you can't bear to budge from the sitting room fire. Such enthusiastic, artistic owners — and you're deep in Hardy country. *Minimum stay two nights.*

Price	£65-£85. Singles £40-£50.
Rooms	2: 1 double, 1 twin sharing bath (let to same party only).
Meals	Supper on a tray £15. Pub next door.
Closed	Christmas & Easter.
Directions	A352 out of Dorchester towards Wareham. Thro' Whitcombe, then next left to W. Knighton. Left again, to New Inn. House next to pub.

🧳	10% off room rate Mon-Thurs. Bottle of wine in room. A pot of homemade jam/marmalade.

	Furse & Rosemary Swann
	Yoah Cottage,
	West Knighton,
	Dorchester DT2 8PE
Tel	+44 (0)1305 852087
Email	roseswann@tiscali.co.uk
Web	www.yoahcottage.co.uk

Entry 174   Map 3

Dorset

Lower Lynch House

On the glorious Isle of Purbeck, between the old stone village of Corfe Castle and Kingston atop a hill, this wisteria-strewn house sits at the end of a long woodland track. Aga-cooked breakfast is served at tables overlooking courtyard and garden; cosy, old-fashioned bedrooms with pale colours and florals are as peaceful as can be. No sitting room, but a small sofa in the double. You are a five-minute drive from the coastal path: a great spot for walkers and peace-seekers. Warm, clean, comfortable B&B – and if you spot wild deer munching on the roses, tell Bron. *Minimum stay two nights.*

Price	From £75.
Rooms	2: 1 twin; 1 double with separate bath.
Meals	Inn 0.75 miles.
Closed	Christmas & New Year.
Directions	A351 from Wareham to Corfe Castle. At end of village fork right on B3069 for Kingston. Left 0.5 miles down track (sign on roadside).

Bron & Nick Burt
Lower Lynch House,
Kingston Hill,
Corfe Castle BH20 5LG
Tel   +44 (0)1929 480089
Email   bronburt@btinternet.com

Entry 179   Map 3

Dorset

The Old Post Office

The stunning coastal path comes past the front door of this restored bungalow on the cliff-top estate. Clamber down to a hidden beach and a short walk will take you to Swanage, or high over Ballard Down with views to the Isle of Wight. Bedrooms are comfortable and sunny, bathrooms are warmed by underfloor heating. Artist Rowena and rare-book dealer David give you much local food at breakfast, in the jolly kitchen (with piano), or on the terrace. Colours are strong and earthy, rugs and cushions bright and colourful, interesting books and art plentiful. Rocking chairs on the veranda are marvellous for a drink at sunset.

Price	£70. Singles £50.
Rooms	2: 1 twin; 1 double with separate bath.
Meals	Pub/restaurant 0.3 miles.
Closed	Rarely.
Directions	A351 to Swanage seafront, then left. Up hill, round one-way. Left into Ballard Way (corner shop on left). Through private estate barrier. House 2nd on right.

 Bottle of wine in your room.

Rowena Bishop
The Old Post Office,
4 Ballard Estate,
Swanage BH19 1QZ
Tel   +44 (0)1929 422041
Email   rowena@outwardbound.plus.com
Web   www.oldpostofficeswanage.co.uk

Entry 180   Map 3

Dorset

Gold Court House

Anthea and Michael have created a mood of restrained luxury and uncluttered, often beautiful, good taste in their Georgian townhouse. Bedrooms are restful in cream with mahogany furniture, beams, armchairs and radios. There's a large drawing room and pretty walled garden in which to relax after a day out. Your hosts are delightful – "they do everything to perfection," says a reader; both house and garden are a refuge. Views are soft and lush yet you are in the small square of this attractive town; the house was rebuilt in 1762 after a great fire, and the Hipwells added their creative spin 12 years ago. *Children over ten welcome.*

Price	£75. Singles from £45.
Rooms	3: 1 double, 1 twin/double; 1 twin/double with separate bath.
Meals	Dinner £20, available in winter. Restaurants 50 yds.
Closed	Rarely.
Directions	From A35, A351 to Wareham. Follow signs to town centre. In North St, over lights into South St. 1st left into St John's Hill; house on far right corner of square.

Use your Sawday's Gift Card here.

Anthea & Michael Hipwell
Gold Court House,
St John's Hill,
Wareham BH20 4LZ
Tel   +44 (0)1929 553320
Email info@goldcourthouse.co.uk
Web   www.goldcourthouse.co.uk

Entry 181   Map 3

Dorset

Bering House

Fabulous in every way. Renate's attention to detail reveals a love of running B&B: the fluffy dressing gowns and bathroom treats, the biscuits, fruit and sherry. She and John are welcoming, enthusiastic, delightful. Expect pretty little sofas, golden bath taps, a gleaming breakfast table, a big sumptuous suite with fine views across sparkling Poole harbour, Brownsea Island and the Purbeck Hills. Breakfasts are served on blue and white Spode china, among the birds and the breezes on summery days. Fresh fruit, Parma ham, smoked salmon, kedgeree: the choice is superb. An immaculate harbourside retreat.

Price	£80–£90. Singles by arrangement.
Rooms	2: 1 twin/double; 1 suite (twin/double) & kitchenette.
Meals	Pub 400 yds. Restaurant 500 yds.
Closed	Rarely.
Directions	From A35 & A350 at Upton, B3068 south to Hamworthy & Rockley Park. 1.5 miles on at pub on left, right into Lake Rd; under bridge; 2nd left down Branksea Ave. House last on left.

Late checkout (12pm). Free pick-up from local bus/train station. 10% off stays of 5 or more nights.

Renate & John Wadham
Bering House,
53 Branksea Avenue,
Hamworthy,
Poole BH15 4DP
Tel   +44 (0)1202 673419
Email johnandrenate1@tiscali.co.uk

Entry 182   Map 3

Dorset

7 Smithfield Place

Valerie adores large mirrors – which she paints and distresses herself – rich fabrics, real wood, dainty antiques. She also delights in looking after guests, so no detail is missed in her elegant home, from the gorgeous bathroom to a 'full works' breakfast – taken in the spanking new breakfast room or on a sunny patio. Built in 1880 as a worker's cottage, the house sits on a quiet cul-de-sac off Winton's thriving high street, two miles from Bournemouth town centre with easy public transport. The garden is lit up in spring by blooming camellias and cherry blossom, and the whole house sparkles – as does your charming hostess.

Price	£70. Singles £50.
Rooms	1 double.
Meals	Packed lunch £15. Pub/restaurant 100 yds.
Closed	Christmas.
Directions	M27 to New Forest, on to A31, then exit A338 Bournemouth. Exit to A3049, up to r'bout, 3rd exit still on A3049. 1.5 miles, right into Wimborne Rd, then left into Smithfield Pl.

10% off room rate Mon-Thurs.

Valerie Johns
7 Smithfield Place,
Winton,
Bournemouth BH9 2QJ
Tel   +44 (0)1202 520722
Email   valeriejohns@btinternet.com
Web   www.smithfieldplace.co.uk

Entry 183   Map 3

Dorset

Thornhill

Here is a pretty Thirties' thatched house, with peaceful views from every window… of fields, woods and two landscaped acres. Sara and John encourage the wildlife on their patch; you may spot a deer on the lawn. Inside are patterned fabrics and old-fashioned candlewick covers, pastel walls and polished antiques. All is neat, tidy, spacious and spotless, and Sara pays attention to detail: a toothbrush for the forgetful, fruit and chocolates in the rooms, a choice of teas. Walkers can stride out straight from the door, gardeners will be happy here – and bridge players, if they come on a Thursday!

Price	From £60. Singles from £30.
Rooms	3: 1 double, 1 twin, 1 single, all sharing 2 baths. Possible use of separate bath.
Meals	Pub/restaurant 400 yds.
Closed	Rarely.
Directions	From Wimborne B3078 towards Cranborne. Right to Holt. After 2 miles Thornhill on right, 200 yds beyond Old Inn.

John & Sara Turnbull
Thornhill,
Holt,
Wimborne BH21 7DJ
Tel   +44 (0)1202 889434
Email   scturnbull@lineone.net

Entry 184   Map 3

Dorset

Crawford House

Below, the river Stour winds through the valley and under the medieval, nine-arched bridge. Above, an Iron Age hill fort; between is Crawford House. It's an elegant Georgian house in an acre of walled garden, soft and pretty inside with an easy, relaxed atmosphere. Carpeted bedrooms are homely and warm, with long curtains; one room has four-poster twin beds with chintz drapes. The sun streams through the floor-to-ceiling windows of the downstairs rooms, and charming 18th- and 19th-century oil paintings hang in the dining room. Visit the Isle of Purbeck coastline – a World Heritage Site.

Price	From £65. Singles £35.
Rooms	3: 1 twin/double; 1 twin with separate bath; 1 twin with separate shower.
Meals	Pub 2 miles.
Closed	Mid-October to mid-April.
Directions	A350 north; after entering Spetisbury, 1st gateway immed. on left after crossroads (B3075).

10% off stays Mon-Thurs.

Andrea Lea
Crawford House,
Spetisbury,
Blandford Forum DT11 9DP
Tel   +44 (0)1258 857338
Email andrea@lea8.wanadoo.co.uk

Entry 185   Map 3

Dorset

Launceston Farmhouse

Farmhouse chic in the most glorious of surroundings. Sarah has named her bedrooms after the fields, and they are an exquisite marriage of contemporary and traditional: rococo beds and mirrors, curtains of iridescent silk, heavenly colours. Two rooms have roll tops in the room itself; every bathroom is seductive. Downstairs is an open-plan living area with a scattering of sofas, a charming bay window, an open fire, and candles for dinner – farm-sourced and deliciously rustic. Sarah, who was born in this listed house, is full of enthusiasm and ideas; son Jimi's farm tours are a must. Amazing value. *Children over 12 welcome.*

Ethical Collection: Food. See page 430.

Price	From £75. Singles from £50.
Rooms	6: 4 doubles, 2 twins.
Meals	Dinner, 2-3 courses, £20-£25 (Monday & Friday only). Pub 1 mile.
Closed	Rarely.
Directions	From Salisbury, A354 to Blandford Forum. Left at Tarrant Hinton. First village is Tarrant Launceston; house is on right.

10% off double room rate Mon-Thurs.

Sarah Worrall
Launceston Farmhouse,
Tarrant Launceston,
Blandford Forum DT11 8BY
Tel   +44 (0)1258 830528
Email info@launcestonfarm.co.uk
Web   www.launcestonfarm.co.uk

Entry 186   Map 3

Dorset

The Old Rectory

Walk all day on Cranborne Chase, return for tea at The Old Rectory, then stroll off for a meal at the much-fêted pub down the road… What could be nicer? Vicky's brick-and-flint Victorian house is in the middle of the village, yet feels wonderfully peaceful in its ten-acre grounds. Bedrooms are simple, comfortable and restful; bathrooms clean and functional. The drawing and dining rooms have the warm, gracious air of a much-loved and lived-in home, family portraits hang on the walls, the furniture is polished, the spaniel is friendly and big windows overlook sweeping lawns and summer terrace.

Price	£80.
Rooms	2: 1 double, 1 twin.
Meals	Pub within walking distance.
Closed	Christmas.
Directions	16 miles south west of Salisbury on A354 Blandford Forum road. Farnham is signed off main road; house is in Farnham opposite Museum pub.

10% off stays of 2 or more nights.

Vicky Forbes
The Old Rectory,
Farnham,
Blandford Forum DT11 8DE
Tel   +44 (0)1725 516474
Email   forbescopper@compuserve.com
Web   www.theoldrectorydorset.co.uk

Entry 187   Map 3

Dorset

Manor Barn

What was once an L-shaped cow shed is now a rather smart self-contained barn – attached to the main house and with views to an Iron Age hill. Relax in a roomy and beamed sitting room with squashy sofas, white walls, a wood-burning stove; down a corridor are two restful bedrooms with delightful linen and huge fluffy pillows. It is all very rustic-contemporary. A huge breakfast is brought to you, and kind Carolyn will cook a delicious, locally sourced supper if you want a night in with a DVD. Perfect for friends or families and you have complete independence. *Children over eight welcome.*

Price	£96. Singles £63.
Rooms	2 twins/doubles.
Meals	Dinner £20-£35. Light supper £10-£15. Pub in village & more within 3 miles.
Closed	Rarely.
Directions	South on A350 from Shaftesbury; right at sign 'Child Okeford 3 miles'. Just before village, drive is on left, opposite 30 ft high hedge.

Bottle of wine in your room.

Carolyn Sorby
Manor Barn,
Upper Street, Child Okeford,
Blandford Forum DT11 8EF
Tel   +44 (0)1258 860638
Email   carisorby@btinternet.com
Web   www.manorbarnbedandbreakfast.co.uk

Entry 188   Map 3

Dorset

Stickland Farmhouse

Charming Dorset... and a soft, delightful thatched cottage in an enviably rural setting. Sandy and Paul have poured love into this listed farmhouse and garden, the latter bursting with lupins, poppies, foxgloves, clematis, delphiniums. Sandy gives you delicious breakfasts with homemade soda bread from the Aga. Cottagey bedrooms have crisp white dressing gowns and lots of books and pictures – one room opens onto your own seating area in the garden. You are in a village with a good pub, and Cranbourne Chase, rich in barrows and hill forts, is close by. *Children over ten welcome. Minimum stay two nights at weekends in summer.*

Price	£65–£70. Singles £50.
Rooms	3: 2 doubles, 1 twin.
Meals	Pub 3-minute walk.
Closed	Never.
Directions	Leave Blandford for SW, cross river Stour. Hard right after Bryanston school for W. Stickland. Down North St, right signed W. Houghton. House 150 yds on left with 5-bar gate.

Sandy & Paul Crofton–Atkins
Stickland Farmhouse,
9 West Street, Winterborne Stickland,
Blandford Forum DT11 0NT
Tel   +44 (0)1258 880119
Email   sandysticklandfarm@tiscali.co.uk
Web   www.sticklandfarmhouse.co.uk

Entry 189   Map 3

Dorset

The Old Forge, Fanners Yard

Tim and Lucy are tangibly happy in this beautifully restored forge. It was built in the 1700s; the wheelwright and carriage-builder from the local estate used to work here. Tim has beautifully restored the cosy gypsy caravan which has super views and a picnic table outside. The attic bedrooms are snug, with Lucy's quilts, country antiques and sparkling bathrooms. Delicious Aga-cooked breakfasts include eggs from their own free-strutting hens, organic sausages and bacon, home-grown jams, apple juice straight from the orchard. The Downs beckon walkers; warm corners invite readers. Utterly genuine.

Price	From £75.
Rooms	3: 1 double, 1 family. Gypsy caravan: 1 double with separate shower & wc (20 yds).
Meals	Pub/restaurant 1 mile.
Closed	Rarely.
Directions	From Shaftesbury, A350 to Compton Abbas. House 1st on left before Compton Abbas sign. Left; entrance on left.

 Local food/produce in your room. Homemade biscuits.

Tim & Lucy Kerridge
The Old Forge, Fanners Yard,
Compton Abbas,
Shaftesbury SP7 0NQ
Tel   +44 (0)1747 811881
Email   theoldforge@hotmail.com
Web   www.theoldforgedorset.co.uk

Entry 190   Map 3

Dorset

Rose Cottage

You are buried deep in a quiet corner here, just perfect for long walks: return to a wood-burner and a cup of tea in a beamed sitting room with plenty of sofas and books — no dull TV. Bedrooms are light and charming with chintzy curtains and fabulous views over the pretty garden; loll in big beds with cushions and crisp white sheets. Breakfast is a fairly flexible, mostly organic treat with Rose Cottage honey, served in an elegant yellow-walled dining room with gleaming furniture and dollops of morning sunshine; delicious dinner includes home-grown vegetables. Amanda, warm and welcoming, looks after you very well indeed.

Price	From £70. Singles £45. Child £15.
Rooms	2: 1 twin/double; 1 twin/double with separate bath/shower.
Meals	Dinner, 3 courses, £20. Supper, 1 or 2 courses, & packed lunch available. Pub/restaurant 1 mile.
Closed	Christmas.
Directions	From Shaftesbury A350 north. Right for Wincombe & Donhead St Mary. After 2 miles 2nd right. Watery Lane 100 yds on left, house 200 yds on right, drive thro' field gate.
	10% off room rate Mon-Thurs. Free pick-up from local bus/train station.

	Giles & Amanda Vardey
	Rose Cottage,
	Watery Lane, Donhead St Mary,
	Shaftesbury SP7 9DF
Tel	+44 (0)1747 828449
Email	amanda@rosecottage.uk.com
Web	www.rosecottage.uk.com

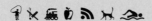

Entry 191   Map 3

Dorset

Lawn Cottage

In a quiet village in the Blackmore Vale, the path to this spacious cottage is lined with tulips and vegetables. Easy-going June is a collector of pretty things; fine sketches and watercolours, antiques and china plates blend charmingly with soft colours and zingy kilims. Sunny, cosy bedrooms are delightful in toile de Jouy with books and flowers; and there are toys in the downstairs bunk room. You breakfast in an airy, contemporary kitchen/dining room or out in the cottage garden; the tiny sitting room is a perfect snug. Visit Sherborne for its abbey, castle and smart shops; walk from the gate to Duncliffe Woods.

Price	£60. Singles £50.
Rooms	3: 1 twin/double, 1 bunk room; 1 double sharing family bath.
Meals	Pub/restaurant 1 mile.
Closed	Rarely.
Directions	A30 towards Sherborne for 3 miles. Left opp. Kings Arms Inn. 1 mile to Stour Row, then left. 2nd house on left after Village Hall.
	Bottle of wine and homemade cheese sables for guests staying 2 or more nights.

	June Watkins
	Lawn Cottage,
	Stour Row,
	Shaftesbury SP7 0QF
Tel	+44 (0)1747 838719
Email	enquiries@lawncottagedorset.co.uk
Web	www.lawncottagedorset.co.uk

Entry 192   Map 3

Dorset

Gorse Farm House

Wendy is a generous soul and throws open her lovely house; you are free to wander the garden, grab a book and laze in the sunny conservatory or settle into the snug and watch TV. Upstairs find a light-filled, peaceful bedroom with dreamy views over fields, a bowl of sweets, dainty china and more books; a shiny new bathroom is just across the landing. Lee is a sculptor and his work peeps out from clever planting around the garden: find a seat on the veranda or near the natural pond and listen to the birds. Breakfast on local sausages, bacon and free-range farm eggs then tackle some fabulous walks and cycles straight from the door.

Price	From £60. Singles £40.
Rooms	1 twin/double with separate bath.
Meals	Pub/restaurant 2 miles.
Closed	Christmas.
Directions	West of Sturminster Newton, south off A357 signed Hazlebury Bryan. 0.5 miles Rivers Corner, left signed Fifehead St Quintin. 0.5 miles bear right at sign for Fifeheads. House 0.25 miles on left.

 Free pick-up from Gillingham bus/train station (20-minute drive).

Wendy Dickenson
Gorse Farm House,
Fifehead St Quintin,
Sturminster Newton DT10 2AW
Tel   +44 (0)1258 475343
Email   contactus@gorsefarmhousebb.co.uk
Web   www.gorsefarmhousebb.co.uk

Entry 193   Map 3

Dorset

Old Causeway Bakery

In an unpretentious hamlet, a quirky gem. Inside, abundant flower arrangements and bold colours – deep green and cerise – glow alongside oils, prints and antiques dotted around; bookcases bow with the weight of walking guides. In the self-contained bakery wing is a theatrical boudoir (think gold drapes and chaise longue). The main house bedrooms are more serene though still eclectic, with antiques and tapestry-upholstered headboards; bathrooms are super throughout. Full English breakfasts are all locally sourced, and can be had whenever you like. Come prepared to cuddle Henry and Bertie – the friendly resident dogs.

Price	£85-£95. Bakery Wing £100-£120. Singles £75-£85.
Rooms	3: 2 doubles. Bakery Wing: 1 double.
Meals	Pub 30 yds.
Closed	Rarely.
Directions	From Sturminster Newton B3092 Blandford; right at lights, then left signed Hazelbury Bryan. 4 miles into village centre, right after pub. House immed. on left.

 10% off room rate Mon-Thurs. 10% off stays of 2 or more nights.

Sandra Williams & Simon Boggon
Old Causeway Bakery,
Hazelbury Bryan,
Sturminster Newton DT10 2BH
Tel   +44 (0)1258 817228
Email   sandrasimonbw@btinternet.com
Web   www.oldcausewaybakery.co.uk

Entry 194   Map 3

Dorset

Golden Hill Cottage

Deep in the countryside lies Stourton Caundle and this charming thatched cottage. The sitting room, traditionally furnished with antiques, paintings and coal fire, is all yours if you stay, along with a carpeted twin room and small shower up a private stair. Anna, courteous and kind, brings you splendid platefuls of local bacon and sausage, homemade jams and Dorset honey for breakfast; nothing is too much trouble for these owners. There are glorious walks from the village, a good pub that serves food and real ales, and Sherborne, Montacute and Stourhead for landscape, culture and history.
Babes in arms welcome.

Price	£66–£80. Singles £40.
Rooms	1 twin & sitting room.
Meals	Pubs/restaurants within 3 miles.
Closed	Rarely.
Directions	From Sherborne, A352 to Dorchester; after 1 mile, left onto A3030; on to far end of Bishops Caundle, left to Stourton Caundle; after sharp left into village street, house 200 yds on right.

 10% off stays of 2 or more nights Mon-Thurs.

Anna & Andrew Oliver
Golden Hill Cottage,
Stourton Caundle,
Sturminster Newton DT10 2JW
Tel   +44 (0)1963 362109
Email   anna@goldenhillcottage.co.uk
Web   www.goldenhillcottage.co.uk

Entry 195   Map 3

Dorset

Holt Cottage

The house stands on high ground and the views are fabulous and panoramic. Richard and Annabel give you a big welcome and two super suites in the cottage a step away. One upstairs, one down, each has its own sitting room, and private entrance too so you can come and go as you please. All is sparkling, light and inviting, with elegant prints on the walls. Bedrooms have wonderful mattresses, good linen and fresh flowers; find fluffy white towels and lots of potions in immaculate bathrooms. Breakfast by the Aga in the large beamed farmhouse kitchen: fresh fruit salad, local bacon and sausages and eggs from Annabel's wandering hens.

Ethical Collection: Food. See page 430.

Price	From £80. Singles £60.
Rooms	Cottage: 1 double & sitting room; 1 twin/double & sitting room.
Meals	Pub/restaurant 1 mile.
Closed	Rarely.
Directions	From Sherborne, A352 south. After 1 mile, left onto A3030 Blandford road. In Bishops Caundle, left at Murco garage. House 1 mile on left.

 10% off stays of 2 or more nights Mon-Thurs. Pick-up from local bus/train station.

Richard & Annabel Buxton
Holt Cottage,
Alweston,
Sherborne DT9 5JF
Tel   +44 (0)1963 23014
Email   annabelbuxton@hotmail.com
Web   www.holtcottagedorset.com

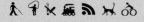

Entry 196   Map 3

Dorset

Avalon Townhouse

You'll feel lucky to end up at Paul and Nicky's smart Edwardian townhouse just a few minutes' walk from the station. A large, high-ceilinged sitting room has a cosy fire, sash windows, paintings and prints, and a baby grand piano if you fancy showing off. Bedrooms nod to the contemporary and are as neat as a pin, with beech furniture and satin throws and cushions; bathrooms are spanking new and filled with pleasant things in bottles. Wander down in the morning to a menu bursting with local food and a bit of 'interactive time' with Paul and his Aga. Antiques, medieval buildings and music in the Abbey await. Perfect town B&B.

Price	£80–£90. Singles £70–£80.
Rooms	3 doubles.
Meals	Pub/restaurant 300 yds.
Closed	Never.
Directions	A30 to Sherborne. Come off A30 heading south for train station. House 300 yds from station.

10% off room rate Mon–Thurs. 10% off stays of 2 or more nights.

Paul & Nicky Aleman
Avalon Townhouse,
South Street,
Sherborne DT9 3LZ
Tel   +44 (0)1935 814748
Email   enquiries@avalontownhouse.co.uk
Web   www.avalontownhouse.co.uk

Entry 197   Map 3

Dorset

Windrush Farm

Fun to eat in the light farmhouse kitchen with its Aga, polished oak table, and rag-rolled dresser full of colourful plates. Upstairs, too, is delightful – creaky floors, sloping ceilings and a maze of corridors brightened by new Zoffany wallpapers. Pretty bedrooms are in soft colours; everywhere there are paintings, prints and photos. On colder evenings, your charming hosts will light a fire for you in the guest sitting room – lived-in and snug with artwork and piles of books – while for summer there's a scented rambler-strewn garden and a terrace with the loveliest views. Bustling Sherborne is a ten-minute drive.

Price	From £75. Singles from £45.
Rooms	2: 1 double with separate bath; 1 twin sharing bath (2nd room let to same party only).
Meals	Dinner £25. Pub/restaurant 1 mile.
Closed	Christmas.
Directions	A357 Wincanton-Templecombe; Right at 2nd turn Stowell, opp. entrance to Horsington House. On for approx. 1 mile, then steep hill; pass church on left. House on left after 0.5 miles.

Richard & Jenny Gold
Windrush Farm,
Stowell,
Sherborne DT9 4PD
Tel   +44 (0)1963 370799
Email   jennygold@hotmail.co.uk
Web   www.windrushfarmbedandbreakfast.com

Entry 198   Map 3

Durham

Durham University

Delightful Durham, curved around by the Wear, its cathedral dominating, its colleges open now for you to be at the student heart of things. Traditionalists will go for Castle College, almost dwarfed by the cathedral: sweeping stairway, grand dining hall, ancient treasures. The Bishop's Suite is properly plush, the student quarters obviously less so, but it's hugely atmospheric. Or Hatfield College, a stone's throw below, more redbrick, with simple, comfortable rooms. Outside the city, around the Botanic Gardens, more choice in purpose-built colleges of many persuasions. Easy to get to, plenty of breathing space.

Durham

Vane House

In the attractive market town of Barnard Castle is this historic home, sympathetically restored by Diana. A writer, broadcaster and keen gardener, she is also an engaging and generous host; Bruno, her characterful terrier, will smile at you too. The light open-fired sitting room where you breakfast is lined with fascinating books; relax awhile, or drift outside in summer, to find a peaceful spot among the roses. Bedrooms, in lavender or terracotta, have fine linen, robes, antiques and good art; soak in the roll top bath or nip downstairs for a shower. Stroll into town, visit castles and cathedrals, discover the beauties of Teesdale.

Price	Doubles £75-£85. Twins £70-£80. Singles £28-£39.
Rooms	600 twins & singles across 5 colleges. Some rooms share showers.
Meals	Breakfast included. Pubs/restaurants within walking distance.
Closed	Mid-Jan to mid-March; May/June; Oct/Nov; Christmas. A few rooms available throughout year.
Directions	Website booking. Free parking at most colleges.

Price	£70-£80. Singles £40-£50.
Rooms	2: 1 double with separate bath; 1 twin with separate shower.
Meals	Pubs/restaurants 500 yds.
Closed	November-Easter.
Directions	From Darlington or A1(M), A67 for Barnard Castle via Piercebridge; after 15 miles A67 becomes 'Galgate'; Vane House on left facing the last green.

10% off room rate Mon-Thurs. 10% off stays of 2 or more nights.

	University Rooms Durham University, Durham
Web	www.durhamrooms.co.uk

	Diana Collecott Vane House, 57 Galgate, Barnard Castle DL12 8EN
Tel	+44 (0)1833 631261
Email	stay@vanehousebedandbreakfast.co.uk
Web	www.vanehousebedandbreakfast.co.uk

Entry 199   Map 12

Entry 200   Map 12

Durham

The Coach House

There's so much to gladden your heart – the cobbled courtyard that evokes memories of its days as a coaching inn, the river running through the estate, the drawing room's log fire, the delicious breakfasts, the blackberry crumbles with cream... and Peter and Mary, your kind, unstuffy, dog-adoring hosts (they have four well-behaved ones). All your creature comforts are attended to in this small, perfect, English country house: lined chintz, starched linen, cushioned window seats, cut flowers, heated towel rails. Friendly, delightful, and the perfect stepping stone to Scotland or the south.

Price	£85. Singles £50.
Rooms	2: 1 twin/double; 1 twin/double with separate bath.
Meals	Dinner, 3 courses, £25. Pub/restaurants within 3 miles.
Closed	Rarely.
Directions	A1(M) to Scotch Corner. A66 west for 8 miles until Greta Bridge turn-off. House on left just before bridge. Front door is near right-hand corner of courtyard.

Peter & Mary Gilbertson
The Coach House,
Greta Bridge,
Barnard Castle DL12 9SD
Tel   +44 (0)1833 627201
Email info@coachhousegreta.co.uk
Web   www.coachhousegreta.co.uk

Entry 201   Map 12

Essex

Emsworth House

Unexpectedly tranquil is this 1937 vicarage, with wide views over the Stour and some wonderful light for painting. Penny, an artist, is a flexible and generous host and you can laze or picnic in her two-acre garden. This is Constable country – great for walking; you are near to Frinton beach and golf, sailing and riding. Return to comfy sofas and chairs, open fires and good books, and redecorated bedrooms with a country feel and the odd African throw or splash of colour. There's heaps of lovely art and a garden full of birds. Penny has camp beds and high chairs and a can-do attitude. Great fun.

Price	From £60. Singles from £45.
Rooms	3: 1 double, 1 twin; 1 double with separate bath.
Meals	Pub/restaurant 0.5 miles.
Closed	Rarely.
Directions	A12-A120 (to Harwich) & left to B1035; right at TV mast to Bradfield, 2 miles; house on right. Manningtree Station 5 miles. A14-A137-B1352, house on left.

10% off room rate Mon-Thurs.

Penny Linton
Emsworth House,
Ship Hill, Station Road, Bradfield,
Manningtree CO11 2UP
Tel   +44 (0)1255 870860
Email emsworthhouse@hotmail.com
Web   www.emsworthhouse.co.uk

Entry 202   Map 10

Essex

Bromans Farm

The island of Mersea is surprisingly secluded, and Bromans Farm is in a most tranquil corner; the sea murmurs across the Saltings where Brent geese wheel and Constable skies stretch. The house began in 1343 – nearly as old as the exquisite village church; the Georgians added their bit, but the venerable beams shine through. Ruth and Martin are charming and give you a very pretty bedroom in yellow and blue, a superb bathroom off the landing, log fires in the snug sitting room, homemade breakfast jams at a beautiful antique table, and tea from Grandmother's blue and white china. Wild walks beckon and the garden is much-loved.

Essex

Caterpillar Cottage

Traditional brick and clapboard, dormer windows, tall chimneys – this looks like the real thing. But the 'converted farm building' in the grounds of Patricia's former grand house is brand new! Filled with fine furniture, family photographs and *objets* from far-flung travels, it invites relaxation. The double-height, vaulted sitting room brims with sofas and books, logs crackle on chilly nights and bedrooms are simple and comfortable with decent-sized bathrooms. Patricia, a lively grandmother, adores children while her big garden promises home-grown fruit and tranquillity.

Price	£70-£80. Singles £40.
Rooms	1 twin/double with separate bath.
Meals	Pub 0.5 miles.
Closed	Rarely.
Directions	From Colchester B1025, over causeway, bear left. After 3 miles, pass Dog & Pheasant pub; 3rd right into Bromans Lane. House 1st on left.

Free pick-up from local bus/train station.

Ruth Dence
Bromans Farm,
East Mersea CO5 8UE
Tel +44 (0)1206 383235
Email ruth.dence@homecall.co.uk
Web www.bromansfarm.co.uk

Entry 203   Map 10

Price	From £65. Singles from £35.
Rooms	2: 1 triple; 1 double with separate bath/shower.
Meals	Packed lunch available. Pubs 50 yds.
Closed	Rarely.
Directions	A12 to A1124. In Fordstreet, cottage through gateway shared with Old House, opposite Old Queens Head pub. 88 bus stops at the gate.

10% off stays of 3+ nights. Box of handmade chocolates from village.

Use your Sawday's Gift Card here.

Patricia Mitchell
Caterpillar Cottage,
Fordstreet, Aldham,
Colchester CO6 3PH
Tel +44 (0)1206 240456
Mobile +44 (0)7776 202713
Email bandbcaterpillar@tiscali.co.uk

Entry 204   Map 10

Essex

Brook Farm

Large low Georgian windows fill the house with light, unpretentious family pieces warm the bedrooms and the stunning carved crossbeam in the largest is late-medieval. Anne, country lover and B&B-er, has farmed here for over 30 years; outbuildings dot the yard, sheep and horses roam the acres. In Anne's sitting room logs fill the copper and hunting prints line the walls – no TV, but magazines and books aplenty – and you breakfast (deliciously) at a long table with fine antique benches. The handsome bright farmhouse oozes history and a faded country charm – yet is 30 minutes from Stansted.

Price	£70–£80. Singles £35–£45.
Rooms	3: 1 twin; 1 double, 1 family room, each with separate bath.
Meals	Packed lunch £3–£5. Pubs within 2 miles.
Closed	Rarely.
Directions	House on B1053, 500 yds south of Wethersfield.

Anne Butler
Brook Farm,
Wethersfield,
Braintree CM7 4BX
Tel   +44 (0)1371 850284
Email   abutlerbrookfarm@aol.com
Web   www.brookfarmwethersfield.co.uk

Entry 205   Map 9

Essex

32 The Hythe

The Thames barge in all her glory: the Gibbs' garden runs almost into the river Blackwater where these majestic old craft are moored and the mudflats are a birdwatcher's dream. Summer breakfast on the deck – local smoked kippers and free-range eggs – watching the barges sail up the river is a rare treat. Beneath wide limpid skies this sensitively extended fisherman's cottage looks out to 12th-century St Mary's at the back where Kim and Gerry ring the Sunday bells. It's immaculate and comfortable inside, an inspired mix of modern and antique lit by myriad candles, among other romantic touches. *Children over 14 welcome.*

Price	£80. Singles £70.
Rooms	2: 1 double; 1 double with separate bath.
Meals	Pub 100 yds.
Closed	Christmas & Boxing Day.
Directions	From A12 to Maldon. House on The Hythe by river, signed for the river. Past St Mary's church then right at the bottom. House at end of road on right.

Kim & Gerry Gibbs
32 The Hythe,
Maldon CM9 5HN
Tel   +44 (0)1621 859435
Email   gibbsie@live.co.uk
Web   www.thehythemaldon.co.uk

Entry 206   Map 10

Essex

Fourteen

White linen, white walls, nautical touches, a private sauna: a wow of a place for sybarites, walkers, watersporters and designers. Architects Mike and Diana have created a super-sleek home in boaty Burnham with gorgeous views across the marshes. Pull up through the tall white gates and enter the inner sanctuary. The blissful bedroom is privately on the ground floor, off its own sitting room with a large flat screen, and the indoor pool kept at a tempting 28 degrees; the lovely hosts live above. There's a fragrant patio – all yours – and a pontoon ahead, and at weekends you can be ferried across the river. Stupendous.

Price	£100. Singles £75.
Rooms	1 twin/double & sitting room.
Meals	Dinner, 2 courses with wine, £20. Pubs/restaurants 100 yds.
Closed	Christmas & Boxing Day.
Directions	B1010 into Burnham, from High St right into Shore Rd at clock tower. Left through Anchor Hotel car park & straight ahead at white gates into Fourteen.

10% off stays of 2 or more nights. Bottle of champagne for bookings of 2 nights or more.

	Diana Bailey
	Fourteen,
	The Quay,
	Burnham-on-Crouch CM0 8AT
Tel	+44 (0)1621 782002
Email	diana@baileylewis.co.uk

Entry 207   Map 10

Gloucestershire

Steep Meadow

An understated exterior belies the charm of Helen and John's modern home. Built into the hillside, bedrooms give a hare's-eye view of woods and wildlife; the guest sitting room above, with its wall of sliding glass, is a comfortable eyrie peering proudly over the Forest of Dean. Recycled local wood and bricks warm the light and generous bedrooms; gleaming bathrooms have homemade soaps. Meals from the Aga-top are a treat: eggs, bacon, sausages, pork, and honey from the Meadow's lively menagerie. There are wonderful walks from the door and Abergavenny, with its magnificent food festival in September, is a 30-minute drive.

Ethical Collection: Environment; Food. See page 430.

Price	£72. Singles £46.
Rooms	2 doubles.
Meals	Dinner, 2 courses, £14; 3 courses, £17. Pub/restaurant 400 yds.
Closed	Rarely.
Directions	A4136 from Monmouth towards Coleford. Right immediately after Staunton 30mph signs. At fork in road (150 yds) right up steep hill; house 1st on left.

Pig and chicken keeping advice. Lifts to walking start points. 10% off repeat stays.

	Helen Theophilus
	Steep Meadow,
	Staunton,
	Coleford GL16 8PD
Tel	+44 (0)1594 832316
Email	helen@steepmeadow.co.uk
Web	www.steepmeadow.co.uk

Entry 208   Map 7

Gloucestershire

Frampton Court

Deep authenticity in this magnificent Grade I-listed house. The manor of Frampton-on-Severn has been in the family since the 11th century and although Rollo and Janie look after the estate, it is Gillian who greets you on behalf of the family and looks after you (very well). Exquisite examples of decorative woodwork and, in the hall, a cheerful log fire; perch on the Mouseman fire seat. Bedrooms are traditional with antiques, panelling and long views. Beds have fine linen, one with embroidered Jacobean hangings. Stroll around the ornamental canal, soak up the old-master views. An architectural masterpiece.

Price	£110-£150.
Rooms	3: 1 twin/double, 1 double, 1 four-poster.
Meals	Dinner £29. Pub across the green. Restaurant 3 miles.
Closed	Rarely.
Directions	M5 junc. 13 west A38 south, then B4071. Left down village green, 400 yds. 2nd turning left, between two chestnut trees & through ornamental gates in wall.

10% off room rate Mon-Thurs. Champagne for bookings of 2 nights or more.

	Rollo & Janie Clifford
	Frampton Court,
	The Green, Frampton-on-Severn,
	Gloucester GL2 7EX
Tel	+44 (0)1452 740267
Email	framptoncourt@framptoncourtestate.co.uk
Web	www.framptoncourtestate.co.uk

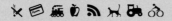

Entry 209   Map 8

Gloucestershire

Grove Farm

Boards creak and you duck, in a farmhouse of the best kind: simple, small-roomed, stone-flagged, beamed, delightful. The walls are white, the furniture is good and there are pictures everywhere. In spite of great age (16th century), it's light, with lots of windows. You'll be fed well, too; the 400 acres are farmed organically and Penny makes a grand breakfast – continental at busy times. Stupendous views across the Severn estuary to the Cotswolds, the Forest of Dean on the doorstep and woodland walks, carpeted with spring flowers. And there is simply no noise – unless the guinea fowl are in voice.

Price	£60-£70. Singles £35.
Rooms	2: 1 double; 1 twin/double with separate bath.
Meals	Packed lunch £4. Pub 2 miles.
Closed	Rarely.
Directions	2 miles south of Newnham on A48, opp. turn for Bullo Pill, large 'pull-in' with phone box on right; turn here; follow farm track to end.

	Penny & David Hill
	Grove Farm,
	Bullo Pill,
	Newnham GL14 1DZ
Tel	+44 (0)1594 516304
Email	davidandpennyhill@btopenworld.com
Web	www.grovefarm-uk.com

Entry 210   Map 8

Gloucestershire

Astalleigh House

The views from here to the Malvern Hills are worth the journey alone, but you also get bright, softly-coloured bedrooms with outrageously snuggly beds, the floatiest goose down, and compact bathrooms with generous towels and Body Shop goodies. There's a sitting room with pale walls, lots of books and magazines, jazzy striped cushions on a comfy sofa and interesting paintings of Northumberland – you can flop here happily. Affable Harriet gives you eggs from their hens and delicious sausages and bacon from the local butcher to set you up for grand walks; this is a good romantic escape for those with outdoor tastes.

Price	From £75. Singles £50. Child £15.
Rooms	2: 1 double, 1 family.
Meals	Pub/restaurant 0.5 miles.
Closed	Christmas & New Year.
Directions	M5, junc. 8, M50 junc. 1 north A38. Then 2nd left Ripple, Uckinghall, Equine Hospital, left at x-roads. House 1st on left. Train to Cheltenham, Gloucester or Pershore.

Harriet & Keith Jewers
Astalleigh House,
School Lane, Ripple,
Tewkesbury GL20 6EU
Tel +44 (0)1684 593740
Email jewers@jewers.freeserve.co.uk
Web www.astalleighhouse.co.uk

Entry 211 Map 8

Gloucestershire

The Court

Just off Chipping Campden high street this huge honey-hued Jacobean house has been in the family since it was built in 1624 by Sir Baptist Hicks. Dogs sound the alarm when you knock… step inside to find a relaxed and faded splendour. Delicate ornaments sit on exquisite antiques, family portraits and spectacular oils line the walls; bedrooms, up winding stairs, have comfortable beds, books, a mix of beautiful and functional furniture and breathtaking views of rooftops or gardens. Jane's friendly housekeeper cooks your Aga breakfast – eggs and jams are from the garden. The walking is superb; Hidcote and Kiftsgate are close.

Price	£45–£70.
Rooms	4: 2 family suites; 1 double, 1 family suite, each with separate bath.
Meals	Pub/restaurant 30 yds.
Closed	Christmas, Easter, Whitsun bank holiday & half term.
Directions	Oxford A34 to Moreton-in-Marsh & Chipping Campden, then right into High St, right signed Shipston. Round one way system left into Calf Lane; 1st house on left.
	10% off stays of 2 or more nights.

Jane Glennie
The Court,
Calf Lane,
Chipping Campden GL55 6JQ
Tel +44 (0)1386 840201
Email j14glennie@aol.com
Web www.thecourtchippingcampden.co.uk

Entry 212 Map 8

Gloucestershire

The Old School

Comfortable, warm and filled with understated style is this 1854 Cotswold stone house. Wendy and John are generous, beds are enormous, linen is laundered, towels and robes are thick and fluffy. Your own mini fridge is carefully hidden and lighting is well thought-out. Best of all is the upstairs sitting room: a chic, open-plan space with church style windows letting the light flood in and super sofas, good art, lovely fabrics. A wood-burner keeps you toasty, Wendy is a grand cook and all is flexible. A gorgeous, relaxing place to stay – on the A44 but peaceful at night – where absolutely nothing is too much trouble.

Price	£96. Singles £70.
Rooms	4: 3 doubles, 1 twin/double.
Meals	Dinner, 4 courses, £32. Supper, 2 courses, £18. Supper tray £12. Pub 0.5 miles.
Closed	Rarely.
Directions	From Moreton, A44 for Chipping Norton & Oxford. Little Compton 3.5 miles; stay on main road, then right for Chastleton village. House on corner, immed. left into drive.

10% off stays of 2 or more nights.

Use your Sawday's Gift Card here.

Wendy Veale & John Scott-Lee
The Old School,
Little Compton,
Moreton-in-Marsh GL56 0SL
Tel   +44 (0)1608 674588
Email   wendy@theoldschoolbedandbreakfast.com
Web   www.theoldschoolbedandbreakfast.com

Entry 213   Map 8

Gloucestershire

Windy Ridge House

Americans love Windy Ridge. It's comfortable, it's cosy, it's run by a cheerful staff and it's well positioned for touring the Cotswolds. Nick's father was in construction and built this in traditional style using the finest timbers and stone; refurbishment sees brand-new carpets for bedrooms, stairs and landings. There's a green marble bathroom with mirrored walls, a proper four-man lift, a pine-panelled drawing room and polished things at every turn. Take a book to a velveteen sofa and help yourself from the honesty bar; visit the arboretum, the prize-winning gardens and the summer heated pool.

Price	From £90. Singles from £70.
Rooms	4: 2 doubles; 1 double, 1 twin/double each with separate bath.
Meals	Pub 100 yds.
Closed	Rarely.
Directions	From Stow, north for Broadway on A424 for 2 miles to Coach & Horses pub. Opp., right by postbox & 30mph signs down single-track lane. Entrance 100 yds down on left, bear left up drive.

10% off stays of 3 or more nights.

Use your Sawday's Gift Card here.

Nick & Jennifer Williams
Windy Ridge House,
Longborough,
Moreton-in-Marsh GL56 0QY
Tel   +44 (0)1451 830465
Email   nick@windy-ridge.co.uk
Web   www.windy-ridge.co.uk

Entry 214   Map 8

Gloucestershire

Wren House

Barely two miles from Stow-on-the-Wold, this peaceful house sits charmingly on the edge of a tiny hamlet. Built before the English Civil War, Kiloran spent two years stylishly renovating it; the results are a joy. Downstairs, light-filled, elegant rooms with glowing rugs on pale Cotswold stone; upstairs, delicious bedrooms, spotless bathrooms and a doorway to duck. Breakfast in the vaulted kitchen is locally sourced and organic, where possible, and the well-planted garden, in which you are encouraged to sit, has far-reaching views. Explore rolling valleys and glorious gardens; Kiloran can advise. *Children over six welcome.*

Ethical Collection: Food. See page 430.

Price	£90–£100. Singles from £70.
Rooms	2: 1 twin/double; 1 twin/double with separate bath & shower.
Meals	Pubs/restaurants 1 mile.
Closed	Rarely.
Directions	A429 between Stow & Moreton; turn to Donnington; 400 yds, bear left uphill; 100 yds, sign on right in wall beside The Granary Cottage with parking at rear thro' 5-bar gate.

 10% off stays of 3 or more nights Mon-Thurs.

 Use your Sawday's Gift Card here.

Kiloran McGrigor
Wren House,
Donnington,
Stow-on-the-Wold GL56 0XZ
Tel   +44 (0)1451 831787
Email   enquiries@wrenhouse.net
Web   www.wrenhouse.net

Entry 215   Map 8

Gloucestershire

Clapton Manor

Karin and James's 16th-century manor is as all homes should be: loved and lived-in. And, with three-foot-thick walls, flagstoned floors, sit-in fireplaces and stone-mullioned windows, it's gorgeous. The enclosed garden, full of birdsong and roses, wraps itself around the house. One bedroom has a secret door that leads to a fuchsia-pink bathroom; the other room, smaller, is wallpapered in a honeysuckle trellis and has wonderful garden views. Wellies, dogs, barbours, log fires… and breakfast by a vast Tudor fireplace on homemade bread and jams and eggs from the hens. A happy, charming family home.

Price	From £95. Singles £85.
Rooms	2: 1 double, 1 twin/double.
Meals	Pub/restaurants within 15-min. drive.
Closed	Rarely.
Directions	A429 Cirencester-Stow. Right signed Sherborne & Clapton. In village, pass grassy area to left, postbox in one corner; house straight ahead on left on corner, facing down hill.

    10% off stays of 2 or more nights Mon-Thurs (Nov-Mar).

Karin & James Bolton
Clapton Manor,
Clapton-on-the-Hill GL54 2LG
Tel   +44 (0)1451 810202
Email   bandb@claptonmanor.co.uk
Web   www.claptonmanor.co.uk

Entry 216   Map 8

Gloucestershire

Rectory Farmhouse

Once a monastery, now a farmhouse with style. Passing a development of converted farm buildings to reach the Rectory's warm Cotswold stones makes the discovery doubly exciting. More glory within: Sybil, a talented designer, has created something immaculate, fresh and uplifting. A wood-burner glows in the sitting room, bed linen is white, walls cream; beds are superb, bathrooms sport cast-iron slipper baths and power showers and views are to the church. Sybil used to own a restaurant and her breakfasts – by the Aga or in the conservatory under a rampant vine – are a further treat.

Gloucestershire

Sherborne Forge

You are in a quiet Cotswolds corner, in your own restored cottage across the garden from the owner's 17th-century house, and overlooking Sherborne Brook. Walk in to a large living space with a high beamed ceiling, comfy sofas, bright rugs, antiques, flowers, books and a dining table and chairs. You have your own small kitchen for toast and tea; Karen brings over a delicious organic breakfast, served on a private terrace on sunny mornings. Your bedroom has pretty fabrics and fine linen; the bathroom has a big tub for long soaks. Fish for trout in the brook, head off for glorious walks and bike rides… this is a sanctuary.

Price	From £93. Singles £60.
Rooms	2 doubles.
Meals	Pubs/restaurants 1 mile.
Closed	Christmas & New Year.
Directions	B4068 from Stow to Lower Swell, left just before Golden Ball Inn. Far end of gravel drive on right.

Price	From £95. Singles £70.
Rooms	Cottage: 1 double, sitting room & kitchenette.
Meals	Pub/restaurant 3 miles.
Closed	Never.
Directions	A429 at Northleach; A40 towards Oxford. 3 miles, left signed Clapton & Sherborne. After 1 mile, left signed Farmington & Turkdean. 400 yds past houses, right before 30mph exit sign. 100 yds down small lane to house.

	Sybil Gisby
	Rectory Farmhouse,
	Lower Swell,
	Cheltenham GL54 1LH
Tel	+44 (0)1451 832351
Email	rectoryfarmhouse@yahoo.com

	Karen Kelly
	Sherborne Forge,
	Number 1 Sherborne,
	Cheltenham GL54 3DW
Tel	+44 (0)1451 844286
Email	karen.j.kelly@btinternet.com
Web	www.sherborneforge.co.uk

Entry 217   Map 8

Entry 218   Map 8

Gloucestershire

Westward

Susie and Jim are highly organised and efficient, juggling farm, horses and B&B. She's also a great cook (Leith trained). The grand, but cosy, house sits above Sudeley Castle surrounded by its own 600 acres; all bedrooms look west to long views. Colours, fabrics and furniture are in perfect harmony, beds and linen are inviting, and the easy mix of elegant living and family bustle is delightful. There's tea on the terrace in summer and by a log fire in winter... your hosts delight in sharing this very English home. Wonderful walks, Cheltenham, Cotswold villages, fabulous restaurants and pubs are near.

Price	From £90. Singles from £60.
Rooms	3: 1 double, 2 twins/doubles.
Meals	Pubs/restaurants 1 mile.
Closed	December/January.
Directions	From Abbey Sq., Winchcombe, go north; after 50 yds, right into Castle St. Follow for 1 mile; after farm buildings, right for Sudeley Lodge; follow for 600 yds. House on right; first oak door.

Susie & Jim Wilson
Westward,
Sudeley Lodge, Winchcombe,
Cheltenham GL54 5JB

Tel	+44 (0)1242 604372
Email	westward@haldon.co.uk
Web	www.westward-sudeley.co.uk

Entry 219   Map 8

Gloucestershire

The Courtyard Studio

This new first-floor studio, attractive in reclaimed red brick, is reached via its own wrought-iron staircase; you are beautifully private. The friendly owners live next door, and will cook you a delicious breakfast in the house, or leave you a continental one in your own fridge. Find a clever, compact, contemporary space with a light and uncluttered living area, a mini window seat opposite two very comfortable boutique hotel style beds, fine linen, wicker armchair, and a patio area for balmy days. A 20-minute walk brings you to the centre of Cheltenham and you're a two-minute canter from the races. *Minimum stay two nights.*

Price	£75.
Rooms	1 twin.
Meals	Restaurants/pubs within 1 mile.
Closed	Rarely.
Directions	From racecourse r'bout on A435 towards town centre, right on to Cleevelands Drive (telephone and old postbox), 300 metres on left, drive thro' brick portal gateway. No 1 is in left corner.

10% off stays of 2 or more nights. Free pick-up from local bus/train station.

John & Annette Gill
The Courtyard Studio,
1 The Cleevelands Courtyard,
Cleevelands Drive, Cheltenham GL50 4QF

Tel	+44 (0)1242 573125
Mobile	+44 (0)7901 978917
Email	courtyardstudio@aol.com

Entry 220   Map 8

Gloucestershire

5 Ewlyn Road

In a bustling suburb of Cheltenham, Barbara's red-brick villa remains firmly unmodernised. The whiff of beeswax fills the air and Barbara looks after you with old-fashioned ease; the front room has an open fire where you can read a book or chat. Your bedroom is peaceful, the bed is firm, and the white cotton sheets robustly pressed; the clean and purposeful bathroom is shared but not noticeably. In the warm parlour Barbara gives you freshly squeezed orange juice, best Gloucester Old Spot bacon, sausage and free-range eggs – have it outside the sunny back door in summer. Authentic, great value B&B.

Price	£60. Singles £30.
Rooms	1 twin sharing bath (& separate shower).
Meals	Pubs/restaurants 5-minute walk.
Closed	Rarely.
Directions	From A40, signs to Stroud. Up Bath Road past shops; at mini r'bout bear left, then left signed Emmanuel Church. House 2nd on right; front door to side.

Barbara Jameson
5 Ewlyn Road,
Cheltenham GL53 7PB
Tel   +44 (0)1242 261243

✕ 🚂 🐾

Entry 221   Map 8

Gloucestershire

Hanover House

The former home of Elgar's wife, in an early-Victorian terrace in Cheltenham's heart, is warm, elegant, inviting and surprisingly peaceful. There are big trees all around and the river Chelt laps at the foot of the garden. Inside, a graceful period décor is enlivened by golden retriever Sophie and exuberant splashes of colour; the delectable drawing room, with pale walls and a trio of arched windows, is the perfect foil for paintings, books and rugs. Bedrooms have vivid Indian throws, bathrooms are simply stylish, breakfasts are superb. Best of all are Veronica and James: musical, well-travelled, irresistible.

Price	£90–£100. Singles £70.
Rooms	3: 1 double; 1 double, 1 twin each with separate bath.
Meals	Pubs/restaurants 200 yds.
Closed	Rarely.
Directions	In Cheltenham town centre, 200 yds from bus & coach station; 800 yds from railway station. Parking available.

Veronica & James Ritchie
Hanover House,
65 St George's Road,
Cheltenham GL50 3DU
Tel   +44 (0)1242 541297
Email   info@hanoverhouse.org
Web   www.hanoverhouse.org

✕ 🚂 📶 🐾

Entry 222   Map 8

Gloucestershire

St Annes

Step straight off the narrow pavement into a sunny hall and a welcome to match. Iris worked in tourism for years and lives here with antique restorer Greg, two smiling children and Rollo the dog. They've also made this pretty 17th-century house in the centre of a captivating village (some road noise) as eco-friendly as possible. The biggest and most beautiful bedroom has a four-poster and a bathroom down the hall; the smallish double and the twin rooms will charm you. Farmers' market breakfasts are a warm, cosy, stylish feast. As for Painswick, it is known as 'the Queen of the Cotswolds'.
Min. two nights at weekends April-Sept.

Ethical Collection: Environment; Food. See page 430.

Price	£65. Singles £40.
Rooms	3: 1 double, 1 twin; 1 four-poster with separate bath.
Meals	Packed lunch £5. Restaurants/pubs in village.
Closed	Rarely.
Directions	A46 Stroud to Painswick; in Painswick, left after lights; house 3rd door on right. Bus: from Cheltenham & Stroud.

	Iris McCormick St Annes, Gloucester Street, Painswick GL6 6QN
Tel	+44 (0)1452 812879
Email	greg.iris@btinternet.com
Web	www.st-annes-painswick.co.uk

Entry 223   Map 8

Gloucestershire

Nation House

Three cottages were knocked together to create this wisteria-clad, listed village house, now a terrific B&B. Beams are exposed, walls are pale and hung with prints, floors are close-carpeted, the sitting room is formally cosy and quiet. Smart, comfortable bedrooms have patchwork quilts, low beams and padded seats at lattice windows; the bathroom is spotless and the small shower room gleaming. In summer, breakfast in the conservatory on still-warm homemade bread, local bacon and sausages, Brenda's preserves. The village is a Cotswold treasure, with two good eating places and with many walks from the door.

Price	£75-£85. Singles £50.
Rooms	3: 1 family for 3; 2 doubles sharing bath (let to same party only).
Meals	Pubs 50 yds.
Closed	Rarely.
Directions	From Cirencester A419 for Stroud. After 7 miles right to Bisley. Left at village shop. House 50 yds on right.

10% off Mon-Thurs, bottle of wine in room, or free pick-up from local station.

Use your Sawday's Gift Card here.

	Brenda & Mike Hammond Nation House, George Street, Bisley GL6 7BB
Tel	+44 (0)1452 770197
Email	nation.house@homecall.co.uk

Entry 224   Map 8

Gloucestershire

Well Farm

Perhaps it's the gentle, unstuffy attitude of Kate and Edward. Or the great position of the house with its glorious views across the valley. Whichever, you'll feel comforted and invigorated by your stay. It's a real family home and you get both a fresh, pretty bedroom that feels very private and the use of a comfortable, book-filled sitting room opening to a pretty courtyard: Kate is an inspired gardener. Sleep soundly on the softest of pillows, wake to the deep peace of the countryside and the delicious prospect of eggs from their own hens, local sausages and good bacon. The area teems with great walks.

Price	From £80.
Rooms	1 twin/double & sitting room.
Meals	Dinner from £20. Pubs nearby.
Closed	Rarely.
Directions	Directions on booking and on website.

Kate & Edward Gordon Lennox
Well Farm,
Frampton Mansell,
Stroud GL6 8JB
Tel +44 (0)1285 760651
Email kategl@btinternet.com
Web www.well-farm.co.uk

Entry 225   Map 8

Gloucestershire

Forwood Farm

Strong old bones and quiet contemporary design make for a pale, restful atmosphere at Forwood, the oatmeal, cream and caramel base brightened by scatter cushions, patterned rugs and modern art. Rose has flair and is enjoying reviving the big garden and its stone terraces. Home-grown fruit and eggs are served with local bacon in the pale blue breakfast room: rustic chest on original oak floorboards, wood-burner and fresh flowers, French windows onto a pretty courtyard. Lovely bedrooms with super modern showers, too. Walk out onto National Trust common land or to pure-Cotswold Minchinhampton for pubs and other antique fleshpots.

Price	£80. Singles £45.
Rooms	3 twins/doubles.
Meals	Packed lunch for walkers £7. Pub/restaurant 0.5 miles.
Closed	Never.
Directions	Directions on booking.

10% off room rate Mon-Thurs.

Rose Evans
Forwood Farm,
Forwood, Minchinhampton,
Stroud GL6 9AB
Tel +44 (0)1453 731620
Email rose@forwoodfarm.com
Web www.forwoodfarm.com

Entry 226   Map 8

Gloucestershire

Drakestone House

A treat by anyone's reckoning. Utterly delightful people with wide-ranging interests (ex-British Council and college lecturing; arts, travel, gardening) in a manor-type house full of beautiful furniture. The house was born of the Arts and Crafts movement: wooden panels painted green, a log-fired drawing room for guests, handsome old furniture, comfortable proportions, good beds with proper blankets. The garden's massive clipped hedges, Monterey pines and smooth, great lawn are impressive, as is the whole place – and the views stretch to the Severn Estuary and Wales.

Price	£90. Singles £49.
Rooms	3: 1 twin/double, 1 double, 1 twin, all with separate bath/shower.
Meals	Dinner £35. BYO. Pub/restaurant under 1 mile.
Closed	Christmas & New Year.
Directions	B4060 from Stinchcombe to Wotton-under-Edge. 0.25 miles out of Stinchcombe village. Driveway on left marked, before long bend.

Hugh & Crystal Mildmay
Drakestone House,
Stinchcombe,
Dursley GL11 6AS
Tel   +44 (0)1453 542140

🍴 🚂 🐕 📶

Entry 227   Map 8

Gloucestershire

Lodge Farm

A plum Cotswolds position, a striking garden, a rolling programme of improvements, exceptional linen – there are plenty of reasons to stay here. Then there are your flexible hosts, who can help wedding groups, give you supper en famille next to the Aga or something smart and candlelit round the dining-room table: perfect for a house party. The sitting room has flowers, family photographs and lots of magazines; sometimes home-produced lamb for dinner, always excellent coffee at breakfast, homemade bread and their own free-range eggs. Peace and quiet lovers will delight, yet you are a short walk from Tetbury.

Price	£70-£80. Singles from £60. Family suite £95.
Rooms	4: 2 twins/doubles; 1 twin/double, 1 family suite with shared bath.
Meals	Dinner, 2-3 courses, £15-£25. Pub/bistro 2.5 miles.
Closed	Rarely.
Directions	From Cirencester A433 to Tetbury, right B4014 to Avening. After 250 yds, left onto Chavenage Lane. Lodge Farm 1.3 miles on right; left of barn on drive.

Robin & Nicky Salmon
Lodge Farm,
Chavenage, Tetbury GL8 8XW
Tel   +44 (0)1666 505339
Email   nsalmon.lodgefarm@btinternet.com
Web   www.lodgefarm.co.uk

🐓 🍴 🚂 🐕 📶 🐈 🏊 🚲

Entry 228   Map 8

Gloucestershire

Le Mesuage

On a steep hill in old Tetbury, sunshine for the senses behind a blue door. Warm smiling Sarah, ex-royal service, invites you in to three intriguing storeys and a plant-filled courtyard at the back. The sitting room is contemporary/comfy, the bedrooms are quirky and serene: lemon and grey cushions on a perfect white bed, a gilt-framed picture, a perspex armchair, a tiny chandelier. All is spotless, fresh, artistic and delightful. Sarah, who once ran a restaurant in France, loves Slow food and the simple life so breakfasts and dinners are a treat. Walk the Cotswolds, book a tour of Highgrove, discover Tetbury's charms.

Price	£80. Singles £50.
Rooms	3: 2 doubles; 1 twin with separate bath.
Meals	Dinner, 4 courses with wine, £35. Packed lunch £10. Pubs/restaurants 300 yds.
Closed	Christmas.
Directions	Cheltenham-Cirencester A4365, then A433 to Tetbury market square. Gumstool Hill 1st left after traffic lights. Ask about parking.

10% off stays of 3 or more nights. Local food/produce in your room.

Sarah Champier
Le Mesuage,
26 Gumstool Hill,
Tetbury GL8 8DG
Tel +44 (0)1666 500478
Email unknownlegend@btinternet.com
Web www.lemesuage.co.uk

Entry 229   Map 3

Gloucestershire

107 Gloucester Street

Slip through gates into a narrow courtyard of potted shrubs and honey-coloured Cotswold stone. This modest Georgian merchant's house is three minutes from the charming town centre yet blissfully quiet. Inside: buttery colours, well-loved antiques, soft uncluttered spaces. Restful, understated bedrooms are small, chic and spotless. Kitchen breakfasts overlook the sheltered garden – a verdant spot for relaxing in summer. For evenings, a creamy first-floor sitting room with a small log fire. Ethne and her ex-army husband are full of fun and good humour – very special.

Price	£75. Singles £50.
Rooms	2: 1 double, 1 twin.
Meals	Hotel 300 yds & restaurants 8-minute walk.
Closed	Christmas & Easter. (Enquire by email only in February.)
Directions	Directions on booking.

10% off stays of 2 or more nights.

Brendan & Ethne McGuinness
107 Gloucester Street,
Cirencester GL7 2DW
Tel +44 (0)1285 657861
Email ethnemcg@onetel.com
Web www.107gloucesterstreet.co.uk

Entry 230   Map 8

Gloucestershire

Ewen Wharf

Life, colour and warmth fill Fiona's pretty early 19th-century wharf keeper's cottage, snoozing in a tranquil corner of the Cotswolds. A log fire blazes in the cosy low-beamed sitting room, a little Norfolk terrier wags enthusiastically, porcelain marches proudly over shelves and you may recognise art by Fiona's father-in-law – creator of the famous Guinness advertisements. A pleasure to take tea in the well-tended garden, slumber deeply in plump, comfortable beds, chat to Fiona over bacon and eggs from the local farm. Stride out on the Thames Path or stroll to the village pub. Such a peaceful home – and good value too.

Price	£70–£75. Singles £45.
Rooms	2: 1 twin/double, 1 twin sharing bath (let to same party only).
Meals	Pub/restaurant 1 mile.
Closed	Christmas & New Year.
Directions	From Cirencester follow signs to south west and Tetbury. 2 miles, left onto A429 to Kemble. After 1 mile, left to Ewen. House on right before bridge.

Fiona Gilroy
Ewen Wharf,
Kemble,
Cirencester GL7 6BP
Tel +44 (0)1285 770469
Email fmgilroy@tiscali.co.uk
Web www.ewenwharf.co.uk

Entry 231   Map 8

Gloucestershire

Lady Lamb Farm

Light pours into perfectly proportioned rooms through windows hung with velvet and chintz; Jeanie and James, farmers, inventors, built the honey-stone house years ago and have kept their Cotswold dream ship-shape. Light bedrooms are a good size and have attractive furniture and pretty flowery fabrics. Aga breakfasts are scrumptious and served in the striped dining hall with wood-burner, country art and views to the garden: locally cured bacon, fruit and eggs from the chickens that strut on the manicured lawn. Great for fishing, cycling and golf; Kelmscott Manor, Bibury, Burford and Buscot are close by too.

Price	From £75. Singles £45.
Rooms	2: 1 twin; 1 twin/double with separate bath.
Meals	Pubs/restaurants 1-4 miles.
Closed	Christmas & New Year.
Directions	Farm 1 mile on right from Meysey Hampton crossroads going towards Fairford on A417.

10% off stays of 3 or more nights.

Jeanie Keyser
Lady Lamb Farm,
Meysey Hampton,
Cirencester GL7 5LH
Tel +44 (0)1285 712206
Email jeanie@ladylambfarm.com
Web www.ladylambfarm.com

Entry 232   Map 8

Gloucestershire

The Old Rectory

English to the core — and to the bottom of its lovely garden, with a woodland walk and plenty of quiet places to sit. You sweep into the circular driveway to a yellow labrador welcome. This beautiful 17th-century high gabled house is comfortably lived-in with an understated décor, antiques, creaky floorboards and a real sense of history. The bedrooms, one with a garden view, have very good beds, a chaise longue or an easy chair; bathrooms are vintage but large. Caroline is calm and competent and serves breakfasts with organic eggs and local bacon at the long polished table in the rich red dining room. A special place.

Price	£80–£95. Singles from £50.
Rooms	2: 1 double, 1 twin/double.
Meals	Pub 200 yds.
Closed	December/January.
Directions	South through village from A417. Right after Masons Arms. House 200 yds on left, through stone pillars.

Roger & Caroline Carne
The Old Rectory,
Meysey Hampton,
Cirencester GL7 5JX
Tel +44 (0)1285 851200
Email carolinecarne@cotswoldwireless.co.uk
Web www.meyseyoldrectory.co.uk

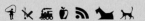

Entry 233   Map 8

Gloucestershire

Kempsford Manor

On the edge of the Cotswolds, this 17th-century village manor house is surrounded by large hedges and mature trees. Crunch up the gravelled drive to find floor-to-ceiling windows, dark floors with patterned rugs, wood panelling, a piano and a library. Spacious bedrooms have super garden views; one comes with a Chinese theme, a mix of rugs and blankets and a pretty quilt. Bathrooms are functional and old-fashioned. Beautifully tended gardens (snowdrops are special here) lead to an orchard and a canal walk; stoke up on Zehra's homemade muesli and bread and return for dinner — vegetables are home-grown. *Garden open for NGS.*

Price	£60–£70. Singles £40.
Rooms	3: 2 doubles, 1 single sharing 2 baths.
Meals	Dinner by arrangement. Pub 200 yds.
Closed	Never.
Directions	A419 Cirencester-Swindon; Kempsford is signed with Fairford. Right into village, past small village green; on right, through stone columns. Glass front door, by a fountain.

10% off stays of 3 or more nights. Stay 3 nights, 4th free.

Zehra I Williamson
Kempsford Manor,
High Street, Kempsford,
Fairford GL7 4EQ
Tel +44 (0)1285 810131
Email info@kempsfordmanor.com
Web www.kempsfordmanor.com

Entry 234   Map 8

Gloucestershire

Little Smithy

Minutes from the M4, the farming village is fairly quiet and your little cottage with mullioned windows completely private. Your front door opens into a hallway which runs the length of the building: at one end, the creamy twin with bright red bedspreads and sparkling bathroom next door, at the other, your L-shaped sitting room with an electric wood-burner. Upstairs is the comfy double and another smart bathroom; all is as neat as a pin. Joanna gives you breakfast in the main house, or on warm days in the garden: eggs from next door's hens, homemade bread and marmalade. Right on the Cotswold Way so perfect for walkers.

Price	£75. Singles £60.
Rooms	2 doubles.
Meals	Pub/restaurant 1 mile.
Closed	Christmas & Easter.
Directions	Bath A46 north. Cross M4 signed Stroud, then almost immed. 1st turning on right. After Compass Inn, 2nd turning on right into village. Past church; house 1st on right after left-hand bend.

10% off stays of 2 or more nights. Free pick-up from local bus/train station.

	Joanna Bowman
	Little Smithy,
	Tormarton,
	Badminton GL9 1HU
Tel	+44 (0)1454 218412
Email	richardbowman@uk2.net
Web	www.littlesmithy.com

Entry 235   Map 3

Gloucestershire

The Moda House

A fine house and a big B&B, but one that retains a deeply homely feel; Duncan and Jo are hugely well-travelled and have filled it with pictures and artefacts from all over the world. Bedrooms differ (three are in a neat annexe) but all are cosy and well decorated with lovely colours, good fabrics, pocket sprung mattresses and bright bathrooms with thick towels. Breakfast is a truly local feast and will set you up for fabulous walks (you are a mile from the Cotswold Way), there's a basement sitting room with comfy armchairs and lots of books, and you have the bustling town to explore with its shops and restaurants.

Price	From £82. Singles from £65.
Rooms	10: 7 doubles, 3 singles.
Meals	Pubs/restaurants within 0.25 miles.
Closed	Never.
Directions	Exit M4 at junction 18. Follow A46 northbound. Turn left and follow A432 into town centre. House is at top of High Street.

	Duncan & Jo MacArthur
	The Moda House,
	1 High Street,
	Chipping Sodbury BS37 6BA
Tel	+44 (0)1454 312135
Email	enquiries@modahouse.co.uk
Web	www.modahouse.co.uk

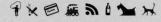

Entry 236   Map 3

Vinegar Hill Pottery

A sylvan setting, stylish pottery, a young and talented family. The cobalt blues and rich browns of David's ceramics fill the old stables of a Victorian manor house. Take pottery courses (one hour to a long weekend) or just enjoy the creative Mexican-inspired décor. A narrow staircase spirals up to a modern loft: crisp whites, cathedral ceiling spiked with sunny windows, brilliant shower. The ground-floor garden suite has a patio, a sitting room, an unusual painted bed and optional children's beds. Lucy brings breakfast to your room. After which, stroll to the beach: stretch out and you almost touch the Isle of Wight.

Price	From £75. Singles £55.
Rooms	2: 1 double, 1 suite (2 extra beds).
Meals	Pub/restaurant 0.25 miles.
Closed	Rarely.
Directions	A339 towards Christchurch. Left onto B3058. Next right into Manor Road, round bend into Barnes Lane. After Baptist church, Vinegar Hill is 3rd on right.

	Lucy Rogers
	Vinegar Hill Pottery,
	Vinegar Hill,
	Milford on Sea SO41 0RZ
Tel	+44 (0)1590 642979
Email	info@davidrogerspottery.co.uk
Web	www.davidrogerspottery.co.uk

Entry 237   Map 3

Bay Trees

Step in from the village street and you find yourself in a striking hall where the guest book perches on the music stand! Comfortable bedrooms have just been refurbished, the double with French windows opening to a lush suntrap of a garden – a wonderful surprise – full of arbours and weeping willow and a brook at the end with a seat for two. Breakfasts are gourmet here, served in the conservatory overlooking the magnolia. Robert, humorous and down-to-earth, makes you feel at ease the moment you arrive. The shingle beach with views to the Isle of Wight is a sprint away. *Minimum stay two nights at weekends.*

Price	£80–£130. Singles from £50.
Rooms	4: 1 double, 1 four-poster; 1 triple, 1 single sharing bath (2nd room let to same party only).
Meals	Restaurants/pubs 100 yds.
Closed	Rarely.
Directions	From Lymington follow signs for Milford-on-Sea (B3058). On left, just past village green.

 10% off stays of 3 or more nights Mon-Thurs.

	Robert Fry
	Bay Trees,
	8 High Street, Milford-on-Sea,
	Lymington SO41 0QD
Tel	+44 (0)1590 642186
Email	rp.fry@virgin.net
Web	www.baytreebedandbreakfast.co.uk

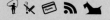

Entry 238   Map 3

Hampshire

Pepperbox House

Expect charming British hospitality in this quaint 1650s brick house on Beaulieu's high street, a perfect base for exploring the New Forest. Thick oak beams from the shipyard at nearby Buckler's Hard support a low ceiling in the dining room, cosy with its polished table and oil painting; step through an original wood door to a winding staircase which curls up to an airy twin and sweet double under the eaves. Jane's garden is brimming with honeysuckle, clematis, climbing roses, a lovely place to relax after a day spent stomping the park's myriad trails. End with a traditional English meal and a sound sleep: homely, well cared-for, a treat.

Hampshire

Home Close

The setting is gorgeous, surrounded by the New Forest – walks start from the gate. The house, once a farm belonging to the Beaulieu estate, is now home to friendly Sally and Bob. You sleep in a sunshine-yellow bedroom overlooking the lovely garden, there are Lloyd Loom chairs for reading or TV, bottled water, proper milk, homemade shortbread. A generous breakfast, sometimes with home-baked bread, is taken in the pretty blue dining room at a solid oak table, from where you can watch the comings and goings of the birds beneath the arbour. Perfect for exploring the New Forest or a day trip to the Isle of Wight.

Price	£70-£80. Singles £45-£60.
Rooms	2: 1 double, 1 twin with shared bath.
Meals	Dinner, 2 courses, £17.50; 3 courses, £22. Picnic lunch £7.50-£10. Pub/restaurant 0.25 miles.
Closed	Rarely.
Directions	B3056 from Lyndhurst. Left into Beaulieu, right into High Street. House about 500 yds on left.

Price	From £80.
Rooms	1 double.
Meals	Packed lunch £7. Pubs/restaurants within 7 miles.
Closed	Christmas, New Year & occasionally.
Directions	M27 junc. 2. A326, then B3054 signed Beaulieu 1.1 miles from New Forest cattle grid, down gravel track signed Home Close & Vanguard. Left past cottage to gate.

Jane Skinner
Pepperbox House,
54 High Street,
Beaulieu SO42 7YD
Tel +44 (0)1590 612728
Email jane@pepperboxhouse.co.uk
Web www.pepperboxhouse.co.uk

Sally Brearley
Home Close,
Hill Top,
Beaulieu SO42 7YR
Tel +44 (0)1590 612287
Email homeclose@talktalk.net
Web www.homeclosebedandbreakfast.co.uk

Entry 239 Map 3

Entry 240 Map 3

Hampshire

Sandy Corner

Stride straight onto open moorland from this smallholding on the edge of the New Forest — a great place for anyone who loves walking, cycling, riding, wildlife and the great outdoors. And there's plenty of room for wet clothes and muddy boots. Cattle graze within ten feet of the window, you may hear the call of a nightjar in June, Dartford warblers nest nearby, happy hens cluck around the yard. Sue also keeps a horse, two cats, a few sheep. You have a little guest sitting room, lovely fresh bedrooms, your own spot in the garden and a marvellous, away-from-it-all feel. You can walk to one pub; others are nearby.

Price	From £78. Singles from £50.
Rooms	2 doubles.
Meals	Packed lunch £8.
	Pub within walking distance, restaurant 2.5 miles.
Closed	Rarely.
Directions	On A338, 1 mile S of Fordingbridge, at small x-roads, turn for Hyde & Hungerford. Up hill & right at school for Ogdens; left at next x-roads for Ogdens North; on right at bottom of hill.

Sue Browne
Sandy Corner,
Ogdens North,
Fordingbridge SP6 2QD
Tel   +44 (0)1425 657295

Entry 241   Map 3

Hampshire

Yew Tree House

A charming papier-mâché cat welcomes you at the front door, setting the tone for this artistic, tranquil house. The views, the house and the villagers are said to have inspired Dickens, who escaped London for the peace of the valley. The exquisite red brick was there 200 years before him; the rare dovecote, to which you may have the key, 300 years before that. Thoughtful hosts, interesting to talk to, have created a house of understated elegance: a yellow-ochre bedroom with Descamps bed linen, cashmere/silk curtains designed by their son, a view onto an enchanting garden, a profusion of flowers. Great value.

Price	£70. Singles by arrangement.
Rooms	2: 1 twin;
	1 double with separate bath.
Meals	Pub in village.
Closed	Rarely.
Directions	From A30 west of Stockbridge for 1.5 miles, left at minor x-roads. After 2 miles left at T-junc. House on left at next junc. opp. Greyhound.

 Use your Sawday's Gift Card here.

Philip & Janet Mutton
Yew Tree House,
Broughton,
Stockbridge SO20 8AA
Tel   +44 (0)1794 301227
Email   pandjmutton@onetel.com

Entry 242   Map 3

Hampshire

Brymer House

Complete privacy in a B&B is rare. Here you have it, a 12-minute walk from town, cathedral and water meadows. Relax in your own half of a Victorian townhouse immaculately furnished and decorated and with a garden to match — all roses and lilac in the spring. Fizzy serves sumptuous breakfasts, there's a log fire in the guests' sitting room and fresh flowers abound — guests have been delighted. You are also left with an 'honesty box' so you may help yourselves to drinks. Bedrooms are small and elegant, with antique mirrors, furniture and bedspreads; bathrooms are warm and spotless. *Children over seven welcome.*

Price	£75–£80. Singles £54–£60.
Rooms	2: 1 double, 1 twin.
Meals	Pubs/restaurants nearby.
Closed	Christmas.
Directions	M3 junc. 9; A272 Winchester exit, then follow signs for Winchester Park & Ride. Under m'way, straight on at r'bout signed St Cross. Left at T-junc.

Guy & Fizzy Warren
Brymer House,
29-30 St Faith's Road, St Cross,
Winchester SO23 9QD
Tel   +44 (0)1962 867428
Email   brymerhouse@aol.com
Web   www.brymerhouse.co.uk

Entry 243   Map 4

Hampshire

Mulberry House

Deep into Jane Austen country, among ancient apple trees and rose bushes, is Mulberry House — the red-brick stable block of Old Alresford House. Peter and Sue are charming, and so is their home, filled with interesting pictures, fresh flowers and family photos. Private, quietly elegant guest rooms share a sitting room and kitchenette; the one in the eaves overlooks a pretty courtyard where a fountain plays. The dining room is elegant, but in fine weather you breakfast beneath the wisteria and vine-hung pergola on home-laid eggs and homemade jams. Comfortably English with a lovely garden.

Ethical Collection: Food. See page 430.

Price	£80. Singles £60.
Rooms	2: 1 double, 1 twin/double.
Meals	Pubs/restaurants within 10-minute walk.
Closed	Rarely.
Directions	M3 exit 9, signs to Alresford. In town centre, left onto B3046 to church on right. Then right into Colden Lane. House is 3rd on right through field gate.

Sue & Peter Paice
Mulberry House,
Colden Lane, Old Alresford,
Alresford SO24 9DY
Tel   +44 (0)1962 735518
Email   suepaice@btinternet.com
Web   www.mulberryhousebnb.com

Entry 244   Map 4

Hampshire

The Threshing Barn

You are on the edge of the rolling Meon valley, the approach through hedge-lined lanes is bucolic and the beautifully restored barn sits on a conservation award-winning farm run by John. Choose between a colourful and homely double in the main house or independence in the glorious bothy – a beamed and light space with a double walk-in shower. Find fresh flowers, good mattresses and feather and down pillows. All guests are greeted with tea and scones, breakfast is a local or home-grown extravaganza (check out Emma's borage honey) and views are to one of the tallest village church spires in Hampshire.

Price	£85–£95. Singles £60.
Rooms	3: 1 double, 1 single with shared bath (let to same party only). Bothy: 1 twin/double.
Meals	Packed lunch £7–£8. Pub 2 miles.
Closed	Rarely.
Directions	A272 Winchester to Petersfield. After A32 & A272 crossing, continue 0.8 miles towards Petersfield. Then left up Stocks Lane, 0.5 miles to the house.

10% off stays of 2 or more nights Mon-Thurs. Farm tour by John.

	Emma Bird
	The Threshing Barn,
	Stocks Lane, Privett GU34 3NZ
Tel	+44 (0)1730 828382
Email	emmacbird@stocksfarmprivett.co.uk
Web	www.thethreshingbarn.co.uk

Entry 245   Map 4

Hampshire

Little Shackles

Gaze upon the pretty Arts and Crafts house from the comfort of the hammock or solar-heated pool: this is a charming place to stay. Rosemary advises on local gardens to visit (her own two acres are also special) and is the loveliest of hosts. Your bedroom has an elegant country air – firm beds with feather toppers, new armchairs and a new TV – and a spring-like bathroom with fluffy bathrobes and views to green fields. Breakfast is plentiful; dinner, at the lovely old drover's pub down the sleepy lane, is a simple treat. Within the South Downs National Park so the walks are marvellous, and Goodwood and Portsmouth are close.

Price	£70. Singles £40.
Rooms	2: 1 twin/double, 1 single sharing bath (2nd room let to same party only).
Meals	Packed lunch from £7. Pub 0.5 miles.
Closed	Rarely.
Directions	From London A3 take A272 junc. Petersfield, right at r'bout. 1st right into Kingsfernsden Lane, over level crossing into Reservoir Lane. Right into Harrow Lane. House 2nd driveway on right.

	Rosemary & Martin Griffiths
	Little Shackles,
	Harrow Lane,
	Petersfield GU32 2BZ
Tel	+44 (0)1730 263464
Email	martgriff@btinternet.com

Entry 246   Map 4

Hampshire

Orchard Barn

Escape to a private country bolthole submerged in the South Downs' rolling AONB countryside. Caroline has transformed the old clapperboard stables into a very large, high-vaulted suite complete with oak floors, wood-burner, smart leather sofas and striking king-size bed: all yours to enjoy, as are the new National Park's splendid walks and cycling trails. Caroline brings cooked breakfasts to your door, to eat inside or on the sunny patio; on prior request she can also whip up anything from nursery food to three-course meals of seasonal, local produce. A glorious getaway in southeast England's finest countryside.

Price	From £90.
Rooms	Stable: 1 suite.
Meals	Supper from £25. Pub 1.2 miles.
Closed	Christmas, New Year & January.
Directions	From centre of Petersfield, A272 towards Winchester. After 1.4 miles, left after Seven Stars pub, signed Ramsdean. On for 1.2 miles. House on right.

Late checkout (12pm). Free pick-up from local bus/train station.

Caroline Wyld
Orchard Barn,
Ramsdean, Petersfield GU32 1RU
Mobile   +44 (0)7795 035590
Email   info@orchardbarn.co.uk
Web   www.orchardbarn.co.uk

Entry 247   Map 4

Hampshire

Mizzards Farm

The central hall is three storeys high, its vaulted roof open to the rafters. This is the oldest part of this lovely, wisteria-clad, mostly 16th-century farmhouse: kilims and fine antiques look splendid with old flagstones and wooden floors. There's a drawing room for musical evenings and an upstairs conservatory from which you can see the garden with its lake, outdoor chess and Harriet's sculptures. The four-poster is luxuriously kitsch with electric curtains, the other bedrooms are traditional and fresh. Come in the summer for occasional mini Glyndebournes on the lawn. *Children over eight welcome. Min. two nights.*

Price	£80-£90. Singles by arrangement.
Rooms	3: 1 double, 1 twin, 1 four-poster.
Meals	Pubs 0.5 miles.
Closed	Christmas & New Year.
Directions	From A272 at Rogate, turn for Harting & Nyewood. Cross humpback bridge; drive signed to right after 300 yds.

Harriet & Julian Francis
Mizzards Farm,
Rogate, Petersfield GU31 5HS
Tel   +44 (0)1730 821656
Email   francis@mizzards.co.uk

Entry 248   Map 4

Hampshire

Land of Nod

A 1939 house of character with hosts to match and one of the greatest gardens in the book... seven tended acres within 100 acres of woodland. There are azaleas and camellias, specimen trees, croquet, tennis, a white wisteria 40 years old – and orchids: Jeremy's passion. Breakfast in the chinoiserie dining room – the allegorical tableau is charming, the needlework on the walls dates from 1901. No sitting room, but bedrooms are spacious, with views over the garden; original baths have vast taps. Flexible breakfasts are locally sourced, with seasonal fruit and preserves from the garden. *Children over ten welcome.*

Price	From £80. Singles from £50.
Rooms	2: 1 twin; 1 twin with separate bath.
Meals	Restaurants 5-minute drive.
Closed	Rarely.
Directions	South on A3 to lights at Hindhead. Straight across & after 400 yds, right onto B3002. On for 3 miles. Entrance (signed) on right in a wood.

Bottle of wine in your room.

Jeremy & Philippa Whitaker
Land of Nod,
Headley,
Bordon GU35 8SJ
Tel   +44 (0)1428 713609
Email pwhitaker100@hotmail.com

Entry 249   Map 4

Hampshire

The Manor House

Gracious yet informal, a crisp Regency house in this little corner of Hampshire where Jane Austen wrote most of her books. Clare, or Vera, her enthusiastic housekeeper, will spoil you, even collect you from the station if you come without a car. Bedrooms are airy and light – the twin has deep windows and faces south across the garden – with space for chairs or a sofa, family paintings and antiques; bathrooms are smart. Eat a delicious breakfast of homemade bread, Cumbrian bacon and local sausages in the elegant dining room where French windows overlook glorious lawns, herbaceous borders and mature trees.

Price	£85. Singles £55.
Rooms	2: 1 double, 1 twin.
Meals	Pub 0.25 miles.
Closed	Never.
Directions	West at r'bout on A31 north of Alton, B3004 for Alton, Bordon & Holybourne. Over railway; 1st right into Holybourne. After 300 yds road dips; up hill and at top left into Church Lane; 100 yds on left up 2nd gravel drive without gate.

10% off room rate Mon-Thurs. Free pick-up from local bus/train station.

Clare Whately
The Manor House,
Holybourne,
Alton GU34 4HD
Tel   +44 (0)1420 541321
Email clare@whately.net
Web   www.manor-house-holybourne.co.uk

Entry 250   Map 4

Hampshire

Little Cottage

Just 45 minutes from Heathrow but the peace is deep, the views are long and the wildlife thrives – watch fox and deer, hear the rare nightjar. Chris and Therese grow many of their own vegetables and fruit, source meat locally and give you superb home cooking; guests have a lovely sitting room with an eclectic mix of modern and antique furniture, and a pretty terrace overlooks the garden. Bedrooms are all ground-floor, fresh and light, the double has distant views; perfect for walkers and those who seek solace from urban life but don't want to go too far. *Minimum stay two nights at weekends. Children over 12 welcome.*

Ethical Collection: Food. See page 430.

Price	£70-£80. Singles £50.
Rooms	3: 1 twin/double, 1 double, 1 single.
Meals	Dinner from £15. Pub 1.5 miles.
Closed	Christmas, New Year & occasionally.
Directions	B3011 from A30 in Hartley Wintney for 1.5 miles. Cottage just before the continuous double white line down the middle of road becomes a single line.

10% off room rate.

Chris & Therese Abbott
Little Cottage,
Hazeley Heath, Hartley Wintney,
Hook RG27 8LY
Tel   +44 (0)1252 845050
Email info@little-cottage.co.uk
Web   www.little-cottage.co.uk

Entry 251   Map 4

Herefordshire

Bunns Croft

The timbers of the medieval house are probably 1,000 years old. Little of the structure has ever been altered and it is an absolute delight: stone floors, rich colours, a piano, dogs, books and cosy chairs – all give a homely, warm feel. Cruck-beamed bedrooms are snugly small, the stairs are steep – this was a yeoman's house – and the twin's bathroom has its own sweet fireplace. The countryside is 'pure', too, with 1,500 acres of National Trust land five miles away. Anita is charming, loves to look after her guests, grows her own fruit and vegetables and makes fabulous dinners. Just mind your head.

Ethical Collection: Food; Community. See page 430.

Price	£70-£80. Singles £35.
Rooms	4: 1 twin; 1 double, 2 singles, sharing bath (let to same party only).
Meals	Dinner, 3 courses, £25. Pub 5 miles.
Closed	Rarely.
Directions	From Leominster, A49 towards Ludlow; 4 miles to village of Ashton, then left. House on right behind postbox after 1 mile.

Jar of homemade jam or marmalade to take home. In summer six eggs from garden hens.

Anita Syers-Gibson
Bunns Croft,
Moreton Eye,
Leominster HR6 0DP
Tel   +44 (0)1568 615836

Entry 252   Map 7

Herefordshire

Staunton House

This handsome Georgian rectory with light, colourful and well-proportioned rooms brims with beautiful furnishings. The original oak staircase leads to peaceful bedrooms with comfortable beds; the blue room looks onto garden and pond. It's a house that matches its owners – quiet, traditional and country-loving. Wander through the lovely garden, drive to Hay or Ludlow, stride some ravishing countryside, play golf near Offa's Dyke; return to Rosie and Richard's lovely home to relax in their drawing room before enjoying a delicious dinner in the elegant dining room. You will be well tended here.

Price	From £80. Singles from £50.
Rooms	2: 1 double, 1 twin/double.
Meals	Dinner, 2-3 courses, £20-£25. Pub/restaurant 2.5 miles.
Closed	Rarely.
Directions	A44 Leominster-Pembridge; right to Shobdon. After 0.5 miles, left to Staunton-on-Arrow; at x-roads, over into village. House opp. church, with black wrought-iron gates.

Rosie & Richard Bowen
Staunton House,
Staunton-on-Arrow, Pembridge,
Leominster HR6 9HR
Tel   +44 (0)1544 388313
Email   rosbown@aol.com
Web   www.stauntonhouse.co.uk

Entry 253   Map 7

Herefordshire

Hall's Mill House

Quiet lanes bring you to this most idyllic spot – a stone cottage in a light and open valley. The sitting room is snug with wood-burner and sofas but the kitchen is the hub of the place – delicious breakfasts and dinners are cooked on the Aga. Grace, chatty and easy-going, obviously enjoys living in her modernised mill house. Rooms are small, fresh, with exposed beams and slate sills; only the old mill interrupts the far-reaching, all-green views. Drift off to sleep to the sound of the Arrow burbling by – a blissful tonic for walkers and nature lovers. Great value, too. *Children over four welcome.*

Price	£55-£60. Singles £27.50-£30.
Rooms	3: 1 double; 1 double, 1 twin, sharing bath.
Meals	Dinner from £15. Pub/restaurant 3 miles.
Closed	Christmas.
Directions	A438 from Hereford. After Winforton, Whitney-on-Wye & toll bridge, sharp right for Brilley. Left fork to Huntington, over x-roads & next right to Huntington. Next right into 'No Through Road', then 1st right.

Grace Watson
Hall's Mill House,
Huntington,
Kington HR5 3QA
Tel   +44 (0)1497 831409

Entry 254   Map 7

Herefordshire

Garnstone House

Come for peace and quiet in the Welsh Marches, good food and lovely, humorous, down-to-earth hosts. The atmosphere is easy, and the furniture a lifetime's accumulation of eclectic pieces and pictures and prints of horses, hounds and country scenes. After dinner and good conversation, climb the picture-lined stairs to a comfortingly carpeted bedroom – either a twin or a double – and a bathroom that is properly old-fashioned. Delicious breakfasts, good dinners and a stunning garden to explore – the variety and colour of the springtime flowers are astonishing and the clematis is a glory.

Price	From £80. Singles from £40.
Rooms	1 twin/double with separate bath.
Meals	Dinner from £25. Pub/restaurant 1 mile.
Closed	Rarely.
Directions	A480 from Hereford; after 10 miles, right onto B4230 for Weobley. After 1.75 miles, right onto level tarmac private road; 2nd on left over cattle grid.

	Dawn & Michael MacLeod
	Garnstone House,
	Weobley HR4 8QP
Tel	+44 (0)1544 318943
Email	macleod@garnstonehouse.co.uk
Web	www.garnstonehouse.co.uk

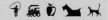

Entry 255   Map 7

Herefordshire

Winforton Court

Dating from 1500, the Court is dignified in its old age – undulating floors, great oak beams, thick walls. It is a dramatic, colourful home with exceptional timber-framed bedrooms; one room has an Indian-style bathroom and huge roll top bath, the suite a sitting area with two sofas. You also have a roomy guest sitting room and a small library for restful evenings. Your hosts are delightful and spoil you with decanters of sherry and bedside chocolates; the long room gallery seats up to 25 – great for family get-togethers. Visit Hay, walk down to the Wye or relax in the splendid garden. *Fishing can be arranged.*

Price	£85-£115. Singles from £70.
Rooms	3: 1 double, 1 four-poster, 1 four-poster suite.
Meals	Pub/restaurant 2-minute walk.
Closed	20-30 December.
Directions	From Hereford, A438 into village. Past Sun Inn, house on left with a green sign & iron gates.

	Bottle of local cider or chocolates for birthday, honeymoon or anniversary.

	Jackie Kingdon
	Winforton Court,
	Winforton HR3 6EA
Tel	+44 (0)1544 328498
Email	jackie@winfortoncourt.co.uk
Web	www.winfortoncourt.co.uk

Entry 256   Map 7

Lower House

A luxuriant garden in a magical valley; strike out for the Black Mountains from the door. The house, itself a forest of old timber, is almost lost within the garden. It is old, but restored with affection. Stairs twist and creak, the unexpected awaits you. Irresistible bedrooms are panelled or timber-clad; bathrooms are new. There's a handsome room downstairs where you eat breakfast (plentiful, delicious), play the piano or read by the fire. Nicky and Pete are kind and generous, steeped in good taste and this exquisite project, next to Offa's Dyke path and on the Welsh border. One of the best! *Minimum stay two nights.*

Ethical Collection: Environment; Food. See page 430.

Price	From £85.
Rooms	2: 1 double; 1 double with separate bath/shower.
Meals	Pubs/restaurants in Hay-on-Wye, 1 mile.
Closed	Rarely.
Directions	East through Hay on B4348 for Bredwardine. On the edge of Hay, right into Cusop Dingle; 0.75 miles, old mill house on left; drive on right, across stone bridge over stream.

Nicky & Peter Daw
Lower House,
Cusop Dingle,
Hay-on-Wye HR3 5RQ

Tel	+44 (0)1497 820773
Email	nicky.daw@btinternet.com
Web	www.lowerhousegardenhay.co.uk

Entry 257   Map 7

Tinto House

Bang in the centre of Hay-on-Wye, opposite the clock tower, amid a sea of bookshops, this beautiful Georgian townhouse brims with period features and original art. John and Karen have decorated their home with love: in the dining room, John's eye-catching paintings set off oak antiques, bookshelves, a fireplace; bedrooms bear mementos of France; one room holds art exhibitions. The garden, on the Wye's banks, is resplendent with roses and sculptures. Breakfast on local sausages and home-grown fruit compotes before hitting the Brecon Beacons or Hay's independent shops. Perfect for lovers of outdoor and armchair pursuits.

Price	£80–£90. Singles £50–£70.
Rooms	4: 2 doubles, 1 twin; 1 double with separate bath.
Meals	Packed lunch £5. Pub/restaurant 100 yds.
Closed	Christmas & New Year.
Directions	From Hereford A438 towards Brecon. After 19 miles left at Clyro to Hay (1 mile). Cross river; right at T-junc. House 100 yds on right facing clock tower.

Karen Clare
Tinto House,
13 Broad Street,
Hay-on-Wye HR3 5DB

Tel	+44 (0)1497 821556
Email	tintohouse@tiscali.co.uk
Web	www.tinto-house.co.uk

Entry 258   Map 7

Herefordshire

Ty-Mynydd

Six miles over open heathland from Hay-on-Wye, it is a remote, precipitous approach up the mountainside to Ty-Mynydd, and this renovated, stone-flagged farmhouse is absolutely gorgeous. Sheep graze the hillside, the views are simply the best and the garden is colourful, informal, delightful. Turn on the taps and taste water straight from your hosts' own mountain stream; awake to bacon and eggs produced in the fields around you (this is a working organic farm). The lovely young family give you two sweetly restful rooms on the ground floor, one with 'that view', and a simple country bathroom. The sunsets are magical.

Ethical Collection: Environment; Food.
See page 430.

Price	From £80. Singles £60.
Rooms	2 doubles sharing bath (2nd room let to same party only).
Meals	Pubs 6-8 miles.
Closed	Christmas & New Year.
Directions	From Hay on A438, 1st left after Swan Hotel; 6 miles uphill to open heath under Hay Bluff; 2nd right signed Capel Y Ffin; 1 mile, signed.

	N Spenceley
	Ty-Mynydd,
	Llanigon,
	Hay-on-Wye HR3 5RJ
Tel	+44 (0)1497 821593
Email	nikibarber@tiscali.co.uk
Web	www.tymynydd.co.uk

Entry 259   Map 7

Herefordshire

Ladywell House

Snuggling in the Golden Valley, wrapped by ancient oaks and a deep peacefulness, a wonderful place to relax. The whitewashed Edwardian dower house is welcoming and informal with understated good taste: soft colours, family paintings, antiques. The four-poster bedroom is regal, the twin fresh in blues and creams, and bathrooms are stylish and spoiling (one with a corner spa bath). A superb locally sourced breakfast with homemade bread is usually served in the conservatory; tea, cakes and drinks can be taken to the garden's Breeze House. Sarah and Charles are warm and generous; this is very much 'open house'.

Ethical Collection: Environment; Food.
See page 430.

Price	From £60. Singles from £50.
Rooms	2: 1 four-poster; 1 twin with separate bath.
Meals	Bistro 5-minute drive. Pub 12-minute drive.
Closed	Occasionally.
Directions	From A465 Hereford to Abergavenny, B4348 to Hay-on-Wye. Go 6.5 miles then left to Michaelchurch Escley & Vowchurch. After approx. 1 mile house opposite tall fir tree.

	Charles & Sarah Drury
	Ladywell House,
	Turnastone,
	Vowchurch HR2 0RE
Tel	+44 (0)1981 550235
Email	sarah@ladywellhouse.com
Web	www.ladywellhouse.com

Entry 260   Map 7

Herefordshire

Burghill Grange

A big, happy, friendly, family house. Harriet and John have sandblasted beams, waxed elm floors, uncovered some fine 18th-century ceilings and put in three smart bathrooms. Your sitting room is cosy – bright with fire, bold fabrics and interesting books; enjoy home-laid eggs, fresh bread, delicious coffee and sausages from Ludlow while looking over the peaceful garden and pond. A first-floor double is calm and uncluttered, the others beamed and large with great views to church tower and orchards; bathrooms have chunky roll tops, big towels and organic bubbles and creams. Handy for Hay, golf, antiques and the Brecons.

Price	£90. Singles from £35.
Rooms	3: 1 double; 1 twin/double with separate shower; 1 twin with separate bath.
Meals	Occasional dinner £20. Pubs/restaurants 1-4 miles.
Closed	Rarely.
Directions	A4103 north of Hereford, then A4110 north to Cannon Pyon. After 2 miles, after Portway sign, left to Burghill. After Burghill sign, house 1st on left.

Harriet Gordon
Burghill Grange,
Burghill,
Hereford HR4 7SE
Tel +44 (0)1432 761016
Email enquiries@burghillgrange.com
Web www.burghillgrange.com

Entry 261 Map 7

Herefordshire

Moor Court Farm

The buildings, about 500 years old, ramble and enfold both gardens and guests. Buff Orpingtons potter and cluck, there are sheep in the fields, owls and bats in the oast house and all feels deeply rural. This authentic idiosyncratic farmhouse is efficiently managed by Elizabeth, busy farmer's wife, and Peter. Elizabeth cooks for the shoots and her forte are traditional British dinners made from the best local produce: make the most of home-produced meat and home-grown vegetables. Bedrooms are cottagey, the four-poster one with views to the Malvern Hills; new shower rooms are promised.

Price	From £60. Singles £35.
Rooms	3: 1 four-poster, 2 twins.
Meals	Dinner, 3 courses, from £19.
Closed	Rarely.
Directions	From Hereford, east on A438. A417 into Stretton Grandison; 1st right past village sign, through Holmend Park. Bear left. House on left.

Elizabeth & Peter Godsall
Moor Court Farm,
Stretton Grandison,
Ledbury HR8 2TP
Tel +44 (0)1531 670408
Email elizabeth@moorcourtfarm.co.uk
Web www.moorcourtfarm.co.uk

Entry 262 Map 7

Herefordshire

Caradoc Court

Down the long drive, past the grand pillars and the Wellingtonia pines, to a lovely Jacobean manor, former seat of the Viscounts Scudamore. In 2009 the Handbys arrived, created four uncluttered, soft-carpeted bedrooms for guests and are mindfully making their mark on the place. Be wowed by impressive fireplaces and mullioned windows, massive oak roof trusses and polished sleigh beds, billiard room, ballroom and 12 wooded, landscaped acres, high on a bluff overlooking the Wye. The vistas are superb, the peace is restorative, the breakfasts are exemplary and there's a civilised pub at the end of the drive.

Price	From £95. Singles £75-£90.
Rooms	4: 3 doubles, 1 twin.
Meals	Pub 500 yds.
Closed	Christmas & New Year.
Directions	From Ross-on-Wye, A49 to Hereford. After 0.5 miles, right to Sellack. Follow lane for 2 miles to Lough Pool pub. Entrance gates to drive just past pub, on right.

John Handby
Caradoc Court,
Sellack,
Ross-on-Wye HR9 6LS
Tel +44 (0)1989 730257
Email kathy@caradoccourt.co.uk
Web www.caradoccourt.co.uk

Entry 263   Map 7

Hertfordshire

Homewood

Lutyens built this wonderful 1901 house for his mother-in-law, Lady Lytton. It is set down a long drive in six acres of gardens and fields, and architectural peculiarities abound. Samantha has applied her considerable artistic skills to the interior. The double bedroom has a pretty stencilled floor while the formal reception rooms are most elegant, their unusual colour schemes offsetting magnificent antiques, tapestries and chinoiserie. Your hosts give you an excellent breakfast, can converse in a clutch of languages, will book tables and taxis if required. And their pets are happy to welcome yours.

Price	£80. Suite from £100. Singles £50.
Rooms	3: 1 double, 1 family suite for 4. 1 double with separate shower also available.
Meals	Occasional dinner, with wine, £30 (min. 4). Pub 15-minute drive.
Closed	20 December-3 January.
Directions	Into Knebworth B197, into Station Rd (becomes Park Lane); 300 yds after m'way bridge, left into public footpath; 300 yds; bear left through gates; house at end.

Samantha Pollock-Hill
Homewood,
Old Knebworth SG3 6PP
Tel +44 (0)1438 812105
Email sami@homewood-bb.co.uk
Web www.homewood-bb.co.uk

Entry 264   Map 9

Isle of Wight

Gotten Manor

Such character, such style – miles from the beaten track, bordered by beautiful stone barns. There's a refreshing simplicity to this unique Saxon house where living space was above, downstairs was for storage. Romantic bedrooms, one hidden up a steep open stair, have limewashed walls, wooden floors, A-frame beams, sofas. You sleep on a French rosewood bed and you bathe in a roll top tub in the room – wallow by candlelight with a glass of wine. The garden bursts with magnificent fruit trees; Caroline's breakfasts include smoked salmon and smoothies. Rustic perfection, ancient peace. *Minimum stay two nights at weekends.*

Ethical Collection: Environment; Food. See page 430.

Price	£70-£100. Singles by arrangement.
Rooms	2 doubles.
Meals	Pub 1.5 miles.
Closed	Rarely.
Directions	0.5 miles south of Chale Green on B3399. After village, left at Gotten Lane. House at end of lane.

	Caroline Gurney-Champion
	Gotten Manor,
	Gotten Lane, Chale PO38 2HQ
Tel	+44 (0)1983 551368
Email	as@gottenmanor.co.uk
Web	www.gottenmanor.co.uk

Entry 265   Map 4

Isle of Wight

Northcourt

A glorious Jacobean house with matchless grounds: 15 acres of pathed terraced gardens, exotica and subtropical flowers. The house, too, is magnificent, with 80 rooms, its big, comfortable guest bedrooms in two wings. The library houses a full-size snooker table (yes, you may use it), there's a chamber organ in the hall, and in the vast music room a grand piano (yours to play). The dining room has separate tables and delightful Nina Campbell wallpaper. Step back in time – in a quiet, untouristy village in lovely downland, this large house is very much a family home, and the perfect base for walkers and garden lovers.

Price	£65-£100. Singles £45-£57.50.
Rooms	6 twins/doubles.
Meals	Occasional light meals. Pub 3-minute walk thro' gardens.
Closed	Rarely.
Directions	From Newport, into Shorwell; down steep hill, under rustic bridge & right opp. thatched cottage. Signed. From Brighstone left on bend after Crown Inn & village shop.

15% off stays of 3 or more nights.

	John & Christine Harrison
	Northcourt,
	Shorwell PO30 3JG
Tel	+44 (0)1983 740415
Email	christine@northcourt.info
Web	www.northcourt.info

Entry 266   Map 4

Isle of Wight

The Old Rectory

This old rectory dates to 1868: it comes in gothic style with arched windows and was influenced by the work of Ruskin and Pugin. Selina and Jon are perfect foils to the grandeur of their refurbished home. Both were teachers – he art, she music – and Jon's paintings cover the walls. Elsewhere, you'll find a tiled entrance hall, French windows that open onto a lawned garden and a red dining room for delicious communal breakfasts. Bedrooms upstairs are just the ticket with lots of books, fresh fruit and lovely linen; bathrooms are a little dated but spotless. The coast is close for cliff-top walks.

Price	£90–£110. Singles from £60.
Rooms	3: 2 doubles, 1 twin/double.
Meals	Dinner £25–£30. Packed lunch £10. Pubs a few hundred yds.
Closed	Never.
Directions	From Ventnor take the Whitwell road. 1 mile. Pass Whitwell village hall on right; house is on left immediately before church.

Jon & Selina Hepworth
The Old Rectory,
Ashknowle Lane,
Whitwell PO38 2PP
Tel   +44 (0)1983 731242
Email   info@oldrectory1868.co.uk
Web   www.oldrectory1868.co.uk

Entry 267   Map 4

Kent

Hartlip Place

The house resonates with a faded, funky grandeur. Family portraits and mahogany pieces, a drawing room to die for, an antique table shimmering with hyacinths, sash windows with sweeping views, happy dogs, chirpy peacocks, a garden intricate and special. After a candlelit dinner, up the circular stair to a colonial-style bedroom (or delightful four-poster) with garden views, decanter for sherry, old-fashioned bathroom and – big treat – real winter fire. John is unflappable and a touch mischievous, Gillian cooks, daughter Sophie greets – you'll like the whole family. *Children over 12 welcome.*

Price	From £90. Singles £50.
Rooms	2: 1 four-poster; 1 twin/double with separate bath.
Meals	Dinner £25. Pub 1 mile.
Closed	Christmas & New Year.
Directions	From Dover, M2 to Medway Services. Into station, on past pumps. Ignore no exit signs. Left at T-junc., 1st left & on for 2 miles. Left at next T-junc. House 3rd on left.

3 nights for 2 Mon-Thurs.

Gillian & John Yerburgh & Sophie & Richard Ratcliffe
Hartlip Place,
Place Lane, Sittingbourne ME9 7TR
Tel   +44 (0)1795 842323
Email   hartlipplace@btinternet.com
Web   www.hartlipplace.co.uk

Entry 268   Map 5

Kent

Dadmans

Once the dower house to Lynsted Park, Dadmans sits in a parkland setting with nearby orchards and grazing cattle and sheep. Your breakfast eggs are laid by rare-breed hens and there is local produce for dinner, served in the dining room on gleaming mahogany or in the Aga-warmed kitchen. Lovely bedrooms have patterned fabrics, indulgent beds, fresh flowers and good bathrooms. Outside there are ancient trees, walled gardens and lots of newly planted species including a nuttery; Doddington Place with its gardens and summer opera is a five-minute drive. *Over fours welcome. Minimum two nights at weekends April-Sept.*

Price	£85. Singles by arrangement.
Rooms	2: 1 twin; 1 double with separate bath.
Meals	Dinner, 4 courses, £35. Supper from £15. Pubs/restaurants nearby.
Closed	Rarely.
Directions	M20 junc. 8, then east on A20; left in Lenham towards Doddington. At The Chequers in Doddington, left; house 1.7 miles on left before Lynsted.

Free pick-up from local bus/train station.

	Amanda Strevens
	Dadmans,
	Lynsted, Sittingbourne ME9 0JJ
Tel	+44 (0)1795 521293
Email	amanda.strevens@btopenworld.com
Web	www.dadmans.co.uk

Entry 269   Map 5

Kent

7 Longport

A delightful, unexpected hideaway bang opposite the site of St Augustine's Abbey and a five-minute walk to the Cathedral. You pass through Ursula and Christopher's elegant Georgian house to emerge in a pretty courtyard, on the other side of which is the self-contained cottage. Downstairs is a cosy sitting room with pale walls, tiled floors and plenty of books, and a clever, compact wet room with mosaic tiles. Then up steep stairs to a swish bedroom with crisp cotton sheets on a handmade bed and views of magnolia and ancient wisteria. You breakfast in the main house or in the courtyard on sunny days. Perfect.

Ethical Collection: Food. See page 430.

Price	£80-£90. Singles £60.
Rooms	Cottage: 1 double & sitting room.
Meals	Restaurants 5-minute walk.
Closed	Rarely.
Directions	Follow ring road around Canterbury. Signs for Sandwich A257, at St George's r'bout turn for Dover. After 300 yds left for Sandwich. At mini r'bout, left; house on left just before corner. No car parking; public car park nearby.

10% off stays of 2 or more nights.

Use your Sawday's Gift Card here.

	Ursula & Christopher Wacher
	7 Longport,
	Canterbury CT1 1PE
Tel	+44 (0)1227 455367
Email	ursula.wacher@btopenworld.com
Web	www.7longport.co.uk

Entry 270   Map 5

Kent

14 Westgate Grove

Slap bang in the city, overlooking the river Stour and within strolling distance of the cathedral... step through the understated door and you will be astonished. Pippa is an interior designer, her husband an architect, and bedrooms are cool, smooth and fresh with good lighting, smart fabrics and pretty flowers. Bathrooms dazzle with rain showers, Brazilian black slate and the fluffiest of towels; don't feel guilty – it's rainwater heated by solar panels. On warm days you breakfast in the rosy-walled garden with its ancient vines, olives, lemons, mimosa; for cooler evenings there is an outdoor fireplace. Lovely.

Price	£80–£100.
Rooms	2: 1 double; 1 double with separate bath.
Meals	Pub/restaurant 50 yds.
Closed	Rarely.
Directions	Centre of Canterbury, on river by the Westgate Towers.

Pippa Clague
14 Westgate Grove,
Canterbury CT2 8AA

Tel	+44 (0)1227 769624
Mobile	+44 (0)7815 107032
Email	pippa@clague.plus.com

Entry 271   Map 5

Kent

Great Weddington

The listed house of perfect proportions was built by a Sandwich brewer of ginger beer. The décor is delicious, the bedrooms desirable and cosy, the bathrooms snug and spotless, and Katie fills the rooms with flowers; she also arranges the flowers for Canterbury Cathedral. Dinner is followed by coffee and chocolates in the drawing room – rich fabrics, shelves of books, fine watercolours, much-loved antiques. Outside, stunning hedges and lawns and a terrace for tea in the summer. An enchanting home in a farmland setting, and the area hums with history. *Minimum stay two nights at weekends April-September. Pets by arrangement.*

Price	£100–£120. Singles £85–£120.
Rooms	2 twins/doubles.
Meals	Dinner (occasionally), 4 courses, £37.50 (excluding Sunday).
Closed	Christmas & New Year.
Directions	From Canterbury, A257 for Sandwich. On approach to Ash, stay on A257 (do not enter village), then 3rd left at sign to Weddington. House 200 yds down on left.

Katie & Neil Gunn
Great Weddington,
Ash, Canterbury CT3 2AR

Tel	+44 (0)1304 813407
Email	greatweddington@hotmail.com
Web	www.greatweddington.co.uk

Entry 272   Map 5

Kent

Park Gate

Peter and Mary are a generous team and their conversation is informed and easy. Behind the wisteria-clad façade are two sitting rooms (one with chesterfield, one with wood-burner), ancient beams and polished wood. Bedrooms are freshly comfortable with gorgeous views over the garden to the fields beyond; bathrooms gleam, meals are delicious. More magic outside: croquet, tennis and thatched pavilions, wildlife and roses and a sprinkling of sheep to mow the paddock. The house has a noble history: Sir Anthony Eden lived here and Churchill visited during the war. Great value, and convenient for the Channel Tunnel.

Price	£80. Singles £40.
Rooms	3: 2 twins/doubles; 1 single with separate shower.
Meals	Dinner, 3 courses, £25. Pubs/restaurants 1 mile.
Closed	Christmas, New Year & January.
Directions	A2 Canterbury to Dover road; Barham exit. Through Barham to Elham. After Elham sign 1st right signed Park Gate 0.75 miles. Over brow of hill; house on left.

Bottle of wine with dinner on first night.

Peter & Mary Morgan
Park Gate,
Elham,
Canterbury CT4 6NE
Tel   +44 (0)1303 840304
Email   marylmorgan@hotmail.co.uk

Entry 273   Map 5

Kent

West End House

The very smart red-bricked Georgian house, formerly the village surgery, is now a gorgeous retreat; there's a deeply peaceful and rural feel, yet you are near to Dover and Canterbury. Choose between complete independence in the spacious suite at the 'North End' of the house, or the Tulip room in the main house. Lovely easy-going Lynne gives you homemade cake when you arrive, and delicious breakfasts (including smoked salmon and scrambled eggs) in an elegant family dining room with garden views. Bedrooms are crisp and pretty in shades of blue and green, mattresses are excellent and bathrooms have scented goodies.

Price	£65-£95. Singles £45-£65.
Rooms	2: 1 double & sitting room; 1 suite for 2 with sitting room & kitchen.
Meals	Dinner, 3 courses, £25. Pub 800 yds.
Closed	Christmas & New Year.
Directions	A2 towards Dover. Follow signs for Coldred. With the green on left, take right fork for Eythorne. House is on left after village sign.

Bottle of wine. Checkout at 12pm with snack for journey.

Lynne Backhouse
West End House,
Coldred Road, Eythorne,
Canterbury CT15 4BE
Tel   +44 (0)1304 830594
Email   lynne_backhouse@yahoo.co.uk
Web   www.westendhousekent.co.uk

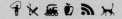

Entry 274   Map 5

Kent

Bunkers Hill

You are high on the North Downs, in this AONB, surrounded by Jacob sheep and fine views. Nicola, immensely kind and keen for guests to feel at home, gives you breakfast – eggs from her hens – in a delightful garden room with a variety of colourful plants. Nicola loves her garden and there is a summerhouse tucked away at the bottom with an enchanting outlook. Find an oak-panelled sitting room, cosy with a wood-burner, and one big guest bedroom, pretty with pale colours, period furniture and lovely garden views; the bathroom has a shower and Victorian cast-iron bath. Glorious gardens lie close by.

Price	£80. Singles £55.
Rooms	1 twin with separate bath & shower.
Meals	Pub within walking distance.
Closed	November–February.
Directions	From M20 junc. 8, A20 east for Ashford. At Lenham, left to Warren St. On for 1 mile. Harrow pub on right. Bear left. After 300 yds, 3-way junc. sharp left. House 4th on left.

Nicola Harris
Bunkers Hill,
Lenham ME17 2EE
Tel +44 (0)1622 858259

Entry 275　Map 5

Kent

The Linen Shed

A weatherboard house with a winding footpath to the front door and a pot-covered veranda out the back: sit here and nibble something delicious and homemade while you contemplate the pretty garden with its gypsy caravan. Vickie, wreathed in smiles, has created a 'vintage' interior: find wooden flooring, reclaimed architectural pieces, big old roll tops, a mahogany loo seat. Bedrooms (two up, one down) are painted in the softest colours, firm mattresses are covered in fine linen, cotton or linen dressing gowns wait patiently in the smart bathrooms. Food is seriously good here, and adventurous – try a seaside picnic hamper!

Ethical Collection: Food. See page 430.

Price	From £70. Singles from £60.
Rooms	3: 2 doubles with separate bath/shower; 1 double with shared bath.
Meals	Dinner from £20. Picnic hamper from £15. Pub/restaurant 300 yds.
Closed	Rarely.
Directions	M2, junc. 7; A2 for Canterbury. 1st immediate turnoff (100 yds) for Boughton, after 1 mile at T-junc. left. After 1 mile, left at phone box. House further along.
	10% off stays of 2 or more nights. Free pick-up from local bus/train station.

Vickie Hassan
The Linen Shed,
104 The Street, Boughton-under-Blean,
Faversham ME13 9AP
Tel +44 (0)1227 752271
Email bookings@thelinenshed.com
Web www.thelinenshed.com

Entry 276　Map 5

Kent

Hoo Farmhouse

Jane and Nicolas are keen shrimpers – let them take you to Minnis Bay and cook your catch for supper! Passionate about the coastline and the area, Jane is also a generous hostess, baking cakes for your arrival and giving you greengages and flowers from the garden. Bedrooms are big and sunny and have Georgian skirting boards and elegant sash windows; new bathrooms have soaps from Provence. The large Georgian-fronted house, surrounded on three sides by garden and rosy-brick outbuildings, has pale classic colours within, a breakfast conservatory, a drawing room with a fire – and a cathedral down the road.

Ethical Collection: Food. See page 430.

Price	£90. Singles £65.
Rooms	2 twins/doubles.
Meals	Supper, 2 courses, £12.50. Dinner, 3 courses, £25. Pub 1 mile.
Closed	Rarely.
Directions	A28 from Canterbury to Sarre, then A253 to Ramsgate. 4th exit at Monkton r'bout onto Willets Hill. Left at mini r'bout. House 0.75 miles on left.

	Jane Irwin
	Hoo Farmhouse,
	Monkton Road, Minster,
	Ramsgate CT12 4JB
Tel	+44 (0)1843 821322
Email	stay@hoofarmhouse.com
Web	www.hoofarmhouse.com

✗ 🚂 📡 ⚬

Entry 277   Map 5

Kent

Orchard Barn

Alison knows how to spoil (big beds, bread from the mill, home-grown soft fruit, homemade jams), David knows the wildlife, and they both love doing B&B. The big beautiful barn has been sympathetically restored, its middle section left open to create a stunning covered courtyard: find soaring beams, a comfortable leather sofa, fresh flowers. You get two snug, carpeted bedrooms up in the eaves – pale beams, bright colours, and a sweet bath (or shower) room. A delightful village, the ancient port of Sandwich nearby and egrets, kingfishers, swallows and squirrels a walk away. Superb. *Children over seven welcome.*

Price	£70-£80. Singles from £45.
Rooms	2: 1 double, 1 twin/double.
Meals	Pubs/restaurants within 1.5 miles.
Closed	20 December-3 January.
Directions	A258 Sandwich to Deal. 1st right after Worth sign into Felderland Lane; 0.5 miles concealed entrance on left, opp. black barn.

 10% off stays of 3 or more nights.

	David & Alison Ross
	Orchard Barn,
	Felderland Lane,
	Worth CT14 0BT
Tel	+44 (0)1304 615045
Email	orchardbarnworth@googlemail.com
Web	www.orchardbarn-worth.co.uk

✗ 🚂 📡 🐕

Entry 278   Map 5

Kent

Beaches

A proper seaside townhouse on The Strand, facing Walmer Green and the sea. But no fierce landlady inside – just cheery Rosie and two sleek, cool bedrooms, one on the ground floor, one on the first. Both are light, bright and fresh, dressed mainly in pale colours but with colourful headboards and cushions, and with comfy chairs for admiring views. Bathrooms are funky in a nautical way, there's a super little garden for breakfast on sunny days, and good restaurants close by. Start your day with eggs Benedict, cinnamon brioche, fresh croissants, good coffee. The perfect English seaside treat. *Minimum stay two nights for singles.*

Price	£80-£90. Singles £65-£75.
Rooms	2 doubles.
Meals	Breakfast or picnic brunch for the beach. Pubs/restaurants 0.5 miles.
Closed	Last 2 weeks in July.
Directions	From Deal station or town centre, south along Victoria Road passing Deal Castle. Then on to The Strand which opens onto Walmer Green. House opposite bandstand.

Rosanna Lillycrop
Beaches,
34 The Strand,
Walmer, Deal CT14 7DX
Tel   +44 (0)1304 369692
Email   enquiries@beaches.uk.com
Web   www.beaches.uk.com

Entry 279   Map 5

Kent

Kingsdown Place

Wow. A huge white villa set in stunning terraced gardens running down to the sea; on clear days you can see France! Tan has renovated both house and garden with panache: works of modern art festoon the walls, statues lurk and all is contemporary inside. Upstairs are neat bedrooms: one four-poster with long views, and, up a spiral staircase in the loft, a fabulous, very private bedroom with a sitting room and terrace. All have Conran mattresses and white linen. Breakfast on scrambled eggs and smoked salmon or the full works; take it outside on the terrace in good weather. Seaside chic.

Price	£90-£120. Singles £75.
Rooms	3: 1 double & sitting room & terrace; 1 double, 1 four-poster each with separate bath & sitting room.
Meals	Packed lunch £10. Dinner £25. Restaurant 500 yds. Pub 0.5 miles.
Closed	Christmas & New Year.
Directions	Through Kingsdown village towards sea; at high flint wall on right, turn right, through gateway, then 3rd gateway on left.
🧳	Bottle of wine in your room.

Tan Harrington
Kingsdown Place,
Upper Street,
Kingsdown CT14 8BT
Tel   +44 (0)1304 380510
Email   tan@tanharrington.com

Entry 280   Map 5

Kent

Alkham Court Farmhouse

An enchanting lane leads up, up to the farm: the glorious Kent valleys unfurl below. Wendy and Neil, locals born and bred, have built the house from scratch and thrown open their lives to share with all those lucky enough to stay. Luscious big bedrooms, two on the ground floor, have embroidered throws, dreamy mattresses, private entrances, sherry, chocolates and fresh flowers. Wake to farmers' market breakfasts and homemade muffins in a panorama-filled, toasty-warm 'Oak Room' from which you may never move, so deep are its seductions. Hens potter, cats purr, dogs doze, a hot tub burbles and the Tunnel is a ten-minute drive.

Kent

Woodmans

No traffic noise, just blissful peace – and you're no more than a short hop to Canterbury. Your cosy ground-floor bedroom has its own entrance via a lovely garden with far-reaching views. Tuck into local bacon and eggs (from Sarah's own rescued hens) in the breakfast room with its old pine table, dresser and flowers – or decide to be lazy and let Sarah bring it to your room. You can eat delicious dinner here too, perhaps after some hearty walking on the Wye Downs with its magnificent Chalk Crown and far-reaching views to Dungeness and the coast. *Babies welcome but cot not available.*

Price	£95–£120. Singles £70–£80.
Rooms	3 doubles.
Meals	Lunch £5. Packed lunch £7. Simple supper £4. Restaurant 0.5 miles.
Closed	Rarely.
Directions	M20 London to Dover. Past junc. 13; after tunnel in hill, left. Left at r'bout, then 1st left into Alkham Valley Rd. 2 miles, right into Meggett Lane. House just before top of hill, on right.

10% off room rate Mon–Thurs.

Price	£75. Singles £40.
Rooms	1 double.
Meals	Dinner, 3 courses, £24.50. Packed lunch £6.50. Pub/restaurant 1 mile.
Closed	Rarely.
Directions	From M20, junc. 9. Signed Wye & Kennington A28. Right for Wye, over level crossing, thro' village. At x-roads left to Canterbury. Hassell St 2nd on left; house 4th on left with signed gate.

Late checkout (12pm). Bottle of house wine with dinner if requested.

Wendy Burrows
Alkham Court Farmhouse,
Meggett Lane,
Alkham, Dover CT15 7DG

Tel	+44 (0)1303 892056
Email	wendy.burrows@alkhamcourt.co.uk
Web	www.alkhamcourt.co.uk

Entry 281   Map 5

Sarah Rainbird
Woodmans,
Hassell Street,
Hastingleigh, Ashford TN25 5JE

Tel	+44 (0)1233 750250
Mobile	+44 (0)7836 505575
Email	sarah.rainbird@googlemail.com

Entry 282   Map 5

Kent

The Old Rectory

On a really good day (about once every five years) you can see France. But you'll be more than happy to settle for the superb views over Romney Marsh, the Channel in the distance. The big, friendly house, built in 1850, has impeccable, elegant bedrooms and good bathrooms; the large, many-windowed sitting room is full of books, pictures and flowers from the south-facing garden. Marion and David are both charming and can organise transport to Ashford International for you. It's remarkably peaceful – perfect for walking (right on the Saxon Shore path), cycling and birdwatching. *Children over ten welcome.*

Price	£65–£75. Singles £45.
Rooms	2: 1 twin; 1 twin with separate bath/shower.
Meals	Pubs within 4 miles.
Closed	Christmas & New Year.
Directions	M20, exit 10 for Brenzett & Hastings on A2070. After 6 miles, right for Hamstreet; immed. left; in Hamstreet, left B2067. After 1.5 miles, left (Ash Hill); 700 yds on right.

	Marion & David Hanbury
	The Old Rectory,
	Ruckinge,
	Ashford TN26 2PE
Tel	+44 (0)1233 732328
Email	oldrectory@hotmail.com
Web	www.oldrectoryruckinge.co.uk

Entry 283　Map 5

Kent

Lamberden Cottage

Down a farm track find two 1780 cottages knocked into one, with flagstone floors, a cheery wood-burner in the guest sitting room and welcoming Beverley and Branton. There's a traditional country-cottage feel with pale walls, thick oak beams, soft carpeting and very comfortable bedrooms (the twin has a child's bedroom adjoining); views from all are across the Weald of Kent. Wander the lovely gardens to find your own private spot, sip a sundowner on the terrace, eat well in the family dining room on home-grown vegetables and fruit. Near to Sissinghurst, Great Dixter and many historic places.

Price	From £65. Singles from £50.
Rooms	2: 1 double, 1 twin (twin has adjoining room for children).
Meals	Dinner, 2 courses, £20. Pub/restaurant 0.75 miles.
Closed	Christmas & New Year.
Directions	From Tenterden A28 to Hastings. 2.5 miles Rolvenden. 2.5 miles to junc. A268 right to Sandhurst. 300 yds Sandhurst sign on left. 20 yds right down farm track. House 80 yds on left.

	Beverley & Branton Screeton
	Lamberden Cottage,
	Rye Road,
	Sandhurst, Cranbrook TN18 5PH
Tel	+44 (0)1580 850743
Email	thewalledgarden@lamberdencottage.co.uk
Web	www.lamberdencottage.co.uk

Entry 284　Map 5

Kent

The Tower House

Peacefully back from the road, a stroll from the antique shops of Tenterden, is a delightful Georgian house with a turreted tower, an Edwardian folly. The box-lined path to the door sets the tone: this is a very well-cared for and hospitable home. Pippa collects vintage china, Mike is the gardener, both delight in meeting people and ensure your stay is happy. Deeply comfortable bedrooms, the biggest at the back, have antique iron beds and romantic white furnishings, flowers and delicious linen. A sofa'd guest sitting room, a gazebo in the garden, homemade blackcurrant jelly at breakfast, Sissinghurst a short drive. Perfect!

Kent

Ramsden Farm

A truly interesting and comfortable house, with south-facing views across the Wealds; charming Sally has renovated these former farm buildings with flair. Unhurried breakfasts are eaten in the huge kitchen with a lemon-coloured Aga and floor to ceiling glass doors opening on to a wooden deck; spill outside on warm days. After a hearty walk you can doze in front of a tree-devouring inglenook; find lovely sunny bedrooms too, with more of that view from each, tip-top mattresses and hand embroidered duvet covers. Sparkling bathrooms have Travertine marble and underfloor heating. Spoiling. *Self-catering in cottage.*

Price	£70–£90. Singles £60.		Price	From £75.
Rooms	2: 1 double; 1 double with separate shower.		Rooms	3: 1 double, 1 twin; 1 double with separate bath.
Meals	Pubs/restaurants 200 yds.		Meals	Pub 1 mile.
Closed	Christmas.		Closed	Rarely.
Directions	Junc. 8 on M20 to Sutton Valence, then Tenterden. Tower House on right (Tower very visible).		Directions	From Benenden on B2086 towards Rolvenden, Dingleden Lane on right after 1 mile. House is 3rd on left.

 Lift to and from local pub or restaurant. A bottle of Sally's famous Benenden Sauce.

Pippa Carter
The Tower House,
27 Ashford Road,
Tenterden TN30 6LL
Tel   +44 (0)1580 761920
Email   pippa@towerhouse.biz
Web   www.towerhouse.biz

Sally Harrington
Ramsden Farm,
Dingleden Lane,
Benenden TN17 4JT
Tel   +44 (0)1580 240203
Email   sally@ramsdenfarmcottage.co.uk
Web   www.ramsdenfarmcottage.co.uk

Entry 285   Map 5

Entry 286   Map 5

Kent

Pullington Barn

Up a private drive and straight in to a vast, beamed expanse of bright light, warm colours, beautiful pictures and a cheery welcome from Gavin and Anne in their converted barn. There are endless books to choose: settle in the comfortable drawing room with its grand piano. Or sit in the pretty south-facing garden on a fine day; on the other side, views from the orchard spread over oast houses and church spires. Bedrooms (one on the ground floor) are both a good size with comfortable mattresses, co-ordinated bed linen and feather pillows. You breakfast soundly on local goodies; stride out for lovely country walks from the door.

Price	From £75. Singles £50.
Rooms	2: 1 double, 1 twin.
Meals	Pub/restaurant 0.5 miles.
Closed	Christmas.
Directions	A228 out of Tunbridge Wells. A21 to The Weald Garden of England r'bout. A262 to Sissinghurst. Right to Benenden.

Gavin & Anne Wetton
Pullington Barn,
Benenden TN17 4EH
Tel +44 (0)1580 240246
Email anne@wetton.info
Web www.wetton.info/bandb

Entry 287   Map 5

Kent

Barclay Farmhouse

Lynn's breakfasts are fabulous: fresh fruits, warm croissants, banana bread, eggs en cocotte. The weatherboarded guest barn may be in perfect trim but has a been-here-for-ever feel; you have a country-cosy dining room for breakfast or playing cards, a patio for summer, a big peaceful garden, a bird-happy pond. Gleaming bedrooms have brocade bedspreads, French oak furniture, chocolates, slippers, flat-screen TVs; shower rooms are in perfect order. Couples, honeymooners, garden lovers – many would love it here (but no children: the pond is deep). Warm-hearted B&B, and glorious Sissinghurst nearby. *Min. stay two nights at weekends in high season.*

Price	£85. Singles from £60.
Rooms	Barn: 3 doubles.
Meals	Pubs/restaurants 1 mile.
Closed	Rarely.
Directions	From Biddenden centre, south on A262: Tenterden road. 0.7 miles, bear right (signed Par3 Golf, Vineyard & Benenden). Immed. on right.

 Locally made chocolate truffles, Kingsdown water, towelling slippers in room.

Lynn Ruse
Barclay Farmhouse,
Woolpack Corner,
Biddenden TN27 8BQ
Tel +44 (0)1580 292626
Email info@barclayfarmhouse.co.uk
Web www.barclayfarmhouse.co.uk

Entry 288   Map 5

Kent

22 Lansdowne Road

Built in 1861, the house in leafy Tunbridge Wells "has never been as Victorian as it is now". So says Harold, whose devotion to Victoriana knows no bounds. Deep colours, rich velvets, marble tables, authentic wallpapers, tasselled lamps, portraits of Queen Victoria, tea and scones by the fire... be prepared to take a serious step back in time. Bedrooms are simple in comparison: ruched chintz in the ground-floor double, damask in the twin below – and a door to the conservatory. Bathrooms have large mirrors and brand new fittings, breakfast is a locally sourced spread. Those in search of heritage will marvel. *Off-road parking.*

Kent

Swan Cottage

A delightful Georgian townhouse in Tunbridge Wells, just near the Pantiles with its covered walkways between shops, coffee houses and spas. Your genial host is an artist, his studio can be seen through the glass wall in the open-plan dining room and his engaging pen and ink drawings dot every wall. Bedrooms have plenty of space, are comfortable and contemporary with big sash windows and fresh flowers; bathrooms are roomy, light and white, one with rooftop views. In summer there's a little patio for local sausages and eggs at a pink table under the magnolia tree. And the High Street is at the bottom of the road.

Price	£80–£120. Singles £80.
Rooms	3: 1 double, 1 twin/double; 1 studio with shower, kitchenette & separate wc.
Meals	Dinner, 2 courses, £20. Pubs/restaurants within 5-min. walk.
Closed	January.
Directions	From A21 to Tonbridge A26 to T. Wells centre. Grosvenor Rd one-way system left onto Victoria Rd. Onto Garden Rd, right onto Lansdowne Rd.

Price	£85. Singles £50.
Rooms	2: 1 twin/double; 1 single with separate bath.
Meals	Pubs/restaurants 200 yds.
Closed	Rarely.
Directions	From railway station follow High Street for 300 yds, left up Little Mt Sion. House faces you at top of hill. Parking in garage at bank of house on request.

Bottle of wine with dinner on first night.

6 greeting cards of your choice drawn by your host David Gurdon.

Use your Sawday's Gift Card here.

	Harold Brown
	22 Lansdowne Road,
	Tunbridge Wells TN1 2NJ
Tel	+44 (0)1892 533633
Email	haroldmbrown@hotmail.com
Web	www.thevictorianbandb.com

	David Gurdon
	Swan Cottage,
	17 Warwick Road,
	Tunbridge Wells TN1 1YL
Tel	+44 (0)1892 525910
Email	swancot@btinternet.com
Web	www.swancottage.co.uk

Entry 289 Map 5

Entry 290 Map 5

Kent

40 York Road

A smart Regency townhouse, slap bang in the centre of Royal Tunbridge Wells and a five-minute walk from the delightfully preserved Pantiles. Patricia will enjoy cooking for you – in another life she served up delights for hungry skiers coming off the French mountains. She is a gentle presence and leaves you to come and go as you please; guests have a comfortable sitting room and bright, spotless bedrooms that are quieter than you may think. In the summer you may breakfast outside in the pretty courtyard garden before wandering into town for the cluster of great little shops and restaurants. *Children over 12 welcome.*

Price	From £74. Singles from £44.
Rooms	2 twins/doubles.
Meals	Supper £13. Dinner, 4 courses with wine, £25. Picnic available. Pub/restaurant nearby.
Closed	23 December–2 January.
Directions	From M25 junc. 5 onto A21, then A26 thro' Southborough to Tunbridge Wells. Sign for Lewes, then 4th road left. Halfway along, on left. Car parks nearby, from £3.50 per 24 hours.

🧳 Bottle of wine with dinner on first night.

Patricia Lobo
40 York Road,
Tunbridge Wells TN1 1JY
Tel +44 (0)1892 531342
Email yorkrd@uwclub.net
Web www.yorkroad.co.uk

Entry 291 Map 5

Kent

Charcott Farmhouse

The 1750 tile-hung brick farmhouse is very much a family home; if you don't come expecting an immaculate environment you should enjoy it here. You share a pretty sitting room in the old bakehouse with the original beams and bread oven, and bedrooms are simple and unfussy, with traditional fabrics and country views. Ginny is charming while Nicholas – a tad eccentric for some – is highly knowledgeable about the area and a brilliant chef. Breakfast is an unrushed, happy affair with heaps of homemade bread and marmalade and free-range eggs from the family flock. You can come and go as you please.

Price	From £65. Singles from £50.
Rooms	3: 2 twins; 1 twin with separate bath.
Meals	Pub 5-minute walk.
Closed	Rarely.
Directions	B2027 0.5 miles north of Chiddingstone Causeway. Equidistant between Tonbridge & Edenbridge. Look for signs to Greyhound pub.

🧳 Sherry & biscuits in your room. Homemade jam or marmalade to take home.

Nicholas & Ginny Morris
Charcott Farmhouse,
Charcott, Leigh,
Tonbridge TN11 8LG
Tel +44 (0)1892 870024
Mobile +44 (0)7714 023021
Email charcottfarmhouse@btinternet.com

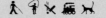

Entry 292 Map 5

Kent

Merzie Meadows

You get your own suite in this lovely ranch-style house with huge windows, pergolas groaning with climbers, and a Mediterranean-style swimming pool in the twittering garden. Pamela is just as light and bright: she keeps horses and hens and gives you locally sourced breakfasts. Your bedroom has a contemporary, uncluttered feel and is beautifully dressed in pale colours with pretty fabrics and a super bed, your own sitting room looks onto the garden and the bathroom is sleek with Italian marble and plump towels. All is peaceful; garden and nature lovers will adore it here. *Minimum stay two nights at weekends April-September.*

Price	£90–£95.
Rooms	1 suite for 2-3.
Meals	Pub 2.5 miles.
Closed	Mid-December to February.
Directions	A229 Maidstone to Hastings road, then B2079 for Marden. 1st right into Underlyn Lane, 2.5 miles, large Chainhurst sign, right onto drive.

Free pick-up from local train station.

Use your Sawday's Gift Card here.

Pamela Mumford
Merzie Meadows,
Hunton Road, Marden,
Maidstone TN12 9SL
Tel   +44 (0)1622 820500
Mobile +44 (0)7762 713077
Web   www.merziemeadows.co.uk

Entry 293   Map 5

Kent

Reason Hill

Brian and Antonia's 200-acre fruit farm is perched on the edge of the Weald of Kent, with stunning views over orchards and oast houses. The farmhouse has 17th-century origins (low ceilings, wonky floors, stone flags) and a conservatory for sunny breakfasts; colours are soft, antiques gleam and the mood is relaxed. The roomy twin has a bay window and armchairs, the pretty double looks over the garden. Come in spring for the blossom, summer for the fresh fruit and veg from the garden and anytime for a break – the Greensand Way runs along the bottom of the farm, you are close to Sissinghurst Castle and 45 minutes from the Channel Tunnel.

Price	£75–£80.
Rooms	3: 1 twin; 1 double with separate shower, 1 single sharing shower (let to same party only).
Meals	Pubs within 3 miles.
Closed	Christmas & New Year.
Directions	From Maidstone A229 for Hastings. After 4.5 miles, right at lights on B2163. In Coxheath, left up Westerhill Rd, 0.2 miles then right into private road; through fruit trees to Reason Hill.

Brian & Antonia Allfrey
Reason Hill,
Linton,
Maidstone ME17 4BT
Tel   +44 (0)1622 743679
Email   antonia@allfrey.net
Web   www.reasonhill.co.uk

Entry 294   Map 5

Kent

The Limes

A three-minute motor from 'the loveliest castle in the world' (magnificent Leeds, on two islands) is a well-renovated, oak-beamed, inglenook'd and thoroughly refurbished Wealdon hall house overlooking the village green. Your hostess greets you with a lovely bright smile and ushers you in to an immaculate interior traditionally decorated with a crisp, modern slant – and bedrooms that delight in fine fabrics and bedding. (Sonia has her own bed linen business so you are assured of the best.) The breakfast buffet is equally splendid: fresh, organic, and served, on warm days, on the sun-trap terrace.

Price	From £90. Singles from £75.
Rooms	2 doubles.
Meals	Pubs/restaurant a short walk.
Closed	Christmas & New Year.
Directions	M20 exit 7 for Maidstone. At 2nd r'bout, signs for Bearsted. Past r'way station on left, past shops. House 50 yds on left overlooking green.

 10% off stays of 2 or more nights. Free pick-up from local bus/train station.

Sonia Ashdown
The Limes,
The Green,
Bearsted, Maidstone ME14 4DR
Tel   +44 (0)1622 730908
Email   info@limesonthegreen.co.uk
Web   www.limesonthegreen.co.uk

Entry 295   Map 5

Lancashire

Challan Hall

The wind in the trees, the boom of a bittern and birdsong. That's as noisy as it gets. On the edge of the village, delightful Charlotte's former farmhouse overlooks woods and Lake Haweswater; deer, squirrels and Leighton Moss Nature Reserve are your neighbours. The Cassons are well-travelled and the house, filled with a colourful mish-mash of mementos, is happily and comfortably traditional. Expect a sofa-strewn sitting room, a smart red and polished-wood dining room and two freshly floral bedrooms. Morecambe Bay and the Lakes are on the doorstep – come home to lovely views and stunning sunsets.

Price	£70. Singles from £40.
Rooms	2: 1 twin/double; 1 twin/double with separate bath.
Meals	Packed lunch available. Pubs 1 mile.
Closed	Rarely.
Directions	M6 exit 35 to Carnforth, past railway station to Warton. Turn left signed Silverdale. After 2.5 miles T-junc., turn right, past golf club on left. Further 1 mile, house on right.

Charlotte Casson
Challan Hall,
Silverdale LA5 0UH
Tel   +44 (0)1524 701054
Email   cassons@btopenworld.com
Web   www.challanhall.co.uk

Entry 296   Map 11

Lancashire

Northwood

A super stretch of golden beach with sand dunes is just across the road and delightful Lytham is a couple of miles away. The Victorian façade conceals light, lofty rooms mixing vintage and modern: bold wallpaper on odd walls, huge displays of flowers, original artwork. Your hosts happily find babysitters, advise on restaurants (then drive you there) and offer you maple syrup pancakes at breakfast, along with other treats. Bedrooms are generous: find coir carpets, baskets of plump blankets and towels, lovely colours and DVDs to watch on wet days. The whole place has an informal, warm and happy family vibe.

Price	£80. Family £90. Singles from £75.
Rooms	2: 1 double, 1 double/family room.
Meals	Restaurants 5-minute walk.
Closed	Christmas & New Year.
Directions	M6 exit 32 then M55 to Blackpool. Follow signs for Lytham St Annes then St Annes. Head for the promenade.

Free pick-up from local train station. Fridge full of beverages. Late checkout.

Shannon Kuspira
Northwood,
24 North Promenade,
St Annes on Sea FY8 2NQ
Tel   +44 (0)1253 782356
Email   skuspira@hotmail.com
Web   www.24northwood.co.uk

Entry 297   Map 11

Lancashire

Sagar Fold House

In a spectacular setting, a 17th-century dairy and two perfect studios, one up, one down. Private entrances lead to big beamed spaces that marry immaculate efficiency with unusual beauty – very here and now. A gorgeous Indian doorframe serves as a bedhead upstairs, soft colours and contemporary touches lift the spirit, plentiful books and DVDs entertain you and a continental breakfast is supplied – homemade and organic whenever possible. Now gaze over the Italian knot garden, which ties in lines of a lovely landscape. Take walks in deeply peaceful countryside; top-notch places to eat are an easy drive.

Price	£80.
Rooms	2: 1 double, 1 studio, each with kitchenette.
Meals	Continental breakfast in fridge. Pubs/restaurants 1-2 miles.
Closed	Rarely.
Directions	A59 through centre of Whalley. At 2nd mini r'bout left to Mitton; 3 miles, Three Fishes pub on left. Right to Whitewell Chaigely; 1 mile, left to Whitewell Chaigely; 0.5 miles, 3rd drive left to house.

Local food/produce in your room.

Helen & John Cook
Sagar Fold House,
Higher Hodder,
Clitheroe BB7 3LW
Tel   +44 (0)1254 826844
Email   helencook14@hotmail.co.uk
Web   www.sagarfoldhouse.co.uk

Entry 298   Map 12

Lancashire

Peter Barn Country House

Wild deer roam – this is the Ribble Valley, an AONB that feels like a time-locked land. In this former 18th-century tithe barn, where old church rafters support the big yet cosy guest sitting room, you settle in among plump sofas, log fire and flat-screen TV. Bedrooms, too, are on the top floor – nicely private. The Smiths couldn't be more helpful and breakfast is a feast: jams and muesli are homemade, stewed fruits are from the gardens. Step outside: Jean has transformed a field into a riot of colour and scent, there are pretty corners, a meandering stream and water lilies bask in still pools. *Minimum stay two nights.*

Price	£66–£72. Singles £38.
Rooms	3: 1 double, 1 twin/double; 1 double with separate bath.
Meals	Restaurants/pubs 1.5 miles.
Closed	Christmas & New Year.
Directions	M6 junc. 31, A59 to Clitheroe. Through Clitheroe to Waddington. Through village 0.5 miles, left on Cross Lane for 0.75 miles, past Colthurst Hall, house on left.

 10% off stays of 3 or more nights.

Jean & Gordon Smith
Peter Barn Country House,
Cross Lane/Rabbit Lane,
Waddington, Clitheroe BB7 3JH
Tel +44 (0)1200 428585
Email jean@peterbarn.co.uk
Web www.peterbarn.co.uk

Entry 299   Map 12

Leicestershire

White House Fields Farm

A house with a very pretty front – Georgian with a leaded porch and sash windows – but you arrive at the back, past rather modern farm buildings. You have your own entrance from the courtyard garden into a light, beamed, pale ochre bedroom brightened with fresh flowers and soothing with linen and goose down. This is a comfortable, lived-in home with no pretensions – but Charlotte gives you very special food indeed, either a smart affair in the dining room or a kitchen supper with her young family: often home-reared organic pork or chicken and garden vegetables. Close to Derby, Nottingham and East Midlands Airport, yet peaceful.

Price	£85–£90. Singles £60–£65.
Rooms	1 double.
Meals	Dinner, 3 courses with coffee & wine, £25. Pub/restaurant 0.5 miles.
Closed	Christmas & New Year.
Directions	M1 junc. 23a. Head towards East Midlands Airport, follow signs to Breedon on the Hill. Left signed Worthington. House 0.5 miles on right.

 Bottle of wine with dinner on first night. Late checkout (12pm).

Charlotte Meynell
White House Fields Farm,
Worthington,
Ashby de la Zouch LE65 1RA
Tel +44 (0)1332 862312
Email charlottemeynell@btinternet.com
Web www.whff.co.uk

Entry 300   Map 8

Leicestershire

Curtain Cottage

A pretty village setting for this cottage on the main street, next door to Sarah's interior design shop. You have your own entrance by the side and through a large garden, which backs onto fields with horses and the National Forest beyond. A conservatory is your sitting room: wicker armchairs, wooden floors, a contemporary take on the country look. Bedrooms are light and fresh, linen from The White Company on sumptuous beds, slate-tiled bathrooms, stunning fabrics. Breakfast is anything, anytime, full English or fresh fruit and croissants from the local shop – all is delivered to you. Perfect privacy.

Price	£80. Singles £55.
Rooms	2: 1 double, 1 twin.
Meals	Pubs/restaurants 150 yds.
Closed	Rarely.
Directions	Gravel driveway to left of Barkers Interiors Design Showroom on Main Street. From car park, access to cottage thro' gate into garden at rear of showroom.

 Glass of wine each night of your stay.

 Use your Sawday's Gift Card here.

Sarah Barker
Curtain Cottage,
92-94 Main Street,
Woodhouse Eaves LE12 8RZ
Tel   +44 (0)1509 891361
Email   sarah@curtaincottage.co.uk
Web   www.curtaincottage.co.uk

Entry 301   Map 8

Leicestershire

The Grange

Behind the mellow brick exterior (Queen Anne in front, Georgian at the back) is a warm family home. Log fires brighten chilly days and you are greeted with kindness and generosity by Mary and Shaun, whose young family includes two sweet dogs. Big, beautifully quiet bedrooms, one in the attic, are hung with strikingly unusual wallpapers and furnished with excellent beds and pretty antiques, bathrooms are simple yet impeccable and there's a fireplace in the big, flagstoned hall decorated with sporting prints and deeds. The garden has a treehouse and is large enough to roam.

Price	£70. Singles £45.
Rooms	2: 1 twin, 1 double.
Meals	Pubs/restaurants 0.5-1.5 miles.
Closed	Christmas & New Year.
Directions	M1 exit 20; A4304 towards Market Harborough. 1st left after Walcote marked 'Gt Central Cycle Ride'; 2 miles, then right into Kimcote, pass church on left. On right after Poultney Lane.

Shaun & Mary Mackaness
The Grange,
Kimcote LE17 5RU
Tel   +44 (0)1455 203155
Email   shaunandmarymac@hotmail.com
Web   www.thegrangekimcote.co.uk

Entry 302   Map 8

Leicestershire

The Gorse House

Passing cars are less frequent than passing horses – this is a peaceful spot in a pretty village. The lasting impression of this 17th-century cottage is of lightness, brightness and space. There's a fine collection of paintings and furniture, everything gleams and oak doors lead from dining room to guest sitting room. Country style bedrooms are fresh, the largest with three views. The garden was designed by Bunny Guinness, the stables accommodate up to six horses and it's strolling distance to a good pub dinner. The house is filled with laughter and the Cowdells are terrific hosts who absolutely love having guests to stay.

Price	From £60. Singles £32.50.
Rooms	3: 1 double, 1 family for 3. Stable: 1 triple & kitchenette.
Meals	Packed lunch £5. Pub 75 yds.
Closed	Rarely.
Directions	From A46 Newark-Leicester; B676 for Melton. At x-roads, straight for 1 mile; right to Grimston. There, up hill, past church. House on left, just after right-hand bend at top.

R L Cowdell
The Gorse House,
33 Main Street, Grimston,
Melton Mowbray LE14 3BZ

Tel	+44 (0)1664 813537
Email	cowdell@gorsehouse.co.uk
Web	www.gorsehouse.co.uk

Entry 303   Map 9

Lincolnshire

The Barn

Simon and Jane, the nicest people, have farmed for 30 years and love having guests to stay. Breakfasts are entirely local or homemade, home-grown and delicious; there are endless extras and nothing is too much trouble. In this light-filled barn conversion find old beams, new walls and good antiques; a brick-flanked fireplace glows and heated floors keep toes warm. Above the high-raftered main living/dining room is a comfy, good-sized double; in the adjoining stables, two further rooms, a crisp feel, sparkling showers, restful privacy. Views are to sheep-dotted fields and the village is on a 25-mile cycle trail.

Price	£70. Singles £50.
Rooms	3: 1 double, 1 twin/double; 1 single with separate bath/shower.
Meals	Supper, 2 courses, £17.50. Dinner, 3 courses, £25. BYO. Pubs in village & 2 miles.
Closed	Rarely.
Directions	Midway between Lincoln & Peterborough. From A15, in Folkingham, turn west into Spring Lane next to village hall; 200 yds on right.
	10% off stays of 2nd night Mon-Thurs (Apr-Oct).

Simon & Jane Wright
The Barn,
Spring Lane, Folkingham,
Sleaford NG34 0SJ

Tel	+44 (0)1529 497199
Email	sjwright@farming.co.uk
Web	www.thebarnspringlane.co.uk

Entry 304   Map 9

Lincolnshire

The White House

The smart wisteria-clad Georgian house stands right by the village green of this conservation village. Victoria and David, passionate about the place, have filled the rooms with gorgeous things: interesting books in the library, etchings and watercolours, a fine moulded fireplace, and English and Chinese porcelain. Each bedroom, too, is striking, one with an antique four-poster canopied in green silk. Bathrooms are fresh and appealing. There are sitting rooms with fires for winter and afternoon tea in the pretty walled garden in summer. Your hosts can also suggest good places for eating out.

Price	£70. Singles £45.
Rooms	2: 1 twin/double; 1 four-poster (with adjoining room if required) with separate bath.
Meals	Pub/restaurant in village.
Closed	Rarely.
Directions	A15 to Folkingham; on village green.

Victoria & David Strauss
The White House,
25 Market Place, Folkingham,
Sleaford NG34 0SE
Tel   +44 (0)1529 497298
Email   victoria.strauss@btinternet.com
Web   www.bedandbreakfastfolkinghamlincolnshire.co.uk

Entry 305   Map 9

Lincolnshire

Belvoir Vale Cottage

The Vale of Belvoir is gloriously quiet and you are just 200 yards from the Viking Way. Kindly Norman and Suzie have restored two old roadside cottages, charmingly; the emphasis is on warmth, lovely colours, beautifully arranged fresh flowers, good food and gorgeous views over the pretty garden to Belvoir Castle. Bedrooms and bathrooms are a good size and have thick carpets and new windows to let in the sunshine; expect big, comfortable beds, fluffy towels, crisp white linen. Start the day with a full English or undyed haddock with poached eggs; you'll be truly spoiled. *Children welcome if rooms let to one party.*

Price	£70-£90. Singles from £50.
Rooms	3: 1 twin/double & sitting room; 1 twin/double, 1 double.
Meals	Dinner from £25. Packed lunch available. Pubs/restaurants 1.2 miles.
Closed	Rarely.
Directions	A52 Nottingham-Grantham. At Sedgebrook x-roads, turn for Stenwith & Woolsthorpe. After 1.5 miles cross double bridges - private car park 300 yds.

10% off room rate Mon-Thurs. Local Belvoir cordials in room. Free pick-up from local bus/train station.

Suzie & Norman Davis
Belvoir Vale Cottage,
Stenwith, Woolsthorpe-by-Belvoir,
Grantham NG32 2HE
Tel   +44 (0)1949 842434
Email   reservations@belvoirvale-cottage.co.uk
Web   www.belvoirvale-cottage.co.uk

Entry 306   Map 9

Lincolnshire

Churchfield House

The little house was built in the sixties; inside glows with character and charm. Bridget is an interior decorator whose eye for detail and sense of fun will delight you. A snug bedroom sports fresh checks in creams and greens, firm mattress, down pillows, interesting pictures, even a gilt-trimmed copy of a Louis XIV chair. The bathroom is small but spotless, and there's a conservatory mood to the warm red, stone-tiled dining room, where glass doors open to a large, lush garden in summer. You're close to a good golf course, Bridget cooks and chats with warmth and humour – this is a gem.

Price	£60. Singles £40.
Rooms	1 twin with separate bath.
Meals	Dinner, 2 courses, from £18. Pubs/restaurants 3 miles.
Closed	Christmas & New Year.
Directions	A607 Grantham to Lincoln road. On reaching Carlton Scroop, 1st left for Hough Lane. Last house on left.

Bridget Hankinson
Churchfield House,
Carlton Scroop,
Grantham NG32 3BA
Tel   +44 (0)1400 250387
Email   info@churchfield-house.co.uk
Web   www.churchfield-house.co.uk

Entry 307   Map 9

Lincolnshire

Brills Farm

There aren't many hills in Lincolnshire, but Sophie and Charlie's early Georgian farmhouse is at the top of one of them. Built of warm brick, near a Roman settlement site, it shines with country elegance and charm, subtle colours and antique furniture. The drawing and dining rooms, filled with fresh flowers, overlook the valley, the beautiful, airy bedrooms have goose down duvets and lovely linen. The Whites are a delightful, young couple with a flourishing family (Sophie is a professional cook and event rider), enthusiastic and hospitable they will give you innovative dinners, and bacon from their own pigs. *Children over 12 welcome.*

Price	£90-£100. Singles £55-£60.
Rooms	3: 2 doubles, 1 twin/double.
Meals	Supper £20. Dinner £30. Packed lunches £10. Pubs 5-minute drive.
Closed	Christmas & New Year.
Directions	A46 Newark-Lincoln. Exit Brough, Norton Disney & Stapleford. Right at T-junc.; 0.5 miles; 1st left onto lane; 0.75 miles; wide gravel entrance, on right before hill (unsigned).

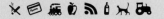 10% off room rate Mon-Thurs, excluding July and August.

Charles & Sophie White
Brills Farm,
Brills Hill, Norton Disney,
Lincoln LN6 9JN
Tel   +44 (0)1636 892311
Email   admin@brillsfarm-bedandbreakfast.co.uk
Web   www.brillsfarm-bedandbreakfast.co.uk

Entry 308   Map 9

Lincolnshire

Ryelands House

Farmer Mike and charming Caroline built this large red-brick and slate house on their land and are much committed to the Countryside Stewardship programme; hang out of your bedroom window to watch waders, even deer, round the nearby pond. Inside is warm with underfloor heating, and spacious. Your bedroom has a boutique hotel feel in shades of cream and brown, while two beautifully-lit sitting rooms are smoothly uncluttered and have comfortable armchairs. Pedal along those lovely flat lanes after breakfast, head to Lincoln and its cathedral or Horncastle for antiques; walk to the local pub for excellent bar food.

Price	From £70. Singles from £50.
Rooms	1 twin/double & sitting room.
Meals	Packed lunch from £5. Restaurant 0.5 miles.
Closed	Christmas & New Year.
Directions	A15 Lincoln, Sleaford turn. Left at Mere onto B1178 for 3 miles; over staggered x-roads into Potterhanworth. At T-junc. right for 100 yds; left onto Barff Road, 0.5 miles, driveway on left.

Michael & Caroline Norcross
Ryelands House,
Barff Road, Potterhanworth,
Lincoln LN4 2DU
Tel   +44 (0)1522 793563
Email   norcross@ukfarming.co.uk
Web   www.ryelands-house.co.uk

Entry 309   Map 9

Lincolnshire

Baumber Park

Lincoln red cows and Longwool sheep surround this attractive rosy-brick farmhouse – once a stud that bred a Derby winner. The old watering pond is now a haven for frogs, newts and toads; birds sing lustily. Maran hens conjure delicious eggs and charming Clare, a botanist, is hugely knowledgeable about the area. Bedrooms are light and traditional, not swish, with mahogany furniture; two have heart-stopping views. Guests have their own wisteria covered entrance, sitting room with a log fire, dining room with local books and the lovely garden to roam. This is good walking, riding and cycling country; seals and rare birds on the coast.

Price	£62-£66. Singles from £35.
Rooms	3: 2 doubles; 1 twin with separate bath.
Meals	Pubs 1.5 miles.
Closed	Christmas & New Year.
Directions	From A158 in Baumber take road towards Wispington & Bardney. House 300 yds down on right.

Home-grown produce, as in season and available.

Use your Sawday's Gift Card here.

Mike & Clare Harrison
Baumber Park,
Baumber,
Horncastle LN9 5NE
Tel   +44 (0)1507 578235
Email   mail@baumberpark.com
Web   www.baumberpark.com

Entry 310   Map 9

Lincolnshire

The Grange

Wide open Lincolnshire farmland on the edge of the Wolds. This immaculately kept farm has been in the family for five generations; their award-winning farm trail helps you explore. Listen to birdsong, catch the sun setting by the trout lake, have supper before the fire in a dining room whose elegant Georgian windows are generously draped. Sarah is a young and energetic host and offers you delicious homemade cake on arrival. Comfortable bedrooms have spick and span bath or shower rooms and fabulous views that stretch to Lincoln Cathedral. A delightful couple running good farmhouse B&B.

Price	From £65. Singles from £45.
Rooms	2 doubles.
Meals	Supper from £18. Dinner from £22. BYO. (No meals during summer.) Pub/restaurant 1 mile.
Closed	Christmas & New Year.
Directions	Exit A157 in East Barkwith at War Memorial, into Torrington Lane. House 0.75 miles on right after sharp right-hand bend.

10% off room rate Mon-Thurs.

Use your Sawday's Gift Card here.

Sarah & Jonathan Stamp
The Grange,
Torrington Lane,
East Barkwith LN8 5RY
Tel   +44 (0)1673 858670
Email   sarahstamp@farmersweekly.net
Web   www.thegrange-lincolnshire.co.uk

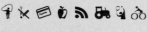

Entry 311   Map 9

Lincolnshire

The Manor House

One guest's summing up reads: "Absolutely perfect — hostess, house, garden and marmalade." Delightful Ann — interested in horses, food, photography, people — makes you feel immediately at home. You have the run of downstairs: all family antiques, fresh flowers and space. Chintzy, carpeted bedrooms have dreamy views of the lovely sweeping gardens and duck-dabbled lake; dinners are adventurous and delicious: game casserole, ginger meringue bombe... Perfect stillness at the base of the Wolds and a pretty one-mile walk along the route of the old railway that starts from the front door. Very special, great value.

Price	From £70. Singles £50.
Rooms	2: 1 double, 1 twin.
Meals	Dinner from £20. BYO. Pub/restaurant 2 miles.
Closed	Christmas.
Directions	From Wragby A157 for Louth. After approx. 2 miles, at triple road sign, right. Red postbox & bus shelter at drive entrance, before graveyard.

Ann Hobbins
The Manor House,
West Barkwith LN8 5LF
Tel   +44 (0)1673 858253
Mobile   +44 (0)7751 891274

Entry 312   Map 9

Lincolnshire

Knaith Hall

This intriguing place, medieval church at its gate, dates from the 16th century. Lawns slope down to the river Trent; daffodils, lambs, a passing barge and waterfowl pattern the serenity. And the skyscapes are terrific; at night, a distant power station shines, enhancing that 'great rurality of taste' referred to in Pevsner. Indoors, diamond-paned windows, a domed dining room and fine furniture are softened by an easy décor and a log fire. An appealing family house, with a relaxed atmosphere. Your own room is comfortable and restful with the very best of old-fashioned bedding.

Price	From £70. Singles £40.
Rooms	2: 1 double with separate shower, 1 twin with separate bath.
Meals	Dinner, 3 courses with wine, £20. Pub 4 miles.
Closed	Rarely.
Directions	Knaith 3 miles south of Gainsborough on A156 Lincoln–Gainsborough road. After Knaith signs, look for white gateposts on west side with sign for St Mary's Church.
	House drink per person for each night of stay. Free pick-up from local train station.

John & Rosie Burke
Knaith Hall,
Knaith,
Gainsborough DN21 5PE
Tel   +44 (0)1427 613005
Mobile +44 (0)7796 881328
Email   jandrburke@aol.com

Entry 313   Map 9

Lincolnshire

The Old Farm House

Hidden in the Lincolnshire Wolds, an 18th-century, ivy-covered house – and Nicola's father still farms the fields beyond the ha-ha. The stone-flagged, terracotta-washed hall gives a hint of warm colours to come; creamy walls show off tawny fabrics, prints and antiques; the beamed sitting/breakfast room has a big, rosy brick inglenook fireplace and tranquil views. Such a welcoming, tucked-away place, hopping with pheasant but just a 10-15-minute drive from shops, golf and racing in the nearby towns. Excellent value, and perfect if you fancy privacy and space. *Children over eight welcome.*

Price	£75. Singles £55.
Rooms	2: 1 double; 1 triple with separate bath.
Meals	Pub 2 miles.
Closed	Christmas, New Year & occasionally.
Directions	M180 exit 5; A18 signed Louth. Past airport; 2.5 miles after junction of A46 take right signed Hatcliffe. House is third on right, before village.

Nicola Clarke
The Old Farm House,
Low Road, Hatcliffe,
Grimsby DN37 0SH
Tel   +44 (0)1472 824455
Email clarky.hatcliffe@btinternet.com
Web   www.oldfarmhousebandbgrimsby.co.uk

Entry 314   Map 13

Norfolk

Glebe Farmhouse

Two miles south of Burnham, and a five-minute stroll from post office and delightful pub, is a charming farmhouse with a sun-drenched terrace and a child-friendly garden. Mary and Jeremy give you TV-free bedrooms that are large, peaceful and cosy, log fires in a family sitting room you are welcome to share and wonderful breakfasts in the big bright farmhouse kitchen with cream Aga. How lovely to come home to books, paintings, flowers and well-cushioned sofas after a wild walk on Holkham Beach... and a real fire in one bedroom, for a modest extra charge.

Price	From £75. Singles from £40.
Rooms	2: 1 double, 1 twin/double. Extra fold-up bed for child & cot.
Meals	Pub 5-minute walk.
Closed	Rarely.
Directions	A148 King's Lynn to Cromer, north onto B1355 just west of Fakenham. 6.5 miles to North Creake. Right after red phone box, then 300 yds. On right.

Mary & Jeremy Brettingham Smith
Glebe Farmhouse,
Wells Road, North Creake,
Fakenham NR21 9LG
Tel   +44 (0)1328 730133
Email enquiries@glebe-farmhouse.co.uk
Web   www.glebe-farmhouse.co.uk

Entry 347   Map 10

Norfolk

1 Leicester Meadows

Up among 13 acres of wild meadow and woodland – not another building in sight. It's all so relaxed and unhurried: barn owls roosting in the outhouse, hens strutting the garden, geese pottering up from the pond. The 19th-century cottages, once the home of workers on the Holkham estate, have been imaginatively restored and enlarged. (Bob was an architect, Sara an art teacher; both are immensely friendly and helpful.) Polished wood and old brick are topped with bright rugs; paintings and ceramics engage the eye; steep stairs take you up to the bedrooms – one large, contemporary and elegant, the other cosy and fun.

Price	From £65. Singles from £50.
Rooms	2: 1 double; 1 twin/double. (Additional small room available.)
Meals	Supper from £18. Pub 1 mile.
Closed	Rarely.
Directions	Off A148 near Fakenham; B1355 dir. Burnham Market. In S. Creake, left by flint bus shelter, right into Avondale Rd; 1 mile, taking left fork. At bottom of hill, house set back 100 yds on left.

Bob & Sara Freakley
1 Leicester Meadows,
South Creake,
Fakenham NR21 9NZ
Tel   +44 (0)1328 823533
Email rf@freakley.com
Web   www.leicestermeadows.com

Entry 348   Map 10

Manor House

Eclectic African art and enormous photos of wildlife decorate this elegant, early Victorian manor house just 20 minutes from the coast. Lorna is great fun and loves to share her interesting home; she moved here from Cape Town and has named the spacious, luxurious bedrooms af____ ____ favourite African haunts. _____amorous bathrooms are spotless a____ ____me complete with snazzy scents a____ ____owelling slippers. Breakfast is Aga cool____d: organic sausages and bacon, croissant____ eggs from the hens. Birdwatchers and w____kers love it here; bring your horse too and____orna will ride with you on the sandy nort____ ____orfolk beaches.

Price	£79-____ ____37. Family suite £137.
Rooms	3: 1____ ouble, 1 suite, 1 f____ ily suite for 4.
Meals	Pa____ ed lunch £5-£10. Supper, 2____ ____urses, £15. Pub 200 yds.
Closed	R____ ____ely.
Directions	F____ ____m Fakenham A1067 for 5 miles, ____en right to G. Ryburgh. On ____ntering village, cross bridge. Manor House on right behind brick & flint wall. Automatic gates.

 Bottle of wine in your room.

Lorna McFarlane
Manor House,
Station Road, Great Ryburgh,
Fakenham NR21 0DX

Tel	+44 (0)1328 829788
Email	manorhousenorfolk@gmail.com
Web	www.northnorfolkbandb.co.uk

Entry 349   Map 10

Norfolk

The Close

A large, creeper-clad, Victorian ho____ ____n the middle of the village, with____ ____ooth lawn, mature trees, curved ____ ____ceous border and a stream (sou____ ____ the river Wensum). Bedr____ ____ with a garden view, are large, ____ and airy, with a mix of antique and contemporary furniture, flowers, comfortable sofas with floral cushions; shower rooms are spotlessly tiled. You breakfast on home-baked bread and the local butcher's finest at a huge mahogany table in the dining room. Val and Rory know their patch well, so do ask: this is wonderful walking countryside and you are near the coast; Sandringham and Houghton, too.

Price	From £85. Singles £60.
Rooms	2 doubles.
Meals	Pub/restaurant 200 yds.
Closed	Rarely.
Directions	King's Lynn A148 to Fakenham. After about 12 miles, through East Rudham. Right immed. after village green at post office. House 100 yds along on right. Map provided on booking.

Valerie McGouran
The Close,
Station Road,
East Rudham PE31 8SU

Tel	+44 (0)1485 528925
Email	rorymcgouran@hotmail.com
Web	www.closenorfolk.com

Entry 350   Map 10

Norfolk

Bagthorpe Hall

Ten minutes from Burnham Market, yet here you are immersed in peaceful countryside. Tid is a pioneer of organic farming and the stunning 700 acres include a woodland snowdrop walk. Gina's passions are music, dance and gardens and she organises open days and concerts for charity. Theirs is a large, elegant house with a fascinating hall mural chronicling their family life; bedrooms – one with a tiny en suite shower room – have big comfy beds and lovely views. Breakfasts are delicious with local sausages and bacon, homemade jams and raspberries from the garden. Birdwatching, cycling and walking are all around. *Stabling available.*

Price	£80–£85. Singles from £50.
Rooms	3: 1 double; 1 double with separate shower; 1 twin with separate bath.
Meals	Pubs/restaurants 2 miles.
Closed	Rarely.
Directions	King's Lynn A148 to Fakenham. In East Rudham, The Crown on right, take next left: Bagthorpe Road. Continue 3.5 miles to Bagthorpe. Past cottages, then farm on left, wood on right, white gates on right set back from trees. At top of drive.

Gina Morton
Bagthorpe Hall,
Bagthorpe, Bircham,
King's Lynn PE31 6QY
Tel   +44 (0)1485 578528
Email   gina@bagthorpehall.co.uk
Web   www.bagthorpehall.co.uk

Norfolk

Meadow House

Hand-made oak banisters, period furniture, a mass of ornaments: this new-build is beautifully traditional. Breakfast is served in the drawing room, where you find a warm, sociable atmosphere with squashy sofas and comfy chairs for anytime use. One bedroom is cosy and chintzy, one is larger and more neutral; brand-new bathrooms gleam. Amanda knows B&B, does it well, and plans to grow vegetables once her land is tamed. There are footpaths from the door and plenty to see, starting with Walpole's Houghton Hall, a short walk. A bucolic setting for a profoundly comfortable stay, perfect for country enthusiasts.

Price	£70. Singles £40.
Rooms	2 twins/doubles.
Meals	Packed lunch £5–£7. Pub/restaurant 1 mile.
Closed	Rarely.
Directions	From King's Lynn, A148 for Cromer. 3 miles after Hillington, 2nd of 2 turnings right to Harpley (no signpost) opp. Houghton Hall sign. 200 yds on; over x-roads, house 400 yds on left.

Amanda Case
Meadow House,
Harpley,
King's Lynn PE31 6TU
Tel   +44 (0)1485 520240
Mobile   +44 (0)7890 037134
Email   amandacase@amandacase.plus.com

Norfolk

Litcham Hall

For the whole of the 19th century this was Litcham's doctor's house; the red-brick Hall is still at the centre of the community. The big-windowed guest bedrooms look onto the stunning gardens with yew hedges, a lily pond and herbaceous borders. This is a thoroughly English home with elegant proportions – the hall, drawing room and dining room are gracious and beautifully furnished. The hens lay the breakfast eggs, the garden fills the table with soft fruit in season and John and Hermione are friendly and most helpful. There's a sitting room for guests. *Children & pets by arrangement.*

Price	£70-£90. Singles by arrangement.
Rooms	3: 2 doubles; 1 twin with separate bath.
Meals	Pub/restaurant 3 miles.
Closed	Christmas.
Directions	From Swaffham, A1065 north for 5 miles, then right to Litcham on B1145. House on left on entering village. Georgian red-brick with stone balls on gatepost.

John & Hermione Birkbeck
Litcham Hall,
Litcham,
King's Lynn PE32 2QQ
Tel +44 (0)1328 701389
Email hermionebirkbeck@hotmail.com
Web www.litchamhall.co.uk

Entry 353   Map 10

Norfolk

Manor House Farm

In the private stable wing and next door cottage of this traditional Norfolk farmhouse, surrounded by four acres of lovingly tended gardens, are beautiful fresh rooms with wildly comfortable beds and their own sitting room opening onto the garden. Expect antiques, colourful rugs and fresh flowers. Breakfast, served in the elegant dining room of the main house, is home-grown and delicious: fruit, eggs from the Welsummer hens, bacon and sausages from their happy pigs. Libby and Robin have won conservation awards for the farm – and the North Norfolk coast is 20 minutes away. *Gardens open for NGS. Children over ten welcome.*

Price	£90-£100. Singles £50-£65.
Rooms	2: 1 double, 1 twin/double.
Meals	Restaurant 1.5 miles.
Closed	Rarely.
Directions	A1065 Swaffham-Fakenham road. 6 miles on, through Weasenham. After 1 mile, right for Wellingham. House on left, next to church.

 Free-range eggs on departure.

Elisabeth Ellis
Manor House Farm,
Wellingham, Fakenham,
King's Lynn PE32 2TH
Tel +44 (0)1328 838227
Email libby.ellis@btconnect.com
Web www.manor-house-farm.co.uk

Entry 354   Map 10

Norfolk

The Old Rectory

A stately place indeed: a venerable English rectory replete with period furniture, art, history, well-bred hosts (he shoots, she rides) and, in the expansive grounds, a ruined chapel, lake, croquet lawn and pool. Breakfast is served on the terrace in summer. You dine by candlelight on local game and the kitchen garden's offerings, then settle in the Georgian drawing room by the rocking horse. Sleep in the Coach House where plush beds have beautiful linen, warm throws and beaded cushions; dogs can stay in the stables. A rare chance to experience the best of British country life. *Riding & shooting can be arranged.*

Price	£75-£95. Singles £60-£80.
Rooms	3: Coach House, 1 double, 1 twin/double, 1 twin.
Meals	Dinner, 2 courses, £25; 3 courses, £35. Pub 1 mile. Restaurant 5 miles.
Closed	Never.
Directions	From Stone Ferry bypass, take road to Oxborough. 0.5 miles before Oxborough Hall, right down Ferry Road. House is 0.5 miles on left.

 10% off room rate Mon-Thurs. Cake in your room, to eat or take home.

	Veronica de Lotbiniere
	The Old Rectory,
	Ferry Road, Oxborough,
	King's Lynn PE33 9PT
Tel	+44 (0)1842 814215
Email	onky.del@btinternet.com
Web	www.oldrectoryoxboroughbandb.co.uk

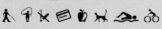

Entry 355   Map 9

Norfolk

Carrick's at Castle Farm

A comfortable, and jolly, mix of farmhouse B&B — rare-breed cattle, tractors, a large, warm-bricked house — and a rather swish interior. Both Jean and John are passionate about conservation and the protection of wildlife, and here you have absolute quiet for birdwatching, fishing, shooting or walking; recover in the drawing room with its books and lovely river views from long windows. Bedrooms are large, light and well thought-out with great bathrooms and binoculars, food is home-grown or local, and there is coffee and cake, or wine, when you arrive. The pretty garden leads down to the River Wensum and a footpath.

Ethical Collection: Environment; Food; Community. See page 430.

Price	From £85. Singles £55.
Rooms	4: 2 doubles; 1 double, 1 twin each with separate bath (let to same party only).
Meals	Dinner, 3 courses, £25. BYO. Pub 0.5 miles.
Closed	Never.
Directions	From Norwich A47 to Dereham (don't go into Dereham). B1147 to Swanton Morley. In village, take Elsing Road at Darby's pub; farm drive 0.5 miles on left.

10% off room rate Mon-Thurs. Late checkout (12pm).

Use your Sawday's Gift Card here.

	Jean Wright
	Carrick's at Castle Farm,
	Castle Farm, Swanton Morley,
	Dereham NR20 4JT
Tel	+44 (0)1362 638302
Email	jean@castlefarm-swanton.co.uk
Web	www.carricksatcastlefarm.co.uk

Entry 356   Map 10

Norfolk

Norfolk Courtyard

Walk straight in through French doors to your own, underfloor-heated room in the courtyard; privacy from the main house where young and friendly Simon and Catherine live. The rooms are decorated in soft colours, mattresses are perfect, cotton sheets are smooth and your handsome bathroom has limestone tiles – all rather luxurious. A table in the corner is beautifully laid for your continental breakfast (take it outside on good days) and you have a fridge to cool a bottle. There is a big attic room in one barn where you can play table tennis or read a book. Stunning walks await on the coast. *Minimum stay two nights (peak season).*

Price	£70–£85. Singles from £50.
Rooms	4: 3 doubles, 1 twin.
Meals	Pub/restaurant 0.5 miles.
Closed	Never.
Directions	From Fakenham take Norwich road for 10 minutes. Take Foulsham turning at the large water tower. House is first on left.

Chilled bottle of wine. Late checkout (12pm).

Simon & Catherine Davis
Norfolk Courtyard,
Westfield Farm, Foxley Road,
Foulsham, Dereham NR20 5RH
Tel   +44 (0)1362 683333
Email   info@norfolkcourtyard.co.uk
Web   www.norfolkcourtyard.co.uk

Entry 357   Map 10

Norfolk

Holly Lodge

The whole place radiates a lavish attention to detail, from the spoilingly comfortable beds to the complimentary bottle of wine. It's perfect for those who love their privacy: these three snug guest 'cottages' have their own entrances as well as smart iron bedsteads and rugs on stone tiles, neat little shower rooms and tapestry-seat chairs, and books, music and TVs. Enjoy the Mediterranean garden with pond and decking in summer, the handsome conservatory and the utter peace. Your hosts are delightful: ex-restaurateur Jeremy who cooks enthusiastically, ethically and with panache, and Canadian-raised Gill.

Price	£90–£120. Singles £70–£100.
Rooms	3 cottages for 2.
Meals	Dinner, 3 courses with wine, £19.50. Pubs/restaurants 1 mile.
Closed	Rarely.
Directions	From Fakenham A148, Fakenham-Cromer road; 6 miles; left at Crawfish pub. Signs to Thursford Collection, past village green; 2nd drive on left.

10% off stays Sun-Thurs. Bottle of wine in your room.

Jeremy Bolam
Holly Lodge,
Thursford Green NR21 0AS
Tel   +44 (0)1328 878465
Email   info@hollylodgeguesthouse.co.uk
Web   www.hollylodgeguesthouse.co.uk

Entry 358   Map 10

Norfolk

Burgh Parva Hall

Sunlight bathes the Norfolk longhouse on summer afternoons; the welcome from the Heals is as warm. The listed house is all that remains of the old village of Burgh Parva, deserted after the Great Plague. It's a handsome house and warmly inviting... old furniture, rugs, books, pictures and Magnet the terrier-daschund. Large guest bedrooms face the sunsets and the garden annexe makes a sweet hideaway, especially in the summer. Breakfast eggs are from the garden hens, vegetables are home-grown, fish comes fresh from Holt and the game may have been shot by William. Settle down by the fire and tuck in.

Price	£60-£80. Singles from £40.
Rooms	3: 1 double, 1 twin; 1 twin with separate bath.
Meals	Dinner £23. BYO. Pub/restaurant 4 miles.
Closed	Rarely.
Directions	Fakenham A148 for Cromer. At Thursford B1354 for Aylsham. Just before Melton, speed bumps, left immed. before bus shelter; 1st house on right after farmyard.

Judy & William Heal
Burgh Parva Hall,
Melton Constable NR24 2PU
Tel   +44 (0)1263 862569
Email   judyheal@dsl.pipex.com

Entry 359   Map 10

Norfolk

Stable Cottage

In the park of a privately owned village, one of Norfolk's finest Elizabethan houses, Heydon Hall. In the Dutch-gabled stable block, fronted by Cromwell's Oak, is this cottage – fresh, sunny and enchanting. Each room is touched by Sarah's warm personality and love of beautiful things; seagrass floors and crisp linen, toile de Jouy walls and pretty china. Bedrooms are cottagey and immaculate, there are fresh fabrics, baskets of treats in the bathrooms (one has a roll top bath) and delicious food on your plate (golden yolked eggs from Sarah's own hens and fruit from the kitchen garden). 20 minutes from the coast.

Price	£80. Singles £45.
Rooms	2 twins/doubles.
Meals	Occasional dinner, 3 courses, £20. BYO. Pub 1 mile.
Closed	Christmas.
Directions	From Norwich, B1149 for 10 miles. 2nd left after bridge, for Heydon. 1.5 miles, right into village, over cattle grid, into park. Pass Hall on left, cottage in front of you; left over cattle grid and into stable yard.

Sarah Bulwer-Long
Stable Cottage,
Heydon Hall, Heydon NR11 6RE
Tel   +44 (0)1263 587343
Mobile   +44 (0)7780 998742

Entry 360   Map 10

Norfolk

Cleat House

In a quiet residential area, but with the bustle of town a short walk away, this is an attractive brick and mock-timber Edwardian seaside villa built by a wealthy London merchant. Sumptuous bedrooms have original fireplaces and sash windows, upbeat fabrics and original art, and an eclectic mix of antique and vintage furniture. The guests' sitting room is superbly equipped: an honesty bar, games, cards, books and guides to help you plan trips. Rob and Linda greet you with homemade treats and serve a tasty breakfast at separate tables – try Linda's dish of the day. You're very well cared for here. *Min. two nights at weekends.*

Price	£80–£130. Singles £70–£100.
Rooms	3: 2 suites; 1 suite with separate bath.
Meals	Pubs/restaurants within 0.5 miles.
Closed	Occasionally.
Directions	Off A148 onto A1082, at r'bout left, then right into Church St. 1st left into The Boulevard, 2nd left into North St. Montague Rd at the end of North St.

Bottle of wine in your room. 10% off room rate Mon-Thur (Nov-Apr) 2 or more nights.

Rob & Linda Ownsworth
Cleat House,
7 Montague Road,
Sheringham NR26 8LN
Tel +44 (0)1263 822765
Email roblinda@cleathouse.co.uk
Web www.cleathouse.co.uk

Entry 361   Map 10

Norfolk

Incleborough House

A listed, mellow-bricked 17th-century house which faces a pretty, bird-filled, walled garden. Nick and Barbara have done a terrific restoration job and give you sumptuous bedrooms with huge beds, beautiful linen, super views, shining contemporary bathrooms, chocolates and wine. There's an elegant sitting room for tea and cakes, with an open fire and books to read. Breakfast at white linen-topped tables in the conservatory is a treat – try slow-baked marmalade ham with poached eggs. You are only 300 yards from the sea and the local walks are fabulous. *Minimum stay two nights at weekends; check for late availability.*

Price	£165–£210. Singles £123.75–£157.50.
Rooms	4: 3 doubles, 1 twin/double.
Meals	Occasional dinner, with wine, £25. Restaurant 100 yds.
Closed	Never.
Directions	From Sheringham head for Cromer. In East Runton, 1st right into Felbrigg Road. House 200 yds on left behind oak trees.

Free pick-up from local bus/train station. 10% off any 2+ night stays, Mon-Thurs.

Nick & Barbara Davies
Incleborough House,
Lower Common, East Runton,
Cromer NR27 9PG
Tel +44 (0)1263 515939
Email enquiries@incleboroughhouse.co.uk
Web www.incleboroughhouse.co.uk

Entry 362   Map 10

Norfolk

The Old Rectory

Conservation farmland all around; acres of wild heathland busy with woodpeckers and owls; the coast two miles away. Relax in the spacious drawing room of this handsome 17th-century rectory and friendly family home, set in four acres of grounds. Fiona loves to cook and bakes her bread daily, food is delicious, seasonal and locally sourced, jams are homemade. Comfortable bedrooms have *objets* from diplomatic postings and the spacious suite comes with mahogany furniture and armchairs so you can settle in with a book. Super views, friendly dogs, tennis in the garden and masses of space.

Price	From £55. Singles £35
Rooms	2: 1 suite; 1 double with separate bath & shower.
Meals	Dinner from £15. Pubs 2 miles.
Closed	Rarely.
Directions	From Norwich A1151 for Stalham. Just before Stalham, left to Happisburgh. Left at T-junc.; 3 miles; 2nd left after E. Ruston church, signed byway to Foxhill. Right at x-roads; 1 mile on right.

10% off room rate Mon-Thurs.

Peter & Fiona Black
The Old Rectory,
Ridlington NR28 9NZ
Tel   +44 (0)1692 650247
Email   blacks7@email.com
Web   www.oldrectory.northnorfolk.co.uk

Entry 363   Map 10

Norfolk

Manor Farmhouse

A family buzz and candlelight in the farmhouse where you eat, peace in the 17th-century barn where you stay. All rooms lead off its charming, stylish, vaulted sitting room with cosy winter fire. You have a modern four-poster and a tiny shower on the ground floor, then two narrow staircases to two beautifully dressed bedrooms upstairs – small, quirky, fun, with a tucked-up-in-the-roof feel. Come for a sunny courtyard, billiards in the old stable, fresh flowers, lovely hosts, gorgeous food – and you may come and go as you please. Great value, a perfect rural retreat. *Children over seven welcome.*

Price	From £50. Singles from £40.
Rooms	3: 1 double, 1 twin/double, 1 four-poster.
Meals	Dinner, 3 courses, £17.50. BYO. Pubs 1 mile.
Closed	Christmas & New Year.
Directions	From Norwich, A1151 & A149 almost to Stalham. Left for Walcott. At T-junc. left again. 1 mile on, right for H'burgh. Next T-junc., right. Next T-junc., left. Road bends right, sign by wall.

10% off stays of 4 nights Mon-Thurs. Norfolk handmade soap.

David & Rosie Eldridge
Manor Farmhouse,
Happisburgh NR12 0SA
Tel   +44 (0)1692 651262
Email   manorathappisburgh@hotmail.com
Web   www.northnorfolk.co.uk/manorbarn

Entry 364   Map 10

Norfolk

Sloley Hall

A grand and gracious yellow-brick Georgian house with formal gardens, tree-studded parkland and glorious views from every window. It has also been beautifully renovated, with flagstoned floors, Persian rugs, gleaming circular tables and vases of garden-grown flowers. Your hosts are delightful – Barbara and Simon were married here and are charmingly easy-going and helpful. A huge light-flooded dining room is perfect for breakfast; the drawing room is comfy but uncluttered in pinks, with a marble fireplace and long views. Bedrooms are large and elegant with sumptuous bed linen, and generous bathrooms glow with warmth.

Price	£70-£90. Singles from £50.
Rooms	3: 1 suite; 1 double with separate shower; 1 twin with separate bath. Extra child bed available.
Meals	Pubs/restaurants 2-4 miles.
Closed	Rarely.
Directions	From Norwich ring road, B1150 through Coltishall & Scottow. Right after Three Horseshoes pub (byway to Sloley); across staggered junc., 1st drive on right.

10% off room rate Mon-Thurs. Free pick-up from local bus/train station.

Barbara Gorton
Sloley Hall,
Sloley,
Norwich NR12 8HA
Tel   +44 (0)1692 538582
Email babsgorton@hotmail.com
Web   www.sloleyhall.com

Entry 365   Map 10

Norfolk

Manor House

Sally looks after you beautifully, in her elegant house on the edge of the marshes, nudged by an atmospheric ruined church. Restful bedrooms up steepish stairs have colour from floral fabrics, paintings and prints, and a connecting sitting space with books, guides, fresh flowers and TV; mattresses are firm and bathrooms sparkle. Bacon and sausages come from their own farm shop, jams and marmalades are deliciously homemade. The Weavers' Way runs past the door, there's birdwatching too, and you may come and go as you please. A lovely spot from which to explore the lesser known bits of the Broads. *Over sevens welcome.*

Price	£80-£90. Singles £40.
Rooms	2: 1 double with separate bath; 1 twin sharing bath (let to same party only).
Meals	Packed lunch £6.50. Pub 3 miles.
Closed	Christmas, New Year & February.
Directions	A47 for Great Yarmouth. After Acle, right to Halvergate. Into village, past pub on right, 3rd right to Tunstall. After 0.5 miles, farmhouse on left before ruined church.

10% off stays of 3 or more nights.

Sally More
Manor House,
Tunstall Road, Halvergate, Acle,
Norwich NR13 3PS
Tel   +44 (0)1493 700279
Email smore@fsmail.net
Web   www.manorhousenorfolk.co.uk

Entry 366   Map 10

Norfolk

Washingford House

Tall octagonal chimney stacks and a Georgian façade give the house a stately air. In fact, it's the friendliest of places to stay and Paris gives you a delicious, locally sourced breakfast including plenty of fresh fruit. The house, originally Tudor, is a delightful mix of old and new. Large light-filled bedrooms have loads of good books and views over the four-acre garden, a favourite haunt for local birds. Bergh Apton is a conservation village seven miles from Norwich and you are in the heart of it; perfect for cycling and the twelve Wherryman's Way circular walks are close by. *Children over 12 welcome.*

Norfolk

The Buttery

Down a farm track, a treasure: your own thatch-and-flint octagonal dairy house perfectly restored by local craftsmen and as neat as a new pin. You get a jacuzzi bath, a little kitchen and a fridge stocked with delicious bacon and ground coffee so you can breakfast when you want; take it to the sun terrace in good weather. The sitting room is terracotta-tiled and has a music system, a warming fire and a sofabed for those who don't want to tackle the steep wooden stair to the snug bedroom on the mezzanine. You may walk from the door into parkland and woods, or try your hand at tennis or fishing. Lovely!

Price	£65-£75. Singles £35-£45.	Price	£80-£95.
Rooms	2: 1 twin/double; 1 single with separate bath.	Rooms	Cottage: 1 double, sitting room & small kitchen.
Meals	Pubs/restaurants 4-6 miles.	Meals	Pub 10-minute walk.
Closed	Rarely.	Closed	Rarely.
Directions	A146 from Norwich to Lowestoft for 4 miles. Right after Gull Pub, signed Slade Lane. First left, then left at T-junc. for 1 mile. Straight over x-roads; house on left past post office.	Directions	From A47 Barnham Broom & Weston Longville x-roads, south towards Barnham Broom. After 150 yds, 1st farm track on right. Left at T-junc., left again, house on left.

Bottle of wine in your room. 10% off stays of 3 or more nights Mon-Thurs.

Bottle of wine.

Paris & Nigel Back
Washingford House,
Cookes Road, Bergh Apton,
Norwich NR15 1AA
Tel +44 (0)1508 550924
Email parisb@waitrose.com
Web www.washingford.com

Deborah Meynell
The Buttery,
Berry Hall, Honingham,
Norwich NR9 5AX
Tel +44 (0)1603 880541
Email thebuttery@paston.co.uk
Web www.thebuttery.thesiliconworkshop.com

Entry 367 Map 10

Entry 368 Map 10

38 St Giles

No expense spared here in this high-ceilinged, elegantly windowed town house: silk curtains in ravishing colours, handmade mattresses, plump goose down pillows and duvets, sumptuous linen, bathrobes, smart gadgetry, and thick towels in gorgeous bathrooms with L'Occitane treats. Breakfast on freshly baked croissants, porridge with caramelised apples, fruit and yogurt, or the full works – much will be locally sourced by Jeanette and William. Leave the car behind: you are slap bang in the right place here for languid strolls to the theatre, cathedral, historic market, interesting shops and good restaurants.

Price	£110–£160. Singles £90–£120.
Rooms	5: 3 doubles, 1 suite, 1 single.
Meals	Packed lunch £5. Light supper from £5. Pub/restaurant 50 yds.
Closed	23–27 December.
Directions	From inner ring road in Norwich, up Grape's Hill and at roundabout turn left onto St Giles Street. House is 200 yds down hill on right.

10% off stays of 2 or more nights.

Jeanette Bennett & William Cheeseman
38 St Giles,
St Giles Street,
Norwich NR2 1LL
Tel   +44 (0)1603 662944
Email booking@38stgiles.co.uk
Web www.38stgiles.co.uk

Entry 369   Map 10

Sallowfield Cottage

In a beautifully remote part of Norfolk is a hospitable house crammed with treasures: gorgeous prints and paintings, polished family pieces, leather fender seats by the drawing room fire. One bedroom, not huge but handsome, has a Regency-style canopied bed and decoration to suit the house (1850); another room is on the ground floor. Drift into the garden to find hedged rooms and a jungly pond with a jetty on which you breakfast (deliciously): magical in spring and summer. Caroline gives you the best, her lovely lurchers add to the charm, and if you have friends locally she can do lunch for up to ten. *Over nines welcome.*

Price	£65. Singles £40.
Rooms	3: 1 double, 1 twin; 1 double with separate bath.
Meals	Lunch £15. Dinner from £25. Pub 2.5 miles.
Closed	Christmas & New Year.
Directions	A11 Attleborough-Wymondham, Spooner Row sign. Over x-roads beside Three Boars pub. 1 mile; left at T-junc. to Wymondham for 1 mile. Rusty barrel on left, turn into farm track.

Caroline Musker
Sallowfield Cottage,
Wattlefield, Wymondham,
Norwich NR18 9NX
Tel   +44 (0)1953 605086
Email caroline.musker@tesco.net
Web www.sallowfieldcottage.co.uk

Entry 370   Map 10

Norfolk

College Farm

Stunning Jacobean panelling in the dining room: from 1349 until the Dissolution of the Monasteries the house was a college of priests. Lavender has done B&B for years, single-handedly looks after her house and its stupendous maze of rooms, serves wonderful breakfasts before the wood-burner and makes every stay a delight. Old-fashioned rooms are large and lived-in, two of the bathrooms are tiny and all have lovely views over the garden with its rare Ice Age ponds, or pingos. Come for history and architecture, and fine food and hospitality; Lavender has led a fascinating life and loves meeting people. *Over sevens welcome.*

Norfolk

Home Hall

On a small lane, fronted by roses, this late Georgian house with six chimneys has been superbly brought back to life by charming Wendy and David. Resplendently Art Deco, their home glows with oak panelling, intriguing lights and luxury; it was once lived in by a well-known author – the little drawing room has a collection of his books. Period themed bedrooms are spoiling with embroidered linen, beautiful fabrics and chocolates on the pillow; bathrooms are grand. Wake to homemade bread, sausages, eggs from the hens; dinner is an organic home-grown feast. Cream teas, creative courses and landscaped gardens are in the offing. *Over 12s welcome.*

Price	From £70. Singles £35.
Rooms	3: 1 twin, 1 twin/double; 1 double with separate bath. Extra shower available.
Meals	Afternoon tea included. Pub 1 mile.
Closed	Rarely.
Directions	From Thetford, A1075 north for Watton. After 9 miles, left to Thompson at 'Light Vehicles Only' sign. After 0.5 miles, 2nd left at red postbox on corner. Left again, house at end.

Lavender Garnier
College Farm,
Thompson,
Thetford IP24 1QG
Tel   +44 (0)1953 483318
Email   collegefarm83@amserve.net

Price	From £90. Singles from £50.
Rooms	3: 1 single; 2 doubles each with separate bath.
Meals	Packed lunch £6. Dinner, 2 courses with wine, from £20. Pub 0.5 miles, pub/restaurant 2 miles.
Closed	Rarely.
Directions	From A11 Thetford, left A1075 towards Watton. After Wretham, right into Gt Hockham. At village green, left, then 2nd left into Vicarage Road. House 1st on left.
🧳	Bottle of wine with dinner on first night for stays of 2 nights or more. 25% off a course.

Wendy Carr
Home Hall,
Vicarage Road,
Great Hockham IP24 1PE
Tel   +44 (0)1953 498985
Email   homehall@btinternet.com
Web   www.homehallbedandbreakfast.com

Entry 371   Map 10

Entry 372   Map 10

Norfolk

Le Grys Barn

Light pours into this 17th-century threshing barn — a jewel of a conversion in peaceful Norfolk. Julie lived in Hong Kong and sells jewellery from Bali. Her house glows with warmth and colour. Glass-topped tables increase the sense of space, Persian carpets beautify beech floors, golden buddhas rest in quiet corners. Across a courtyard, two private beamed and raftered bedrooms are stunningly equipped: guidebooks and glossies, easy chairs and Thai silk, music, flowers and mini fridge. Bathrooms have Italian tiles and breakfast, served on a Chinese altar table, is as delicious as all the rest.

Price	£70-£75. Singles from £45.
Rooms	2: 1 double, 1 twin/double.
Meals	Dinner, 3 courses, £20. BYO. Packed lunch available. Pub 5-minute drive.
Closed	Christmas & New Year.
Directions	From A140 at Long Stratton, Flowerpot Lane to Wacton; at x-roads left by phone box; 500 yds to telegraph pole with sign: left up 'Private Rd', over cattle grid to end of lane.

Julie Franklin
Le Grys Barn,
Wacton Common,
Long Stratton NR15 2UR

Tel	+44 (0)1508 531576
Email	jm.franklin@virgin.net
Web	www.legrys-barn.co.uk

Entry 373   Map 10

Norfolk

Rushall House

Plenty of treats to be had in this light and bright Victorian rectory: blue-shelled eggs for breakfast, homemade cake for tea, and radios, books and sofas in the double bedrooms. The wood-burner warm sitting room is classically decorated with a contemporary touch, airy bedrooms have pale walls, rich fabrics and a grand mix of colours and textiles (Jane's vintage furniture and fabrics are for sale in the courtyard studio). Walk or cycle after breakfast — it's good flat countryside and there are plenty of restorative pubs. Jane and Martin are relaxed hosts, and children will love collecting the eggs.

Ethical Collection: Food. See page 430.

Price	From £65. Singles £40.
Rooms	3: 1 double; 1 double, 1 twin sharing bath/shower.
Meals	Dinner £23. BYO. Pubs/restaurants 0.5-3 miles.
Closed	Rarely.
Directions	Turn off A140 at r'bout to Dickleburgh; right at village store. After two miles pass Lakes Rd & Vaunces Lane, on right. Shortly after z-bend sign, house on right.

Martin Hubner & Jane Gardiner
Rushall House,
Dickleburgh Road,
Rushall, Diss IP21 4RX

Tel	+44 (0)1379 741557
Email	janegardineruk@aol.com
Web	www.rushallhouse.co.uk

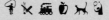

Entry 374   Map 10

Northamptonshire

Coton Lodge

Hidden at the end of a mile-long drive, a handsome, wisteria-clad farmhouse surrounded by enchanting gardens and mature trees. On the farm Joanne and Peter raise rare-breed sheep in the pastures, bantams patrol the orchard and miscanthus grass (an alternative energy crop) grows in the distance. The elegant rooms are filled with light and overlook a gentle valley. Bedrooms are traditional, utterly comfortable and immaculate. Breakfast on the best of local produce and homemade jams – in the conservatory on sunny days. *Children over 12 welcome. Minimum stay two nights at weekends March-September.*

Price	From £90. Singles from £70.
Rooms	3: 2 doubles, 1 twin/double.
Meals	Packed lunch £5. Pub 3 miles.
Closed	Rarely.
Directions	From M1 junc. 18 signs for Crick & W. Haddon. Bypass W. Haddon signs to Guilsborough. After 0.5 miles fork right to Guilsborough, Coton Lodge 0.75 miles on right.

10% off stays of 2 or more nights.

Joanne de Nobriga
Coton Lodge,
West Haddon Road, Guilsborough,
Northampton NN6 8QE
Tel   +44 (0)1604 740215
Email jo@cotonlodge.co.uk
Web   www.cotonlodge.co.uk

Entry 375   Map 8

Northamptonshire

Colledges House

Huge attention to comfort here, and a house full of laughter. Liz clearly derives pleasure from sharing her 300-year-old stone thatched cottage, immaculate garden, conservatory and converted barn with guests. Sumptuous bedrooms have deep mattresses with fine linen, sparkling bathrooms are a good size. The house is full of interesting things: a Jacobean trunk, a Bechstein piano, mirrors and pictures, pretty china, bright fabrics, a beautiful bureau. Cordon Bleu dinners are elegant affairs – and great fun. Stroll around the conservation village of Staverton – delightful. *Children over eight & babes in arms welcome.*

Price	£98-£106. Singles £67.50-£69.50.
Rooms	4: 1 single; 1 double with separate bath. Cottage: 1 double, 1 twin.
Meals	Dinner, 3 courses, £32. Pub 4-minute walk.
Closed	Rarely.
Directions	From Daventry, A425 to Leamington Spa. 100 yds past Staverton Park Conference Centre, right into village, then 1st right. Keep left, & at 'Give Way' sign, sharp left. House immed. on right.

10% off stays of 2 or more nights for double occupancy only.

Liz Jarrett
Colledges House,
Oakham Lane, Staverton,
Daventry NN11 6JQ
Tel   +44 (0)1327 702737
Email liz@colledgeshouse.co.uk
Web   www.colledgeshouse.co.uk

Entry 376   Map 8

Northamptonshire

The Vyne

Weighed down by wisteria, this 16th-century cottage rests in a honey-hued conservation village on the cusp of Oxfordshire. Beams and wonky lines abound; rooms are filled with good antiques and eclectic art. The spacious twin is enchanting, tucked under the rafters, its beds decorated in willow-pattern chintz, its walls glinting with gilded frames; the double has a Georgian four-poster and a sampler-decorated bathroom that's a quick flit next door. Warm and charming, Imogen not only works in publishing but is a dedicated gardener and Cordon Bleu cook – enjoy supper in her sunny secluded garden. *Babies welcome.*

Northamptonshire

Bridge Cottage

A truly restful place: sip a glass of wine on the decking down by the Willowbrook; rolling green countryside envelops you, the cattle are drinking peacefully, kingfishers flash by and you may see a red kite (borrow some binoculars). Inside find beautiful bedrooms with sloping ceilings, the purest cotton sheets and proper blankets; bathrooms are thickly towelled and full of lovely lotions and bubbles. Rules are few, breakfast is local and scrumptious and served in the friendliest kitchen facing that heavenly view, there's a tranquil conservatory for a quiet read, and Judy and Rod look after you very well indeed.

Price	£75. Singles from £45.
Rooms	2: 1 twin; 1 four-poster with separate bath.
Meals	Supper £20. Dinner £30. BYO. Pub 2-minute walk.
Closed	Christmas & New Year.
Directions	M40 exit 11. A422 to Northampton, left onto B4525. 2 miles, left to Thorpe Mandeville. 3 miles, left to Culworth. After Culworth, right to Eydon.

Late checkout (12pm).

Price	From £80. Singles from £40.
Rooms	4: 1 double, 2 twins; 1 double with separate bath.
Meals	Pub/restaurant 2 miles.
Closed	Rarely.
Directions	From south A1 to Peterborough junc. A605 signed Oundle & Northampton for 4 miles. At 1st r'bout right thro' Fotheringhay, then Woodnewton. House 1st on left on bridge.

	Imogen Butler
	The Vyne,
	High Street, Eydon,
	Daventry NN11 3PP
Tel	+44 (0)1327 264886
Mobile	+44 (0)7974 801475
Email	Imogen@ibutler2.wanadoo.co.uk

Entry 377   Map 8

	Judy Colebrook
	Bridge Cottage,
	Oundle Road, Woodnewton,
	Peterborough PE8 5EG
Tel	+44 (0)1780 470779
Email	enquiries@bridgecottage.net
Web	www.bridgecottage.net

Entry 378   Map 9

Northumberland

Matfen High House

Bring the wellies – and jumpers! You are 25 miles from the border and the walking is a joy. Struan and Jenny are amusing company, love sporting pursuits and will drive you to Matfen Hall for dinner. The sturdy stone house of 1735 is a lived-in, pretty place to stay: the en suite bedrooms have fine fabrics and good pictures, the bathrooms are stocked with fluffy towels and the drawing room promises books and choice pieces. Breakfasts are superb (local bacon and sausages and Struan's bread and marmalade) and the countryside is stunning. Hadrian's Wall and the great castles (Alnwick, Bamburgh) beckon.

Bog House

It's too quiet for some townies – and thank goodness! If you've had it with bustle, bury yourself in the depths of Northumberland, two miles from Hadrian's Wall. Here is an immaculate barn conversion that's mercifully free from the usual modern furniture; what you have is a contemporary, airy feel and an open-raftered space stuffed with antiques. Rosemary has created a stunning place. Breakfast is later at weekends and sausages are local, bread is freshly baked. The peace here is total; you have your own entrance and may come and go as you please. An indulgent, wonderful retreat. *Children over 12 welcome.*

Price	£70–£75. Singles £35–£40.
Rooms	4: 1 double, 1 twin; 1 double, 1 twin sharing bath.
Meals	Packed lunch £4.50. Restaurant 2 miles.
Closed	Rarely.
Directions	A69 at Heddon on the Wall, onto B6318; 500 yds, right to Moorhouse; right at next junc. signed Brewery & visitor centre; past Hadrian Pet Hotel; 300 yds, right, opp. cottages.

10% off room rate Mon-Thurs.

Struan & Jenny Wilson
Matfen High House,
Matfen,
Corbridge NE20 0RG
Tel   +44 (0)1661 886592
Email struan@struan.enterprise-plc.com

🐟🍴🚂🐕🐈

Entry 379   Map 12

Price	£90. Singles £45–£50.
Rooms	2: 1 twin; 1 double with separate bath.
Meals	Dinner £20. Pubs/restaurants 15-minute drive.
Closed	Rarely.
Directions	A68; 3 miles north of Corbridge, right onto B6318. After 3.5 miles, left signed Moorhouse. On for 1 mile, right; left to Bog House after 1 mile. Last farm on left.

Bottle of wine with dinner on first night. Late breakfast (11 am) Sat/Sun.

Use your Sawday's Gift Card here.

Rosemary Stobart
Bog House,
Matfen NE20 0RF
Tel   +44 (0)1661 886776
Email rosemary.stobart@btinternet.com
Web www.boghouse-matfen.co.uk

🚶🍴🐦🐕

Entry 380   Map 16

Northumberland

The Hermitage

A magical setting, three miles from Hadrian's wall, in a house full of friendship and comfort. Through ancient woodland, up the drive, over the burn and there it is: big, beautiful and Georgian. Interiors are comfortable country-house, full of warmth and charm; bedrooms, carpeted, spacious and delightful, are furnished with antiques, paintings and superb beds; bathrooms have roll top baths. Outside are lovely lawns, a walled garden, wildlife, and breakfasts on the terrace in summer. Katie — who was born in this house — looks after you brilliantly. *Guests back please by 11pm. Over sevens & babes in arms welcome.*

Price	From £85. Singles from £50.
Rooms	3: 1 double, 1 twin; 1 twin with separate bath.
Meals	Pub 2 miles.
Closed	October-February.
Directions	7 miles north of Corbridge on A68. Left on A6079 for 1 mile, then right through lodge gates with arch. House 0.5 miles down drive.

Simon & Katie Stewart
The Hermitage,
Swinburne,
Hexham NE48 4DG
Tel +44 (0)1434 681248
Email katie.stewart@themeet.co.uk

Entry 381   Map 16

Northumberland

The Old Vicarage

Come for the tiny village, the ancient church, and a gentler way of life in this stone built, wisteria-covered former vicarage. Light pours in to an elegant drawing room with large open fire, chintzy chairs and sofa, soft rugs, beautiful antique furniture and pictures. Bedrooms are comfortingly traditional, with crisp white sheets, squishy pillows, thick curtains and white bathrooms. Margaret gives you a grand breakfast in a toasty warm conservatory overlooking the garden; wander down to the river or to have a peek at the church, which dates from 1080! Newcastle, Alnwick Garden and stunning beaches are all a short drive away.

Price	£60-£80. Singles £50.
Rooms	3: 1 double; 1 twin, 1 single sharing bath.
Meals	Dinner, 3 courses with wine, £25. Pub 1 mile.
Closed	Christmas, New Year & Easter.
Directions	6 miles west of Morpeth on B6343, towards Scots Gap and Cambo.

10% off room rate.

Margaret Smart
The Old Vicarage,
Hartburn,
Morpeth NE61 4JB
Tel +44 (0)1670 772562
Email margiecook2001@yahoo.co.uk

Entry 382   Map 16

Northumberland

Shieldhall

The guest rooms are in the charming 18th-century farm buildings, each with its own entrance. Stephen and his sons make and restore antique furniture and rooms are named after the wood used within: Elm, Oak, Mahogany, Pine. Bathrooms are spacious, there's a beautiful sitting room/library and you pop across the courtyard for meals in the main house – once home to the family of Capability Brown. Celia is friendly and attentive and loves cooking, so ingredients are often organic or locally sourced; there's also a secret bar and a small but interesting wine list. Peaceful, hospitable B&B – with fine views.

Northumberland

Thistleyhaugh

Enid thrives on hard work and humour, her passions are pictures, cooking and people and if she's not the perfect B&B hostess, she's a close contender. Certainly you eat well – local farm eggs at breakfast and their own beef at dinner. Choose any of the five large, lovely bedrooms and stay the week; they are awash with old paintings, silk fabrics and crisp white linen. But if you do stray downstairs, past the log fire and the groaning table, there are 720 acres of organic farmland to discover and a few million more of the Cheviots beyond that. Wonderful hosts, house and region.

Price	£80. Singles £60.	
Rooms	3: 1 double, 1 twin, 1 four-poster.	
Meals	Dinner, 4 courses, £25. Pub 7 miles.	
Closed	Rarely.	
Directions	From Newcastle A696 for Jedburgh. 5 miles north of Belsay, right onto B6342. On left after 500 yds (turn into front courtyard).	

Price	£80. Singles £52.50–£75.	
Rooms	5: 3 doubles, 1 twin, 1 single.	
Meals	Dinner, 3 courses, £20. Pub/restaurant 2 miles.	
Closed	Christmas, New Year & January.	
Directions	Leave A1 for A697 for Coldstream & Longhorsley; 2 miles past Longhorsley, left at Todburn sign; 1 mile to x-roads, then right; on 1 mile over white bridge; 1st right, right again, over cattle grid.	

 Guided tour of antique furniture restoration workshops & advice on related subjects.

Celia & Stephen Robinson-Gay
Shieldhall,
Wallington,
Morpeth NE61 4AQ
Tel   +44 (0)1830 540387
Email stay@shieldhallguesthouse.co.uk
Web   www.shieldhallguesthouse.co.uk

Henry & Enid Nelless
Thistleyhaugh,
Longhorsley,
Morpeth NE65 8RG
Tel   +44 (0)1665 570629
Email thistleyhaugh@hotmail.com
Web   www.thistleyhaugh.co.uk

Entry 383   Map 16

Entry 384   Map 16

Northumberland

East Hepple Farmhouse

In the farmhouse sitting room, a wood-burner blazes away in winter. The double, too, has a sitting room, with an original cast-iron range and shelves groaning with books – bibliophile heaven. The peace is so deep in the Coquet valley that you may sleep until the whiff of sizzling local bacon hits your nostrils. Beds are firm, old pine pieces pretty, pillows feathery soft and views over the river to the Simonside hills abundant. Joan and Brian are expert at looking after you, will drive you to dinner and guide you the next day to the beaches, Cragside, Alnwick Castle and fabulous walking. To stay is a treat. *Fishing can be arranged nearby.*

Northumberland

Courtyard Garden

In the county town of Northumberland, with its grand castle and innovative gardens, step directly off the pavement and enter a courtyard surrounded by shrubs and pretty pots; sit out here on sunny days and sip a glass of something cool. Bedrooms (one overlooking the church, the other the garden) are traditional and immaculate; bathrooms, one with a roll top bath, have original wooden floors, thick towels. Friendly Maureen gives you breakfast in the comfortable sitting room at a round Georgian table underneath the window. Explore the town on foot, stride along white beaches, discover more castles; history is all around you.

Price	£65–£70. Singles from £50.	
Rooms	2: 1 double & sitting room; 1 twin (let to same party only).	
Meals	Packed lunch £5. Pubs/restaurants 2.5 miles.	
Closed	Rarely.	
Directions	West from Rothbury on B6341. In Hepple, pass church on left; next right, then immediate hard right into driveway.	

 Bottle of wine in your room.

 Use your Sawday's Gift Card here.

Joan & Brian Storey
East Hepple Farmhouse,
Hepple,
Rothbury NE65 7LH
Tel   +44 (0)1669 640221
Email   joanstorey@coquetdale.net
Web   www.easthepplefarmhouse.co.uk

Entry 385   Map 16

Price	From £70. Singles £50.	
Rooms	2: 1 double, 1 twin/double.	
Meals	Pub/restaurant within 300 yds.	
Closed	Christmas & New Year.	
Directions	A1, Alnwick turnoff A1068. Over r'bout; left at next r'bout B6346. Prudhoe St 1st left. Pass police station; house opp. St Paul's Church.	

Free pick-up from local train station. Organic skin care products.

Maureen Mason
Courtyard Garden,
10 Prudhoe Street,
Alnwick NE66 1UW
Tel   +44 (0)1665 603393
Email   maureenpeter10@btinternet.com
Web   www.courtyardgarden-alnwick.com

Entry 386   Map 16

Northumberland

Bilton Barns

A solidly good farmhouse B&B whose lifeblood is still farming. The Jacksons know every inch of the countryside and coast that surrounds their 1715 home; it's a pretty spot. They farm 400 acres of mixed arable land that sweeps down to the coast yet always have time for guests. Dorothy takes pride in creating an easy and sociable atmosphere – three couples who were introduced to each other one weekend now return for reunions! Bedrooms are big, carpeted, fresh and comfortable, a conservatory leads onto the garden and there's an airy guests' sitting room with an open fire and views to the sea.

Price	£68–£78. Singles £31–£55.
Rooms	3: 1 double, 1 twin, 1 four-poster.
Meals	Packed lunch from £5.
	Pub/restaurant 1.5 miles.
Closed	Christmas & New Year.
Directions	From Alnwick, A1068 to Alnmouth. At Hipsburn r'bout follow signs to station & cross bridge. 1st lane to left, 0.3 miles down drive.

Brian & Dorothy Jackson
Bilton Barns,
Alnmouth,
Alnwick NE66 2TB

Tel	+44 (0)1665 830427
Email	dorothy@biltonbarns.com
Web	www.biltonbarns.com

Entry 387   Map 16

Northumberland

Alnham Farm

Delve deep into the glorious sheep-dotted hills and valleys of the Northumberland National Park to find Jenny's handsome Georgian farmhouse and a dollop of urban chic in bedrooms and bathrooms. Walkers will be in heaven: set off with a tummy full of farmhouse porridge, home-reared sausages and bacon or a smashing Craster kipper. Spot whirling buzzards, the elusive red squirrel, otters if you are lucky; return to the crispest linen, gleaming mahogany, fresh flowers, and a power shower or a soak in a free-standing tub (bubbles and lotions provided). Castles, deep dunes and long white beaches are an easy drive.

Price	£80. Singles £50.
Rooms	2: 1 double, 1 twin/double.
Meals	Pub/restaurant 7 miles.
Closed	December-February.
Directions	From Whittingham, over bridge left to Netherton; 2nd right to Little Ryle & left passing Unthank Farm. Left at T-junc. & down front drive before 1st cottage on left.

Picnic and map for walkers. Bottle of wine in your room.

Jenny Sordy
Alnham Farm,
Alnwick NE66 4TJ

Tel	+44 (0)1669 630210
Email	jenny@alnhamfarm.co.uk
Web	www.alnhamfarm.co.uk

Entry 388   Map 16

Northumberland

Broome

A totally surprising one-storey house, full of beautiful things. It is an Aladdin's cave and sits in the middle of a coastal village with access to miles of sandy beaches. The garden/breakfast room is its hub and has a country cottage feel; enjoy locally smoked kippers here, award-winning 'Bamburgh Bangers' and home-cured bacon from the village butcher. There's also a sun-trapping courtyard full of colourful pots for breakfasts in the sun. Guests have a cheerful sitting/dining room and bedrooms with fresh flowers and good books. Mary is welcoming and amusing and has stacks of local knowledge.

Price	£90–£100. Singles £60–£70.
Rooms	2: 1 double, 1 twin, sharing bath/shower (2nd room let to same party only).
Meals	Pubs/restaurants 2-minute walk.
Closed	1 November–1 April.
Directions	From Newcastle north on A1; right for Bamburgh on B1341. To village, pass 30mph sign & hotel; 1st right at Victoria Hotel. House 400 yds on right.

	Mary Dixon
	Broome,
	22 Ingram Road,
	Bamburgh NE69 7BT
Tel	+44 (0)1668 214287
Mobile	+44 (0)7956 013409
Email	mdixon4394@aol.com

Entry 389   Map 16

Northumberland

West Coates

Slip through the gates of this Victorian townhouse and you're in the country. Two acres of leafy gardens, with shady or sunny spots to relax, belie the closeness of Berwick's centre. As surprising are the indoor pool and hot tub tucked in the corner. From the lofty ceilings and sash windows to the soft colours, paintings and gleaming furniture, the house has a calm, ordered elegance. Bedrooms have antiques and garden views; two have roll top baths; fruit, homemade cakes, flowers welcome you. Warm, friendly Karen is a stunning cook, inventively using local produce and spoiling you.

Price	£90–£120. Singles from £60.
Rooms	3: 1 double, 1 twin/double; 1 twin/double with separate bath/shower.
Meals	Dinner £35. Pub/restaurant 10-minute walk.
Closed	Christmas & New Year.
Directions	From A1 take A6105 into Berwick. House 300 yds on left. Stone pillars at end of drive. Train station 20-minute walk.

	Karen Brown
	West Coates,
	30 Castle Terrace,
	Berwick-upon-Tweed TD15 1NZ
Tel	+44 (0)1289 309666
Email	karenbrownwestcoates@yahoo.com
Web	www.westcoates.co.uk

Entry 390   Map 16

Nottinghamshire

Willoughby House

Past the village pub, through a gate, this three-storey brick farmhouse reflects its owners' skilful interior design. The house brims with tokens of its 18th century past, like meat hooks in the scullery-turned-sitting room, but feels ever so smart. Climb up to Harry's room with its brass bed and toy soldiers over the fireplace; Edward's and George's share raftered loft space and a swish bathroom. Sarah rustles up meals – and cheeses from her market stall – in a dining room embraced by poppy red walls and shutters. Get out on hikes or bikes; round the little village, or Southwell and Newark are close.

Price	£65–£75. Singles £45–£55.
Rooms	3: 1 twin/double; 1 double, 1 twin (let to same party only). 1 double with separate bath/shower.
Meals	Dinner, 2 courses, from £20. Packed lunch £7.50. Pub 3-minute walk; Restaurants within 5 miles.
Closed	Christmas & occasionally.
Directions	1.5 miles off A1, Cromwell & Norwell exit. At Cromwell left to Norwell 1.5 miles. House in village opp. school lane on corner of Willoughby Court.

A chunk of your favourite cheese to take home!

Andrew & Sarah Nesbitt
Willoughby House,
Main Street, Norwell,
Newark NG23 6JN
Tel   +44 (0)1636 636266
Email willoughbybandb@aol.com
Web   www.willoughbyhousebandb.co.uk

Entry 391   Map 9

Nottinghamshire

The Old Vicarage

Jillie's grandmother studied at the Slade and her paintings line the walls; glass and china adorn every surface. This wisteria-clad Victorian vicarage next to the 12th-century church was falling down when the Steeles bought it; now it's an elegant, traditional country home and popular with honeymoon couples. Long windows are generously draped, two of the bedrooms are spacious, baths have claw feet and a number of friendly cats and dogs wait to welcome you. Jerry bakes the bread and all the vegetables come from the garden. Mary Queen of Scots is reputed to have stayed at Langford as guest of the Earl of Shrewsbury!

Price	£75–£85. Singles £50–£55.
Rooms	3: 2 doubles, 1 twin.
Meals	Dinner, for special occasions, £25. Pub/restaurant 1.5 miles.
Closed	Rarely.
Directions	From A1, A46 to Lincoln & left onto A1133 for Gainsborough. Through Langford, 0.5 miles on, then left for Holme. House 100 yds on, on right, by church.

Occasionally fruit & veg from garden to take home. 10% off stays of 3 or more nights.

Jerry & Jillie Steele
The Old Vicarage,
Holme Lane, Langford,
Newark NG23 7RT
Tel   +44 (0)1636 705031
Email jillie.steele@virgin.net
Web   www.langfordoldvicarage.co.uk

Entry 392   Map 9

Nottinghamshire

Compton House

Two minutes from Newark's antique shops and ancient market, seek out this terraced Georgian townhouse where the mayor once lived. Naturally elegant, and overlooking Fountain Gardens, the sunny drawing room has a marble fireplace; Lisa and Mark have filled the place with lovely personal touches. Rooms are named after friends, from plush red-gold Judy's room to Harry's bijou single; the best is Cooper's, with a four-poster bed, a roll top bath through a draped archway and a wall hand-painted by a local artist. Pad down to the sunny basement for Mark's feast of a breakfast. Hotel comforts but a truly personal feel.

Price	£88. Singles from £60.
Rooms	7: 2 doubles, 1 twin/double, 2 twins, 1 four-poster; 1 single with separate shower.
Meals	Packed lunch £6. Buffet lunch £15. Dinner, 2 courses, from £25. Pub/restaurant 0.5 miles.
Closed	Occasionally Christmas.
Directions	From Nottingham A52, join A46 north to Newark. At r'bout 2nd exit. Right at lights, left at next lights then 1st right. House on left.
🧳	Bottle of wine in your room.

Mark & Lisa Holloway
Compton House,
117 Baldertongate,
Newark NG24 1RY
Tel   +44 (0)1636 708670
Email   info@comptonhousenewark.com
Web   www.comptonhousenewark.com

Entry 393   Map 9

Nottinghamshire

Wisteria Court

A listed, terraced cottage in Georgian Southwell – ideal for visiting the Minster. On the road but quiet at night, the modest cottage with a big-house feel is crisply elegant inside. The small, charming bedroom has a Victorian fireplace and pillows to die for; you have your own comfortable guest sitting room with TV, traditionally furnished with rich rugs and cushions. Friendly Lynn treats you to fruit salads, organic eggs, bacon and honeycomb from the farm shop – in the courtyard garden on sunny days. The town is pretty; numerous castles and antique shops are close by. *Children over 12 welcome.*

Ethical Collection: Food. See page 430.

Price	£75. Singles £50.
Rooms	1 twin & sitting room.
Meals	Pubs/restaurants 300 yds.
Closed	Rarely.
Directions	From A1 at Newark A617 towards Southwell. Left after Averham; 3 miles on, approach town, 'Minster spires' in view; sharp right turn, house 200 yds on left.

Lynn McKay
Wisteria Court,
58 Church Street,
Southwell NG25 0HG
Tel   +44 (0)1636 815509
Mobile   +44 (0)7827 734482
Email   susan_lynn@btinternet.com

Entry 394   Map 9

Oxfordshire

Uplands House

Come to be spoiled at this 'farmhouse' built in 1875 for the Earl of Jersey's son. Renovated by a talented couple, it's elegant and sumptuously furnished; expect large light bedrooms, crisp linen, thick towels and long bucolic views from the Orangery where you have tea and cake. Relax here with a book as the sounds and scents of the pretty garden waft by, or chat to charming Poppy while she creates delicious dinner – a convivial occasion enjoyed with your hosts. Breakfast is Graham's domain – try smoked salmon with scrambled eggs and red caviar. You're well placed for exploring but you'll find it hard to leave.

Price	£90–£160. Singles £60–£90.
Rooms	3: 1 double; 1 twin/double, 1 four-poster, each with separate bath.
Meals	Dinner, 2-4 courses, £20–£30. Pub 1.25 miles.
Closed	Rarely.
Directions	M40 junc. 11; thro' Banbury, A422 towards Stratford. Thro' Wroxton; just after 'Upton House' National Trust sign, right single lane drive marked 'Uplands Farm'. 1st drive on right to house.

Drink before dinner.

Use your Sawday's Gift Card here.

Poppy Cooksey & Graham Paul
Uplands House,
Upton,
Banbury OX15 6HJ
Tel   +44 (0)1295 678663
Email   poppy@cotswolds-uplands.co.uk
Web   www.cotswolds-uplands.co.uk

Entry 395   Map 8

Oxfordshire

Buttslade House

Choose between a gorgeous ground-floor retreat across the courtyard, or a very pretty room in the 17th-century farmhouse with its barns and stables. Both have their own sitting rooms with a clever melody of ancient and contemporary styles: Spanish art, antique sofas, bright cushions. Beds have seriously good mattresses, feather and down pillows and crisp white linen; bathrooms are smart and sparkling – one with a Victorian roll top. Diana is lovely and will pamper you or leave you, there's a blissful garden to stroll through, food is fresh and local and it's a hop to the village pub. A fun and stylish treat.

Price	£75. Singles £50.
Rooms	2: 1 double & sitting room; 1 twin & sitting room with separate bath.
Meals	Dinner, 3 courses, £25. Lunch £7. Pub 100 yds.
Closed	Rarely.
Directions	From B4035 look for signs to Wykham Arms. Buttslade is 2nd house beyond pub, going down hill.

10% off room rate Mon-Thurs.
10% off stays of 3 or more nights.

Diana Thompson
Buttslade House,
Temple Mill Road, Sibford Gower,
Banbury OX15 5RX
Tel   +44 (0)1295 788818
Email   janthompson50@hotmail.com
Web   www.buttsladehouse.co.uk

Entry 396   Map 8

Oxfordshire

Gower's Close

All the nooks, crannies and beams you'd expect from an ancient thatched cottage in a Cotswold village... and more besides: good food, lively conversation and lots of inside information about gardens to visit. Judith is a keen gardener who writes books on the subject (her passion for plants is evident from her own glorious garden) and her style and intelligence are reflected in her home. Pretty, south-facing and full of sunlight, the sitting room opens onto the garden and terrace. Bedrooms are light, charming and cottagey; the twin is at garden level. A thoroughly relaxing place to stay.

Price	£75. Singles £50.
Rooms	2: 1 double, 1 twin.
Meals	Dinner, 4 courses, £28 (min. 4 people). Pub/restaurant 100 yds.
Closed	Christmas & New Year.
Directions	In Sibford Gower, 0.5 miles south off B4035 between Banbury & Chipping Campden. On Main Street, same side as church & school.

Judith Hitching & John Marshall
Gower's Close,
Sibford Gower,
Banbury OX15 5RW
Tel   +44 (0)1295 780348
Email   judith@gowersclose.co.uk
Web   www.gowersclose.co.uk

✗ ⚷ ⅍

Entry 397   Map 8

Oxfordshire

Minehill House

Bump your way up the track (mind the car!) to the top of a beautiful hill and a gorgeous family farmhouse with views for miles and young, energetic Hester to care for you. Children will adore the ping-pong table and the trampoline; their parents will enjoy the gleaming old flagstones, vibrant contemporary oils, wood-burning stove and seriously sophisticated food. Rest well in the big double room with its verdant leafy wallpaper and stunning views, and a cubby-hole door to extra twin beds; bathrooms are sparklingly clean and spacious. Bracing walks straight from the door.

Price	£90. Singles from £50.
Rooms	1 double/family.
Meals	Dinner, 3 courses, £30. Supper £15. BYO. Packed lunch available. Pubs 1-5 miles.
Closed	Christmas & New Year.
Directions	From Banbury B4035 to Brailes; after 10 miles take left signed Hook Norton; 0.5 miles, right onto unmarked uphill farm track to house.

 10% off room rate Mon-Thurs.

Hester & Ed Sale
Minehill House,
Lower Brailes,
Banbury OX15 5BJ
Tel   +44 (0)1608 685594
Email   ed_and_hester@lineone.net
Web   www.minehillhouse.co.uk

🐓 ⚷ ⅍

Entry 398   Map 8

Oxfordshire

Home Farmhouse

The house is charming, with low, wobbly ceilings, beams, inglenook fireplaces and winding stairs; the bedrooms, perched above their own staircases like crows' nests, are traditionally furnished and decorated with swathes of flowery chintz. All rooms are faded and full of character; bathrooms are old fashioned and floral curtains embellish one bath. The barn room has a mixture of furniture and its own entrance up old stone steps. The family's travels are evident all over; this super couple run their B&B as a team. Delightful dogs, too – Samson and Goliath. It's all so laid-back you'll find it hard to leave.

Price	£80. Singles £52.
Rooms	3: 1 double, 1 twin/double. Barn: 1 twin/double.
Meals	Dinner £27. Supper £20. Pub 100 yds.
Closed	Christmas.
Directions	M40 junc. 10, A43 for Northampton. After 5 miles, left to Charlton. There, left & house on left, 100 yds past Rose & Crown.

Fruit, chocolates, flapjacks in room. 10% off room rate Mon-Thurs.

Rosemary & Nigel Grove-White
Home Farmhouse,
Charlton,
Banbury OX17 3DR
Tel   +44 (0)1295 811683
Email   grovewhite@lineone.net
Web   www.homefarmhouse.co.uk

Entry 399   Map 8

Oxfordshire

The Old Post House

Great natural charm in the 17th-century Old Post House, where shiny flagstones, rich dark wood and mullion windows combine with warm fabrics, deep sofas and handsome furniture. Bedrooms are big, with antique wardrobes, oak headboards and a comforting old-fashioned feel. The walled gardens are lovely – rich with espaliered fruit trees, and with a pool for sunny evenings. Christine, a well-travelled ex-pat, has a springer spaniel and an innate sense of hospitality; her breakfasts are delicious. There's village traffic but your sleep should be sound. Deddington is delightful. *Children over 12 welcome.*

Price	£80. Singles £52.
Rooms	3: 1 twin/double; 1 double with separate bath, 1 four-poster with separate shower.
Meals	Occasional dinner. Pubs/restaurants in village.
Closed	Rarely.
Directions	A4260 Oxford to Banbury. In Deddington, on right next to cream Georgian house. Park opposite.

Free pick-up from local bus/train station.

Christine Blenntoft
The Old Post House,
New Street,
Deddington OX15 0SP
Tel   +44 (0)1869 338978
Email   kblenntoft@aol.com
Web   www.oldposthouse.co.uk

Entry 400   Map 8

Oxfordshire

Rectory Farm

A general sense of peaceful order pervades at this solid, big house set in a manicured lawn. Inside find large, light bedrooms, floral and feminine, with bold chintz bed covers, draped kidney-shaped dressing tables, thick mattresses; some have garden views, others face the farm buildings. Sink into comfy sofas flanking a huge fireplace in the drawing room, breakfast on local bacon and sausage with free-range eggs, stroll the pretty garden, or grab a rod and try your luck on one of the trout lakes. Elizabeth knows her patch well; walkers can borrow maps, and she can point the way to lovely shops for the dedicated.

Price	From £90. Singles £50–£65.
Rooms	3: 1 double, 1 twin/double; 1 twin/double with separate bath.
Meals	Pub/restaurant 1.5 miles.
Closed	December/January.
Directions	A44 out of Chipping Norton towards Moreton-in-the-Marsh. After 1.5 miles right into Salford. Right at pub, then immediate left uphill past green on right. Left into drive for Rectory Farm, continue 200 yds then left.

Elizabeth Colston
Rectory Farm,
Salford,
Chipping Norton OX7 5YZ
Tel   +44 (0)1608 643209
Email   colston@rectoryfarm75.freeserve.co.uk
Web   www.rectoryfarm.info

Entry 401   Map 8

Oxfordshire

York House

On a country road between villages, surrounded by open garden, lake and trees, is this freshly painted and peaceful house. Its old cottage heart has become a delicious low-ceilinged sitting room with a log fire; new and 'deceptively spacious' is the rest. Ewa, warm, fun and full of good taste, has made it all delightful with swagged curtains, gold embossed antique books, delicate china, ancestral pieces and elegant glass. Bedrooms are comfortable, pretty and traditional. There are stately houses and gardens to visit and gastropubs to try, but if you've come with a party and decide to dine in, Ewa's cooking is a joy.

Price	£80–£140.
Rooms	3: 2 doubles; 1 twin with separate shower. (Extra double available.)
Meals	Dinner £40 (min. 6). BYO. Pubs within 2 miles.
Closed	1 November–1 February.
Directions	Chipping Norton to Churchill. From Churchill, take road to Kingham. 1 mile beyond Churchill, house on right.

Ewa Lewis
York House,
Churchill,
Chipping Norton OX7 6UL
Tel   +44 (0)1608 659341
Email   ewa.lewis@virgin.net

Entry 402   Map 8

Oxfordshire

Fox House

In idyllic stonewalled little Holwell is a big stylish house on a corner – the old village school. Welcoming Susan, who is in the antiques business, gives you two super sitting rooms (one with a friendly wood-burner, the other with a barn window and a heated flagstone floor), two immaculately cosy bedrooms (the twin up, the double down) and serves delectable breakfasts on pretty blue china and jams and juices from the orchard. The garden is open and leads to pasture and horses, the countryside is delicious in every season and footpaths radiate from the door. The Cotswolds at its finest!

Price	£80–£110. Singles from £65.
Rooms	2: 1 double; 1 twin with separate bath (extra room available).
Meals	Packed lunch £6. Dinner, 3 courses, £20. Pubs/restaurants 2 miles.
Closed	Christmas, New Year & January.
Directions	A361 south from Burford over A40. Right at sign for Cotswold wildlife park, then right signed Holwell. First house left on corner.

🧳 10% off room rate Mon-Thurs. Special homemade extra breakfast choices.

Susan Blacker
Fox House,
Holwell,
Burford OX18 4JS
Tel +44 (0)1993 823409
Email susan.blacker@btconnect.com
Web www.foxhouse-rooms.co.uk

Entry 403   Map 8

Oxfordshire

Manor Farmhouse

Helen and John radiate pleasure and good humour in this old Cotswold stone farmhouse, once part of the Blenheim estate (a short walk down the lane). Find comfortable, traditional living with good prints and paintings, venerable furniture and nothing cluttered or overdone. Shallow, curvy, 18th-century stairs lead up to the pretty double; the small bedroom has a challenging spiral stair to a cobbled courtyard. Breakfast is by the stone fireplace and ancient dresser. On warm days have tea in a sheltered corner by the fig tree and pots, and wander in the lovely garden; the village is quiet yet close to Oxford.

Price	£70–£78. Singles from £60.
Rooms	2 doubles, sharing shower room (let to same party only).
Meals	Pub within walking distance.
Closed	Christmas.
Directions	A44 north from Oxford's ring road. At r'bout, 1 mile before Woodstock, left onto A4095 into Bladon. Last left in village; house on right, on 2nd bend in road, with iron railings.

Helen Stevenson
Manor Farmhouse, Manor Road,
Bladon, Woodstock OX20 1RU
Tel +44 (0)1993 812168
Email helstevenson@hotmail.com
Web www.oxtowns.co.uk/woodstock/
manor-farmhouse/

Entry 404   Map 8

Oxfordshire

Caswell House

A handsome 15th-century manor house with an ancient orchard, walled gardens, smooth lawns and a moat brimming with trout. A flagstoned hall leads to a warm sitting room with vast fireplaces and squishy sofas. Spoil yourself in comfortable bedrooms, most with new shower rooms, thick towels, lovely bathroom treats and gorgeous views of the garden through leaded windows. Amanda and Richard are generous and easy-going – a game of snooker is a must! – and seasonal produce is sourced from the farm shop and cooked on the Aga. A great place to relax; for heartier souls there are 450 acres of rolling farmland.

Price	£85. Singles £65.
Rooms	3: 2 doubles, 1 twin/double.
Meals	Pubs/restaurants nearby.
Closed	Rarely.
Directions	A40 Burford to Oxford. Right after 1.8 miles dir. Brize Norton, left at staggered x-roads. Right then left at r'bouts; on for 1.2 miles, house on right.

10% off room rate Mon-Thurs.

Amanda Matthews
Caswell House,
Caswell Lane,
Brize Norton OX18 3NJ
Tel   +44 (0)1993 701064
Email   stay@caswell-house.co.uk
Web   www.caswell-house.co.uk

Entry 405   Map 8

Oxfordshire

Rectory Farm

Come for the happy vibe. It's relaxed and informal here and you are welcomed with tea and homemade shortbread by Mary Anne. The date above the entrance stone reads 1629 and the bedrooms, light and spotless, have beautiful stone-arched mullioned windows. The huge twin with ornate plasterwork overlooks the garden and church; the double, with a carved pine headboard, is cosier; both have good showers and big fluffy towels. A herd of pedigree North Devon cattle are Robert's pride and joy; the family have farmed here for three generations. It's a huge treat to stay. *Minimum stay two nights at weekends & high season.*

Price	£75-£85. Singles £60.
Rooms	2: 1 double, 1 twin.
Meals	Pub 2-minute walk.
Closed	Mid-December to mid-January.
Directions	From Oxford, A420 for Swindon for 8 miles & right at r'bout, for Witney (A415). Over 2 bridges, immed. right by pub car park. Right at T-junc.; drive on right, past church.

10% off stays of 3 or more nights Mon-Thurs.

Mary Anne Florey
Rectory Farm,
Northmoor,
Witney OX29 5SX
Tel   +44 (0)1865 300207
Email   pj.florey@farmline.com
Web   www.oxtowns.co.uk/rectoryfarm

Entry 406   Map 8

Oxfordshire

Oxford University

Oxford at your fingertips – at a fair price. In the city's ancient heart are Wadham and Keble; in leafy North Oxford is small friendly St Hugh's. Keble's sleeping quarters, functional though a good size, stand in stark contrast to the neo-gothic grandeur of its dining hall – pure Hogwarts! Wadham's hall, medieval, soaring, is yet more glorious – with top breakfasts. Its student-simple bedrooms are reached via crenellated cloisters and lovely walled gardens; ask for a room facing the beautiful quad. At St Hugh's: three residences (one historic), a student bar, romantic gardens and a 15-minute walk into town. *12 colleges in total.*

Price	Doubles £88–£110. Twins £60–£100. Singles £30–£75.
Rooms	Wadham: 250. St Hugh's: 200. Keble: 320. All with twins & singles, some with family rooms. Some share showers.
Meals	Breakfast included. Keble: occasional supper £10.20. Restaurants 2-15 minutes' walk.
Closed	Mid-Jan to mid-March; May/June; Oct/Nov; Christmas. A few rooms available throughout year.
Directions	Website booking. On-request parking at St Hugh's & Lady Margaret Hall.

University Rooms
Oxford University,
Oxford
Web   www.oxfordrooms.co.uk

Entry 407   Map 8

Oxfordshire

Cowdrays

Walkers will be happy here and Margaret keeps a much-used stock of plasters. The house is down a quiet lane, there are chickens, geese, dogs and, in the lovely garden – a corner of which is Gertrude Jekyll-inspired – a tennis court. This is a homely, endearingly timeworn sort of place, neither smart nor stylish, but with good furniture, masses of books, clean bathrooms, a little sitting room... even a kitchen area in which to prepare a snack if you prefer not to walk to the historic village's pubs. Birdsong and sunlight find their way into every room: the downstairs room is perfect for wheelchair-users.

Price	£70–£80. Singles £35.
Rooms	5: 2 doubles; 1 twin with separate shower; 1 twin, 1 single sharing bath/shower.
Meals	Packed lunch £7.50. Pubs within 10-minute walk.
Closed	Rarely.
Directions	Off A41, 3 miles from Wantage. Into E Hendred, 3rd right into Orchard Lane; past Plough pub; left into Cat St. House behind wall & gates (immed. on right).

Margaret Bateman
Cowdrays,
Cat Street, East Hendred, Wantage,
Oxford OX12 8JT
Tel   +44 (0)1235 833313
Email   enquiries@cowdrays.co.uk
Web   www.cowdrays.co.uk

Entry 408   Map 4

Oxfordshire

Brook Barn

Not your average country B&B, but a swish interior of light oak, soaring rafters, lots of light and space, and well-travelled charming owners. Bedrooms are of the boutique-hotel breed: good lighting, lots of space for sitting, and beds that you want to climb into there and then; bathrooms vary in size but all have enormous towels and lovely lotions and potions. Breakfast at a time to suit you, either on your terrace, or in the beamed dining room; all is sourced locally and the mushrooms are home grown. Grab a book, stroll round the garden, or find a sofa to flop into downstairs – this is a place to relax.

Price	£100-£225. Singles £80-£135.
Rooms	5: 4 doubles; 1 twin/double with separate bath/shower.
Meals	Dinner from £18.50. Packed lunch £10.50-£19.50. Pub/restaurant 2 miles.
Closed	Christmas.
Directions	Ashbury road out of Wantage. Left to Letcombe Regis, round right-hand bend, 400 yds after cream house, drive on left.

Bottle of wine in your room.

Sarah-Jane & Mark Ashman
Brook Barn,
Letcombe Regis,
Wantage OX12 9JD
Tel   +44 (0)1235 766502
Email   info@brookbarn.com
Web   www.brookbarn.com

Entry 409   Map 3

Oxfordshire

Fyfield Manor

One of the most fabulous houses in Oxfordshire (once owned by Simon de Montfort) with vast water gardens and a water wheel for electricity, created by the Browns. Through the grand wood-panelled hall enter a beamed dining room with high-backed chairs and brass rubbings; you breakfast (local, free-range, organic) through the 12th-century arch... or al fresco. Bedrooms are large, warm and light with snowy bed covers and views. Oxford Park & Ride is nearby, there's walking from the door and delightful Christine has wangled you a free glass of wine in the local pub if you walk or cycle. Superb. *Children over ten welcome.*

Ethical Collection: Environment. See page 430.

Price	£70-£80. Singles £50-£60.
Rooms	2: 1 twin/double; 1 twin/double/family with separate bath.
Meals	Pubs within 1 mile.
Closed	Rarely.
Directions	M4 junc. 8/9; A4130 thro' Henley to Wallingford. Turn off for Benson; continue through village 1 mile. Last house on right, behind 6 foot-high brick wall.

25% discount on pilates or Alexander Technique lesson.

Christine Brown
Fyfield Manor,
Benson,
Wallingford OX10 6HA
Tel   +44 (0)1491 835184
Email   chris_fyfield@hotmail.co.uk
Web   www.fyfieldmanor.co.uk

Entry 410   Map 4

Rutland

Old Rectory

Jane Austen fans will swoon. This elegant 1740s village house was used as Mr Collins's 'humble abode' by the BBC: you breakfast in the beautiful dining room that was 'Mr Collins's hall', and you can sleep in 'Miss Bennett's bedroom'. Victoria is the archetypal English woman – feisty, fun and gregarious – and looks after you beautifully with White Company linen in chintzy old-fashioned bedrooms and (not swish) bathrooms, fruit from the lovely garden and Aga-cooked bacon and eggs. You are near to some pleasant market towns and lovely walking and riding country. Don't forget the smelling salts!

Price	£85. Singles £45.
Rooms	2: 1 twin; 1 double with separate bath.
Meals	Pubs within 3 miles.
Closed	Rarely.
Directions	5 miles NE of Oakham, through Ashwell. Or 7 miles west of A1 from Stretton.

 10% off room rate Mon-Thurs for stays of 2 or more nights.

 Use your Sawday's Gift Card here.

Victoria Owen
Old Rectory,
Teigh,
Oakham LE15 7RT
Tel +44 (0)1572 787681
Email torowen@btinternet.com
Web www.teighbedandbreakfast.co.uk

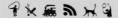

Entry 411   Map 9

Rutland

Old Hall Coach House

A rare and special setting; the grounds of the house meet the edge of Rutland Water, with far-reaching lake and church views. Inside: high ceilings, stone archways, antiques and a conservatory overlooking a year-round stunning garden and croquet lawn. Bedrooms are traditional with modern touches and comfortable; the double and single have super new bathrooms. Rutland is a mini-Cotswolds of stone villages and gentle hills, the lake encourages you to sail, fish, walk or ride, and Georgian Stamford, Burghley House and Belvoir Castle are nearby. Cecilie is a well-travelled, interesting host. *Minimum stay two nights at weekends.*

Price	From £90. Singles from £40.
Rooms	3: 1 double; 1 twin, 1 single, each with separate bath.
Meals	Dinner £30. Pub/restaurant 5-minute walk.
Closed	Occasionally.
Directions	From A1 Stamford bypass A606 for Oakham for 3 miles. Fork left for Edith Weston; past village sign; 1st right, Church Lane; past church, right down hill; on right on left bend.

Bottle of wine with dinner on first night.

Cecilie Ingoldby
Old Hall Coach House,
Edith Weston,
Oakham LE15 8HQ
Tel +44 (0)1780 721504
Email cecilieingoldby@aol.com
Web www.oldhallcoachhouse.co.uk

Entry 412   Map 9

Shropshire

Pinfold Cottage

Heart-warming B&B in a beautiful spot with lots of books, a parrot called Polly and vintage games and toys to add to the merry clutter. Walls are covered in illustrations and some lovely paintings, bedrooms are calm, simple and charming, but the biggest treat is Sue. Generous with her time, spirit and home cooking, she makes her own muesli with fruits and nuts from the garden. Natural sounds are provided by the well-fed birdlife and the trickle of the stream that meanders through the enchanting garden. Breakfasts are healthy and delicious and you'll revel in the peace. Superb value.

Price	£60. Singles £40.
Rooms	2: 1 double, 1 single, each with separate shower. Extra bath available.
Meals	Dinner, 3 courses, from £15. Packed lunch £7. Restaurant 0.5 miles.
Closed	Rarely.
Directions	From Oswestry, A483 from A5 for Welshpool. 1st left to Maesbury; 3rd right at x-roads with school on corner; 1st house on right.

	Sue Barr
	Pinfold Cottage,
	Newbridge,
	Maesbury,
	Oswestry SY10 8AY
Tel	+44 (0)1691 661192
Email	suebarr100@hotmail.com

Entry 413   Map 7

Shropshire

Top Farmhouse

The charming roadside house in little Knockin is 16th-century, magpie-gabled and rambling, the church and pound are 800 years old and Pam is theatrical and fun. Downstairs is attractive, warm and cosy, a lattice of beams dividing the dining room from the sitting room where wine and conversation flow. Upstairs, floors rise, fall and creak, and all is in apple-pie order: beds are of brass, oak and varnished pine, tea trays are filled with treats. A place with a huge heart to which the loyal return — and Pam's breakfasts are as generous as her spirit. Chirk and Powys castles are near. *Children over 11 welcome.*

Price	£65-£75. Singles from £35.
Rooms	3: 1 double, 1 twin, 1 double/family room.
Meals	Packed lunch available. Pub within walking distance.
Closed	Rarely.
Directions	From Shrewsbury, A5 north. Through Nesscliffe & after 2 miles, left to Knockin. Through Knockin, past Bradford Arms. House 250 yds on left.

	Pam Morrissey
	Top Farmhouse,
	Knockin,
	Oswestry SY10 8HN
Tel	+44 (0)1691 682582
Email	p.a.m@knockin.freeserve.co.uk
Web	www.topfarmknockin.co.uk

Entry 414   Map 7

Shropshire

Brimford House

Beautifully tucked under the Breidden Hills, farm and Georgian farmhouse have been in the Dawson family for four generations. Views stretch all the way to the Severn; the simple garden does not try to compete. Bedrooms are spotless and fresh: a half-tester with rope-twist columns and Sanderson fabrics, a twin with Victorian wrought-iron bedsteads, a double with a brass bed, a big bathroom with a roll top bath. Liz serves you farm eggs and homemade preserves at breakfast, and there's a food pub just down the road. Sheep and cattle outdoors, a lovely black lab in, and wildlife walks from the door. Good value.

Price	£60-£75. Singles £40-£60.
Rooms	3: 2 doubles, 1 twin.
Meals	Packed lunch £4.50. Pub 3-minute walk.
Closed	Rarely.
Directions	From Shrewsbury A458 Welshpool road. After Ford, right onto B4393. Just after Crew Green, left for Criggion. House 1st on left after Admiral Rodney pub.

Bottle of sparkling wine, minimum 2-night stay.

Liz Dawson
Brimford House,
Criggion,
Shrewsbury SY5 9AU
Tel +44 (0)1938 570235
Email info@brimford.co.uk
Web www.brimford.co.uk

Shropshire

The Isle

History buffs and nature lovers will delight: these 800 acres are almost enfolded by the River Severn; drive through lion-topped stone pillars to the house, built in about 1682 and extended later. Charming Ros and Edward are truly hands-on: all wood for fires is grown on the estate which also provides eggs, bacon, ham and vegetables – so you eat well! Flop in front of a huge fire in the drawing room with Chinese rug, family antiques and sublime views. Peaceful bedrooms are large and light with pocket-sprung memory mattresses and snazzy, upmarket bathrooms. Super walks, rides and fishing on the estate.

Price	£75-£90. Singles £50-£60.
Rooms	3: 2 doubles; 1 twin with separate bath.
Meals	Packed lunch £5. Dinner £20. Pub/restaurant 4.3 miles.
Closed	Never.
Directions	From Shrewsbury signs for Oswestry & Bicton (B4380). At Four Crosses pub right into Isle Lane. After 0.5 mile drive thro' pillars with lions. Follow B&B signs.

10% off room rate Mon-Thurs. 10% off stays of 2 or more nights.

Use your Sawday's Gift Card here.

Ros & Edward Tate
The Isle,
Bicton,
Shrewsbury SY3 8EE
Tel +44 (0)1743 851218
Mobile +44 (0)7776 257286
Email ros@isleestate.co.uk

Shropshire

Hardwick House

On a quiet street in the heart of Shrewsbury, this fine Georgian house has been in Lucy's family for generations. The dining room with oak panelling and huge fireplace is a lovely space to breakfast – locally sourced with homemade bread; vases of garden flowers are dotted all around this cheerful, family home. Bedrooms are traditional and comfortable with pretty china tea cups; bathrooms are old fashioned. The walled garden is fabulous; take tea in the splendid 18th-century summerhouse. Birthplace of Darwin, this is a fascinating historic town; walk to the abbey, castle, theatre, festivals and great shops. Lucy is delightful.

Price	£75–£95. Singles £55–£65.
Rooms	2: 1 twin/double, 1 twin.
Meals	Pubs/restaurants 150 yds.
Closed	Christmas & New Year.
Directions	Follow signs to town centre. House near St Chad's church. Train: left out of station & up the hill. Staight down Pride Hill, then up into St John's Hill.

10% off room rate Mon-Thurs.

Lucy Whitaker
Hardwick House,
12 St John's Hill,
Shrewsbury SY1 1JJ
Tel   +44 (0)1743 350165
Email   gilesandlucy@btinternet.com
Web   www.hardwickhouseshrewsbury.co.uk

Entry 417   Map 7

Shropshire

Meole Brace Hall

Charles takes B&B to a new state of excellence: come to be spoilt in a heavenly house. The quintessence of English period elegance, it's a sumptuous home rich with polished mahogany and eye-catching wallpapers and fabrics. Bedrooms have comfortable sofas and flat-screen TVs; the Blue Room has an elegant half-tester bed. Sit on the terrace overlooking the manicured gardens: a stream trickles down to the willow pond, a second pond with lion fountains is home to koi carp. All this under the watchful eye of Dolly, the friendly Patterdale cross terrier. A 25-minute stroll from town – but it feels a million miles away.

Price	From £79. Singles from £59.
Rooms	3: 2 doubles, 1 twin.
Meals	Restaurants 1 mile.
Closed	Rarely.
Directions	A5 & A49 junc. (south of bypass), signs to centre. Over 1st mini r'bout, 2nd exit at next; 2nd left into Upper Rd; 150 yds on at bend, left & immed. right into Church Lane. Drive at bottom on left.

Charles Hathaway
Meole Brace Hall,
Shrewsbury SY3 9HF
Tel   +44 (0)1743 235566
Email   hathaway@meolebracehall.co.uk
Web   www.meolebracehall.co.uk

Entry 418   Map 7

Shropshire

Brompton Farmhouse

Surround yourself with calming caramels, beiges and golds in this Georgian farmhouse with a contemporary twist. Phillipa, an interior designer, has worked her magic here and it's all delightfully understated: a large comfortable sitting room with open fire and squishy sofas, bright bathrooms with thick towels, spoiling beds and linen, fresh flowers and gleaming furniture. Outside are acres of National Trust land, beautifully looked after, for walks and picnics. Food is scrumptious and generous; kippers, scrambled eggs and homemade damson jam at breakfast, and farmhouse cooking for supper. *Cookery school; courses to suit all.*

Price	£70–£95. Singles from £55.
Rooms	4 twins/doubles.
Meals	Packed lunch £5. Dinner £25. Restaurants 1.5 miles.
Closed	Christmas & New Year.
Directions	4 miles south of Shrewsbury on A458. In Cross Houses, left after petrol station, signed Atcham. Down lane & right to Brompton; follow to farm.

10% off room rate Mon–Thurs. 10% off stays of 2 or more nights.

Philippa Home
Brompton Farmhouse,
Cross Houses,
Shrewsbury SY5 6LE
Tel +44 (0)1743 761629
Email info@bromptonfarmhouse.co.uk
Web www.bromptonfarmhouse.co.uk

Entry 419   Map 7

Shropshire

Hannigans Farm

High on the hillside, a mile up the drive, the views roll out before you – stunning. Privacy and peace are yours in the converted dairy and barn across the flower-filled yard. Big, carpeted, ground-floor rooms have comfy beds and sofas; one has views that roll towards the setting sun. In the morning Fiona and Alistair, delightful, easy-going and fun, serve you home eggs, sausages from their own pigs and honey from their bees in the book-lined dining room of their farmhouse. Feel free to take tea in the garden with its little hedges and manicured lawns; you'll feel restored in this quiet Shropshire corner.

Price	£80. Singles by arrangement.
Rooms	2 twins.
Meals	Pub 1.25 miles.
Closed	Rarely.
Directions	From Bridgnorth, A458 to Shrewsbury. 0.5 miles after Morville, right onto stone road & follow signs for 1 mile, to farm.

Bowl of fruit in your room.

Use your Sawday's Gift Card here.

Fiona Thompson
Hannigans Farm,
Morville,
Bridgnorth WV16 4RN
Tel +44 (0)1746 714332
Email hannigansfarm@btinternet.com
Web www.hannigans-farm.co.uk

Entry 420   Map 7

Shropshire

Jinlye

Wuthering Heights in glorious Shropshire – and every room with a view. There's comfort too, in the raftered lounge with its huge open fire, the swish dining room for fun breakfasts, the conservatory scented in summer – and the spacious bedrooms with their deep-pile carpets, new mattresses and sumptuous touches... expect faux-marble reliefs, floral sinks, boudoir chairs and spotless *objets*. Sheltered Jinlye sits in lush landscaped gardens surrounded by hills, rare birds, wild ponies and windswept ridges. Kate, Jan and their little papillon dogs look after you professionally and with ease.

Price	£74–£86. Singles £54–£62.
Rooms	6: 3 doubles, 2 twins/doubles, 1 twin.
Meals	Packed lunch on request. Pubs 1 mile.
Closed	Christmas.
Directions	From Shrewsbury A49 to Church Stretton then right towards All Stretton. Once in All Stretton right, immed. past phone box, up a winding road, up the hill to Jinlye.

	Jan & Kate Tory
	Jinlye,
	Castle Hill, All Stretton,
	Church Stretton SY6 6JP
Tel	+44 (0)1694 723243
Email	info@jinlye.co.uk
Web	www.jinlye.co.uk

♿ ✗ ▤ ⟋ 🐾 ⚲

Entry 421   Map 7

Shropshire

Lawley House

A lovely calm sense of the continuity of history and family life emanates from this large, comfortable Victorian home. Jackie and Jim are delightful hosts and great fun. Bedrooms welcome you with flowers, bathrobes, books, duckdown pillows – and stupendous views of the Stretton Hills, even from bed. Tuck into a generous breakfast in the dining room, elegant with family portraits and a grand piano you are welcome to play. Enjoy long hilltop views from the spectacular conservatory or the garden – lush with lupins, sweet peas, delphiniums and 50 types of rose that bloom in profusion. *Children over 12 welcome.*

Price	£50–£70. Singles £40–£55.
Rooms	3: 2 doubles, 1 twin/double.
Meals	Pub/restaurant 1.5 miles.
Closed	Christmas & New Year.
Directions	From Shrewsbury, south on A49. Ignore turn in Dorrington, keep on for 3 miles. 0.5 miles before Leebotwood, right to Smethcott. Follow signs uphill for 2 miles; drive on left just before Smethcott.

10% off room rate Mon-Thurs. Wine & chocolates in fridge for stays of 2+ nights.

	Jackie & Jim Scarratt
	Lawley House,
	Smethcott,
	Church Stretton SY6 6NX
Tel	+44 (0)1694 751236
Email	jscarratt@onetel.com
Web	www.lawleyhouse.co.uk

✗ ⟋

Entry 422   Map 7

Shropshire

Victoria House

A lovely part of England, with great walking on the doorstep, but in this cosy town house you get a few urban treats like a good pub next door and a tea shop below. Breakfast is hearty with organic leanings, there's a little guest sitting room for flopping, and your bedroom is deeply comfortable: posh mattresses, lovely linen, fluffy towels, views over the town to the Longmynd hill range and a Victorian feel with the odd splosh of contemporary chic. Bathrooms are fairly modest and not state-of-the-art, but all are scrupulously fresh, and Linda — a Shropshire lass — looks after you impeccably.

Ethical Collection: Food; Community. See page 430.

Price	£55–£75. Singles £32.50–£45.
Rooms	6: 4 doubles, 1 twin; 1 double with separate shower.
Meals	Packed lunch £5. Pub/restaurant 10 yds.
Closed	Never.
Directions	From Shrewsbury or Ludlow A49 to Church Stretton. Off A49 into Sandford Ave. Left onto High Street, past square, past pub on right. House next door but one to pub.

10% off stays of 2 or more nights.

Linda Smith
Victoria House,
48 High Street,
Church Stretton SY6 6BX
Tel   +44 (0)1694 723823
Email   victoriahouse@fsmail.net
Web   www.bedandbreakfast-shropshire.co.uk

Entry 423   Map 7

Shropshire

The Manor House

House, garden and owner have bags of character: clever Caroline, an interior designer, gives you lots of space to roam. Find ancient beams and salvaged panels, the odd contemporary painting or ceramic, a glowing wood-burner, and bright splashes of colour. Your bedroom is lovely, with a sloping ceiling, fresh white walls and a bang-up-to-date bathroom — all chubby towels and Jo Malone potions. Peaceful breakfasts overlooking the bird-filled garden will set you up for anything and there are plenty of hearty walks from the door, or nearby Ludlow and Church Stretton to explore. *Minimum stay two nights.*

Price	£100. Singles £85.
Rooms	1 double.
Meals	Packed lunch £10. Dinner from £20. BYO. Pub/restaurant 100 yds.
Closed	Christmas & New Year.
Directions	From Ludlow, left off A49 into Church Stretton, up to staggered crossroads, then right. Past schools on right, into All Stretton. Past Yew Tree pub, next council road left, by phone box & postbox & immed. left into drive.

Free drop off within 10 mile radius. Fair trade chocolate in your room.

Caroline Montgomery
The Manor House,
All Stretton SY6 6JU
Tel   +44 (0)1694 724508
Email   caro@manorhouseallstretton.co.uk
Web   www.manorhouseallstretton.co.uk

Entry 424   Map 7

Shropshire

The White Cottage

A narrow road three miles from Bishop's Castle snakes past fields of placid sheep, through farm gates, to the White Cottage and a lovely welcome from Tim and Mary. This is B&B with a difference: your very own stone bothy, once used by drovers, now a light, warm and inviting suite, bright with art and stylish touches. A member of Shropshire's 'Buy Local, Eat Local' scheme, Mary delivers a breakfast basket to your patio deck – or will cook you something scrumptious in her kitchen: scurry up to the cottage for scrambled eggs or devilled kidneys. All around you are country sounds and bucolic beauty.

Price	£80.
Rooms	Bothy: 1 double & kitchen/dining area.
Meals	Pubs/restaurants 3 miles.
Closed	Occasionally.
Directions	From Bishop's Castle, A488 towards Clun. Pass through Colebatch. At next staggered x-roads right. After 0.5 miles, signed gate on right.

10% off room rate Mon-Thurs. Late checkout (12pm).

Mary Wraith
The White Cottage,
Golden Grove, Acton,
Bishop's Castle SY9 5LD
Tel   +44 (0)1588 630330
Email   staying@thewhitecottageacton.co.uk
Web   www.thewhitecottageacton.co.uk

Entry 425   Map 7

Shropshire

The Birches Mill

Just as a mill should be, tucked in the nook of a postcard valley. It ended Gill and Andrew's search for a refuge from the city; it is a treat to share its seclusion and natural beauty where the only sounds are watery ones from the river. The fresh, breezy rooms in the 17th-century part have elegant brass beds, goose down duvets, fine linen and one has an original, very long, roll top bath; the new stone and oak extension blends beautifully and has become a large, attractive twin. Gill and Andrew are affable hosts in their stunning valley of meadowland and woods. *Children over 12 welcome.*

Price	£80-£90. Singles by arrangement.
Rooms	3: 1 double, 1 twin; 1 double with separate bath.
Meals	Packed lunch £6. Pub 3 miles.
Closed	November-March.
Directions	From Clun A488 for Bishops Castle. 1st left, for Bicton. 2nd left for Mainstone, then narrow winding lane for 1.5 miles. Up bank to farm, then 1st right for Burlow. House at bottom of hill on left by river.

5% off stays Mon-Thurs.

Gill Della Casa & Andrew Farmer
The Birches Mill,
Clun,
Craven Arms SY7 8NL
Tel   +44 (0)1588 640409
Email   gill@birchesmill.fsnet.co.uk
Web   www.birchesmill.co.uk

Entry 426   Map 7

Shropshire

Clun Farm House

These young, relaxed owners make a great team. Susan gives you homemade marmalade at breakfast and seasonal produce at dinner, Anthony helps you discover the secrets of the historic village and the heavenly hills. Both are enthusiastic collectors of country artefacts and have filled their listed 15th-century farmhouse with eye-catching things; the cowboy's saddle by the old range echoes Susan's roots. Bedrooms have aged and oiled floorboards, fun florals and bold walls; bathrooms are simple. Walk Offa's Dyke and the Shropshire Way; return to a cosy wood-burner, a warm smile and a delicious dinner. Good value.

Price	From £70. Singles by arrangement.
Rooms	2: 1 double (with extra bunk-bed room); 1 twin/double with separate shower.
Meals	Dinner from £25. Packed lunch £3.50. Pubs/restaurants nearby.
Closed	Occasionally.
Directions	A49 from Ludlow & onto B4368 at Craven Arms, for Clun. In High St on left 0.5 miles from Clun sign.

Anthony & Susan Whitfield
Clun Farm House,
High Street, Clun,
Craven Arms SY7 8JB
Tel   +44 (0)1588 640432
Email   susanwhitfield@talk21.com
Web   www.clunfarmhouse.co.uk

Entry 427   Map 7

Shropshire

Hopton House

Karen looks after her guests with competence and care – she even runs courses on how to do B&B! Relax and enjoy the country views in this fresh, uplifting, converted granary with old beams, high ceilings and a sun-filled dining/sitting room overlooking the hills. Bedrooms are warm and charming, and all have digital radio and good lighting; one has a balcony, another alder wood floors or comfortable sofa. Bathrooms are spoiling: lie back and gaze at the stars from the free-standing bath in the Loft room. Breakfast promises Ludlow sausages, Hopton House hen eggs and homemade jams. Perfect B&B.

Ethical Collection: Environment; Food.
See page 430.

Price	£80–£105. Singles from £60.
Rooms	3 doubles.
Meals	Restaurant 3 miles.
Closed	20-26 December.
Directions	A49 Craven Arms exit, B4368 west. After 1 mile, left signed Hopton Heath. At Hopton Heath x-roads, right over bridge, follow road right. House 2nd on left.

Local food/produce in your room.

Use your Sawday's Gift Card here.

Karen Thorne
Hopton House,
Hopton Heath,
Craven Arms SY7 0QD
Tel   +44 (0)1547 530885
Email   info@shropshirebreakfast.co.uk
Web   www.shropshirebreakfast.co.uk

Entry 428   Map 7

Shropshire

Brick House Farm

From the roadside this looks unexceptional, but once through the gates and into the farmyard with strutting chickens you can see the black and white checked side of this freshly-painted 16th-century longhouse. In the guest sitting room David has kept the walls simple white, restored beams and red tiles, and found a hidden fireplace; warm yourself here on a comfy sofa with a good book. Sleep soundly on smart mattresses, soak in a deep Villeroy & Boch bath, tuck into home-grown lamb for supper at a smart table. The garden seeps into unspoilt countryside with peaceful, grazing horses.

Price	£75.
Rooms	2: 1 double, 1 twin/double, each with separate bath.
Meals	Dinner, 4–5 courses, £25. BYO. Restaurant 4 miles.
Closed	Rarely.
Directions	On A4110, from Leintwardine; house 1st on left, with sandy coloured render, opposite church.

3rd night half price for stays starting on a Sunday.

David Watson
Brick House Farm,
Adforton, Leintwardine,
Craven Arms SY7 0NF
Tel   +44 (0)1568 770870
Email   info@adforton.com
Web   www.adforton.com

Entry 429   Map 7

Shropshire

Upper Buckton

Hayden and Yvonne love their stunning location – which ensures a special stay. Bedrooms are large, with huge beds made to perfection, lovely linen and proper blankets; bathrooms sport robes and treats. Standing in lush gardens that slope peacefully down to millstream, meadows and river, the house has a motte and bailey castle site, a heronry, a point-to-point course and a ha-ha. Yvonne's cooking using local produce is upmarket and creative, Hayden's wine list is a treat – marvellous for walkers returning from a day in the glorious Welsh Borders. *Children by arrangement.*

Price	£84–£100. Singles £57–£65.
Rooms	3: 1 double; 2 twins/doubles each with separate bath.
Meals	Dinner, 4 courses, £30. Pub/restaurant 5 miles.
Closed	Rarely.
Directions	From Ludlow, A49 to Shrewsbury. At Bromfield, A4113. Right in Walford for Buckton, on to 2nd farm on left. Large sign on building.

Guided tour of the heronry when appropriate. 10% off stays of 2 or more nights.

Hayden & Yvonne Lloyd
Upper Buckton,
Leintwardine, Craven Arms,
Ludlow SY7 0JU
Tel   +44 (0)1547 540634
Email   ghlloydco@btconnect.com

Entry 430   Map 7

Shropshire

Lower Buckton Country House

You are spoiled here in house party style; energetic Carolyn – passionate about Slow food – and Henry, are born entertainers. Kick off with homemade cake in the drawing room with its oil paintings, antique furniture and old rugs; return for delicious nibbles when the lamps and wood-burner are flickering. You dine well at a huge oak table (home-reared pork, local cheeses, dreamy puddings) then nestle into the best linen and the softest pillows in your deeply restful bedroom. This is laid-back B&B: play croquet on the lawn, admire stunning views, or just find a quiet spot with a good book. *Cookery courses. Stabling for horses.*

Price	£90.
Rooms	3: 2 doubles; 1 twin/double with separate bath.
Meals	Dinner, 4 courses, £30. BYO wine. Pub/restaurant 4 miles.
Closed	Rarely.
Directions	South through Leintwardine; after 0.25 miles right A4113. At Walford right at x-roads down narrow lane for Buckton. Over river, 2nd house on left, entrance by village green; white gate with postbox in wall.
🧳	Home-grown vegetable goodie bag. Free pick-up from local bus/train station.

Henry & Carolyn Chesshire
Lower Buckton Country House,
Buckton,
Leintwardine SY7 0JU
Tel   +44 (0)1547 540532
Email   carolyn@lowerbuckton.co.uk
Web   www.lowerbuckton.co.uk

Entry 431   Map 7

Shropshire

Walford Court

Come for a break from clock-watching and a spot of fresh air. Large bedrooms delight with the comfiest mattresses on king-size beds, scented candles, books, games and double-end roll top baths – one under a west facing window. Aga-cooked breakfasts include eggs from 'the ladies of the orchard'; candlelit dinners may be served outside on fine evenings. Wander through apple, plum and pear trees, find a motte and bailey, strike out for a long hike. Craig and Debbie are thoughtful and hugely keen on wildlife (you get binoculars) and this is the perfect place to bring a special person – and a bottle of champagne.

Ethical Collection: Environment; Food. See page 430.

Price	£75-£85. Singles £45.
Rooms	3: 1 double; 2 doubles each with sitting room.
Meals	Dinner, 2-3 courses, £15-£25. Packed lunch £6. Lunch in the tea room. Pubs/restaurants 1-3 miles.
Closed	Christmas & Boxing Day.
Directions	A49 N of Ludlow; A4113 to Knighton. Through Leintwardine; right for Walford. There, left for Presteigne, then immed. left. Signs to Walford Court Tea Room.
🧳	Local food/produce in room. Homemade muffins to take away.

Debbie & Craig Fraser
Walford Court,
Walford, Leintwardine,
Ludlow SY7 0JT
Tel   +44 (0)1547 540570
Email   info@romanticbreak.com
Web   www.romanticbreak.com

Entry 432   Map 7

Shropshire

35 Lower Broad Street

You're almost at the bottom of the town, near the river and the bridge. Elaine's terraced Georgian cottage is spotless and cosy; her office doubles as a sitting area for guests with leather armchairs and desk space for workaholics. Upstairs are two good-sized doubles with a country crisp feel, king-size beds and a pretty blue and white bathroom. Walkers, shoppers, antique- and book-hunters can fill up on homemade potato scones, black pudding, organic eggs and good coffee before striding out to explore. This is excellent value B&B: comfortable, clean and can be enjoyed without a car. Perfect for two couples.

Ethical Collection: Food; Community. See page 430.

Price	£70. Singles £45.
Rooms	2 doubles sharing bath & sitting room (let to same party only).
Meals	Pubs/restaurants 100 yds.
Closed	Rarely.
Directions	Right out of railway station, 200 yds to lights. Left onto Corve St, then up to top of hill. At lights, right & follow to Broad St; thro' arch into Lower Broad St. On right towards bottom.

Free pick-up from local train station. Fruit in bedroom.

Use your Sawday's Gift Card here.

	Elaine Downs
	35 Lower Broad Street, Ludlow SY8 1PH
Tel	+44 (0)1584 876912
Email	a.downs@tesco.net
Web	www.ludlowbedandbreakfast.blogspot.com

Entry 433   Map 7

Shropshire

Rosecroft

A pretty, quiet, traditional house with charming owners, well-proportioned rooms and an elegant sitting room. But there's not a trace of pomposity and breakfasts are huge enough to set you up for the day: Pimhill organic muesli, smoked or unsmoked local bacon, black pudding, delicious jams. The garden is a delight to stroll through – in summer you can picnic – and serious walkers are close to the Welsh borders. Bedrooms and bathrooms are polished to perfection, you have fresh flowers, homebaked cakes and biscuits when you arrive, the village has a super pub and Ludlow is five miles away. *Children over 12 welcome.*

Price	£70-£75. Singles £50-£55.
Rooms	2: 1 double; 1 double with separate bath.
Meals	Packed lunch £5. Pub 200 yds.
Closed	Rarely.
Directions	Between Ludlow & Leominster on A49, turn onto B4362 at Woofferton. After 1.5 miles, left into Orleton. Past school & small green, house on right, opp. vicarage.

3 nights for 2, October – 20 March. Free pick-up from local bus/train station.

	Gail Benson
	Rosecroft, Orleton, Ludlow SY8 4HN
Tel	+44 (0)1568 780565
Email	gailanddavid@rosecroftorleton.co.uk
Web	www.stmem.com/rosecroft

Entry 434   Map 7

Shropshire

Timberstone Bed & Breakfast

The house is young, engaging and fun – as are Tracey and Alex. She, once in catering, is a reflexologist and new generation B&Ber. Come for logs in winter, charming bedrooms under the eaves, a double ended or claw-foot bath, chunky beams with a modern feel, pale colours, white cotton... and the Bowen Technique in the garden studio or the relaxing sauna. In the warm guest sitting room – brimming with art – are books, kilims on oak boards, a wood-burner. Eggs come from their hens, breakfasts are special; have an excellent home-cooked supper or head for Ludlow and its clutch of Michelin stars.

Ethical Collection: Environment; Food. See page 430.

Price	£87.50–£100. Singles £45–£70.
Rooms	5: 2 doubles, 1 twin, 1 family. Summerhouse: 1 double (summer only).
Meals	Dinner, 3 courses, £25. Pubs/restaurants 5 miles.
Closed	Rarely.
Directions	B4364 Ludlow-Bridgnorth. After 3 miles, right to Clee Stanton; on for 1.5 miles; left at signpost to Clee Stanton; 1st house on left.

Free local pick-up. Late checkout (12pm).

Use your Sawday's Gift Card here.

	Tracey Baylis & Alex Read
	Timberstone Bed & Breakfast,
	Clee Stanton, Ludlow SY8 3EL
Tel	+44 (0)1584 823519
Email	timberstone1@hotmail.com
Web	www.timberstoneludlow.co.uk

Entry 435   Map 7

Shropshire

Cleeton Court

Rare peace: a tiny lane leads to this part 14th-century farmhouse, immersed in the countryside with views over meadows and heathland. You have your own entrance, and the use of the pretty drawing room, elegantly comfortable with sofas and a log fire. Beamed bedrooms are delightfully furnished, one with a magnificent, chintzy four-poster and a vast bathroom; recline in the cast-iron bath with a glass of wine, gaze on views from the window as you soak. Bring your boots: the walking is superb, and charming Ros gives you a smashing, locally sourced breakfast to get you going. *Children over five welcome.*

Price	From £75. Singles £45–£50.
Rooms	2: 1 twin/double, 1 four-poster.
Meals	Pubs/restaurants 4 miles.
Closed	Christmas & New Year.
Directions	From Ludlow, A4117 for Kidderminster for 1 mile; left on B4364 for Cleobury North; on for 5 miles. In Wheathill, right for Cleeton St Mary; on for 1.5 miles; house on left.

10% off stays of 3 or more nights.

	Rosamond Woodward
	Cleeton Court,
	Cleeton St Mary, Ludlow DY14 0QZ
Tel	+44 (0)1584 823379
Email	roswoodward@talktalk.net
Web	www.cleetoncourt.co.uk

Entry 436   Map 7

Somerset

West Liscombe

Down deep Devon lanes, then up, up, up to the remote farmhouse encircled by footpaths and bridle paths, breezes and green views. Heaven! Inside is comfy, cheery, chintzy and English to the core. Deborah, true country lady and Cordon Bleu cook, was born to do B&B; she runs the Pony Club and welcomes all. The grandfather clock tick-tocks in the sitting room, the silver shines, the log-burner glows, and the guest bedrooms, with books, great beds and posies of flowers, are well-groomed and inviting. Sheep roam the drive, the garden stretches down the valley, Exmoor is 600 yards, the sea is 11 miles.

Price	From £75. Singles £45.
Rooms	2: 1 double; 1 twin with separate bath.
Meals	Lunch £7.50. Dinner £20. Pub 5 miles.
Closed	Rarely.
Directions	In East Anstey village pass school on left; continue 1 mile to Waddicombe, up hill for 50 yds. Postbox in wall, turn right; house 500 yds.

Robert & Deborah Connell
West Liscombe,
Waddicombe,
Dulverton TA22 9RX
Tel   +44 (0)1398 341282
Email deborahconnell@btinternet.com

✗ ⚹

Entry 437   Map 2

Somerset

Emmetts Grange

A superb landscape high on the moor with 900 acres of moorland asking to be discovered – the rugged real deal. This listed country house, at the end of a long drive, is well-loved and lived-in; be greeted by a fox head in the hall and a portrait of an ancestor in wig and ermine. Easy-going, kind Tom and Lucy have boys, dogs, ponies, hens, and raise Red Devon cattle; they are knowledgeable about the area and Lucy is keen on studying the family's genealogy. Bedrooms and bathrooms are large and comfortable with an old-fashioned but bright and colourful feel. Tom is the cook and, not surprisingly, is pretty keen on the local beef.

Price	£80–£120. Singles from £50.
Rooms	4: 2 twins/doubles, 1 twin, 1 four-poster.
Meals	Dinner, 3 courses, £30. Pub 2 miles.
Closed	Christmas, New Year & occasionally.
Directions	M5 exit 27. A361 towards South Molton. 25 miles then right to A399 Ilfracombe. 1 mile, right towards Simonsbath. 6 miles, entrance to Grange on right.

Tom & Lucy Barlow
Emmetts Grange,
Simonsbath, Minehead TA24 7LD
Tel   +44 (0)1643 831138
Email mail@emmettsgrange.co.uk
Web   www.emmettsgrange.co.uk

✗ 📖 📶 🍷 ⚹ 💬

Entry 438   Map 2

Somerset

North Wheddon Farm

Pootle through the vibrant green patchwork of Exmoor National Park and bowl down a pitted track to land in Blyton-esque bliss – a classic Somerset farmyard, crackling with geese and hens, round which is the gentleman farmer's house. Bedrooms are airy and calming with grand views, books, fresh flowers and small, but neat-as-a-pin bathrooms. Bring children and they will be in heaven, with eggs to collect and pigs to pat, or come just for yourself and a bit of indulgence. Food is 'River Cottage' style and much is home reared, the walking is fabulous for miles and kind Rachael sends you off with a thermos of tea.

Price	£75–£80. Singles £38.50.
Rooms	3: 1 double, 1 twin/double; 1 single with separate bath.
Meals	Dinner, 3 courses, £24. Cold/hot packed lunch £7.50–£9.75.
Closed	Rarely.
Directions	From Minehead A396 to Wheddon Cross. Pass pub on right & Moorland Hall on left. North Wheddon is next driveway on right.

| | Rachael Abraham
North Wheddon Farm,
Wheddon Cross TA24 7EX |
|---|---|
| Tel | +44 (0)1643 841791 |
| Email | rachael@go-exmoor.co.uk |
| Web | www.northwheddonfarm.co.uk |

Entry 439   Map 2

Somerset

Glen Lodge

High brick walls and tumbling gardens in the Victorian tanner's house give way to the warm embrace of a wood-burning stove and a giddy rush of intriguing artwork – one painting is by an elephant! Polished oak floors are dotted with oriental rugs, bedrooms are immaculate, bay windows gaze on the Bristol Channel. Meryl and David care about sustainable living – feast on American home baking and fruit from their 21 acres: all is recycled, composted and enjoyed. Surrounded by the woods and wilds of Exmoor National Park yet a short stroll from popular Porlock, you'll revel in comfort, warmth and their passion for life.

Price	£80. Singles £55.
Rooms	5: 1 double; 2 doubles sharing bath; 1 double, 1 twin each with separate bath.
Meals	Packed lunch £8. Dinner £28. Pub/restaurant 0.5 miles.
Closed	Christmas & New Year.
Directions	From Minehead, A39 to Porlock; on entering town, left at church into Parsons Street 0.5 miles up. At 'weak bridge' sign, left over bridge. Gate to house in front.
	20% off stays Mon–Thurs. Free pick-up from local bus/train station.

| | Meryl Salter
Glen Lodge,
Hawkcombe, Porlock TA24 8LN |
|---|---|
| Tel | +44 (0)1643 863371 |
| Email | glenlodge@gmail.com |
| Web | www.glenlodge.net |

Entry 440   Map 2

Somerset

Higher Orchard

A little lane tumbles down to the centre of lovely old Dunster. The village is a two minute-walk yet here you have open views of fields, sheep and sea. Exmoor footpaths start behind the house and Janet encourages explorers, by bike or on foot; ever helpful and kind, she is a local who knows the patch well. The 1860s house keeps its Victorian features, bedrooms are quiet and simple and the double has a view to Blue Anchor Bay and Dunster castle and church. All is homely, with stripped pine, cream curtains, fresh flowers, garden fruit and home-laid eggs for breakfast. *Children & pets by arrangement.*

Ethical Collection: Environment; Food. See page 430.

Price	£70. Singles from £35.
Rooms	3: 1 double, 2 twins/doubles.
Meals	Packed lunch from £3.50. Restaurants 2-minute walk.
Closed	Christmas.
Directions	From Williton, A39 for Minehead for 8 miles. Left to Dunster. There, right fork into 'The Ball'. At T-junc. at end of road, right. House 75 yds on right.

10% off stays Mon-Fri. Lifts to walking start points. Free pick-up.

Janet Lamacraft
Higher Orchard,
30 St George's Street,
Dunster TA24 6RS
Tel   +44 (0)1643 821915
Email   lamacraft@higherorchard.fsnet.co.uk
Web   www.higherorchard-dunster.co.uk

Entry 441   Map 2

Somerset

The Old Priory

The 12th-century priory leans against its church, has a rustic gate, a walled garden, a tumble of flowers. Both house and hostess are dignified, unpretentious and friendly. Here are old oak tables, flagstones, panelled doors, higgledy-piggledy corridors and large bedrooms in the softest colours. But a perfect English house in a sweet Somerset village needs a touch of pepper and relaxed, cosmopolitan Jane adds her own special flair with artistic touches here and there, and books and dogs for company. Dunster Castle towers above on the hill, walks start from the door.

Ethical Collection: Food. See page 430.

Price	£85-£90. Singles by arrangement.
Rooms	3: 1 twin, 1 four-poster; 1 double with separate shower.
Meals	Restaurants/pubs 5-minute walk.
Closed	Christmas.
Directions	From A39 into Dunster, right at blue sign 'Unsuitable for Goods Vehicles'. Follow until church; house adjoined.

Free pick-up from Dunster station. Jar of Exmoor honey & free-range eggs (when available).

Jane Forshaw
The Old Priory,
Priory Green,
Dunster TA24 6RY
Tel   +44 (0)1643 821540
Web   www.theoldpriory-dunster.co.uk

Entry 442   Map 2

Somerset

Wyndham House

A charming Georgian house tucked away in the unspoilt town of Watchet, with its interesting little shops. Susan and Roger will greet you with homemade cake and biscuits, either in their pretty dining room – or in the unexpectedly large and beautiful garden, which overlooks the harbour and small marina. Bedrooms are comfortable and traditional, one overlooking the pretty courtyard and the other with views to Wales. Delicious breakfasts are relaxed affairs accompanied by newspapers; walk it all off in the delightful Quantocks or Exmoor National Park – you are near to both. *Children & dogs by arrangement.*

Ethical Collection: Food.
See page 430.

Price	From £80. Singles from £40.
Rooms	2: 1 twin/double; 1 double with separate shower/bath.
Meals	Pubs/restaurants a short walk.
Closed	Christmas.
Directions	From railway station & footbridge in Watchet, up South Rd (for Doniford). After 50 yds, left into Beverly Drive. House 50 yds on left with gravel parking area.

 10% off room rate. Homemade biscuits & flowers in room.

Susan & Roger Vincent
Wyndham House,
4 Sea View Terrace,
Watchet TA23 0DF
Tel   +44 (0)1984 631881
Email   info@wyndhamhousebb.co.uk
Web   www.wyndhamhousebb.co.uk

Entry 443   Map 2

Somerset

Rock House

Tucked away in an AONB, near the Quantocks and Exmoor, this elegant Georgian house hides behind a tall hedge in a sleepy village. Deborah greets her guests with impeccable manners and scrumptious biscuits; take tea in the drawing room where fresh flowers are beautifully arranged and there are books to read. Bedrooms are well-presented and full of thoughtful touches like fresh milk and a torch; bathrooms have generous towels and Molton Brown lotions. The Rock House fry-up will set you up for miles of walking, or a quick stroll to the top of the pretty garden with its croquet lawn. *Children & pets by arrangement.*

Price	From £80. Singles from £50.
Rooms	2: 1 twin/double; 1 double (extra single bed) with separate bath.
Meals	Pub 100 yds.
Closed	Christmas.
Directions	M5 exit 25, signs to A358 Minehead. Left to Halse. Rock House in middle of village, near pub.

3 nights for the price of 2. 10% off room rate.

Christopher & Deborah Wolverson
Rock House,
Halse,
Taunton TA4 3AF
Tel   +44 (0)1823 432956
Email   dwolverson@rockhousesomerset.co.uk
Web   www.rockhousesomerset.co.uk

Entry 444   Map 2

Somerset

Causeway Cottage

Robert and Lesley are ex-restaurateurs, so guests heap praise on their food, most of which is sourced from a local butcher and fishmonger; charming Lesley is an author, runs cookery courses and once taught at Prue Leith's. This is the perfect, pretty Somerset cottage, with an apple orchard and views to the church across a cottage garden and a field. The bedrooms are light, restful and have a country-style simplicity with their green check bedspreads, white walls and antique pine furniture; guests have their own comfortable sitting room. Easy access to the M5 yet with a rural feel. Very special. *Children over ten welcome.*

Price	£75. Singles by arrangement.
Rooms	3: 1 double, 2 twins.
Meals	Supper from £25. Pub/restaurant 0.75 miles.
Closed	Christmas.
Directions	From M5 junc. 26, West Buckland road for 0.75 miles. 1st left just before stone building. Bear right; 3rd house at end of lane, below church.

Lesley & Robert Orr
Causeway Cottage,
West Buckland,
Taunton TA21 9JZ
Tel   +44 (0)1823 663458
Email causewaybb@talktalk.net
Web   www.causewaycottage.co.uk

Entry 445   Map 2

Somerset

Frog Street Farm House

Through a pastoral landscape, past green paddocks and handsome horses, to a beautiful Somerset longhouse in 130 acres of land. Its heart dates from 1436 and its renovation is remarkable. Louise, who grew up here, and David, brimful of enthusiasm for house and guests, give you three exquisite bedrooms in French country style, and bathrooms romantic and new. Louise will happily chef every night and can host small house parties with ease; much produce comes from the farm and food is one of her passions. Set off on a gorgeous riverside trail, return to great leather sofas and a wood-burning stove. What value!

Price	From £80. Singles from £60. Suite from £130.
Rooms	3: 2 doubles, 1 family suite for 4.
Meals	Dinner, 3 courses, £25. Pubs within 2.5 miles.
Closed	Rarely.
Directions	A358 to Illminster. 1st exit to Hatch Beauchamp. At Hatch Inn left into Station Rd. Left after 0.5 mile; over humpback bridge, Frog St Farm in front.

Bottle of local Somerset cider with dinner on first night.

Louise Farrance
Frog Street Farm House,
Hatch Beauchamp,
Taunton TA3 6AF
Tel   +44 (0)1823 481883
Email frogstreet@hotmail.com
Web   www.frogstreet.co.uk

Entry 446   Map 2

Somerset

Bashfords Farmhouse

A feeling of warmth and happiness pervades the exquisite 17th-century farmhouse in the Quantock hills. The Ritchies love doing B&B even after 15 years, and there's a homely feel with splashes of style – well-framed prints, good fabrics, comfortable sofas. Rooms are pretty, fresh and large and look over the cobbled courtyard or open fields; the sitting room has an inglenook, sofas and books. Charles and Jane couldn't be nicer, know about local walks (the Macmillan Way runs past the door) and love to cook: local meat and game, tarte tatin, homemade bread and jams. A delightful garden rambles up the hill.

Price	£65–£70. Singles £37.50–£40.
Rooms	3: 1 double; 1 double with separate shower; 1 twin with separate bath.
Meals	Dinner £27.50. Supper £22.50. Pub 75 yds.
Closed	Rarely.
Directions	M5 junc. 25. A358 for Minehead. Leave A358 at West Bagborough turning. Thro' village for 1.5 miles. Farmhouse 3rd on left past pub.

Charles & Jane Ritchie
Bashfords Farmhouse,
West Bagborough,
Taunton TA4 3EF

Tel	+44 (0)1823 432015
Email	info@bashfordsfarmhouse.co.uk
Web	www.bashfordsfarmhouse.co.uk

Entry 447   Map 2

Somerset

Parsonage Farm

Breakfast beside the open fire is a feast: homemade bread and jam, eggs from the hens, juices from the orchard, pancakes and porridge from the Aga. This is an organic smallholding and your enthusiastic hosts have added an easy comfort to their 17th-century rectory farmhouse – quarry floors, log fires, books, maps and piano in the cosy sitting room. Suki, from Vermont, has turned a stable into a studio, and her pots and paintings add charm to the décor. Big bedrooms have fresh flowers and tranquil views. Wonderful walking and cycling in the Quantock Hills, and the new Coleridge Way starts down the lane. *Over twos welcome.*

Ethical Collection: Environment; Food; Community. See page 430.

Price	£60–£80. Singles £45–£60.
Rooms	3: 1 double (extra sofabed), 1 twin/double (extra sofabed); 1 double sharing bath.
Meals	Supper £10. Dinner, 2-3 courses, £20–£25. Pub/restaurant 2 miles.
Closed	Christmas.
Directions	A39 Bridgwater-Minehead. 7 miles on, left at Cottage Inn for Over Stowey; 1.8 miles; house on right after church.

Susan Lilienthal
Parsonage Farm,
Over Stowey,
Nether Stowey TA5 1HA

Tel	+44 (0)1278 733237
Email	suki@parsonfarm.co.uk
Web	www.parsonfarm.co.uk

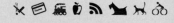

Entry 448   Map 2

Somerset

The Old House

Coleridge is said to have stayed here, and been inspired by the walks; but if the muse fails to strike you, bedrooms are in a private wing and elegant comforts abound. The enormous Coleridge Suite has a sofa, good books, an open fire, views to the beautiful garden and a sleigh bed; nip across your own landing to the bathroom, freshly decorated in blue and white. Sarah's Room is feminine, pink and pretty with white armchairs. Amiable Manor serves breakfast in the dining room or garden: soft fruits, full English, or smoked salmon and scrambled eggs. The quiet village has a bistro and bracing walks are in every direction.

Price	£75-£85. Singles from £60.
Rooms	2: 1 twin/double; 1 suite with separate bath.
Meals	Pub/bistro 50 yds.
Closed	Rarely.
Directions	M5, Bridgwater junc.; follow A39 towards Minehead 8 miles. Left into Nether Stowey; after 300 yds right into courtyard of house.

Ann Scourfield
The Old House,
Nether Stowey TA5 1LJ
Tel   +44 (0)1278 732392
Email   scourfieldfam@yahoo.co.uk
Web   www.theoldhouse-quantocks.co.uk

Entry 449   Map 2

Somerset

Church House

Feel happy in this warm Georgian rectory with sweeping views over gardens, seaside homes and the dramatic Bristol channel. Tony and Jane are great fun, enormously generous and love what they do. Bedrooms are large, pristine and indulgent with goose down duvets as soft as a cloud, swish modern bathrooms, huge towels and thoughtful extras like fluffy hot water bottles and scrumptious biscuits. Breakfasts are a grand feast of eggs from their hens, organic sausages and homemade preserves, all served on delightful china at a long mahogany table. Take the whole house and be cosseted – great for large gatherings.

Price	From £80. Singles from £60.
Rooms	5: 4 doubles, 1 twin.
Meals	Pubs 400 yds.
Closed	Rarely.
Directions	M5 junc. 21, follow signs for Kewstoke. After Old Manor Inn on right, left up Anson Rd. At T-junc. right into Kewstoke Rd. On for 1 mile; church on right; drive between church & church hall.

10% off room rate Mon-Thurs. Free pick-up from local bus/train station.

Jane & Tony Chapman
Church House,
27 Kewstoke Road, Kewstoke,
Weston-super-Mare BS22 9YD
Tel   +44 (0)1934 633185
Email   churchhouse@kewstoke.net
Web   www.churchhousekewstoke.co.uk

Entry 450   Map 2

Somerset

Rolstone Court Barn

A converted Victorian grainstore, full of light, good family furniture, portraits and interesting finds. It's down a narrow lane on the Somerset Levels – fabulous walking country, with rabbits on the lawn and a productive potager. Two prettily decorated bedrooms are under the eaves, the other on the first floor, there's a lovely sitting room with open fire and a smart dining room for delicious breakfasts of organic bacon and sausages. Kathlyn, who extends her welcome to children and dogs, will collect from or deliver to Bristol airport, thus saving you airport parking. An attractive stopover for the Cornwall route.

Ethical Collection: Environment; Food. See page 430.

Price	£75. Singles £45.
Rooms	3: 1 double; 1 double, 1 family room sharing bath/shower.
Meals	Pubs/restaurants 4 miles.
Closed	Rarely.
Directions	M5 junc. 21; north onto A370 towards Bristol. Take 2nd right to Rolstone, then 1st left into Balls Barn Lane. House 3rd & last.

10% off stays of 2 or more nights. Free pick-up from local bus/train station.

	Kathlyn Read
	Rolstone Court Barn,
	Rolstone, Hewish,
	Weston-super-Mare BS24 6UP
Tel	+44 (0)1934 820129
Email	read@rolstone-court.co.uk
Web	www.rolstone-court.co.uk

Entry 451   Map 3

Somerset

Burrington Farm

Can this really be ten minutes from Bristol airport? High in the Mendips, it is blissfully quiet and rural, with fabulous views. A narrow lane takes you to Ros and Barry's 15th-century longhouse – and the kindest of welcomes. Inside are rugs and flagstones, books, paintings and fine old furniture. Guests have a cosy low-beamed snug and bedrooms are charming; you'll need to be nimble to negotiate ancient steps and stairs. For those who prefer a bit more privacy there's a lovely family room in a separate green oak barn – stunningly converted. The garden is enchanting and you are free to roam. *Airport pick-up offered.*

Price	£75–£110.
Rooms	4: 1 double, 1 family; 2 doubles sharing bath (let to same party only).
Meals	Pub 5-minute walk.
Closed	Christmas.
Directions	A368 Bath-Weston-super-Mare, between Blagdon and Churchill. Take Burrington village sign, on to square with school on right. House 4th on left after Parish Rooms, immed. after Stable Cottage.

Pick-up from airport & Yatton station. 10% off stays of 2+ nights.

Use your Sawday's Gift Card here.

	Barry & Ros Smith
	Burrington Farm,
	Burrington BS40 7AD
Tel	+44 (0)1761 462127
Email	bookings@bedandburrington.co.uk
Web	www.bedandburrington.co.uk

Entry 452   Map 3

Somerset

Barton Drove Cottage

Come for the views – on a clear day you can see the Black Mountains. The pretty cottage extension is tucked into the hill so the first-floor drawing room opens directly to the terrace. All is polished and spotless inside: pretty bedrooms have patterned rugs on soft carpets, goose down and crisp linen, fresh flowers, gleaming bathrooms and a loo with a view. Charming, child-friendly, Sarah gives you bacon and sausages from Mendip piggies, eggs from her hens, soft fruit from the garden and maybe pheasant casserole for supper. Roe deer in the field, primroses in the woods, wonderful walking on Wavering Down.

Ethical Collection: Food. See page 430.

Price	£70. Singles £35.
Rooms	2: 1 double; 1 twin with separate bath.
Meals	Dinner from £17.50. Packed lunch £5. Pub 1 mile.
Closed	Rarely.
Directions	From A38 0.5 miles up Winscombe Hill. When road begins to descend, left between houses onto unmade track. Cottage 100 yds on the left.

10% off room rate Mon-Thurs. 3-course dinner for the price of 2 courses.

	Sarah Gunn
	Barton Drove Cottage,
	Winscombe Hill,
	Winscombe BS25 1DJ
Tel	+44 (0)1934 842373
Email	sarahgunn2000@hotmail.com
Web	www.bartondrovecottage.com

Entry 453   Map 3

Somerset

Harptree Court

Linda has softened this rambling 1790 house and imbued it with an upbeat elegance. The rooms are sunny and sparkling with beds and windows dressed in delicate fabrics in perfect contrast to solid antique pieces. On one side of the soaring Georgian windows, 17 acres of parkland with ponds, an ancient bridge and carpets of spring flowers; on the other, the log-fired guest sitting room and extravagant bedrooms. An excellent breakfast sets you up to walk the grounds. One condition of Linda's moving to her husband Charles' family home was that she should be warm! She is, and you will be, too. Relaxing and easy.

Ethical Collection: Food; Community. See page 430.

Price	£95-£120.
Rooms	4: 3 doubles, 1 twin/double.
Meals	Dinner, 2-3 courses, £20-£25. Pub 300 yds.
Closed	Rarely.
Directions	Turn off A368 onto B3114 towards Chewton Mendip. After approx. 0.5 miles, right into drive entrance, straight after 1st x-roads. Left at top of drive.

Free airport parking and pick-up from airport.

	Linda Hill
	Harptree Court,
	East Harptree,
	Bristol BS40 6AA
Tel	+44 (0)1761 221729
Email	bandb@harptreecourt.co.uk
Web	www.harptreecourt.co.uk

Entry 454   Map 3

Somerset

The Tithe Barn

You are in a quiet, well-kept village surrounded by softly rolling hills, but the joys of Bath and Bristol are a short drive away. Down a narrow lane with lawns and orchard on either side, find Stephen and Pauline's pinky-red stone 15th-century tithe barn. You have your own cosy, rather old-fashioned sitting room with a wood-burning stove and a spiral staircase leading to a gallery and upstairs bedrooms, the twin a bit smaller, with views over the lovely garden and one bathroom with a jacuzzi. You breakfast well in the conservatory: smoked salmon, local sausages, home-laid eggs, delicious homemade jams and honey from the garden.

Ethical Collection: Food; Community. See page 430.

Price	£70–£100. Singles £70–£90.
Rooms	3: 2 doubles; 1 twin with separate bath.
Meals	Pubs/restaurants 2 miles.
Closed	Never.
Directions	From Chew Magna on B3130, right after about 2 miles at little white cottage in middle of road. Right in village to Sandy Lane. House 200 yds on right.

10% off room rate Mon–Thurs. Free grazing if you bring your horse on holiday.

Stephen & Pauline Croucher
The Tithe Barn,
Sandy Lane, Stanton Drew,
Bristol BS39 4EL
Tel +44 (0)1275 331887
Email stephen.jcroucher@btinternet.com
Web www.thetithebarnsomerset.co.uk

Entry 455 Map 3

Somerset

numbertwelve

Simple pleasures: after a day exploring England's smallest city or the Mendip Hills, return to tea on the balcony and sunlight glinting on Wells Cathedral. Cathy's family house is spacious, secluded, fantastically located, with a private guest wing. Settle on huge sofas around the sitting room fire; snuggle in new king beds; awaken to Cathedral bells, a south-facing view over the lovely walled garden and kedgeree or corned beef hash. Cathy's art studio is next door and she'll help connect you to the local community: tiny Wells – a five-minute walk – bustles with markets, music, art and life.

Price	£80–£95. Singles £60–£75.
Rooms	2 doubles.
Meals	Pub 0.25 miles. Restaurant 0.5 miles.
Closed	Rarely.
Directions	From Bristol A39, 1st left into College Rd. Round into North Rd, house 150 yds on left. Train station 20-minute drive, bus station 15-minute walk.

Cathy Charles
numbertwelve,
12 North Road,
Wells BA5 2TJ
Tel +44 (0)1749 679406
Email stay@numbertwelve.info
Web www.numbertwelve.info

Entry 456 Map 3

Beryl

A lofty, mullioned, low-windowed home – yet light, bright and devoid of Victorian gloom. Every bedroom has a talking point… an extravagantly draped four-poster here, a vintage cot there, an original bath clad in mahogany reached by a tiny private stair. The flowery rooms in the attic have a 'gothic revival' feel, thanks to arched doorways. Holly, her daughter and her devoted staff serve delicious breakfasts in the sunny dining room, and drinks in the richly elegant drawing room. The old walled garden is full of flowers, roses, ancient figs and espaliered apples: the wonders of Wells lie just below.

Price	£75-£130.
Rooms	11: 3 doubles, 2 twins, 1 twin/double, 2 four-posters, 2 family rooms (1 with four-poster); 1 double with separate shower. Kitchenette.
Meals	Pubs/restaurants within 1 mile.
Closed	Christmas.
Directions	From Wells B3139 for Radstock. Follow signs to Horringtons; after church left into Hawkers Lane, next to bus pull in. At top of lane, past Beryl sign; 500 yds to main gate.

	Holly Nowell
	Beryl,
	Wells BA5 3JP
Tel	+44 (0)1749 678738
Email	stay@beryl-wells.co.uk
Web	www.beryl-wells.co.uk

Entry 457   Map 3

Stoberry House

Super swish B&B in this old coach house surrounded by 26 acres of parkland, but within walking distance of Wells: Frances has thought of everything to soothe you: bedrooms are sumptuous and spoiling – all differently styled, and most are in the main house, but there's one little love nest in a cottage; bathrooms are vamped up and spacious. Breakfast is enormous: fresh fruit, porridge, boiled eggs with soldiers, prunes and berries, ham and salami, pancakes with grilled bacon, whatever you desire. Work it off with a stroll around the gorgeous gardens, and return to a choice of sitting rooms – one 40-foot long.

Ethical Collection: Community. See page 430.

Price	£70-£100. Singles £60-£80.
Rooms	3: 2 doubles, 1 twin/double.
Meals	Dinner, 2-3 courses, £20-£25. Pubs/restaurants 0.5 miles.
Closed	Rarely.
Directions	A39 from Bristol, enter Wells, left into College Rd. Immediately left into Stoberry Park, follow track to Stoberry House at top of park.

A basket of Stoberry homemade goodies to take home.

Use your Sawday's Gift Card here.

	Frances Young
	Stoberry House,
	Stoberry Park,
	Wells BA5 3LD
Tel	+44 (0)1749 672906
Email	stay@stoberry-park.co.uk
Web	www.stoberry-park.co.uk

Entry 458   Map 3

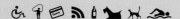

Somerset

Hillview Cottage

Don't tell too many of your friends about this place! It's an unpretentious ex-quarryman's cottage presided over by Catherine, a warm-spirited and cultured host who makes fresh coffee, tells you about the area and can even show you around Wells Cathedral (she's an official guide). This is a comfy tea-and-cakes family home with rugs on wooden floors, antique quilts, an old Welsh dresser and elevated views. The bedrooms have a French feel, the bathroom has an armchair for chatting, and there's a friendly sitting room with an open fire. Glorious walks and excellent value. *Self-catering in Garden Studio.*

Somerset

Manor Farm

Hens, ducks and geese stroll around the pond and the peace is supreme. And there's a magical view of the cathedral: you can walk to Wells across the fields. Ros is a geologist and keen walker, who looks after guests with immense kindness and is happy for folk to linger. The house is ancient and much loved (massive low beams, creaking floorboards), packed with books, pictures and a comfy mishmash of furniture; a log fire fills an inglenook in winter and the suite opens to a walled garden, illuminated at night. Water comes from the spring, breakfast can be a different treat each day – in the lovely warm conservatory in summer. Bliss.

Price	From £70. Singles from £35.
Rooms	2: 1 twin/double, 1 twin sharing bath (2nd room let to same party only).
Meals	Pubs 5-minute walk.
Closed	Rarely.
Directions	From Wells A371 to middle of Croscombe. Right at red phone box & then immed. right into lane. House up on left after 0.25 miles. Straight ahead into signed drive.

Escorted walks. Tour of Wells Cathedral or Wells Bishop's Palace. Late checkout (12pm).

Michael & Catherine Hay
Hillview Cottage,
Paradise Lane, Croscombe,
Wells BA5 3RN
Tel +44 (0)1749 343526
Mobile +44 (0)7801 666146
Email cathyhay@yahoo.co.uk

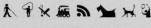

Entry 459   Map 3

Price	£70-£90. Singles from £40.
Rooms	4: 2 doubles; 1 twin/double with separate bath & shower; 1 suite & sitting room.
Meals	Packed lunch & light meals from £5. Pubs/restaurants 1 mile.
Closed	Rarely.
Directions	From Wells, A371 for Shepton Mallet for 1 mile; left onto B3139. In Dulcote, left at stone fountain. House on right after Manor Barn.

Free pick-up from local bus/train station. 10% off stays of 4+ nights.

Use your Sawday's Gift Card here.

Rosalind Bufton
Manor Farm,
Dulcote,
Wells BA5 3PZ
Tel +44 (0)1749 672125
Email rosalind.bufton@talktalk.net
Web www.wells-accommodation.co.uk

Entry 460   Map 3

Somerset

The Coach House

Take a glass of wine to your private courtyard and absorb the peace; or picnic in the lush gardens. In the hamlet of Dulcote, a mile from Wells, is a converted coach house flooded with light, full of character and with the latest mod cons. Downstairs, a black and white zebra theme plays; upstairs (white walls, snowy duvets, soft carpets, high beams) has views that reach to the Mendips. And then there's Karen, full of ideas for your stay, who leaves delicious goodies in your fridge so you can breakfast in your jim-jams. For romantic couples or a girls' weekend, this is B&B at its most luxurious – and so private!

Price	£95.
Rooms	2: 1 double, 1 twin & sitting room, sofabeds, kitchen, shower. (Let to same party only.)
Meals	Pubs within 2 miles.
Closed	Never.
Directions	Directions on booking.

Karen Smallwood
The Coach House,
Little Fountains, Dulcote,
Wells BA5 3NU

Tel	+44 (0)1749 678777
Email	stay@littlefountains.co.uk
Web	www.littlefountains.co.uk

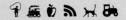

Entry 461   Map 3

Somerset

Claveys Farm

For the artistic seeker of inspiration, not those who thrill to standardised luxury. Fleur is a talented artist, Francis works for English Heritage, both have a passion for art, gardening and lively conversation. Rugs are time-worn, panelling and walls are distempered with natural pigment, bedrooms are better than simple, bathrooms old. From the Aga-warm kitchen of this historic farmhouse come eggs from the hens, oak-smoked bacon from Fleur's rare-breed pigs and homemade bread and jams. Acres of fields, footpaths and woodland for long walks, and a garden for children to adore. Bring your woolly jumpers!

Ethical Collection: Food. See page 430.

Price	£70. Singles £50.
Rooms	2: 1 double/family; 1 twin sharing separate bath.
Meals	Dinner, 3 courses, £25. BYO. Packed lunch £7. Pub in village.
Closed	Rarely.
Directions	At Mells Green on Leigh on Mendip road SW from Mells (NGR ST718452). Past red phone box; house last on right before speed de-restriction signs. If lost, Mells PO, by village pond, has map outside.

Fleur & Francis Kelly
Claveys Farm,
Mells,
Frome BA11 3QP

Tel	+44 (0)1373 814651
Mobile	+44 (0)7968 055398
Email	bandb@fleurkelly.com

Entry 462   Map 3

Somerset

Broadgrove House

Down a long, private lane with views towards Alfred's Tower and Longleat, tranquillity: a 17th-century stone house with a walled cottage garden. Inside is just as special. Beams, flagstones and inglenook fireplaces have been sensitively restored; rugs, pictures, comfy sofas and polished antiques add warmth and serenity. The twin, at the end of the house, has its own sitting room. Breakfast on homemade and farmers' market produce before exploring Stourhead, Wells, Longleat. Sarah, engaging, well-travelled and a great cook, looks after guests and horses with enthusiasm. *Shooting available. Children by arrangement.*

Price	From £80. Singles £50.
Rooms	2: 1 twin & sitting room; 1 double with separate bath.
Meals	Pub/restaurant 1 mile.
Closed	Christmas.
Directions	Directions on booking.

10% off room rate Mon-Thurs.

Sarah Voller
Broadgrove House,
Leighton,
Frome BA11 4PP
Tel +44 (0)1373 836296
Email broadgrove836@tiscali.co.uk
Web www.broadgrovehouse.co.uk

Entry 463   Map 3

Somerset

The Cyder Barn

Somerset cider was once pressed in this cute stone barn – now hugged by honeysuckle. Its beamed cathedral ceiling and new windows enclose a bijou studio for two. Pure pizzazz: spot-lit stone walls, dashing pinks, browns and terracottas on a king-size bed overhung by striped kilims, a swish wet room, and a gravel terrace and table in mature gardens alive with birds and bright colours. Step over to the main farmhouse for breakfast among art and antiques (for dinner, a good restaurant is opposite). Roger will relate the area's history and Jackie can show you her jewellery studio; both are happy, humorous and relaxed.

Price	£80.
Rooms	Barn: 1 twin/double.
Meals	Restaurant opposite.
Closed	Rarely.
Directions	Cottage & barn on Frome-Whatley road: 2nd house on right, past Whatley Village sign.

Free pick-up from local bus/train station.

Jackie Truman
The Cyder Barn,
Park Farm Cottage, Whatley,
Frome BA11 3JU
Tel +44 (0)1373 836703
Mobile +44 (0)7721 579814
Email rwtrumanstamps.jtruman@virgin.net

Entry 464   Map 3

Somerset

Burnt House Farm

Lovers of modern art, clean lines, pale wood and clever lighting will be thrilled, and nature lovers – you are in a deeply rural valley with no roads, and acres of ancient woodland to explore. David, an architect, and charming Elizabeth have transformed their farmhouse into a cool, clean space: tea and cake when you arrive, relaxed breakfasts in a light, slate-floored room with an ash table and contemporary fireplace, big bedrooms with fabulous views in the softest creams, thick mattresses, squishy pillows and a gleaming new bathroom or shower. This feels remote but you are near to Bath, Wells and mystical Glastonbury.

Price	£60–£80. £110 family.
Rooms	3: 1 twin/double; 1 double, 1 twin sharing bath (let to same party only).
Meals	Pub/restaurant 2 miles.
Closed	Christmas & Boxing Day.
Directions	From Bristol A37 to Shepton Mallet and Yeovil until after Gurney Slade. Down hill, then right at chevron posts. Right at Fern Cottage to Burnt House Farm.

10% off room rate Mon-Thurs.

David & Elizabeth Parry
Burnt House Farm,
Burnthouse Drove, Windsor Hill,
Shepton Mallet BA4 4JQ
Tel   +44 (0)1749 840185
Email stay@burnthousedrove.co.uk
Web   www.burnthousedrove.co.uk

Entry 465   Map 3

Somerset

Maplestone

You are in the oldest part of Shepton Mallet, with narrow lanes, tiny cottages and the Babycham factory. Through a charming, walled cottage garden, with views over parkland, find a thick front door and cheerful Donald and Gillian: guests have one end of the weaver's cottages (one bedroom has a separate entrance and its own sitting room) so the feel is private. White walls, pale colours, lovely paintings by Gillian and an eclectic mix of styles give a quirky feel; bedrooms are deeply comfortable and very quiet. Breakfast on local sausages and eggs from Wells' market, explore the town or don your boots. Marvellous.

Price	£70–£80. Singles £55.
Rooms	3: 1 double, 1 twin/double. Cottage annexe: 1 double & sitting room/kitchenette.
Meals	Pubs/restaurants within walking distance.
Closed	Christmas.
Directions	From Bristol A37. In Shepton Mallet, right before Gaymer's Cider down Garston St. At bottom, right up Quarr. House 100 yds on left.

Donald & Gillian Sinclair
Maplestone,
Quarr,
Shepton Mallet BA4 5NP
Tel   +44 (0)1749 347979
Email info@maplestonehall.co.uk
Web   www.maplestonehall.co.uk

Entry 466   Map 3

Somerset

Chalice Hill House

You can see St John's spire poking out over the treetops: vibrant Glastonbury buzzes just below. Fay's contemporary artistic flair mingles naturally with the classical frame of this Georgian house, where grand mirrors, wooden floors, gentle colours and loads of books create an interesting feel. The bedrooms are enchanting, not at all understated: carved oak Slavic sleigh beds, embroidered Indian cotton bedspreads and views of the dovecote, wedding cake tree and Chalice Hill beyond. Weekend breakfasts are leisurely, served with panache (and optional chilli jam!). Exotic, comfortable elegance, a beautiful garden and a lovely hostess.

Price	£100. Singles £75.
Rooms	3: 2 doubles, 1 twin with shower.
Meals	Pubs/restaurants 5-minute walk.
Closed	Rarely.
Directions	From top of Glastonbury High Street, right; 2nd left into Dod Lane. Past Chalice Hill Close; right into driveway.

Fay Hutchcroft
Chalice Hill House,
Dod Lane,
Glastonbury BA6 8BZ
Tel   +44 (0)1458 830828
Email mail@chalicehill.co.uk
Web   www.chalicehill.co.uk

Entry 467   Map 3

Somerset

Westbrook House

David is an interior designer; Keith does gardens – hence this blend of good taste and style in a revamped 1870s house with generous, well-tended grounds. Wander through a young orchard, spot unusual plants, sit on stone benches or a sunny patio; a wildlife meadow contrasts with clipped lawns. Inside, every object has a story (your hosts are full of smiles and stories too): tapestries from India, a mirrored cabinet from an officer's mess, ornate brass lanterns. Light floods into the dining room as you breakfast on local treats – all the while absorbing the peace of this tranquil hamlet, where cows amble calmly down the lane.

Price	From £85. Singles £60.
Rooms	3: 1 double, 1 twin; 1 double with separate bath (let to same party only).
Meals	Dinner £25. Pub/restaurant 4 miles.
Closed	Rarely.
Directions	From Glastonbury A361 to Shepton Mallet. After 2 miles, right for W. Bradley. Signed for W. Bradley; at fork in road, right for Baltonsborough. House on left.

Keith Anderson & David Mendel
Westbrook House,
West Bradley,
Glastonbury BA6 8LS
Tel   +44 (0)1458 850604
Email mail@westbrook-bed-breakfast.co.uk
Web   www.westbrook-bed-breakfast.co.uk

Entry 468   Map 3

Somerset

Chindit House

Inside this light and elegant Edwardian mansion you will find fine architectural features, charming furniture, fresh flowers, vibrant paintings and compelling sculptures. There are long views over garden and town from the large, light sitting room; bedrooms have spoilingly serious mattresses, good art, thick curtains and sleek, contemporary bathrooms. Breakfast is enormous and locally sourced, cakes are homemade. Peter, a sculptor, and Felicity, an art consultant, are easy going and fun. You are a short hop from the town with its lively mix of exotic shops and colourful characters.

Price	£100-£125. Singles £70-£85.
Rooms	4: 2 doubles; 2 singles with shared bath (let to same party only).
Meals	Pubs/restaurants 500 yds.
Closed	Never.
Directions	In the centre of Glastonbury. Left at top of High Street on to Wells Road. House is about 200 yds along on left - just before corner with St Edmunds Road.

10% off room rate Mon-Thurs. Bottle of wine in your room. Late checkout (12pm).

Peter Smith & Felicity Wright
Chindit House,
23 Wells Road,
Glastonbury BA6 9DN
Tel +44 (0)1458 830404
Email enquiries@chindit-house.co.uk
Web www.chindit-house.co.uk

Entry 469 Map 3

Somerset

Church Cottage

Partly clothed in English garden and with views to the church, this 400-year-old cottage has wooden beams, low ceilings and wonky walls. Ignore the modern house on the other side of the road and restore your senses with blue lias flagstones, neutral colours, soft cushions, a flash of Thompson gazelle skin, the whiff of woodsmoke and floppy roses on a scrubbed table. Caroline is artistic and rustles up a fine breakfast in her calm kitchen. Bedrooms are small and simple – pine furniture, cool colours; the Potting Shed is a private, generous nest for two. Miles of walking straight from the door.

Price	£70-£85. Singles £60-£75.
Rooms	2: 1 double. Potting Shed: 1 double.
Meals	Pubs 1 mile.
Closed	Rarely.
Directions	M5 exit 23 to A39. 7 miles; left to Shapwick. Cottage on left next to church.

10% off stays of 3 or more nights Mon-Thurs.

Caroline Hanbury Bateman
Church Cottage,
Station Road, Shapwick,
Bridgwater TA7 9NH
Tel +44 (0)1458 210904
Email caroline@shapwick.fsnet.co.uk
Web www.churchcottageshapwick.co.uk

Entry 470 Map 3

Somerset

Blackmore Farm

Come for atmosphere and architecture: the Grade I-listed manor-farmhouse is remarkable. Medieval stone walls, a ceiling open to a beamed roof, ecclesiastical windows, a fire blazing in the Great Hall. Ann and Ian look after guests and farm (900 acres plus dairy) with equal enthusiasm. Furnishings are comfortable not lavish, bedrooms are cavernous and the oak-panelled suite (with secret stairway intact) takes up an entire floor. Breakfast at a 20-foot polished table in the carpeted but baronial Great Hall, store your bikes in the chapel, visit the calves in the dairy. A rare place. *Farm shop on site.*

Price	£75-£85. Singles £45-£55.
Rooms	4: 1 double, 1 twin, 1 four-poster, 1 suite.
Meals	Pubs/restaurants 5-minute walk.
Closed	Rarely.
Directions	From Bridgwater, A39 west around Cannington. After 2nd r'bout, follow signs to Minehead; 1st left after Yeo Valley creamery; 1st house on right.

10% off room rate Mon-Thurs.

Use your Sawday's Gift Card here.

Ann Dyer
Blackmore Farm,
Cannington,
Bridgwater TA5 2NE
Tel   +44 (0)1278 653442
Email   dyerfarm@aol.com
Web   www.dyerfarm.co.uk

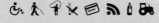

Entry 471   Map 2

Somerset

Huntstile Organic Farm

Catapult yourself into country life in the foothills of the Quantocks, and make that connection between the rolling green hills, the idyllic munching animals and the delicious, organic food on your plate; here it is understood. Lizzie and John buzz with energy in this gorgeous old house with Jacobean panelling and huge walk-in fireplaces, two sitting rooms, sweet and cosy rustic bedrooms, a café, and a restaurant serving their own meat, eggs and vegetables. House parties, weddings, team building, a stone circle for hand-fasting ceremonies – all come under Lizzie's happy and efficient umbrella, and there are woodlands to roam.

Ethical Collection: Environment; Food; Community. See page 430.

Price	From £85. Singles from £49.
Rooms	5: 1 double; 1 double, 1 twin/double sharing bath. Apartment: 1 double, 1 twin with sitting room.
Meals	Dinner £15-£22. Packed lunch £5-£7.50. Pub/restaurant 3 miles.
Closed	22 December-7 January.
Directions	M5 junc. 24, left to N. Petherton. Before entering village right to Goathurst & Broomfield. 2nd right to Goathurst. House 1 mile on right.

10% off room rate Mon-Thurs. Bottle of organic wine with stays of 2 nights.

Lizzie Myers
Huntstile Organic Farm,
Goathurst,
Bridgwater TA5 2DQ
Tel   +44 (0)1278 662358
Email   huntstile@live.co.uk
Web   www.huntstileorganicfarm.co.uk

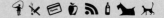

Entry 472   Map 2

Somerset

The Lynch Country House

Peace, seclusion and privacy at this immaculate Regency house in lush Somerset. First-floor bedrooms are traditionally grand, attic rooms are small but bright; those in the coach house have a more modern feel. Deep warm colours prevail, fabrics are flowery and carpets soft green. You'll feel as warm as toast and beautifully looked after. A stone stair goes right to the top where the observatory lets in a cascading light; the flagged hall, high ceilings, long windows and private tables at breakfast create a country-house hotel feel. A lovely garden has a pond, wildlife and a terrace from which to drink it all in.

Somerset

Rectory Farm House

Lavinia has showered love and attention on her early Georgian house and garden in a landscape that has changed little since the 18th century. Beams, sash windows, wood fires and high ceilings are the backdrop for polished family furniture and delightfully arranged flowers. Good-sized bedrooms in lovely restful colours have starched linen, fluffy bathrobes and binoculars for watching the wildlife; the beautiful, peaceful garden draws deer, badgers, foxes, hares. Breakfast is so local it could walk to the table – and includes homemade marmalade and jams. All this and only a mile off the A303!

Price	£70–£100. Singles £60–£70.
Rooms	9: 1 double, 1 twin, 2 four-posters; 1 double (extra single bed) with separate bath. Coach house: 3 doubles, 1 twin.
Meals	Restaurants 5-minute walk.
Closed	Never.
Directions	From London, M3 junc. 8, A303. At Podimore r'bout A372 to Somerton. At junc. of North St & Behind Berry.

Price	From £90. Singles from £65.
Rooms	3: 1 double; 1 twin/double, 1 double sharing bath (let to same party only).
Meals	Dinner £30. Pub 0.5 miles.
Closed	Christmas & New Year.
Directions	From the east, exit A303 on to B3081 for Bruton. After 1 mile, left into Rectory Lane. House 0.25 miles on right.

	Roy Copeland
	The Lynch Country House,
	4 Behind Berry,
	Somerton TA11 7PD
Tel	+44 (0)1458 272316
Email	the_lynch@talk21.com
Web	www.thelynchcountryhouse.co.uk

	Michael & Lavinia Dewar
	Rectory Farm House,
	Charlton Musgrove,
	Wincanton BA9 8ET
Tel	+44 (0)1963 34599
Email	l.dewar@btconnect.com
Web	www.rectoryfarmhouse.com

Entry 473   Map 3

Entry 474   Map 3

Somerset

Bratton Farmhouse

A gorgeous old (1600) house around which strut hens and happy Jacob sheep. Intelligent and generous Suellen has created contemporary, warm interiors and the bedrooms are a joy. One, in the main house, has oak-panelled walls, bucolic views and a vast bed with old French embroidered linen. Another, in a newly converted studio across the courtyard, gives you complete independence with your own stylish sitting room made cosy with a wood-burner; lovers can laze till late in a huge nest of feather and down. Good books and art surround you, breakfasts are delicious and imaginative, and walks are from the door.

Price	From £80. Singles from £50.
Rooms	3: 2 doubles, each with separate bath/shower. Studio: 1 twin/double & sitting room.
Meals	Lunch £10. Dinner, 3 courses, £25. Packed lunch £5. Pub 2 miles.
Closed	Rarely.
Directions	A303 then A371 signed Wincanton & Castle Cary. Follow signs to Castle Cary. After approx. 2.5 miles, right to Bratton Seymour. House 0.4 miles on right.

10% off stays Mon-Thurs. Local food. Late checkout (12pm). Bottle of wine with dinner.

Suellen Dainty
Bratton Farmhouse,
Bratton Seymour,
Wincanton BA9 8BY
Tel   +44 (0)1963 32458
Email   sdainty52@googlemail.com
Web   www.brattonfarmhouse.co.uk

Entry 475   Map 3

Somerset

Yarlington House

A mellow Georgian manor surrounded by impressive parkland, formal gardens, rose garden, apple tree pergola and laburnum walk. Your hosts are friendly and flexible, artists with an eye for detail; her embroideries are everywhere. Something to astound at every turn: fine copies of 18th-century wallpapers, 18th-century fabric around the canopied bed and a bedroom whose Regency striped wallpaper extends across the entire ceiling creating the effect of a Napoleonic tent. There are elegant antiques, proper 50s bathrooms, log fires, a heated pool (summer only) and lovely local walks. Surprising, unique. *Children by arrangement.*

Price	£120. Singles £60.
Rooms	2: 1 double, 1 twin.
Meals	Pubs/restaurants nearby.
Closed	28 July-23 August.
Directions	From Wincanton take A371 to Castle Cary. After Holbrook House take 2nd left, then 3rd right (both signed Yarlington). First stone gateposts on left.

Use of studio area. Tour of house (interesting pictures & furniture) & of garden.

Charles & Carolyn de Salis
Yarlington House,
Yarlington,
Wincanton BA9 8DY
Tel   +44 (0)1963 440344
Email   carolyn.desalis@yarlingtonhouse.com

Entry 476   Map 3

Somerset

Barwick Farm House

A 17th-century farmhouse sitting in ten acres of organically managed land dotted with Dorset sheep, hens and horses. Charming Angela and Robin have limewashed walls in vibrant colours, restored ancient elm boards and exposed the sandstone fireplace lintels in this interesting house full of open fires, books and flowers. Roomy bedrooms have good cotton sheets, comfortable beds and a mishmash of styles; one bathroom, painted bubble-gum pink, has a free-standing bath and views over fields. The Barn is beamed, cosy and pretty. Wake to birdsong and the sizzle of bacon; good walking and cycling start from the door.

Ethical Collection: Environment; Food. See page 430.

Price	£60–£75. Singles from £35.
Rooms	4: 1 double, 1 family suite (1 twin, 1 double sharing bath). Barn: 1 twin, 1 double.
Meals	'Early Bird' packed breakfasts also available. Restaurant 100 yds.
Closed	Rarely.
Directions	A37 to Dorchester; 0.25 miles outside Yeovil, 1st exit off r'bout (opp. Red House pub) following signs to Little Barwick House restaurant. House in fork of road.
	Home-grown produce. Free pick-up from local bus/train station.

	Angela Nicoll
	Barwick Farm House,
	Barwick, Yeovil BA22 9TD
Tel	+44 (0)1935 410779
Email	info@barwickfarmhouse.co.uk
Web	www.barwickfarmhouse.co.uk

Somerset

Farndon Thatch

The bedrooms are country-traditional with touches of luxury, the garden is full of surprises, and the owners – he violinist, she soprano – are delightful. This immaculate reed-thatched cottage has a medieval panelled hall and a smart new elm staircase, a sitting room with low beams and a wood-burner, and an interesting history. New carpets, perfect showers, views over the garden, and roasts, casseroles and crumbles (Jane can be persuaded to do supper on occasions)... life doesn't get much better than this. The house is the last in the village and looks over miles of pretty fields towards Glastonbury Tor.

Price	From £70. Singles by arrangement.
Rooms	2: 1 double; 1 double with separate shower.
Meals	Occasional supper. Pubs/restaurants within 2 miles.
Closed	Christmas, New Year & occasionally.
Directions	From Ilminster r'bout at A30, A358 & A303 intersection, then B3168; signed for Langport, Curry Rival; after 3 miles through Puckington; house last on left.

	Jane & Bob St John Wright
	Farndon Thatch,
	Puckington, Ilminster TA19 9JA
Tel	+44 (0)1460 259845
Email	info@bandbinsomerset.com
Web	www.bandbinsomerset.com

Somerset

Bellplot House

This may not be the trendiest place in the book, but there are good Georgian features and Betty and Dennis to look after you. Step into a quirky interior of stripped floors, yellow walls, a pool table and an honesty bar – help yourself to a drink before heading off to dinner. Bedrooms tend to be large and are furnished in a homely style: warm and spotless, lots of colour, crisp white linen, compact bathrooms, some have sofas, all have TVs. Wake to a delicious locally sourced breakfast in a country-green dining room. You're on the high street, but it's quiet at night. Montacute House and Forde Abbey are both close.

Somerset

Pyle House

Swoop down onto a buttermilk yellow lodge with landscaped gardens hugged by rural Somerset's rolling green fields: it's so well renovated you'd never guess it was an 1800s hunting lodge for Whitestaunton Estate. Past the flagstoned hallway, discover a house of pristine paintwork, valley views, swish bathrooms and immaculate bedrooms. Madeleine loves to cook so expect a breakfast worthy of the fine china it comes on; Michael's pride and joy are his fossil finds – proof of the area's antiquity. It's perfect for walkers: kick boots into the drying room, browse through maps, stroll to the pub for a meal. *Children over ten welcome.*

Price	£89.50–£99.50. Singles £79.50.
Rooms	7: 5 doubles, 1 family room, 1 single.
Meals	Pubs/restaurants within 2 miles.
Closed	Never.
Directions	In centre of Chard, 500 yds from the Guildhall. Car park available.

10% off room rate.

	Betty Jones
	Bellplot House,
	High Street, Chard TA20 1QB
Tel	+44 (0)1460 62600
Email	info@bellplothouse.co.uk
Web	www.bellplothouse.co.uk

Entry 479   Map 2

Price	From £70. Singles £45.
Rooms	3: 1 double, 1 twin/double, 1 suite all with separate shower rooms.
Meals	Pub/restaurant 0.5 miles.
Closed	Christmas & New Year.
Directions	From Chard A30 for Honiton. After 4 miles, right for Howley. 2nd right through stone pillars, signed Pyle, to cream house at end of drive.

10% off stays of 3 or more nights. Drop-off service for coastal walks.

	Madeleine Berry
	Pyle House,
	Whitestaunton, Chard TA20 3DZ
Tel	+44 (0)1460 239268
Email	info@pylehouse.co.uk
Web	www.pylehouse.co.uk

Entry 480   Map 2

Staffordshire

Slab Bridge Cottage

A 19th-century cottage in a quiet setting beside the Shropshire Union Canal. Bedrooms have floral curtains and all is spotless and homely, with open fires, polished copper, silver and brass, old oak furniture, pretty bathrooms and fresh flowers. Eat outside on the terrace overlooking the canal, or on the narrowboat on an evening cruise – but do book! Diana makes her own bread, biscuits, cakes and jams and has four much-loved llamas (very therapeutic). David collects fresh vegetables and salads from the garden, and eggs from the hens on a good day, for delicious breakfasts and dinners.

Price	£65–£70. Singles £45–£50.
Rooms	2: 1 double with separate bath; 1 double with separate shower.
Meals	Dinner £20. Packed lunch £5. Pub 2 miles.
Closed	Christmas & New Year.
Directions	M6 junc. 12; A5 west to r'bout; straight on. 1 mile to Stretton x-roads, right then 1st left (Lapley Lane); 3 miles to small x-roads at white house; left. Cottage 0.5 miles, on right.

Diana Walkerdine
Slab Bridge Cottage,
Little Onn,
Church Eaton ST20 0AU
Tel   +44 (0)1785 840220
Email ddwalkerdine@btinternet.com

Entry 481   Map 8

Staffordshire

Manor House

A working rare-breed farm in an area of great beauty, a Jacobean farmhouse with oodles of history. Behind mullioned windows is a glorious interior crammed with curios and family pieces, panelled walls and wonky floors... hurl a log on the fire and watch it roar. Three rooms have four-posters; one bathroom flaunts rich red antique fabrics. Chris and Margaret are passionate hosts who serve perfect breakfasts (eggs from their own hens, sausages and bacon from their pigs and home-grown tomatoes) and give you the run of a garden resplendent with plants, vistas, tennis, croquet, two springer spaniels and one purring cat. Heaven.

Ethical Collection: Food. See page 430.

Price	£58–£70. Singles £38–£48.
Rooms	4: 3 four-posters, 1 double.
Meals	Pub/restaurant 1.5 miles.
Closed	Christmas.
Directions	From Uttoxeter, B5030 for Rocester. Beyond JCB factory, left onto B5031. At T-junc. after church, right onto B5032. 1st left for Prestwood. Farm 0.75 miles on right over crest of hill, through arch.

10% off room rate Mon–Thurs.

Chris & Margaret Ball
Manor House,
Prestwood, Denstone,
Uttoxeter ST14 5DD
Tel   +44 (0)1889 590415
Email cm_ball@yahoo.co.uk
Web   www.4posteraccom.com

Entry 482   Map 8

Staffordshire

Martinslow Farm

High up in the Peaks, lost to the world, this listed 300-year-old farmhouse once sheltered donkeys... the accommodation has since stepped up a gear. The sitting room, as warm and engaging as Diana herself, is cosy with beams, log-burner and muted chintz. Peaceful bedrooms in the stable block (interconnecting for families) have a country feel: a rocking horse and equine curtains in the Stable (Diana and Richard love country pursuits, dogs and good company), mahogany beds in the Tack Room, carpets in both. Perfect tranquillity, a sheltered patio for great views, and delicious locally sourced food from Diana.

Price	From £80.
Rooms	Stables: 1 double, 1 twin.
Meals	Dinner, 3 courses, £25. Supper £15. Pub 5-minute walk.
Closed	Rarely.
Directions	A523 Leek-Ashbourne. At Winkhill, signs to Grindon. Over x-roads, left at T-junc.; 300 yds; house on right below lane.

10% off stays of 2 or more nights. Bottle of wine in your room.

Richard & Diana Bloor
Martinslow Farm,
Winkhill,
Leek ST13 7PZ
Tel +44 (0)1538 304500
Email richard.bloor@btclick.com
Web www.martinslowfarm.co.uk

Entry 483   Map 8

Staffordshire

Stoop House Farm

Step through a rosy arch from this enchanting 18th-century farmhouse: the view across garden, fields and valley will bowl you over. Inside, oak beams, heated flagged floors, a cast-iron range, a bedroom shot through with olive and gold. In this thriving conservation village (with lovely pub), the farm draws on the latest in green design, while two Andalusian horses share the grounds with sheep, pigs and poultry – expect superb eggs at breakfast! Your warm, lovely hosts, she a midwife, he a climber, share their passion for the outdoors with their guests – and the Peak District National Park lies at your feet.

Price	From £75. Singles £55.
Rooms	1 suite & sitting room.
Meals	Pub 1-minute walk.
Closed	Rarely.
Directions	From Leek A523 towards Ashbourne. At crossroads left B5053. Thro' Onecote, up hill then 2nd right signed Butterton. Thro' village past shop on right, 200 yds, then right fork. House 2nd on right.

Bottle of wine in your room.

Andrea Evans
Stoop House Farm,
Butterton,
Leek ST13 7SY
Tel +44 (0)1538 304486
Email bnfrench@yahoo.co.uk
Web www.stoophousefarm.co.uk

Entry 484   Map 8

Suffolk

The Old Vicarage

Up the avenue of fine horse chestnut trees to find just what you'd expect from an old vicarage: a Pembroke table in the flagstoned hall, a refectory table sporting copies of *The Field*, a piano, silver pheasants, a log fire that warms the sitting room and homemade cake on arrival. The house is magnificent, with huge rooms and passageways. Comfy mattresses are dressed in old-fashioned counterpanes, and the double has hill views. Weave your way through the branches of the huge copper beech to the garden that Jane loves; she grows her own vegetables, keeps hens and cooks a fine breakfast. *Children over seven welcome.*

Price	£70–£80. Singles £45.
Rooms	2: 1 double; 1 twin with separate bath. Extra single room off double (let to same party only).
Meals	Dinner £20. BYO. Packed lunch £6. Pub 1 mile.
Closed	Christmas.
Directions	From Cambridge, A1307 for Haverhill. Left to Withersfield. At T-junc., left. Almost 3 miles on, high yew hedge; at 'Concealed Entrance' sign on left, sharp turn into drive.

🧳	Bottle of wine for stays of 3 or more nights.

	Jane Sheppard
	The Old Vicarage,
	Great Thurlow,
	Newmarket CB9 7LE
Tel	+44 (0)1440 783209
Mobile	+44 (0)7887 717429
Email	s.j.sheppard@hotmail.co.uk

Entry 485   Map 9

Suffolk

The Manse

Unmissable in its coat of rich red paint, the beamed, 16th-century Manse overlooks a historic village green. The owners will present you with a superb breakfast each day, plus homemade cakes or scones for tea, and a fresh posy of garden flowers. Robin, ex-diplomatic service, has a passion for opera; Bridget organises the church choir. The guest quarters are completely private and deliciously cosy; there are polished antiques, fine porcelain and a wood-burning stove, a rose-tumbled garden for breakfast on fine days, and a chivalrous black labrador called Tristan, always happy to take guests for a walk.

Price	£70–£75. Singles from £45.
Rooms	1 twin/double & sitting room.
Meals	Pub/restaurant 2-minute walk.
Closed	Rarely.
Directions	From Bury St Edmunds, A143 to Haverhill; left on to B1066 for Glemsford. 6 miles to Hartest; house on far side of green, opp. red telephone box.

🧳	Decanter of port. Fresh fruit bowl in your room. 10% off stays of 3 or more days.

	Bridget & Robin Oaten
	The Manse,
	The Green,
	Hartest IP29 4DH
Tel	+44 (0)1284 830226
Mobile	+44 (0)7910 857446
Email	robin@oatens.plus.com

Entry 486   Map 10

Suffolk

The Old Manse Barn

A large, lush loft apartment in sleepy Suffolk; this living/eating/sleeping space of blond wood, white walls and big windows has an urban feel yet overlooks glorious countryside. Secluded from the main house, in a timber-clad barn, the style is thrillingly modern: leather sofas, glass dining table, stainless steel kitchenette. Floor lights dance off the walls, CD surround-sound creates mood and you can watch the stars from your bed. Homemade granola, local bread and ham in the fridge – breakfast when you like. There's peace for romance, solitude for work, a garden to sit in and friendly Sue to suggest the best pubs.

Price	From £70.
Rooms	Apartment: 1 double & kitchenette.
Meals	Pubs within walking distance.
Closed	Rarely.
Directions	A134 towards Bury St Edmunds & Sudbury; A1141 Lavenham, left after 1.4 miles towards Cockfield & Stowmarket; house 1.2 miles on right.

Late checkout (12pm). Local food/produce in your room.

Sue & Ian Jones
The Old Manse Barn,
Chapel Road, Cockfield,
Bury St Edmunds IP30 0HE
Tel +44 (0)1284 828120
Email bookings@theoldmansebarn.co.uk
Web www.theoldmansebarn.co.uk

Entry 487 Map 10

Suffolk

16 Bolton Street

The house is 15th century and rests on a quiet street in lovely, bustling Lavenham: part medieval, part Tudor, this is one of England's showpiece towns. Heavy beams, low doorways, books, magazines, fresh flowers and gentle hosts create a warm happy feel; steep oak stairs lead to fresh, cosy bedrooms where patchwork quilts, colourful cushions and handmade curtains abound. Gillian likes nothing better than to spoil her guests with breakfasts of local sausages and bacon, potato cakes, very special mushrooms and fresh fruit. A delightful, relaxed, generous place to stay. *Minimum stay two nights at weekends.*

Price	£80-£90.
Rooms	2: 1 twin/double, 1 double.
Meals	Packed lunch £8. Pubs/restaurants in Lavenham.
Closed	Rarely.
Directions	From market square in Lavenham, pass The Great House Restaurant, then left into Bolton Street. Long pink house at bottom on right. Park outside to unload; Gillian will help with parking.

Gillian de Lucy
16 Bolton Street,
Lavenham CO10 9RG
Tel +44 (0)1787 249046
Email gdelucy@aol.com
Web www.guineahouse.co.uk

Entry 488 Map 10

Suffolk

Milden Hall

Over five generations of Hawkins have lived in this seemingly grand 16th-century hall farmhouse with its smooth wooden floors, enormous windows and vast fireplaces. Bedrooms that range from big to huge are elegantly old-fashioned and filled with fascinating tapestries, wall hangings and lovely furniture. Juliet is a passionate conservationist, full of ideas for making the most of the surrounding countryside, on foot or by bicycle. Expect delicious home-grown bacon, sausages, bantam eggs and fruit compotes for breakfast in the sunny living room, warmed by a wood-burner in the winter. *Self-catering Barn for large groups.*

Ethical Collection: Environment; Food; Community. See page 430.

Price	£65-£90. Singles from £45.
Rooms	3: 2 twins, 1 double/family room, with separate shared bath & 2nd wc.
Meals	Occasional supper from £20. BYO. Pubs/restaurants 2-3 miles.
Closed	Rarely.
Directions	Lavenham, A1141 for Monks Eleigh. After 2 miles, right to Milden. At x-roads, right, Sudbury B1115. Hall's long drive 0.25 miles on left. Train to Sudbury; bus runs past drive.

	Juliet & Christopher Hawkins
	Milden Hall,
	Milden,
	Lavenham CO10 9NY
Tel	+44 (0)1787 247235
Email	hawkins@thehall-milden.co.uk
Web	www.thehall-milden.co.uk

Entry 489   Map 10

Suffolk

Hill House

Nayland is a charming village and this apricot-coloured, listed house sits on a quiet lane. Enter an unusual tunnel hall with flagstones, rugs and fresh flowers, to find a beamed drawing room and an elegant dining room. There are well-polished antiques, good art, and creamy colours dotted with bright chintz; smart, fresh bedrooms have good views over the pretty garden and you get a choice of pillows. Pauline happily shares her home with you and provides generous Aga breakfasts – with homemade bread and preserves. Good walks abound in Constable country; Beth Chatto gardens nearby. *Minimum stay two nights at weekends in summer.*

Price	From £74. Singles from £40.
Rooms	2: 1 twin/double; 1 double with separate bath.
Meals	Pub/restaurant a short walk.
Closed	Christmas & New Year.
Directions	Enter village from A134 into Bear St. Past T-junction into Birch St. 100 yds turn left, house 70 yds uphill on right.

Pick-up from local station.

	Pauline & David Heigham
	Hill House,
	Gravel Hill,
	Nayland CO6 4JB
Tel	+44 (0)1206 262782
Email	heighamhillhouse@hotmail.com
Web	www.heighamhillhouse.co.uk

Entry 490   Map 10

Suffolk

Nether Hall

The River Box borders the garden, you're welcome to use the hard tennis court and the garden cascades with old English roses in summer. This is a charming 16th-century home in a valley made famous by John Constable; make the most of this delightful area. Inside is warmly enticing. Find elegance and period charm in ancient doors and beams, massive open fireplaces in dining and drawing rooms, little windows, chintz and checks on the chairs. Bedrooms are simple and fresh; one is downstairs with its own entrance. Jennie and Patrick immediately put you at ease and the Aga breakfasts are plentiful and delicious.

Suffolk

West Lodge

This beautifully mellowed brick 1600s coach house has the original huge front door and stunning views from the garden over Dedham Vale. There's a comfortable snug for guests with pinky, terracotta walls and a red sofa; go up your own staircase to simple, light and airy bedrooms and old-fashioned, compact bathrooms. Friendly Penny, and ex-chef Paul, will give you local bacon and sausages and very good dinners in a colourful dining room stuffed full of gleaming antiques and silver – or on balmy evenings in the summer house, maybe with a cocktail up in the trees first. *Babes in arms & children over eight welcome. French & Spanish spoken.*

Price	£80-£85. Singles £60.
Rooms	3: 1 double, 1 twin/double; 1 single with separate bath.
Meals	Pubs 1 mile.
Closed	Rarely.
Directions	3 miles from A12, on B1068 between Higham & Stoke by Nayland. On south side of road, 300 yds east of Thorington Street.

Price	£60-£65. Singles £45.
Rooms	3: 2 doubles, 1 family suite.
Meals	Dinner, 3 courses, £18.50; 2 courses, £15. Packed lunch from £8. Pub/restaurant 140 yds.
Closed	Rarely.
Directions	From A12 exit for B1070, at junc. left towards East Bergholt. At Carriers Arms pub (0.8 miles) right. At post office (0.4 miles), right into Cemetery Lane. Entrance to house 80 yds on left.
	10% off stays of 3 or more nights. Early check in, late checkout by arrangement.

Patrick & Jennie Jackson
Nether Hall,
Thorington Street,
Stoke-by-Nayland CO6 4ST
Tel   +44 (0)1206 337373
Mobile   +44 (0)7799 560804
Email   patrick.jackson7@btopenworld.com

Paul & Penny Lewis
West Lodge,
The Street, East Bergholt,
Colchester CO7 6TF
Tel   +44 (0)1206 299808
Email   westlodgebandb@talktalk.net
Web   www.westlodge.uk.com

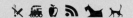

Entry 491   Map 10

Entry 492   Map 10

Suffolk

Poplar Farm House

Only a few miles from Ipswich but down a green lane, this rambling farm house has a pretty, white-washed porch and higgledy-piggledy roof. All light, elegant and spacious with wonderful flowers, art, sumptuous soft furnishings (made by Sally) and quirky sculptures; expect comfortable beds, laundered linen and smart bathrooms. Sally is relaxed and friendly and will give you eggs from her handsome hens, homemade bread, veg from the garden on an artistically laid table. Play tennis, swim, steam in the sauna or book one of Sally's arts and crafts courses, then wander in the woods beyond with beautiful dogs Shale and Rune.

Price	£65. Singles £55.
Rooms	3: 2 doubles, 1 twin with 2 shared bath/shower rooms. Yurt: 1 double.
Meals	Dinner, 3 courses, £15-£25. Packed lunch £7. Pub 1 mile.
Closed	Rarely.
Directions	From Ipswich A1214 signed Colchester. After 2 miles at Holiday Inn turn right (at lights) onto A1071, signed Hadleigh. Poplar Lane is immediately on left. House first on right.
💼	Reductions for stays of 2 or more nights. Free pick-up from local bus/train station.

	Sally Sparrow
	Poplar Farm House,
	Poplar Lane, Sproughton,
	Ipswich IP8 3HL
Tel	+44 (0)1473 601211
Email	sparrowsally@aol.com
Web	www.poplarfarmhousesuffolkbb.eu

Entry 493   Map 10

Suffolk

Mulberry Hall

Delight in the polished oak panelling and uneven tread of this handsome hall house of 1523, once owned by Cardinal Wolsey. Five miles from Ipswich it rambles round corners, is rich in beams and beloved family pieces, and has two winding staircases. Penny gives you tea and cakes in the drawing room, homemade bread and jams for breakfast, soft robes for the bath before bed. In the garden: old roses, pear pergola and mulberry tree. In the bedrooms: leaded windows, soft colours, pretty furnishings. Tennis in the garden, a log fire for chillier days and a boudoir grand for you to play: your gentle hosts give you the best.

Price	From £70. Singles from £40.
Rooms	2: 1 twin; 1 double with separate shower.
Meals	Supper £8-£12. Pubs/restaurants in Ipswich, 5 miles.
Closed	Christmas & New Year.
Directions	5 miles west of Ipswich (off A1071). 300 yds into village on left next to farmyard but before phone box.
💼	10% off stays of 3 or more nights. 10% off room rate Mon-Thurs.

	Penny Debenham
	Mulberry Hall,
	Burstall,
	Ipswich IP8 3DP
Tel	+44 (0)1473 652348
Email	pennydebenham@hotmail.com

Entry 494   Map 10

Suffolk

Haughley House

A timber-framed medieval manor in three acres of garden overlooking farmland. The attractive village is in a conservation area, and your hosts, the Lord of the Manor and his wife, are accomplished cooks and passionate about organic food; they produce their own beef, game, eggs, vegetables and soft fruits. Breakfast is an Aga-cooked feast of homemade bread, Suffolk cured bacon and black pudding, fresh juices and compote; delicious dinners are served in an elegant, silk-lined dining room. You'll find genuine country-house style here with tea and homemade cake on arrival, pretty wallpapers, flowers and a welcoming fire in the hall.

Suffolk

Bealings House

A picture postcard of a setting and a large, beautifully proportioned, Georgian house sitting high in mature parkland. Charming Selina and Jonathan give the whole thing an unpretentious feel and you are encouraged to make yourself at home, but it will be among family memorabilia, grand marble fireplaces, Irish linen, well-trodden floorboards under fading Persian rugs, first class antiques, gilt-framed landscape paintings and bursts of dried flowers. Bedrooms and bathrooms are fearfully old-fashioned and you may need to bring an extra jumper if you are a pampered city-dweller. Quirky, with wonderful grounds.

Price	£90–£100. Singles £60–£65.
Rooms	3: 2 doubles, 1 twin.
Meals	Dinner, 3 courses, £25. Restaurants 12 miles.
Closed	Rarely.
Directions	From A14 exit 49, follow signs to Haughley. Fork left at village green, house 100 yds on left.

 Bottle of wine with dinner on 1st night. 10% off stays of 2 or more nights Sun-Thur.

Price	From £70. Singles from £50.
Rooms	3: 1 double, 1 twin each with separate bath/shower; 1 double with separate bath, sitting room & kitchen.
Meals	Pub/restaurant 1 mile.
Closed	Rarely.
Directions	From Ipswich A12 N. At Woodbridge r'bout, N on A12; after 150 yds left at Seckford Hall Hotel sign. After 1 mile left at T-junc. at bottom of hill; then 1st right. Entrance immed. on right.

	Jeffrey & Caroline Bowden
	Haughley House,
	Haughley IP14 3NS
Tel	+44 (0)1449 673398
Email	bowden@keme.co.uk
Web	www.haughleyhouse.co.uk

	Selina & Jonathan Peto
	Bealings House,
	Great Bealings,
	Woodbridge IP13 6NP
Tel	+44 (0)1394 382631
Email	jonathanpeto@btinternet.com
Web	www.bealingshouse.co.uk

Entry 495 Map 10

Entry 496 Map 10

Suffolk

The Hayloft

Romantics, walkers, birdwatchers and those who need to get away from it all will be in heaven. In the old hayloft is a self-contained and stunningly stylish apartment: a raftered sitting room with a sweeping oak floor, cream sofas and a window to trumpet the view. The bedroom is uncluttered and cosy with a big leather bed, gorgeous linen and feathered bedside lights. Continental breakfast is in the fridge (homemade jams, local honey, their own fruits in summer, home-baked rolls), there are ten idyllic acres of gardens, meadows and wildlife, and bikes to borrow. Farmers' markets and festivals abound. *Ask about midweek three-night deals.*

Price	£120. Singles £80.
Rooms	Studio: 1 double & sitting room.
Meals	Restaurants 4 miles.
Closed	Christmas.
Directions	North of Woodbridge on A12, take road signed Bredfield. At T-junc. with B1078 (3 miles), left, then 1st right into Martins Lane. House on right, gravel parking on left.

 For 2 night stays including Saturday, 3rd night at single rate.

	Adrian & Jane Stevensen
	The Hayloft,
	Valley Farm House, Clopton,
	Woodbridge IP13 6QX
Tel	+44 (0)1473 737872
Email	info@thehayloftsuffolk.co.uk
Web	www.thehayloftsuffolk.co.uk

Entry 497   Map 10

Suffolk

Melton Hall

There's more than a touch of theatre to this beautiful listed house. The dining room is opulent red; the drawing room, with its delicately carved mantelpiece and comfortable sofas, has French windows to the terrace. There's a four-poster in one bedroom, an antique French bed in another (occasional road noise) and masses of fresh flowers and books. The garden includes an orchid and wildflower meadow: a designated County Wildlife Site. River walks, the coast and the Saxon burial site Sutton Hoo are close. Generous Cindy, her delightful children, little dog Snowball and cats Bea and Bubbles, all give a great welcome.

Price	£105–£130. Singles from £60.
Rooms	3: 1 double; 1 double, 1 single sharing bath.
Meals	Dinner, 1-3 courses, £19–£38. BYO. Pubs/restaurants nearby.
Closed	Rarely.
Directions	From A12 Woodbridge bypass, exit at r'bout for Melton. Follow for 1 mile to lights; there, right. Immediately on right.

	Lucinda de la Rue
	Melton Hall,
	Woodbridge IP12 1PF
Tel	+44 (0)1394 388138
Email	cindy@meltonhall.co.uk
Web	www.meltonhall.co.uk

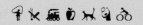

Entry 498   Map 10

Suffolk

The Old Rectory

Through the front door to a generously proportioned and flagstoned hall and a smiling welcome from Christopher. Archways lead down the corridor to the library (cosy with maps, books and open fire) and a tall elegant staircase leads to spacious bedrooms, one with delightful bow windows and a view of the sea. There are sash windows and shutters, pelmets and antiques, heaps of good books. Outside: 20 acres of woodlands, meadows, paddocks, croquet lawn and vegetable garden (walled and wonderful). Walks galore on the Deben Peninsula, music at Snape Maltings; it's Suffolk at its best and peace reigns supreme.

Suffolk

The Old Butchers Shop

Artist Sarah has cleverly converted this old butcher's shop – right on the main street of an undisturbed brick and timber estuary village. Bedrooms – the new ground-floor room is the largest – are pretty and light with proper linen on supremely comfortable beds and views over the garden or fine Norman church. Happy cat Rufus lies comatose in the drawing room amidst gay kilims and bright checks, good pictures and books. Sarah is laid-back and fun and cooks a mean breakfast: homemade yogurt and stewed fruits, local kippers. You're a hop from the sea (birdwatching and walks), and Snape for music lovers.

Ethical Collection: Food; Community. See page 430.

Price	£75. Singles £50.	
Rooms	3: 2 doubles, 1 twin. Extra bed available.	
Meals	Dinner, 3 courses, £30. Supper, 2 courses, £20. Pub 5-minute walk.	
Closed	Occasionally.	
Directions	From A12 Woodbridge bypass A1152. After railway line at r'bout, B1083 for 7 miles to Alderton. Driveway on left after 30mph & Alderton signs.	

 10% off room rate Mon-Thurs. Late checkout (12pm).

Price	£70-£105. Singles from £50.
Rooms	3: 2 twins/doubles; 1 twin/double with separate bath/shower.
Meals	Pubs/restaurants within 5-minute walk.
Closed	Rarely.
Directions	From A12, signs to Orford. Left-hand bend after King's Head pub towards quay. House on opposite side of road with blue door. Park in Market Sq.

	Christopher Langley
	The Old Rectory,
	Alderton,
	Woodbridge IP12 3DE
Tel	+44 (0)1394 410003
Email	clangley@keme.co.uk
Web	www.oldrectoryaldertonbandb.co.uk

Entry 499   Map 10

	Sarah Holland
	The Old Butchers Shop,
	111 Church Street, Orford,
	Woodbridge IP12 2LL
Tel	+44 (0)1394 450517
Email	sarah@oldbutchers-orford.co.uk
Web	www.oldbutchers-orford.co.uk

Entry 500   Map 10

Suffolk

Grange Farm

The tennis court and garden are surrounded by a 12th-century listed moat – this is a glorious old place. Ancient stairs rise and fall all over the 13th-century house, there are sloping floors and honey-coloured beams and a lovely dining room that was once the dairy. Bedrooms are large, comfortable and traditional; the sitting room is cosy with baby grand, log fire, fresh flowers, books, puzzles and games, and the views are to a garden full of birds. Delightful Elizabeth spoils you with homemade cake, local honey, own bread and homemade marmalade for breakfast. Good value, great fun.

Price	£64. Singles £32.
Rooms	2: 1 twin/double, 1 twin, sharing bath.
Meals	Pub 2-mile walk.
Closed	December-March.
Directions	A1120 (Yoxford to Stowmarket) to Dennington. B1116 north for approx. 3 miles. Farm on right 0.9 miles north of Owl's Green & red phone box.

Half a bottle of wine or Aspall apple juice in room on arrival.

Elizabeth Hickson
Grange Farm,
Dennington, Framlingham,
Woodbridge IP13 8BT
Tel +44 (0)1986 798388
Mobile +44 (0)7774 182835
Web www.grangefarm.biz

Entry 501   Map 10

Suffolk

Dunan House

You may get wild mushrooms for breakfast and new-laid eggs, homemade bread and marmalade. This is a relaxed and lovely place to stay, with entertaining hosts and a lively décor: Ann is a potter and her artistry is apparent. Bedrooms are upbeat and attractive, with woven rugs and imaginative and decorative touches, while the delightful family room in the eaves has its own little sitting/sleeping room and long views. It is wonderfully close to the sea with views over the marshes to the river Alde – and beyond. *Min. two nights at weekends; three on bank holidays. See website for availability calendar.*

Price	From £75. Singles from £50.
Rooms	3: 1 twin/double, 1 double, 1 family room for 3.
Meals	Pubs/restaurants 7-minute walk.
Closed	Christmas.
Directions	From A1094 drive towards town from r'bout. First right towards hospital, through 'Private Road' gate. House 100 yds on left, opp. tennis courts.

10% off stays of 2 or more nights, Sun-Thurs (not July-Sept & bank holidays).

Simon Farr & Ann Lee
Dunan House,
41 Park Road,
Aldeburgh IP15 5EN
Tel +44 (0)1728 452486
Email dunanhouse@btinternet.com
Web www.dunanhouse.co.uk

Entry 502   Map 10

Suffolk

Arch House

Arch House stands in three acres of garden, meadow and woodland, in easy reach of Snape Maltings, the Minsmere bird reserve and the sea. It is also home to the delightful and fun-loving Araminta who offers complementary therapies, welcomes children and is happy to babysit. The décor is traditional, the bedrooms colourful, and the elegant drawing/dining room has a boudoir grand piano and a warming log fire. Araminta is a fabulous cook and you eat well in the farmhouse kitchen: bacon and sausages are local, the hens lay your breakfast eggs, vegetables and fruit are home-grown and organic. Wonderful value, too.

Ethical Collection: Food. See page 430.

Price	£55–£70. Singles £30.
Rooms	2: 1 double, 1 twin with separate bath.
Meals	Dinner from £15. BYO. Pub 200 yds.
Closed	Rarely.
Directions	From A12, A1094 into Aldeburgh. Left at r'bout onto B1122 to Leiston. On left, 0.5 miles after Aldringham sign.

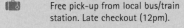 Free pick-up from local bus/train station. Late checkout (12pm).

	Araminta Stewart
	Arch House,
	Aldeburgh Road,
	Aldringham IP16 4QF
Tel	+44 (0)1728 832615
Email	amintys@aol.com
Web	www.archhouse-aldeburgh.com

Entry 503   Map 10

Suffolk

Willow Tree Cottage

Seductively near RSPB Minsmere, medieval castles, fabulous walks and the glorious coast; and Edwardian Southwold with its pier and sandy beach. The evening sun pours into the back of this contemporary cottage with butter yellow walls; you are on the edge of the village but all is quiet with an orchard behind and a bird-filled garden for cups of tea or a drink. No sitting room, but easy chairs in your bedroom face views, your bed is carefully dressed and all sparkles in the bathroom. Caroline is a good cook and breakfast is large (try homemade kedgeree); you can cycle for miles through heath and forest.

Price	£65. Singles £45–£50.
Rooms	1 double.
Meals	Pub/restaurant 1.5 miles.
Closed	Rarely.
Directions	1.5 miles north of Saxmundham on B1121 & 100 yds north off turning to Kelsale. Belvedere Close on left immediately after Cloutings Close, behind White Gables.

Free pick-up from local bus/train station.

	Caroline Youngson
	Willow Tree Cottage,
	3 Belvedere Close,
	Kelsale,
	Saxmundham IP17 2RS
Tel	+44 (0)1728 602161
Mobile	+44 (0)7747 624139

Entry 504   Map 10

Suffolk

Sandpit Farm

Idyllic views of the wide Alde valley from this deeply comfortable, listed farmhouse. The river borders their 20 acres of beautiful meadows, orchard, gardens, tennis court, ponds and remains of brick-lined moat. Be charmed by family antiques and portraits, easy colour schemes, some beams and open fires, and every cossetting thing in the pretty bedrooms, one with its own sitting room. Susie and her Aga will cook a scrumptious breakfast of homemade and local produce. Near the coast, Snape for concerts, great birdwatching, walks and cycling. Peaceful and so relaxing. *Painting classes possible.*

Price	£65–£80. Singles from £50.
Rooms	2: 1 double, 1 twin.
Meals	Pub/restaurant 1.5 miles.
Closed	Rarely.
Directions	From A1120, Yoxford to Stowmarket, east to Dennington; take B1120, Framlingham. First left; house 1.5 miles on left.

Home-grown produce in season to take home. 5% off stays of 3 or more nights.

	Susie Marshall
	Sandpit Farm,
	Bruisyard,
	Saxmundham IP17 2EB
Tel	+44 (0)1728 663445
Email	smarshall@aldevalleybreaks.co.uk
Web	www.aldevalleybreaks.co.uk

Entry 505   Map 10

Suffolk

The Old Methodist Chapel

This converted listed Victorian chapel is full of atmosphere, warm colours and beautiful stained glass windows. Bedrooms have their own entrance and are charming – one, with access to conservatory and courtyard garden, has pale walls, oak floors and beams; the flag-floored Retreat Room sports bright rugs and bedcovers from far-flung places. The chapel is comfortably, cosily cluttered and Jackum is easy-going and interesting. Potions and lotions by your bath, videos, DVDs and music in your room, books and flowers in every corner, and an organic breakfast with famous bacon from Peasenhall. *Minimum stay two nights.*

Price	£75–£95. Singles £50–£65.
Rooms	2: 1 twin; 1 double with separate bath.
Meals	Nearest restaurant directly opposite. More pubs/restaurants within walking distance.
Closed	Rarely.
Directions	From A12 in Yoxford, A1120 signed Peasenhall & Stowmarket. Chapel 200 yds on right.

Free pick-up from local bus/train station. Bottle of wine for 3 or more nights.

	Jackum Brown
	The Old Methodist Chapel,
	High Street,
	Yoxford IP17 3EU
Tel	+44 (0)1728 668333
Email	browns@chapelsuffolk.co.uk
Web	www.chapelsuffolk.co.uk

Entry 506   Map 10

Suffolk

Church Farmhouse

This lovely Elizabethan farmhouse is in a quiet hamlet by an ancient thatched church, but the bird sanctuary at Minsmere, Southwold, Snape Maltings, music and the coast are near for lovely days out. Characterful Sarah, well-travelled and entertaining, is also an excellent cook, so breakfast will be a treat, and occasional dinners are well worth staying in for. Bedrooms are restful and painted in soft colours; beds are supremely comfortable and well dressed in laundered white cotton. There are peaceful views, fresh flowers, lots of books and a calm atmosphere. *Children over 12 welcome. Minimum stay two nights at weekends.*

Price	From £85. Singles from £50.
Rooms	3: 1 double, 1 twin; 1 double with separate bath.
Meals	Dinner £24–£28. Pub/restaurants within 4 miles.
Closed	Christmas.
Directions	A12 for Wangford; left signed Uggeshall; house 1 mile on left before church.

Sarah Lentaigne
Church Farmhouse,
Uggeshall,
Southwold NR34 8BD

Tel   +44 (0)1502 578532
Email   uggeshalljupp@btinternet.com
Web   www.uggeshall.fsnet.co.uk

Entry 507   Map 10

Suffolk

Valley Farm

Soaps and sweeties in baskets, walking and cycle route maps on tap, videos for your TVs: some of the personal touches you'll find at this delightfully unpretentious B&B. The soft brick farmhouse in a lovely corner of Suffolk sits in two acres of new landscaped garden, with a play area for children, a field for kite flying and a wonderful indoor solar-heated pool, shared with the self-catering guests. You get jams from their fruits for breakfast – Jackie and Andrew have a passion for real food – and two friendly and comfortable carpeted bedrooms, each with a spotless new shower. *Minimum stay two nights at weekends.*

Price	£65–£85. Singles £85.
Rooms	2: 1 double, 1 family room for 3-4.
Meals	Pub 1.2 miles.
Closed	Rarely.
Directions	From A144 at Halesworth, B1123 signed Holton & Southwold. Fork left at Holton, on to school, then left. Farm 0.25 miles on left.

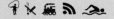 Free pick-up from local bus/train station. 1 hour per day exclusive use of pool.

Jackie Circus
Valley Farm,
Bungay Road, Holton,
Halesworth IP19 8LY

Tel   +44 (0)1986 874521
Email   mail@valleyfarmholton.co.uk
Web   www.valleyfarmholton.co.uk

Entry 508   Map 10

Suffolk

Priory House

A 16th-century Suffolk combination of bricks and beams; drink in the peace of house and garden all day if you wish. The house is friendly and informal with antique furniture and gleaming brass. The guest sitting room has a wood-burning stove, books and comfy sofas; the bedrooms have summer flowers and feather pillows. The heavily timbered dining room was once a cheese room where 'Suffolk Bang' was made; breakfast here on delicious fruit compote, local sausages and bacon, Orford kippers. Plan your days with friendly Rosemary – the Southwold coast is nearby. *Children over ten welcome. Minimum two nights July-October.*

Price	From £80. Singles £40.
Rooms	3: 1 double; 1 double, 1 twin, each with separate bath.
Meals	Pubs/restaurants 8-minute walk.
Closed	Christmas week.
Directions	From Scole, A140, right onto A143 for Gt Yarmouth. After 7 miles, right at Harleston. B1116 to Fressingfield. Pass church & Fox & Goose on left. At top of hill, right, then left into Priory Rd.

Stephen & Rosemary Willis
Priory House,
Priory Road, Fressingfield,
Eye IP21 5PH
Tel   +44 (0)1379 586254
Email   willisbb@clara.co.uk

Entry 509   Map 10

Surrey

Greenaway

An enchanting cottage in an idyllic corner of Chiddingfold. People return time and again – for the house (1545), the garden with dovecote, vegetables, flowers and hens, the glowing interiors, and Sheila and John. The sitting room is inviting with rich colours and textures, and the turning oak staircase leads to bedrooms that are cosy and sumptuous at the same time. Bathrooms are bliss, with deep roll top tubs. Come for gorgeous countryside and walks on the Greensand Way… who would guess London and the airports were so close? Delicious English B&B; readers are full of praise.

Price	£90–£115. Singles from £65.
Rooms	3: 1 double; 1 double, 1 twin sharing bath.
Meals	Hotels within walking distance.
Closed	Rarely.
Directions	A3 to Milford, then A283 for Petworth. At Chiddingfold, Pickhurst Road off green. House 3rd on left, with large black dovecote.

Sheila & John Marsh
Greenaway,
Pickhurst Road,
Chiddingfold GU8 4TS
Tel   +44 (0)1428 682920
Email   jfmarsh@gotadsl.co.uk

Entry 510   Map 4

Surrey

Lower Eashing Farmhouse

A homely place with a lovely walled garden and super hosts; Gillian, who speaks French, German and Spanish, enjoys welcoming people from all over the world. The house, 16th to 19th century, has exposed timbers, books and bold colours. The dining room is red; the guest sitting room – with open fire and decorated with fascinating artefacts from around the world – is big enough for a small company meeting, or a wedding group. Your hosts, who are great fun, run an efficient and caring ship. In the walled garden, sipping tea, the distant rumble of the A3 reminds you how well placed you are for Gatwick and Heathrow.

Price	From £80. Singles from £50.
Rooms	4: 1 twin/double; 1 twin/double with separate bath/shower; 2 singles sharing shower.
Meals	Pub 300 yds.
Closed	Occasionally.
Directions	A3 south. 5 miles after Guildford, Eashing signed left at service station. House 150 yds on left behind white fence.

🧳 Spirits, beer or wine each evening. Free pick-up from local bus/train station.

David & Gillian Swinburn
Lower Eashing Farmhouse,
Lower Eashing,
Godalming GU7 2QF
Tel +44 (0)1483 421436
Email davidswinburn@hotmail.com

Entry 511   Map 4

Surrey

Old Great Halfpenny

It feels as rural as Devon, yet you are perfectly placed for airports and easy access to London, with Guildford a few minutes away. The 16th-century farmhouse sits on a country lane beneath the Pilgrim's Way. Beyond Michael's immaculate gardens roll the Surrey Hills; there are stunning views from every room and glorious walks start from the door. You have your own entrance up fairly steep steps to lovely bedrooms which Alison, an interior designer, has made beautiful with fine fabrics and antique French beds. Wake to the smell of home-baked bread; in summer you breakfast on the terrace. Special.

Price	£75–£85. Singles £65.
Rooms	2 doubles, each with separate bath.
Meals	Pub 0.5 miles.
Closed	Rarely.
Directions	From London, exit A3 before Guildford, signed Burpham. From here 2 miles to house. Ring for detailed directions.

Michael & Alison Bennett
Old Great Halfpenny,
Halfpenny Lane, St Martha,
Guildford GU4 8PY
Tel +44 (0)1483 567835
Mobile +44 (0)7768 745765
Email bennettbird@gmail.com

Entry 512   Map 4

Surrey

Shoelands House

Behind the beautiful brickwork façade, history oozes from carved panel and creaking stair. The dining room, with its cross beams and stunning oak door, dates from 1616; Sarah and Clive know all the history. Ecclesiastical paintings, family photos, embroidered sofas, tapestry rugs; the décor is endearingly haphazard, nothing matches and the house feels loved. Huge bedrooms have papered walls and beams, and big old radiators for heat; old-fashioned bathrooms are carpeted. You are peacefully between Puttenham and Seale villages, just off the 'Hog's Back' – blissfully quiet. Loseley Park, with vine walk and moat, is close.

Price	£85. Singles from £60.
Rooms	2 twins/doubles.
Meals	Occasional supper. Pub/restaurant 1 mile.
Closed	Rarely.
Directions	On Seale-Puttenham road, halfway between Guildford & Farnham, just south of the Hog's Back.

Clive & Sarah Webster
Shoelands House,
Seale,
Farnham GU10 1HL
Tel   +44 (0)1483 810213
Email   clive@clivewebster.co.uk

Entry 513   Map 4

Surrey

High Edser

Ancient wattle and daub, aged timbers and bags of character – it really does ramble. Built in 1532, High Edser sits in 2.5 acres of smooth lawns beyond which lie the village and the Surrey hills. But, unlike many houses of a certain age, this one is light and inviting and has the sort of family clutter that makes you feel at home. Bedrooms are full of character; kind Patrick and Carol leave you plenty of space to gently unfurl. The carved wooden fireplace in the stone-flagged dining room is spectacular, and there's a snug study just for guests. Very peaceful in an AONB, yet close to both airports.

Price	£65-£70. Singles £30-£40.
Rooms	3: 2 doubles, 1 twin, all sharing bath.
Meals	Pub/restaurant 300 yds.
Closed	Rarely.
Directions	From A3, 1st exit after M25, for Ripley. Through Ripley & West Clandon, over dual c'way (A246) onto A25. 3rd right to Shere. There, right to Cranleigh. House 5 miles on left, 1 mile past The Windmill.

10% off room rate Mon-Thurs.

Use your Sawday's Gift Card here.

Patrick & Carol Franklin Adams
High Edser,
Shere Road, Ewhurst,
Cranleigh GU6 7PQ
Tel   +44 (0)1483 278214
Email   carol@highedser.co.uk
Web   www.highedser.co.uk

Entry 514   Map 4

Surrey

Blackbrook House

A large Victorian house sitting in lawns and garden and with a wide gravel drive; this has a rural feel but you are less than two miles from the centre of Dorking. Emma and Rae, both easy-going, give you a super little sitting room with a hidden TV and space to make a cup of tea; both bedrooms are spacious, smart and feminine with floral fabrics, deep pocket sprung mattresses and good linen, bathrooms are tip-top. Breakfast is beautifully presented with cereals, pancakes and maple syrup or the full Monty. Walk it off over lawns, shrubs and woods – or strike out further over National Trust land.

Surrey

Swallow Barn

A squash court, coach house and stables, once belonging to next-door's manor, have become a home of old-fashioned charm. Full of family memories and run by a gentle and hospitable couple, the B&B is excellently placed for Windsor, Wisley and golf courses; close to both airports, too. Lovely trees in the garden, fields and woods beyond, a paddock and a summer pool... total tranquillity, and you can walk to the pub. None of the bedrooms is huge but the beds are firm, the garden views are pretty and the downstairs double has its own sitting room. Breakfasts are both generous and scrumptious. *Children over eight welcome.*

Price	From £80. Singles from £55.
Rooms	2 doubles.
Meals	Pub 0.5 miles.
Closed	Christmas & New Year.
Directions	R'bout outside Dorking A24 intersects A25. A24 0.5 miles. Left into Blackbrook, signed. 1 mile until Plough pub. Turn into pub & up track. House 3rd on left.

Price	From £80. Singles from £50.
Rooms	3: 1 double & sitting room; 1 twin with separate shower. Apple Store: 1 twin.
Meals	Pub/restaurant 0.75 miles.
Closed	Rarely.
Directions	From M25, exit 11, A319 into Chobham. Left at T-junc.; left at mini r'bout onto A3046. After 0.7 miles, right between street light & postbox. House 2nd on left.

	Emma & Rae Burdon
	Blackbrook House,
	Blackbrook,
	Dorking RH5 4DS
Tel	+44 (0)1306 888898
Email	blackbrookbb@btinternet.com
Web	www.blackbrookhouse.org.uk

	Joan & David Carey
	Swallow Barn,
	Milford Green, Chobham,
	Woking GU24 8AU
Tel	+44 (0)1276 856030
Email	swallowbarn@web-hq.com
Web	www.swallow-barn.co.uk

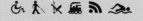

Entry 515   Map 4

Entry 516   Map 4

Sussex

Linacre Lodge

On the edge of the small village of Rudgwick, and originally part of the Baynards Park Estate, this late Victorian lodge house is a relaxed and friendly home. The kitchen is full of historic, Italian James Bond posters and unusual little chairs are found throughout: Laura is a collector and loves having people to stay. Smart, pretty bedrooms include elderflower cordial, flowers, sweets and magazines; one has its own sitting room with children's books and games. There's a huge choice at breakfast: full English or continental. Chris and Laura are keen walkers – borrow maps, order a packed lunch and set off from the door. *Dogs £5.*

Price	£85. Singles £70. Child (over 3) £10.
Rooms	2: 1 double; 1 double & sitting room.
Meals	Packed lunch £6.50. TV supper (homemade pizza & popcorn) £10. Pub/restaurant 2 miles.
Closed	Christmas & New Year.
Directions	A281 Guildford-Horsham. Follow signs off 'A' road into Rudgwick, Past King's Head pub on right; 2nd left on sharp right bend onto Baynard's Lane. House about 0.5 miles on right.
	10% off room rate Mon-Thurs.

Laura Anstead
Linacre Lodge,
Baynards, Rudgwick,
Horsham RH12 3AD
Tel   +44 (0)1403 823522
Email   chrisandlauraanstead@mac.com
Web   www.linacrelodge.co.uk

Entry 517   Map 4

Sussex

Redford Cottage

In a tiny hamlet, a friendly home with much-loved books and very kind hosts. The immense inglenook dates back to 1510 and the garden suite opens to undulating lawns; it is cosy, old-worldly, floral and private, and its sitting room comes with a wood-burner. The barn has the woody spaciousness of a ski chalet and is perfect for friends... old rugs, new pine, games, views and (up steep open stairs) beds tucked under a sloped ceiling. The silence is filled with birdsong and you are surrounded by woodland, wildlife and the rolling South Downs. Breakfasts in the conservatory are a treat. *Minimum stay three nights during Goodwood.*

Price	From £95. Singles from £65.
Rooms	3: 1 suite. Barn: 2 twins/doubles & sitting room.
Meals	Pubs/restaurants 2.5-4 miles.
Closed	Christmas.
Directions	On old A3, north from Petersfield, at Hill Brow right for Rogate, left after 300 yds to Milland. Follow lane through woods for 6 miles; right for Midhurst & Redford. On right, 150 yds beyond Redford sign.

Caroline & David Angela
Redford Cottage,
Redford,
Midhurst GU29 0QF
Tel   +44 (0)1428 741242
Email   redfordcottage@btinternet.com

Entry 518   Map 4

Sussex

The Quag

Buried in a birchwood, The Quag feels remote, yet Midhurst — "the second most attractive town in England" — is only two miles away. Feel private in your own space with a lived-in comfortable bedroom, a bathroom with a chequerboard floor, a wooden-floored sitting room, a useful fridge and separate stairs to the garden and pool. You breakfast in the main house at a long wooden table. Views are to the lawns that run romantically down to the stream, then across to the South Downs; a maze of footpaths cross common land. Mark works for Christie's and Loveday looks after you. A happy, relaxed place.

Sussex

Lyndale House

Come to feel spoiled in a pretty 18th-century merchant's house right in the centre of Midhurst; Trina and David are relaxed and thoughtful and look after you well. Their home is filled with antiques and family heirlooms, and an interesting collection of antique maps reveals all the places they've lived. Cordon Bleu-trained Trina is passionate about good food; breakfasts and dinners are local and organic. Bedrooms are light and fresh, one overlooks the church; bathrooms are smart and sparkling. Sit in the sunny walled garden with a book. A great spot for bikers and hikers. *Minimum stay two nights during Goodwood & Cowdray.*

Price	From £80. Singles £50.
Rooms	1 twin & sitting room.
Meals	Pubs/restaurants nearby.
Closed	Rarely.
Directions	A272 Midhurst-Petersfield; 2 miles from Midhurst, left signed Minsted. Count 7 telegraph poles, then 1st left. White house 1st on right.

Price	From £85. Singles from £65.
Rooms	2: 1 double; 1 twin/double with separate bath/shower.
Meals	Packed lunch from £8. Dinner from £20. Pubs/restaurants 50 yds.
Closed	Rarely.
Directions	From Petersfield A272 to Midhurst, approx. 10 miles. At mini r'bout straight on, then 3rd left. House opposite war memorial and church.

 Homemade chocolates in room. 10% off stays of 2 or more nights.

Loveday & Mark Wrey
The Quag,
Minsted,
Midhurst GU29 0JH
Tel +44 (0)1730 813623
Email beds@wrey.co.uk

Trina Duncan
Lyndale House,
Church Hill,
Midhurst GU29 9NX
Tel +44 (0)1730 813362
Email trinadad48@aol.com
Web www.lyndalehousebandb.co.uk

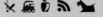

Sussex

West Marden Farmhouse

Bowl down a gentle valley in the South Downs to find a 16th-century farmhouse with beautiful Sussex granaries and barn; the Edney family has farmed the land for generations. Your delightful, helpful hosts, committed to the environment, give you a sitting/dining room with a huge old fireplace, comfortable sofas, oak floor and French windows to the garden. Upstairs is a beamed bedroom with a luxurious feel and a fabulous bathroom (free-standing bath, swish shower) bursting with aromatic soaps and oils. Breakfasts are delicious, the walking is great, Goodwood is a 20-minute drive. *Minimum stay two nights at weekends.*

Price	From £95.
Rooms	1 twin/double.
Meals	Pub 75 yds.
Closed	Christmas.
Directions	West Marden Farmhouse is in centre of village opposite Noredown Way.

Lifts to local walking start points.

Carole Edney
West Marden Farmhouse,
West Marden,
Chichester PO18 9ES
Tel   +44 (0)2392 631761
Email   carole.edney@btinternet.com
Web   www.westmardenfarmhousebandb.co.uk

Entry 521   Map 4

Sussex

Lordington House

Croquet on the lawn in summer, big log fires and woolly jumpers in winter, brilliant food all year round. On a sunny slope of the Ems valley, life ticks by peacefully as it has always done... The house is vast and impressive and a lime avenue links the much-loved garden with the AONB beyond. The 17th-century staircase is a glory, the décor is engagingly old-fashioned: Edwardian beds with firm mattresses and floral bedspreads, carpeted Sixties-style bathrooms, shepherdess wallpapers up and over wardrobe doors. A privilege to stay in a house of this age and character! *Children over five welcome. Dogs by arrangement.*

Price	From £95. Singles from £47.50.
Rooms	4: 1 double; 1 twin/double with separate bath/shower; 1 double, 1 single sharing bath/shower.
Meals	Dinner £25. Packed lunch from £5. Pub 2 miles.
Closed	Rarely.
Directions	Lordington (marked on some maps) west of B2146, 6 miles south of South Harting, 0.5 miles south of Walderton. Enter thro' white railings by letterbox; right after bridge.

Free pick-up from local pubs or stations.

Mr & Mrs John Hamilton
Lordington House,
Lordington,
Chichester PO18 9DX
Tel   +44 (0)1243 375862
Email   hamiltonjanda@btinternet.com
Web   www.lordingtonhouse.com

Entry 522   Map 4

Sussex

Church Gate

Janie has added a conservatory and huge, sunny, Aga kitchen to her 1930s house; she greets with afternoon tea, rustles up tasty home eggs at breakfast, and may even treat guests to home-baked bread or croissants, served on the terrace in summer. The house is adorned with Nigerian musical instruments and Janie's photographs; the bedrooms are fresh with low windows looking onto the garden; lovely soaps in the bath and shower rooms, driftwood lamps in the flagstoned airy sitting room. Set off for nearby Chichester with its theatre and shops, or pretty Itchenor, a mecca for sailors.

Ethical Collection: Food. See page 430.

Price	From £85. Singles from £65.
Rooms	Cottage: 1 double, 1 twin with sitting room.
Meals	Pub within 4 miles.
Closed	Most of the winter months.
Directions	From A27 at Chichester A286 Witterings; 5 miles; at r'bout bear right onto B2179. 0.5 miles right to Itchenor. 1 mile, house opposite church.

Bottle of wine in your room. Local food/produce in your room.

Janie Impey
Church Gate,
Itchenor,
Chichester PO20 7DL
Tel +44 (0)1243 514700
Email janie.allen@btinternet.com
Web www.chichesterbandb.co.uk

Entry 523 Map 4

Sussex

Itchenor Park House

The Duke of Richmond reportedly built Itchenor Park for his French mistress in 1783; it's a listed Georgian house in beautiful formal gardens on a 700-acre farmed estate. It is remote and utterly peaceful, and a path across the fields brings you to Chichester harbour for boat trips and sailing bustle. There are great walks to the beach, too, and around the village. You stay in a cosy self-contained apartment in the wing with a sitting room, kitchenette and wood-burner. And you may enjoy the lovely little walled garden, sheltered from the winds. Susie leaves you breakfast in the fridge. *Ask about body & soul detox breaks.*

Price	From £95. Singles from £60.
Rooms	Apartment: 1 twin/double & sitting room with sofabed & kitchenette.
Meals	Continental breakfast in fridge. Pub 5-minute walk.
Closed	Rarely.
Directions	A27 at Chichester onto A286 towards the Witterings. At Birdham, right at garage onto B2179; 500 yds, right to Itchenor. Driveway on left past church, signed.

Late checkout (12pm). Local food/produce in your room.

Susie Green
Itchenor Park House,
Itchenor,
Chichester PO20 7DN
Tel +44 (0)1243 512221
Email susie.green@lineone.net
Web www.itchenorpark.co.uk

Entry 524 Map 4

Sussex

The Old Manor House

Wild flowers in jugs, old wooden floors and beams, pretty cottagey curtains: Judy's manor house near Chichester has bags of character and she is friendly and chatty. Originally constructed round a big central fireplace, the rooms are all refreshingly simple allowing the original features to shine. Sweet bedrooms up steep stairs have seagrass floors, limed furniture and a skylark or chiff chaff on the doors. Enjoy breakfast by the wood-burner in the dining room: fresh fruit smoothies and an organic full English. Great for horse racing, castle visiting, sailing, theatre and festivals; fantastic walks on the south downs, too.

Price	From £85. Singles from £55.
Rooms	3: 2 doubles; 1 twin/double sharing shower room with owner.
Meals	Pub/restaurant 500 yds.
Closed	Christmas.
Directions	From Arundel, A27 west to Fontwell r'bout.Then A29 towards Bognor Regis, along Westergate Street. House on left with large forecourt.

Judy Wolstenholme
The Old Manor House,
Westergate Street, Westergate,
Chichester PO20 3QZ
Tel   +44 (0)1243 544489
Email   judy@veryoldmanorhouse.com
Web   www.veryoldmanorhouse.com

Entry 525   Map 4

Sussex

Baron's Hall Cottage

A delightful hideaway – your thatched cottage/annexe to listed Well House leads into its own pretty walled garden and has a private entrance. Marilyn's style reflects her warm personality: you have white bedding on a big brass bed, a rich rug on wooden boards, armchairs, a hat stand for clothes and a fine chest of drawers. It's luxurious, cosy and warm, with a shower room to match. Delicious, Aga-cooked, locally sourced breakfasts are served in your own small dining room. Surrounded by farmland and the unspoilt Climping beach just 600 yards away… perfect. *Minimum two nights. Arrivals between 12 noon & 6pm.*

Price	From £85.
Rooms	1 double.
Meals	Pub/restaurants 2-10 minute walk.
Closed	Rarely.
Directions	A259 Littlehampton & Bognor. Left towards sea signed Climping Street & Beach. House 4th on right with private lay-by opposite.

Marilyn Craine
Baron's Hall Cottage,
The Well House, Climping Street,
Climping, Littlehampton BN17 5RQ
Tel   +44 (0)1903 713314
Email   info@baronshall.co.uk
Web   www.baronshall.co.uk

Entry 526   Map 4

Sussex

Castle Cottage

However beautiful the countryside and the walks, you will be most enchanted by what your hosts have achieved. In birdsung woodland is a small house with a separate weather-boarded family barn and a cobbled conservatory. The barn's A-frame roof draws in the light and the front views, and there are perfect decorative touches: Persian carpets, dashing blue paints, a wrought-iron staircase, sculptures, handmade paper, superb lighting. The double in the house has the same magic. But the treehouse upstages all, high in a giant chestnut, with vast bed, veranda, sauna and shower room. Beautifully built… ineffable.

Price	£115–£140.
Rooms	3: 1 double with separate bath/shower. Barn: 1 family suite. Treehouse: 1 double.
Meals	Pubs/restaurants 1.5 miles.
Closed	Rarely.
Directions	From Fittleworth, south on B2138. Right onto Coates Lane; 1 mile, then right onto 'private drive'. Right at castle, right again & immed. left.

Local food/produce in your room.

	Alison Wyatt
	Castle Cottage,
	Coates Castle,
	Petworth RH20 1EU
Tel	+44 (0)1798 865001
Email	alison@castlecottage.info
Web	www.castlecottage.info

Entry 527   Map 4

Sussex

73 Sheepdown Drive

Strolling distance from lovely Petworth, in a cul-de-sac with outstanding valley views, is a modern but traditional tile-hung house with a gorgeous little garden. Friendly charming Angela, vice-president of the National Gardens Scheme, knows all there is to know about the gardens of Sussex. Bedrooms are fresh and simple, with well-dressed beds and good pictures. You take breakfast at a superb Jacobean oak table and can soak up the sunshine from the comfort of the conservatory; then walk down through fields to the pub in Byworth for supper. Handy for Chichester's Theatre, Goodwood and the treasures of Petworth House.

Price	From £60. Singles from £40.
Rooms	2 twins sharing bath & shower.
Meals	Pub/restaurant 10-minute walk.
Closed	Christmas & New Year.
Directions	From Petworth on A283. Sheepdown Drive east of town centre.

	Angela Azis
	73 Sheepdown Drive,
	Petworth GU28 0BX
Tel	+44 (0)1798 342269

Entry 528   Map 4

Sussex

Beauchamp Cottage

In the market town of Petworth, a tucked-away and very private retreat for two. The owners, who live nearby, have sensitively restored the little two-storey cottage with its brewery connections. Up the pine stair, under open rafters, is a light and airy sitting room with wooden floors and sofabed; downstairs, carved antique beds and fine linen, a super shower room and sweet garden views. Breakfast waits for you in the little kitchen with microwave and fridge; enjoy it on the patio. Petworth House (paintings, history, summer concerts in the park) is a mere stroll. *Off-street parking. Minimum stay two nights preferred.*

Price	£85-£105.
Rooms	Cottage: 1 twin/double, sitting room & kitchen area.
Meals	Pub/restaurant 180 yds.
Closed	Christmas.
Directions	In Petworth, follow one-way system to end of East St. Straight ahead onto Middle St; at T-junc. with High St, driveway opposite, thro' arch.

David Parsons
Beauchamp Cottage,
c/o Fairfield House,
High Street, Petworth GU28 0AU
Tel +44 (0)1798 345110
Email beauchampcottage@btinternet.com

Entry 529   Map 4

Sussex

Fitzlea Farmhouse

A wooded track leads to the beautiful, mellow, 17th-century farmhouse with tall chimneys and a cluster of overgrown outbuildings. Wood-panelled walls and ancient oak beams, a vast open fireplace, mullioned windows and deep sofas create an atmosphere of relaxed country-house charm. Maggie welcomes you to a delicious breakfast in her Aga-warm farmhouse kitchen; in spring, the scent of bluebells wafts through open doors. A winding staircase leads to comfortable timbered bedrooms which overlook fields, rolling lawns and woodland where you can stroll in peace. Heavenly. *Children by arrangement.*

Price	£60-£85. Singles by arrangement.
Rooms	3: 1 family room; 1 double, 1 twin, sharing bath.
Meals	Packed lunch available. Pubs/restaurants 2 miles.
Closed	Rarely.
Directions	Directions on booking.

Maggie Paterson
Fitzlea Farmhouse,
Selham,
Petworth GU28 0PS
Tel +44 (0)1798 861429

Entry 530   Map 4

Sussex

Riverhill Lodge

Views, views and more views over gorgeous National Park, from this handsome redbrick house with early Georgian origins. A sunny, airy sitting room with open fire and elegant cream and pink sofas, looks onto the well-planted garden; you breakfast copiously in a cosy terracotta-coloured dining room — cheerful Chris and Jenny serve up homemade bread, eggs from local hens and smoked bacon. Bedrooms are newly prettified in pale, neutral colours, with fresh fabrics and deep mattresses; bathrooms are sleekly up-to-date and toasty warm, with the thickest towels. Walk from the house for miles; the peace and quiet is palpable.

Price	£85-£125.
Rooms	2: 1 double, 1 twin/double.
Meals	Pub 0.75 miles.
Closed	Christmas & occasionally Easter.
Directions	From Petworth go east, past Welldiggers pub on right. 0.5 miles, then left. As road ceases to be a green 'tunnel' (before house on left) take right. Beech hedge on right.

Christopher & Jenny Leaver
Riverhill Lodge,
Riverhill, Fittleworth,
Pulborough RH20 1JY
Tel   +44 (0)1798 343872
Email   bookings@riverhilllodge.co.uk
Web   www.riverhilllodge.co.uk

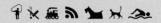

Entry 531   Map 4

Sussex

Arundel Holt Court

In a hillside clearing, in what was once the largest beech forest in the country, the house has an Arts and Crafts feel: dark wood panelling, beams and leaded windows. Contemporary bedrooms in the eaves, duck-egg blue or taupe, come with sparkling bathrooms. One opens onto a sweet single, all have delicious views over the terraced garden and far beyond. Pete and his enthusiastic dogs greet you, happy hens lay eggs for breakfast — served in the splendid dining room — there's a pool to splash in, table tennis and exceptional walks. Return to deep sofas in the drawing room, with a flintstone style mantelpiece and winter fires.

Price	£70-£90. Singles £63-£83.
Rooms	3: 2 doubles; 1 family room with separate bath.
Meals	Dinner, 2-3 courses, £21-£26 (Mon-Thurs only). Pub/restaurant 2.5 miles.
Closed	Christmas, New Year, Easter & occasionally.
Directions	From Petworth, east A272. After 2 miles, left-hand bend, take lane on right signed Bedham. 1.8 miles, then house on left, enter by second gate.

Peter Drummond
Arundel Holt Court,
Bedham, Fittleworth,
Pulborough RH20 1JP
Tel   +44 (0)1798 805426
Email   stay@arundelholtcourt.co.uk
Web   www.arundelholtcourt.co.uk

Entry 532   Map 4

Sussex

Hookwood

On the edge of the village, nudging fields, a lovely 1926 Arts and Crafts house owned by Rose, ex-photojournalist with a sympathetic eye. Colours are natural, textures are friendly, there are maps, magazines and a cheery winter fire. Stylish bedrooms, TV-free, offer you hot water bottles and dressing gowns; characterful bathrooms are cosy and well-kept. Brush – the award-winning terrier – is a darling with children, porridge is from the mill, eggs and bacon from down the road: delightful Rose is passionate about supporting the farmers. Find the path in the far corner of the garden: it takes you all the way to Pulborough!

Price	£80–£90. Singles from £45.
Rooms	3: 1 double; 1 double, 1 single sharing bath.
Meals	Packed lunch £6. Pub/restaurant 10-minute walk.
Closed	Usually mid-January to mid-March.
Directions	From Petworth, A283 towards Fittleworth, then B2138 to Bury & Arundel. Pass The Swan pub. Up hill; slow down. House 5th on left from top of hill.

Rose Beddington
Hookwood,
Tripp Hill, Fittleworth,
Pulborough RH20 1ER
Tel   +44 (0)1798 865047
Email   info@stay-hookwood.co.uk
Web   www.stay-hookwood.co.uk

Entry 533   Map 4

Sussex

Sussex Prairies

A wonderfully friendly, family farm: Paul and Pauline designed the showcase six-acre garden and look after the Shetland sheep, rare-breed pigs and chickens; Pauline is a bundle of creativity inside the farmhouse they built together – her mother sells homemade cakes and farm-reared meat in the tea shop. All are committed to green living. Sleep in country-chic rooms dotted with funky objets d'art, wake to the cock's crow and descend to the light dining room for eggs, sausages and fruit from the farm. Brighton is close, the South Downs on your doorstep. All who love great gardens, good food and fun company will be in clover.

Price	From £95. Singles from £80.
Rooms	3: 2 doubles, 1 twin.
Meals	Restaurant 0.25 miles, pub 1.5 miles.
Closed	Never.
Directions	20 minutes north of Brighton, via M23 & A23; then via B2116 (Wheatsheaf Rd) north & to the east of Henfield. House on right..

10% off stays of 2 or more nights, Mon–Thurs.

Pauline McBride
Sussex Prairies,
Morlands Farm, Wheatsheaf Road,
Henfield BN5 9AT
Tel   +44 (0)1273 495902
Email   morlandsfarm@btinternet.com
Web   www.sussexprairies.co.uk

Entry 534   Map 4

Sussex

Highbridge Mill

Many humorous touches here – a 'No Diving' mat by the bath, a life-size family of pigs on the back lawn – courtesy of Sue and Joffy, your mildly eccentric, extremely charming hosts. The old part of the house – attractive from the rear – was a flour mill (1810-1930) and there's a rusted wheel to prove it; the interiors are joyfully new. A red-Aga kitchen with wrought-iron chandelier, a bright sitting room with an open fire, bedrooms with quilts and happy colours. Gregarious Sue is a grand cook; walk off a very hearty breakfast in acres of garden, meadow and woodland. Huge fun. *Minimum stay two nights.*

Price	£80. Singles £50.
Rooms	2: 1 twin/double; 1 double with separate bath/shower.
Meals	Dinner, 3 courses, £40. Pubs within 10-minute drive.
Closed	1 December-1 April.
Directions	A23, then A272 for Haywards Heath. Pass Ansty Cross pub, downhill towards Cuckfield Rd. Drive to house on right opposite the r'bout sign.

	Sue Clarke
	Highbridge Mill,
	Cuckfield Road, Ansty,
	Haywards Heath RH17 5AE
Tel	+44 (0)1444 450881
Mobile	+44 (0)7850 271606
Web	www.highbridgemill.com

Entry 535   Map 4

Sussex

Holy Well Barn

A sanctuary for those who wish to be alone in lush countryside, and who want a big TV too! A smartly converted old store house has a bedroom on the ground floor, all soaring beams and vaulted ceiling, with a coffee cream scheme, faux fur bed throw and a comfy sofa. Through a latched door find a sweet, snug bathroom, with robes and Harding soaps. Up the little stairs to a galleried space (not for giants!) for a hamper of goodies and a fridge. Breakfast is brought to you, the only sound is the little steam railway and birdsong, and you have your own terrace for sunny days. You are on 400 acres of organic farm. Romantic.

Price	From £90. Singles from £70.
Rooms	1 double.
Meals	Pub/restaurant 1.9 miles.
Closed	Rarely.
Directions	From Haywards Heath take B2028 to Lindfield. Drive out of Lindfield past church, take 2nd turning on right (Stonecross Lane). Left into Keysford Lane; driveway immediately on right.

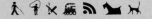	Biscuits and fresh fruit in your room. Bottle of wine for stays of 2 or more nights.

	Sophie Blaker
	Holy Well Barn,
	Keysford Lane, Lindfield,
	Haywards Heath RH16 2QT
Tel	+44 (0)1444 484438
Email	info@holywellbarn.com
Web	www.holywellbarn.com

Entry 536   Map 4

Sussex

Little Lywood

On the ground floor you feel nicely private; the bathroom is a couple of steps from your door. The softly-lit, unfussy room, which overlooks the drive and is well back from the road, has a pine dressing table, rattan chairs, matching curtains and duvet covers, and fresh flowers. You breakfast in the old part of this Elizabethan forester's cottage; a super dining room with small mullioned windows and ancient timbers – Jeannie and Nick will leave you to come and go as you please. Within easy reach of the Ashdown forest and Sussex's great gardens; the one here is lovely, too.

Price	£70. Singles £50.
Rooms	1 double with separate bath.
Meals	Pubs 2.5 miles.
Closed	Rarely.
Directions	From Haywards Heath, B2028 to Lindfield. House on left, 1.5 miles after passing church at north end of Lindfield.

	Jeannie & Nick Leadsom
	Little Lywood,
	Ardingly Road,
	Lindfield RH16 2QX
Tel	+44 (0)1444 892571
Email	nick@nleadsom.plus.com

Entry 537 Map 4

Sussex

The Grange

There's a time-worn feel to this dreamy home. Books are stuffed into shelves, walls are decorated with years of paintings and carved African hippos guard the stairs. The mainly-Queen-Anne rectory in a secluded spot beside the church feels wonderfully timeless with its oak stairs, antique swords, ancient tapestry and comfy old-fashioned sitting room (all yours). Bedrooms are traditional and have lovely views over the garden; there's a small single room attached to one. Few modern innovations here but Bunny looks after you beautifully and there's marvellous walking in Ashdown Forest: this is Pooh Bear country.

Price	From £75. Singles £50.
Rooms	2: 1 double & sitting room (with single room attached); 1 double with separate bath.
Meals	Pubs/restaurant 200 yds.
Closed	Occasionally.
Directions	In centre of Hartfield, take road (Church Street) between The Haywagon & The Anchor pubs. Pass church on left; house is beyond church, on left.

	Bunny & James Murray Willis
	The Grange,
	Hartfield TN7 4AG
Tel	+44 (0)1892 770259
Email	bunnymw@hotmail.co.uk

Entry 538 Map 5

Sussex

Old Whyly

Breakfast in a light-filled, chinoiserie dining room – there's an effortless elegance to this manor house, once home to one of King Charles's Cavaliers. Bedrooms are atmospheric, one in French style. The treats continue outside with a beautiful flower garden annually replenished with 5,000 tulips, a lake and orchard, a swimming pool and a tennis court – fabulous. Dine under the pergola in summer: food is a passion and Sarah's menus are adventurous with a modern slant. Glyndebourne is close so make a party of it and take a divine 'pink' hamper, with blankets or a table and chairs included. Sheer bliss.

Price	£90–£140. Singles by arrangement.
Rooms	3: 2 twins/doubles; 1 twin/double with separate bath.
Meals	Dinner, 3 courses, £30. Hampers £35. Pub/restaurant 0.5 miles.
Closed	Rarely.
Directions	0.5 miles past Halland on A22, south from Uckfield; 1st left off Shaw r'bout towards E. Hoathly; on for 0.5 miles. Drive on left with postbox; central gravel drive.

Sarah Burgoyne
Old Whyly,
London Road, East Hoathly BN8 6EL
Tel +44 (0)1825 840216
Email stay@oldwhyly.co.uk
Web www.oldwhyly.co.uk

Entry 539 Map 5

Sussex

Hailsham Grange

Come for elegance and ease. Noel welcomes you into his lovely Queen 'Mary Anne' home (1701-1705) – set back from the road in a town where they still hold two cattle markets a week. No standing on ceremony here, despite the décor: classic English touched with chinoiserie in perfect keeping with the house. Busts on pillars, swathes of delicious chintz, books galore and bedrooms a treat: a sunny double and a romantic four-poster. Summery breakfasts are served on the flagged terrace, marmalades and jams on a silver salver. The town garden, with its box parterre and bank of gothic summer house, is an equal joy.

Price	£95–£120. Singles from £70.
Rooms	4: 1 double, 1 four-poster. Coach house: 2 suites.
Meals	Pub/restaurants 300 yds.
Closed	Rarely.
Directions	From Hailsham High St, left into Vicarage Rd. House 200 yds on left. Park in adjacent coach yard.

 Use your Sawday's Gift Card here.

Noel Thompson
Hailsham Grange,
Hailsham BN27 1BL
Tel +44 (0)1323 844248
Email noel@grange.co.uk
Web www.hailshamgrange.co.uk

Entry 540 Map 5

Sussex

Ocklynge Manor

On top of a peaceful hill, a short stroll from Eastbourne, find tip-top B&B in an 18th-century house with an interesting history – ask Wendy! Now it is her home, and you will be treated to home-baked bread, delicious tea time cakes and scrummy jams – on fine days you can take it outside. Creamy carpeted, bright and sunny bedrooms, all with views over the lovely walled garden, create a mood of relaxed indulgence and are full of thoughtful touches: dressing gowns, DVDs, your own fridge. Breakfasts are superb and there's a chintzy, comfy sitting room just for guests: this is a very spoiling, nurturing place.

Price	£80–£90. Singles from £50.
Rooms	3: 1 twin, 1 suite for 3; 1 double with separate shower.
Meals	Pub 5-minute walk.
Closed	Rarely.
Directions	From Eastbourne General Hospital, over r'bout on A2021. 1st right to Kings Avenue; up hill to T-junc. Cream house faces you on right.

Wendy Dugdill
Ocklynge Manor,
Mill Road,
Eastbourne BN21 2PG
Tel   +44 (0)1323 734121
Email   ocklyngemanor@hotmail.com
Web   www.ocklyngemanor.co.uk

Entry 541   Map 5

Sussex

Globe Place

A listed 17th-century house beside the church in a tiny village, ten minutes from Glyndebourne. Alison – a former chef to the Beatles – is a great cook and can provide you with a delicious and generous hamper, and tables and chairs too. Willie is a former rackets champion who gives tennis coaching; there's a court in the large, pretty garden, and a pool. Relax by the inglenook fire in the drawing room after a walk on the Cuckoo Trail or the South Downs, then settle down to a great supper – local fish, maybe, with home-grown vegetables. An easy-going, fun and informal household. *Children over 12 welcome.*

Price	£80–£100. Singles £45.
Rooms	6: 2 doubles, 1 twin each with separate bath; 2 singles sharing baths (let to same party only). Cottage: 1 twin/double with drawing room.
Meals	Dinner £25. BYO wine. Hamper £35. Pub 10-minute drive.
Closed	Christmas.
Directions	From Boship r'bout on A22, A267. 1st right to Horsebridge; immed. left to Hellingly. Pass church, left into Mill Lane. Next to church. Park at top of drive, enter at back.

Alison & Willie Boone
Globe Place,
Hellingly BN27 4EY
Tel   +44 (0)1323 844276
Email   aliboone@globeplace.plus.com
Web   www.globeplace.co.uk

Entry 542   Map 5

Sussex

Netherwood Lodge

The whiff of the log fire, the scent of fresh flowers and a smattering of chintz over calm, uncluttered interiors will please you in this single-storey coach house: engaging Margaret may give you homemade cake or scones in an elegant sitting room with views over the pretty garden. Cosy bedrooms are beautifully dressed and chic with wool carpets, silk and linen curtains, oak furniture and gloriously comfortable beds. You eat well, much is locally sourced and homemade for the flexible, award-winning breakfasts. This is a quiet part of East Sussex, ideal for walking, National Trust properties and Glyndebourne.

Sussex

St Benedict

You can walk to town from here: the house, in a conservation area, has been restored by Stephen using the original 1880 floor plans. Lovers of Victoriana will swoon: find hand-printed wallpapers, gleaming mahogany, Persian rugs, Dutch marquetry furniture, coal fires in winter, decorative objects and artwork galore. Bedrooms are both extremely comfy with brass beds, eiderdowns and squishy pillows; wake to devilled kidneys, kedgeree, smoked haddock, all delivered by the working dumb waiter. Stephen will play the piano should you wish, or you can borrow a book from the lovely library and head for the summer house in the long garden.

Price	From £100. Singles from £80.
Rooms	2: 1 twin; 1 double with separate bath.
Meals	Pub/restaurant 1 mile.
Closed	Rarely.
Directions	A22 towards Eastbourne. Left at Golden Cross between BP garage and antique shop. 0.5 miles, right at T-junc. then sharp right into unmade lane. House 2nd on left.

Loaf of homemade bread and pot of homemade marmalade, jam or lemon curd.

Margaret Clarke
Netherwood Lodge,
Muddles Green, Chiddingly,
Lewes BN8 6HS
Tel +44 (0)1825 872512
Email netherwoodlodge@hotmail.com
Web www.netherwoodlodge.co.uk

Entry 543 Map 5

Price	£80. Singles £50.
Rooms	2 doubles each with separate bath.
Meals	Dinner £25. Packed lunch £10. Pub/restaurant 0.5 miles.
Closed	Rarely.
Directions	From Hastings, west A27 Marine Parade until London Rd, St L. on Sea. Right (signed London) away from sea. Take 5th on left, just before disused church. At top of hill, over junc. beside St John's Church, house 100 yds, on left.

Free pick-up from local bus/train station. Late checkout (12pm).

Stephen Groves
St Benedict,
81 Pevensey Road,
St Leonards on Sea TN38 0LR
Tel +44 (0)1424 434973
Email stephen.groves@zen.co.uk
Web www.victorian-bed-and-breakfast.com

Entry 544 Map 5

Sussex

Swan House

Effortless style drifts through the beamed rooms of this boutiquey B&B in a 1490s bakery, from a roaring inglenook fireplace to an honesty bar in a mock bookcase – all run by relaxed creative hosts Brendan and Lionel. Bedrooms hold surprises: Elizabethan frescoes, an old pulley for bags of flour, a window seat, seashell mosaics and handmade soaps. Step out into lively Old Hastings, wander down to see fishing boats tucked in for the night or find an antiques bargain. Seagulls herald the new day: pick a morning paper; breakfast like kings on organic croissants and local kippers (dinners also on request). Unique.

Price	£115–£145. Singles £70–£95.
Rooms	4: 3 doubles, 1 suite.
Meals	Restaurants 2-minute walk.
Closed	Christmas.
Directions	In Hastings Old Town, close to seafront, a 20-minute walk from Hastings town centre and train station.

25% off room rate Mon-Thurs.

	Brendan McDonagh
	Swan House,
	1 Hill Street,
	Hastings TN34 3HU
Tel	+44 (0)1424 430014
Email	res@swanhousehastings.co.uk
Web	www.swanhousehastings.co.uk

Entry 545   Map 5

Sussex

Appletree Cottage

An enviable position facing south for this old hung-tile farmer's cottage, covered in roses, jasmine and wisteria; views are over farmland towards Fairlight Glen. Jane will treat you to tea and cake when you arrive – either before a warming fire in the drawing room, or in the garden in summer. Both bedrooms are sunny, spacious, quiet and traditional, one with gorgeous garden views. Breakfast well on apple juice from their own apples, homemade jams and marmalade, local bacon. Perfect for walkers with a footpath at the front gate, but birdwatchers will be happy too, and you are near the steam railway at Bodium.

Price	£80. Singles £50.
Rooms	2: 1 twin; 1 double with separate bath.
Meals	Pub/restaurant 0.5 miles.
Closed	Rarely.
Directions	A21 towards Hastings. Left at B2089 towards Rye. 0.25 miles beyond Cripps Corner left at Beacon Lane. Right at farm track at top of hill - house is 1st on left (second drive).

10% off stays of 2 or more nights.

	Jane & Hugh Willing
	Appletree Cottage,
	Beacon Lane, Staplecross,
	Robertsbridge TN32 5QP
Tel	+44 (0)1580 831724
Email	appletree.cottage@hotmail.co.uk
Web	www.appletreecottagestaplex.com

Entry 546   Map 5

Sussex

Wellington House

A stroll away from the gardens of Great Dixter is a warm, comfortable, charming B&B. Behind the Victorian red-brick façade the Brogdens have worked an informal magic, giving guests a cosy sitting room and two big peaceful bedrooms above. These are creamy-walled and carpeted, with comfy mattresses, antique bed linen, pristine shower rooms and good toiletries. Fanny is passionate about food, bakes her own bread, grows her own peaches – a treat; Vivian is a charmer. Visit Bodiam by river boat, comb Camber Sands, explore Rye, revel in Dixter... and return to tea and homemade cakes in the garden.

Price	From £80. Singles from £50.
Rooms	2 doubles.
Meals	Supper, 2 courses, from £18; 3 courses, from £22 (min. 4). Pubs within 2 miles.
Closed	Christmas & New Year.
Directions	Follow brown tourist signs in Northiam village for Great Dixter House & Gardens to Dixter Rd. House at main road end, next to opticians.

Glass of wine at dinner. Late checkout.

Fanny & Vivian Brogden
Wellington House,
Dixter Road, Northiam,
Rye TN31 6LB
Tel   +44 (0)1797 253449
Email   fanny@frances14.freeserve.co.uk
Web   www.wellingtonhousebandb.co.uk

Entry 547   Map 5

Sussex

Boonshill Farm

A glorious farmhouse with a duck pond, brick and weatherboard outbuildings, flouncing flower beds and charming Lisette, a garden designer from London. Large bedrooms have big wide floor boards and inviting beds, decorative gates for headboards, reclaimed windows for mirrors and a delicious rusticity. Bathrooms could appear in *Country Living* (and have!); views are green from every window. Outside are acre of lawns, a wildflower garden, hens and handsome Berkshire pigs; organic breakfasts are outstanding. A bucolic retreat ten minutes from Rye, in rolling Sussex hills: open the door and walk for miles.

Price	£80-£100. Singles £50-£80. Child £20.
Rooms	2: 1 double, 1 twin. Extra child bed.
Meals	Pub 1 mile.
Closed	Rarely.
Directions	Grove Lane opposite The Bell in Iden. Down lane for 1 mile, then left immediately before oast house, down track. Go past Boonsfield Farm; Boonshill at end of track, on left, white gate.

Lisette Pleasance
Boonshill Farm,
Grove Lane, Iden,
Rye TN31 7QA
Tel   +44 (0)1797 280533
Email   boonshillfarm@yahoo.co.uk
Web   www.boonshillfarm.co.uk

Entry 548   Map 5

Warwickshire

Hardingwood House

Close to Birmingham and the NEC and with a theatrical, Tudor feel. Denise, warm and delightful, spoils guests with big bedrooms, dressing rooms, good linen and deep gold-tapped baths. There are books, flowers, antique clocks and plush sofas; tapestry and velvet curtains frame leaded windows; dark timbers and reds and pinks abound. The 1737 barn is immaculate inside and out: the kitchen gives onto a stunning patio, while bedrooms have views to garden or fields. Much rural charm — and there's a self-catering cottage for two if you like your independence. *Advance booking essential.*

Price	£80. Singles from £60.
Rooms	3: 1 double, 2 twins.
Meals	Pub 1 mile.
Closed	Rarely.
Directions	M6 junc. 4; A446 for Lichfield. Into right lane & 1st exit towards Coleshill. From High St, into Maxstoke Lane. After 4 miles, right. 1st drive on left.

Denise Owen
Hardingwood House,
Hardingwood Lane,
Fillongley, Coventry CV7 8EL
Tel   +44 (0)1676 542579
Email   denise@hardingwoodhouse.fsnet.co.uk

Entry 549   Map 8

Warwickshire

Park Farm House

Fronted by a circular drive, the warm red-brick farmhouse is listed and old — it dates from 1655. Linda is friendly and welcoming, a genuine B&B pro, giving you an immaculate guest sitting room filled with pretty family pieces. The bedrooms sport comfortable mattresses, mahogany or brass beds, blankets on request, bathrobes, flowers, magazines, DVDs. A haven of rest from the motorway (morning hum only) this is in the heart of a working farm yet hugely convenient for Birmingham, Warwick, Stratford, Coventry. You may get their own beef at dinner and the vegetables are home-grown.

Price	£79. Singles from £48.
Rooms	2: 1 double, 1 twin.
Meals	Dinner, 3 courses, from £25. Supper £19. Pub/restaurant 1.5 miles.
Closed	Rarely.
Directions	M6 & M69 exit 2; B4065 through Ansty to Shilton; left at lights then next left. Over bridge and right to Barnacle; through village. Left at brick wall signed Spring Road. House at end.

Linda Grindal
Park Farm House,
Barnacle,
Shilton, Coventry CV7 9LG
Tel   +44 (0)2476 612628
Web   www.parkfarmguesthouse.co.uk

Entry 550   Map 8

Warwickshire

Mows Hill Farm

From the chocolate labradors in the flagstoned kitchen to the cattle munching in their stalls this late-Victorian farmhouse is a proper working farm of 1,300 acres that has been in the family for generations. Lynda and Edward give you an elegant and comfortable sitting and dining room with field views, loads of books and magazines, family portraits and an open fire. Breakfast on homemade bread and jams, fruit salad, home-reared bacon, just-laid eggs – in the conservatory looking onto the garden in the summer. Bedrooms have cotton sheets, armchairs for flopping and cosy bathrobes. A warm, family home. *Children over ten welcome.*

Price	£80-£90. Singles from £55.
Rooms	2: 1 twin/double; 1 double with separate bath.
Meals	Pub/restaurant 3 miles.
Closed	Rarely.
Directions	A3400 Hockley Heath; B4101 (Spring Lane); left into Umberslade Rd. At 2nd triangle, keep right & onto Mows Hill Rd; 0.25 miles on right.

10% off room rate Mon-Thurs.

Lynda Muntz
Mows Hill Farm,
Mows Hill Road, Kemps Green,
Tanworth in Arden B94 5PP
Tel   +44 (0)1564 784312
Email   mowshill@farmline.com
Web   www.b-and-bmowshill.co.uk

Entry 551   Map 8

Warwickshire

Salford Farm House

Beautiful within, handsome without. Thanks to subtle colours, oak beams and lovely old pieces, Jane has achieved a seductive combination of comfort and style. A flagstoned hallway and an old rocking horse, ticking clocks, beeswax, fresh flowers: this house is well-loved. Jane was a ballet dancer, Richard has green fingers and runs a fruit farm and farm shop nearby – you may expect meat and game from the Ragley Estate and delicious fruits in season. Bedrooms have a soft, warm elegance and flat-screen TVs, bathrooms are spotless and welcoming, views are to garden or fields. Wholly delightful.

Ethical Collection: Food; Community.
See page 430.

Price	£90. Singles £45.
Rooms	2 twins/doubles.
Meals	Dinner £25. Restaurant 2.5 miles.
Closed	Rarely.
Directions	A46 from Evesham or Stratford; exit for Salford Priors. On entering village, right opp. church, for Dunnington. House on right, approx. 1 mile on, after 2nd sign on right for Dunnington.

Jane & Richard Beach
Salford Farm House,
Salford Priors,
Evesham WR11 8XN
Tel   +44 (0)1386 870000
Email   salfordfarmhouse@aol.com
Web   www.salfordfarmhouse.co.uk

Entry 552   Map 8

Warwickshire

Cross o' th' Hill Farm

Stratford in 12 minutes on foot, down a footpath across a field: from the veranda you can see the church where Shakespeare is buried. There's been a farm on this rural spot since before Shakespeare's time but part of the house is Victorian. Built around 1860, it's full of light, with wall-to-ceiling sash windows, glass panelling in the roof, large uncluttered bedrooms and smart, newly decorated bathrooms. The garden, full of trees and birds, dates from the same period – there's even a sunken croquet lawn. Decima grew up here; she and David are gentle hosts, and passionate about art and architecture.

Ethical Collection: Food. See page 430.

Price	£90-£95. Singles £65-£70.
Rooms	3: 2 doubles; 1 double with separate bath/shower.
Meals	Pubs/restaurants 20-minute walk.
Closed	20 December-1 March.
Directions	From Stratford south on A3400 for 0.5 miles, 2nd right on B4632 for Broadway Rd for 500 yds. 2nd drive on right for farm.

	Decima Noble
	Cross o' th' Hill Farm,
	Broadway Road,
	Stratford-upon-Avon CV37 8HP
Tel	+44 (0)1789 204738
Email	decimanoble@hotmail.com
Web	www.crossothhillfarm.com

Entry 553   Map 8

Warwickshire

Drybank Farm

Behind the high, red-brick face of the farmhouse lies a cool, spacious hall, where Angela – warm and friendly – welcomes you in. Honey-coloured beams, a big sitting room overlooking the garden with cheerful fabrics and fresh flowers make for a perfectly serene feel, and the countrified bedrooms and bathrooms are reassuringly traditional; the separate bakery is quietly private and you can breakfast here à deux, or join the others in the main house. Shooting, riding and golf can all be arranged – and even RSC seats, tickets permitting. Return to a deep bath, a fluffy dressing gown and a feather duvet.

Price	From £85. Singles £60.
Rooms	2: 1 twin/double, 1 suite.
Meals	Supper £20-£35. Packed lunch from £7. Pub 0.5 miles.
Closed	Christmas.
Directions	A422 from Stratford to Ettington; thro' village, past Chequers pub on left. Right at x-roads; house on left over brow of hill.

Bottle of wine in your room.

	Angela Winter
	Drybank Farm,
	Fosseway, Ettington,
	Stratford-upon-Avon CV37 7PD
Tel	+44 (0)1789 740476
Email	drybank@btinternet.com
Web	www.drybank.co.uk

Entry 554   Map 8

Warwickshire

Sequoia House

A cat snoozes by the Aga in this smart Victorian townhouse – an easy stroll from Stratford and a civilised base for exploring Shakespeare country. Step into a pretty tiled hallway and discover high ceilings, deep bays, generous landings, handsome flagstones, a homely sitting room. The easygoing Evanses (Welsh-born) downsized from the hotel they used to run here, and are happy to treat just a few guests: trouser presses and piles of towels mingle with fine old furniture in immaculate rooms. A walkway runs past cricket grounds straight into town. Hotel touches but a warmly personal welcome, and so wonderfully convenient.

Price	£125. Singles £85.
Rooms	6 doubles.
Meals	Pub/restaurant 100 yds.
Closed	Christmas & New Year.
Directions	From M40 (junc. 15) to Stratford (signed). Enter town, then signed A3400 Shipston. Cross River Bridge, then 2nd exit off traffic island. House 100 yds on right.

10% off room rate for 2 or more nights Mon-Thurs.

Jean Evans
Sequoia House,
51 Shipston Road,
Stratford-upon-Avon CV37 7LN
Tel   +44 (0)1789 268852
Email   reservations@sequoia-house.co.uk
Web   www.sequoia-house.co.uk

Entry 555   Map 8

Warwickshire

The Bakehouse

Red-bricked and mellow on the outside, a lavishly romantic bolthole within. Find beautifully upholstered armchairs, a rose-soft sofa laden with tapestry cushions, an embellished repro mirror with a fun French flourish, plentiful glossy mags and little gilt-framed pictures, and a wood-burner that belts out the heat… and that's just the sitting room. The bedroom is spacious and light, with immaculate carpeting, dark beams and a view onto the neighbouring farmyard and gardens. There's a tiny courtyard for guests and Shoshana is warm and generous. Comfort, character and style, minutes from Stratford and its theatres.

Price	From £70.
Rooms	1 double (extra single available).
Meals	Restaurant/pub next door.
Closed	Never.
Directions	From Stratford-upon-Avon, Shipston road then right to Broadway B4632 for 3 miles. Signed Lower Quinton on left.

Shoshana Kitchen
The Bakehouse, Magdalen House,
The Green, Lower Quinton,
Stratford-upon-Avon CV37 8SG
Tel   +44 (0)1789 721792
Email   info@cotswoldbakehouse.co.uk
Web   www.cotswoldbakehouse.co.uk

Entry 556   Map 8

Warwickshire

Machado Gallery

Artists and artisans have lived in this red-brick village house since 1746 – and it has never looked finer. Sue, a well-travelled sculptor and designer, has spent 21 happy years filling her home with art and natural light: skylights gulp sunshine into the fire-warmed sitting room; carved Russian windows frame daylight; bedrooms – one with a private patio, another a Juliet balcony – have pretty linen and super bathrooms. Wake to coffee and homemade bread, then sit out by the garden pond or browse the studio gallery. The village pubs are close; Warwick, the Cotswolds and Stratford-on-Avon beckon.

Price	£70-£95.
Rooms	3: 2 doubles, 1 twin/double.
Meals	Lunch £6-£12. Packed lunch available. Occasional dinner £15. Pub 50 yds. Restaurant 100 yds.
Closed	Rarely.
Directions	M40 junc. 15, A429 to Stow for 1 mile. Left into Barford Village. Cross Norman bridge & mini r'bout under the cedar tree. House 10 yds on left.

 10% off room rate Mon-Thurs.

Sue Machado
Machado Gallery,
9 Wellesbourne Road,
Barford,
Warwick CV35 8EL
Tel   +44 (0)1926 624061
Web   www.machadogallery.co.uk

Entry 557   Map 8

Warwickshire

Blackwell Grange

Thatch barns and stables dated 1604, and wonderfully creative touches at a Cotswold farmhouse revived by a talented third generation. Didi, interior designer, has introduced patterned silks and restored antiques to creaking floorboards and flagstones; elegant bedrooms have dressing gowns, fine linen, indulgent treats; bathrooms are luxurious. You breakfast on home-produced eggs and sausages, and fruits from the grandparents' orchard. Pictures of the family's racehorses dot the sitting room, while views from mullioned windows reach over charming gardens to pedigree livestock. Ideal for theatre goers, walkers and garden lovers.

Price	£85-£95. Singles from £60.
Rooms	2: 1 double, 1 twin/double.
Meals	Pubs 1-1.5 miles.
Closed	Christmas & occasionally.
Directions	From Stratford-on-Avon, A3400 Oxford. After 5 miles right by church in Newbold on Stour; follow signs to Blackwell. Right on entering Blackwell. Entrance at end of village road beyond thatched barn.

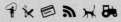 10% off stays Mon-Thurs. Local and homemade food/produce in your room

William & Didi Vernon Miller
Blackwell Grange,
Blackwell,
Shipston-on-Stour CV36 4PF
Tel   +44 (0)1608 682357
Email   didi@blackwellgrange.co.uk
Web   www.blackwellgrange.co.uk

Entry 558   Map 8

Warwickshire

The Old Manor House

An attractive 16th-century manor house with beautiful landscaped gardens sweeping down to the river Stour. The beamed double has oak furniture and a big bathroom; the old-fashioned twin and single are in a private wing. There is a large and elegant drawing and dining room whose antiques, contemporary art and open fire are for visitors to share. Jane prepares first-class breakfasts, and in warm weather you can have tea on the terrace: pots of tulips in spring, old scented roses in summer, meadow land beyond. A comfortable, lived-in family house with Stratford and the theatre close by. *Children over seven welcome.*

Price	£85–£90. Singles from £50.
Rooms	3: 1 double with separate bath; 1 twin, 1 single sharing bath (2nd room let to same party only).
Meals	Restaurants nearby.
Closed	Rarely.
Directions	From Stratford, A422 for 4 miles for Banbury. After 4 miles, right at r'bout onto A429 for Halford. There, 1st right, down hill on Queen's Street. House with black & white timbers straight ahead after 150 yds.

Jane Pusey
The Old Manor House,
Halford,
Shipston-on-Stour CV36 5BT

Tel	+44 (0)1789 740264
Email	info@oldmanor-halford.fsnet.co.uk
Web	www.oldmanor-halford.co.uk

Entry 559   Map 8

Warwickshire

Yew Tree Farm

Pristine gravel courtyard, softly weathered stone, mullioned windows, pleached limes: a charming house. Colefax and Fowler'd rooms brim with exquisite china, portraits and furniture; the gleaming dining table is acres long. Chat by the fire with Lady Hereford, or retreat to the top-floor sitting room. The pretty twin room in the attic is particularly full of chintzy character; the mahogany four-poster room has a smart new bathroom and is beautifully done. Outside, pheasants strut around formal gardens full of sweet peas. Visit the Whichford potteries, return to creature comforts and visual delights.

Price	£105. Singles £55.
Rooms	3: 1 four-poster, 1 twin, 1 single each with separate bath.
Meals	Pub 0.5 miles.
Closed	Rarely.
Directions	Chipping Norton, Great Rollright. Third turning to Whichford. Then 1st turning to Ascott. Down hill and straight into drive.

Susan Hereford
Yew Tree Farm,
Ascott,
Shipston-on-Stour CV36 5PP

Tel	+44 (0)1608 684115
Email	susanhereford@tiscali.co.uk
Web	www.yewtreeascott.co.uk

Entry 560   Map 8

Warwickshire

Oxbourne House

Hard to believe the house is new, with its beamed ceilings, fireplaces and antiques. Bedrooms are fresh, crisp, cosy and cared for, the family room with an 'in the attic' feel; lighting is soft, beds excellent, bath and shower rooms attractive and warm, and views far-reaching. In the garden are tennis, sculpture and Graeme's rambler-bedecked pergola. Wake to birdsong and fresh eggs from their own hens; on peaceful summer nights, watch the dipping sun. Posy and Graeme are hugely likeable and welcoming and the excellent village pub is just down the road. A most comforting place to stay. *Dogs by arrangement.*

Ethical Collection: Food; Community. See page 430.

Price	£65-£85. Singles from £45.
Rooms	3: 1 double, 1 family room; 1 twin/double with separate bath.
Meals	Dinner from £20. Pub 5-minute walk.
Closed	Rarely.
Directions	A422 from Stratford-upon-Avon for Banbury. After 8 miles, right to Oxhill. Last house on right on Whatcote Road.

10% off stays of 3 or more nights.

Use your Sawday's Gift Card here.

Graeme & Posy McDonald
Oxbourne House,
Oxhill,
Warwick CV35 0RA
Tel   +44 (0)1295 688202
Email   graememcdonald@msn.com
Web   www.oxbournehouse.com

Entry 561   Map 8

Warwickshire

Shrewley Pools Farm

A charming, eccentric home and fabulous for families, with space to play and animals to see: sheep, bantams and pigs. A fragrant, romantic garden, too, and a fascinating house (1640), all low ceilings, aged floors and steep stairs. Timbered passages lead to large, pretty, sunny bedrooms (all with electric blankets) with leaded windows and polished wooden floors and a family room with everything needed for a baby. In a farmhouse dining room Cathy serves sausages, bacon, and eggs from the farm, can do gluten-free breakfasts and is happy with teas for children. Buy a day ticket and fish in the lake.

Price	From £55. Singles from £40.
Rooms	3: 1 family room (& cot). 1 twin, 1 single sharing bath (let to same party only).
Meals	Packed lunch £4. Child's high tea £4. Pub/restaurant 1.5 miles.
Closed	Christmas.
Directions	From M40 junc. 15, A46 for Coventry. Left onto A4177. 4.5 miles to Five Ways r'bout. 1st left, on for 0.75 miles; signed, opp. Farm Gate Poultry: track on left.

10% discount for members of armed forces. Free pick-up from local bus/train station.

Cathy Dodd
Shrewley Pools Farm,
Five Ways Road, Haseley,
Warwick CV35 7HB
Tel   +44 (0)1926 484315
Mobile   +44 (0)7818 280681
Email   cathydodd@hotmail.co.uk

Entry 562   Map 8

Warwickshire

Marston House

A generous feel pervades this lovely family home; Kim's big friendly kitchen is the hub of the house. She and John are easy-going and kind and there's no standing on ceremony. Feel welcomed with tea on arrival, delicious homemade breakfasts, oodles of interesting facts about what to do in the area. The house is big and sunny; old rugs cover parquet floors, soft sofas tumble with cushions and sash windows look onto the smart garden packed with interesting plants and birds. Bedrooms are roomy, traditional and supremely comfortable. A special place with a big heart and great walks straight from the house.

Ethical Collection: Food; Community. See page 430.

Price	£85-£100. Singles from £60.
Rooms	2: 1 twin/double with separate bath; 1 twin/double with separate shower.
Meals	Kitchen supper, 3 courses, £29.50. Dinner, in dining room, £35 (min. 4). Pub 5-minute walk.
Closed	Rarely.
Directions	M40 exit 11. From Banbury, A361 north for 7 miles; Byfield village sign, left into Twistle Lane; on to Priors Marston; 5th house on left with cattle grid, after S-bend.
	10% off stays Mon-Thurs. Bottle of house wine with dinner.

Kim & John Mahon
Marston House,
Byfield Road, Priors Marston,
Southam CV47 7RP
Tel   +44 (0)1327 260297
Email   kim@mahonand.co.uk
Web   www.ivabestbandb.co.uk

Entry 563   Map 8

Wiltshire

Sarum College

This is very much a working, educational institution – not a luxurious B&B – but the setting in The Close is stunning: there are several museums with art and architecture from medieval to Georgian, you can listen to the choir sing at Evensong, stroll around the cloisters, or wander to good theatre and restaurants. Bedrooms are plain and comfortable, bathrooms functional and neat as a pin, there's a sitting room (no frills, but a magnificent view of the Cathedral) with TV if you want it, and a chapel you are welcome to attend. Food is hearty: they run courses here so at times it may be busy.

Price	£105. Singles £80.
Rooms	7: 3 doubles, 4 twins.
Meals	Lunch £10. Packed lunch £5. Dinner £10. (Rates for groups negotiable.) Pub/restaurant 100 yds.
Closed	Christmas & New Year.
Directions	In Salisbury's Cathedral Close, 10-minute walk from train & bus stations. From New Street or Crane Street, enter The Close at High St gate, then left.
	10% off stays of 2 or more nights.

Linda Cooper
Sarum College,
19 The Close,
Salisbury SP1 2EE
Tel   +44 (0)1722 424800
Email   hospitality@sarum.ac.uk
Web   www.sarum.ac.uk

Entry 564   Map 3

Wiltshire

85 Exeter Street

You are so central here that you can wander into town on foot (having parked by the house or walked from the station). Susan's Georgian house, facing the cathedral close, is on a main road but the bedrooms sit very quietly at the back and the upstairs drawing room has a lovely view of the spire. Enjoy a good breakfast of fresh fruit, local bacon and sausages, and homebaked bread downstairs at one big table. Bedrooms are simple and traditional: William Morris curtains, a five-foot bed and a shower cabinet in one, a single bed with a spare roll-out bed in the other. Good, solid city B&B. *French & German spoken.*

Price	From £80. Singles from £65.
Rooms	2: 1 double; 1 twin with separate bath/shower.
Meals	Pubs/restaurants nearby.
Closed	Rarely.
Directions	Ring road round Salisbury to south of city; past r'bout to Southampton; at next r'bout (Exeter St r'bout), 3rd exit on to Exeter St (signed Old George Mall). No 85 near city centre. Park opp. house; ask for permit on arrival.

🧳 10% off stays of 2 or more nights.

Susan Orr–Ewing
85 Exeter Street,
Salisbury SP1 2SE
Tel +44 (0)1722 417944
Email info@85exeterstreet.co.uk
Web www.85exeterstreet.co.uk

Wiltshire

Old Stoke

As pretty as thatched cottages come. This lovely old farmhouse is edged by an AONB filled with birdsong and wildlife, yet you are close to Salisbury. Guests have a book-filled sitting room with Dorset cream walls and pretty chairs and sofas to collapse onto: upstairs are fresh bedrooms with bright fabrics on headboards and window cushions, feathery beds and sparkling bathrooms. Tracie is charming and cooks well; good wholesome food using eggs from her own hens, vegetables from the garden and delicious flapjacks or cake for tea. Stroll down the fecund garden to a meadow and the river. *Children over eight welcome.*

Price	£65–£70. Singles £45.
Rooms	2: 1 twin/double; 1 double with separate bath.
Meals	Dinner £17.50–£22.50. Packed lunch £6. Pub 1 mile.
Closed	December-February.
Directions	SW from Salisbury on A354; right at Coombe Bissett dir. Bishopstone. 2nd left after White Hart, signed Stoke Farthing. In hamlet, sharp bend to right, 2nd house on left. Parking to left of house.

🧳 Bottle of wine with dinner on first night.

Tracie Pickford
Old Stoke,
Stoke Farthing, Broad Chalke,
Salisbury SP5 5ED
Tel +44 (0)1722 780513
Email stay@oldstoke.co.uk
Web www.oldstoke.co.uk

Wiltshire

Manor Farm

Two children, two cats, 22 chickens, 25 sheep, a burgeoning young garden and a greenhouse to die for: Katie looks after it all with energy and good humour, and goes the extra mile for her guests. Dating from the 1600s, it's a house with a history – and today combines luxury with simplicity. Be cheered by an elegant sitting room with a real fire, a suite with thick feather pillows and a big comfy bed, a bathroom with taupe towels and Neal's Yard bubbles, a breakfast, delivered to your private quarters, of local and home-grown delights, an iPod dock and DVDs on request. And there's a room to store your bicycles and boots!

Price	£80. Singles £50.
Rooms	1 suite.
Meals	Supper tray £15. Packed lunch £10. Pub within walking distance.
Closed	Christmas & lambing time.
Directions	A354 Coombe Bissett, 1st right to Broadchalke. 5 miles to village. Left opp. pub, 0.25 miles, church on right. Road bends 90° right. On apex straight on, then left. House 2nd left.

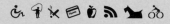

Bottle of wine in your room.

Katie Jowett
Manor Farm,
Broad Chalke,
Salisbury SP5 5DW
Tel   +44 (0)1722 780230
Email info@manorfarmbroadchalke.co.uk
Web   www.manorfarmbroadchalke.co.uk

Entry 567   Map 3

Wiltshire

Dowtys

This beautifully converted Victorian dairy farm has fabulous views over the Nadder valley. Peaceful, private bedrooms have original beams, antiques and big Vi-Spring beds – the ground-floor one has its own sitting room; bathrooms are smart. The guest sitting room has a contemporary feel with frameless windows, wood-burner, sliding oak doors and underfloor heating. Have breakfast in the old milking parlour, now the dining room, or on the terrace, sit beneath the espaliered limes in the immaculate garden, dip into the National Trust woods. Footpaths start from the gate and Willi and Di are happy to help with outing plans.

Price	£75-£85. Singles from £55.
Rooms	3: 1 double; 1 double, 1 twin each with separate bath/shower.
Meals	Packed lunch on request. Pub 0.25 miles.
Closed	Christmas & New Year.
Directions	B3089 approaching Dinton from east (Barford St Martin). Take 1st turn right after village sign & 30mph, signed Wylye. 100 yds; 1st right up Dowtys Lane to house.

Di & Willi Verdon-Smith
Dowtys,
Dowtys Lane, Dinton,
Salisbury SP3 5ES
Tel   +44 (0)1722 716886
Email dowtys.bb@gmail.com
Web   www.dowtysbedandbreakfast.co.uk

Entry 568   Map 3

Wiltshire

Little Langford Farmhouse

A rare treat to have your milk fresh from the cow – the Helyers have pedigree cattle. The bedrooms of this rather grand Victorian-gothic farmhouse are large and pretty with period furniture and crisp linen; there are impressive countryside views, a baby grand and a billiard room. Everything is elegant and polished yet cosy, and terrace doors are thrown open for delicious al fresco breakfasts in summer. The farm, part of which is an SSSI, is treasured for its glorious walks, wild flowers and butterflies, and the Helyers are immensely welcoming. *Minimum stay two nights at weekends. Children by arrangement.*

Price	£78-£80. Singles £58-£70.
Rooms	3: 1 double, 1 twin/double; 1 twin with separate shower.
Meals	Pub/restaurant 1.75 miles.
Closed	December/January.
Directions	Exit A303 junc. A36, Salisbury. 2 miles; right for The Langfords. In Steeple L, right for Hanging L. At T-junc. opp. village hall, left for Little Langford. House 0.75 miles on left.

10% off stays of 2 or more nights.

Use your Sawday's Gift Card here.

Patricia Helyer
Little Langford Farmhouse,
Little Langford,
Salisbury SP3 4NP
Tel +44 (0)1722 790205
Email bandb@littlelangford.co.uk
Web www.littlelangford.co.uk

Entry 569   Map 3

Wiltshire

The Duck Yard

Independence with your own terrace, your own entrance and your own sitting room. Peaceful too, at the end of the lane, with a colourful cottage garden, a summerhouse and roaming hens and ducks. Harriet makes wedding cakes, looks after guests and cheerfully rustles up fine meals at short notice; breakfasts promise delicious homemade bread. Your carpeted bedroom and aquamarine bathroom are tucked under the eaves; below is a sitting room cosy with wood-burner, books and old squashy sofas, leading to a terrace. Good for walkers – maps are supplied and you may even borrow a dog. *Reflexology available: book in advance.*

Price	£70. Singles £50.
Rooms	1 twin/double & sitting room.
Meals	Dinner, 3 courses, £25. Packed lunch £7. Pub 2 miles.
Closed	Christmas & New Year.
Directions	A303 to Wylye, then for Dinton. After 4 miles left at x-roads, for Wilton & Salisbury. On for 1 mile, down hill, round sharp right bend, signed Sandhills Rd. 1st low red brick building on left. Park in space on left.

25% off room rate Mon-Thurs. Late checkout (12pm).

Harriet & Peter Combes
The Duck Yard,
Sandhills Road, Dinton,
Salisbury SP3 5ER
Tel +44 (0)1722 716495
Mobile +44 (0)7729 777436
Email harriet.combes@googlemail.com

Entry 570   Map 3

Wiltshire

The Mill House

In a tranquil village next to the river is a house surrounded by water meadows and wilderness garden. Roses ramble, marsh orchids bloom and butterflies shimmer. This 12-acre labour of love is the creation of ever-charming Diana and her son Michael. Their home, the time-worn 18th-century miller's house, is packed with country clutter – porcelain, foxes' brushes, ancestral photographs above the fire – while bedrooms are quaint and flowery, with firm comfy beds; organic breakfasts are served at small tables. Diana has lived here for many many years, and has been doing B&B for 27 of them! *Children over eight welcome.*

Price	From £90. Singles from £60.
Rooms	5: 3 doubles, 1 family room; 1 twin with separate bath.
Meals	Pub 5-minute walk.
Closed	Never.
Directions	From A303 take B3083 at Winterbourne Stoke to Berwick St James. Go through village, past Boot Inn & church. Turn left into yard just before the sharp left bend. Coming from A36 (B3083), house 1st on right.

Diana Gifford Mead & Michael Mertens
The Mill House,
Berwick St James,
Salisbury SP3 4TS
Tel +44 (0)1722 790331
Web www.millhouse.org.uk

Entry 571   Map 3

Wiltshire

The Old School House

Charmingly cluttered, sparklingly clean, this 1860 village house is filled with light, beautiful objects and lovely pieces of furniture. Find a comfy chair in the snug with its loaded book shelves on art, gardening and travel – Darea's passions. Your chintzy bedrooms (the double is larger) have wooden arched beams, excellent mattresses and a newly decorated bathroom with oatmeal tiles. Breakfast is in the smart kitchen with its humming black Aga: good sausages and bacon, local eggs. A little south-facing courtyard has colourful pots and a bench for idle gazing; Stonehenge, Longleat and Stourhead beckon.

Price	£70-£80. Singles £40-£50.
Rooms	2: 1 double, 1 twin sharing bath (let to same party only).
Meals	Pub 0.5 miles.
Closed	Rarely.
Directions	From London exit 303 at first Wylye turn off signed A36 Warminster, Salisbury. Right fork, right at T-junc., then immediate left into Wylye village. Past pub, church & shop & house immediately after.

Darea Browne
The Old School House,
Wylye,
Warminster BA12 0QR
Tel +44 (0)1985 248228
Email dareabrowne@aol.com

Entry 572   Map 3

Wiltshire

Manor Farm

Could this be everyone's idea of a country B&B? A lovely old mellow-stone farmhouse (1500s) in a quaint little village with delightful, friendly hosts, three gorgeous dogs and a huge organic vegetable garden. Inside, it is family-friendly not spanking-smart, comfortable, colourful and easy-going. Your quarters at one end of the house have a big family room on the floor above the guest breakfast/sitting room; family pictures and photographs bring the walls to life, boots huddle discreetly behind a screen, two lived-in sofas lie in wait. You can even book a flight in Bertie's microlight for a different view of Wiltshire.

Price	From £70. Singles from £45.
Rooms	1 family room with separate bath.
Meals	Packed lunch £5-£8. Pub within 3 miles.
Closed	Christmas.
Directions	From London & Stonehenge, A303. After A350 junc. pass Esso garage, turn immediately left, then sharp right signed West Knoyle. House 1st on right at bottom of hill.

10% off room rate Mon-Thurs.

Frances & Bertie Grotrian
Manor Farm,
West Knoyle,
Warminster BA12 6AG
Tel   +44 (0)1747 830380
Email   bertiegrotrian@yahoo.co.uk
Web   www.englishfarmhouse.co.uk

Entry 573   Map 3

Wiltshire

Oaklands

A comfortable townhouse, a south-facing garden, two dear dogs and a lovely old Silver Cross pram sitting under the stairs. It was the first house in Warminster to have a bathroom; the bathrooms have multiplied since and the interiors have had a delightful makeover – easy to see why this spacious 1880s house has been in the family forever. Andrew and Carolyn, relaxed and charming, serve delicious breakfasts in the beautiful new conservatory at the drawing room end. Bedrooms, desirable and welcoming, overlook churchyard and trees; fresh fabrics, soft colours, cosy bathroom, family antiques. And restaurants are a stroll.

Price	£65-£85. Singles from £55.
Rooms	3: 2 doubles, 1 twin/double (rooms can interconnect).
Meals	Occasional dinner (min. 4). Pub/restaurant 0.5 miles.
Closed	Christmas & rarely.
Directions	From Warminster centre direction Salisbury. On right, opp. end of St John's churchyard.

10% off room rate.

Carolyn & Andrew Lewis
Oaklands,
88 Boreham Road,
Warminster BA12 9JW
Tel   +44 (0)1985 215532
Email   apl1944@yahoo.co.uk
Web   www.stayatoaklands.co.uk

Entry 574   Map 3

Wiltshire

The Limes

Through the electric gates, past the gravelled car park and the pretty, box-edged front garden and you arrive at the middle part of a 1620 house divided into three. The beams, stone mullions and leaded windows are charming, and softly spoken Ellodie is an exceptional hostess. Light bedrooms have pretty curtains and fresh flowers, tiled bathrooms have good soaps and thick towels, logs glow in the grate, and breakfasts promise delicious Wiltshire bacon, prunes soaked in orange juice and organic bread. You are on the busy main road leading out of Melksham – catch the bus to Bath from right outside the door.

Price	£78-£88. Singles £48-£53.
Rooms	3: 2 twins/doubles, 1 single.
Meals	Dinner £20-£25. BYO.
	Packed lunch £6. Pub 1.5 miles.
Closed	Rarely.
Directions	Leave Melksham on A365 to Bath. After Victoria Motors, sharp right at school sign, brown gates will open slowly. Park on right, follow path to house.

10% off stays Mon-Thurs & for 3-night stays over a weekend.

Ellodie van der Wulp
The Limes,
Shurnhold House, Shurnhold,
Melksham SN12 8DG
Tel   +44 (0)1225 790627
Mobile   +44 (0)7974 366892
Email   ellodie@ukonline.co.uk

Entry 575   Map 3

Wiltshire

Alcombe Manor

Down a maze of magical lanes discover this hamlet and its 17th-century manor house: a deeply romantic hideaway with panelling, wooden floors, a couple of medieval windows, deep sofas, log fires, a galleried hall, shelves of books and plenty of places to sit. A fine oak staircase leads to large, light bedrooms, reassuringly old-fashioned; carpeted floors creak companionably and every ancient leaded window has a dreamy garden view... five acres of English perfection, no less, with topiary and a stream dashing through. Your hosts are kind and helpful, the peace is palpable, and you are just five miles from Bath.

Price	From £80. Singles £50.
Rooms	3: 2 twins, each with separate bath/shower; 1 single sharing bath.
Meals	Occasional dinner. Pubs nearby.
Closed	Rarely.
Directions	M4 junc. 17; A4 to Bath through Box; right for Middle Hill & Ditteridge; 200 yds, left signed Alcombe. Up hill for 0.5 miles, fork right; 200 yds on left.

Simon & Victoria Morley
Alcombe Manor,
Box,
Corsham SN13 8QQ
Tel   +44 (0)1225 743850
Mobile   +44 (0)7887 855634
Email   morley@alcombemanor.co.uk

Entry 576   Map 3

Wiltshire

Puckshipton House

An intriguing name, Puckshipton: it means Goblin's Barn. The house is deep in the lush countryside of the Vale of Pewsey, reached by a long tree-lined drive. You stay in the Georgian end, with a private entrance that leads to a Regency-blue hall. Rooms are stylish and uncluttered, an attractive mix of old and new with good beds, crisp linen and bathrooms that are cossetting, one with a roll top bath. The dining and sitting rooms have wood-burners both. James, a forester, and Juliette have young children, a walled garden and a thatched hen house from which to fetch your breakfast egg.

Ethical Collection: Environment; Food. See page 430.

Price	£80. Singles £50.
Rooms	2: 1 four-poster; 1 twin/double with separate bath/shower.
Meals	Pubs/restaurant 5-minute drive.
Closed	Christmas.
Directions	Devizes A342 towards Rushall; left to Chirton, right to Marden & through village. On for 0.25 miles; right into private drive.

Free pick-up from local bus/train station. 10% off stays of 3 or more nights. Flexible checkout.

Juliette & James Noble
Puckshipton House,
Beechingstoke,
Pewsey SN9 6HG
Tel   +44 (0)1672 851336
Web   www.puckshipton.co.uk

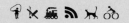

Entry 577   Map 3

Wiltshire

Upper Westcourt

Long views down Pewsey Vale, a stroll to the pub, bedrooms looking onto a beautiful garden. This is a relaxed, light-filled house surrounded by farmland that stretches away to Somerset, between Pewsey Downs and Martinsell Hill. Inside are rich curtains, polished old furniture, photographs and paintings; bedrooms and bathrooms are sunny with florals, pictures and books; drawing room sofas demand to be sunk into before a winter log fire; breakfasts may include fresh fruits and tomatoes from the garden. Come for traditional good taste and charming, welcoming, well-organised hosts.

Price	£75-£85. Singles £45-£55.
Rooms	3: 1 twin/double; 1 twin, 1 single sharing separate bath (single let to same party only).
Meals	Pubs within walking distance.
Closed	Christmas & Easter.
Directions	A346 or A338 to Burbage. In High St, turn west to Westcourt, over bypass and at sharp left-hand bend, right (signed 'No Through Road'). 250 yds on left.

10% off stays of 2 or more nights Mon-Thurs.

Peter & Carolyn Hill
Upper Westcourt,
Burbage,
Marlborough SN8 3BW
Tel   +44 (0)1672 810307
Email   prhill@onetel.com
Web   www.upperwestcourt.co.uk

Entry 578   Map 3

Wiltshire

Westcourt Farm

Rozzie and Jonny left London to restore a medieval, Grade II* cruck truss hall house (beautifully) amid wildflower meadows, hedgerows, ponds, geese and hens. Delightful people, they love to cook and can spoil you rotten. Rooms are freshly decorated, crisp yet traditional, the country furniture is charming and the architecture fascinating. Bedrooms have comfortable beds and fine linen, bathrooms are spot-on, there's a lovely light drawing room and a barn for meetings and parties. Encircled by footpaths and fields, Westcourt is the oldest house in a perfect village, two minutes from a rather good pub.

Wiltshire

Fisherman's House

Ducks shoot the rapids of the Kennet river as it flows past the lawns of this exquisitely situated home – bliss to sit out here with binoculars on a warm day. Built in 1812 it looks every inch a doll's house, but charming Heather adds a deft human touch. Elegant breakfasts are served in the Edwardian style conservatory, there's a delightful guests' sitting room with an open fire and, upstairs, three sumptuously decorated bedrooms that face the garden and river; time slips by effortlessly here. Many people come to visit the crop and stone circles and Bath and Marlborough are a hop away.

Price	£80. Singles £40.
Rooms	2: 1 twin with separate bath; 1 double with separate shower.
Meals	Pub/restaurant in village.
Closed	Christmas & New Year.
Directions	A338 Hungerford-Salisbury; after 4 miles signed Shalbourne; through village & fork left at pub; 150 yds, 2nd drive on right.

Price	£85. Singles £40-£50.
Rooms	3: 1 double; 1 twin, 1 single sharing bath.
Meals	Lunch/packed lunch from £5. Pub 500 yds.
Closed	Rarely.
Directions	From Hungerford, A4 for Marlborough. After 7 miles, right for Stitchcombe, down hill (bear left at barn) & left at T-junc. On entering village, house 2nd on left.

	Jonny & Rozzie Buxton
	Westcourt Farm,
	Shalbourne,
	Marlborough SN8 3QE
Tel	+44 (0)1672 871399
Email	rozzieb@btinternet.com
Web	www.westcourtfarm.com

	Heather Coulter
	Fisherman's House,
	Mildenhall,
	Marlborough SN8 2LZ
Tel	+44 (0)1672 515390
Email	heathercoulter610@btinternet.com
Web	www.fishermanshouse.co.uk

Entry 579   Map 3

Entry 580   Map 3

Wiltshire

Blue Barn

Jackie's gorgeous home is along a byway and surrounded by a lovely garden and paddocks with sweeping views. Through an avenue of trees you glimpse the stunning timber-framed green oak farmhouse. You have independence in your own annexe with a light and airy L-shaped sitting room, tartan sofa, lots of pictures, comfy chairs and a French daybed for an extra guest. Jackie brings your locally sourced breakfast here and you eat round a farmhouse table. The twin bedroom is fresh and pretty with rose-covered chintz headboards; the shower room spotless. You are right on the Ridgeway for fabulous walking.

Price	£80. Singles £40-£55.
Rooms	1 twin & sitting room. Extra beds available.
Meals	Pub 1 mile.
Closed	Never.
Directions	A346 Marlborough-Swindon. Turn for Ogbourne St George. Right after Crown Inn, continue to 'No Through' sign. At Ridgeway, left, then continue until Blue Barn. M4 motorway 5 miles.

Jacqueline Palmer
Blue Barn,
Ogbourne St George,
Marlborough SN8 2NT
Tel   +44 (0)1672 841082
Email jax@capalmer.co.uk
Web   www.blue-barn.co.uk

Entry 581   Map 3

Wiltshire

Glebe House

The rogues' gallery of photographs up the stairs says it all: Glebe House is quirky and fun. Friendly Ginny spoils guests rotten with pressed linen and sociable dinners served on Wedgewood china. Charming, cosy and comfortable are the bedrooms, one with an Indian theme; delightful is the drawing room with its landscape oils, Bechstein piano and rugs from all over Asia; settle into a coral sofa and roast away by the fire. Breads, marmalades and jams are homemade, beautiful views shoot off down the valley, the garden trills with hundreds of birds and Mr Biggles (the grey parrot) chats by the Aga.

Ethical Collection: Environment; Food; Community. See page 430.

Price	£80. Singles £45.
Rooms	2: 1 double, 1 twin.
Meals	Dinner, 3 courses, from £25 (BYO). Pub 4 miles.
Closed	Christmas.
Directions	From Devizes-Chippenham A342. Follow Chittoe & Spye Park. On over crossroads onto narrow lane. House 2nd on left.

10% off stays of 2 or more nights. Bottle of wine with dinner on first night.

Ginny Scrope
Glebe House,
Chittoe,
Chippenham SN15 2EL
Tel   +44 (0)1380 850864
Email gscrope@aol.com
Web   www.glebehouse-chittoe.co.uk

Entry 582   Map 3

Wiltshire

The Coach House

In an ancient hamlet a few miles north of Bath, an impeccable conversion of an early 19th-century barn. Bedrooms are fresh and cosy with sloping ceilings; the drawing room is elegant with porcelain and chintz, its pale walls the ideal background for striking displays of fresh flowers. Sliding glass doors lead to a south-facing patio... then to a well-groomed croquet lawn bordered by flowers, with vegetable garden, tennis court, woodland and paddock beyond. Helga and David are delightful and there's lots to do from here; the splendours of Bath, Castle Combe and plenty of good golf courses are all near.

Price	£70-£80. Singles £35-£45.
Rooms	2: 1 double with separate bath/shower; 1 twin/double let to same party only.
Meals	Dinner, 3 courses, from £20. Pubs/restaurants 1 mile.
Closed	Rarely.
Directions	From M4 junc. 17, A350 for Chippenham. A420 to Bristol (east) & Castle Combe. After 6.3 miles, right into Upper Wraxall. Sharp left opp. village green; at end of drive.

🧳 Bottle of wine with dinner. Late checkout (12pm).

Helga & David Venables
The Coach House,
Upper North Wraxall,
Chippenham SN14 7AG
Tel   +44 (0)1225 891026
Email   david@dvenables.co.uk
Web   www.upperwraxallcoachhouse.co.uk

🛎 🚂 🐂 🔊 🐕 🎭

Entry 583   Map 3

Wiltshire

Cadwell Hill Barn

Elizabeth is a dynamo at interior design and gardens. The result: a stunningly converted barn hugged by exuberant greenery and packed with interesting fabrics, lampshades, paintings and hand-made chandeliers. A fluffy cat basks in sunlight that filters into the raftered upstairs sitting room; down in the dining area an inglenook fireplace and Persian rugs give an elegant, cosy feel. Bedrooms are calm, soft spaces, one with its own sitting room; bathrooms have heaps of good lotions and Neal's Yard soaps. Countryside rolls into the distance, the local village has a lively community and you're five minutes from the M4.

Price	£70-£90. Singles £40.
Rooms	4: 1 double, 1 suite; 1 double, 1 single sharing separate bath (let to same party only).
Meals	Pub/restaurant 1.5 miles.
Closed	Christmas.
Directions	M4, A46 towards Bath, junc. 18. About 1 mile, then left signed West Littleton. Through village, pass green and St James' church, then on for further 0.3 miles; house on right.

🧳 10% off room rate. Bottle of wine with dinner on first night. Late checkout (12pm).

Elizabeth Edwards
Cadwell Hill Barn,
West Littleton,
Chippenham SN14 8JE
Tel   +44 (0)1225 891122
Email   maesdewi@uk2.net
Web   www.cadwellhillbarn.co.uk

🛎 🚂 🔊 🐕

Entry 584   Map 3

Wiltshire

Manor Farm

Farmyard heaven in the Cotswolds. A 17th-century manor farmhouse in 550 arable acres; horses in the paddock, dozing dogs in the yard, tumbling blooms outside the door and a perfectly tended village, with duck pond, a short walk. Beautiful bedrooms are softly lit, with muted colours, plump goose down pillows and the crispest linen. Breakfast in front of the fire is a banquet of delights, tea among the roses is a treat, thanks to charming, welcoming Victoria. This is the postcard England of dreams, with Castle Combe, Lacock, grand walking and gardens to visit. *Children over 12 welcome.*

Price	From £80. Singles from £43.
Rooms	3: 2 doubles; 1 twin with separate bath.
Meals	Pubs nearby.
Closed	Rarely.
Directions	From M4 A429 to Cirencester (junc. 17). After 200 yds, 1st left for Grittleton; there, follow signs to Alderton. Farmhouse near church.

Victoria Lippiatt-Onslow
Manor Farm,
Alderton,
Chippenham SN14 6NL

Tel	+44 (0)1666 840271
Email	victoria.lippiatt@btinternet.com
Web	www.themanorfarm.co.uk

Entry 585   Map 3

Wiltshire

Manor Farm

The road through the sleepy Wiltshire village brings you to a Queen Anne house with a *petit château* feel, enfolded by a tranquil garden with tulip meadow, groomed lawns and... hens! Inside is as lovely; watercolourist Clare is a perfectionist behind the scenes and is charming. The bedroom is elegant and cosy, its soft-painted panelled walls hung with good pictures, its sash windows beautifully dressed. Scrumptious, all-organic breakfasts are served in a butter-yellow kitchen; the eclectically furnished drawing room, shared among guests, has a real fire and a delightful lived-in, family feel.

Price	£90. Singles by arrangement.
Rooms	1 double.
Meals	Pub 200 yds.
Closed	Christmas & New Year.
Directions	M4 exit 17. North on A429 for Malmesbury, right on B4042. Right after 3 miles to Little Somerford. Past pub, right at crossroads, 50 yds on, house behind tall wall.

10% off room rate Mon–Thurs.

Clare Inskip
Manor Farm,
Little Somerford,
Chippenham SN15 5JW

Tel	+44 (0)1666 822140
Mobile	+44 (0)7970 892344
Email	clareinskip@hotmail.com

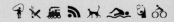

Entry 586   Map 3

Wiltshire

Bullocks Horn Cottage

Up a country lane to this hidden-away house which the Legges have turned into a haven of peace and seclusion. Liz loves fabrics and mixes them with flair, Colin has painted a colourful mural – complete with macaws – in the conservatory. Bedrooms are quiet with lovely views, the sitting room with log fire has large comfy sofas, and the garden, which has been featured in various magazines, is exceptional. Home veg and herbs and local seasonal food are used at dinner which, in summer, you can eat in the cool shade of the arbour, covered in climbing roses and jasmine. *Children over 12 welcome.*

Ethical Collection: Food. See page 430.

Price	From £80. Singles from £40.
Rooms	2: 1 twin; 1 twin with separate bath.
Meals	Dinner £20-£25. BYO. Pub 1.5 miles.
Closed	Christmas.
Directions	From A429, B4040 through Charlton, past Horse & Groom. 0.5 miles, left signed 'Bullocks Horn No Through Road'. On to end of lane. Right then 1st on left.

	Colin & Liz Legge
	Bullocks Horn Cottage,
	Charlton,
	Malmesbury SN16 9DZ
Tel	+44 (0)1666 577600
Email	bullockshorn@clara.co.uk
Web	www.bullockshorn.co.uk

Entry 587   Map 3

Wiltshire

Westhill House

A large Regency house in the centre of this market town; you are on the edge of the marvellous Cotswolds. Vivacious Brenda, well-travelled and a collector of art, has filled her home with bold colours, eclectic paintings, beautiful glass and ceramics; the elegant drawing room has an open fire and the dining room is dramatically red. Bedrooms come in creams and blues, beds are new, wine glasses and corkscrew await; bathrooms are contemporary and indulgent with fluffy towels. Be greeted with tea and cake, try French toast with fruit and maple syrup for breakfast, or full English. Marked walking trails run from the door.

Price	£75-£105. Singles £60-£90.
Rooms	3 doubles.
Meals	Pubs/restaurants within 5 miles.
Closed	Rarely.
Directions	Exit 15 off M4, A419 to Cirencester. Take A361 Burford, Highworth exit. Left at lights in Highworth onto Cricklade Road. House on right immed. after Oak Drive. Black wrought iron gate.

	10% off room rate Mon-Thurs. Free pick-up from local bus/train station.

	Brenda Haywood
	Westhill House,
	Cricklade Road,
	Highworth SN6 7BL
Tel	+44 (0)1793 764219
Email	info@westhillhouse.net
Web	www.westhillhouse.net

Entry 588   Map 3

Worcestershire

Harrowfields

Tucked just off the high street this compact cottage is massively comfortable and stylish too: contemporary colours and old beams, great books and a homely feel. The bedroom is large enough to lounge in with a good sofa, an antique brass bed, crisp linen and your own cosy wood-burner; in the shower room the spoiling continues – and there are lovely garden views. Susie and Adam (who cooks) are natural and charming, hens cluck around outside, breakfast is local and seasonal, you can walk for miles or just to the pub. Young, romantic couples will be in heaven here; uncork the wine, light the fire, turn up the music.

Worcestershire

Lower End House

They've piled on the chic here, in this timber-framed hall house: wide floorboards, wood-burners, leather sofas, all cleverly mixed with bold fabrics, antler chandeliers and cowhide rugs. The listed Cyder Mill is equally stylish, and private stairs lead to its romantic suite. Lavish, warm bedrooms have the best mattresses and Siberian goose down; some have handmade wallpaper, one an explosion of beams, another an antique brocade sofa. Bathrooms will tempt you to preen: carved stone basins, the thickest towels. Foodies will enjoy breakfast in the Cookery School, and walkers have the beautiful Malvern Hills nearby.

Price	£75. Singles from £55.
Rooms	1 double.
Meals	Pubs in village.
Closed	Rarely.
Directions	Enter Eckington from Bredon (M5 junc. 9). Turn 1st right by village shop. House on left before Anchor pub.

Free pick-up from local bus/train station.

Use your Sawday's Gift Card here.

Susie Alington & Adam Stanford
Harrowfields,
Cotheridge Lane,
Eckington WR10 3BA
Tel +44 (0)1386 751053
Email susie@harrowfields.co.uk
Web www.harrowfields.co.uk

Entry 589   Map 8

Price	£125–£185. Singles £65.
Rooms	9: 3 twins/doubles; 2 singles with shared bath. Cyder Mill: 3 doubles, 1 suite.
Meals	Supper trays from £12.50. Packed lunch from £10. Pubs in village.
Closed	Never.
Directions	From Pershore, left onto A4104 signed Upton. Left to Eckington on B4080, then 1st right in village into Drakesbridge Road; continue then right into Manor Road.

Local food/produce in your room, including Cookery School foodie goody bag.

Jane Harber
Lower End House,
Manor Road,
Eckington WR10 3BH
Tel +44 (0)1386 751600
Email info@lowerendhouse.co.uk
Web www.lowerendhouse.co.uk

Entry 590   Map 8

Worcestershire

Bidders Croft

Completely rebuilt in 1995 from 200-year-old bricks, this solid house has a hand-carved mahogany hall pillar, oak-framed loggias and an enormous conservatory where you eat overlooking the garden, orchard, field and the Malvern Hills. Traditional bedrooms with padded headboards and dressing tables are warm and comfortable; bathrooms are spick and span. Bill and Charlotte give you a log fire, books and magazines in the drawing room, an Aga-cooked breakfast and candlelit dinner with home-grown vegetables and fruit. The hills beckon walkers, the views soar and you're near the Malvern theatres.

Price	£79-£89. Singles £49-£55.
Rooms	2: 1 twin with separate bath; 1 double with separate shower.
Meals	Dinner, 4 courses, £29.50 (for min. 4). Pub/restaurant 250 yds.
Closed	Christmas & New Year.
Directions	From Upton-upon-Severn, A4104 dir. Little Malvern & Ledbury. After 3 miles, pass Anchor Inn on right; drive is 250 yds on left, house signed.

 Bottle of vintage Cava for bookings of 2 or more nights.

Use your Sawday's Gift Card here.

Bill & Charlotte Carver
Bidders Croft,
Welland,
Malvern WR13 6LN
Tel   +44 (0)1684 592179
Email carvers@bidderscroft.com
Web   www.bidderscroft.com

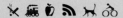

Worcestershire

The Birches

Thoughtful Katharine is attentive; Edward puts you at ease humming a jolly tune. Come and go as you please from this self-contained annexe, spotless and contemporary. French windows lead to a pretty terrace, then to a charming garden opening to fields and views of the Malverns. Though the house is easily accessible, the tranquillity is sublime; plenty of spots to sit and ponder the view back to the timber-framed house. Hens pottering on the lawn lay eggs for breakfast, served – in your room – with local bacon and sausages, and bread from Ledbury's baker. Wander further for abundant leafy walks and lovely Regency Malvern.

Price	£70. Singles £50.
Rooms	1 double.
Meals	Pub/restaurant 0.3 miles.
Closed	Never.
Directions	From Ledbury A449, signed Malvern. After 1 mile right onto A438. After 3 miles, crossroads; left, then after 1 mile right into Birts Street. House on right after 0.25 miles.

10% off room rate Mon-Thurs.

Katharine Litchfield
The Birches,
Birts Street, Birtsmorton,
Malvern WR13 6AW
Tel   +44 (0)1684 833821
Email katharine-thebirches@hotmail.co.uk
Web   www.the-birchesbedandbreakfast.co.uk

Worcestershire

Old Country Farm

Ella's passion for this remote, tranquil place – and the environment in general – is infectious. She believes the house was once home to a Saxon chief. Certainly, it has beams dating from 1400; now it's a rambling mix of russet stone and colour-washed brick, with a warm and delightfully cluttered kitchen, wooden floors, lovely rugs. Friendly, low-ceilinged bedrooms are simple and rustic. Ella's parents collected rare plants and the garden is full of hellebores and snowdrops; roe deer and barn owls flit about in the surrounding woods. A wonderful retreat for nature lovers, birdwatchers and walkers.

Ethical Collection: Environment; Food.
See page 430.

Price	£60–£90. Singles £35–£55.
Rooms	3: 1 double; 1 double with separate bath; 1 double with separate shower.
Meals	Pubs/restaurants 3 miles.
Closed	Rarely.
Directions	From Worcester A4103 for 11 miles; B4220 for Ledbury. After leaving Cradley, left at top of hill for Mathon, right for Coddington; house 0.25 miles on right.

Ella Grace Quincy
Old Country Farm,
Mathon,
Malvern WR13 5PS
Tel   +44 (0)1886 880867
Email   ella@oldcountryhouse.co.uk
Web   www.oldcountryhouse.co.uk

Entry 593   Map 8

Worcestershire

The Hayloft

Beams galore – and photos too. Dennis is a photographer and your bedroom walls are lined with his colourful works; you get a jolly comfortable bed, posh robes, snazzy bathrooms with candles, plump towels and views across rolling fields. All is peaceful here: wake to a sizzling full English from cheery Maureen, with proper black pudding and homemade jams. You are near the Wychavon Way and the Droitwich Canal for walking, boating and birdwatching, but you could just pootle round the garden which slides down the hill into the countryside, or bubble gently in the hot tub. Excellent value, hearty suppers, lovely people.

Price	£70–£80. Singles from £40.
Rooms	2: 1 double; 1 double with separate bath.
Meals	Dinner, 2–3 courses, £15–£20. Packed lunch £5. Pubs/restaurants 2–3 miles.
Closed	Rarely.
Directions	From Droitwich take the A442 Kidderminster road. After approximately 1 mile turn left into Doverdale Lane. Upper Hall is half a mile on right on the hill top.
📷	Dennis's expert advice on digital cameras and Photoshop editing techniques.

Maureen & Dennis Alton
The Hayloft,
Upper Hall, Hampton Lovett,
Droitwich WR9 0PA
Tel   +44 (0)1905 772819
Email   maureen@hayloftbandb.com
Web   www.hayloftbandb.com

Entry 594   Map 8

Worcestershire

Brook Farm

A wonderful lost-in-the-country feel here with dogs bounding to greet you, a herd of cats lounging around and donkeys looking on. The farmhouse is surprisingly large: you get one end, Sarah and William have the other, so there's a private feel. Big armchairs and sofas are made for sprawling, a wood-burner keeps you shiver-free and there are masses of lovely books; you can have a ploughman's supper here if you want. Sleep soundly in a charming bedroom with fresh flowers, wake (with tea in bed if you like) to scrambled eggs and smoked trout. There are eight acres of woodland to explore and footpaths from the garden.

Ethical Collection: Environment.
See page 430.

Price	From £70. Singles £55.
Rooms	2: 1 double;
	1 double with separate bath.
Meals	Supper, ploughman's platter,
	£25 for 2. Pub/restaurant 2 miles.
Closed	Rarely.
Directions	From Tenbury Wells for Leominster.
	Right on bend after Pembroke House
	pub. At T-junc. left, 2 miles. At
	T-junc. right. Approx. 0.5 miles.
	House on left on right-hand bend
	opp. white railings, next to postbox.
	Late checkout (12pm). Free pick-up
	from local bus/train station.

Sarah & William Wint
Brook Farm,
Berrington,
Tenbury Wells WR15 8TJ
Tel +44 (0)1584 819868
Email sarah@brookfarmberrington.com
Web www.brookfarmberrington.com

Entry 595   Map 7

Yorkshire

Sunnybank

A Victorian gentleman's residence just a short walk up the hill from the centre of bustling *Last of the Summer Wine* Holmfirth, still with its working Picturedrome cinema (touring bands too), arts and folk festivals, restaurants and shops. Peter and Anne look after you beautifully. Big peaceful bedrooms are a fresh mix of contemporary, Art Nouveau and Art Deco pieces, caramel cream velvets and silks, spoiling bathrooms and lovely views. A full choice Yorkshire breakfast will set you up for a lazy stroll round the charming gardens, or a brisk yomp through rural bliss. *Minimum stay two nights at weekends.*

Price	£65-£90. Singles from £55.
Rooms	3: 2 doubles, 1 twin/double
	(with extra single bed).
Meals	Supper snacks £12. Packed lunch
	£12. Pubs/restaurants 500 yds.
Closed	New Year & occasionally.
Directions	A6024 signed Glossop out of
	Holmfirth centre. Take right in
	between Ashley Jackson Studio &
	Worthingtons into Upperthong
	Lane. House is first drive on right
	after St John's Church.

Peter & Anne White
Sunnybank,
78 Upperthong Lane,
Holmfirth HD9 3BQ
Tel +44 (0)1484 684857
Email info@sunnybankguesthouse.co.uk
Web www.sunnybankguesthouse.co.uk

Entry 596   Map 12

Yorkshire

Thurst House Farm

This solid Pennine farmhouse, its stone mullion windows denoting 17th-century origins, is English to the core. Your warm, gracious hosts give guests a cosy and carpeted sitting room with an open fire in winter; bedrooms are equally generous, with inviting brass beds, antique linen and fresh flowers. Outside: clucking hens, two friendly sheep and a hammock in a garden with beautiful views. Tuck into homemade bread, marmalade and jams at breakfast, and good traditional English dinners, too – just the thing for walkers who've trekked the Calderdale or the Pennine Way. *Children over eight welcome.*

Price	£80. Singles by arrangement.
Rooms	2: 1 double, 1 family room.
Meals	Dinner, 4 courses, £25 (BYO). Packed lunch £5. Restaurants within 0.5 miles.
Closed	Christmas & New Year.
Directions	Ripponden on A58. At brown Beehive sign, right up Royd Lane 100 yds before lights; right at T-junc. opp. Beehive Inn; on for 1 mile. House on right, gateway on blind bend, reverse in.

David & Judith Marriott
Thurst House Farm,
Soyland, Ripponden,
Sowerby Bridge HX6 4NN
Tel   +44 (0)1422 822820
Email judith@thursthousefarm.co.uk
Web   www.thursthousefarm.co.uk

Entry 597   Map 12

Yorkshire

Ponden House

Bump your way up to Brenda's sturdy house, high on the wild Pennine Way. The spring water makes wonderful tea and the house hums with interest and artistic touches. Comfy sofas are jollied up with throws, there are homespun rugs and hangings, paintings, plants and a piano. Feed the hens, plonk your boots by the Aga, chat with your lovely leisurely hostess as she turns out fab home cooking; food is a passion. Bedrooms are exuberant but cosy, it's great for walkers and there's a hot tub under the stars (bookable by groups in advance). Good value with a lived-in, homely feel.

Price	£65–£75. Singles from £45.
Rooms	3: 2 doubles; 1 twin sharing bath.
Meals	Occasional dinner, 3 courses, £18. Packed lunch £6. Pub/restaurant 3 miles.
Closed	Rarely.
Directions	From B6142 for Colne. Pass through Stanbury village, then past Old Silent Inn. Access by Ponden reservoir.

Brenda Taylor
Ponden House,
Stanbury,
Haworth BD22 0HR
Tel   +44 (0)1535 644154
Email bjt@pondenhouse.co.uk
Web   www.pondenhouse.co.uk

Entry 598   Map 12

Yorkshire

Pickersgill Manor Farm

A sparkling welcome, immaculate bedrooms, spectacular views. So you'll forgive the ramshackle yard: this is a working farm! The handsome new farmhouse stands high on the moors, criss-crossed by the Millennium Way. Lisa seduces you with Italian coffee and homemade cake, then shows you the rest: lovely big bedrooms; a guest sitting room with books, games and wood-burning stove; bathrooms with Neal's Yard potions and stacks of white towels. Delicious breakfasts are for walkers – sausages from their pigs, eggs from their hens – and are fun. If you time it right, you'll be cuddling new-born lambs.

Price	£70. Singles £50.
Rooms	2: 1 double, 1 family.
Meals	Supper £13. Packed lunch £6.50. Afternoon tea £8.50. Pub/restaurant 1.5 miles.
Closed	Rarely.
Directions	A65 from Ilkley, then A6034 to Silsden Moor. On top of hill right into Cringles Lane. After 1.5 miles, left into Low Lane. After 0.5 miles, left when you see B&B sign.

Half a dozen farm eggs.

Lisa Preston
Pickersgill Manor Farm,
Low Lane,
Silsden Moor BD20 9JH
Tel   +44 (0)1535 655228
Email   pickersgillmanorfarm@tiscali.co.uk
Web   www.pickersgillmanorfarm.co.uk

Entry 599   Map 12

Yorkshire

Braythorne Barn

Great independence here with your own entrance. Inside are paintings, fine furniture, colourful fabrics and rugs; floors are light oak, windows and doors are hand-crafted and sunlight dances around the rooms. Both bedrooms are understatedly luxurious with beautiful rafters, glorious views, a fresh country feel. Bathrooms have Molton Brown toiletries and plump towels; the guest sitting room is gorgeous. Visit charming Harrogate or walk the Priests Way. Hens in the field, great breakfasts – perhaps brandy-soaked fruit compote… a rural idyll with a contemporary twist. *Children over 12 welcome. Minimum stay two nights.*

Price	£85-£95. Singles from £65.
Rooms	2: 1 twin; 1 double with separate shower.
Meals	Pubs/restaurants 2-4 miles.
Closed	Rarely.
Directions	From Pool-in-Wharfedale, A658 over bridge towards Harrogate. 1st left to Leathley; right opp. church to Stainburn (1.5 miles). Bear left at fork; house next on left.

Petrina Knockton
Braythorne Barn,
Stainburn,
Otley LS21 2LW
Tel   +44 (0)113 284 3160
Email   trina@home-relocation.co.uk
Web   www.braythornebarn.co.uk

Entry 600   Map 12

Yorkshire

Brandymires

The Wensleydale hills lie framed through the windows of the time-warp bedrooms; no TV, no fuss, just calm. In the middle of the National Park, this is a glorious spot for walkers. Gail and Ann bake their own bread and make jams and marmalade, and their delicious, well-priced dinners are prepared with fresh local produce and served at your own table. Two bedrooms, not in their first flush of youth, have four-posters; all have the views. If you're arriving by car, take the 'over-the-top' road from Buckden to Hawes for the most stunning countryside. *Minimum stay two nights. Children over eight welcome.*

Ethical Collection: Food. See page 430.

Price	£56. Singles £33.
Rooms	3: 1 twin, 2 four-posters, all sharing 2 bath/shower rooms (each floor can be let to same party only, by arrangement.)
Meals	Dinner, 4 courses, £19.50 (not Thursday). Pubs/restaurant 5-minute walk.
Closed	November–February.
Directions	300 yds off A684, on road north out of Hawes, signed Muker & Hardraw. House on right.

Choice of any bottle of wine from list with first dinner.

Gail Ainley & Ann Macdonald
Brandymires,
Muker Road,
Hawes DL8 3PR
Tel   +44 (0)1969 667482

Yorkshire

Cliffe Hall

What remains is the Victorian section of an earlier mansion, added by Richard's family in 1858. Inside is a beautifully proportioned and charming family home: huge reception rooms, plasterwork ceilings, acres of sofas, family portraits, floor to ceiling shelves of books. Bedrooms are large, sunny, traditional and uncontrived, bathrooms carpeted and twin beds super-comfy; large windows look onto the glorious grounds that run down to the river Tees. Breakfast on local organic bread and eggs and seasonal fruit from the garden. A special place with a soft, timeless grandeur and a big welcome.

Ethical Collection: Food; Community. See page 430.

Price	From £80. Singles from £40.
Rooms	2 twins/doubles, each with separate bath.
Meals	Pub 1 mile.
Closed	Rarely.
Directions	From A1, exit 56. North for 4.2 miles on B6275. Into drive (on left before Piercebridge); 1st right fork. Darlington Station 7 miles.

10% off stays of 2 or more nights.

Caroline & Richard Wilson
Cliffe Hall,
Piercebridge, Darlington DL2 3SR
Tel   +44 (0)1325 374322
Mobile +44 (0)7785 756380
Email   petal@cliffehall.co.uk

Yorkshire

Hill Top

Books, magazines, bath essences, biscuits by the bed – and the charming, warm and welcoming Christina. Her pretty, listed, limestone farmhouse dates from 1820 and is deceptively big. Ivory walls are a perfect foil for some good furniture and paintings; the sitting room overlooks the charming garden and has a cosy fire. Bedrooms are comfy and conventional; food is fresh, interesting and as homemade as possible. Far-reaching views over rolling countryside in this AONB where waterfalls, moorland and castles beckon. Handy for Scotland or the south. *Babes in arms & children over ten welcome.*

Price	£80. Singles £40.
Rooms	2: 1 twin; 1 twin sharing bath (let to same party only).
Meals	Dinner, 2-3 courses, £15-£20. Pub/restaurant 1.5 miles.
Closed	Christmas & New Year.
Directions	From Scotch Corner west on A66. Approx. 7 miles on, down hill. Left to Newsham. Through village; 2nd left opp. sign on right for Helwith. House on right, name on gate.

	Christina Farmer
	Hill Top,
	Newsham, Richmond DL11 7QX
Tel	+44 (0)1833 621513
Email	plow67@btinternet.com

Entry 603   Map 12

Yorkshire

Manor House

It's the handsomest house in the village. Annie – warm, intelligent, fun – invites you in to spacious interiors elegantly painted and artfully cluttered. Tall shuttered windows and a big open fire, candles in glass sconces and heaps of flowers, soft wool carpets and charming fabrics: a genuinely relaxing family home. The bedroom is a sunny retreat with green views on two sides and a bathroom with a French country feel; fittings are vintage but spotless. Stride the Dales or discover Georgian Richmond, a hop away; return to a simple, delicious supper, with veg from the garden and eggs from the hens. *Note: peacocks in village!*

Price	£90. Singles £40.
Rooms	1 double.
Meals	Supper, 2 courses, £18. Pubs 1 mile.
Closed	Christmas, New Year & Easter.
Directions	From A1, A66 Scotch Corner towards Brough. After 5 miles, slip road to Ravensworth. In village, right at Bay Horse pub; up steep hill to x-roads then right. In Gayles, left at telephone box into Middle St. House 3rd on left.

	Annabel Burchnall
	Manor House,
	Middle Street, Gayles, Richmond DL11 7JF
Tel	+44 (0)1833 621578
Email	annieburchnall@hotmail.com

Entry 604   Map 12

Yorkshire

The Orangery

Sweep into the estate of grand Aske Hall. Through the electric gates into a large walled garden and there is the 18th-century Orangery, with stunning views from every window. It has been recently, and beautifully, renovated. Inside is as warm as toast, scented with fresh flowers and beeswax, aglow with antique runners, ornate clocks, fine paintings, mirrors and porcelain. There's a big open fire with a marble surround, a single bedroom on the ground floor and two country-house bedrooms upstairs; be soothed by soft carpets, low lights, tasteful chintz. Handsome Richmond is a mile away: quite a treat.

Price	From £110. Singles £60.
Rooms	3: 1 double, 1 twin; 1 single with separate shower.
Meals	Supper £20. Pubs/restaurants 2 miles.
Closed	Christmas.
Directions	From A1 at Scotch Corner, onto A66 west. After 2 miles, left onto B6274 signed Gilling West. Through village, after 0.5 miles right through gates; follow signs for The Orangery.

Bottle of wine with dinner on first night.

Susan Zetland
The Orangery,
Aske,
Richmond DL10 5HE
Tel   +44 (0)1748 823222
Email suezet@aske.co.uk
Web   www.aske.co.uk

Entry 605   Map 12

Yorkshire

Lovesome Hill Farm

Who could resist home-reared lamb followed by sticky toffee pudding? This is a working farm and the Pearsons the warmest people imaginable; even in the mayhem of the lambing season they greet you with homemade biscuits and Yorkshire tea. Their farmhouse is as unpretentious as they are: chequered tablecloths, cosy and simple bedrooms (four in the old granary, one in the cottage) with garden and hill views, and a proper Victorian-style sitting room. You have easy access to the A167 and are brilliantly placed for the Moors and Dales. Good for walkers, families, business people.

Price	£70-£80. Singles £40-£50. Gate Cottage: £80-£90.
Rooms	5: 1 twin, 1 double, 1 family room, 1 single. Gate Cottage: 1 double.
Meals	Dinner, 2-3 courses, £17.50-£23. BYO. Packed lunch £5. Pub 4 miles.
Closed	Rarely.
Directions	From Northallerton, A167 north for Darlington for 4 miles. House on right, signed.

Tour of the working farm.

John & Mary Pearson
Lovesome Hill Farm,
Lovesome Hill,
Northallerton DL6 2PB
Tel   +44 (0)1609 772311
Email lovesomehillfarm@btinternet.com
Web   www.lovesomehillfarm.co.uk

Entry 606   Map 12

Yorkshire

Mill Close

Country-house B&B in a tranquil spot among fields and woodland; spacious, luxurious and with your own entrance through a flower-filled conservatory. Beds are large and comfortable, there's a grand four-poster with a spa bath, and sconces for flickering candle light. Be spoiled by handmade chocolates, fluffy robes, even your own 'quiet' fridge. A blue and cream sitting room has an open fire – but you are between the National Park and the Dales so walks are a must. Start with one of Patricia's famous breakfasts: bacon and sausages from the farm, smoked haddock or salmon, homemade jams. Bliss.

Price	£80–£95. Singles £45–£65.
Rooms	3: 2 doubles, 1 four-poster.
Meals	Pubs/restaurants 2 miles.
Closed	Christmas & New Year.
Directions	Follow the brown tourist signs from the village of Patrick Brompton on A684. Farm is 1 mile from village.

 Bottle of wine for stays of 3 or more nights.

Patricia Knox
Mill Close,
Patrick Brompton,
Bedale DL8 1JY
Tel   +44 (0)1677 450257
Email pat@millclose.co.uk
Web   www.millclose.co.uk

Entry 607   Map 12

Yorkshire

Braithwaite Hall

Immerse yourself in fascinating history at this working hill farm in the gorgeous Dales; the house belongs to the National Trust and parts go back to 1301. Lovely, unfussy Charles and Vicky farm hundreds of acres but look after you with substantial breakfasts (eggs from their hens, homemade bread and jams) and super bedrooms with long views and fine furniture. The house is worth exploring: an oak staircase dating back to 1667, stone flagging, wood panelling, enormous fireplaces. The village is tickety-boo pretty, Richmond is near, and you straddle the pretty Dales and the wild Moors for bracing walks and birdwatching.

Price	£65–£95. Singles £65.
Rooms	3: 1 double, 1 four-poster; 1 twin with separate bath.
Meals	Pub 1.5 miles.
Closed	December/January.
Directions	A6108 Leyburn towards Middleham, then towards East Witton. Braithwaite 1.5 miles on left, head east, from top of village green.

Charles & Vicky Duffus
Braithwaite Hall,
East Witton,
Leyburn DL8 4SY
Tel   +44 (0)1969 640287
Email info@braithwaitehall.co.uk
Web   www.braithwaitehall.co.uk

Entry 608   Map 12

Yorkshire

Park House

The soundtrack could be *Perfect Day*: a scenic drive, delicious cake on arrival, undisturbed peace in the converted estate house – partly built with stone from next door's stunning Cistercian Jervaulx Abbey, owned by your hosts. Antique gems stand out among leather bucket chairs, splashes of colour brighten a neutral palette, guest bedrooms are luxurious. Try Carol's bacon, egg and maple crumpets for breakfast – the menu lists local suppliers. Leave pets and children at home but take boots and binoculars for the glorious scenery of Wensleydale: an AONB and a fitting backdrop to a perfect country stay.

Price	From £75. Singles from £55.
Rooms	4: 3 doubles, 1 twin.
Meals	Packed lunch £5-£8. Restaurant 1.25 miles.
Closed	Never.
Directions	House is midway between Masham & Leyburn, about 25 minutes off A1. Full directions given on booking.

Entrance to Jervaulx Abbey. Taxi service to & from local award-winning restaurant.

Ian & Carol Burdon
Park House,
Jervaulx, Masham,
Ripon HG4 4PH
Tel +44 (0)1677 460184
Email ba123@btopenworld.com
Web www.jervaulxabbey.com

Entry 609   Map 12

Yorkshire

Low Sutton

Judi's biscuits are a sweet welcome, Steve has a twinkle in his eye: they're B&B pros. Wood fires in the vast dining/sitting room and cosy snug burn fuel from their own copse; good insulation and underfloor heating keep the homely rooms comfy. Curl up in a soft white robe with a book, or wallow in the sparkling bathrooms – one is solar-heated (more greenie points!). There are six acres to explore with ponies, sheep, dogs and chickens; taste the fruit keen cook Judi jams up for breakfast and expect good dinners with veggies from the garden. Country delights from abbeys to markets are in easy reach. *Minimum stay two nights.*

Ethical Collection: Environment; Food.. See page 430.

Price	£70. Singles £50.
Rooms	2 doubles.
Meals	Packed lunch £5. Dinner £20. Pub/restaurant 1.5 miles.
Closed	Rarely.
Directions	From Ripon A6108 through Masham towards Leyburn. 1.5 miles outside Masham left into Sutton Lane. House 0.25 miles on left.

10% off stays of 2 or more nights. Home produced gift to take away.

Judi Smith
Low Sutton,
Masham,
Ripon HG4 4PB
Tel +44 (0)1765 688565
Email info@lowsutton.co.uk
Web www.lowsutton.co.uk

Entry 610   Map 12

Yorkshire

Laverton Hall

Rachel and Christopher have swapped their Fulham B&B for the 'big house' of Laverton, just half an hour from Harrogate. There's space, beauty, history (it's 400 years old), three walled gardens and comfort in great measure: feather pillows, thick white towels, all is in apple-pie order. Sumptuous breakfasts are followed by a Cordon Bleu dinner overlooking the garden. The sunny guest sitting room is elegant and charming, the cream and white twin and the snug little single have long views to the river. The area is rich with abbeys and great houses, and then there are the glorious Dales to be explored.

Price	£95. Singles £60.
Rooms	2: 1 twin/double, 1 single.
Meals	Supper, 3 courses, £28.
	Pubs/restaurants 2 miles.
Closed	Christmas.
Directions	Leave Ripon on Pateley Bridge Rd. 0.25 miles, right at Garden Centre to Galphay. Through Galphay, 0.5 miles, right at T-junc. to Kirkby Malzeard; 0.5 miles, left to Laverton; 0.5 miles, last house on right.

Rachel Wilson
Laverton Hall,
Laverton,
Ripon HG4 3SX
Tel   +44 (0)1765 650274
Mobile   +44 (0)7711 086385
Email   rachel.k.wilson@hotmail.co.uk

Entry 611   Map 12

Yorkshire

Lawrence House

A classically elegant, comfortable house run with faultless precision by John and Harriet – former wine importer and interior decorator respectively. The house is listed, and Georgian, the garden is formal, flagged and herbaceous, the position – by the back gate to Fountains Abbey and Studley Royal, overlooking long meadow and parkland – is supreme. There's a linen-sofa'd drawing room just for guests, and the promise of a very good dinner. Bedrooms and bathrooms are in a private wing: light, well-proportioned, full of special touches. Relaxed, peaceful and timeless. *Golf, riding & clay pigeon shooting can be arranged.*

Price	£120. Singles £80.
Rooms	2: 1 twin/double, 1 twin.
Meals	Dinner £30. Pub/restaurant 1 mile.
Closed	Christmas & New Year.
Directions	A1 to Ripon. B6265 & Pateley Bridge road for 2 miles. Left into Studley Roger. House last on right.

John & Harriet Highley
Lawrence House,
Studley Roger,
Ripon HG4 3AY
Tel   +44 (0)1765 600947
Email   john@lawrence-house.co.uk
Web   www.lawrence-house.co.uk

Entry 612   Map 12

Yorkshire

Mallard Grange

Perfect farmhouse B&B. Hens, cats, sheepdogs wander the garden, an ancient apple tree leans against the wall, guests unwind and feel part of the family. Enter the rambling, deep-shuttered 16th-century farmhouse, cosy with well-loved family pieces, and feel at peace with the world. Breakfast is generous – homemade muffins, poached pears with cinnamon and a sizzling full Monty. A winding steep stair leads to big, friendly bedrooms, two cheerful others await in a converted 18th-century smithy and Maggie's enthusiasm for this glorious area is as genuine as her love of doing B&B. *Minimum stay two nights at weekends.*

Price	£75–£90. Singles from £70.
Rooms	4: 1 double, 3 twins/doubles.
Meals	Pubs/restaurants 10-minute drive.
Closed	Christmas & New Year.
Directions	B6265 from Ripon for Pateley Bridge. Past entrance to Fountains Abbey. House on right, 2.5 miles from Ripon.

 10% off room rate Mon-Thurs (please telephone to book offer).

	Maggie Johnson
	Mallard Grange,
	Aldfield,
	Ripon HG4 3BE
Tel	+44 (0)1765 620242
Email	maggie@mallardgrange.co.uk
Web	www.mallardgrange.co.uk

Entry 613   Map 12

Yorkshire

Lavender House

House and owners, a warm and genuine couple, glow from within. Saving Lavender from dereliction, Bill and Barbara lavished care on original doors but removed the servants' bells; brought up five children (oh for that maid!); refurbished after the whirlwind years. The place has enormous charm: a glamorous sitting room in white damask, a classic dining room in green and mahogany for convivial organic breakfasts, a funky-comfy conservatory onto the cottage garden, one huge modern bedroom, one smaller in country style, a Victorian bathroom. Walk in to the soaring cathedral or out to ineffable Fountains Abbey and the lyrical Dales.

Price	£80. Singles £60.
Rooms	2 doubles each with separate bath.
Meals	Pub/restaurant 0.25 miles.
Closed	Christmas, New Year & Easter.
Directions	From Ripon market square, north towards Thirsk. Left at 1st set of lights, Coltsgate Hill; right at 2nd roundabout. Continue until allotments on left, then right onto College Road.

 10% off stays of 2 or more nights. Free pick-up from local bus/train station.

	Bill & Barbara Cross
	Lavender House,
	28 College Road,
	Ripon HG4 2HA
Tel	+44 (0)1765 605469
Email	billcross12@hotmail.com
Web	www.lavendersbluedillydilly.co.uk

Entry 614   Map 12

Yorkshire

Fountains House

Warm stone under a terracotta roof: Fountains is a house full of sunshine on the edge of the village. Fat sofas and charmingly grouped pictures make the elegant sitting room an inviting spot to spend an evening, while the fresh, pretty bedrooms promise a good sleep (in spite of a little road noise in the room at the front). The twin has a garden view, the bathrooms are lovely. Your hosts, friendly and hospitable without being intrusive, give you fresh fruit, homemade bread and a piping hot fry-up at breakfast, and if you become addicted to Gill's wonderful jams and marmalades, you can buy a jar to take home.

Price	£76-£82.
Rooms	2: 1 double, 1 twin.
Meals	Pubs 3-minute walk.
Closed	Rarely.
Directions	From A61 Harrogate Ripon road, turning for Burton Leonard at garage. In village, house on right, 500 yds. From A1 junc. 48. Signed for Burton Leonard. Thro' village, past green, house 200 yds on left.

Clive & Gill King
Fountains House,
Burton Leonard,
Harrogate HG3 3RU
Tel   +44 (0)1765 677537
Email   info@fountainshouse.co.uk
Web   www.fountainshouse.co.uk

Entry 615   Map 12

Yorkshire

The Old Rectory

Once the residence of the Bishops of Whitby this elegant rectory has a comfortable lived-in air. Both Turner and Ruskin stayed here and probably enjoyed as much good conversation and comfort as you will. Bedrooms are pretty, traditional and with grand views; the drawing room is classic country house with a fine Venetian window and an enticing window-seat. The graceful, deep pink dining room looks south over a large garden of redwood and walnut trees – some are 300 years old. Caroline will give you a generous breakfast; wander at will to find an orchard, tennis court and croquet lawn. *Children over five welcome.*

Price	From £68. Singles from £40.
Rooms	2: 1 double with separate bath & dressing room; 1 twin/double with separate bath & shower.
Meals	Pub opposite.
Closed	Rarely.
Directions	Take A168 (Northallerton road) off A19; over r'bout; left into village; house opp. pub, next to church.

Bottle of wine in your room.

Tim & Caroline O'Connor-Fenton
The Old Rectory,
South Kilvington,
Thirsk YO7 2NL
Tel   +44 (0)1845 526153
Mobile   +44 (0)7981 329764
Email   ocfenton@talktalk.net

Entry 616   Map 12

Yorkshire

Shallowdale House

Phillip and Anton have a true affection for their guests so you will be treated like angels. Sumptuous bedrooms dazzle in yellows, blues and limes, acres of curtains frame wide views over the Howardian Hills, bathrooms are gleaming and immaculate. Breakfast on the absolute best; fresh fruit compote, dry-cured bacon, homemade rolls – and walk it off in any direction straight from the house. Return to an elegant drawing room, with a fire in winter, and an enticing library. Dinner is out of this world and coffee and chocolates are all you need before you crawl up to bed. Bliss. *Children over 12 welcome.*

Ethical Collection: Food. See page 430.

Price	£95–£117.50. Singles £75–£97.50.
Rooms	3: 2 twins/doubles; 1 double with separate bath/shower.
Meals	Dinner, 4 courses, £35.
Closed	Christmas & New Year.
Directions	From Thirsk, A19 south, then 'caravan route' via Coxwold & Byland Abbey. 1st house on left, just before Ampleforth.

	Anton van der Horst & Phillip Gill
	Shallowdale House,
	West End,
	Ampleforth YO62 4DY
Tel	+44 (0)1439 788325
Email	stay@shallowdalehouse.co.uk
Web	www.shallowdalehouse.co.uk

Entry 617   Map 12

Yorkshire

Cundall Lodge Farm

Ancient chestnuts, crunchy drive, sheep grazing, hens free-ranging. This four-square Georgian farmhouse could be straight out of Central Casting. Homely rooms of damask sofas and bright wallpapers have views to Sutton Bank's White Horse or the river Swale, spotless bedrooms are inviting – family furnishings, fresh flowers, Roberts radios – and tea and oven-fresh cakes welcome you. This is a working farm and the breakfast table groans with free-range eggs, homemade jams and local bacon. The garden and river walks guarantee peace, and David and Caroline are generous and delightful. *Children over ten welcome.*

Ethical Collection: Food; Community. See page 430.

Price	£80–£95.
Rooms	3: 2 doubles; 1 twin/double.
Meals	Packed lunch £5. Pubs/restaurants 2 miles.
Closed	Christmas & January.
Directions	Exit junc. 49 A1(M) onto A168 (Thirsk). Turn off 1st junc. for Cundall. Turn right at the Crab & Lobster. 2 miles on left.

10% off stays Mon–Thurs.

	Caroline Barker
	Cundall Lodge Farm,
	Cundall,
	York YO61 2RN
Tel	+44 (0)1423 360203
Email	info@lodgefarmbb.co.uk
Web	www.cundall-lodgefarm.co.uk

Entry 618   Map 12

Yorkshire

The Chantry

The Chantry is a listed building in a village setting, lived in by Diana and Nigel – warm, humorous and engaging. A member of the Slow Food movement in York, and half Lebanese by birth, Diana reflects her culture in her cooking; her big ramshackle kitchen is the heart of this house. Bedrooms have space and high ceilings and an old-fashioned décor while bathrooms are swisher; the mood is comfy, warm, authentic, historic, and ever so gently eccentric. Pull yourself away from the suntrap terrace and sally forth into town: York, history-rich, is a sturdy walk (or a 20-minute bike ride) away.

Yorkshire

Corner Farm

Coffee and scones on arrival? You get a lovely welcome here! This peaceful farmhouse is so well insulated it's snug and warm even on the coldest day. With York so close and stunning estates nearby, this is a cosy nest from which to explore the area – or just the village pub. Bathrooms are swish and bedrooms are light, fresh and comfortable: cast-iron beds, fine sheets, cute satin cushions. Much-loved Dexters graze on six acres – Tim and Sharon are aiming for self-sufficiency – and apples from the orchard are pressed for your breakfast, flexibly served and with lots of choice, including home-laid eggs.

Price	£70. Singles £50.
Rooms	2: 1 double, 1 twin.
Meals	Dinner £20. Pubs 200 yards, restaurant 0.5 miles.
Closed	Rarely.
Directions	From York take Bishopthorpe Road. Enter Bishopthorpe, left into Chantry Lane after Bishopthorpe Palace. Last house on right.

10% off stays of 2 or more nights.

Price	£75. Singles £50.
Rooms	2: 1 double, 1 twin.
Meals	Packed lunch £4. Pub 100 yds.
Closed	Rarely.
Directions	From York A1079 (6.5 miles). Through two roundabouts, at Kexby left. then on for 0.9 miles. Left for Low Catton, then into village. House 0.8 miles on right.

10% off stays of 2 or more nights.

	Diana Naish
	The Chantry,
	Chantry Lane, Bishopthorpe,
	York YO23 2QF
Tel	+44 (0)1904 709767
Mobile	+44 (0)7850 912203
Email	diananaish@athomecatering.freeserve.co.uk

	Sharon Stevens
	Corner Farm,
	Low Catton,
	York YO41 1EA
Tel	+44 (0)1759 373911
Email	info@cornerfarmyork.co.uk
Web	www.cornerfarmyork.co.uk

Entry 619   Map 12

Entry 620   Map 13

Yorkshire

The Mount House

A dollop of stylish fun in the rolling Howardian Hills (an AONB), Kathryn and Nick's redesigned village house is light, airy and filled with gorgeous things – from good antiques to splashy modern art and fresh flowers. The ground-floor twin with white cast-iron beds has its own cosy book-filled sitting room; the sunny upstairs double has views across the roof tops to open countryside. Kathryn, a devoted foodie, will spoil you at breakfast – supper too, if you wish – sometimes in the pretty garden. Discover Nunnington Hall, Castle Howard, old market towns and great walking; only 20 minutes from York too. Super.

Price	From £90. Singles from £55.
Rooms	2: 1 double; 1 twin & sitting room.
Meals	Dinner, 2-4 courses, £20-£35. Pub/restaurant 200 yds.
Closed	Rarely.
Directions	North from York, left off A64 through Flaxton & Sheriff Hutton. Follow signs to Terrington. First gateway on right after sharp right bend as you enter village.

Kathryn Hill
The Mount House,
Terrington,
York YO60 6QB
Tel   +44 (0)1653 648206
Email   mount.house@clayfox.co.uk
Web   www.howardianhillsbandb.co.uk

Entry 621   Map 13

Yorkshire

Hunters Hill

The moors lie behind this elegant stone farmhouse, five yards from the National Park, in farmland and woodland with fine views… the position is marvellous and you can walk from the door. The house is full of light and flowers; bedrooms are pretty but not overly grand, and look onto valley or church. The lovely lived-in drawing room displays comfortable old sofas, paintings and fine furniture; rich colours, hunting prints and candles at dinner create a warm and cosy feel. The family has poured a good deal of affection into this tranquil house and the result is a home that's happy, charming and remarkably easy to relax in.

Price	£80. Singles from £50.
Rooms	2: 1 twin/double; 1 twin/double with separate bath.
Meals	Dinner, 3 courses, £30. Pub/restaurant 500 yds.
Closed	Rarely.
Directions	From A170 to Sinnington. On village green, keep river on left, fork right between cottages, sign to church. Up lane, bearing right up hill. House past church beyond farm buildings.

Jane Otter
Hunters Hill,
Sinnington,
York YO62 6SF
Tel   +44 (0)1751 431196
Email   ejorr@tiscali.co.uk

Entry 622   Map 13

Yorkshire

No. 54

The welcome tea and homemade cakes set the tone for your stay; this is a happy place. No 54 was once two cottages on the Duncombe estate; now it's a single house and Lizzie has made the most of the space. Buttermilk walls, be-rugged flagged floors, country furniture, open fires and a stylish lack of clutter. A single-storey extension has been fashioned into three extra bedrooms around a secluded courtyard. Thoughtful extras – a Roberts radio, fresh milk, hot water bottles – make you feel looked after, and the breakfasts will fuel the most serious of walks. Make a house party and bring your friends!

Price	£90. Singles from £45.
Rooms	4: 2 doubles, 1 twin; 1 single with separate shower.
Meals	Dinner, 2-3 courses, £28-£35. Restaurants 10-minute walk.
Closed	Christmas & New Year.
Directions	A170 to Helmsley; right at mini r'bout in centre, facing The Crown; house 500 yds along A170, on right.

Lizzie Would
No. 54,
Bondgate,
Helmsley YO62 5EZ
Tel   +44 (0)1439 771533
Email   lizzie@no54.co.uk
Web   www.no54.co.uk

Entry 623   Map 13

Yorkshire

West View Cottage

In a village packed with thatched houses is Valerie's – gorgeous, 17th-century and fronted by cottage flowers, with a bench at the side to take advantage of the views; they reach for miles. The hall is high-raftered with a stunning chandelier, the little dining room has exquisite oak panelling; there's no sitting room but a sofa in your bedroom, reached via the patio, beautifully self-contained. Fabulous curtains, an ornate brass bed, a funky bathroom – comfortable luxury in an unusual space. History and abbeys abound, the North Yorks Moors lie across the field, and bright friendly Valerie knows the area inside out.

Price	£80-£90. Singles £59.
Rooms	1 double.
Meals	Pubs/restaurants 2 miles.
Closed	Rarely.
Directions	Helmsley A170 towards Pickering. After 1 mile, left towards Pockley. House on right.

Valerie & Greg Lack
West View Cottage,
Pockley,
Helmsley YO62 7TE
Tel   +44 (0)1439 770526
Email   westview.cottage@btinternet.com
Web   www.westviewcottage.info

Entry 624   Map 13

Yorkshire

Brickfields Farm

Down a long peaceful track but just a stone's throw from bustling Kirkbymoorside is this walker's paradise. Friendly Janet sends you off to the North Yorks Moors with maps and information – and a tasty breakfast, served at separate tables in the conservatory overlooking guinea fowl and sheep. Bedrooms are in the main house or in the long low barn or converted cow shed, and all are lovely; a French vintage bed, antiques, heavy curtains, sprung mattresses, fresh flowers, a hidden fridge. Bathrooms have big open showers, thick towels and generous lotions and bubbles. *Not suitable for children.*

Price	£85-£125.
Rooms	7: 1 twin. Barn: 4 suites. Cow shed: 1 suite, 1 four-poster suite.
Meals	Pub/restaurant 1 mile.
Closed	Rarely.
Directions	A170 east from Thirsk to Kirkbymoorside; continue past r'bout for 0.5 miles. Right into Kirkby Mills, signed. House 1st right along small lane.

6 breakfast eggs: extra fresh, free-range.

Janet Trousdale
Brickfields Farm,
Kirkby Mills,
Kirkbymoorside YO62 6NS
Tel   +44 (0)1751 433074
Email   janet@brickfieldsfarm.co.uk
Web   www.brickfieldsfarm.co.uk

Entry 625   Map 13

Yorkshire

Flamborough Rigg Cottage

Even in the North York Moors it's rare to find a spot so remote – rarer still to find such luxury in an 1820s farmhouse set in fields of lambs. Philip and Caroline know how to delight guests with brilliant bathrooms, crisp linen, delicious meals from home-grown produce. They've melded modern touches with handsome antiques, like contemporary art around a grandfather clock in the vaulted dining room – it works. One bedroom has a sitting area; the others have French doors to an orchard garden; all gaze over hills that cry out for walking. Dogs are welcome, Whitby coast is ten miles, and there's fine food and company to round off the day.

Price	From £85. Singles £65.
Rooms	3 doubles (1 with sitting room).
Meals	Supper platter £15. Dinner, 3 courses, from £20. Pub 2 miles.
Closed	Rarely.
Directions	Leave Pickering passing the Steam Railway towards Newton upon Rawcliffe and Stape. Go through Newton in to Stape. 500 yards past phone box turn left, keep left. House 4th property along.

10% off stays of 2 or more nights. Late checkout (12pm).

Philip & Caroline Jackson
Flamborough Rigg Cottage,
Middlehead Road, Stape,
Pickering YO18 8HR
Tel   +44 (0)1751 475263
Email   enquiries@flamboroughriggcottage.co.uk
Web   www.flamboroughriggcottage.co.uk

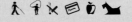

Entry 626   Map 13

Yorkshire

Thorpe Hall

Arrive and listen: nothing, bar the wind in the trees and the odd seagull; the eye gathers glimmering sea and mighty headland, the final edge of the moors. Are there still smugglers? The wonderful house smells of polish and flowers, the panelled drawing room breathes history. Angelique, a delight, has furnished it all, including the TV-free bedrooms, with an eclectic mix of old and new and some fun (a framed transport caff poster in the breakfast room). She's hung contemporary art on ancient walls and has made a veg patch with young Phoebe. David helps with breakfast when he's not globetrotting. The very opposite of stuffy.

Price	£80-£90.
Rooms	7: 3 doubles; 3 doubles, 1 twin sharing separate bath & shower rooms.
Meals	Pub within 0.25 miles.
Closed	Occasionally.
Directions	Scarborough, A171 Whitby. After 15 miles right at junc. for Fylingthorpe & Robin Hood's Bay. In centre of Fylingthorpe, right onto Middlewood Lane, house on left before ford.

 Late checkout (12pm).

Angelique Russell
Thorpe Hall,
Middlewood Lane, Fylingthorpe,
Whitby YO22 4TT
Tel +44 (0)1947 880667
Email thorpehall@googlemail.com
Web www.thorpe-hall.co.uk

Entry 627 Map 13

Yorkshire

Holly Croft

Huge kindness and thoughtful touches (hot water bottles, lifts to the pub, cake and tea on arrival) make this home special. The décor is Edwardian plush – wallpapers striped and floral, curtains lavish – and the comforts indisputable. The double has an elaborate floral-and-rose headboard with matching drapes, there are bathrobes in fitted wardrobes, big showers and generous breakfasts – own jams, Yorkshire teas, kippers if you choose – served at the polished mahogany table. After a bracing cliff-top walk return to a homely sitting room overlooking the garden. Wonderful Whitby is 20 minutes away.

Price	From £75. Singles from £45.
Rooms	2: 1 twin; 1 double with separate bath.
Meals	Dinner by arrangement (4+ only). Pub 600 yds.
Closed	Rarely.
Directions	A171 from Scarborough to Whitby; at Scalby x-roads, by tennis courts, take road on right. Signed 500 yds on right.

 10% off room rate Mon-Thurs.

🎁 Use your Sawday's Gift Card here.

John & Christine Goodall
Holly Croft,
28 Station Road, Scalby,
Scarborough YO13 0QA
Tel +44 (0)1723 375376
Email christine.goodall@tesco.net
Web www.holly-croft.co.uk

Entry 628 Map 13

Yorkshire

The Wold Cottage

Drive down through mature trees, and a proper entrance with signs to an elegant Georgian Manor house in 300 glorious acres. Inside find a light and cheerful guest sitting room with thick carpets and plenty of sofas, a dining room with heartlifting views across the landscaped gardens, and gorgeous original features: fan-lights, high ceilings and broad staircases. Bedrooms in the house are sumptuous and comfortable, two in the barn are as neat as a pin. You are warmed by straw bale heating, food is local and delicious: an award-winning Yorkshire breakfast will set you up for discovering the unspoilt Wolds.

Ethical Collection: Environment; Food. See page 430.

Price	£100–£120. Singles £60–£75.
Rooms	5: 1 double, 2 twins. Barn: 1 family room, 1 four-poster.
Meals	Supper £25. Wine from £12.95.
Closed	Rarely.
Directions	A64 onto B1249. Through Foxholes to Wold Newton. In village, take road between pond & pub; signed on right.

Local food/produce in your room. Local chocolates and water in room.

Katrina Gray
The Wold Cottage,
Wold Newton,
Driffield YO25 3HL
Tel   +44 (0)1262 470696
Email katrina@woldcottage.com
Web   www.woldcottage.com

Entry 629   Map 13

Yorkshire

Low Penhowe

With the Turners at the helm, you are on a safe ship. They see to everything so perfectly – the crispness of the breakfast bacon, the freshness of the eggs from their hens, the homemade bread, the bowls of flowers, the fire in the guest drawing room. Traditional, comfortable bedrooms face south and overlook the garden – lap up the views in summer while birds soar and twitter, Christopher's Highland cattle peer over the fence and the chickens strut and scratch. Castle Howard and the North Yorks Moors are in front of you and all around are abbeys, castles, rivers, ruins and woods. *Children over ten welcome.*

Ethical Collection: Environment; Food; Community. See page 430.

Price	£80–£99. Singles £65.
Rooms	2: 1 double; 1 twin/double with separate bath.
Meals	Packed lunch £6. Pubs 1.5 miles.
Closed	Christmas & New Year.
Directions	A64 at Whitwell on the Hill, right for Kirkham. Over crossing & Derwent, pass Kirkham Priory & Stone Trough Inn. Right at T-junc., left for Burythorpe, over x-roads, 700 yds; right up drive.

Bottle of house wine for a minimum 2-night stay.

Christopher & Philippa Turner
Low Penhowe,
Burythorpe,
Malton YO17 9LU
Tel   +44 (0)1653 658336
Email lowpenhowe@btinternet.com
Web   www.bedandbreakfastyorkshire.co.uk

Entry 630   Map 13

Yorkshire

Dowthorpe Hall

Caroline is lovely, cooking is her passion and she trawls the county for the best; fish and seafood from Hornsea, Dexter beef, game from the local shoot; her fruits and veg are home-grown. All is served in a sumptuous Georgian dining room by flickering candlelight, after which you retire to a comfortable drawing room; this is a marvellously elegant, and happy, house. Sleep peacefully on a luxurious mattress, wake to the aroma of bacon, sausages, eggs and home-baked bread. There are acres of gorgeous garden to roam – orchards, pathways, potager and pond – and a trio of historic houses to visit.

Price	£80–£90. Singles £50.
Rooms	2: 1 twin/double; 1 double with separate bath.
Meals	Dinner £25. Pubs 0.25-5 miles.
Closed	Never.
Directions	North on A165 for Bridlington, through Ganstead & Coniston. On right, white railings & drive to Dowthorpe Hall.

1 night free for stays of 5 nights or more. Bottle of wine with dinner on 1st night.

John & Caroline Holtby
Dowthorpe Hall,
Skirlaugh,
Hull HU11 5AE
Tel   +44 (0)1964 562235
Email   john.holtby@farming.co.uk
Web   www.dowthorpehall.com

Entry 631   Map 13

Guernsey

Seabreeze

Maggie's house – the most southern on Guernsey – comes with enormous views: Herm and Sark glistening in the water under a vast sky. The breakfast terrace is hard to beat, there are sofas in the conservatory, cliff-top paths for fabulous walks, a beach for picnics in summer. The house started life as HQ for French pilots flying seaplanes in WWI; these days warm, rustic interiors make for a great island base. It's not grand, just very welcoming with rooms that hit the spot: pretty linen, bathrobes, super showers, fresh flowers. You can hire bikes locally, then spin up the lane to a Michelin-starred restaurant. Brilliant.

Price	£70–£80. Singles from £40.
Rooms	3: 1 twin/double, 1 twin/double with kitchen & balcony, 1 single.
Meals	Pubs/restaurants 500 yds & 0.5 miles.
Closed	Rarely.
Directions	South from St Peter Port for 3 miles. Through Fermain village, then left at lights for Jerbourg Point. Keep left at Hotel Jerbourg and last house on right along cliff top lane, keeping sea on left.

10% off room rate. Late checkout (12pm). Local food/produce in your room.

Maggie Talbot-Cull
Seabreeze,
Jerbourg Point GY4 6BN
Tel   +44 (0)1481 237929
Email   seaplane@mail.com
Web   www.guernseybandb.com

Entry 632   Map 4

Scotland

Photo: istockphoto.com

Aberdeenshire

Ardneidly Steading

Near a conservation village in rugged open countryside, the granite former steading conceals an entrancing interior. Walls are white or café au lait, timbers are reclaimed, and art, antiques and textiles add personality; there's a designer wood-burner in the split-level living room and games for the grandchildren. Mandy and Colin make their own jams, grow their own food and create perfect breakfasts on the Aga; Mandy loves house, garden and guests in equal measure. Two peaceful bedrooms, simple and stylish, are up a private stair; bathrooms are delicious. Wildlife, biking, hiking, castles by the hatful. Heaven!

Price	£75. Singles £50.
Rooms	2: 1 double, 1 twin.
Meals	Supper £18. Packed lunch from £5. Pub/hotel 1 mile.
Closed	Rarely.
Directions	From Aberdeen, A944 west; 2 miles past Dunecht right. Follow signs to Monymusk. Through village. After 0.5 miles, left at crossroads. House second on left.

🧳 For a stay of 3 nights, supper on 3rd night.

Mandy Hamilton
Ardneidly Steading,
Monymusk AB51 7HX
Tel   +44 (0)1467 651222
Email   info@ardneidlysteading.co.uk
Web   www.ardneidlysteading.co.uk

Entry 633   Map 19

Aberdeenshire

Woodend House

Elegant riverside living at a fishing lodge by the river Dee – one of the most magnificent settings in Scotland. Outside, a wild, wonderful garden; inside, beautiful wallpapers, fabrics and rugs. The dining hall leads to the kitchen with an Aga, the drawing room has dreamy river views, the large bedrooms ooze comfort and more fabulous views, and the bathrooms have old cast-iron baths and fine toiletries. Breakfast and dinner are local, seasonal and first-class. All this, and a fishing hut and a secure rod room for salmon and sea trout fishing in season. *Minimum stay two nights.*

Price	£110. Singles £80.
Rooms	3: 1 double, 1 twin; 1 twin with separate bath.
Meals	Dinner, 4 courses, £30. Packed lunch £5-£10. Pub 2 miles.
Closed	Christmas, New Year & occasionally.
Directions	4 miles west of Banchory on A93. Entrance to drive on south side of road.

Miranda & Julian McHardy
Woodend House,
Trustach, Banchory AB31 4AY
Tel   +44 (0)1330 822367
Email   miranda.mchardy@woodend.org
Web   www.woodend.org

Entry 634   Map 19

Aberdeenshire

Lys-na-Greyne House

Peace, tranquillity and a natural welcome – one of the loveliest places in this book. Expect a sweeping stair, sun-streamed rooms, log fires and the most comfortable beds in Scotland. Your room may be huge – two are; one with a dressing room and a balcony, all with family antiques, bathrobes, fine linen… and views of river, field, forest and hill where osprey and lapwing glide. Meg picks flowers and organic vegetables from the garden and her food is delicious; David is an enthusiastic naturalist and can advise on walking and wildlife. Nearby, golf, fishing and castles by the hatful.

Ethical Collection: Community. See page 430.

Price	£90. Singles from £45.
Rooms	3: 2 twins/doubles; 1 twin/double with separate bath/shower. Extra shower available.
Meals	Dinner £25-£28.50. Pub/bistro 15-minute walk.
Closed	Rarely.
Directions	From Aboyne, A93 west for Braemar. Just before 30mph sign, left down Rhu-na-Haven Rd. House 400 yds on, 4th gateway on right.

Fresh flowers in room.

David & Meg White
Lys-na-Greyne House,
Rhu-na-Haven Road,
Aboyne AB34 5JD
Tel   +44 (0)1339 887397
Email   meg.white@virgin.net

Entry 635   Map 19

Aberdeenshire

Lynturk Home Farm

The stunning drawing room, with pier-glass mirror, ancestral portraits and enveloping sofas, is reason enough to come, while the food, served in a candlelit, deep-sage dining room, is delicious, with produce from the farm. You're treated very much as friends here and your hosts are delightful. It's peaceful, too, on the Aberdeenshire Castle Trail. The handsome farmhouse has been in the family since 1762 and you can roam the surrounding 300 acres of rolling hills. Inside, good fabrics and paints, hunting prints and some lovely family pieces. "A blissful haven," says a reader. *Fishing, shooting & golf breaks.*

Price	From £80. Singles £50.
Rooms	3: 2 twins/doubles; 1 double with separate bath.
Meals	Dinner, 4 courses, £30. Pub 1 mile.
Closed	Rarely.
Directions	20 miles from Aberdeen on A944 (towards Alford); thro' Tillyfourie, then left for Muir of Fowlis & Tough; after Tough, 2nd farm drive on left, signed.

Bottle of wine with dinner on first night. Late checkout (12pm).

John & Veronica Evans-Freke
Lynturk Home Farm,
Alford AB33 8DU
Tel   +44 (0)1975 562504
Mobile   +44 (0)7773 389793
Email   lynturk@hotmail.com

Entry 636   Map 19

Aberdeenshire

Old Mayen

Follow narrow lanes crowded by beech trees and hedges, through high rolling hills and fast flowing rivers to this beautiful house perched next to a farm and overlooking the unspoilt valley below. You get classic country-house style in elegant bedrooms, spoiling bathrooms, a book-filled sitting room, cut flowers and a delicious candlelit dinner by a roaring fire. Fran and Jim are infectiously enthusiastic and kind; breakfasts are a moveable feast (outside in good weather) and the garden hums with birds. A fine retreat for tired and jaded souls – and there are castles, distilleries and gardens to visit.

Price	£90. Singles £50.
Rooms	2: 1 double; 1 double with separate shower.
Meals	Dinner £25. Supper £18. Packed lunch £8.
Closed	Rarely.
Directions	From A96, A97 to Banff. After crossing river Deveron (9 miles), left onto B9117; 3 miles, on left behind thick beech hedge.

Pre-dinner drink and house wine with dinner. 10% off stays of 2 or more nights.

James & Fran Anderson
Old Mayen,
Rothiemay,
Huntly AB54 7NL
Tel   +44 (0)1466 711276
Email oldmayen@tiscali.co.uk

Entry 637   Map 19

Aberdeenshire

Balwarren Croft

Thirty acres at the end of a farm track, a field of Highland cattle, mixed woodland, ancient dykes, a lochside full of birdlife, a herb garden with 200 varieties and a burn you may follow down the hill. Hazel and James, warm, friendly, quietly passionate about green issues, came to croft 25 years ago and the whole place is a delight: cathedral roof, shiny wooden floors, cashmere blankets, sparkling bathrooms, log fires, a decanter of whisky. And superb breakfasts and dinners: eggs from their hens, beef from their cattle. A beautiful, uplifting and peaceful place in glorious countryside. *Cream teas £3.50.*

Price	£68-£85. Singles £45-£50.
Rooms	2: 1 twin, 1 double.
Meals	Dinner, 3 courses, £25. Pub/restaurant 10 miles.
Closed	Rarely.
Directions	North from Aberchirder on B9023. Right at Lootcherbrae (still B9023); 2nd left for Ordiquhill. After 1.7 miles, right at farm track opp. Aulton Farm; last croft up track.

10% off stays of 2 or more nights. Guided tour and informal talk of the herb garden.

Hazel & James Watt
Balwarren Croft,
Ordiquhill, Banff AB45 2HR
Tel   +44 (0)1466 751688
Email balwarren@tiscali.co.uk
Web   www.balwarren.com

Entry 638   Map 19

Angus

Newtonmill House

The house and grounds are in perfect order; the owners are warm, charming and discreet. This is a little-known part of Scotland, with glens and gardens to discover; fishing villages, golf courses and deserted beaches, too. Return to a cup of tea in the sitting room or summerhouse, a wander in the lovely walled garden, and a marvellous supper of local produce; Rose grows 20 varieties of potato and her hens' eggs make a great hollandaise! Upstairs are crisp sheets, soft blankets, feather pillows, fresh flowers, homemade fruit cake and warm sparkling bathrooms with thick towels. Let this home envelop you in its warm embrace.

Angus

Ethie Castle

Amazing. A listed Pele tower that dates to 1300 and which once was home to the Abbot of Arbroath, murdered in St Andrews on Henry VIII's orders. His private chapel remains, as does his secret stair. As for the rest of the house: turret staircases, beautiful bedrooms, a 1500s ceiling in the Great Hall, a Tudor kitchen with a walk-in fireplace that burns night and day. Kirstin has breathed new life into the house; the garden is now complete – and something of a show-stopper. Lunan Bay, one of Scotland's most glorious beaches, is at the end of the road. There's a loch too.

Price	£96-£110. Singles from £60.		Price	From £95. Singles from £75.
Rooms	2: 1 twin; 1 double with separate bath.		Rooms	3: 1 four-poster; 1 twin/double, 1 double, both with separate bath/shower.
Meals	Dinner, 4 courses, from £32. Supper, 2 courses, from £22. BYO. Packed lunch £10. Pub 3 miles.		Meals	Dinner, 4 courses with wine, £30. Packed lunch up to £10. Pub/restaurant 3 miles.
Closed	Christmas.		Closed	Rarely.
Directions	Aberdeen-Dundee A90, turning marked Brechin & Edzell B966. Heading towards Edzell, Newtonmill House is 1 mile on left, drive marked by pillars and sign.		Directions	North from Arbroath on A92; right after Shell garage for Auchmithie; left at T-junc.; on for 2 miles; at BT phone box, private road to Ethie Barns in front.

One free supper for stays of 3 or more nights (November-May).

Use your Sawday's Gift Card here.

	Rose & Stephen Rickman Newtonmill House, Brechin DD9 7PZ			Kirstin de Morgan Ethie Castle, Inverkeilor, Arbroath DD11 5SP
Tel	+44 (0)1356 622533		Tel	+44 (0)1241 830434
Email	rrickman@srickman.co.uk		Email	kmydemorgan@aol.com
Web	www.newtonmillhouse.co.uk		Web	www.ethiecastle.com

Entry 639   Map 19

Entry 640   Map 16+19

Argyll & Bute

Sithe Mor House

Terrific views from this lovely house on the shores of Loch Awe; its own bay and jetty below, acres of sky above and a winning pair at the helm. Patsy ensures all runs smoothly and John, a former oarsman of repute and the first man to row each way across Scotland, sweeps you along with joie de vivre. With ornate plasterwork, antlers and oils, lofty domed ceilings in the bedrooms and loch views, this 1880s house combines a baronial feel with massive luxury in bathrooms, beds and fabrics. Stay for home-grown and local dinners, borrow a kilt, marvel at the Oxford and Cambridge boat race memorabilia. *Minimum stay two nights.*

Price	£118.
Rooms	2: 1 double, 1 twin/double.
Meals	Dinner, 4 courses, £35. Supper £25. Restaurants/pub 0.5-3 miles.
Closed	Rarely.
Directions	A82 from Glasgow; A85 from Tyndrum. At Taynuilt, left onto B845 to Kilchrenan village. After 1 mile, single track 'No Through Road' to Taychreggan. House is last on left.

Patsy & John Cugley
Sithe Mor House,
Kilchrenan,
Loch Awe PA35 1HF
Tel   +44 (0)1866 833234
Email   patsycugley@hotmail.com
Web   www.sithemor.com

Entry 641   Map 17

Argyll & Bute

Ardnacross Farm

The Forresters' Aberdeen Angus cattle farm borders Mull's stunning coastline, where eagles, whales, red deer and otters leap, swoop, breach and soar. The farmhouse is wonderfully homely: the dining room with a huge antique table, family silver and open fire; the guest room (reached by private stairs) with a pretty patterned bedspread and floral curtains. The Scottish breakfast with Ardnacross eggs and porridge is hearty. Tobermory has everything from very good fish and chips and pleasant restaurants to an excellent theatre and festival; you can catch a boat trip to Iona or Staffa too. A beautiful slice of island Scotland.

Price	£70.
Rooms	1 double.
Meals	Pubs/restaurants 5 miles.
Closed	Christmas & New Year.
Directions	15 miles from Craignure & 11 miles from Fishnish ferry terminals. Right from either on Tobermory road. House half way between Salen and Tobermory on right.

Picnic lunch using local & farm produce.

Rory & Penelope Forrester
Ardnacross Farm,
Aros,
Isle of Mull PA72 6JS
Tel   +44 (0)1680 300262
Email   enquiries@ardnacross.com
Web   www.holidaycottages-mull.co.uk

Entry 642   Map 17

Argyll & Bute

Dun Na Mara

Twenty paces from the door, past the standing stone, a sweep of private beach and dazzling views to Mull. The Arts & Crafts house has been given a minimalist makeover by Mark and Suzanne — ex-architects and friendly, caring, interesting hosts. The result is a spotless, luminous interior of sumptuous beds, quilted throws, cream bucket chairs, sensual bathrooms, colourful cushions and sea views from three bedrooms. Breakfast on porridge with toasted almonds and honey, kedgeree, devilled kidneys, the full Scottish works; end the day with sherry in the little sitting room, DVDs, beautiful art and books. *Children over 12 welcome.*

Price	£95–£115. Singles £50–£70.
Rooms	7: 5 doubles, 2 singles.
Meals	Pubs 3 miles.
Closed	Christmas & New Year.
Directions	North from Oban on A828; over Connel Bridge; north for two miles; house signed left just after lay-by, before Benderloch village.

Mark & Suzanne McPhillips
Dun Na Mara,
Benderloch,
Oban PA37 1RT

Tel	+44 (0)1631 720233
Email	stay@dunnamara.com
Web	www.dunnamara.com

Entry 643   Map 17

Argyll & Bute

Barndromin Farm

Jamie and Morag run a cheerful, busy farmhouse that opens its arms to guests; hens cluck around the farmyard and Jamie will happily share his knowledge of butterflies, wild flowers and mushrooms. Bedrooms are carpeted and comfy with flowery duvets and Morag's art. There are places to flop in the elegant drawing room and a polished table for breakfast — tuck into croissants, bacon, sausages, black pudding, farm eggs. Set on the hillside with spectacular views over Loch Feochan, you can fish, walk, ride, spot grouse, otters, deer, red squirrels and rare butterflies. Gorgeous. *Children over ten welcome. Minimum stay two nights at weekends.*

Price	£75–£85. Singles £40–£50.
Rooms	2: 1 twin; 1 double with separate bath.
Meals	Pub/restaurant 4–6 miles.
Closed	December–February.
Directions	6 miles south of Oban on A816 to Lochgilphead. Take 2nd entrance on left 200 yds after Knipoch Hotel.

10% off room rate Mon–Thurs, 2 or more nights only.

Jamie & Morag Mellor
Barndromin Farm,
Knipoch,
Oban PA34 4QS

Tel	+44 (0)1852 316297
Email	mogsmellor@hotmail.co.uk
Web	www.knipochbedandbreakfast.com

Entry 644   Map 17

Argyll & Bute

Glenmore

A pleasing buzz of family life and no need to stand on ceremony. The house was built in 1854 but it's the later 30s additions that set the style: carved doorways, red-pine panelling, Art Deco pieces, oak floors, elaborate cornicing and a curvy stone fireplace. Alasdair's family has been here for 140 years and much family furniture remains. One of the huge doubles is arranged as a suite with a single room and a sofabed; bath and basins are chunky 30s style with chrome plumbing. From the organic garden and the house there are magnificent views of Loch Melfort with its bobbing boats; you're free to come and go as you please.

Price	£70–£90. Family suite £85–£160. Singles £45–£60.
Rooms	2: 1 family suite; 1 double with separate bath/shower.
Meals	Pub 0.5 miles, restaurant 1.5 miles.
Closed	December/January.
Directions	From A816 0.5 miles south of Kilmelford; then on to Glenmore. House signed (both directions). Past Lodge House at bottom of drive; on for 0.25 miles to big house.

Free pick-up from local bus/train station. Bottle of wine in your room.

Melissa & Alasdair Oatts
Glenmore,
Kilmelford,
Oban PA34 4XA
Tel   +44 (0)1852 200314
Email oatts@glenmore22.fsnet.co.uk
Web   www.glenmorecountryhouse.co.uk

Entry 645   Map 17

Argyll & Bute

Melfort House

Enter a wild landscape of hidden glens, ancient oak woods and rivers that tumble to a blue sea. Find a big beautiful house with views straight down the loch, aglow with exquisite fabrics and polished antiques, fine oak floors and paintings and prints. Bedrooms have upholstered beds in soft plaids, delicious colours, superb views; bathrooms have huge towels and Aaron Aromatics. Yvonne and Matthew are brilliant at looking after you: fresh fruit at breakfast, Stornoway black pudding, chilli omelettes, tattie scones from the Aga. Sally forth with boots or bikes, come home to a dram and a roaring log fire. Argyll at its finest.

Price	£95–£115. Singles from £65. £15 for sofabed.
Rooms	3: 2 twins/doubles, 1 suite.
Meals	Dinner, 3 courses, from £30. Packed lunch £7. Pub/restaurant 400 yds.
Closed	Rarely.
Directions	From Oban take A816 south, signed Campbeltown. After 14 miles, go thro' Kilmelford, then right to Melfort. Follow road & bear right after bridge.

Yvonne & Matthew Anderson
Melfort House,
Kilmelford,
Oban PA34 4XD
Tel   +44 (0)1852 200326
Email relax@melforthouse.co.uk
Web   www.melforthouse.co.uk

Entry 646   Map 14

Argyll & Bute

Corranmor House

A radiant setting on the Ardfern peninsula. Barbara and Hew are as committed to their guests as they are to their 400-acre farm – and are charming and interesting in equal measure. In a red dining room sparkling with silver they treat you to goose, mutton and lamb from the farm, or fish from local landings. Breakfasts too are delicious. Old-fashioned bedrooms are exceptionally private – the double, with kitchen, across the courtyard, the suite with the cosy log-fired sitting room. Wander and admire; the eye always comes to rest on the water and boats of Loch Craignish and the Sound of Jura.

Price	£80–£135. Singles £50.
Rooms	2: 1 double & sitting room; 1 family suite & sitting room.
Meals	Dinner, 3 courses and cheese, £30; with lobster £45. Pubs/restaurants 0.75 miles.
Closed	1 December–3 January; 4th week of August.
Directions	From A816, B8002 to Ardfern, & through village; 0.75 miles past church, long white house high on right. Right by Heron's Cottage, up drive.

Hew & Barbara Service
Corranmor House,
Ardfern,
Lochgilphead PA31 8QN
Tel   +44 (0)1852 500609
Email   corranmorhouse@aol.com

Entry 647   Map 14

Argyll & Bute

Achamore House

No traffic jams here, tucked between the mainland and Islay. Despite its grandeur – turrets, Arts & Crafts doors, plasterwork ceilings – Achamore is not stuffy and neither is Don, your American host. A coastal skipper, he can take you to sea, or over to other islands in his boat. Find warm wood panelling and light-washed rooms, huge bedrooms with shuttered windows, oversize beds, heavy antiques; all have iPods and music. You get the run of the house – billiard room, library, large lounge, TV room (great for kids). With 50 acres of gardens and a quiet beach it's ideal for big parties or gatherings.

Price	£90–£130. Singles from £35.
Rooms	9: 2 doubles, 1 family room; 2 doubles sharing bath; 2 twins/doubles sharing bath; 2 singles sharing bath.
Meals	Pub/restaurant 1 mile.
Closed	December/January.
Directions	Uphill from ferry landing, turn left at T-junc.; 1 mile, stone gates on right, signed; house at top of drive.

Free pick-up from ferry port.

Don Dennis & Emma Rennie
Achamore House,
Isle of Gigha PA41 7AD
Tel   +44 (0)1583 505400
Email   gigha@atlas.co.uk
Web   www.achamorehouse.com

Entry 648   Map 14

Ayrshire

Langside Farm

Your hosts have gentle intelligence and humour and are squeaky green in their family home: local (much organic) produce promises fine breakfasts and suppers; water comes from a private spring and you are kept cosy by a biomass woodchip boiler. Inside, a well-proportioned Georgian elegance – the main part dates back to 1745 – fresh contemporary artwork (some Elise's) and a snug kitchen. Deep red sofas, pale striped walls, books and lamps draw you in; pretty bedrooms have a period feel and long views. There's good walking and golf nearby. Chat in the kitchen, sit by the fire, make yourselves truly at home.

Ethical Collection: Environment; Food; Community. See page 430.

Price	£79. Singles from £49.50.
Rooms	2: 1 twin, 1 four-poster.
Meals	Packed lunch £5.50. Dinner £24.50. BYO. Restaurant 8 miles.
Closed	January, February & November.
Directions	Langside Farm is 0.7 miles from the Dalry end of the B784. The B784 links the B780 Dalry-Kilbirnie road to the A760 Kilbirnie-Largs road. Rail to Dalry or Glengarnock.

Free transport to Braidwoods, our local 'Michelin Star' restaurant.

Nick & Elise Quick
Langside Farm,
Dalry KA24 5JZ
Tel   +44 (0)1294 834402
Email mail@langsidefarm.co.uk
Web   www.langsidefarm.co.uk

Entry 649   Map 14

Ayrshire

The Carriage House

An avenue of limes, 250 acres of parkland, rhododendrons, wellingtonia – what a view to wake to! Luke's family have owned the estate and castle for 900 years. Their stylishly converted Carriage House, with its ochre walls, cobbled courtyard and delightful drawing room, is full of light and comfortable good taste: polished floors, handsome antiques, family photographs, contemporary fabrics. Aga-cooked breakfasts are taken in a huge kitchen with views of pottering hens. Tennis court, swimming pool, country walks: this is an elegant place to unwind. The Borwicks are confident and keen hosts.

Price	£90. Singles £55.
Rooms	3: 1 double, 1 twin/double, 1 twin.
Meals	Pubs/restaurants 3-7 miles.
Closed	Rarely.
Directions	From Beith enter Dalry on A737. First left (signed Bridgend Industrial Estate); uphill through houses, past farm on right at top of hill. First right into Blair Estate.

Luke & Caroline Borwick
The Carriage House,
Blair, Dalry KA24 4ER
Tel   +44 (0)1294 833100
Email office@blairtrust.co.uk
Web   www.blairestate.com

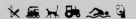

Entry 650   Map 14

Ayrshire

Heughmill

Five acres of fields and lawn with free-range hens that kindly donate for breakfast and views to the sea. The house is just as good, surrounded by old stone farm buildings, with climbing roses and a small burn tumbling through. Inside, a lovely country home with tapestries in an airy hall, an open fire in the sitting room and a terrace that sits under a vast sky. Country-house bedrooms are stylishly homely. Two have the view, one has an old armoire, another comes with a claw-foot bath; all have delightful art. Julia sculpts, Mungo cooks breakfast on the Aga. Rural Ayrshire waits, yet you are close to the airport.

Price	£65–£80. Singles on request.
Rooms	3: 2 twins/doubles, 1 twin.
Meals	Pubs/restaurants within 2 miles.
Closed	Christmas & New Year.
Directions	3 miles south of Kilmarnock, turn east down B730 for Tarbolton. After 0.75 miles, right onto narrow road signed Ladykirk. House is 250 yds on right.

	Mungo & Julia Tulloch
	Heughmill,
	Craigie, Kilmarnock KA1 5NQ
Tel	+44 (0)1563 860389
Email	mungotulloch@hotmail.com
Web	www.stayprestwick.com

Entry 651   Map 14

Clackmannanshire

Kennels Cottage

Live the dream: tour Scotland by classic car. Sandy does Triumphs, Austin Healeys, convertible Beetles. Tanya spoils you, with big crisp beds, huge white towels, elegant blinds, orchids and oriental touches. The old gamekeeper's cottage is a stunningly fresh, stylish and immaculate place, all white walls, white sofas, books, paintings and the odd flash of gold. In the morning, feast on local bacon, Fair Trade coffees and eggs from their hens served at one convivial table. Take a picnic to the garden, wander through what was the Dollarbeg estate, replete with pheasant and deer... totally unwind.

Price	£70–£80. Singles £50.
Rooms	3 doubles.
Meals	Packed lunch £10. Pub 2 miles.
Closed	December/January.
Directions	From Dollar take B913 towards Blairingone. House 2 miles from Dollar just before Blairingone.

	10% off room rate Mon-Thur. 10% off mini tour package (classic car hire plus b&b).

	Tanya Worsfold & Sandy Stewart
	Kennels Cottage,
	Dollarbeg, Dollar FK14 7PA
Tel	+44 (0)1259 742186
Email	tanya.worsfold@btinternet.com
Web	www.guesthousescotland.co.uk

Entry 652   Map 15

Dumfries & Galloway

Knockhill

Fabulous Knockhill: stunning place, stunning position, a country house full of busts and screens, oils and mirrors, chests and clocks, rugs and fires. In the intimate drawing room, full of treasures, floor-to-ceiling windows look down the wooded hill. Fine stone stairs lead to country-house bedrooms that are smart yet homely: headboards of carved oak or padded chintz, books and views. Come for a grand farming feel and delicious Scottish meals; the Morgans are the most unpretentious and charming of hosts. Mellow, authentic, welcoming – an enduring favourite.

Price	£88–£90. Singles £54–£64.
Rooms	2: 1 twin; 1 twin with separate bath.
Meals	Dinner £26. Pub 5 miles.
Closed	Rarely.
Directions	From M74 junc. 19, B725 for Dalton. Right by church in Ecclefechan, signed Hoddam Castle. After 1.2 miles right at x-roads towards Lockerbie. 1 mile on, right at stone [not whitewashed] lodge cottage. At top of long drive.

	Yda & Rupert Morgan
	Knockhill,
	Lockerbie DG11 1AW
Tel	+44 (0)1576 300232
Mobile	+44 (0)7813 944107
Email	morganbellows@yahoo.co.uk

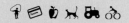

Entry 653   Map 15

Dumfries & Galloway

Applegarth House

Here is an old peaceful manse at the top of the hill, right next door to the church, with a 12th-century motte; the views from the pretty garden stretch for miles around. The house is a good size, with original pine floors and sweeping stairs. Off the large and light landing are three bedrooms with warm carpets, shuttered windows and glorious garden and country views. Let the tawny owls lull you to sleep then wake to freshly stewed fruits and excellent porridge. There are paths to wander through the flower beds, statues to admire and endless wildlife; a perfect stop off point for a trip north or south.

Price	£84–£88. Singles from £54.
Rooms	3: 2 twins; 1 double with separate bath.
Meals	Supper, 2 courses, £20. BYO. Hotel restaurant 1.5 miles.
Closed	Rarely.
Directions	M74 junc. 17 to Lockerbie, B7076 for Johnstonebridge. 1st right after 1.5 miles; after 100 yds left over m'way bridge. After 1 mile, right at T-junc., then 2nd left to church. Next to church. Do not use satnav.
	10% off stays of 2 or more nights. Free pick-up from local bus/train station.

	Frank & Jane Pearson
	Applegarth House,
	Lockerbie DG11 1SX
Tel	+44 (0)1387 810270
Mobile	+44 (0)7732 127779
Email	jane@applegarthtown.demon.co.uk

Entry 654   Map 15

Dumfries & Galloway

Chipperkyle

Sink into the sofas without worrying about creasing them; this beautiful Scottish-Georgian family home has not a hint of formality, and the sociable Dicksons put you at your ease. Sitting and dining rooms connect through a large arch; there are family pictures, rugs on wooden floors and a log fire. Upstairs: a cast-iron bed dressed in good linen, striped walls, flowered curtains, lots of books and windows with views – this wonderful house just gets better and better. There are 200 acres, dogs, cats, donkeys and hens, and you can walk, play golf, visit gardens, sail or cycle – in magnificent countryside.

Price	£96.
Rooms	2: 1 double; 1 twin with separate bath/shower. Cot available.
Meals	Dinner available for groups. Pub 3 miles.
Closed	Christmas.
Directions	A75 Dumfries ring road for Stranraer. Approx. 12 miles to Springholm & right to Kirkpatrick Durham. Left at x-roads, after 0.8 miles, up drive on right by white lodge.

Late checkout (12pm).
50% off 4th night.

Use your Sawday's Gift Card here.

Willie & Catriona Dickson
Chipperkyle,
Kirkpatrick Durham,
Castle Douglas DG7 3EY
Tel   +44 (0)1556 650223
Email special_place@chipperkyle.co.uk
Web   www.chipperkyle.co.uk

Entry 655   Map 11

Dumfries & Galloway

The House on the Shore

Impossible not to be wowed by this incredible shoreline setting with views across the Solway Firth. The 1,250-acre estate has been in Jamie's family for generations; he and Sheri are excellent hosts and love their dower house with its rich and varied woodland and wildlife, formal gardens and stupendous views. Grand but with a family feel, this is old country house style at its best with rugs on polished floors, paintings, open fires and fresh flowers. The farm produces its own meat, an enormous walled kitchen garden is being restored, and a peach tree fruits abundantly; you'll eat well. Very special.

Price	£80-£100. Singles £30-£55.
Rooms	2: 1 double, 1 twin.
Meals	Dinner, 3 courses, £25 (BYO). Pub/restaurant 2 miles.
Closed	Rarely.
Directions	A710 Dumfries towards Dalbeatie. Left in Kirkbean. First right, second left at top of hill, 0.5 miles down private drive then left to the house.

10% off room rate Mon-Thurs.

Jamie & Sheri Blackett
The House on the Shore,
Arbigland, Kirkbean,
Dumfries DG2 8BQ
Tel   +44 (0)1387 880717
Email sheri@arbigland.com
Web   www.arbiglandestate.co.uk

Entry 656   Map 11

Dumfries & Galloway

Chlenry Farmhouse

Handsome in its glen; a traditional family farmhouse full of old-fashioned comfort with charming, well-travelled owners and friendly dogs. In peaceful bedrooms with leafy views, solid antiques jostle with tasselled lampshades, flowers, bowls of fruit, and magazines on country matters. There are capacious bath tubs (with soft, peaty water) and suppers for walkers – the Southern Upland Way passes close by. Breakfasts are properly fortifying, evening meals can be simple or elaborate, often with game or fresh salmon. Many Galloway gardens and golf courses wait to be discovered; return to a snug sitting room with an open fire.

Price	From £75. Singles £50.
Rooms	3: 1 twin/double with separate bath; 1 double, 1 twin with shared bath.
Meals	Supper, £17.50. Dinner, 4 courses, £30. Packed lunch £6. Pub 1.5 miles.
Closed	Christmas, New Year & occasionally.
Directions	A75 for Stranraer. In Castle Kennedy, right opp. Esso station. Approx. 1.25 miles on, after right bend, right signed Chlenry. Down hill, 300 yds on left.
	Drink & wine with dinner. Plate of fruit in bedroom. Use of internet.

David & Ginny Wolseley Brinton
Chlenry Farmhouse,
Castle Kennedy, Stranraer DG9 8SL
Tel   +44 (0)1776 705316
Email wolseleybrinton@aol.com
Web   www.chlenryfarmhouse.com

Entry 657 Map 14

Dunbartonshire

Finglen House

The Campsie Hills rise behind (climb them and you can see Loch Lomond), the Fin Burn takes a two-mile tumble down the hill into the garden, and herons and wagtails can be spotted from the breakfast table. All this 40 minutes from Glasgow. Sabrina's designer flair gives an easy, graceful comfort to the whole house: good beds in stylish rooms, proper linen, French touches, eclectic art, cast-iron baths and cream-painted wooden floors. A fresh, elegant drawing room with log fire is yours to share. Douglas, a documentary film maker, knows the Highlands and Islands well; he and Sabrina are fun and good company.

Price	£80. Singles £50.
Rooms	2: 1 double; 1 double with separate bath.
Meals	Pub 5-minute drive.
Closed	Christmas & New Year.
Directions	A81 from Glasgow right on A891 at Strathblane. 3 miles on, in Haughhead, look for a wall & trees on left, & turn in entrance signed Schoenstatt. Immed. left to house.

Sabrina & Douglas Campbell
Finglen House,
Campsie Glen G66 7AZ
Tel   +44 (0)1360 310279
Email sabrina.campbell@btinternet.com
Web   www.finglenhouse.com

Entry 658 Map 15

Dunbartonshire

Ashfield House

Up a sweeping drive to an imposing front door, and a wonderful welcome from Hermione. The grandfather clock ticks in the hall, logs blaze in the drawing room, landscapes dot the walls... the old-school interiors of this very friendly Georgian home are filled with ancestral artefacts and interesting tales. A brass bedstead is topped with an embroidered spread, the larger double has a walnut panelled dressing room, and you wake to delicious breakfasts of local goodies and eggs from Hermione's hens. He and she, travellers both, know Scotland inside out – and you can walk to Loch Lomond! Hikers and golfers rejoice.

Price	£95. Singles £80.
Rooms	2: 1 double; 1 double with separate bath.
Meals	Pub 1.5 miles.
Closed	Rarely.
Directions	Between Balloch & Gartocharn. From Glasgow A82 to Balloch. Right on to A811 for 2 miles. Past garden centre entrance on left before high grey wall among trees.

Hermione & Hugh Spencer
Ashfield House,
Gartocharn G83 8NB
Tel   +44 (0)1389 752805
Email hughandhermione@hotmail.com

Entry 659   Map 15

Edinburgh

24 Saxe Coburg Place

A ten-minute walk from the centre of Edinburgh, this 1827 house stands in a quiet, Georgian square with a central communal garden. The three simple bedrooms are on the garden level and are self-contained with their own entrance; find comfortable beds, good lighting, handsome antiques and a small kitchen for making tea and coffee. Bathrooms are spotless and one has Paris metro tiling in white and green. Excitingly you can nip over the road to the refurbished Victorian Baths for a swim, sauna or workout in the gym; return to a generous continental breakfast served in the little hall – or on the pretty terrace in summer.

Price	£90-£120. Singles £48-£55.
Rooms	3: 1 double, 1 twin/double, 1 single.
Meals	Continental breakfast. Restaurants/pubs 5-minute walk.
Closed	Rarely.
Directions	From George St, down Frederick St. Over 3 sets of lights, left at bottom of hill. Right up Clarence St. At junc. over to Saxe Coburg St. Saxe Coburg Place is at end. Ask about parking.

Diana McMicking
24 Saxe Coburg Place,
Edinburgh EH3 5BP
Tel   +44 (0)131 315 3263
Email diana@saxecoburgplace.co.uk
Web   www.saxecoburgplace.co.uk

Entry 660   Map 15

Edinburgh

7 Gloucester Place

A cantilevered staircase in walnut and mahogany, a soaring hand-painted cupola: the classic Georgian townhouse is five minutes from Princes Street. Rooms are cosy yet immaculate, sprinkled with paintings and decorative things from travels to far-flung places. Bedrooms are comfy, traditional and well-stocked with books and radio (and there are Z-beds for children). Bag the south-facing double with its stunning Art Deco bathroom and garden views. Naomi is pretty relaxed and happy to chat to you about the local music and art scene, or to leave you in peace. An interesting and hospitable place to unwind.

Price	£90–£110. Singles from £50.
Rooms	3: 1 double; 1 double with separate bath; 1 double with separate shower. Extra child beds.
Meals	Pubs/restaurants 300 yds.
Closed	Christmas & rarely.
Directions	From George St (city centre), down Hanover St, across Queen St at lights. Left into Heriot Row, right onto India St, then left.

	Naomi Jennings
	7 Gloucester Place,
	Edinburgh EH3 6EE
Tel	+44 (0)131 225 2974
Email	naomijennings@hotmail.com
Web	www.stayinginscotland.com

Entry 661   Map 15

Edinburgh

10 London Street

A Roman X marks this special spot: a beautiful Georgian terraced house in Edinburgh's world heritage New Town, home to descendants of Scots author John Gibson Lockhart. Step into a family home of period elegance and charming informality: accept a sherry by the fire in the sash-windowed drawing room (with baby grand piano), chat with Pippa and Hugh over breakfast bagels, sleep undisturbed in 'Beauregard' with its lovely views and paintings. Or pick 'Gibson' for its off-courtyard privacy and self-catering option. The best of Edinburgh is a stroll away, good buses zip you further afield, but at night-time all is quiet.

Price	£85–£120.
Rooms	2 doubles (one with self-catering option).
Meals	Pub/restaurant 500 yds.
Closed	Rarely.
Directions	In the centre of Edinburgh, 10-minute walk from Edinburgh Waverly (main train & bus station, airport bus terminal station).

10% off stays of 2 or more nights. Late checkout (12pm).

	Pippa Lockhart
	10 London Street,
	Edinburgh EH3 6NA
Tel	+44 (0)131 556 0737
Email	pippa@hjlockhart.co.uk
Web	www.londonstreetaccommodation.co.uk

Entry 662   Map 15

Edinburgh

21 India Street

Portraits of the Macpherson clan beam down upon you at delicious breakfast served in a sunny and elegant dining room. In this house of great character you are cared for by Zandra, who offers guests the Laird's Room with its half-tester and the (smaller) Patio Room with its own front entrance. And it's just a hop and a skip up the majestic cobbled streets of New Town to Princes Street and the centre. Zandra plays the Scottish harp, loves to cook, has two beautiful black labs and has written about her life as wife of a clan chieftain – read up about it all in the spacious drawing room.

Price	£95-£145. Singles £69-£105.
Rooms	2: 1 double, 1 twin.
Meals	Restaurants close by.
Closed	Rarely.
Directions	Down South Queensferry Rd; left at Y-junc.; at 2nd Y-junc. left into Craig Leith Rd. Thro' Stockbridge, over lights at bridge; 3rd right into Royal Circus; sharp right thro' Circus Gdns; left into India St. Garage parking.

Signed copy of *A strange & Wild Place* written by hostess.

Zandra Macpherson of Glentruim
21 India Street,
Edinburgh EH3 6HE
Tel +44 (0)131 225 4353
Email zandra@twenty-one.co.uk
Web www.twenty-one.co.uk

Entry 663 Map 15

Edinburgh

11 Belford Place

Guests love Susan's modern townhouse above the Water of Leith. A golden retriever wags his welcome in the wooden-floored entrance, a picture-lined staircase winds upward. Outside, New Zealand flax bursts into flower while herons and foxes share an exquisite sloping garden. Handsome rooms offer china cups and floral spreads; dazzling bathrooms have Molton Brown goodies. Taste Stornoway black pudding at the gleaming breakfast table – there are simple box lunches if you're on the trot. You hear owls at night yet you're a hop from the city, with free parking and a bus stop nearby. *Minimum stay two nights in August.*

Price	£70-£120.
Rooms	3: 1 double, 2 twins/doubles.
Meals	Packed lunch £10. Pub 200 yds. Restaurants 10-minute walk.
Closed	Christmas.
Directions	From city centre to Belford Rd; Belford Pl 1st left after Travelodge Hotel. House down hill opp. Edinburgh Sports Club. Free parking. No 13 bus passes top of lane to city centre.

Bottle of wine and chocolates in your room on arrival.

Susan Kinross
11 Belford Place,
Edinburgh EH4 3DH
Tel +44 (0)131 332 9704
Email suekinross@blueyonder.co.uk
Web www.edinburghcitybandb.com

Entry 664 Map 15

Edinburgh

12 Belford Terrace

Leafy trees, a secluded garden, a stone wall and, beyond, a quiet riverside stroll. Right on the doorstep of the Modern Art and Dean galleries with Edinburgh's theatres and restaurants just a 15-minute walk, this Victorian end terrace, beside Leith Water, oozes an easy-going elegance, helped by Carolyn's laid-back but competent manner. Garden level bedrooms have their own entrance and are big and creamy with stripy fabrics, antiques, sofas and huge windows. (The single has a *Boys Own* charm.) Carolyn spoils with crisp linen, books and biscuits and a delicious, full-works breakfast. After a day in town, relax on the sunny terrace.

Price	£70–£100. Singles from £40.
Rooms	3: 1 double, 1 twin/double; 1 single with separate shower.
Meals	Pub/restaurants within 10-min walk.
Closed	Christmas.
Directions	From Palmerston Place through 2 sets of lights, downhill on Belford Rd past the Travelodge. Immed. left is Belford Terrace. Limited free parking, 2-minute drive.

Fresh flowers and bottle of wine in your room.

	Carolyn Crabbie
	12 Belford Terrace,
	Edinburgh EH4 3DQ
Tel	+44 (0)131 332 2413
Mobile	+44 (0)7785 303396
Email	carolyncrabbie@blueyonder.co.uk

Entry 665   Map 15

Edinburgh

Wallace's Arthouse Scotland

The apartment door swings open to a world of white walls, smooth floors, modern art, acoustic jazz, and smiling Wallace with a glass of wine – well worth the three-storey climb up this old Assembly Rooms building. Wallace – New York fashion designer and arts enthusiast, Glasgow-born, not shy – has created a bright, minimalist space sprinkled with humour and casual sophistication. Bedrooms capture light and exude his inimitable style; the kitchen's narrow bar is perfect for a light breakfast. Leith is Edinburgh's earthy side with its docks and noisy street life, but fine restaurants abound and the centre is close. Memorable.

Price	£95. Singles £85.
Rooms	2 doubles.
Meals	Pubs/restaurants 10 yds.
Closed	December.
Directions	From Princes St, follow Leith Walk to the foot and left along Gt. Junction St. Then 1st right along Henderson St to Water of Leith traffic lights. Right along Bernard St; at the next lights right into Constitution St.

10% off room rate Mon-Thurs. Late checkout (12pm).

	Wallace Shaw
	Wallace's Arthouse Scotland,
	41-4 Constitution Street,
	Edinburgh EH6 7BG
Tel	+44 (0)131 538 3320
Email	cawallaceshaw@mac.com
Web	www.wallacesarthousescotland.com

Entry 666   Map 15

Edinburgh

2 Fingal Place

An elegant house on a Georgian terrace. The leafy park lies opposite (look upwards to Arthur's Seat). Bustling theatres, shops and the university are a stroll away, yet this is a very quiet house. Your hostess is sometimes away so you may be looked after by a housekeeper, but when at home Gillian can help plan your trips – or cater for celebrations and graduations with lunch and dinner; it's entirely flexible. Downstairs at garden level, the bedrooms have mahogany antique beds, floral curtains and bathrooms with good towels. Noodle the Llasa Apso and Gillian's cat will welcome you. *Parking metered 8.30-5.30pm weekdays.*

Edinburgh

20 Blackford Road

A 20-minute stroll from the Royal Mile is a substantial Victorian house with relaxed hosts and a touch of old-world luxury. From a cushioned window seat you gaze onto a lovely wildlife-filled walled garden where you can eat out on a warm day; breakfasts, though not cooked, are superb. Bedrooms, one up, one down, are tranquil and serene, with delicately papered walls and lush toile de Jouy; the drawing room, with cream sofas, soft lights, drinks tray and beautiful books, is elegant yet cosy. Lucas the rescue greyhound completes the picture – of a happy, charming place to stay. *Minimum stay two nights in August.*

Price	£80-£115 (£90-£130 during Festival). Singles from £55 (from £65 during Festival).	Price	£70-£100. Singles from £60.
Rooms	2: 1 twin (with single room attached), 1 twin.	Rooms	2: 1 twin/double, 1 twin, each with separate bath.
Meals	Pubs/restaurants 100 yds.	Meals	Restaurants 500 yds.
Closed	22-27 December.	Closed	Christmas & New Year.
Directions	From centre, Lothian Rd to Tollcross (clock) & Melville Drive. At 2nd major lights, right into Argyle Place; immed. left into Fingal Place.	Directions	A720 city bypass, take Lothianburn exit to city centre. Continue for 2.5 miles on Morningside Rd; right into Newbattle Terrace; 2nd left into Whitehouse Loan. Immed. right into Blackford Road. House at end on left.

	Gillian Charlton-Meyrick		John & Tricia Wood
	2 Fingal Place,		20 Blackford Road,
	The Meadows,		Edinburgh EH9 2DS
	Edinburgh EH9 1JX	Tel	+44 (0)131 447 4233
Tel	+44 (0)131 667 4436	Email	enquiries@grangebandb.co.uk
Email	gcmeyrick@fireflyuk.net	Web	www.grangebandb.co.uk
Web	www.fingalplace.co.uk		

Entry 667   Map 15

Entry 668   Map 15

Edinburgh

1 Albert Terrace

A warm-hearted home with a lovely garden, an American hostess and two gorgeous Siamese cats. You are 20 minutes by bus from Princes Street yet the guests' sitting room overlooks pear trees and clematis and the rolling Pentland Hills. Cosy up in the winter next to a log fire; in summer, take your morning paper onto the terrace above the sunny garden. Books, fresh flowers, interesting art and ceramics and – you are on an old, quiet street – utter, surprising peace. Bedrooms are colourful, spacious and bright, one with an Art Deco bathroom and views over the garden. Clarissa is arty, easy, generous and loves having guests.

Price	£75–£90. Singles £50.
Rooms	3: 1 double; 1 double, 1 single sharing bath.
Meals	Pubs/restaurants nearby.
Closed	Rarely.
Directions	From centre of Edinburgh, A702 south, for Peebles. Pass Churchill Theatre (on left), to lights. Albert Terrace 1st right after theatre. Metered parking on street, but non-metered area nearby.

Clarissa Notley
1 Albert Terrace,
Edinburgh EH10 5EA
Tel   +44 (0)131 447 4491
Email   canotley@aol.com

Entry 669   Map 15

Edinburgh

Craigbrae

Half a mile down a narrow winding lane and you wash up at the old stone farmhouse, with huge windows overlooking fields. The house has been recently renovated so there's a lovely new bathroom in New England style and bedrooms that ooze tranquillity and thoughtful touches. Your hosts are hospitable and great fun; the drawing room is warm, cosy and homely; there are books, china, family pieces and good oil paintings. Edinburgh is 15 minutes by train from the village, the airport 12 minutes by taxi or car. And there's a pretty garden that catches the sun with plenty of places to sit.

Price	£70–£90. Singles from £40.
Rooms	3: 1 double; 2 twins/doubles sharing 2 bath/shower rooms.
Meals	Pubs/restaurants 2 miles.
Closed	Christmas.
Directions	Please ask for directions when booking.

Louise & Michael Westmacott
Craigbrae,
Kirkliston, Edinburgh EH29 9EL
Tel   +44 (0)131 331 1205
Email   louise@craigbrae.com
Web   www.craigbrae.com

Entry 670   Map 15

Inveresk House

Cromwell stayed here, and plotted his siege of Edinburgh Castle; the house oozes history. The magnificent main rooms are furnished with ornate antiques, squashy sofas in chintzes, flowers, gilt, mirrors, seriously gorgeous rugs and Alice's own vibrant art. Bedrooms and bathrooms, on the expected scale, come with vintage radiators, huge beds, good old-fashioned comfort. Musicians will be happy — there are two baby grands. Come for Inveresk (a conservation village), golf (the course at Musselburgh is the oldest in the world), interesting conversation and history by the hatful. Edinburgh is a bus hop away.

Letham House

Sweep down the rhododendron-lined drive to enter a magical, secret world. This fine, early 17th-century mansion has elegant staircases, resplendent fabrics, gleaming antiques and roaring fires; generous, people-loving Barbara and Chris just want you to enjoy it all. They give you complete privacy and tranquillity in stunning south-facing bedrooms; the views over mature trees and impeccable parkland are the stuff of dreams. Eat robustly, sleep peacefully, indulge yourself in gorgeous bathrooms; this is a nurturing retreat. You won't want to leave, but there are beaches and golf nearby; Edinburgh is beyond.

Price	£100–£140. Singles £65.
Rooms	3: 1 double, 1 twin, 1 family room.
Meals	Pubs/restaurants in Musselburgh.
Closed	Rarely.
Directions	From Edinburgh, A199 (A1) to Musselburgh. There, signs to Inveresk. At top of Inveresk Brae, sharp right into cul-de-sac. 2nd opening on right, opp. gates with GM on them, bear right past cottages to house.

Price	£140–£190. Singles £55–£95.
Rooms	5: 2 doubles, 2 twins/doubles; 1 suite with separate bath.
Meals	Dinner, 3 courses, £35. Packed lunch £10. Pubs/restaurants 1 mile.
Closed	Rarely.
Directions	From A1 south, exit at Oak Tree junc. Follow signs for Haddington (B6471). Turn immediately right after 40mph signs, through large stone pillars. Straight down drive.

 10% off room rate Mon-Thurs. 10% off stays of 2 or more nights.

Alice & John Chute
Inveresk House,
3 Inveresk Village, Musselburgh
EH21 7UA
Tel +44 (0)131 665 5855
Email chute.inveresk@btinternet.com
Web www.invereskhouse.com

Barbara Sharman
Letham House,
Haddington EH41 3SS
Tel +44 (0)1620 820055
Email stay@lethamhouse.com
Web www.lethamhouse.com

Entry 671   Map 15

Entry 672   Map 15

Edinburgh & the Lothians

Eaglescairnie Mains

Wildlife thrives: eight acres of conservation headland have been created and wildflower meadows planted on this 350-acre working farm... you'd never guess Edinburgh was so close. The Georgian farmhouse sits in lovely gardens, its peace uninterrupted. There's a traditional conservatory for locally sourced breakfasts, a perfectly gracious drawing room (coral walls, rich fabrics, log fire) for wintery nights, and beautiful big bedrooms full of books and kind extras. Barbara is warm and charming, Michael's commitment to the countryside is wide-ranging; follow signed farm walks to the pub in Gifford.

Ethical Collection: Environment; Community. See page 430.

Price	£70–£80. Singles from £45.
Rooms	3: 2 doubles, 1 twin.
Meals	Pub 1 mile.
Closed	Christmas.
Directions	From A1 at Haddington, B6368 south for Bolton & Humbie. Right immed. after traffic lights on bridge. 2.5 miles on through Bolton, at top of hill, left for Gifford. Entrance 0.5 miles on left.

Barbara & Michael Williams
Eaglescairnie Mains,
Gifford, Haddington EH41 4HN
Tel   +44 (0)1620 810491
Email   williams.eagles@btinternet.com
Web   www.eaglescairnie.com

Entry 673   Map 16

Edinburgh & the Lothians

Glebe House

Gwen has lavished a huge amount of time and love on her 1780s manse. The perfect Georgian family house with all the well-proportioned elegance you'd expect, it is resplendent with original features – fireplaces, arched glass, long windows – that have appeared more than once in interiors magazines. Bedrooms are light and airy with pretty fabrics and lovely linen. The beach is a stone's throw away, views are leafy-green, and golfers have over 21 courses to choose from. There's also a fascinating sea bird centre close by – yet you are 30 minutes from Edinburgh! Regular trains take you to the foot of the castle.

Price	£90–£100. Singles by arrangement.
Rooms	3: 1 double, 1 twin, 1 four-poster.
Meals	Restaurants 2-minute walk.
Closed	Christmas.
Directions	From Edinburgh, A1 for Berwick. Left onto A198, follow signs into North Berwick. Right into Station Rd signed 'The Law', to 1st x-roads; left into town centre; house on left behind wall.

Gwen & Jake Scott
Glebe House,
Law Road, North Berwick EH39 4PL
Tel   +44 (0)1620 892608
Email   gwenscott@glebehouse-nb.co.uk
Web   www.glebehouse-nb.co.uk

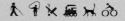

Entry 674   Map 16

Edinburgh & the Lothians

Highfield House

Although much of it is grand, there's a relaxed feel to this 18th-century manse house, where Jillian and Hugh enjoy having guests. Treat yourself to a quiet time in the large, light sitting room with family photos, books and paintings, comfy sofas by the fire and a sunny window seat. Bedrooms are softly painted in yellows and blues, beds have good mattresses and bathrooms are spotless. Breakfast on old favourites, or haggis and black pudding, in a dining room with oodles of sunlight and Hugh's oil-clad ancestors watching; home cooking in the evening is candlelit and cosy – or catch the train into town. *Dogs extra charge.*

Price	£76–£80. Singles £50.
Rooms	2 twins/doubles.
Meals	Packed lunch £6. Dinner £15–£25. Pub/restaurant 3 miles.
Closed	Christmas.
Directions	A71 from Edinburgh. 5 miles beyond city bypass left onto B7031 to Kirknewton. Next right then cross railway line. House is on left at top of hill.

10% off stays of 2 or more nights. Bottle of wine in your room.

Jillian & Hugh Hunter Gordon
Highfield House,
Kirknewton EH27 8BJ
Tel   +44 (0)1506 881489
Email jill@hunter-gordon.co.uk
Web   www.highfield-h.co.uk

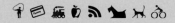

Entry 675   Map 15

Fife

Blair Adam

If staying in a place with genuine Adam features is special, how much more so in the Adam family home! They've been in this corner of Fife since 1733: John laid out the walled garden, son William was a prominent politician, Sir Walter Scott used to come and stay... you may be similarly inspired. The house stands in a swathe of parkland and forest overlooking the hills and Loch Leven, with big, friendly, light-flooded rooms filled with intriguing contents. The pretty bedroom is on the ground floor and you eat in the private dining room or with the family in the kitchen – you choose.

Price	From £100. Singles from £50.
Rooms	1 twin.
Meals	Dinner, with wine, £25. Restaurants 5 miles.
Closed	December/January.
Directions	From M90 exit 5, B996 south for Cowdenbeath. Right for Maryburgh, through village, right through pillars onto drive, under bridge, then 0.5 miles on up to house.

10% off stays of 2 or more nights.

Keith & Elizabeth Adam
Blair Adam,
Kelty KY4 0JF
Tel   +44 (0)1383 831221
Mobile +44 (0)7986 711099
Email   adamofblairadam@hotmail.com

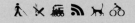

Entry 676   Map 15

Fife

Greenlaw House

With superb views towards the Lomond Hills, Debbie's bright, warm converted farm steading will please you the moment you step in. The oak-floored sitting room has Afghan rugs, sofas around a log-burner, a grand piano; step onto the decked area for summer sun. In all the rooms is a medley of modern and antique, and fascinating art. The ground-floor bedroom has a lovely old chest and books; the more lived-in upstairs one has the view. Debbie loves to cook: kedgeree, porridge with cream, organic eggs, local honey. Falkland Palace, hunting haunt of the Stuart kings, is close; there are wonderful walks and sea eagles soar.

Price	£60-£75. Singles £40-£50.
Rooms	2: 1 double; 1 double with separate bath.
Meals	Dinner £15-£30. Restaurants 15-minute drive.
Closed	Christmas & New Year.
Directions	B937 north off A91, at Trafalgar junc. turn towards Newburgh. After exactly 1 mile right onto tarmac road. Third house at top.

Bottle of champagne for bookings of 2 nights or more. Late checkout (12pm).

Debbie Butler
Greenlaw House,
Braeside, Collessie,
Cupar KY15 7UX
Tel   +44 (0)1337 810236
Email butlerjackson@googlemail.com

Entry 677   Map 15

Fife

18 Queen's Terrace

Hard to imagine you're in the heart of St Andrews, a mere five-minute walk from the centre; it's so peaceful. Jill's stylishly traditional home shows off her good taste, from the light, restful drawing room to the elegant dining room full of sunlight and flowers. Big bedrooms exude comfort, with their delicious beds and crisp linens; bathrooms flourish Arran Aromatics. Jill, gracious and generous, is a mine of information on art, gardens and walks, and serves you scrumptious breakfasts. In summer you can relax on the terrace and admire the water garden – and the birds. *Children over 12 welcome.*

Price	From £90. Singles £65-£70.
Rooms	3: 2 doubles, 1 twin.
Meals	Dinner, 3 courses with wine, £30-£35.
Closed	Rarely.
Directions	Into St Andrews on A917; pass Old Course Hotel. Right at 2nd mini r'bout, left through arch at 2nd mini r'bout. 250 yds, right into Queens Gardens. Right at T-junc. On left opp. church.

Jill Hardie
18 Queen's Terrace,
St Andrews KY16 9QF
Tel   +44 (0)1334 478849
Email stay@18queensterrace.com
Web   www.18queensterrace.com

Entry 678   Map 15+19

Fife

Kinkell

An avenue of beech trees patrolled by guinea fowl leads to the house. If the sea views and the salty smack of St Andrews Bay air don't get you, step inside and have your senses tickled. The elegant drawing room has two open fires, rosy sofas, a grand piano – gorgeous. Bedrooms and bathrooms are immaculate, sunny and warm. There's great cooking too; Sandy and Frippy excel in the kitchen and make full use of local produce. From the front door head down to the beach, walk the wild coast, jump on a quad bike, try your hand at clay pigeon shooting. All this and wonderful hosts. *Online booking available.*

Price	£90. Singles from £55.
Rooms	3 twins/doubles.
Meals	Dinner £30. Restaurants in St Andrews, 2 miles.
Closed	Rarely.
Directions	From St Andrews, A917 for 2 miles for Crail. Driveway in 1st line of trees on left after St Andrews.

 Use your Sawday's Gift Card here.

Sandy & Frippy Fyfe
Kinkell,
St Andrews KY16 8PN
Tel   +44 (0)1334 472003
Email   fyfe@kinkell.com
Web   www.kinkell.com

Entry 679   Map 16+19

Fife

Falside Smiddy

The old smithy sits right on a bend (peaceful at night) but city dwellers won't mind. Saved from dereliction by Rosie and musical, chatty Keith, it is a home you are invited to share. Expect fresh flowers, maps on walls, books, boots and interesting ephemera – not for style seekers but this place is interesting and different. Small rooms have homemade biscuits and hat stands for clothes, bath and shower rooms are spotlessly clean. Rosie cooks a truly good breakfast and turns berries into jams, and the wood-burner makes winters cosy. Lovely walks from the door to the sea and you are close to golf courses.

Price	£65–£70. Singles £45.
Rooms	2 twins.
Meals	Restaurants 4 miles.
Closed	Occasionally.
Directions	From St Andrews, A917 for Crail. After 4 miles, ignore turning for Boarhills, & continue to small river. Over bridge; house 2nd on left.

10% off stays of 2 or more nights. Late checkout (12pm).

Rosie & Keith Birkinshaw
Falside Smiddy,
Boarhills,
St Andrews KY16 8PT
Tel   +44 (0)1334 880479
Email   rosiebirk@btinternet.com

Entry 680   Map 16+19

Fife

Westbourne Cottage

Be charmed by Roger and Joan's stone cottage in a pretty conservation village with winding narrow roads. Pale colours, natural timber and honey-coloured sofas are offset by copper pieces, colour splashes and striking art. Off the garden, in an annexe beautifully renovated by their architect daughter, is your bedroom – fresh, contemporary, spacious and bright. In the vaulted kitchen an original bee hole makes a pretty window – and you can breakfast on the patio in summer. There's a lively local art festival in August, Fife's coastal path is superb and you can eat lobster straight off the boats, cooked in a cabin at Crail.

Price	£70-£80. Singles £60-£70.
Rooms	1 double.
Meals	Pub/restaurant 1 mile.
Closed	Christmas & New Year.
Directions	A92 to Kirkcaldy, A915 & A917 to Anstruther, then B9131 at St Andrews & A917 at Anstruther. After a mile left to Kilrenny, then 2nd right, 1st house on left.

10% off stays of 2 or more nights.

Roger & Joan Brown
Westbourne Cottage,
14 Main Street, Kilrenny,
Anstruther KY10 3JL
Tel   +44 (0)1333 310039
Email   enjoyyourstay@westbournecottage.co.uk

Entry 681   Map 16

Highland

The Grange

A Victorian townhouse with its toes in the country: the mountain hovers above, the loch shimmers below and the garden slopes steeply to great banks of rhododendrons. Bedrooms, the one in the turret with a sumptuous new bathroom, are large, luscious, warm and inviting: crushed velvet, beautiful blankets, immaculate linen — all ooze panache. Expect decanters of sherry, ornate cornices, a Louis XV bed and a superb suite with contemporary touches. Elegant breakfasts are served at glass-topped tables; Joan's warm vivacity and love of B&B means guests keep coming back. And just a 10-minute walk into town.

Price	£110-£118.
Rooms	3: 2 doubles, 1 suite.
Meals	Restaurants 12-minute walk.
Closed	Mid-November to Easter.
Directions	A82 Glasgow-Fort William; 1 mile after 30mph sign into Fort William, turn right up Ashburn Lane, next to Ashburn guesthouse. House on left at top.

50% off 4th night.

Joan & John Campbell
The Grange,
Grange Road,
Fort William PH33 6JF
Tel   +44 (0)1397 705516
Email   info@thegrange-scotland.co.uk
Web   www.thegrange-scotland.co.uk

Entry 682   Map 17

Highland

Tigh An Dochais

An arresting, award-winning, 'see-through' house, quite unlike its neighbours, on a strip of land between the town road and the rocky shoreline, with stunning views out the back across the bay to mountains and islands. Huge windows and a cathedral ceiling allow light to flood in to an oak-floored sitting room with a wood-burner and modern art. Gliding glazed doors in crisp luxurious bedrooms open to larchwood verandas – and the shore! Bathrooms are toasty underfoot. Neil meets, greets, cooks, bakes: try black pudding from Stornoway at breakfast; superb fish, shellfish and game for supper. Irresistible B&B.

Price	£80–£85. Singles £70–£75.
Rooms	3: 2 doubles, 1 twin/double.
Meals	Dinner, 4 courses, £22–£25. BYO. Packed lunch £5. Pub/restaurant 200 yds.
Closed	Rarely.
Directions	Leave Skye Bridge & follow A87 to Broadford. After 6 miles pass Hebridean Hotel on left, house is 200 yds further up A87 on right.

	Neil Hope
	Tigh An Dochais,
	13 Harrapool,
	Isle of Skye IV49 9AQ
Tel	+44 (0)1471 820022
Email	hopeskye@btinternet.com
Web	www.skyebedbreakfast.co.uk

Entry 683   Map 17

Highland

The Berry

Drive through miles of spectacular landscape then bask in the final approach down a winding single-track road to Allt-Na-Subh — just five houses overlooking the loch. Joan, who is friendly and kind, prepares delicious meals in her Rayburn-warmed kitchen – the hub of this character-filled house. Inside is fresh and light with stylish bedrooms — one up, one down; the sitting room has a log fire and stunning views. Eat fish straight from the boats, stride the hills and spot golden eagles, red deer and otters. The perfect place for naturalists and artists, or those seeking solace. A hidden gem. *Skye is a 20-minute drive.*

Price	£65. Singles from £35.
Rooms	2: 1 double with separate shower; 1 double sharing bath.
Meals	Dinner, 3 courses with wine, £30. Packed lunch £7. Pub 20-min drive.
Closed	Rarely.
Directions	From A87 at Dornie follow signs for Killilin, Conchra & Salachy. House 2.7 miles on left.

	Joan Ashburner
	The Berry,
	Allt-Na-Subh,
	Dornie,
	Kyle of Lochalsh IV40 8DZ
Tel	+44 (0)1599 588259

Entry 684   Map 17

Highland

Duncraig Castle

The original owner built the station at Duncraig purely to bring his friends to the castle; Suzanne, open and friendly, is just as keen to share her grand country house. Wood fires blaze, stunning views are of open sea and high mountain, and the rooms are vast. Expect tartan carpet, tiger skins, dark wood panelling and floor to ceiling windows; suits of armour and heraldic pennants hang theatrically on your route to the dining room. Bedrooms are huge, comfortable and velvety with whisky, glassses and shortbread set by all the well-made beds. Walks are marvellous, and you can eat freshly caught langoustines at Plockton Inn.

Price	From £89. Singles £44.50.
Rooms	3 doubles.
Meals	Restaurant 1.2 miles.
Closed	Never.
Directions	Directions on booking and on website.

Suzanne Hazeldine
Duncraig Castle,
Plockton IV52 8TZ
Tel   +44 (0)1599 544295
Email   suzanne@duncraigcastle.co.uk
Web   www.duncraigcastle.co.uk

Entry 685   Map 17

Highland

Aurora

The perfect spot for walkers and climbers (single-track roads, lochs, rivers and mountains) and the perfect B&B for groups: three smart, uncluttered bedrooms have flexible sleeping arrangements and spick and span shower rooms. The guest sitting room is light and airy with binoculars, books to borrow, maps and a small fridge for your wine – stay put for glorious sunsets and views to Harris. Breakfast time is generously bendy and Thomas cooks delicious suppers; salads and herbs are home-grown. There's a drying room and bike storage, but those wanting to relax will love it here too. *Minimum stay two nights. Over 12s welcome.*

Ethical Collection: Environment; Food. See page 430.

Price	£70–£90. Singles £65–£75.
Rooms	3: 1 double, 2 twins/doubles (extra single bed).
Meals	Packed lunch £6. Dinner, 2 courses, £20. BYO. Pub/restaurant within 0.5 miles.
Closed	Occasionally November–March.
Directions	From Inverness A9 north, signed 'Wester Ross Coastal Trail'. Left at Garve A832. Left at Kinlochewe A896. In Shieldaig at Heron sign 1st right; house 4th on left.
	Packed lunch 1st full day. Supper for stays 3 or more nights (Oct-Apr).

Ann Barton
Aurora,
Shieldaig, Torridon IV54 8XN
Tel   +44 (0)1520 755246
Email   info@aurora-bedandbreakfast.co.uk
Web   www.aurora-bedandbreakfast.co.uk

Entry 686   Map 17

Highland

Tanglewood House

Down a steep drive through stunning landscape to this modern, curved house on the shore of Loch Broom – and distant views of the old fishing port of Ullapool. The drawing room is filled with antiques, fine fabrics, original paintings, flowers and a grand piano; bask in the views from the floor-to-ceiling window. Bedrooms are delightful: bold colours, crisp linen, proper bath tubs with fluffy towels. Anne gives you just-squeezed orange juice and eggs from her hens for breakfast, and delicious dinners; explore the wild garden then stroll to the rocky private beach for a swim in the loch. Superb. *Minimum stay two nights.*

Price	£96–£110. Singles £73-£80.
Rooms	3: 1 double, 2 twins.
Meals	Dinner, 4 courses, £36. BYO. Packed lunch £9. Pubs in village 0.5 miles.
Closed	Christmas, New Year & Easter.
Directions	On outskirts of Ullapool from Inverness on A835, left immed. after 4th 40mph sign. Take cattle grid on right & left fork down to house.

	Anne Holloway
	Tanglewood House,
	Ullapool IV26 2TB
Tel	+44 (0)1854 612059
Email	anne@tanglewoodhouse.co.uk
Web	www.tanglewoodhouse.co.uk

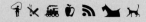

Entry 687   Map 17

Highland

The Old Ferryman's House

This former ferryman's house is small, homely and delightful, and just yards from the river Spey with its spectacular mountain views. Explore the countryside or relax in the garden with a tray of tea and homemade treats; plants tumble from whisky barrels and pots and you can spot red squirrels. The sitting room is cosy with a wood-burning stove and lots of books (no TV). Generous Elizabeth, a keen traveller who lived in the Sudan, cooks delicious and imaginative meals: herbs & some veg from the garden, eggs from her hens, heathery honeycomb, homemade bread and preserves. An unmatched spot for explorers, and very good value.

Price	£58. Singles £29.
Rooms	3: 1 double, 1 twin, 1 single, sharing 1 bath & 2 wcs.
Meals	Dinner, 3 courses, £21. BYO. Packed lunch £6.50.
Closed	Occasionally in winter.
Directions	From A9, follow main road markings through village, pass golf club & cross river. Or turn off B970 to Boat of Garten. House on left, just before river.

	Elizabeth Matthews
	The Old Ferryman's House,
	Boat of Garten PH24 3BY
Tel	+44 (0)1479 831370

Entry 688   Map 18

Highland

Craigiewood

The best of both worlds: the remoteness of the Highlands (red kites, wild goats) and Inverness just four miles. The landscape surrounding this elegant cottage exudes a sense of ancient mystery augmented by these six acres – home to woodpeckers, roe deer and glorious roses. Inside, maps, walking sticks, two cats and a lovely, family-home feel – what you'd expect from delightful owners. Bedrooms, old-fashioned and cosy, overlook a garden reclaimed from Black Isle gorse. Gavin is experimenting with solar panels, and runs garden tours: he can take you off to Inverewe, Attadale, Cawdor and Dunrobin Castle. Warm, peaceful, special.

Price	£76-£80. Singles £40-£50.
Rooms	2 twins.
Meals	Pub 2 miles.
Closed	Christmas & New Year.
Directions	A9 north over Kessock Bridge. At N. Kessock junc. left to r'bout to Kilmuir. After 0.25 miles, right to Kilmuir; left at top of road. Pass Drynie Farm, then right; house 1st left.

 Use your Sawday's Gift Card here.

Araminta & Gavin Dallmeyer
Craigiewood,
North Kessock, Inverness IV1 3XG
Tel   +44 (0)1463 731628
Email   2minty@craigiewood.co.uk
Web   www.craigiewood.co.uk

Entry 689   Map 18

Highland

The Farmhouse

This freshly painted Victorian cottage is up a tree-lined driveway. Barbara's new home glows with art, antique rugs, a dazzling chandelier and French linen curtains; the kitchen has a magnificent dresser stocked with colourful pottery and comfortable armchairs in a warm spot by the wood-burner. The master bedroom sports smart linen, large feather pillows and a spotless bathroom. You get great home baking, and Barbara's creative energy will soon transform the garden, too. Highland views and the wildlife are spectacular, the mountain air is clean; this is a great escape.

Price	£60-£80. Singles from £40.
Rooms	2: 1 double; 1 twin with separate bath.
Meals	Dinner, 4 courses, from £30. Pub 3.5 miles.
Closed	Christmas & New Year.
Directions	From Inverness follow signs to Beauly. After approx. 8 miles, right to Kirkhill. Follow road signed Beauly. House 1 mile on right.

🧳   Late checkout (12pm).

Barbara Turner
The Farmhouse,
Kirkhill Beauly IV5 7PF
Tel   +44 (0)1463 831379
Mobile +44 (0)7099 807468
Email   mlbtuk@googlemail.com

Entry 690   Map 18

Highland

Knockbain House

This is a well-loved farm, its environmental credentials supreme, and David and Denise are warm and interesting. A beautiful setting, too: landscaped gardens, a 700-acre farm (cows, lambs, barley) and rolling countryside stretching to Cromarty Firth. A grandfather clock ticks away time to relax, by floor-to-ceiling windows and a wood-burner in the antiques-filled sitting room; over a breakfast or dinner of home-grown foods; with a drink on the pond-side terrace; in bedrooms with new bathrooms and stunning views. Revel in the birds, walks and your hosts' commitment to this glorious unspoilt nature. *Babes in arms & over tens welcome.*

Price	£70–£90. Singles £25–£60.
Rooms	2: 1 double, 1 twin.
Meals	Dinner, 3 courses with wine, £30. Packed lunch £5. Pubs/restaurants 1 mile.
Closed	Rarely.
Directions	From Dingwall, A834 past County Buildings & police station. After 200 yds, first left Blackwells Street. Narrow road to farm road, 300 yds then over cattle grid up driveway.

David & Denise Lockett
Knockbain House,
Dingwall IV15 9TJ
Tel   +44 (0)1349 862476
Email davidlockett@avnet.co.uk
Web   www.knockbainhouse.co.uk

Entry 691   Map 18

Highland

Wemyss House

The peace is palpable, the setting overlooking the Cromarty Firth is stunning. Take an early morning stroll and spot buzzards, pheasants, rabbits and roe deer. The deceptively spacious house with sweeping maple floors is flooded with light and fabulous views, big bedrooms are warmly decorated with Highland rugs and tweeds, there's Christine's grand piano in the living room, Stuart's handcrafted furniture at every turn, and a sweet dog called Bella. Aga breakfasts include homemade bread, preserves and eggs from happy hens. Dinners are delicious; Christine and Stuart are wonderful hosts.

Ethical Collection: Food. See page 430.

Price	From £90.
Rooms	3: 2 doubles, 1 twin.
Meals	Dinner, 4 courses, £35. Restaurants 15-minute drive.
Closed	Rarely.
Directions	From Inverness, A9 north. At Nigg r'bout, right onto B9175. Through Arabella; left at sign to Hilton & Shandwick; right towards Nigg; past church; 1 mile, right onto private road. House on right.

Bottle of wine with dinner on first night.

Use your Sawday's Gift Card here.

Christine Asher & Stuart Clifford
Wemyss House,
Bayfield, Tain IV19 1QW
Tel   +44 (0)1862 851212
Email stay@wemysshouse.com
Web   www.wemysshouse.com

Entry 692   Map 18

Highland

Linsidecroy

Heaven in the Highlands with stunning valley and mountain views. The house, built in 1863 was part of the Duke of Sutherland's estate; Robert, a factor, first set eyes on it 20 years ago and now it is home. A sublime renovation gives you walls of books, valley views and an open fire in the airy drawing room. Super bedrooms come with rugs, crisp linen, books galore and fresh flowers. There are two terraces, one for breakfast, one for pre-dinner drinks; all around you Davina's remarkable garden is taking shape. You can fish and walk, play some golf, or head north to Tongue through Britain's wildest land. Magical.

Price	£80. Singles £50.
Rooms	2: 1 double, 1 twin.
Meals	Hotel 6 miles.
Closed	Christmas, Easter & occasionally.
Directions	A836 west out of Bonar Bridge. After 4 miles, left onto A837. Cross Shin river, then left towards Rosehall & Lochinver, 1.5 miles, double wooden gates on right. House is 150 yds up drive.

Robert & Davina Howden
Linsidecroy,
Invershin, Lairg IV27 4EU
Tel   +44 (0)1549 421255
Mobile   +44 (0)7776 259768
Email   howden@linsidecroy.wanadoo.co.uk

Entry 693   Map 18

Highland

St Callan's Manse

Fun, laughter and conversation flow in this warm and happy home. You share it with prints, paintings, antiques, sofas, amazing memorabilia, three dogs, nine ducks, 14 hens and 1,200 teddy bears of every size and origin. Snug bedrooms have pretty fabrics, old armoires, flower-patterned sheets and tartan blankets; your sleep will be sound. Caroline cooks majestic breakfasts and dinners; Robert, a fund of knowledgeable anecdotes, can arrange just about anything. All this in incomparable surroundings: 60 acres of sheep-strewn land plus glens, forests, buzzards, deer and the odd golden eagle. A gem. *Dogs by arrangement.*

Price	£80. Singles £65.
Rooms	2: 1 double with separate bath; 1 double with separate shower.
Meals	Dinner, 2-4 courses, £15-£25. BYO. Pub/restaurant in village, 1.5 miles.
Closed	March & occasionally.
Directions	From Inverness, A9 north. Cross Dornoch bridge. 14 miles on, A839 to Lairg. Cross small bridge in Rogart; sharp right uphill, for St Callan's church. House 1.5 miles on, on right, next to church.
	Free pick-up from local bus/train station. Local food/produce in your room.

Robert & Caroline Mills
St Callan's Manse,
Rogart IV28 3XE
Tel   +44 (0)1408 641363
Email   caroline@rogartsnuff.me.uk

Entry 694   Map 21

Moray

Westfield House

Sweep up the drive to the grand home of an illustrious family: Macleans have lived here since 1862. Inside find polished furniture and burnished antiques, a tartan-carpeted hall, an oak stair hung with ancestral oils. John farms 500 acres while Veronica cooks sublimely; dinner is served at a long candelabra'd table, with vegetables from the vegetable garden. A winter fire crackles in the guest sitting room, old-fashioned bedrooms are warm and inviting (plump pillows, fine linen, books, lovely views), the peace is deep. A historic house in a perfect setting, run by the most charming people.

Price	£80. Singles from £40.
Rooms	3: 1 twin; 1 twin with separate bath & shower; 1 single with separate bath.
Meals	Dinner, 3 courses, £25. Pub 3 miles.
Closed	Rarely.
Directions	From Elgin, A96 west for Forres & Inverness; after 2.5 miles, right onto B9013 for Burghead; after 1 mile, signed right at x-roads. Cont. to 'Westfield House & Office'.

	John & Veronica Maclean
	Westfield House,
	Elgin IV30 8XL
Tel	+44 (0)1343 547308
Email	veronica.maclean@yahoo.co.uk

Entry 695   Map 18

Moray

Blervie

The Meiklejohn coat of arms flies from the flagpole, an apple's throw from the orchard in which King Malcolm met his death. Blervie is a small 1776 mansion, "a restoration in progress", its finely proportioned rooms crammed with fresh flowers and splendid things to catch the eye. A large dresser swamped in china, a piano in the hall, books everywhere and the sweet smell of burnt beech from grand marble fireplaces. Big bedrooms have comfy old sofas at the feet of four-posters and a frayed charm; bathrooms are eccentrically old-fashioned. Fiona and Paddy enjoy country pursuits and like to dine with their guests.

Price	£80.
Rooms	2 four-posters, each with separate bath. Extra single bed.
Meals	Dinner, 4 courses, £28. Pubs/restaurants 2-5 miles.
Closed	Christmas & New Year.
Directions	From A96 to Forres. South at clocktower, straight across r'bout onto B9010. Pass hospital; exactly 1 mile on, left at Mains of Blervie sign. Right at farm. (Do not use satnav.)

	Paddy & Fiona Meiklejohn
	Blervie,
	Forres IV36 2RH
Tel	+44 (0)1309 672358
Email	meiklejohn@btinternet.com

Entry 696   Map 18

Perth & Kinross

Grenich Steading

Perched above silvery Loch Tummel is Lindsay's award-winning renovation of a once derelict barn. Inside, blue-and-white Portuguese tiles, seagrass matting and a wood-burning stove. You get a kitchen, dining and sitting room so you can self-cater too (minimum one week). Gaze upon mountain-to-loch views, walk in the unspoilt glen or visit the theatre at Pitlochry. Lindsay loves nurturing both garden and guests; her two Scottish deerhounds are welcoming too. The sunsets are fabulous, and there's so much to do you'll barely be inside. *Children over eight welcome. Minimum stay two nights at weekends May-October.*

Price	From £80. Singles £60.
Rooms	2: 1 double; 1 twin sharing bath & sitting room (2nd room let to same party only).
Meals	Dinner, with wine, £30 (Oct-Mar only). Pub 0.75 miles.
Closed	Rarely.
Directions	From A9 north of Pitlochry for Killiecrankie. Left, B8019 for Tummel Bridge to Loch Tummel Inn. After 0.75 miles, right at sign, then up forestry road for 0.5 miles.

Lindsay Morison
Grenich Steading,
Strathtummel,
Tummel Bridge,
Pitlochry PH16 5RT
Tel   +44 (0)1882 634332
Mobile +44 (0)7502 199163

Entry 697   Map 15+18

Perth & Kinross

Beinn Bhracaigh

Here is a solid Victorian villa, with later wings, built for an Edinburgh family in the 1880s, when Pitlochry was hailed as the Switzerland of the North. Ann and Alf, generous hosts, have swept through with the cream paint and all is spanking new. Expect soft lighting, gleaming wooden floors, silk flowers, bowls of pot pourri and scented candles. The lounge is comfy and has an honesty bar with over 50 malt whiskies, good-sized bedrooms have excellent mattresses, padded headboards and views to the Tummel Hills, bathrooms are all new with thick towels and lovely lotions. Breakfast is a huge, imaginative feast.

Price	£70-£90. Singles from £55.
Rooms	10: 4 doubles, 6 twins/doubles.
Meals	Dinner £22.50-£30 (for special occasions only). Pubs/restaurants within 10-minute walk.
Closed	23-28 December.
Directions	From A9, turn for Pitlochry. Under railway bridge, then right at scout hut & up East Moulin Road. 2nd left into Higher Oakfield; house almost immediately on left.

Ann & Alf Berry
Beinn Bhracaigh,
14 Higher Oakfield,
Pitlochry PH16 5HT
Tel   +44 (0)1796 470355
Email info@beinnbhracaigh.com
Web   www.beinnbhracaigh.com

Entry 698   Map 15+18

Perth & Kinross

Rock House

Prepare to fall hopelessly in love. Hard to know here, high above Loch Tay, whether the views are more beautiful outside or in. The cathedral ceiling in the sitting room allows light to soar upwards, there's a striking collection of modern art and an unfussy style: white sofas, painted furniture, and, here and there, a bit of quirky fun or a perfect antique. Sleep deeply in beds piled with linen cushions, soft woollen throws and cotton ticking, wake to grape and mint salad, Irish bread, kedgeree or anything else you want... Roland and Penny are passionate about their house, the land, and real food. *Minimum stay two nights.*

Price	£120. Singles £85.
Rooms	2 doubles.
Meals	Dinner, 2-3 courses, £25-£35. Packed lunch £12. Pub/restaurant 2.2 miles.
Closed	Rarely.
Directions	From Aberfeldy, A827 dir. Kenmore. At Loch Tay where main road turns sharp right, cont. along narrow road signed Acharn. Follow loch side for 2.2 miles. At top of hill, house on right.

Roland & Penny Kennedy
Rock House,
Achianich, Kenmore,
Aberfeldy PH15 2HU
Tel	+44 (0)1887 830336
Email	rockhouse@lochtay.co.uk
Web	www.lochtay.co.uk

Entry 699   Map 15+18

Perth & Kinross

Mackeanston House

They grow their own organic fruit and vegetables, make their own preserves, bake their own bread. Likeable and energetic – Fiona a wine buff and talented cook, Colin a tri-lingual guide – your hosts are hospitable people whose 1690 farmhouse combines informality and luxury in peaceful, central Scotland. Light-filled bedrooms have soft carpets, pretty fabrics, fine antiques; one has a canopied bed, a double shower (with a seat if you wish it) and a bath that overlooks fields. In the conservatory with views to Stirling Castle you may dine on salmon from the Teith and game from close by. *Local & battlefield tours.*

Price	£96-£100. Singles £58-£60.
Rooms	2: 1 double, 1 twin/double.
Meals	Dinner £30. Pub 1 mile.
Closed	Christmas.
Directions	From M9, north, junc. 10 onto A84 for Doune. After 5 miles, left on B826 for Thornhill. Drive on left after 2.2 miles, right off farm drive.

Bottle of wine on 1st night of min. 2-night stay (dinner, B&B).

Fiona & Colin Graham
Mackeanston House,
Doune,
Stirling FK16 6AX
Tel	+44 (0)1786 850213
Email	info@mackeanstonhouse.co.uk
Web	www.mackeanstonhouse.co.uk

Entry 700   Map 15

Perth & Kinross

Old Kippenross

Pink since 1715 (a signal to Jacobites that the house was a safe haven), Old Kippenross rests in a wooded valley overlooking the river Allan – spot herons, dippers and otters. The Georgian part was built above the 500-year-old Tower House, and its rustic white-vaulted basement embraces dining room and sitting room, strewn with soft sofas and Persian rugs. Upstairs there are deeply comfortable sash-windowed bedrooms and warm, well-equipped bathrooms stuffed with towels. Sue and Patrick (who is an expert on birds of prey) are welcoming; breakfast and dinner are delicious. *Children over ten welcome. Dogs by arrangement.*

Price	£95. Singles £62.50.
Rooms	2: 1 double, 1 twin.
Meals	Dinner £28. BYO. Pub 1.5 miles.
Closed	Rarely.
Directions	M9 exit 11, B8033 for Dunblane. 500 yds, right over dual c'way, thro' entrance by stone gatehouse. Down drive, 1st fork right after bridge. House along gravelled drive.

Bottle of wine with dinner on first night. Salmon & trout fishing on river Allan.

	Sue & Patrick Stirling-Aird
	Old Kippenross,
	Dunblane FK15 0LQ
Tel	+44 (0)1786 824048
Email	kippenross@hotmail.com

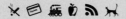

Scottish Borders

Fauhope House

Near to Melrose Abbey and the glorious St Cuthbert's Walk, this solid 1890s house is immersed in bucolic bliss. Views soar to the Eildon Hills through wide windows with squashy seats; all is luxurious, elegant, fire-lit and serene with an eclectic mix of art. Bedrooms are warm with deeply coloured walls, thick chintz, pale tartan blankets and soft carpet; bathrooms are modern and pristine. Breakfast is served with smiles at a flower-laden table and overlooking those purple hills. A short walk through the garden and over a footbridge takes you to the interesting town of Melrose, with shops, restaurants and its own theatre.

Price	From £90. Singles from £60.
Rooms	3 twins/doubles.
Meals	Pub/restaurant 0.5 miles.
Closed	Rarely.
Directions	From A7, through Gattonside; at end of village, at sign on left 'Monkswood', immed. left; right up drive.

	Ian & Sheila Robson
	Fauhope House,
	Gattonside, Melrose TD6 9LY
Tel	+44 (0)1896 823184
Mobile	+44 (0)7816 346768
Email	info@fauhopehouse.com

Scottish Borders

Skirling House

An intriguing house with 1908 additions, impeccably maintained. The whole lovely place is imbued with the spirit of Scottish Arts & Crafts, augmented with Italianate flourishes. Colourful blankets embellish chairs; runners soften flagged floors; the carvings, wrought-ironwork and rare Florentine ceiling are sheer delight. Upstairs, a more English comfort holds sway: carpets and rugs, window seats and wicker, fruit and flowers. Bob cooks the finest local produce, Isobel shares a love of Scottish contemporary art and both look after you beautifully. Outside: 25,000 trees have been planted and grand walks from the door.

Price	£110–£120. Singles £60.
Rooms	5: 3 doubles, 1 twin, 1 twin/double.
Meals	Dinner £32. Pubs/restaurants 2 miles.
Closed	Christmas & January/February.
Directions	From Biggar, A702 for Edinburgh. Just outside Biggar, right on A72 for Skirling. Big wooden house on right opp. village green.

	Bob & Isobel Hunter
	Skirling House,
	Skirling, Biggar ML12 6HD
Tel	+44 (0)1899 860274
Email	enquiry@skirlinghouse.com
Web	www.skirlinghouse.com

Entry 703   Map 15

Scottish Borders

Lessudden

A treat to stay in a great and historic tower house in the heart of the Scottish Borders. Your generous hosts give you big cosy bedrooms (one ground floor with an old-fashioned bathroom, one upstairs with a view), and a spacious sitting room with fine old rugs, heaps of books and a log fire. Memorable meals are served at a polished oak refectory table beneath the gaze of Sir Walter Scott's uncle and aunt, who used to live here. The 1680s white-stone stairwell is unique, the décor is traditional and homely, the living is relaxed and Alasdair and Angela care for their guests as open-heartedly as they do their cats, dogs, horses and hens.

Ethical Collection: Food. See page 430.

Price	£100. Singles £70.
Rooms	2: 1 double; 1 twin with separate bath.
Meals	Dinner, 3-4 courses, £25. Pub 0.5 miles.
Closed	Rarely.
Directions	North on A68 to St Boswells. Right opp. Buccleuch Arms Hotel, on through village; left up drive immed. beyond turning to golf course.

10% off stays of 3 or more nights.

	Alasdair & Angela Douglas-Hamilton
	Lessudden,
	St Boswells TD6 0BH
Tel	+44 (0)1835 823244
Email	alasdaird@lineone.net
Web	www.lessudden.com

Entry 704   Map 16

Scottish Borders

New Belses Farm

Once lost by Lord Lothian in a game of backgammon, this Georgian farmhouse is safe in current hands. Delightful Helen divides her time between helping on the farm, gardening and caring for sundry pets, fan-tail doves, hens (fox permitting), family and guests. Bedrooms glow in a harmony of old paintings, lush chintzes and beautiful antiques; beds are extra long, towels snowy white. It's like home, only better. Discover great Border towns, stunning abbeys, fishing on the Tweed. Enjoy an excellent dinner locally then back to plump sofas by the log fire. Heaven.

Ethical Collection: Food. See page 430.

Price	From £80.
Rooms	2: 1 double, 1 twin.
Meals	Pubs/restaurants 3.5-5 miles.
Closed	Christmas.
Directions	From Jedburgh, A68 for Edinburgh. Left after 3.5 miles to Ancrum; B6400 Ancrum to Lilliesleaf road; right after 4 miles, down drive (signed).

10% off stays of 2 or more nights.

Peter & Helen Wilson
New Belses Farm,
Ancrum, Jedburgh TD8 6UR
Tel   +44 (0)1835 870472
Mobile   +44 (0)7710 277020
Email   wilson699@totalise.co.uk

Entry 705   Map 16

Stirling

The Moss

Rozie loves fishing and Jamie keeps bees; they live in a charming listed house full of lovely things and are great hosts. Outside are 28 acres where deer prune the roses, pheasants roam and a garden seat sits with its toes in the water. Generous bedrooms are very private in their own wing and have big beds with feather pillows, books, flowers and long views to pastures and moorland. Expect walking sticks and the bell of HMS Tempest in the porch, rugs in the hall and smart sofas in the log-fired drawing room. Breakfast comes fresh from the Aga and is delivered to a big oak table, from which there are yet more views.

Price	£90. Singles £45.
Rooms	3: 1 twin; 2 doubles sharing bath (2nd room let to same party only).
Meals	Pubs/restaurants within 2 miles.
Closed	Rarely.
Directions	4 miles west of Blanefield. Half a mile after Beech Tree Inn turn left off A81. After 300 yds, over bridge, 1st entrance on left.

Jamie & Rozie Parker
The Moss,
Killearn G63 9LJ
Tel   +44 (0)1360 550053
Mobile   +44 (0)7787 123599
Email   themoss@freeuk.com

Entry 706   Map 15

Stirling

Quarter

This stately 1750s house commands views across Stirling's lush countryside and comes complete with crunching gravel drive and original ceiling dome. It was owned by the same family for generations until Pippa arrived, taking over its high ceilings, period features, sash windows. Pad your way upstairs to three comfortable bedrooms and bathrooms, brightened with a floral touch. Breakfast is a grand affair at a polished table; pecking hens provide the eggs and Pippa is determined to restore the kitchen garden to its former glory. The house is cocooned in extensive grounds and you've easy access to Stirling, Edinburgh and Perth. *Dogs by arrangement.*

Price	£90. Singles £45.
Rooms	3: 1 double, 1 twin/double, 1 twin.
Meals	Pub/restaurant 4 miles.
Closed	Christmas.
Directions	Stirling, exit 9 off the M9. From roundabout take A872 towards Denny, after exactly 2 miles turn left (200 yds past Wellsfield Farm) through grey pillars up to house.

Fruit and fresh flowers in your room. Free pick-up from local bus/train station.

Pippa Maclean
Quarter,
Denny FK6 6QZ
Tel   +44 (0)1324 825817
Email   pippa@edmonstone.com
Web   www.quarterstirling.com

Entry 707   Map 15

Stirling

Blairhullichan

So much to do here in the National Park: woodland walks, cycle tracks, your own fishing bay on the edge of Loch Ard, a private island to wade out to for picnics. The tranquil house sits high on a slope with fabulous loch views from the drawing room, comfortable with window bay, big fireplace and stacks of books. Reassuringly old-fashioned bedrooms have new mattresses and crisp linen; bathrooms have good towels and lotions. Be charmed by the 'Highlands in miniature' – plus resident labradors and welcoming Bridget, who gives you a grand breakfast and the best of her local knowledge. *Minimum stay two nights.*

Price	£75-£80. Singles £40.
Rooms	3: 1 double with sitting room, 1 twin; 1 double with sep. bath/shower.
Meals	Dinner, with wine, £25-£35. Restaurant 10 miles.
Closed	Rarely.
Directions	A81 to Aberfoyle; at Bank of Scotland, onto B829 to Kinlochard; on for 4.5 miles, pass Macdonald Hotel; left at shop, road becomes unpaved, pass wooden house on right. On left, signed.

Bottle of wine with dinner on first night. Late checkout (12pm).

John & Bridget Lewis
Blairhullichan,
Kinlochard,
Aberfoyle FK8 3TN
Tel   +44 (0)1877 387341
Email   jablewis@aol.com
Web   www.blairhullichan.net

Entry 708   Map 15

Stirling

Cardross

Dodge the lazy sheep on the long drive to arrive (eventually!) at a sweep of gravel and lovely old Cardross, in a gorgeous setting with its 15th-century tower. Bang on the enormous old door and either Archie or Nicola (plus labradors and Jack Russells) will usher you in. And what a delight it is; light and space, long views, exquisite furniture, wooden shutters, towelling robes, fresh flowers, crisp linen, a cast-iron period bath – and that's just the bedrooms. It all feels warm, kind and generous, the drawing room is vast, the house is filled with character and the Orr Ewings can tell you all the history. *Young people over 14 welcome.*

Price	£100–£110. Singles £50–£55.
Rooms	2: 1 twin; 1 twin with separate bath.
Meals	Occasional dinner £28. Pubs/restaurants 2.5–6 miles.
Closed	Christmas & New Year.
Directions	A811 Stirling-Dumbarton to Arnprior; B8034 towards Port of Menteith; 2 miles, then cross Forth over humpback bridge. Drive with yellow lodge 150 yds from bridge on right. 1st exit on right from drive.

Archie & Lady Orr Ewing
Cardross,
Port of Menteith,
Kippen FK8 3JY

Tel	+44 (0)1877 385223
Email	cardrossestate@googlemail.com
Web	www.cardrossholidayhomes.com

Entry 709   Map 15

Western Isles

Kinloch

Meander across the flower-filled machair to the wide open spaces of South Uist – home to waders, hen harriers, corncrakes and talkative Wegg. The house, built 20 years ago, is comfy with books, photos, easy chairs, pictures and angling paraphernalia. Bedrooms – the upstairs double the best – have patchwork and pine and a general junk-shop chic; views across the loch are enormous, sunrises are spectacular. Wegg loves cooking, especially barbecued fish and game; his breakfasts and dinners are sociable occasions and you are surrounded by a clever acre of garden. Nature lovers will adore it. *Shoes off at the front door!*

Price	£76. Singles £38.
Rooms	3: 1 twin/double; 1 twin/double, 1 single both with separate bath.
Meals	Dinner £22. Packed lunch £8. Restaurant 5 miles.
Closed	Rarely.
Directions	30 mins from Benbecula airport; 30 mins from Lochboisdale ferry; 45 mins from Lochmaddy.

Wegg Kimbell
Kinloch,
Grogarry,
Isle of South Uist HS8 5RR

Tel	+44 (0)1870 620316
Email	wegg@kinlochuist.com
Web	www.kinlochuist.com

Entry 710   Map 20

Western Isles

Pairc an t-Srath

Richard and Lena's lovely home overlooks the beach at Borve, another absurdly beautiful Harris view. Inside, smart simplicity abounds: wooden floors, white walls, a peat fire, colourful art. Airy bedrooms fit the mood perfectly: trim carpets, chunky wood beds, Harris tweed throws, excellent shower rooms (there's a bathroom, too, if you want a soak). Richard crofts, Lena cooks, perhaps homemade soup, venison casserole, wet chocolate cake with raspberries. Views from the dining room tumble down hill, so expect to linger over breakfast. You'll spot otters in the loch, while the standing stones at Callanish are unmissable.

Price	£100. Singles from £50.
Rooms	4: 2 doubles, 1 twin, 1 single.
Meals	Dinner, 3 courses, £35. Restaurant 3 miles, pub 7 miles.
Closed	Rarely.
Directions	South from Tarbet ferry and first house on left in village; or north from Leverburgh ferry and last house on right.

Lena & Richard MacLennan
Pairc an t-Srath,
Borve,
Isle of Harris HS3 3HT
Tel   +44 (0)1859 550386
Email   info@paircant-srath.co.uk
Web   www.paircant-srath.co.uk

Entry 711   Map 20

Western Isles

Broad Bay House

In a wild landscape, 21st-century sophistication and style. Built in 2007, the house rises on graceful flights of decking above the beach. On an otherwise deserted shore, there is a villa right next door – but it disappears the moment you're inside. A stunning hall leads to a vaulted living room, whose windows face the waves on three sides... wow! More intimate boutique hotel than B&B – subtle lighting, oak doors, original art – Broad Bay House has been designed with sheer, unadulterated comfort in mind. Ian and Marion are considerate, generous, flexible hosts and the food, served at candlelit tables, is heavenly.

Price	£129–£170.
Rooms	4: 2 doubles, 2 twins/doubles.
Meals	Dinner, 3 courses, £35. Packed lunch £10. Pub/restaurant 7 miles.
Closed	Rarely.
Directions	A867 from Stornoway towards Barvas & Ness. On edge of Stornoway, right onto B895. After 6 miles, house on right, between Back & Gress.

Use your Sawday's Gift Card here.

Ian Fordham
Broad Bay House,
Back, Stornoway,
Isle of Lewis HS2 0LQ
Tel   +44 (0)1851 820990
Email   stay@broadbayhouse.co.uk
Web   www.broadbayhouse.co.uk

Entry 712   Map 20

Wales

Anglesey

North Stack

Perched on the extreme north-westerly tip of Wales, high on a cliff overlooking the Irish sea, this 200-year-old fog signal station in an RSPB Reserve is special indeed. You must leave your car in the warden's car park and be taken in a 4x4 across the mountain. Once there, do not expect shops and restaurants, just fabulous views from the dining room, great food, quiet cosy sitting areas, wonderful walks (perhaps to the lighthouse and its little café), seagulls flying at your level and you may spot a dolphin. Bedrooms are simple and attractive with pine furniture and views to the sea. *Application for brochure essential.*

Price	£75. Singles £40.
Rooms	2: 1 double with separate shower; 1 twin sharing bath. (Let to same party only.)
Meals	Dinner, 3 courses, £25. Wine available or BYO.
Closed	October–March.
Directions	On Holyhead seafront, take upper road on left. After 2 bridges, Warden's House at Breakwater Country Park on left. Phone to be collected. If coming by train or ferry, ring from station.

Philippa Jacobs
North Stack,
c/o 4 Lower Park Street,
Holyhead LL65 1DU

Tel	+44 (0)1407 761252
Mobile	+44 (0)7772 324461
Email	northstack@hotmail.com

Entry 713   Map 6

Anglesey

Cleifiog

Liz moved here for the view: you can see why. The creamy Georgian monks' hospice, later an 18th-century customs house, looks across to the whole Snowdon massif — spectacular with the Menai Strait between; the masts of Beaumaris Bay chink in the wind. As well as being a keen gardener, Liz paints and exhibits; her bold, striking pictures are dotted through the house. Big, bright, elegant rooms, are sprinkled with tapestries, antique samplers and fresh flowers. Be charmed by the welcome, the soft linens, the ample breakfasts and the wonderful soft sea air. *Children over three welcome. Minimum stay two nights at weekends.*

Price	£75–£95. Singles £45–£65.
Rooms	3: 2 twins/doubles, 1 suite.
Meals	Pub/restaurant 200 yards.
Closed	Christmas & New Year.
Directions	A55 over Britannia Bridge to Anglesey. A545 to Beaumaris. Past 2 left turns, house is 5th on left facing the sea. Bus stop outside.

 Bottle of wine in your room.

Liz Bradley
Cleifiog,
Townsend,
Beaumaris LL58 8BH

Tel	+44 (0)1248 811507
Email	liz@cleifiogbandb.co.uk
Web	www.cleifiogbandb.co.uk

Entry 714   Map 6

Carmarthenshire

The Drovers

The ice-cream pink Georgian townhouse looks good enough to eat – as do the leek and cheese cakes; Jill is a superb cook. A fabulous Welsh hospitality pervades this B&B, along with antiques, gas log fires and peaceful, cosy rooms. Downstairs areas are spacious, with a rambling hotel feel; sunny bedrooms are laced with books and Sanderson wallpapers; bathrooms come in contemporary white and cream, stocked with spoiling towels. Over breakfast (relaxed, delicious, locally sourced) you gaze through deep sash windows onto the town square; order a packed lunch and head for the hills. *Minimum stay two nights at weekends in high season.*

Price	£65-£80. Singles from £45.
Rooms	3: 2 doubles, 1 twin/double.
Meals	Dinner, 3 courses, £20.
	Packed lunch £5. Inns 50 yds.
Closed	Christmas & New Year.
Directions	In town centre, opposite the fountain.

10% off room rate Mon-Thurs.

	Jill Blud
	The Drovers,
	9 Market Square,
	Llandovery SA20 0AB
Tel	+44 (0)1550 721115
Email	jillblud@aol.com
Web	www.droversllandovery.co.uk

Carmarthenshire

Mandinam

On a heavenly bluff at the edge of the Beacons, beneath wheeling red kites and moody Welsh skies, lies Mandinam, the 'untouched holy place'. Delightful artistic Marcus and Daniella are its guardians, and they look after you as friends. Be charmed by bold rugs on wooden floors, weathered antiques, lofty ceilings, fires... and scrumptious meals in the red dining room. The serene four-poster room has a small gallery with a sofa; the large, rustic coach house room is plain with simple furnishings and shower, a wood-burner and a terrace. Watch the sun go down, revel in the peace and wonderful views.

Ethical Collection: Environment; Food; Community. See page 430.

Price	£70-£80. Singles by arrangement.
Rooms	2: 1 four-poster.
	Coach house: 1 twin/double.
	Self-catering in Shepherd's Hut.
Meals	Lunch or picnic from £7.50.
	Dinner, with wine, £25.
	Restaurants/pubs 2 miles.
Closed	Christmas.
Directions	Left at Llangadog shop; 50 yds, right for Myddfai. Past cemetery, 1st right for Llanddeusant; 1.5 miles, left thro' woods. Or, by train to Llangadog.

Bottle of wine with dinner. Free pick-up from local train station. Maps drawn for walkers.

	Daniella & Marcus Lampard
	Mandinam,
	Llangadog SA19 9LA
Tel	+44 (0)1550 777368
Email	iolo@onetel.com
Web	www.mandinam.com

Carmarthenshire

Plas Alltyferin

Wisteria-wrapped and, in parts, delightfully creaky, this Georgian family house sits in 270 beautiful acres. The breakfast room has the original panelling and the bedrooms have an old-fashioned charm. Not the place for you if you like spotlessness and state-of-the-art plumbing, but the views across the ha-ha to the Norman hill fort are timelessly lovely and the welcome is heartfelt. Gerard and Charlotte are the easiest, kindest and dog-friendliest of hosts. You're close to the gardens of Aberglasney and the National Botanical Gardens – and, most importantly, a lovely gastropub! *Children over ten welcome. Ballooning arranged.*

Price	£60–£70. Singles £35–£40.
Rooms	2: 1 twin; 1 twin with separate bath.
Meals	Pubs/restaurants within 2 miles.
Closed	September & occasionally.
Directions	From Carmarthen A40 east to Pont-ar-gothi. Left before bridge & follow narrow lane for approx. 2 miles keeping to right-hand hedge. House on right, signed. Call for precise details.

10% off stays of 3 or more nights. Late checkout (12pm).

Use your Sawday's Gift Card here.

Charlotte & Gerard Dent
Plas Alltyferin,
Pont-ar-gothi, Nantgaredig,
Carmarthen SA32 7PF
Tel   +44 (0)1267 290662
Email   dent@alltyferin.co.uk
Web   www.alltyferin.co.uk

Entry 717   Map 6

Carmarthenshire

Sarnau Mansion

Listed and Georgian, the house has its own water supply. Play tennis and revel in 16 acres of beautiful grounds complete with pond, walled garden and woodland with nesting red kites. Bedrooms are simply furnished in heritage colours; bathrooms are big. The oak-floored sitting room with chesterfields has French windows onto the garden, the dining room is simpler with separate tables and there's good, fresh home cooking from Cynthia. One mile from the A40, you can hear a slight hum of traffic if the wind is from that direction. You are 15 minutes from the National Botanic Garden of Wales. *Children over five welcome.*

Price	£70–£80. Singles £50.
Rooms	3: 2 doubles, 1 twin.
Meals	Dinner, 3 courses, around £20. BYO. Pub 1 mile.
Closed	Rarely.
Directions	From Carmarthen A40 west for 4 miles. Right for Bancyfelin. After 0.5 miles, right into drive on brow of hill.

10% off stays of 4 or more nights.

Cynthia & David Fernihough
Sarnau Mansion,
Llysonnen Road, Bancyfelin,
Carmarthen SA33 5DZ
Tel   +44 (0)1267 211404
Email   fernihough@so1405.force9.co.uk
Web   www.sarnaumansion.co.uk

Entry 718   Map 6

Carmarthenshire

Treetops B&B

Would you like to fly in my beautiful balloon? More B in B – Bed in Basket – than B&B. Don't arrive early morning or evening as chances are the place may have disappeared. Your smiling, nonagenarian host is sprightly with a twinkle in her eye and while her feet are firmly on the ground, she has high ideals. This is for lovers of the outdoors who don't mind heights, draughts, sleeping standing up, sharing with strangers, the odd bit of noise as things heat up, waking up snagged in a tree – so make sure you book as it's obviously going to be a popular choice. Great views and sure to be a soaraway success – it could really take off.

Ceredigion

Broniwan

Carole and Allen keep cattle and chickens on their organic farm and their perfect kitchen garden is prolific. With huge warmth and a tray of cakes they invite you into their cosy, ivy-clad house. Downstairs find natural colours and the odd vibrant flourish of local art, a wood-burner and lots of books – a literary weekend can be arranged; upstairs bedrooms and bathrooms are simple and old-fashioned. The wonderful garden with views to the Preseli hills has a water lily pond and is full of birds. Food is delicious and home-grown, coastal paths are close, the National Botanic Garden of Wales and Aberglasney are a 45-minute drive.

Price	Sky high.
Rooms	Just the one.
Meals	Pie in the sky, basket meals.
Closed	No, open.
Directions	Anywhere the wind blows.

Price	£66-£70. Singles £35.
Rooms	2: 1 double; 1 double with separate bath.
Meals	Dinner £25-£30. BYO. Restaurant 7-8 miles.
Closed	Rarely.
Directions	From Aberaeron, A487 for 6 miles for Brynhoffnant. Left at B4334 to Rhydlewis; left at Post Office & shop, 1st lane on right, then 1st track on right.

	Eileen Dover
	Treetops B&B,
	No fixed address,
Tel	No
Email	At my age? No thank you!
Web	Ditto

	Carole & Allen Jacobs
	Broniwan,
	Rhydlewis,
	Llandysul SA44 5PF
Tel	+44 (0)1239 851261
Email	broniwan@btinternet.com
Web	www.broniwan.com

Ceredigion

Ffynnon Fendigaid

Arrive through rolling countryside – birdsong and breeze the only sound; within moments you will be sprawled on a leather sofa admiring modern art and wondering how a little bit of Milan arrived here along with Huw and homemade cake. A place to come and pootle, with no rush; you can stay all day to stroll the fern fringed paths through the acres of wild garden to a lake and a grand bench, or opt for hearty walking. Your bed is big, the colours are soft, the bathrooms are spotless and the food is local – try all the Welsh cheeses. Wide beaches are minutes away, red kites and buzzards soar above you. Pulchritudinous.

Price	From £70. Singles from £40.
Rooms	2 doubles.
Meals	Dinner, 2–3 courses, £15–£18. Packed lunch £6. Pub 1 mile.
Closed	Rarely.
Directions	From A487 Cardigan & Aberystwth coast road, take B4334 at Brynhoffnant towards Rhydlewis. 1 mile to junc. where road joins from right & lane to house on left.

Bottle of wine on first night (either at dinner or in your room).

Huw Davies
Ffynnon Fendigaid,
Rhydlewis,
Llandysul SA44 5SR
Tel +44 (0)1239 851361
Email ffynnonf@btinternet.com
Web www.ffynnonf.co.uk

Entry 721   Map 6

Conwy

Pengwern Country House

The steeply wooded Conwy valley snakes down to this stone and slate gabled property set back from the road in Snowdonia National Park. Inside has an upbeat traditional feel: a large sitting room with floor-to-ceiling bay windows and pictures by the Betws-y-Coed artists who once lived here. Settle with a book by the wood-burner; Gwawr and Ian know just when to chat and when not. Bedrooms have rough plastered walls, colourful fabrics and super bathrooms, one with a double-ended roll top and views of Lledr Valley. Breakfast on fruits, yogurts, herb rösti, soda bread – gorgeous. *Minimum stay two nights.*

Price	£72–£84. Singles from £62.
Rooms	3: 1 double, 1 four-poster, 1 twin/double.
Meals	Pubs/restaurants within 1.5 miles. Packed lunch £5.50.
Closed	Christmas & New Year.
Directions	From Betws-y-Coed, A5 towards Llangollen for 1 mile. Driveway on left, opposite small stone building.

Gwawr & Ian Mowatt
Pengwern Country House,
Allt Dinas,
Betws-y-Coed LL24 0HF
Tel +44 (0)1690 710480
Email gwawr.pengwern@btopenworld.com
Web www.snowdoniaaccommodation.co.uk

Entry 722   Map 7

Conwy

Lympley Lodge

The solid Victorian exterior belies a surprising interior. Welcoming Patricia, a former restorer, has brought together a gorgeous collection of furniture, while her meticulous paintwork adds light and life to her seaside home. Above is the Little Orme; below, across the main coast road, the sweep of Llandudno Bay. Bedrooms strike the perfect balance between the practical and the exotic; all have crisp linen, rich fabrics, fresh flowers, lovely views. There's an elegant sitting room for guests, a stunning dining room with a Renaissance feel and breakfasts full of local and homemade produce. Wonderful.

Denbighshire

Plas Efenechtyd Cottage

Efenechtyd means 'place of the monks' but there's nothing spartan about Dave and Marilyn's handsome brick farmhouse: breakfasts of local sausages, eggs from their hens, salmon fish cakes with mushrooms and homemade bread, are served at a polished table in the dining room with exotic wall hangings from Vietnam and Laos. Light bedrooms have a clear, uncluttered feel, excellent mattresses and good linen; bathrooms are surprisingly bling and warm as toast with plump towels. Motor or walk to Ruthin with its windy streets and interesting shops, or strike out for Offa's Dyke with a packed lunch; this is stunning countryside.

Price	£80. Singles £50-£55.
Rooms	3: 2 doubles, 1 twin.
Meals	Restaurants/pubs 5-minute drive.
Closed	Mid-December to end of January.
Directions	From Llandudno Promenade, turn right and follow B5115 (Colwyn Bay) up the hill. Pass right turn for Bryn Y Bia. House entrance (board on side of building) on right.

Price	From £65. Singles £45.
Rooms	3: 2 doubles, 1 twin.
Meals	Packed lunch £6. Pub 1.6 miles.
Closed	Rarely.
Directions	From Ruthin follow signs for Bala. Straight over mini r'bout onto B5105. 1st left after 1 mile. Right at T-junc.; house 50 yds on right.

 Welsh cakes and a jar of our jam or marmalade to take home.

Patricia Richards
Lympley Lodge,
Colwyn Road, Craigside,
Llandudno LL30 3AL
Tel   +44 (0)1492 549304
Email patricia@lympleylodge.co.uk
Web   www.lympleylodge.co.uk

Dave Jones & Marilyn Jeffery
Plas Efenechtyd Cottage,
Efenechtyd,
Ruthin LL15 2LP
Tel   +44 (0)7540 501009
Email info@plas-efenechtyd-cottage.co.uk
Web   www.plas-efenechtyd-cottage.co.uk

Entry 723   Map 7

Entry 724   Map 7

Denbighshire

Castle House

Charlie and Angie's happy home stands high on the hill with huge views floating off across the valley. It's knee deep in Denbigh history: lawns run down to medieval town walls, a castle built by Edward I stands beyond the woods and Robert Dudley's ruined cathedral (he the lover of Elizabeth I) occupies the back garden. As for the house, it's grand and fit for a king yet warm and homely; find parquet floors, rococo ceilings, roaring fires, the odd grand piano. Bedrooms are vast, bathrooms divine, as is Angie's cooking (delicious breakfasts and dinners, sinful cream teas). A great base for walkers and culture vultures.

Price	£135-£150. Singles from £85.
Rooms	3: 1 four-poster, 1 double, 1 twin.
Meals	Dinner: 3 courses, £25; 5 courses, £32.50.
Closed	Christmas
Directions	A525 for Denbigh town centre. Left at r'about; left again at T-junct.; then right at next T-junc. and immediately left. Follow track left (not straight on) up to house.

10% off stays Mon-Thurs (excl. Jun, Jul, Aug). Free pick-up from local bus/train station.

Charlie & Angie Hobson
Castle House,
Plas Castell, Bull Lane,
Denbigh LL16 3SN
Tel   +44 (0)1745 816860
Email stay@castlehousebandb.co.uk
Web   www.castlehousebandb.co.uk

Entry 725   Map 7

Flintshire

Golden Grove

Huge, Elizabethan and intriguing – Golden Grove was built by Sir Edward Morgan in 1580. The Queen Anne staircase, oak panelling, faded fabrics and fine family pieces are enhanced by jewel-like colour schemes: rose-pink, indigo, aqua. In summer the magnificent dining room is in use; in the winter the sitting room fire counters the draughts. The two Anns are charming and amusing, dinners are delicious and the family foursome tend the garden – beautiful, productive and well-kept. They also find time for a nuttery and a sheep farm as well as their relaxed B&B. Many return to this exceptional place.

Price	£100. Singles £60.
Rooms	3: 1 double; 1 double, 1 twin, each with separate bath.
Meals	Dinner £30. Pubs within 2 miles.
Closed	November-February.
Directions	Turn off A55 onto A5151 for Prestatyn. At Texaco before Trelawnyd, right. Branch left immed. over 1st x-roads; right at T-junc. Gates 170 yds on left.

Ann & Mervyn and Ann & Nigel
Steele-Mortimer
Golden Grove,
Llanasa, Holywell CH8 9NA
Tel   +44 (0)1745 854452
Email golden.grove@lineone.net
Web   www.golden-grove-estate.co.uk

Entry 726   Map 7

Flintshire

Plas Penucha

Swing back in time with polished parquet, tidy beams, a huge Elizabethan panelled lounge with books, leather sofas and open fire – a cosy spot for tea in winter. Plas Penucha – 'the big house on the highest point in the parish' – has been in the family for 500 years. Airy, old-fashioned bedrooms have long views across the garden to Offa's Dyke and one has a shower in the corner. The L-shaped dining room has a genuine Arts & Crafts interior; outside, rhododendrons and a rock garden flourish. Beyond is open countryside and St Asaph, with the smallest medieval cathedral in the country.

Price	From £68. Singles from £35.
Rooms	2: 1 double, 1 twin.
Meals	Dinner £18.50. Packed lunch £4.50. Pub 2 miles.
Closed	Rarely.
Directions	From Chester, A55, B5122 left for Caerwys. 1st right into High St. Right at end. 0.75 miles to x-roads & left, then straight for 1 mile. House on left, signed.

10% off stays of 2 or more nights. Late checkout (12pm).

Nest Price
Plas Penucha,
Peny Cefn Road,
Caerwys, Mold CH7 5BH
Tel   +44 (0)1352 720210
Email info@plaspenucha.co.uk
Web   www.plaspenucha.co.uk

Entry 727   Map 7

Gwynedd

Abercelyn Country House

The 1729 rectory comes with rhododendron-rich grounds, an immaculate kitchen garden and a mountain stream. In spite of the rugged setting Abercelyn is a genteel retreat. Shutters gleam, logs glow and bedrooms are spacious and light with smart bathrooms and luscious views. You are well looked after: the drawing room overflows with outdoor guides, Ray orchestrates adventure trips to Snowdonia National Park and Lindsay cooks a great breakfast with eggs from their own hens. Bala Lake is a ten-minute stroll – or you can strike off round it for the whole 14 miles – bracing indeed! *Guided walks & canoeing.*

Ethical Collection: Environment; Food; Community. See page 430.

Price	£76-£90. Singles £55-£60.
Rooms	3: 2 doubles, 1 twin/double.
Meals	Pub 10-minute drive. Restaurant 15-minute walk; free return taxi service.
Closed	Rarely.
Directions	On A494 Bala-Dolgellau road, 1 mile from centre of Bala, opp. Llanycil Church. Bus service: Wrexham - Bala - Llanycil - Dolgellau - Bamouth.

Stay 4 or more nights for a guided walk (half day) with a mountain guide.

Ray & Lindsay Hind
Abercelyn Country House,
Llanycil, Bala LL23 7YF
Tel   +44 (0)1678 521109
Email info@abercelyn.co.uk
Web   www.abercelyn.co.uk

Entry 728   Map 7

Gwynedd

Dolgadfa

Gasp at the beauty of the road to Dolgadfa, every bend revealing yet another perfect frame of southern Snowdonia – the gentle prelude to the ragged peaks. The youthful Robertsons' slice of this bliss is unexpectedly luxurious. The deep limpid river winds past the listed guest barn where bedrooms – one with stone steps straight onto the riverside garden – are fresh and country-cosy, with gingham curtains and all the trimmings. A bright living room with roaring fire, sofas and Welsh oak floor is yours, and Louise does a fine breakfast. For a couple or a party, a superb place. *Fishing & shooting available.*

Price	£80.
Rooms	3: 1 double, 1 twin; 1 double with separate bath.
Meals	Pub/restaurant in village, 1 mile.
Closed	Christmas.
Directions	B4401; after Llandrillo, 2nd right. Single track road; over bridge; at T-junc. left, on for 1.5 miles; 2nd farmhouse on left. White gate.

Fishing & packed lunch for stays of 2 or more nights.

Louise Robertson
Dolgadfa,
Llandderfel, Bala LL23 7RE

Tel	+44 (0)1678 530469
Email	dolgadfa@btinternet.com
Web	www.dolgadfa.co.uk

Entry 729   Map 7

Gwynedd

Bryniau Golau

Under clear skies, there are few more soul-lifting views: the long lake and miles of Snowdonia National Park. Each generous room is beautifully furnished – traditional with a contemporary twist, and more glorious views to the garden and lake. Katrina, friendly and adaptable, spoils you with open fires in the sitting room, goose down duvets on the beds, spa baths, underfloor heating and scrumptious breakfasts that set you up for the day. Linger on the lawn, perhaps with a drink as the sun sets, and try your hand at fly fishing or white water rafting. A wonderful place for a house party – and the walking is superb.

Price	£80-£90. Singles £55-£65.
Rooms	3: 2 four-posters, 1 twin/double.
Meals	Supper available. Pubs/restaurants within 2 miles.
Closed	Rarely.
Directions	From Bala B4391; 1 mile, B4403 Llangower. Pass Bala Lake Hotel; look for sign showing left turn; 20 yds after tree, sign on right; left up hill, over cattle grid; 1st on right.

10% off room rate Mon-Thurs. Bottle of wine in your room.

Katrina le Saux
Bryniau Golau,
Llangower, Bala LL23 7BT

Tel	+44 (0)1678 521782
Email	katrinalesaux@hotmail.co.uk
Web	www.bryniau-golau.co.uk

Entry 730   Map 7

Gwynedd

The Old Rectory on the lake

The drive to get here is fantastic and the approach truly beautiful – The Old Rectory waits for you on the other side of the lake. The owners are full of enthusiasm for their fabulous B&B and spoil guests rotten – comfy beds with smooth Egyptian cotton sheets, binoculars for bird spotting and luxurious baths. There are views from every window to the luminous lake, and you can climb Cadair Idris from the front door. Return, weak-limbed, to a delicious, home-cooked meal taken in the airy Orangery and… maybe a wallow in the hot tub under the stars sipping a glass of champagne. *Min. two nights at weekends; three on bank holidays.*

Price	£100. Singles £70.
Rooms	3 doubles.
Meals	Dinner £27.50. Pub 4 miles.
Closed	Rarely.
Directions	A470 from Dolgellau. A487 from Cross Foxes Inn, then B4405 (signposted Tywyn). Follow along lakeside; turn right at head of lake and cont. 0.25 miles. House illuminated by blue lights at night.

Use your Sawday's Gift Card here.

Ricky Francis
The Old Rectory on the lake,
Talyllyn LL36 9AJ
Tel   +44 (0)1654 782225
Email   enquiries@rectoryonthelake.co.uk
Web   www.rectoryonthelake.co.uk

Entry 731   Map 7

Gwynedd

Y Goeden Eirin

A little gem tucked between the sea and the mountains, an education in Welsh culture, and a great place to explore wild Snowdonia, the Llyn pensinsula and the dramatic Eifl mountains. Inside presents a cosy picture: Welsh-language and English books share the shelves, paintings by contemporary Welsh artists enliven the walls, an arty 70s décor mingles with sturdy Welsh oak in the bedrooms – the one in the house the best – and all bathrooms are super. Wonderful food is served alongside the Bechstein in the beamed dining room – the welcoming, thoughtful Eluned and John have created an unusually delightful space.

Ethical Collection: Environment; Food.
See page 430.

Price	£80–£100. Singles from £60.
Rooms	3: 2 doubles, 1 twin.
Meals	Dinner, 4 courses, £28. Wine from £14. Packed lunch £12. Pub/restaurant 0.75 miles.
Closed	Christmas, New Year & occasionally.
Directions	From Caernarfon onto Porthmadog & Pwllheli road. A487 thro' Bontnewydd, left at r'bout, signed Dolydd. House 0.5 miles on right, last entrance before garage on left.
	Bottle of wine with dinner on first night.

Use your Sawday's Gift Card here.

John & Mrs Eluned Rowlands
Y Goeden Eirin,
Dolydd, Caernarfon LL54 7EF
Tel   +44 (0)1286 830942
Email   john_rowlands@tiscali.co.uk
Web   www.ygoedeneirin.co.uk

Entry 732   Map 6

Monmouthshire

Allt-y-bela

It's a rare treat to come here. This beautiful, late medieval farmhouse sits in its own secret valley and is reached down a narrow lane. Built between 1420 and 1599, Allt-y-bela is now perfectly presented for the 21st century; find conviviality and warmth among soaring beams and period furniture. The dining room has an enormous log fire for delicious and social eating; and there's a super farmhouse kitchen if you want to be more involved. Bedrooms soothe with limewashed walls, fabulous beds, no TV and stunning art. Peace, privacy and an amazing garden in deep yet accessible countryside. Exceptional. *Minimum two nights.*

Price	£125.
Rooms	2 doubles.
Meals	Farmhouse supper £30. Other meals by arrangement. Pubs/restaurants 3 miles.
Closed	Rarely.
Directions	A449 towards Usk, then B4235 to Chepstow. After 200 yds, unsigned right turn. Follow for 0.5 miles; left into 'No Through Road', follow for 0.5 miles.

	William Collinson & Arne Maynard Allt-y-bela, Llangwm Ucha, Usk NP15 1EZ
Mobile	+44 (0)7892 403103 (unreliable)
Email	bb@alltybela.co.uk
Web	www.alltybela.co.uk

Entry 733   Map 7

Monmouthshire

Upper Red House

Head down the lane and land in deepest Monmouthshire surrounded by orchard, paddocks and woodland. Teona cares deeply about wildlife and countryside and her 17th-century organic farm has ponies, sheep, peafowl and honey bees; six ponds attract birds and insects and you can book a tour of the farm. Up steep wooden stairs are limewashed rustic bedrooms with beams, lots of books, no TV, beautiful views; the attic rooms are up more little stairs. Bathrooms are simple, one with an old roll top tub. After a good vegetarian breakfast at the long kitchen table stride off to Offa's Dyke and revel in the silence.

Ethical Collection: Environment; Food; Community. See page 430.

Price	£75-£85. Singles £35-£45.
Rooms	4: 1 double en suite; 1 double, 2 singles sharing bath (let to same party only).
Meals	Vegetarian packed lunch £6. Pubs/restaurants 3.5 miles.
Closed	Rarely.
Directions	From Monmouth B4233 through Rockfield to Hendre. Left after Rolls Golf Course entrance; after 1.5 miles 1st right; after 0.75 miles 1st left; old house on right.
	Free farm & wildlife tour. Local food/produce in your room. Late checkout (12pm).

	Teona Dorrien-Smith Upper Red House, Llanfihangel-Ystern-Llewern, Monmouth NP25 5HL
Tel	+44 (0)1600 780501
Email	upperredhouse@mac.com
Web	www.upperredhouse.co.uk

Entry 734   Map 7

Monmouthshire

Penpergwm Lodge

On the edge of the Brecon Beacons, a large and lovely Edwardian house. Breakfast round the mahogany table, relax by the fire in the sitting room with books to read and piano to play. The Boyles have been here for years and pour much of their energy into three beautiful acres of parterre and potager, orchard and flowers. Bedrooms are gloriously traditional – ancestral portraits, embroidered bed covers, big windows, good chintz – with garden views; bathrooms are a skip across the landing. A pool and tennis for the sporty, two summer houses for the dreamy, a good pub you can walk to. Splendid, old-fashioned B&B.

Price	£70-£75. Singles £40.
Rooms	2 twins, each with separate bath.
Meals	Pub within walking distance.
Closed	Rarely.
Directions	A40 to Abergavenny; at big r'bout on SE edge of town, B4598 to Usk for 2.5 miles. Left at King of Prussia pub, up small lane; house 200 yds on left.

Use your Sawday's Gift Card here.

Catriona Boyle
Penpergwm Lodge,
Abergavenny NP7 9AS
Tel   +44 (0)1873 840208
Email   boyle@penpergwm.co.uk
Web   www.penplants.com

Entry 735   Map 7

Pembrokeshire

Hayston

Calm, friendly dogs greet you in the courtyard of this attractive Pembrokeshire farmhouse surrounded by pretty bantams and barns. Nicky and Johnny's home is a relaxed place; rooms have a comfortable, faded grandeur and the garden has lovely spots to sit. Eat in the deep-red beamed dining room with books, flowers and a big log fire; supper is often local lamb or fish direct from the fisherman. Sleep in cottagey bedrooms in the house, one with a garden view, or up stone steps in your own sunny coach house. Castles, surfing championships, stunning beaches and brilliant coastal walks will bring you back.

Price	£70. Singles £35.
Rooms	3: 1 twin with separate bath; 1 single with shared bath (let to same party only). Coach house: 1 double.
Meals	Occasional dinner from £12. Pubs/restaurants 3 miles.
Closed	Christmas.
Directions	B4319 from Pembroke thro' St Petrox. After right turn to St Twynnells, 2nd left (no through road). Hayston 1st farm on right.

 10% off stays of 2 or more nights.

Nicola Rogers
Hayston,
Merrion,
Pembroke SA71 5EA
Tel   +44 (0)1646 661462
Email   haystonhouse@btinternet.com
Web   haystonfarmhouse.co.uk

Entry 736   Map 6

Pembrokeshire

Penfro

This is fun — idiosyncratic and a tad theatrical, rather than conventional and uniformly stylish. The Lappins' home is a tall, impressive Grade II*-listed Georgian affair, formerly a ballet school. Judith's taste — she's also a WW1 expert — is eclectic verging on the wacky and she minds that guests are comfortable and well-fed. You eat communally, and very well, at the big scrubbed table in the flagged, Aga-fired kitchen at garden level... the garden's big and beautiful so enjoy its conversational terrace and hammocks. And discuss which of the three very characterful bedrooms will suit you best, plumbing and all!

Ethical Collection: Food. See page 430.

Price	£65-£90. Singles from £45.
Rooms	3: 1 double; 1 double, 1 twin each with separate bath.
Meals	Packed lunch from £8. Pub 250 yds.
Closed	Rarely.
Directions	A4075 Pembroke; 2 miles to mini r'bout. Straight ahead, down hill, bear right. Right lane past castle; T-junc. bear right. Road widens by Chapel Pembroke Antique Centre. House on right.

Penfro jam or similar. Subsequent visits of 2 or more nights £5 per night discount.

Judith Lappin
Penfro,
111 Main Street, Pembroke SA71 4DB
Tel +44 (0)1646 682753
Email info@penfro.co.uk
Web www.penfro.co.uk

Entry 737   Map 6

Pembrokeshire

Furzehill Farm

In 140 acres of conservation-run land stands Val and Paul's recently built farmhouse — a hospitable and characterful place for families and walkers to stay. The Aga-driven kitchen is the hub and Paul does you a grand breakfast — and something tasty and local for supper too. Find hunting prints, a modern leather sofa and a brick-surround open fire in the sitting room, and cosy carpeted bedrooms upstairs, one with a shower, two sharing a jazzy jacuzzi. Ask about riding weekends — this is a horsey household — and don't miss the Cresselly Arms down the road, on the bird-rich Cleddau Estuary. Heavenly beaches, too.

Ethical Collection: Environment; Food. See page 430.

Price	£60-£90. Singles from £30.
Rooms	3: 1 family for 4/5; 1 double, 1 room with bunk beds, sharing separate bath.
Meals	Dinner, 3 courses, £18. Supper from £12. Packed lunch £5. Pub/restaurant 3 miles.
Closed	Christmas.
Directions	A40 to Canaston Bridge; A4075 for Pembroke. Rt at Crosshands; after sharp bend, left for Cresswell Q.; left at T-junc. for C. Quay; 2nd entrance on left.

10% off stays of 2 or more nights.

E V Rees
Furzehill Farm,
Martletwy, Narberth SA67 8AN
Tel +44 (0)1834 891480
Email val@furzehillfarm.com
Web www.furzehillfarm.com

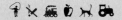

Entry 738   Map 6

Pembrokeshire

Knowles Farm

The Cleddau estuary winds its way around this 1,000-acre organic farm – its lush grasses feed the cows that produce milk for the renowned Rachel's yoghurt. Your hosts love the area, are passionate about its conservation and let you come and go as you please; picnic in the garden, wander through bluebell woods, discover a pond – dogs love it too! Gini rustles up scrumptious, candlelit dinners; food is fully organic or very local (five miles!). You have your own entrance to bedrooms which are old-fashioned but well-maintained, with comfy beds, fresh flowers and glorious views. Traditional, real-farmhouse B&B.

Price	From £70.
Rooms	3: 2 doubles; 1 twin with separate bath.
Meals	Supper from £12. Dinner, 4 courses, £22. Packed lunch £6. Pub 1.5 miles, restaurant 3 miles.
Closed	Rarely.
Directions	A4075 to Cressely; turn right. Follow signs for Lawrenny to first x-roads; straight over; next x-roads right; 100 yds on left.

Glass of wine with dinner, or evening of first night if dining out.

Virginia Lort Phillips
Knowles Farm,
Lawrenny SA68 0PX
Tel   +44 (0)1834 891221
Email   ginilp@lawrenny.org.uk
Web   www.lawrenny.org.uk

Pembrokeshire

Boulston Manor

A lush descent through ancient woodland, with tantalising glimpses of open water, takes you to the ivy-clad 1790s house and a great place to stay. A country-house drawing room with veranda and Cleddau views is yours to use; soft sofas, horsey pictures, fresh flowers and a grand piano set the tone. Perfectly refurbished bedrooms and bathrooms are roomy and glamorous: yards of thick fabrics, dazzling white linen, stone fireplaces, marble tiling, and, in one, a jucuzzi with the grandest parkland views. Generous Jules and Rod are lively and fun, you will eat good, local food and there's miles of walking in the National Park.

Price	£60–£100.
Rooms	3 doubles.
Meals	Supper £15. Dinner from £25.
Closed	Never.
Directions	From Salutation Square (County Hotel) Haverfordwest, take Uzmaston Road past Popes Garage. Through Uzmaston, past Goodwood (signed Boulston). Continue for 1.5 miles and follow Boulston signs.

Roderick Thomas
Boulston Manor,
Haverfordwest SA62 4AQ
Tel   +44 (0)1437 764600
Email   info@boulstonmanor.co.uk
Web   www.boulstonmanor.co.uk

Pembrokeshire

Pentower

Curl up with a cat and watch the ferries – or sometimes a porpoise – coasting to Ireland; French windows open onto the terrace and a glorious vista. Mary and Tony are welcoming; they've done an excellent restoration on the turreted 1898 house, keeping its quarry tiled floors, decorative fireplaces and impressive staircase. Spotless bedrooms are light and airy, with large showers; the Tower Room has the views. There's a tiled dining/sitting room for full English (or Welsh) breakfasts – also with views, a 'temple' in the garden for summer, Fishguard is a short stroll, and the stunning coastal path nearby.

Price	£75–£80. Singles £45.
Rooms	3: 2 doubles, 1 twin.
Meals	Packed lunch £5. Pubs/restaurants 500 yds.
Closed	Occasionally.
Directions	A40 to Fishguard town; at r'bout, 2nd exit onto Main Street. Before sharp left bend, right fork onto Tower Hill; 200 yds on, through house gates.

Homemade Welsh recipe cakes. Bottle of wine for stays of 2 or more nights.

Tony Jacobs & Mary Geraldine Casey
Pentower,
Tower Hill, Fishguard SA65 9LA
Tel   +44 (0)1348 874462
Email   sales@pentower.co.uk
Web   www.pentower.co.uk

Entry 741   Map 6

Pembrokeshire

Merton Hall

In front of this intriguing triple-peaked Victorian house lies manicured parkland; behind, a wild, wonderful hill offering stunning sea views. Nigel and Rowena are busy refurbishing Dinas's 'Ty Hen' (Old House), which was pieced together over centuries. Family heirlooms (with matching anecdotes) and naval prints and paintings give the sitting room a certain charm; the dining area's bay windows overlook distant gorse-covered hills. On sunny mornings, join the birds for breakfast in a pretty wisteria-strewn courtyard. You can walk to Aberbach cove, explore Preseli hills, return to comfortable beds and capable, caring hosts.

Price	£75–£90. Singles £45–£55.
Rooms	2: 1 double, 1 twin/double.
Meals	Pub 0.75 miles; restaurants 3.5 miles.
Closed	Christmas, New Year & occasionally.
Directions	From Fishguard, A487 towards Cardigan. After 3 miles enter Dinas Cross. Left down track just after 30 limit sign. House is on left after 50 yds.

Bottle of wine for stays of 2 or more nights.

Rowena Corlett
Merton Hall,
Dinas Cross, Newport SA42 0XN
Tel   +44 (0)1348 811223
Email   info@mertonhall.co.uk
Web   www.mertonhall.co.uk

Entry 742   Map 6

Powys

Llangattock Court

Built in 1690 and mentioned in Pevsner as an 'outstanding example of a country house in this style', this is indeed grand and sits in the middle of the sleepy village, surrounded by a large garden. Both bedrooms are a good size (one has a big French bed and a small shower room) with lovely antiques and a fresh feel; views from one soar across to the Black Mountains. Breakfast in style in the enormous dining room overlooked by framed relatives, stroll through the rose garden, visit a castle or historic house, walk to the local pub for dinner. Morgan is a painter; some of his paintings are on display.

Powys

Ty'r Chanter

Warmth, colour, children and activity: this house is fun. Tiggy welcomes you like family; help collect eggs, feed the lambs or the pony, drop your shoes by the fire. The farmhouse and barn are stylishly relaxed; deep sofas, tartan throws, heaps of books, views to the Brecon Beacons and Black Mountains. Bedrooms are soft, simple sanctuaries with Jo Malone bathroom treats. Children's rooms zing with murals; toys, kids' sitting room, sandpit – child heaven. Walk, fish, canoe, book-browse in Hay or stroll the estate. Homemade cakes, whisky to help yourself to: fine hospitality.

Price	£50-£80. Singles £45.
Rooms	2: 1 double, 1 suite with four-poster & twin.
Meals	Restaurants/pubs within 1 mile.
Closed	Christmas & New Year; 1-2 weeks October.
Directions	From A465 B4777 into Gilwern, follow signs to Crickhowell. In Legar, left at Vine Tree Inn. Pass Horse Shoe Inn on right; after 60 yds right, then right again 50 yds beyond church signed to Dardy. 1st on left.
	10% off room rate Mon-Thurs. Free pick-up from local bus/train station.

Price	£90. Singles £55.
Rooms	4: 1 double; 1 double with separate bath/shower; 2 children's rooms.
Meals	Packed lunch £8. Pub 1 mile.
Closed	Christmas.
Directions	From Crickhowell, A40 towards Brecon. 2 miles left at Gliffaes Hotel sign. 2 miles, past hotel, house is 600 yds on right.

	Polly Llewellyn Llangattock Court, Llangattock, Crickhowell NP8 1PH
Tel	+44 (0)1873 810116
Email	morganllewellyn@btinternet.com
Web	www.llangattockcourt.co.uk

	Tiggy Pettifer Ty'r Chanter, Gliffaes, Crickhowell NP8 1RL
Tel	+44 (0)1874 731144
Email	tiggy@tyrchanter.com
Web	www.tyrchanter.com

Entry 743   Map 7

Entry 744   Map 7

Powys

The Old Store House

Unbend here with agreeable books, chattering birds, and twinkling Peter, who asks only that you feel at home. Downstairs are a range-warmed kitchen, a sunny conservatory overlooking garden, ducks and canal, and a charmingly ramshackle sitting room with a wood-burner, sofas and a piano — no babbling TV. Bedrooms are large, light and spotless, with more books, soft goose down, armchairs and bathrooms with views. Breakfast, without haste, on toothsome scrambled eggs, local bacon and sausages, blistering coffee. Bliss — but not for those who prefer the comfort of rules. Walk into the hills from the back door. *Self-catering available.*

Powys

Hafod Y Garreg

A unique opportunity to stay in the oldest house in Wales — a fascinating, 1402 cruck-framed hall house, built for Henry IV as a hunting lodge. Informal Annie and John have filled it with a charming mix of Venetian mirrors, Indian rugs, pewter plates, gorgeous fabrics and oak furniture. Dine by candlelight in the fabulous dining room — maybe pheasant pie with chilli jam and hazelnut mash: delicious. Bedrooms are luxurious and comfortable with Egyptian cotton bed linen. Reach the Grade II*-listed house by a bumpy track across gated fields crowded with chickens, cats, goats… a special, secluded and relaxed place.

Price	£75. Singles £37.50.
Rooms	4: 3 doubles, 1 twin.
Meals	Packed lunch £4. Pub/restaurant 0.75 miles.
Closed	Rarely.
Directions	From Brecon, Abergavenny A40. After 1 mile, left for Llanfrynach B4558. Cross narrow stone bridge. House is 1.3 miles on right.

Pick-up from local bus/train station.

Price	£78. Singles from £70.
Rooms	2 doubles.
Meals	Dinner, 3 courses, £23. BYO. Pubs/restaurants 2.5 miles.
Closed	Christmas.
Directions	From Hay-on-Wye, A479 then A470 to B. Wells. Through Llyswen, past forest on left, down hill. Next left for Trericket Mill, then immed. right & up hill. Straight through gate across track to house.

	Peter Evans
	The Old Store House,
	Llanfrynach LD3 7LJ
Tel	+44 (0)1874 665499
Email	oldstorehouse@btconnect.com
Web	www.theoldstorehouse.co.uk

	Annie & John McKay
	Hafod Y Garreg,
	Erwood, Builth Wells LD2 3TQ
Tel	+44 (0)1982 560400
Email	john-annie@hafod-y.wanadoo.co.uk
Web	www.hafodygarreg.co.uk

Entry 745 Map 7

Entry 746 Map 7

Powys

Trericket Mill Vegetarian Guesthouse

Part guest house, part bunk house, all very informal – all Grade II*-listed. The dining room has been created amid a jumble of corn-milling machinery: B&B guests, campers and bunkers pile in together to fill hungry bellies with Nicky and Alistair's delicious and plentiful veggie food from a chalkboard menu. Stoves throw out the heat in the flagstoned living rooms with their comfy chairs; the bedrooms are simple pine affairs. Set out to explore from here on foot, horseback, bicycle or canoe; lovers of the outdoors looking for good value and a planet-friendly bias will be in heaven.

Ethical Collection: Environment; Food. See page 430.

Price	£64–£75. Singles £42–£55.
Rooms	3: 2 doubles, 1 twin.
Meals	Dinner, 3 courses, £18.75. BYO. Simple supper £8.50. Pub/restaurant 2 miles.
Closed	Christmas & occasionally in winter.
Directions	12 miles north of Brecon on A470. Mill set slightly back from road, on left, between Llyswen & Erwood. Train to Llandrindod Wells; bus to Brecon every 2 hrs will drop at mill on request.

Bottle of fair trade wine.

Alistair & Nicky Legge
Trericket Mill Vegetarian Guesthouse,
Erwood, Builth Wells LD2 3TQ
Tel   +44 (0)1982 560312
Email   mail@trericket.co.uk
Web   www.trericket.co.uk

Entry 747   Map 7

Powys

Rhedyn

Come here if you need to remember how to relax. Such an unassuming little place, but with real character and soul: great comfort too with exposed walls in the bedrooms, funky lighting, pocket sprung mattresses, lovely books to read, and calm colours; bathrooms are modern and delightfully quirky. But the real stars of this show are Muiread and Ciaran: wonderfully warm, enthusiastic and engaging, with a passion for good, local food and a desire for more self-sufficiency – pigs and bees are planned next. This is a totally tranquil place, with agreeable walks through the Irfon valley and bog snorkelling too!

Price	£70. Singles £60.
Rooms	3 doubles.
Meals	Dinner, 3 courses, £25. Packed lunch £7.50. Pub/restaurant 1 mile.
Closed	Rarely.
Directions	From Builth Wells follow A483 towards 'Garth'. Pass Cilmery village, Rhedyn signpost is one mile on right. House is in middle of field.

Use your Sawday's Gift Card here.

Muiread & Ciaran O'Connell
Rhedyn,
Cilmery, Builth Wells LD2 3LH
Tel   +44 (0)1982 551944
Email   info@rhedynguesthouse.co.uk
Web   www.rhedynguesthouse.co.uk

Entry 748   Map 7

Powys

The Old Vicarage

Blessed are those who enter... especially devotees of Victoriana. The house, designed by Sir George Gilbert Scott, is a delight. Your host, charming and fun, ushers you in to a rich confection of colours, dark wood and a lifetime's collecting: splendid brass beds, cast-iron radiators, porcelain loos, sumptuous bedspreads and a garden with grotto, waterfall and rill. Dine by candle or gas light (the food is superb), ring the servants' bell for early morning tea. You are on the English side of Offa's Dyke: look north to the heavenly Radnorshire hills, south to all of Herefordshire. *Minimum stay two nights weekends & bank holidays.*

Price	From £98.
Rooms	3: 2 doubles, 1 twin.
Meals	Dinner, 4 courses, £34. Pub 10-minute drive.
Closed	Rarely.
Directions	B4355, between Presteigne & Knighton; in village of Norton, immed. north of church.

10% off stays of 2 or more nights (subject to availability).

Paul Gerrard
The Old Vicarage,
Norton, Presteigne LD8 2EN
Tel   +44 (0)1544 260038
Email   paul@nortonoldvic.co.uk
Web   www.oldvicarage-nortonrads.co.uk

Entry 749   Map 7

Powys

The Old Vicarage

Come for vast skies, forested hills and quilted fields that stretch for miles. This Victorian vicarage is a super base: smart, welcoming, full of comforts. You get a log fire in a cosy sitting room, a super-smart dining room with long country views and fancy bedrooms that spoil you all the way. Tim's food is just as good. Local suppliers are noted on menus, but much is grown in the garden, where chickens run free. Resist laziness and take to the hills – the Kerry Ridgeway is on your doorstep as is Powis Castle – for glorious walking, then home and afternoon tea. *Children over 12 welcome.*

Ethical Collection: Environment. See page 430.

Price	£95. Singles £65.
Rooms	4: 1 twin/double, 2 doubles, 1 family suite.
Meals	Dinner, 3 courses, £30. Packed lunch available. Pub 1 mile.
Closed	Rarely.
Directions	A483, 3.5 miles from Newtown towards Llandrindod Wells, left on sharp right bend, house first on left.

25% off stays of 2 or more nights.

Tim & Helen Withers
The Old Vicarage,
Dolfor, Newtown SY16 4BN
Tel   +44 (0)1686 629051
Email   tim@theoldvicaragedolfor.co.uk
Web   www.theoldvicaragedolfor.co.uk

Entry 750   Map 7

Powys

Talbontdrain

Way off the beaten track, remote and wild, sits a white-painted stone farmhouse. The Cambrian mountains stretch to the south, the river Dovey lies in the vale below and kind Hilary knows all the walks and can sort special routes for you. She cooks a hearty breakfast too, or a farmhouse supper, and gives you colourful bedrooms – not swish, but with everything you need. There are photographs of garden plants, a pianola, and furniture in such a mix of styles that it all gives a feeling of great informality. The peace is deep – even the cockerel stays quiet until a respectable time – and walkers will adore it.

Price	£56–£66. Singles £28.
Rooms	4: 1 double, 1 family room for 3; 1 twin/double, 1 single sharing shower.
Meals	Dinner, 2 courses & coffee, £18. Packed lunch £6.
Closed	Christmas & Boxing Day.
Directions	Leaving Machynlleth on A489, 1st right signed Forge. In Forge bear right to Uwchygarreg up 'dead end'. 3 miles, pass phone box on left, up steep hill. House on left at top.
💼	Free entry to the Centre for Alternative Technology if staying 2 or more nights.

Hilary Matthews
Talbontdrain,
Uwchygarreg, Machynlleth SY20 8RR
Tel   +44 (0)1654 702192
Email   hilary@talbontdrain.co.uk
Web   www.talbontdrain.co.uk

Entry 751   Map 7

Swansea

Blas Gwyr

Sleepy Llangennith was once a well-kept secret – now walkers, riders, surfers and beach lovers of all ages flock. Tucked back from the bustling bay is an extended 1700s cottage with a boutique hotel facelift. All is simple but stylish: bedrooms are modern and matching with tiled floors and contemporary paintings; bathrooms come with warm floors and fluffy towels. Everything from the bedspread to the breakfast is local: make sure you try the lavabread. After a day at sea, fling wet gear in the drying room and linger over a coffee on the front deck, or walk to the pub for a sun-kissed pint. Bliss. *Welsh spoken.*

Price	£100–£110. Singles £85.
Rooms	4: 1 double, 1 double (with sofabed), 1 twin/double, 1 suite for 2-4.
Meals	Packed lunch £5. Dinner £20 (Friday/Saturday, for groups of 6+). Pub 150 yds.
Closed	Never.
Directions	M4 junc. 47, 2nd exit, A483. Next 2 r'bouts 3rd exit, A484. Dual c'way then r'bout, 1st left, B4296. Right at lights. On to Llangennith, pass pub; mini r'bout, right, then immed. right.
💼	10% off room rate Mon-Thurs.

Dafydd & Kerry James
Blas Gwyr,
Plenty Farm, Llangennith,
Swansea SA3 1HU
Tel   +44 (0)1792 386472
Email   info@blasgwyr.co.uk
Web   www.blasgwyr.co.uk

Entry 752   Map 2

Wrexham

The Garden House

Unbelievable that a few years ago this was bare farmland. Simon and Susie have worked magic: Simon building the handsome brick house, his mother transforming the land into a symphony of lawns, boxed hedges, hideaways, a bridged pond with views to the river, sculptures here and there, hordes of hydrangeas, a greenhouse for afternoon tea. One of Simon's passions is art and antiques so inside is equally creative: the smart double room in the main house and separate Orangery suite are bursting with artworks and original pieces. Eat in the wonderfully chaotic family kitchen or walk to the pub, wake to a dawn chorus, revel in the enthusiasm of it all.

Price	£100. Singles £60.
Rooms	2: 1 double with sitting area. Orangery: 1 double with sitting room, 2 singles.
Meals	Supper £20-£30. Pub/restaurant 0.75 miles.
Closed	Occasionally.
Directions	A483 to Chester, turn on to A539 (Whitchurch). Turn right on A528; right by Cross Foxes pub. Follow Gardens sign. House 0.75 miles on right.

Simon Wingett
The Garden House,
Erbistock, Wrexham LL13 0DL
Tel   +44(0)1978 781149
Email   art@simonwingett.com
Web   www.simonwingett.com

Entry 753   Map 7

Wrexham

Worthenbury Manor

Homemade bread and Hepplewhite! This is a good, solid house of generous proportions and your hosts live in part of it. Wallow in antique oak four-posters in rose-carpeted chandeliered bedrooms, full of comfort (books, games and flowers adding a cosy touch) and breakfast on fresh fruit (some from the garden) local bacon and sausages. Ian, history buff and former chef, is gentle, thoughtful and looks after you properly; dinner is quite an occasion. The listed house is close to Chester yet in a quiet, birdsung setting; the original building was enlarged in the 1890s in the William and Mary revival style.

Price	£60-£85. Singles £38-£49.
Rooms	2: 1 four-poster; 1 four-poster with separate bath.
Meals	Dinner, 3 courses, £25. Lunch £15.
Closed	December-February.
Directions	Between A525 Whitchurch to Wrexham & A41 Whitchurch to Chester, on B5069 between Bangor-on-Dee (Bangor-is-y-coed) and Malpas. Manor on right before bridge.

3 nights for price of 2. Half bottle wine with dinner for stays of 2+ nights.

Use your Sawday's Gift Card here.

Elizabeth & Ian Taylor
Worthenbury Manor,
Worthenbury LL13 0AW
Tel   +44 (0)1948 770342
Email   enquiries@worthenburymanor.co.uk
Web   www.worthenburymanor.co.uk

Entry 754   Map 7

Becoming a member of Sawday's Travel Club opens up hundreds of discounts, treats and other offers at over 700 of our Special Places to Stay in Britain and Ireland, as well as 50% discount on all Sawday's books.

Where you see the ▮▮ symbol in this book it means the place has a special offer for Club members. It may be money off your room price, a bottle of wine or a basket of home-grown produce. The offers for each place are within each entry and on our website. These were correct at the time of going to print, but owners reserve the right to change the listed offer. Latest offers for all places can be found on our website, www.sawdays.co.uk.

Membership is only £25 per year. To join the Travel Club visit www.sawdays.co.uk/bookshop/travel_club.

The small print

You must mention that you are a Travel Club member when booking, and confirm that the offer is available. Your Travel Club card must be shown on arrival to claim the offer. Sawday's Travel Club cards are not transferable. If two cardholders share a room they can only claim the offer once. Offers for Sawday's Travel Club members are subject to availability. Alastair Sawday Publishing cannot accept any responsibility if places fail to honour offers; neither can we accept responsibility if a place changes hands and drops out of the Travel Club.

Photo left: Mallard Grange, entry 613
Photo right: Sagar Fold House, entry 298

Many of you may want to stay in environmentally friendly places. You may be passionate about local, organic or home-grown food. Or perhaps you want to know that the place you are staying in contributes to the community? To help you we have launched our Ethical Collection, so you can find the right place to stay and also discover how each owner is addressing these issues.

The Collection is made up of places going the extra mile, and taking the steps that most people have not yet taken, in one or more of the following areas:

• **Environment** Those making great efforts to reduce the environmental impact of their Special Place. We expect more than energy-saving light bulbs and recycling – in this part of the Collection you will find owners who make their own natural cleaning products, properties with solar hot water and biomass boilers, the odd green roof and a good measure of green elbow grease.

• **Community** Given to owners who use their property to play a positive role in their local and wider community. For example, by making a contribution from every guest's bill to a local fund, or running pond-dipping courses for local school children on their farm.

• **Food** Awarded to owners who make a real effort to source local or organic food, or to grow their own. We look

for those who have gone out of their way to strike up relationships with local producers or to seek out organic suppliers. It is easier for an owner on a farm to produce their own eggs than for someone in the middle of a city, so we take this into account.

How it works

To become part of our Ethical Collection owners choose whether to apply in one, two or all three categories, and fill in a detailed questionnaire asking demanding questions about their activities in the chosen areas. You can download a full list of the questions at www.sawdays.co.uk/about_us/ethical_collection/faq/

We then review each questionnaire carefully before deciding whether or not to give the award(s). The final decision is subjective; it is based not only on whether an owner ticks 'yes' to a question but also on the detailed explanation that accompanies each 'yes' or 'no' answer. For example, an owner who has tried as hard as possible to install solar water-heating panels, but has failed because of strict conservation planning laws, will be given some credit for their effort (as long as they are doing other things in this area).

We have tried to be as rigorous as possible and have made sure the questions are demanding. We have not checked out the claims of owners before making our decisions, but we do trust them to be honest. We are only human, as are they, so please let us know if you think we have made any mistakes.

The Ethical Collection is still a new initiative for us, and we'd love to know what you think about it – email us at ethicalcollection@sawdays.co.uk or write to us. And remember that because this is a new scheme some owners have not yet completed their questionnaires – we're sure other places in the guide are working just as hard in these areas, but we don't yet know the full details.

Ethical Collection in this book

On the entry page of all places in the Collection we show which awards have been given.

A list of the places in our Ethical Collection is shown below, by entry number.

Environment

24 • 32 • 45 • 49 • 59 • 69 • 75 • 77 • 81 • 84 • 101 • 109 • 127 • 134 • 140 • 162 • 208 • 223 • 257 • 259 • 260 • 265 • 356 • 410 • 428 • 432 • 435 • 441 • 448 • 451 • 472 • 477 • 489 • 577 • 582 • 593 • 595 • 610 • 629 • 630 • 649 • 673 • 686 • 716 • 728 • 732 • 734 • 738 • 747 • 750

Community

29 • 77 • 81 • 109 • 115 • 158 • 252 • 356 • 423 • 433 • 448 • 454 • 455 • 458 • 472 • 489 • 500 • 552 • 561 • 563 • 582 • 602 • 618 • 630 • 635 • 649 • 673 • 716 • 728 • 734

Photo: Tom Germain

Food

5 • 24 • 29 • 32 • 39 • 45 • 49 • 56 • 59 • 69 • 75 • 77 • 81 • 86 • 98 • 102 • 106 • 109 • 112 • 115 • 116 • 127 • 128 • 134 • 151 • 158 • 159 • 160 • 161 • 186 • 196 • 208 • 215 • 223 • 244 • 251 • 252 • 257 • 259 • 260 • 265 • 270 • 276 • 277 • 339 • 356 • 374 • 394 • 423 • 428 • 432 • 433 • 435 • 441 • 442 • 443 • 448 • 451 • 453 • 454 • 455 • 462 • 472 • 477 • 482 • 489 • 500 • 503 • 523 • 552 • 553 • 561 • 563 • 577 • 582 • 587 • 593 • 601 • 602 • 610 • 617 • 618 • 629 • 630 • 649 • 686 • 692 • 704 • 705 • 716 • 728 • 732 • 734 • 737 • 738 • 747 • 750

Ethical Collection online

There is stacks more information on our website, www.sawdays.co.uk. You can read the answers each owner has given to our Ethical Collection questionnaire and get a more detailed idea of what they are doing in each area. You can also search for properties that have awards.

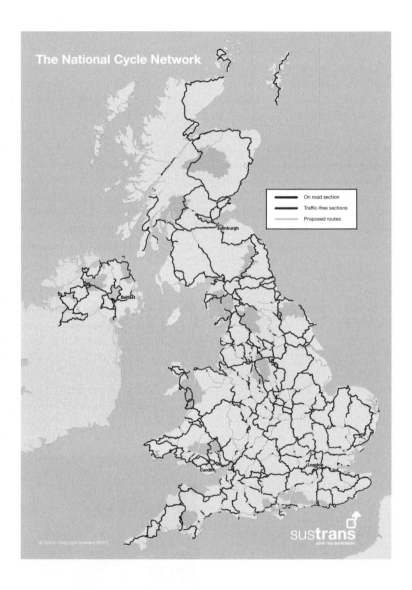

For route information see www.sustrans.org

National Cycle Network
These Special Places are
within two miles of the NCN.

Quick reference indices

Wheelchair-accessible
At least one bedroom and bathroom accessible for wheelchair users. Phone for details.

Stay all day
You can stay all day at these places if you wish.

On a budget?
These places have a double room for £70 or under.

Quick reference indices

Quick reference indices

List of titles:	RRP	Discount price
British Bed & Breakfast	£14.99	£9.74
British Bed & Breakfast for Garden Lovers	£14.99	£9.74
British Hotels and Inns	£14.99	£9.74
Pubs & Inns of England & Wales	£15.99	£10.39
Venues	£11.99	£7.79
Cotswolds	£9.99	£6.49
Devon & Cornwall	£9.99	£6.49
Wales	£9.99	£6.49
Ireland	£12.99	£8.44
French Bed & Breakfast	£15.99	£10.39
French Self-Catering	£14.99	£9.74
French Châteaux & Hotels	£14.99	£9.74
French Vineyards	£19.99	£12.99
Paris	£9.99	£6.49
Green Europe	£11.99	£7.79
Italy	£14.99	£9.74
Portugal	£11.99	£7.79
Spain	£14.99	£9.74
Morocco	£9.99	£6.49
India	£11.99	£7.79
Go Slow England	£19.99	£12.99
Go Slow France	£19.99	£12.99
Go Slow Italy	£19.99	£12.99
Eat Slow Britain	£19.99	£12.99

*postage and packaging is added to each order

How to order:
You can order online at: www.sawdays.co.uk/bookshop/
or call: **+44(0)1275 395431**

Alastair
Sawday's
Special Escapes
Self-catering in the UK

A whole week self-catering in Britain with your friends or family is precious, and you dare not get it wrong. To whom do you turn for advice and who on earth do you trust when the web is awash with advice from strangers? We launched Special Escapes to satisfy an obvious need for impartial and trustworthy help – and that is what it provides. The criteria for inclusion are the same as for our books: we have to like the place and the owners. It has, quite simply, to be 'special'. The site, our first online-only publication, is featured on www.thegoodwebguide.com and is growing fast.

Cosy cottages • Manor houses
Tipis • Hilltop bothies
City apartments and more

www.special-escapes.co.uk

Your passport to a choice of Special Places to Stay

Sawday's Gift Cards can be used at a whole array of bed and breakfasts, hotels, self-catering places and pubs with rooms scattered across the British Isles. You may fancy a night in a country house which towers majestically over the River Usk, or perhaps a weekend in a splendid Georgian mansion in the Cotswolds. Stay in a garret above a legendary London coffee house or sample a stunning barn conversion in the depths of Northumberland.

Wherever you choose as a treat for yourself, friends or a loved one we know it will be fun, unusual, maybe even eccentric and definitely life affirming. A perfect present.

They are available in six denominations – £25, £50, £75, £100, £150 and £200, and come in attractive packaging, which includes a series of postcards and a printed booklet featuring all the participating places.

You can purchase Gift Cards at: www.sawdays.co.uk/gift-cards/ or you can order them by phone: +44(0)1275 395431.

You can also view the full list of participating places on our website www.sawdays.co.uk and search by this symbol: 🎁

1 Norfolk

The Old Rectory

2 A stately place indeed: a venerable English rectory replete with period furniture, art, history, well-bred hosts (he shoots, she rides) and, in the expansive grounds, a ruined chapel, lake, croquet lawn and pool. Breakfast is served on the terrace in summer. You dine by candlelight on local game and the kitchen garden's offerings, then settle in the Georgian drawing room by the rocking horse. Sleep in the Coach House where plush beds have beautiful linen, warm throws and beaded cushions; dogs can stay in the stables. A rare chance to experience the best of British country life. *Riding & shooting can be arranged.*

4 Price	£75-£95. Singles £60-£80.
5 Rooms	3: Coach House, 1 double, 1 twin/double, 1 twin.
6 Meals	Dinner, 2 courses, £25; 3 courses, £35. Pub 1 mile. Restaurant 5 miles.
7 Closed	Never.
8 Directions	From Stone Ferry bypass, take road to Oxborough. 0.5 miles before Oxborough Hall, right down Ferry Road. House is 0.5 miles on left.

9 10% off room rate Mon-Thurs. Cake in your room, to eat or take home.

Veronica de Lotbiniere
The Old Rectory,
Ferry Road, Oxborough,
King's Lynn PE33 9PT
Tel +44 (0)1842 814215
Email onky.del@btinternet.com
Web www.oldrectoryoxboroughbandb.co.uk

11

12 Entry 355 Map 9

Norfolk

Carrick's at Castle Farm

A comfortable, and jolly, mix of farmhouse B&B – rare-breed cattle, tractors, a large, warm-bricked house – and a rather swish interior. Both Jean and John are passionate about conservation and the protection of wildlife, and here you have absolute quiet for birdwatching, fishing, shooting or walking; recover in the drawing room with its books and lovely river views from long windows. Bedrooms are large, light and well thought-out with great bathrooms and binoculars, food is home-grown or local, and there is coffee and cake, or wine, when you arrive. The pretty garden leads down to the River Wensum and a footpath.

Ethical Collection: Environment; Food; Community. See page 430. 3

Price	From £85. Singles £55.
Rooms	4: 2 doubles; 1 double, 1 twin each with separate bath (let to same party only).
Meals	Dinner, 3 courses, £25. BYO. Pub 0.5 miles.
Closed	Never.
Directions	From Norwich A47 to Dereham (don't go into Dereham). B1147 to Swanton Morley. In village, take Elsing Road at Darby's pub; farm drive 0.5 miles on left.

10% off room rate Mon-Thurs. Late checkout (12pm).

Use your Sawday's Gift Card here. 10

Jean Wright
Carrick's at Castle Farm,
Castle Farm, Swanton Morley,
Dereham NR20 4JT
Tel +44 (0)1362 638302
Email jean@castlefarm-swanton.co.uk
Web www.carricksatcastlefarm.co.uk

Entry 356 Map 10